The Michigan Historical Reprint Series

Reprints from the collection of the University of Michigan University Library

The Scholarly Publishing Office
the University of Michigan
University Library

BRYANT & STRATTON'S COUNTING HOUSE BOOK-KEEPING:

CONTAINING A

COMPLETE EXPOSITION OF THE SCIENCE OF ACCOUNTS,

IN ITS APPLICATION TO

THE VARIOUS DEPARTMENTS OF BUSINESS;

INCLUDING

COMPLETE SETS OF BOOKS

IN

WHOLESALE AND RETAIL MERCHANDISING,

FARMING, SETTLEMENT OF ESTATES.

FORWARDING, COMMISSION,

BANKING, EXCHANGE, STOCK BROKERAGE, ETC.

WITH FULL EXPLANATIONS AND APPROPRIATE REMARKS ON THE CUSTOMS OF TRADE; AND EXAMPLES OF THE MOST IMPORTANT BUSINESS FORMS IN USE.

BY

H. B. BRYANT, AND H. D. STRATTON,

FOUNDERS OF THE INTERNATIONAL CHAIN OF COMMERCIAL COLLEGES, LOCATED IN THE PRINCIPAL CITIES OF THE U. S. AND THE DOMINION OF CANADA,

AND

S. S. PACKARD,

RESIDENT PRINCIPAL OF THE NEW YORK CITY MERCANTILE COLLEGE, 18 AND 19 COOPER INSTITUTE.

IVISON, BLAKEMAN, TAYLOR & COMPANY,

NEW YORK: CHICAGO:

PREFACE.

IN 1859, the authors of the present treatise perfected arrangements for the publication of a series of works on Bookkeeping which should comprise three books, and constitute a progressive treatment of the subject· commencing with the most simple formulas and illustrations, adapted to the comprehension of beginners, and proceeding, in the natural order of development, to the more complex and intricate questions which arise in the exigencies of business, requiring in their adjustment, maturity of thought, and a thorough knowledge of the principles governing business record.

In pursuance of this plan they issued in the summer of 1860, the intermediate book of the series, known as the "High School" edition, which embraced, with other matter, the first 185 pages of the present treatise; and in the year following, the primary, or "Common School" edition, comprising 192 pages 12mo, and adapted to class and private instruction, for the lower grades of schools and beginners. At the same time, the final book of the series, the "Counting House" edition, was announced as forthcoming "in a few months." Two years have elapsed since this announcement, the greater portion of which time has been faithfully spent in carrying out the original purpose which culminates in the work before the reader.

This unexpected delay has been the source of much regret and annoyance to us, as well as of solicitude to our friends,—if we are permitted to judge from the frequent inquiries which have encountered us on every hand—but it has been *unavoidable;* and here we rest our defense.

It is one thing to evolve a general theory of debits and credits, which, having a mathematical basis, and clearly defined limits, may, with carefully selected, and ingeniously arranged material, be fashioned into symmetrical proportions, which will both please the eye, and captivate the understanding, and quite another to take up the actual occurrences of a multifarious and extensive business, and, without discarding any details which may seem to destroy the symmetry of a preconceived theory, so fashion the whole as not only to dispose of each item composing the daily routine in such a manner as to make apparent its ultimate bearing upon the grand result, but to keep these recurring facts so well in hand, as that each shall be made to work out its own separate mission, without encroachment or self-stultification.

The first two books of this series were intended mainly to teach the *theory* of Accounts; and while great care was taken that the transactions should be such as usually occur in the departments of business represented, they were selected more with a view to establish the student in the grand fundamental principles of the science, than to exhibit the peculiar forms of entry variously employed in business. That this was the proper course we are fully confident, not only from our own experience in this special department of instruction, but from the oft-repeated assurances of competent teachers and educationists in all parts of the country.

In the "Common School" edition we aimed to give the plainest instruction, accompanied by the most simple illustrations, avoiding as far as possible any fine-spun theories, or elaborate discussions upon points not likely to be understood and appreciated by the class of minds to which the work was addressed. In the higher edition we deemed it our privilege to enter upon the general discussion with more freedom of expression, and less regard to the undefined prejudices against metaphysical reasoning which marks the indolent, no less than the timid mind. The general theories there assumed, and more or less elaborately enforced, were, in some essential particulars, original and novel, and were put forth with a good degree of timidity, not on account of any fears as to their truthfulness or consistency, but as to the prudence of venturing upon the untried sea of authorship against a tide of opposing precedents, which although they may have been disturbed by collision with the innovations of recent authors were surely not destroyed.

But if the natural distrustfulness with which these general propositions were made public was then admissable, the thorough test which a three years' use of the book in the hands of teachers, who are in the habit of, thinking for themselves, has afforded, would render any farther hesitancy or special pleading, not only uncalled for but puerile. This satisfactory ordeal has afforded us no occasion for changing any of our positions, or even of qualifying the deductions which seemed naturally to grow out of them. And so we have embodied them in the present treatise as affording the best possible preparation for a clear understanding of the more practical features presented in the last half of the work, and which constitute its chief characteristics.

PREFACE.

These sets have been carefully prepared with a view, not only to illustrate the features of the various departments of business, but to afford the most extensive application of the science of Accounts. In preparing this portion of the work, we have drawn without stint upon the experience of business men; having to this end visited many of the first establishments of the country, and had access to all such books and documents as could in any manner aid us in presenting the true aspects of business. And we take this occasion to return our sincere thanks to those gentlemen—whom we would be proud to name—who have so generously afforded us these invaluable facilities; and whose kind suggestions have served as a perpetual inspiration in the prosecution of our labor.

Our aim has been to make the book, in the truest sense, *practical;* and while we esteem, at their full value, the necessary abstractions which enter into the discussion of general principles, and which have not been spared in the theoretical part, experience has taught us that with the majority of learners the shortest and most effectual method of inculcating theory is to make a proper application of its principles to practical results. Especially is this true of Bookkeeping, a science so thoroughly susceptible of illustration; and the beauties of which are in no way so clearly shown as in the practical forms of business through which its theories are enforced.

In selecting from the numerous callings of business life those best adapted to our purpose, we have endeavored to secure as great a variety of record as possible, while we have had direct reference to the probable future wants of the student. Without desiring to make the book cumbersome, or to place it beyond the reach of the many on account of price, we have nevertheless endeavored to treat each separate subject with fullness and fidelity; choosing rather to limit variety than to accept the alternative of superficiality. This purpose, we feel assured, will be appreciated by that large and worthy class of young men who are willing to undergo the necessary ordeal of study to prepare themselves for first-class positions; and we are free to say that an earnest desire to meet the wants of such has had much to do in giving direction to our efforts.

In preparing the practical sets we have been actuated by two leading impulses, viz., to exhibit the most approved forms of business record, as they exist in *actual practice*, and to combine the best features in each department, with such improvements as our own experience and observation dictate.

We have endeavored to present the transactions in their natural order, that the student's practice may, as far as possible, assimilate to the actual business routine, and enable him to appreciate the practical bearing of each entry. If some of the sets seem to be tedious in their length and repetition, the advantage afforded by such discipline will more than outbalance the labor; which can be, at best, but a slight indication of the more responsible duties of the Counting Room.

It is true that no book hitherto published on this subject has required of the student such an extent of mental labor; and we feel assured that this fact, instead of interdicting its favorable reception with an intelligent public will rather add to its claims. The great foe to true progress in all ages has been mental slothfulness; and so prone are we all to this condition—so willing to let others do our thinking—that we are constantly in need of some impelling force which shall develop the dormant faculties, and enable us to realize the true idea of EDUCATION.

We have little faith in the "learning-made-easy" method of treating a science so eminently worthy of the best mental efforts, and requiring in its application such thorough comprehension as well as such nice distinctions. To understand it at all, the student must *think for himself;* and in order that he may not forget this part of his duty, we have endeavored to prescribe at proper intervals his appropriate mental tasks.

If he will follow them out carefully and faithfully to the end, producing through the regularly prescribed processes the specified results, he will never have occasion to regret the time and labor thus spent, and can make no mistake in reckoning his knowledge of Bookkeeping as among the most valuable of his acquisitions.

BRYANT, STRATTON, & PACKARD.

NEW YORK, July 1, 1863.

A SHORT ADDRESS,

RESPECTFULLY DEDICATED TO THE YOUNG MEN OF THE COUNTRY.

Every human life has its purpose, as every thing in nature its uses; and, however much the desire may grow to evade the responsibilities which rest on each individual soul, or to absorb them in the general application to the race, or to whatever extent we may throw ourselves upon the soothing thought—

> "There is a Divinity that shapes our ends,
> Rough-hew them how we will;"—

still ever within the heart there lives a consciousness that, in the duties of life, every one must answer for himself, and not another. This very consciousness is the key-note of existence, lending to life its charms, and to society its surest safeguard. We desire to accept it as the basis of a few suggestions, which we think not out of place in this connection.

Let us come, then, directly to the point: What is *your* purpose in life, and how do you hope to accomplish it? Do you desire riches? You have but to stretch forth your hand and take them. Honor? It is yours for the asking. Fame? Many less noble and talented have won it, and so may you. Friends? They will come of their own accord, if you get but the others. There is, indeed, a wonderful potency in the human will, and an efficiency in human hands scarce dreamed of by the brightest visionary. But let us separately consider these desires, and the avenues which lead to their consummation.

1. Riches.

It is folly to contend against this desire, even on moral grounds; as he who would be able to make the clearest case, would still fail in convincing *himself* that a "reasonable" share of this world's goods would necessarily disqualify him for the highest state of human enjoyment. Even the Prophet, speaking through inspiration, as positively denounces poverty as its opposite; and the world has yet to see a philosopher, of whatever school, who would not make *himself* an exception to any rule which would constitute the getting of riches a moral wrong. The possession of wealth is, in itself, neither good nor bad. It is only the *use* of money which circumscribes its moral tendencies. Even the Bible—that highest text-book of morality—does not denounce riches *per se*. It is not money, but the *love* of it which is called "the root of all evil." To desire riches, then, is no evil. On the other hand, we consider it to be not only legitimate, morally speaking, but highly commendable. The possession of wealth not only adds to one's importance in the community, but places within his power almost limitless opportunities to do good. There is not an enterprise, having for its object the bettering of human condition, that does not depend, in the greatest measure, for its usefulness, upon money. Through its potency, states are inhabited, churches erected, knowledge diffused, the avenues of commerce kept open, industry rewarded, genius fostered, and the refining influences of civilization strengthened and perpetuated. The acquisition of wealth, then, for the good it may do, is a worthy purpose of life. How shall it be accomplished? If one may judge by the flaming advertisements which disgrace the columns of our daily papers, there is no method which ingenuity can devise, or rascality concoct, that is not resorted to for this end; and the world will probably never be so good or so wise, this side of the millennium that such will not be the case. To become *suddenly* rich, is the passion of the age; and if one out of every ten thousand, who run the gauntlet of this mad ambition, succeeds, the nine thousand nine hundred and ninety-nine disastrous failures are lost sight of in the dazzling effulgence of that one success. Like policy-dealers, who blind the eyes of willing victims to the almost inevitable result of their folly, by dwelling alone upon the magnificence of coveted but inaccessible prizes, so the deluded and deluding followers of mammon cheat their own better judgment in the wild pursuit of impossible fortunes, expecting, despite experience to the contrary, by some grand *coup d'etat* to surprise the strongholds of wealth, and take her captive.

It is not thus that sensible people seek to grow rich, nor thus that we would prescribe the means. Our suggestions on this head, though possessing not the freshness of novelty, nor the charm of mystery, shall be to the point. The three prerequisites to this enviable and attainable condition are: *honesty, industry,* and *frugality;* three homely virtues, whose names are as "familiar in our mouths as household words," and which are as necessary to our personal comfort and self-respect as is the condition they would bring about. We are, in truth, the architects of our own fortune; and this is the sweetest consideration of all. That which has become ours by patient, honest, unremitting endeavor, will be appreciated, and we shall the better know how to dispose of it. Again, true riches cannot be wholly measured by any known financial standard. Wealth is a purely comparative condition, and its extent has less to do with the number and significance of the figures composing its total than the relation which those figures bear to the real necessities of life. He who has enough for his own immediate wants—who owes no man any thing, and is not fostering in his own heart a brood of extravagant desires, is "comfortably rich." He who has more than this, is, to that extent, *wealthy.* To such a position, it is not only the privilege but the duty of every young man to aspire; for not only will the coveted prize repay all his exertions, but every well-meant endeavor will bring its own immediate reward in developing the internal resources, in raising the standard of self-respect, in enlarging the capacities of enjoyment, and in begetting the self-consciousness of having performed one's part and lot in the world.

2. Honor.

To be esteemed of men, is also a commendable desire; and, next to riches, is it the ruling passion of life. It is, in fact, to this end that most men desire riches. That position in life, however, which is the mere contingency of wealth, will not repay the effort necessary to acquire it. To be *truly* esteemed of men, is to be the possessor of qualities which money cannot buy. To be worthy of that esteem, is the highest social position attainable in this life. How shall it be reached? Everybody has heard that "honesty is the best policy;" and the truth of the maxim is substantiated in every phase of human history: but if no higher moral ground than this were possible, we should despair of ever witnessing a correct standard of honor. Honesty which springs from motives of *policy,* deserves not the name. It is akin to that bastard friendship begotten of selfishness, and is not entitled to a place on the list of virtues. To be truly honorable, all actions must spring from pure motives, and pure motives can rest only on correct principles. So we come down to the position that *correct principles* alone can produce that "noblest work of God"—an honest man. But how is one to judge of correct principles? We might answer as most moral instructors would: Go to the Bible. The answer would not be amiss; and yet, there is planted within every human breast a little monitor, the pure instincts of which are as unerring as truth itself. An appeal to conscience will invariably settle the little perplexing questions which sometimes become so inwrought in the very constitution of moral actions as to threaten the utter destruction of all safeguards. It is through neglect of this appeal that so many hundreds of names are yearly added to that dishonored catalogue of "ruined young men." The *first* step in a wrong direction is always the most difficult. One such step, unrepented of, is a sure precursor to a course of infamy. No young man, at the beginning of his career, coolly premeditates a life of dishonor; but, having once launched upon the tide, he is like the impotent boatman who permits his craft to drift into the rapids of Niagara. Occasionally one such, in his swift descent toward the awful chasm, may strike upon a friendly rock, as did poor Avery; but, as in his case, the relief will be but temporary, and the wild hopes of rescue will only add pangs to the certainty of destruction. Honesty *is* the best policy; and better than that, it is as the right hand of God, a "present help in every time of need."

3. Fame.

This is an empty bubble, at best, though men have willingly yielded up their lives to secure the heritage for their children. It has been truly said that "some men are born great, others achieve greatness, while others have it thrust upon them." As, in this country, the first of these conditions is impossible and the last inaccessible by any human effort, there remains but the process of achievement for those who desire to be famous. It will be apparent to the most careless observer, that the very existence of fame is dependent upon its opposite, as the existence of a mountain would be impossible without its contiguous plain or valley. As the height of a mountain is estimated by the distance of its summit from "the level of the sea," so is the extent of a man's fame measured by his relative distance above the level of society. He who would court

Fame, then, must not be content to do *as well* as others. Negative virtues count as nought in such a contest and no one who has not the positive qualities of energy and perseverance can hope for success in this endeavor.

4. Friends.

Sentimentalists talk of friendship as self-created connoisseurs in art point out the beauties of an Italian 1scape, or a boarding-school miss would apostrophize "a love of a bonnet." So widely prevalent is the disgust which these sickly views of the noblest of human sentiments have produced, that we are fast becoming infidels on this point; and no opinion is more common or more freely expressed than that "friendship is but a name." We are not willing to accept this conclusion, for many reasons. First, history proves its fallacy; and next, to yield this point, would be to strike from the world every living virtue; for if pure, unselfish friendship does not exist, then truth has no abiding-place, and love, the sum of all the virtues, would be without foundation. It is the privilege of every young man to contribute to a healthier sentiment in this regard, first by deserving friends, and next by enjoying them. By *friends* we mean not those summer birds who twitter about the opening petals of our joy, and sing in the branches of our prosperity, while the warm sun gives life, and the soft breezes stir the tender foliage. Flatterers are not friends, how musical soever may be the sweet cadences of their adulation. Those, and those only, are our friends in the mirror of whose hearts the angles of incidence and reflection are rendered equal from a surface unruffled by pride or any selfish quality—who can tell us of our faults as they would point out a malady which threatened to undermine our health—not for the gratification it may give them, or the mortification us, but that efficient means may be taken for its eradication. As a father affords the strongest proof of love for his child by inflicting pain that good may follow, so the surest test of friendship is a fealty to our good which will not shrink from any duty towards us, however unpleasant, or liable to be misconstrued. Again, society is not so depraved as we are apt to think, and men *will* learn to put a true estimate on character, entirely independent of extraneous considerations. Beauty and symmetry have charms, even to those who are themselves most uncomely; and if one desires the acquisition of such friends as will not desert when most their friendship is needed, the surest method of obtaining them is not to seek by flattery and fawning, or at the expense of one particle of self-respect, but to *deserve* by a life and character which must force them into the ranks. One friend thus secured is worth a thousand flatterers who live in the sunshine and die in the storm.

We have thus briefly reviewed some of the important desires which actuate young men in adopting rules of conduct which are to regulate their lives. Let us, a little more explicitly, consider the points which bear upon

The Choice of Vocation.

Very few young men before fairly starting in life have any decided predeliction for a special calling. It is true that the organ of hope, which so preponderates in the earlier stages of life, draws extravagant pictures of what we shall be "when we are men;" but even this ambition changes with the shifting panorama which produced it; and we run in imagination, through the entire category of professions and positions, impelled alone by the distant halo, which in our youthful wonder, surrounds the objects of our envious regard.

It is, perhaps, as well that this is so; for no decision abstractly made, and without experience to give it force, would bind our riper judgment, if not in accordance with it. Besides, it is absolutely impossible thus to dispose of our future selves. For instance, it is one of the peculiar and fascinating doctrines of our republic, that the highest positions of honor and emolument are open to its children. It is common when referring to the humblest scion of the humblest stock—"the unwashed democracy"—to remark, "Here may be a future president," or, "Disguised in that torn and faded apparel is an embryo governor;" and history is not wanting in examples to prove that, in this country at least, the end of human success can never be estimated from its beginning. The accident of birth has no weight in deciding destiny. Suppose, then, reasoning from this basis, every ambitious young man should say: "There is nothing in my birth, position, or constitution which can stand in the way of my elevation to the presidential chair; it is worthy of my best efforts, and I will not rest until that purpose is accomplished." The very supposition proclaims its own folly. It is true that all aspirations of this kind may be legitimate; but, considering how few presidents are chosen in each generation, the chances for such preferment are even less than that of obtaining the chief prize in a lottery scheme by the purchase of a single ticket. A great man—one who was himself nearer to the realization of this fond dream than any other who failed—has left on record a sentiment which does him more honor than would the office he coveted. It is appropriate here: "I would rather be *right* than president." If this be the ruling ambition in life, the accident of *place*—for it is, at best, but an accident—will be valued only as it can be made best to subserve the higher purposes of existence. "I was once called upon," said a popular divine, "by a conscientious member of my church who confided to me the secret wish of his heart to become a preacher of the Gospel. He was a banker, able, consistent, and prosperous, and he desired my advice as to the propriety of forsaking his chosen vocation, that he might the more effectually win souls to Christ. 'Preach the Gospel,' I said to him, 'by all means! Preach it daily and hourly; but do not forsake your business. Your counter is your best pulpit, and the sermons which speak through the common transactions of life have efficacy such as seldom follows the exhortations of those who make a profession of Theology, and are *paid* to preach the Gospel.' " There is common sense as well as sound theology in such advice; and so we would say to every ambitious young man: Be not so careful concerning the particular line of your duties, as you are to make your position the means of scattering blessings around you.

Again, young men are apt to be impatient of preferment, and to place a higher estimate on the intrinsic value of their services than the state of the market will warrant. "I have one objection," said a shrewd business man to us, "to employing graduates of Commercial Colleges. They are apt to think when their preliminary studies are finished, that they know all that is worth learning, and to value their services accordingly. This remark does not apply alone to the graduates of colleges, however truthful it may be in this application. It indicates a constitutional weakness which, like the measles and whooping-cough is quite sure to visit us all at some stage of life. If the disease can be forced outward, or, as physicians say, "driven to the surface," it may be of short duration and leave the system in better condition than before the attack; but if it "strikes in," much skill and courage is required to take the patient safely through.

Of one thing aspirants for position and preferment may rest assured, that the business world will put an estimate on every man entirely independent of his own self-valuation, and in strict accordance with his merits. The universal law of "supply and demand" is as inexorable in prescribing social position as in regulating the markets; and the surest way to attain to a certain desirable point is to cultivate those qualities which are essential to its duties. That detestable cowardice which whines at the "fickleness of fortune," and lays such serious charges at the door of an "unappreciating public," should be purged from every heart. Whoever would win for himself a place must expect to contest the ground, inch by inch, using each obstacle overcome as a stepping-stone to his own advancement.

Above all, let us earnestly beseech you, do not *wait* for something in the future which, to your unpractised eye, promises greater reward than that which is at present attainable. If, by a well-directed effort, you can secure the starting-point which you most desire, as congenial to your tastes, and, in your judgment possessing the germ of success, strike out boldly and fearlessly. Should you fail in this, do not despair, but turn your attention to the next most desirable object. There is nothing so hopeful of future success as *present employment.* Never be idle. There is always something for willing hands to do; and no class of persons have less favor with right-thinking men than those who are "out of employment."

Do not set your heart upon city life. It is a mistaken idea which seems to have taken possession of certain young men reared in the country, that the surest road to wealth and distinction leads through the metropolis. It is true that the majority of those who are eminent for wealth or talent in the large cities are country born; but they compose a meagre share of that almost ceaseless tide of influx which is daily swelling the ranks of the restless horde of adventurers clamorous for something to do—any thing to obtain a foothold in the city. It is true that young men are wanted in every avenue of city life, and that without them the very channels of commerce would become stagnant; but there is already an over supply of those "to the manner born," while beyond the limits of city life there are fields of adventure, and enterprises of industry, actually suffering for strong hands and stout hearts. Besides, there are no qualifications which would secure eminence in city life, that may not be made equally productive, if not more so, in less populous districts. In all large commercial centers, every department of industry is filled with competitors, a few only of whom can, in the nature of the case, stand at the head of their business. In the country, competition is less severe, and appreciation assumes a more genial type. In large cities, the eternal strife necessary not only to obtain position and wealth, but to *retain* them, tends to selfishness and moroseness, shuts out the nobler heart-qualities, fossilizes the affections, and makes men recreant to their own better natures. We do not say that this is so, necessarily; but the commonest observation will substantiate its essential truth.

In conclusion, we would say to the young men, and particularly to such as are about entering upon busy life: Be in earnest. Whatever is worthy of your attention at all, is entitled to your best energies of thought and action. Do not despise the day of small things. If you would be sure of success in any department of life, earn it. Do not place a false estimate upon yourself, but accept the estimate of others as the safest standard upon which to act. Never despair of obtaining what you desire, and have a right to possess. Seek to rise upon your own merits, rather than through the favor of friends. Do not defer action, in hopes of some better starting-point in the future. In whatever you do, act from principle, appealing to your own conscience, and the revealed Word for decision in every doubtful case.

If, by adhering to all these requirements you should at length fail of riches, honor, fame and friends, you may still have the consciousness of a life well spent, and an eternal reward.

INTRODUCTION.

[1] BOOK-KEEPING is the faithful and systematic record of business transactions.

[2] All business transactions consist in an exchange of values; and hence, [3] Book-keeping is the science by which these exchanges are recorded and their results shown.

[4] There are two methods of Book-keeping in general use, distinguished as *Single* and *Double* Entry. Both of these methods may be made to show the same general results, but [5] the latter is conceded to be greatly superior, both from its better facilities for developing results, and its more excellent tests for determining the correctness of the work.

[6] The characteristic feature of Double Entry may be inferred from its distinctive title. [7] Each transaction must be entered to two or more Ledger accounts, as two or more persons or things are affected thereby.

[8] The three main books used in Double Entry are the Day Book, Journal and Ledger. [9] The Day Book and Journal are sometimes combined in one.

[10] The number and character of the auxiliary books depend somewhat on the nature and extent of the business, but more on the amount and kind of information desired. Of these we shall speak more fully hereafter.

[11] THE DAY BOOK

Is the book of original entry, and contains a consecutive history of the transactions in the date and order of their occurrence. [12] It should be plain, concise, and unequivocal in its statements; neither confusing the mind by redundancy of language, nor leaving room for improper inferences from lack of sufficient explanation. [13] As the records in this book are supposed to be made when the transactions and all the circumstances connected therewith are fresh in the mind, it is the only book allowed in court, in cases of litigation. [14] Its importance, from this fact, and also on account of its being the basis of all the results shown by the other books, cannot be overrated.*

* There is, perhaps, no one thing leading more directly to unpleasant and mischievous results than the lack of clearness in the original record of transactions. So palpable is this fact to the minds of many experienced business men, that they insist upon putting in black and white every thing which may affect the interests of any party, however remote; writing out all contracts in full, and even preserving the *figures* upon which all agreements are based. We cannot too strongly commend this practice, either in connection with the Day Book, or in a book kept for the purpose. Much of the difficulty growing out of misunderstandings would be readily avoided by reference to all the circumstances affecting agreements; and particularly if these circumstances are written down *at the time* of such agreements.

[15] The Journal

Is distinct from the Day Book, insomuch as its special use is to decide upon the proper debits and credits involved in each transaction, preparatory to their entry upon the Ledger. [16] It is sometimes combined with the Day Book, and sometimes omitted entirely, [17] its labor being performed mentally. Its essential character and convenience, however, are not to be questioned, [18] and the improvements which have been instituted in its form have rendered it not only important as an interpreter, but valuable for labor-saving purposes.

[19] The Ledger

Is the merchant's encyclopedia. All other books of the series are subservient and tributary to this. [20] Here are shown the results of all the transactions, arranged under distinct and appropriate heads, called accounts. [21] Each account has two sides, a Dr. and a Cr., each governed by well-defined conditions, and showing certain important facts bearing upon the general result.

FORM OF THE PRINCIPAL BOOKS.

We give below the usual forms of the three principal books, showing their characteristic records of the same transaction :

1.—Day Book.

New York, January 1, 1859.

Check-mark.	*Statement of transaction.*	*Dollars.*	*Cents*
√	Bought of James Monroe, on account, 500 Bbls. Flour @ $10	5000	
	2 (*Date*)		
√	Sold Andrew Jackson, for cash, 100 Bbls. Flour @ $10.50	1050	

2.—Journal.

New York, January 1, 1859.

Page of Ledger.	*Ledger Titles.*	*Dr. Dollars.*	*Dr. Cents.*	*Cr. Dollars.*	*Cr. Cents.*
1	Merchandise Dr.	5000			
2	To James Monroe			5000	
	2 (*Date*)				
2	Cash Dr.	1050			
1	To Merchandise			1050	

3.—Ledger.

Date — *Dr.* — MERCHANDISE. — *Cr.* — 1

Month.	*Day.*	*Explanation or Opposite Ledger Title*	*Page of Journal.*	*Dollars.*	*Cents.*	*Month.*	*Day.*	*Explanation or Opposite Ledger Title*	*Page of Journal.*	*Dollars.*	*Cents.*
1859 *Jan.*	1	To James Monroe	1	5000		1859 *Jan.*	2	By Cash	1	1050	

JAMES MONROE. — 2

Month.	*Day.*	*Explanation or Opposite Ledger Title*	*Page of Journal.*	*Dollars.*	*Cents.*	*Month.*	*Day.*	*Explanation or Opposite Ledger Title*	*Page of Journal.*	*Dollars.*	*Cents.*
						1859 *Jan.*	1	By Mdse.	1	5000	

CASH. — 3

Month.	*Day.*	*Explanation or Opposite Ledger Title*	*Page of Journal.*	*Dollars.*	*Cents.*	*Month.*	*Day.*	*Explanation or Opposite Ledger Title*	*Page of Journal.*	*Dollars.*	*Cents.*
1859 *Jan.*	2	To Mdse.	1	1050							

MERCANTILE TERMS.

LEDGER ACCOUNTS.

[22]Every person, species of property or cause, which enters into the transaction, producing a debit or credit, is designated by a *name*, which appears upon the Ledger, and is known as an Account. Each account has two sides, one of which ([23]the left-hand side) is called Debtor, and the other, ([24]the right-hand side,) Creditor.

DEBITS AND CREDITS.

[25]These terms are contradistinctive, and are used to denote the relation in which persons, property and causes stand to the business. [26]In every transaction the sum of these must be equal. Various authors and teachers have spent much effort, and exhausted both time and ingenuity to bring these terms to the test of some general and "infallible" rule; while others have gone so far in the opposite direction as to insist that the items of which they are composed "would form a list of incongruous facts, having no object in common." Their true significance and use can be ascertained in no way so well as by noting particularly their application to the various objects and causes which enter into each transaction. [27]Each Ledger account, by the use of these terms, is made to show an important result of itself.

INTRODUCTION.

Resources and Liabilities.

[28]Any kind of value belonging to the concern is a Resource, and [29]any debt owing by the concern is a Liability.

[30]Cash

Is the title to designate money. [31]The Cash account in the Ledger is debited with all receipts of cash, and [32]credited with all disbursements. [33]The difference between the two sides must, at any time, exhibit a resource of the exact amount of cash on hand. [34]It will be evident that the credit side of Cash account cannot exceed the debit, as more cash cannot be paid out than has been received.

Bills Receivable.

[35]By this title is meant all written obligations of whatever form,* in our possession, for which a certain specified amount is to be *received.* [36]The Bills Receivable account is debited with notes received, and [37]credited with those disposed of, or in any manner canceled. [38]The excess, if any, must be on the debit side, and will indicate that portion of our resources consisting in notes.

Bills Payable.

[39]By this term is meant the written obligations of the concern, for which a specified amount is to be *paid.* Under this head are placed, on the credit side, [40]our notes and acceptances issued, and on the debit side, [41]such of them as have been redeemed. [42]The difference, if there be any, must exhibit our outstanding notes, or our liability on unredeemed paper.

Merchandise.

[43]This term may be more or less general in its application, according as it embraces a larger or smaller variety of property. It usually implies all property purchased or owned by the concern for purposes of traffic, and *remaining in store.* It generally embraces all such

---

* There are, in common use, two forms of written obligations known as "negotiable paper." One is called a *note*, and the other a *draft*, or *acceptance*. They are precisely similar in their legal effect and value, differing only in *form*, from the different circumstances of their origin. A Note originates with the *payer*, and is a voluntary promise to pay, thus:—

NOTE.

$1000.

18 Cooper Institute, New York, *July* 1, 1859.

Sixty days after date I promise to pay S. S. Packard, or order, one thousand dollars, for value received.

H. B. Bryant.

A Draft originates with *the person on whose account the payment is to be made*, being in the form of a request thus:—

DRAFT.

$1000.

New York, *July* 1, 1859.

Sixty Days after date pay to H. D. Stratton, or order, one thousand dollars, value received, and charge to the account of

S. S. Packard.

To H. B. Bryant,
18 Cooper Institute, *New York.*

To make the latter equivalent to the former, it is necessary that the person on whom it is drawn, or of whom the request is made, should respond, which he does by writing across the face "Accepted," and signing his name This is now as virtually a "promise to pay" as the other, and there is no commercial difference between the two.

property, [44] unless the merchant, being curious to know his gains or losses on a particular kind, opens a separate account with that particular kind, under its own special title. [45] This account, or any of its correlative titles, is debited with the cost of the property represented, and [46] credited with its returns. As this kind of property has no standard or stipulated value, like cash and notes, but is usually bought at one price and sold at another, it will be evident that the difference between its sides cannot represent an exact resource; but, rather, [47] the debit showing its cost, and the credit its proceeds, the difference must be a gain or a loss. [48] [49] This is the case, provided we reckon with the proceeds from sales the real value of that which remains unsold.

Real Estate.

[50] This relates to such property as houses and lands, and [51] the account is similar in its objects and teachings to that of Merchandise.

Bank Stock, Railroad Stock, etc.*

[52] Accounts of this kind are not dissimilar to Merchandise and Real Estate, inasmuch as stocks of all kinds are bought and sold at their *market* value, rather than the value written on their face.

Shipment or Adventure.

[53] When property is sent away to be sold by an agent for us we should distinguish it from our merchandise in store by giving it a significant name, such as "Shipment to Buffalo," or "Shipment to A," our agent, or "Adventure" to the place sent. All such accounts are debited with their entire cost, and credited with their proceeds, the difference being a gain or loss. Should we desire to show the result of our business, before receiving advice from our agent, it is proper to reckon this property as a resource at its cost. [54] This is but another name for Merchandise, and is used to distinguish between property *in* store and *out of* store.

Personal Accounts.

[55] Accounts representing personal indebtedness, and designated by the proper names of such persons as sustain relations of debtor and creditor to the concern, are capable of showing either resources or liabilities. [56] They are debited with such sums as, from time to time, the persons may become indebted to the concern, or the concern has paid them, and [57] credited with what they have paid the concern, or the concern may have become indebted to them. [58] An excess of debits in a personal account will thus show a resource, and [59] an excess of credits, a liability.

Stock.

Beginners are apt to misapprehend the term "Stock," supposing it to relate to some kind of property, or rather to property in general. Such is its common signification, but [60] when used as a Ledger title, it means simply the proprietor of the business, or the *stock*-holder. [61] There would be no valid objection to using the proprietor's name instead; [62] but as no real

---

* For a full description of Stocks, please refer to page 185.

good would result from the change, authors, teachers and practical accountants have been content to accept the term which custom has suggested.

This account is usually the first opened in the Ledger, and is important to show [63] the net investment. It is generally credited with the whole investment, and debited with such liabilities as the concern assumes to pay for the proprietor. The difference is the net investment, or what the concern owes the proprietor. [64] It is not customary to use this account during the business, except for the purpose of recording subsequent investments; but it will appear evident to any studious mind that [65] it would be philosophically correct to credit the account with *any* increase of resources, either from actual investment, or from the gains of the business, *just as often as such increase occurs;* as also to debit it with amounts drawn out by the proprietor for his private purposes. [66] Such a course, however, would be attended with many difficulties, and we would, by no means, recommend its adoption; particularly as the same result is achieved with much less labor by the usual method.

From the foregoing remarks we gather the following

GENERAL PRINCIPLES.

I.

The person or persons investing in the business should be credited, under some title, for all such investments, and also for his or their share of the gains. On the other hand, he or they should be debited for all liabilities assumed by the concern for him or them, for all sums withdrawn by him or them from the business, and for such losses as he or they are entitled to share.

II.

Cash account should be debited for all cash receipts, and credited for all disbursements.

III.

Merchandise, and all species of property bought upon speculation, should be debited, under some appropriate head, with the cost of the property represented, and credited with its proceeds.

IV.

Bills Receivable account should be debited with other people's notes, acceptances and other written obligations when they become ours, and credited when they are paid, or otherwise disposed of.

V.

Bills Payable account should be credited with *our* notes, acceptances, or written promises to pay when they are issued, and debited when they are paid or redeemed.

VI.

Personal accounts, such as the names of persons, banks, or other institutions competent to sue or be sued, should be debited under their proper titles when they become indebted to us, or we get out of their debt, and credited when we become indebted to them, or they get out of our debt.

VII.

All expenses, of whatever name, should be debited with the outlay, and all causes, of whatever kind, producing us value, should be credited, under some name, for the amount thus produced.

The foregoing principles are all embraced in the following simple

Formula.

DEBIT WHAT COSTS THE CONCERN VALUE, AND CREDIT WHAT PRODUCES THE CONCERN VALUE.

QUESTIONS FOR REVIEW.

Appropriate answers to all the following questions may be found in the foregoing remarks. The student should be able to give them without hesitation before proceeding to the main portion of the work. The teacher will, of course, exercise his own judgment as to the thoroughness of this review, and not confine himself necessarily to these questions.

1. What is book-keeping? 2. In what do business transactions consist? 3. What has book-keeping to do with the exchange of values? 4. How many methods of book-keeping are there, and how are they distinguished? 5. Which is the better method, and for what reason? 6. What is the characteristic feature of Double Entry? 7. Why must each transaction be entered twice on the Ledger? 8. What are the three main books in Double Entry? 9. Which two are sometimes combined in one? 10. Upon what do the number and character of auxiliary books depend? 11. Describe the Day Book. 12. What should be the character of Day Book expressions? 13. Why is the Day Book alone produced in court? 14. What other importance has it? 15. What is the special use of the Journal? 16. Is it ever omitted? 17. When such is the case, how is its labor performed? 18. Why is the Journal an important book? 19. What is the character of the Ledger? 20. What is shown in the Ledger? 21. How many sides has each account, and what are they? 22. What is an account? 23. Which is the debit side of an account? 24. Which the credit? 25. How are the terms *debit* and *credit* used? 26. What is a sure condition of debits and credits? 27. What importance is attached to Ledger accounts by the use of debits and credits? 28. What is a Resource? 29. What is a Liability? 30. What is meant by the term Cash? 31. For what is Cash account debited? 32. For what credited? 33. What is shown by the difference between the sides? 34. Why cannot the credit side of Cash be the larger? 35. What is meant by Bills Receivable? 36. For what is Bills Receivable account debited? 37. For what credited? 38. What does the difference show? 39. What is meant by Bills Payable? 40. For what is Bills Payable account credited? 41. For what debited? 42. What is shown by the difference? 43. What is usually implied by the term Merchandise? 44. What exceptions are there to this general application? 45. What is Merchandise account debited with? 46. With what credited? 47. What is shown by the difference? 48. Is this always the case? 49. When is it? 50. What is meant by Real Estate? 51. How is the account kept? 52. Wherein are accounts with Bank Stock, Railroad Stock, etc., similar to Merchandise? 53. What is meant by Shipment, or Adventure? 54. Wherein do such accounts differ from Merchandise? 55. What are shown by personal accounts? 56. With what are they debited? 57. With what credited? 58. What does an excess of debits in a personal account show? 59. An excess of credits? 60. What is meant by the term Stock? 31. Would there be any valid objection to using the proprietor's name instead? 62. Why is not this done? 63. What does Stock account show? 64. Is it customary to use this account during business? 65. Would it be improper to do so? 66. Why is it not done?

The student should either commit to memory the seven General Principles laid down, or satisfy the teacher that he fully understands them. It is impossible that he should be able to proceed without the knowledge which they convey.

PLAN OF THE WORK.

THE design of this book, as its title-page imports, is to supply accountants, teachers, and advanced students with appropriate instruction in the principles and application of Book-keeping.

The first four Sets—with their intermediate "Exercises for the Learner"—are devoted mainly to the *theory* of Accounts; and, although each Set is distinct in itself, the same business is continued throughout the whole, with such changes in proprietorship, and such varieties of success and adversity as are necessary to a thorough illustration of the exigencies of business.

The *practical* series commences with Set V., which illustrates an Importing and Jobbing business, the transactions and most of the forms of which were obtained from one of the first establishments of the kind in the city of New York.

The changing of Single to Double Entry which follows, comprises a most important feature, and is introduced in the body of the work, that its lessons may be the more thoroughly understood and appreciated.

The Farmer's Set introduces a new form of Journal and Ledger, which may be used as well in connection with other departments of business.

The Administrator's Set, aside from illustrating the business of an adminstrator or executor, affords a beautiful application of the different theories of recording the transactions of an agent; and will serve well as a brief review of the preceding instructions.

The Commission and Forwarding Sets are among the most practical in the book, having been prepared mainly by an experienced Accountant, whose thorough acquaintance with all the phases of the business has enabled him to cover the exigencies in a manner at once conclusive and satisfactory.

The Banking Set is, by far, the most elaborate in detail, and the most extended both in theory and application of all the departments shown. It has been prepared with great care, and meets the approval of the first bankers in the country, as affording the best exposition of Banking, as it is conducted in our inland cities, which has ever been made public. It is scarcely possible that any person should write up the transactions of this Set understandingly, without obtaining a fair knowledge of the business.

This Set is appropriately followed by a short series of transactions in Exchange and Stock Brokerage, illustrating the main characteristics of these departments of Finance.

The short treatise on Commercial Calculations, which close the work, contains some valuable practice for the student.

SET I.

DAY-BOOK, JOURNAL, AND LEDGER:

REPRESENTING THE BUSINESS OF A SINGLE PROPRIETOR.

BUSINESS PROSPEROUS.

INSTRUCTIONS FOR SET I.

It should be the first care of every student to mark his own progress, not by the ***extent*** of his studies, but by the amount of useful information secured. Particularly should he be careful, in entering upon a new department of study, to thoroughly comprehend each progressive step in the unfolding of its principles, that in their application, he will be enabled to constantly keep in view the ***result*** of his labor. There is no science more liable to be gone over by the easy process of *copying*, than that of Book-keeping, as it is presented in the majority of text books. It is essentially a science of *forms*—or, more properly, its principles are best shown through forms, which, being submitted, offer serious temptations to the mere copyist. We have endeavored to avoid this evil as far as possible, and have, therefore, left for the student plenty of brain-work, which, if he honestly performs, must advance him in the science. The general instructions given in connection with this set will apply with equal force to the succeeding work. They should, therefore, be properly heeded.

To the majority of learners the following forms, and the order of entry to be observed, will be immediately apparent; but for the benefit of those who may not observe so readily, and to follow out the original plan of this work—to divest the study of Accounts of even the appearance of mystery—we give the following brief exposition.

In writing up this first set, it will be well to employ loose paper. If it cannot be obtained readily properly ruled, let the student rule it for himself. This exercise will be found highly serviceable. First, copy the Day Book, observing well the form and expression. Do not *copy* the footings of the money column from the book, but perform the addition without assistance. First add the columns *upwards*, and then prove the result by adding *downwards*. Careful accountants usually write the amount in pencil and carry forward. This is to avoid ink erasures, in case any of the additions should prove, on examination, to be incorrect. The *best* accountants are generally those who do the least *scratching* in their books.

In *journalizing* the transactions, the careful student will always keep the Ledger in view, as the process is simply deciding how the accounts shall stand on the Ledger. Let the decision be made, in every case, in accordance with the principles laid down. In this set the transactions are the most simple that could be suggested, each requiring but one debit and one credit entry. Let the *check-mark* (✓) be made opposite the Day Book entry, [2]*immediately* upon its being journalized—never *before.*

Transferring to the Ledger is called [3]"posting." If the transactions are properly journalized, the labor of posting is simply mechanical. It requires great care, however, and constant watchfulness, and nothing is more common with new beginners than errors in posting. [4]As these errors must all be found and corrected before he can progress, the student will find discretion to be the better part of valor, and, after confusing his brains and sharpening his wits as a detective for a few days, will come to the conclusion that errors are much more easily *avoided* than *detected.*

Commence with the first account indicated on the Journal, and write it as a heading in the Ledger.* See if the amount opposite be in the debit or credit Journal column, and enter it

---

* It is customary and proper always to open as the first accounts in the Ledger, [5]Stock, or the Partners. Some houses, desiring to keep the particular interests of the partners, or the conditions of the copartnership from the public, or from the knowledge of any parties except themselves, keep a private Stock Ledger, to which even the book-keeper has no access. In such cases the books are kept as Stock books, with but one account to represent the capital.

on the corresponding side in the Ledger, using as an expression [6]the opposite journal entry. For example, suppose the journal entry to be "Cash Dr. To Merchandise." This expression implies, of course, that Cash is to be debited, and Merchandise credited. Under Cash account in the Ledger, on the *debit* side we say, "To Merchandise;" and carry the amount to the money column. Also, under Merchandise account on the *credit* side, we say, "By Cash," and carry the amount into the credit column. [7]It is not really necessary that any expression should be made in the Ledger, as the *fact* which we are after is expressed by the *figures.* However, [8]the expression properly made is suggestive of the transaction, and hence is rarely ever omitted by accountants. In posting from the Journal, be careful to enter in the column at the left of the account, and directly opposite, the *page* of the Ledger to which the amount is posted, [9]*immediately after* the amount is entered in the Ledger, but *never before.**

There is nothing in business that pays better than *system;* and it should be rigidly enforced at every step. No legislative body can be properly conducted without an "order of business," much less the intricate machinery of business itself. Let each student feel, therefore, that his success in life will depend, in a great measure, upon his habits of order, and let him be as careful in observing the minute essentials in these exercises, as though his reputation depended upon it. Learners are too apt to think that in these initiatory steps no impor tance should be attached to neatness and accuracy, as no real financial results depend upon them; and, thus reasoning, adopt slovenly habits, which may follow them through life. It is a pungent truth, that "Whatever is worth doing at all, is worth doing well," and nowhere will the sentiment better apply than in the work before us. It is scarcely to be expected that the beginner should be able to carry out his instructions so fully at the first as to avoid entirely the "errors and omissions" which even more experienced persons have to guard against with watchfulness and care; but if he makes each error a lesson which shall preclude its own repetition, his progress will be real as well as apparent, and the study of what he at first considered an abstract and difficult science will become as a pleasant pastime, and infinitely more profitable.

It will be well in all these primary exercises, and until the student is so thoroughly drilled in the principles as to be beyond the recurrence of the little perplexing errors which so much annoy, to employ loose paper ruled for the purpose, and continue to write and re-write all the books, until the proper results are satisfactorily achieved. This kind of *practice* is what is needed to fasten *theory*, and fit one for the more arduous toil of actual business.

Our earnest advice, then, is to attach importance to the most minute instructions bearing either upon principles or arrangement, and, under no circumstances, to progress more rapidly than the subject is fully understood.

---

* This instruction will, of course, apply only to cases where the post-mark is used also as a check mark It is customary with some accountants, in order to facilitate the labor of posting, to enter opposite the Journal entries, *before posting*, the page of the Ledger to which each entry is *to be* posted; and to indicate the *fact* of posting by an additional post-mark. In this case, of course, the *check mark* and not the Ledger page, is subject to the above restriction.

DAY BOOK, SET I.

NEW YORK, JANUARY 1, 1859.

Entry	Rate	Items	$	cts
H. B. Bryant invests in business this day Cash amounting to			5000	
//				
He also owes Peter Cooper on %, which is to be paid from the business .			500	
3				
Bought of Wilson G. Hunt, for Cash,				
400 yds. English Broadcloths	@ $3 . .	$1200		
200 yds. Domestic Cassimeres	@ $1 . .	200	1400	
5				
Sold Digby V. Bell, for Cash,				
200 yds. Broadcloth	@ $4		800	
6				
Sold H. D. Stratton, on %				
10 yds. Broadcloth	@ $4		40	
9				
Bought of Francis & Loutrel, on our note at 90 days,				
50 reams extra Foolscap	@ $3.50 . .	$175		
20 do Superfine Letter	@ 3.00 . .	60	235	
10				
Accepted Peter Cooper's draft on us at 10 days' sight, favor of W. H. Beebe			500	
12				
Sold S. S. Packard, on his note at 60 days,				
10 reams Foolscap	@ $4.00 . .	$40.00		
5 do Letter	@ 3.50 . .	17.50	57	50
14				
Bought, on our note at 40 days,				
250 yds. Black French Cloths	@ $4		1000	
//				
Paid Cash for Set of Books for use of store			20	
16				
Sold R. C. Spencer, for Cash,				
5 reams Foolscap	@ $3.75		18	75
18				
Sold E. G. Folsom, on %				
20 reams Foolscap	@ $4.00	$80		
10 do Letter	@ 3.50	35	115	
22				
Received Cash of H. D. Stratton, on %			20	
23				
Paid our acceptance, favor of W. H. Beebe, in Cash			500	
25				
Sold J. T. Calkins, for Cash,				
150 yds. Black French Cloths	@ $4.50		675	
28				
Bought of J. D. Comstock, on %				
4 dozen Soft Hats	@ $24		96	
31				
Paid Cash as follows:				
For Clerk Hire		$60		
For Rent of Store, one month		100		
For Gas Bill		4	164	
			11141	25

JOURNAL,—SET I.

NEW YORK, JANUARY 1, 1859.

	Dr.		*Cr.*	
CASH Dr.	5000			
To STOCK			5000	
"Stock" is the title chosen to represent the person investing; in this case, H. B. Bryant. It is credited with the investment according to *Principle* 1. Cash is here *received* by the concern, and is made Dr., according to *Principle* 2.				
//				
STOCK Dr.	500			
To PETER COOPER			500	
Stock is debited for the liability assumed by the concern, *Prin.* 1. Peter Cooper is credited, because the concern has assumed to pay him a certain amount, and is, therefore, indebted to him. *Prin.* 6.				
3				
MERCHANDISE Dr.	1400			
To CASH			1400	
Merchandise *cost* $1,400, and is debited, *Prin.* 3. Cash was *paid* for merchandise, and is credited, *Prin.* 2.				
5				
CASH Dr.	800			
To MERCHANDISE			800	
Cash is debited for its receipts, *Prin.* 2. Merchandise is credited for its proceeds, *Prin.* 3.				
//				
H. D. STRATTON Dr.	40			
To MERCHANDISE			40	
H. D. Stratton Dr., *Prin.* 6. Merchandise Cr., *Prin.* 3.				
9				
MERCHANDISE Dr.	235			
To BILLS PAYABLE			235	
Merchandise Dr., *Prin.* 3. Bills Payable Cr., *Prin.* 5.				
10				
PETER COOPER Dr.	500			
To BILLS PAYABLE			500	
Peter Cooper is here made Dr. because we have *canceled* our indebtedness to him by promising to pay the amount to another person whom he has authorized to receive it, *Prin.* 6. Bills Payable is credited for our new liability thus assumed, *Prin.* 5. (For the form of the draft see note on page 15.) The only change wrought in our affairs by this transaction is the transfer of a liability from a personal account to a note. We must now meet this obligation at its maturity, or be disgraced by having our paper protested.				
12				
BILLS RECEIVABLE Dr.	57	50		
To MERCHANDISE			57	50
Bills Receivable Dr., *Prin.* 4. Merchandise Cr., *Prin.* 3.				
	8532	50	8532	50

JOURNAL,—SET I.

NEW YORK, JANUARY 14, 1859.

		Dr.		Cr.	
	Amounts brought forward, ...	8532	50	8532	50
	— // —				
1	MERCHANDISE Dr.	1000			
2	To BILLS PAYABLE			1000	
	Merchandise Dr., *Prin.* 3. Bills Payable Cr., *Prin.* 5.				
	— 15 —				
2	EXPENSES Dr.	20			
1	To CASH			20	
	Expenses Dr., *Prin.* 7. Cash Cr., *Prin.* 2.				
	— 16 —				
1	CASH Dr.	18	75		
1	To MERCHANDISE			18	75
	Cash Dr., *Prin.* 2. Merchandise Cr., *Prin.* 3.				
	— 18 —				
2	E. G. FOLSOM Dr.	115			
1	To MERCHANDISE			115	
	E. G. Folsom Dr., *Prin.* 6. Merchandise Cr., *Prin.* 3.				
	— 22 —				
1	CASH Dr.	20			
1	To H. D. STRATTON			20	
	Cash Dr., *Prin.* 2. H. D. Stratton Cr., *Prin.* 6.				
	— 23 —				
2	BILLS PAYABLE Dr.	500			
1	To CASH			500	
	Bills Payable Dr. *Prin.* 5. Cash Cr., *Prin.* 2.				
	— 25 —				
1	CASH Dr.	675			
1	To MERCHANDISE			675	
	Cash Dr., *Prin.* 2. Merchandise Cr., *Prin.* 3.				
	— 28 —				
1	MERCHANDISE Dr.	96			
2	To J. D. COMSTOCK			96	
	Merchandise Dr., *Prin.* 3. J. D. Comstock Cr., *Prin.* 6.				
	— 31 —				
2	EXPENSE Dr.	164			
1	To CASH			164	
	Expense Dr., *Prin.* 7. Cash Cr., *Prin.* 2.				
		11141	25	11141	25

LEDGER,—SET I.

Dr. (*Liabilities assumed for the Proprietor and Amounts drawn out.*) Stock. (*Capital invested by the Proprietor.*) Cr.

Date			Fol.	$	cts.	Date			Fol.	$	cts.
1859 Jan.	1	To Peter Cooper	1	500		1859 Jan.	1	By Cash	1	5000	
								Invested [illegible]			
								Drawn out [illegible]			
								Net Investment $[illegible]			

Dr. (*Money received.*) Cash. (*Money disposed of.*) Cr.

Date			Fol.	$	cts.	Date			Fol.	$	cts.
1859 Jan.	1	To Stock	1	5000		1859 Jan.	3	By Mdse.	1	1400	
"	5	Mdse.	1	800		"	15	Expense.	2	20	
"	16	"	2	18	75	"	23	Bills Payable	2	500	
"	22	H. D. Stratton	2	20		"	31	Expense	2	164	
"	25	Mdse.	2	675				2084			
		Received 6513 75									
		Disbursed 2084									
		Cash on hand $4429 75									

Dr. (*Our % against him.*) Peter Cooper. (*His % against us.*) Cr.

Date			Fol.	$	cts.	Date			Fol.	$	cts.
1859 Jan	10	To Bills Payable *Canceled*	1	500		1859 Jan.	1	By Stock *Canceled*	1	500	

Dr. (*What Mdse. has cost.*) Merchandise. (*What Mdse. has produced.*) Cr.

Date			Fol.	$	cts.	Date			Fol.	$	cts.
1859 Jan.	3	To Cash	1	1400		1859 Jan.	5	By Cash	1	800	
"	10	Bills Payable	1	235		"	6	H. D. Stratton	1	40	
"	14	" "	2	1000		"	12	Bills Rec'ble	1	57	50
"	28	J. D. Comstock	2	96		"	16	Cash	2	18	75
		Cost 2731				"	20	E. G. Folsom	2	115	
		Proceeds 1706 25				"	25	Cash	2	675	
		*Net Cost** $1024 75						1706 25			

Dr. (*Our % against him.*) H. D. Stratton. (*His % against us.*) Cr.

Date			Fol.	$	cts.	Date			Fol.	$	cts.
1859 Jan	6	To Mdse.	1	40		1859 Jan.	22	By Cash	2	20	
		40									
		20									
		He owes us $20									

* This phrase may not seem, at first view, properly significant; but we apprehend that it is truthful, nevertheless. For, although it may not be true that the difference between the cost of merchandise and the proceeds of a certain portion sold exhibits the *net cost* of that which remains unsold, yet that difference does express what we lack so far, in receiving as much as we have paid for merchandise; therefore, we say it has really *cost* us this difference. If this amount should express the cost over proceeds, *with the property all disposed of*, it would represent a *loss;* but as there is yet actual value in that which remains unsold, we can safely anticipate farther proceeds equal to that value. When this is shown, as it will be in the final exposition, the difference between the cost and the returns will be the *gain* or *loss*.

LEDGER,—SET I.

Dr. (*Our Notes Redeemed.*) Bills Payable. (*Our Notes Issued.*) Cr.

Date			Fo.	Amount	Date			Fo.	Amount
1859 Jan.	23	To Cash	2	500	1859 Jan.	9	By Mdse.	1	235
					"	10	Peter Cooper	1	500
					"	14	Mdse.	2	1000
							Issued 1735		
							Redeemed 500		
							Our Notes outstanding $1235		

Dr. (*Others' Notes received.*) Bills Receivable. (*Others' Notes disposed of.*) Cr.

Date			Fo.	Amount	Date			Fo.	Amount
1859 Jan.	12	To Mdse.	1	57 50					
		Notes on hand $57 50							

Dr. (*Outlay.*) Expense. Cr.

Date			Fo.	Amount	Date			Fo.	Amount
1859 Jan.	15	To Cash	2	20					
"	31	"	2	164					
		Incidental Expenses $184							

Dr. (*Our % against him.*) E. G. Folsom. (*His % against us.*) Cr.

Date			Fo.	Amount	Date			Fo.	Amount
1859 Jan.	20	To Mdse.	2	115					
		He owes us $115							

Dr. (*Our % against him.*) J. D. Comstock. (*His % against us.*) Cr.

Date			Fo.	Amount	Date			Fo.	Amount
					1859 Jan.	28	By Mdse.	2	96
							We owe him $96		

GENERAL STATEMENT.

AFTER posting all our transactions to the Ledger, in accordance with the principles laid down, we are enabled to deduce therefrom the following result:—

Trial Balance.—Face of Ledger.

Dr.					Cr.	
500		*Assumed by the Concern,*	STOCK	*Invested as capital*	5000	
6513	75	*Received*	CASH	*Paid out*	2084	
500		*Our % against him*	PETER COOPER	*His % against us*	500	
2731		*Cost*	MERCHANDISE	*Returns from sales*	1706	25
40		*Our % against him*	H. D. STRATTON	*His % against us*	20	
500		*Our notes redeemed*	BILLS PAYABLE	*Our notes issued*	1735	
57	50	*Others' notes received*	BILLS RECEIVABLE,	*Others' notes disposed of*		
184		*Outlay*	EXPENSE			
115		*He owes us*	E. G. FOLSOM,			
			J. D. COMSTOCK	*We owe him*	96	
11141	25		*Equilibrium*		11141	25

The above statement is called a "Trial Balance," for the reason most apparent; [10]it is a *trial* to ascertain if the debits and credits of the Ledger are equal, or *balance.* [11]It does not, as some suppose, prove the Ledger to be absolutely correct, as there are many circumstances under which the Ledger may balance, and yet be wrong. [12]This form of Trial Balance, however, is so nearly a test, that, under ordinary circumstances, it may be considered satisfactory. [13]By observing the footings you will see that they exactly agree with those of the Journal, which could rarely be the case if any of the Journal entries were omitted to be posted; [14]and as the footings of the Journal columns also tally with that of the Day Book, we must be satisfied that all the original entries have found their way into the Ledger. [15]This leaves but two chances of error in the accounts, viz.: from improper Journal entries, or from posting to the wrong accounts in the Ledger.

[16]It will be seen that, in order to afford this additional test, we have found it necessary to carry into the Trial Balance the *total footings* of the Ledger. [17]If we desired only to test the balance of our Ledger, this would not be necessary, as will be seen from the following example:

[18]Trial Balance.—Differences of Ledger Accounts.

		Dr.		Cr.
STOCK	*Net investment*			4500
CASH	*Amount on hand*	4429	75	
MERCHANDISE	*Net cost*	1024	75	
H. D. STRATTON	*He owes us*	20		
BILLS PAYABLE	*Our outstanding notes*			1235
BILLS RECEIVABLE	*Others' notes on hand*	57	50	
EXPENSE	*Incidental expenses*	184		
E. G. FOLSOM	*He owes us*	115		
J. D. COMSTOCK	*We owe him*			96
	Equilibrium	531		5831

ACCOUNT OF STOCK.

Here we have a test of equal debits and credits quite as satisfactory as the other, and much more brief, [19] upon the principle of *cancellation;* that is, permitting a debit to offset a credit of the same amount, and *vice versa.* These forms have each its peculiar advantages, and [20] accountants have found it very convenient at times to combine them in one. This latter method is exemplified in another portion of the work.

We will now turn our attention more particularly to the object and sphere of the Ledger. [21] The important consideration with the business man, is to keep his resources and liabilities constantly in view. [22] He is thus enabled to estimate, not only theoretically, but practically, the degree of his prosperity. [23] A Ledger properly kept will show, at any time, all resources having a real or fixed value, and all liabilities of whatever kind. There is a class of resources, however, that cannot be determined from the Ledger. [24] This embraces all property purchased on speculation or subject to fluctuation in price. [25] The real value of such property can be ascertained only by actual appraisal.

[26] By reference to the Ledger, in Set I., it will be seen that the only property represented which is subject to fluctuation or speculation, is Merchandise. Had we sold our merchandise for the same price for which we purchased it, [27] the difference between the sides would show the value of that remaining unsold, reckoning it at the cost price; or had we credited Merchandise account with only the cost price of that which was sold, the difference would also show the value of that remaining unsold. But we have adopted the usual plan of crediting the Merchandise account with its *proceeds* from sales, and as it was previously debited with its *cost,* [28] the difference will fail to represent the amount on hand in the exact amount of the discrepancy between the cost and the proceeds from sales: and as we have no means of knowing what this discrepancy is, [29] our only method of ascertaining the value of unsold merchandise, is to go to our shelves and estimate by actual inspection. [30] This process is called "taking an inventory," or "taking an account of stock."

This we now proceed to do, with the following result:

INVENTORY.

Merchandise remaining unsold, Jan. 31, 1859.

		$	cts
190 yards English Broadcloths.	@ $3 . . .	570	
200 do Domestic Cassimeres	@ $1 . . .	200	
100 do Black French Cloths	@ $4 . . .	400	
4 dozen Soft Hats	@ $24 . . .	96	
15 reams Extra Foolscap	@ $3.50 . .	52	50
5 do Letter Paper	@ $3 . . .	15	
		1333	50

We have now sufficient data to enable us to ascertain the exact condition of our affairs on the 31st of January, and to show us, beyond a reasonable doubt, how much has been gained or lost in the month's transactions.

In the statements which follow, such forms have been adopted as would seem to place the facts aimed at in boldest relief, having little reference to symmetry of arrangement, which will be more fully appreciated when the truths inculcated are better comprehended.

It is hoped that the instructions given in this treatise will enable each student to originate his own forms, as well as to detect the truth, in whatever garb it may be clothed.

Statement of Resources.

	1. *Taken from the Ledger.*				
CASH	Amount received	6513	75		
	Amount paid out	2084			
	Balance on hand			4429	75
H. D. STRATTON	Our account against him	40			
	His account against us	20			
	He owes us			20	
BILLS RECEIVABLE	Others' notes received, and on hand			57	50
E. G. FOLSOM	He owes us			115	
	2. *Taken from Inventory.*				
MERCHANDISE	Value of that unsold			1333	50
	Total Resources			5955	75

Statement of Liabilities.

	Taken from the Ledger.				
BILLS PAYABLE	Our Notes issued,	1735			
	" redeemed,	500			
	" outstanding,			1235	
J. D. COMSTOCK	We owe him			96	
STOCK	Amount invested for the proprietor,	5000			
	" assumed for "	500			
	Net investment			4500	
	Total Liabilities, (less unappropriated gains)			5831	

From these statements it appears that the Total Resources of the concern are........ $5955 75
And the Total Liabilities (as shown)........ 5831
Leaving an excess of........ $124 75

It is plain that this *excess* of resources must have accumulated during the business, as at the commencement the resources and liabilities were shown to be equal, upon the principle that the concern owed "Stock" or the proprietor for his net investment. Upon the same principle Stock should be credited with the increase or gain, and, as we have before intimated, it would be proper to do so at any time when such increase or gain can be ascertained. Should we now credit Stock with this excess—$124.75—it will equalize our resources and liabilities, and place the proprietor's account in the same relative position to the business which it occupied at the commencement, viz.: as showing the net investment.

The fact most clearly demonstrated thus far, then, is that, whether apparent or not, the difference between the resources of a concern and its *outside* liabilities is what the concern is owing to the proprietor, or his real net investment, and should be equal to the excess of credits of Stock or Partners' accounts, when those accounts are made to show their adequate results.

This will be more plainly seen in the following schedules:

At the Commencement of Business.

Resources.			*Liabilities.*		
Cash	5000		Peter Cooper	500	
			Stock	4500	
	5000			5000	

On the 31st of January.

Resources.			*Liabilities.*		
Cash	4429	75	J. D. Comstock	96	
Bills receivable	57	50	Bills Payable	1235	
H. D. Stratton	20		Stock	4624	75
E. G. Folsom	115				
Merchandise	1333	50			
	5955	75		5955	75

It will now be evident that [31] when the real condition of any concern can be ascertained, it must exhibit equal resources and liabilities; and that, if at any time during the business this fact is not apparent, it is only from some temporary cause or convenience. Let us see if this cause can be ascertained.

By reference to the statement showing the resources and liabilities of the concern on the 31st of January, it will be seen that all the open Ledger accounts are there represented except Merchandise and Expense. It is true that the amount of merchandise on hand, as shown by the inventory, is reckoned among the resources, but this had nothing whatever to do with the Mercha dise account in the Ledger. Why were these two accounts omitted? [32] Evidently because they were not necessary in showing the resources and liabilities. What then do they show? [33] The debit of Merchandise account shows the cost of merchandise, and the credit the proceeds from sales. If to these proceeds we add the *anticipated* proceeds of that remaining unsold, we shall have the total in value of what has been produced by merchandise. From this amount if we deduct its *cost*, we shall get the *gain* on merchandise; or, if the cost be *more* than the proceeds, the excess will be the *loss.*

The credit side of merchandise account, or the proceeds from sales is	$1706	25
The inventory of merchandise unsold, or the anticipated proceeds is.	1333	50
Making Total Proceeds..................................	3039	75
The debit side or cost of merchandise is........................	2731	
Which, deducted from the proceeds, shows a gain of..............	$308	75

It would now seem, at first view, that we must have made in business, $308.75, and such would be the case if we had incurred no further expenses than what appear on the debit side of our Merchandise account. Now, if we dissect the items which make up our Expense account ($184), we shall find that, of that amount, $20 was paid for a set of books, in which to record our business transactions, and the balance, $164, for store rent and clerk hire. [34]It is reasonable to suppose that all these expenses were incurred to facilitate the purchase and sale of merchandise, as that is the only property we have dealt in; and, such being the case, would it not have been proper to debit Merchandise account with these items, instead of Expense? Had this method been pursued, our gains on merchandise would appear to be $184 less than they now show. Our gains in business would thus be reduced to $124.75, which, it will be seen, exactly agrees with the excess of resources already shown. [35]Inasmuch, therefore, as we choose to exhibit our contingent expenses under special titles, such as "Expense," we must not forget that the amounts thus taken from the legitimate accounts for which the cost was incurred, thereby forcing such account to show an excessive gain, must ultimately be used to cancel that excess. This fact will be more apparent by the following

Statement of Losses and Gains.

MERCHANDISE	Returns from Sales	1706	25		
	Anticipated returns (mdse. unsold) . .	1333	50		
	Total Returns	3039	75		
	Cost	2731			
	Gain on Merchandise			308	75
EXPENSE	Outlay	184			
	No Returns				
	Loss on Expenses			184	
	Net Gain			124	75

From the foregoing schedules, it will be readily seen that [36]there are two classes of accounts,* [37]from one of which can be ascertained the *resources* and *liabilities* of the concern, and from the other, the unappropriated *gains* and *losses*. We learn, moreover, that whenever the resources and liabilities of a concern can all be shown they *must be equal;* and that, [38]if at any time these are not apparent on the Ledger, it is from the use of certain temporary accounts for the purpose of containing the gains and losses of the business, until such time as it may be convenient or desirable to distribute them under their proper accounts.

As we shall need frequently to refer to these two classes, and desire them in their application to be thoroughly understood, we will denominate them REAL and REPRESENTATIVE, with the simple definition that [39]*Real* accounts are such as exhibit, from an excess of debits or credits, real *resources* or *liabilities*, and [40]*Representative* such as represent the stockholder or stockholders, by exhibiting such *gains* or *losses* as are ultimately to be carried to his or their proper accounts. [41]When it is further understood that all gains in business must appear, either in an *increase* of *resources*, or a *decrease* of *liabilities;* and that all losses must appear, either in a *decrease* of *resources*, or an *increase* of *liabilities*, it will be sufficiently plain that the two classes of accounts we have named, must always run exactly parallel.

* Formerly authors and teachers were accustomed to divide accounts into *three* classes, under various titles So far as we know to the contrary, the credit of first reducing this number to *two*, and of giving substantial reasons for the division in clear and satisfactory analyses, belongs to THOMAS JONES, author of "Book-keeping and Accountantship," published in 1853. Mr. Jones distinguishes by the appellative terms "Primary" and "Secondary," classifying "Stock" or Partners' accounts with those which *do not* show resources or liabilities.

We will now make a practical application of these lessons, in restoring our Ledger to its proper condition. By referring to the Stock account, you will see that it has remained unchanged since the commencement of the business; while we know, from the foregoing statements, that the business itself has changed in a material sense. You may remember that [42]Stock account was opened for the purpose of showing the net capital or investment. [43]It answered this purpose thoroughly at the start, and would do so even now, if the capital or investment had remained the same. But such is not the case, and consequently, Stock account fails of its full mission in just the amount of the fluctuation of invested capital. We have already shown, by two processes, what this fluctuation is, and it is now [44]with a view to restoring Stock account to its normal condition, that we "close up" the Ledger accounts, exhibiting the grand result by the balances of resources and liabilities. We wish this process distinctly noted, as the entire theory we have sought to advance is herein practically demonstrated.

QUESTIONS FOR REVIEW.

GENERAL INSTRUCTIONS.

1. Why should the student keep the Ledger in view when journalizing? 2. When should the check-mark (✓) be made in the Day Book, and where? 3. What is transferring to the Ledger called? 4. Why is it necessary to observe care in posting? 5. What is the first account opened in the Ledger? 6. When an account is posted to the Ledger what expression should be made? 7. Is it necessary that *any* expression should be made? 8. Of what should the Ledger expression be suggestive? 9. When should the page of the Ledger to which an amount is posted be entered in the Journal, and where?

GENERAL STATEMENT.

10. Why is a Trial Balance so called? 11. Does the Trial Balance prove the Ledger to be absolutely correct? 12. Is the test afforded by the Trial Balance usually satisfactory? 13. What test is afforded proving all the Journal entries to have been posted? 14. What to prove that all the original entries have been journalized? 15. When these precautions are used, how many chances are there for errors which may escape the Trial Balance test? 16. What must be the condition of the Trial Balance which affords these tests? 17. Would it be necessary to carry the *total footings* into the Trial Balance did we not desire this additional security? 18. Can a correct Trial Balance be had which will contain simply the *balances* of the Ledger accounts? 19. Upon what principle is this effected? 20. Are these two forms of Trial Balance ever combined in one? 21. What is the important consideration with the business man in connection with his accounts? 22. What does this enable him to do? 23. What will a Ledger properly kept show at any time? 24. What kind of resources cannot be shown from the Ledger? 25. How is the real value of such property ascertained? 26. Is there any property of this kind represented in Set I., and what is it? 27. What will the difference in the sides of Merchandise account show, if debited and credited with the same value? 28. When the Merchandise account is debited with the cost of merchandise, and credited with its proceeds, how much will the difference between the sides fail of showing the value of merchandise unsold? 29. When the account is so kept what is our only method of ascertaining the value of merchandise unsold? 30. What is the process called? 31. When the real condition of a concern is stated, what must it exhibit? 32. In the statement of resources and liabilities on page 29, why were not the Ledger accounts of Expense and Merchandise taken cognizance of? 33. What is shown by these accounts? 34. Is there any similarity in these accounts? 35. What must be borne in mind with reference to the nature of such special accounts as Expense? 36. How many classes of accounts are there? 37. What can be learned from each? 38. When the resources and liabilities of a concern do not show to be equal, what must be the reason? 39. What accounts are called Real? 40. What Representative? 41. How is it shown that these two classes of accounts run exactly parallel? 42. For what purpose is Stock account opened? 43. Why does not Stock account perpetually represent the net investment? 44. For what purpose is it necessary to close up certain of the Ledger accounts?

CLOSING THE LEDGER.

This phrase is much more technical than descriptive; and, although the process may be easily learned, experience has taught us that [1] the great difficulty in the matter with learners is to be able clearly to understand the *object* to be attained by "Closing the Ledger." We will endeavor to explain.

[2] To "close up" an account in the Ledger is to put an end to its *current* condition. This may be for a temporary purpose only, or it may be final. [3] In closing a *Real* account, if the sides be equal, it is necessary only to add up the two sides, and draw red lines underneath the amounts of each. The account thus becomes canceled, and, so far as our business is affected, is as though it had never been. [4] If the sides be *not* equal, and we desire to close the account, for the purpose of showing the result, we enter upon the *smaller side*, in red ink, an amount which will make it equal to the larger side. This will, of course, be the difference between the sides, or the *excess* of the larger, and must be shown as such, either in a continuation of the same account, or in another account of the same import. The balance thus shown will be either a *resource* or a *liability*. If the sides of a *Representative* account be equal, and the proceeds all shown, it is also closed by adding up the debit and credit columns, and drawing red lines underneath; [5] if *unequal*, the excess will be entered on the smaller side in red ink, and will represent a *gain* or a *loss*. The columns will then be added, as in the other case.

So much for the *process*. Let us now ascertain *for what purpose* the Ledger accounts are closed at all, and each step will then suggest its own philosophy. We have already shown that [6] just as soon as the invested capital begins to fluctuate or change in value, Stock account ceases to represent the real interest of the proprietor. [7] This is simply because the gains and losses are not carried to Stock account *when they occur*, but are allowed to remain in the Representative accounts. [8] As often, therefore, as we wish to show what is the proprietor's interest in the business, or what the concern is owing him, we must take these gains and losses from his Representative accounts, and carry them to the Stock account. We do this by "closing up" the accounts, and transferring their balances. [9] The usual method is to open a general account, called "Profit and Loss," or "Loss and Gain," and first transfer to it all the gains and losses. [10] This enables us to get the net gain or the net loss in one amount, which we carry to Stock; [11] if it be a net gain, it will go to the credit side of the account, increasing the investment; [12] if a loss, to the debit side, decreasing the investment.

[13] This can all be accomplished without disturbing the *Real* accounts. [14] If, however, it is desired to show in a tabular form the resources and liabilities of the concern, we can easily do so by opening an account for this purpose called "Balance," and close the Real accounts into it. [15] Or if we wish to show an era in our business, we can close up these accounts, and bring the balances down, as shown in the Ledger which follows.

[16] The object, then, of closing the Ledger accounts is to restore the proprietor's account to the same relative position towards the business which it occupied at the commencement, viz., as showing the net investment, or net interest of the proprietor.

[17] An entry in red ink on the Ledger, denotes that the amount thus written is *to be transferred*, either to some other account, or to another position under the same account. It also shows that the entry is *first* made in the Ledger, not having passed through the usual preliminary books of entry. [18] Red ink entries are *always* transferred to the *opposite side* from where they first appear, [19] for the reason that they indicate an excess of that side.

ORDER OF CLOSING.

In closing the Ledger accounts, for the purposes of a general exposition of affairs, the following order should be observed:

1.

[20] Open an account with "Loss and Gain," (if not already opened,) and another with "Balance;" [21] the former to exhibit the *losses* and *gains*, and [22] the latter the *resources* and *liabilities*.

2.

[23] Ascertain from the inventory if any property remains unsold; and, if so, credit each account for which such property was originally debited with the value of that unsold, making the entry *in red ink*, "By Balance," and transferring the amount directly to the debit side of Balance account, making this entry *in black ink*, "To Merchandise," or "To Real Estate," or any other account from which the amount is transferred. [24] The Ledger accounts will each show, now, one of the four following results, viz: a Resource, a Liability, a Gain, or a Loss.

3.

[25] Omitting Stock account, (or Partners' accounts,) commence with the first account in the Ledger. First ascertain which of the above results it shows, and make the closing entry accordingly. If the difference represent a resource, or a liability, enter upon the smaller side, *in red ink*, "*To*," or "*By* Balance," as the case may be, and transfer the amount *in black ink* to the opposite side of Balance account. If the difference represent a gain or loss, enter on the smaller side in red ink, "To" or "By Loss and Gain," and transfer the amount, in the same manner to Loss and Gain account. Close all the accounts (except Stock or Partners') and transfer the balances as directed. [26] The Loss and Gain account will now show, on the debit side, all the losses, and on the credit side, all the gains, the difference being the net gain or net loss. [27] The Balance account will show on the debit side all the resources, and on the credit side all the liabilities, (excepting the result of Stock or Partners' accounts,) the difference being the real interest or present investment of the proprietor or proprietors.

4.

[28] Take a "Second Trial Balance," or a Trial Balance of the remaining open accounts: Stock or Partners', Loss and Gain, and Balance. [29] If the balances have been properly transferred the debits and credits of these accounts, taken together, must be equal.

5.

[30] Close the Loss and Gain account into Stock, or, if it be a partnership business, into the partners' accounts, dividing the gain or loss according to agreement. [31] The Stock or Partners' accounts will now show the original investment, increased by the gain, or decreased by the loss; the difference being the *present* net investment. [32] As the Balance account shows the same thing, they must, of course, agree.

6.

[33] Close Stock account (or Partners' accounts) into Balance account, which must equalize that account, it showing now, [34] on one side the total resources, and on the other the total liabilities, and presenting in the most condensed form, the exact present condition of the business.

The student will please observe this order in making the closing entries which follow. It will be seen that this Ledger presents the same accounts as the preceding, and differs only in having disposed of the gains and losses. The balances of the *Real* accounts (except Stock) agree with the Trial Balance, showing balances on page 27, while the *Representative* accounts have ceased to exist, their results being exhibited in the Stock account.

Dr. Stock. Cr.

Date			Fo.	$	cts.	Date			Fo.	$	cts.
1859 Jan.	1	To Peter Cooper	1	500		1859 Jan.	1	By Cash	1	5000	
"	31	*Balance*	2	4624	75	"	31	Loss and Gain	4	124	75
				5124	75			5124 75 / 500 / 4624 75		5124	75
						Feb.	1	By Balance		4624	75

Dr. Cash. Cr.

Date			Fo.	$	cts.	Date			Fo.	$	cts.
1859 Jan.	1	To Stock	1	5000		1859 Jan.	3	By Mdse.	1	1400	
"	5	Mdse.	1	800		"	15	Expense	2	20	
"	16	Mdse.	2	18	75	"	23	Bills Payable	2	500	
"	22	H. D. Stratton	2	20		"	31	Expense 2084	2	164	
"	25	Mdse.	2	675		"	31	*Balance*		4429	75
		6513 75 / 2084 / 4429 75		6513	75					6513	75
Feb.	1	To Balance		4429	75						

Dr. Peter Cooper. Cr.

Date			Fo.	$	cts.	Date			Fo.	$	cts.
1859 Jan.	10	To Bills Payable	1	500		1859 Jan.	1	By Stock	1	500	

Dr. Merchandise. Cr.

Date			Fo.	$	cts.	Date			Fo.	$	cts.
1859 Jan.	3	To Cash	1	1400		1859 Jan.	5	By Cash	1	800	
"	10	Bills Payable	1	235		"	6	H. D. Stratton	2	40	
"	14	" "	2	1000		"	12	Bills Receivable	2	57	50
"	28	J. D. Comstock 2731	2	96		"	16	Cash	3	18	75
"	31	*Loss and Gain*		308	75	"	20	E. G. Folsom	3	115	
						"	25	Cash	3	675	
						"	31	*Balance*		1333	50
				3039	75			3039 75 / 2731 / 308 75		3039	75
Feb.	1	To Balance		1333	50						

Dr. H. D. Stratton. Cr.

Date			Fo.	$	cts.	Date			Fo.	$	cts.
1859 Jan.	6	To Mdse.	1	40		1859 Jan.	22	By Cash	2	20	
						"	31	*Balance Inv.*		20	
		40 / 20 / 20		40						40	
Feb.	1	To Balance		20							

Dr. Bills Payable. Cr.

Date			Fo.	$	cts.	Date			Fo.	$	cts.
1859 Jan.	23	To Cash	2	500		1859 Jan.	9	By Mdse.	1	235	
"	31	*Balance*		1285		"	10	Peter Cooper	1	500	
						"	14	Mdse.	2	1000	
				1735				1735 / 500 / 1235		1735	
						Feb.	1	By Balance		1235	

LEDGER, SET I.—CLOSED.

Bills Receivable.

Dr.						Cr.					
1859						1859					
Jan.	12	To Mdse.	1	57	50	*Jan.*	31	*By Balance.*		57	50
		To Balance		57	50						

Expense.

Dr.						Cr.					
1859						1859					
Jan.	15	To Cash	2	20		*Jan.*	31	*By Loss and Gain.*		184	
"	31	"	2	164							
				184						184	

E. G. Folsom.

Dr.						Cr.					
1859						1859					
Jan.	20	To Mdse.	2	115		*Jan.*	31	*By Balance*		115	
Feb.	1	To Balance		115							

J. D. Comstock.

Dr.						Cr.					
1859						1859					
Jan.	31	*To Balance*		96		*Jan.*	28	By Mdse.	2	96	
						Feb.	1	By Balance		96	

Loss and Gain.

Dr.						Cr.					
1859						1859					
Jan.	31	To Expense		184		*Jan.*	31	By Mdse.		308	75
"	31	*Stock*		124	75						
				308	75					308	75

Balance.

Dr.						Cr.					
1859						1859					
Jan.	31	To Mdse.		1333	50	*Jan.*	31	By Bills Payable		1235	
"	31	Cash		4429	75	"	31	J. D. Comstock		96	
"	31	H. D. Stratton		20		"	31	Stock		4624	75
"	31	Bills Receivable		57	50						
"	31	E. G. Folsom		115							
				5955	75					5955	75

GENERAL REMARKS.

By referring to the Balance account in the preceding Ledger, we shall find [35]a full statement of the resources and liabilities of our concern on the 31st of January. Should we desire to open a new set of books on the 1st of February, [36]we have all the necessary information for that purpose; or we can represent the state of our affairs in our present Ledger, [37]simply by bringing down the balances showing resources and liabilities under their separate accounts, instead of transferring them to Balance account. [38]This we have done. It will now be evident that [39]there was no actual necessity of opening a Balance account; the only object in doing so was [40]to exhibit, *under one title*, the resources and liabilities. [41]In practice, this account is rarely ever exhibited on the Ledger, but [42]its contents are shown in a separate Balance Sheet, various forms of which we have given elsewhere in this work.

It is often a matter of wonder to the new student in Accounts why the difference between the sides of Stock account, being transferred to Balance account, should equalize it. A moment's thought will dispel the mystery. [43]Before closing any of the accounts in the Ledger, we ascertain by the Trial Balance that our debits and credits are equal, and we take care, in every step, to keep them so; for whenever we debit any account, we credit some other account with the same amount, and *vice versa.* In "closing up" the Ledger, we call this process "transferring;" but it is exactly [44]equivalent to posting. Let us see if this is not so.

[45]The first entry of this kind was to *credit* Merchandise and *debit* Balance with the property unsold. So far as this affected our Merchandise account, it was equivalent to selling the merchandise, and receiving therefor an absolute resource, which we have called "Balance," but which *is* Merchandise, reckoned at its true value. We can now treat our Merchandise account as if the property were all disposed of. This we do, in fact, by representing the difference between the sides as a *gain.* We now *debit* Merchandise account with this gain, and *credit* Loss and Gain, preserving, as before, our fundamental rule of "equal debits and credits." We pursue this policy with all the accounts, transferring always to the opposite side from that on which the closing entry is made, and thus maintaining a perpetual equilibrium. [46]The balances which we transfer to Loss and Gain account might, with equal propriety, be carried directly to Stock account, but that [47]it is desirable to exhibit, in one amount, the net gain or loss during the business. It will be borne in mind, that the balancing or closing of an account is simply [48]upon the principle of cancellation. The account is made to "balance" only [49]by taking away the *excess.* But that excess appears [50]elsewhere, and *on the same side* of the Ledger. These balances of gains, losses, resources, and liabilities are thus transferred to the two accounts, "Loss and Gain" and "Balance," thus exhibiting in the former, all the gains and losses, and in the latter all the resources and liabilities. This leaves, except the Stock account, but these two accounts open, which, taken together, must have equal debits and credits, [51]as we have never failed in each step to produce this result. The Stock account, as it now stands, shows [52]the capital at *commencing*, and the Balance account [53]the capital at *closing.* There must, of course, be a discrepancy between these two accounts, [54]exactly equal to the gain or loss in business. Now as the gains and losses are all shown in the Loss and Gain account, [55]the difference between the sides being the net gain or loss, it follows that this difference must exactly equal the discrepancy between the capital at commencing, and the capital at closing; or, in other words, between the Stock and Balance accounts. If, then, we close the Loss and Gain account into Stock, we shall have exhibited in Stock account, [56]first, the capital at commencing, and next, the gain or loss during business, which, together, must equal the

capital at closing. [57] The Balance account showing all the resources, and all the outside liabilities at closing, must represent the same amount; and hence, the balance of either transferred to the other, must equalize the sides.

This is usually one of the most difficult points of comprehension in the student's path, but all such difficulties give way readily to a little momentum of reason and determination.

It will be apparent that throughout the discussion thus far, we have drawn a marked distinction between the *proprietor* and the *business.* It is necessary that this distinction be clearly apprehended before we proceed farther; as, if there is any thing peculiar in this treatise, it will be found to emanate from this recognition.* The great fact to which we refer, is strikingly apparent in the first entry upon our books, which was to credit Stock with the investment. Now if we inquire *who* credits Stock, we shall be forced to the conclusion that there is a party represented here, entirely distinct from stock, or the proprietor; as it would be sheer nonsense to express the fact that a man owes *himself.* The person competent to construct a system of philosophy on such a basis, would be able to show how a man might lift himself by his own boot-straps, or get rich by taking money from one pocket and putting it in the other. The fact clearly stated is, that the books represent [58] the *concern,* and not the proprietor, and the account opened with "Stock" is precisely [59] the same as that opened with any other person, except that the *final settlement* with Stock will not take place until the business ceases, or he withdraws from it. If Stock account, then, shows an excess of credits, [60] it is as much a liability as Peter Cooper's account, and must eventually be canceled by payment as well. To make this still more plain, let us see in what light Stock himself views it. Suppose the investment in this enterprise is only one among many which he has made. Suppose he has, also, a mill, wherein he has invested $10,000; and a tannery where he has invested $15,000. How will he keep an account with these three distinct concerns in his private books? According to the principles of accounts, he will charge the mill, the tannery, and the store, each with its cost, or the amount invested in it. He does this upon the principle of holding these concerns responsible for such investment, and upon the full expectation that they will eventually pay him what they thus owe. Our reasons for crediting Stock on the books of the store (which is the concern here represented) will now be sufficiently apparent, and the attentive student cannot fail to see that this credit is as much a liability of the concern as any credit on our books.

If there be still any doubt as to the correctness of this position, let us dissipate it, at once, by analyzing the second entry in the preceding series of transactions. The first entry, according to our theory, gave us a resource in cash of $5000, and a liability to Stock of the same amount. The second entry, which we propose now to consider, created a new liability to Peter Cooper of $500, but, at the same time, reduced the former liability to Stock in the same amount; so that the relative position of our resources and liabilities was not changed. The reason for this entry was this: Stock was owing Peter Cooper $500, which he did not

---

* All authors whom we have consulted—and "their name is legion"—agree that "Stock," as a Ledger title, represents the proprietor, or as some few elegantly express it, "the *owner of the books;*" while not one among them attempts to give a reason for crediting this account with the investment, except that it is used to represent the capital; and of all the *rules* given, both fallible and "infallible," for journalizing, no one attempts to apply such rules to the first, or opening entry. Now, it is impossible, grammatically, that the same set of books should, at the same time, represent two distinct and opposite interests. All the expressions used in the books purport to emanate from some person or persons having a common interest in the transactions, and all the entries, of whatever nature, must necessarily be the exponent of the same interests. A pronoun in the first person, either expressed or understood, cannot properly represent two separate and distinct parties in the same sentence, or the same discussion. So, if it be necessary, in crediting Stock for the original investment to assume a position *distinct* from Stock, the same necessity must exist, with equal force, through all the subsequent entries. The more this position is studied, the more apparent will be its truthfulness.

care to pay from his private funds. He reasons thus: I have $5000 which I can invest in this business, but I also owe Peter Cooper $500, which is not yet due. Now I will invest this capital upon the condition that this liability be paid by *the concern* when it matures. The concern accepts this proposition, and first credits Stock with his investment, and next debits him with the amount *assumed* for him. The liability to Peter Cooper is now transferred from Stock's private books to those of this concern, and the concern's liability to Stock is decreased to the extent of the new liability thus assumed.

EXERCISES FOR THE LEARNER.

FIRST SERIES.

It is hoped that the preceding exercises in their fullness of explanation and illustration will enable the student to carry successfully through a series of transactions embracing the same general principles. The following memoranda will comprise a month's business, and the student is required to write up therefrom all the books represented in the preceding series. The form and arrangement of the books he will of course gather from the examples given; and he will find no point of difficulty which has not been fully discussed in connection with Set I. These exercises will require him to study well the form of expression in the Day Book, and the principles which govern the Journal, and will afford an excellent test of his proficiency in what he has passed over. The great objection to be urged against published text books in this science is, that too little is left for the mind of the student. There is a wide difference between *copying* the forms in Accounts and *originating* them; and hence we have followed each exemplified set of books, with a series of transactions embracing the same principles—which the student is required to put in proper form in the various books—and giving the *result* of the entries which he is required to produce. If we are not greatly mistaken, this will be found the most useful portion of the work, and should, under no circumstances, be omitted.

Memoranda.

Jan. 1st, Commenced business with a cash capital of $6000. 2d, Bo't of E. R. Felton, for cash, 100 bbls. Flour, @ $8. 3d, Sold W. E. Crocker on %, 20 bbls. Flour, @ $8.50. 4th, Bo't on our note, @ 30 days, of C. S. Sill, 20 pieces Calico, @ $3; 10 do. figured Silks, @ $9. 5th, Sold E. C. Packard, for cash, 30 bbls. Flour, @ $8.25. 6th, Paid cash for set of Books for use of store, $15. 7th, Bo't of E. P. Selmser, for cash, 200 bbls. Genesee Flour, @ $9; paid Drayage on same, in cash, $3. 10th, Sold Hiram A. Pryor on his note @ 30 days, 100 bbls. Genesee Flour, @ $9.50. 12th, Sold W. H. Clark, for cash, 10 pieces Calico, @ $3.75. 15th, Paid Cash for repairing store, $15. 16th, Bo't of J. D. Williams, on %, 50 pieces Merrimac Prints, @ $5. 17th, Sold R. C Spencer, on %, 25 pieces Merrimac Prints, @ $5.35. 20th, Sold R. W. Hoadley, for cash, 50 bbls. Genesee Flour, @ $9.50. 21st, Received Cash, in full, of W. E. Crocker's %. 22d, Paid J. D. Williams Cash on %, $100. 25th, Paid Clerk hire in full to Feb. 1, $50. 27th, Sold E. B. Rockwell, on %, 50 bbls. Genesee Flour, @ $10. 29th, Received Cash on % of E. B. Rockwell, $250. 31st, Paid Store rent, in cash, $100.

INVENTORY.*

Mdse. remaining unsold Jan. 31st.

50 bbls. Flour,	@ $10		$500
10 pieces Calico,	@ 3		30
25 do Merrimac Prints,	@ 5		125
10 do figured Silks,	@ 9		90
			$745

If these accounts are properly kept, the first Trial Balance and the Balance Account will each represent the following statement:

First Trial Balance.

		Stock	6000	
7180		Cash	2883	
3003		Merchandise	2513	75
		Bills Payable	150	
180		Expense		
950		Bills Receivable		
100		J. D. Williams	250	
170		W. E. Crocker	170	
133	75	R. C. Spencer		
500		E. B. Rockwell	250	
12216	75		12216	75

Balance Account.

Resources			*Liabilities.*		
Cash	4297		Bills Payable	150	
Merchandise	745		J. D. Williams	150	
Bills Receivable	950		Stock	6075	75
R. C. Spencer	133	75			
E. B. Rockwell	250				
	6375	75		6375	75

* The student will please ascertain if this is correct.

QUESTIONS FOR REVIEW.

CLOSING THE LEDGER.

1. What is the chief difficulty with learners in closing the Ledger? 2. What is the effect of "closing up" an account? 3. How is a *Real* account closed when the sides are equal? 4. How, when unequal? 5. How is a *Representative* account closed when the sides are unequal? 6. At what stage of the business does Stock account cease to represent the proprietor's interest? 7. Why is this? 8 How can we at any time ascertain the proprietor's interest? 9. What is the usual method of carrying gains and losses to Stock account? 10. What is the advantage of opening a "Loss and Gain" account? 11. To which side of Stock account are gains carried, and how do they affect that account? 12. To which side are losses carried, and how do they affect the account? 13. Can the gains and losses be thus disposed of, without disturbing the *Real* accounts? 14. What is the object of opening a "Balance" account? 15. How can we dispose of the amounts properly carried to Balance account, if we wish merely to show an era in our business? 16. What, then, is the prime object in closing the Ledger accounts? 17. What does an entry in *red ink* on the Ledger denote? 18. How are red ink entries always transferred? 19. Why transferred to the *opposite* side?

ORDER OF CLOSING.

20. What is the first step in closing the Ledger? 21. What results are shown by the "Loss and Gain" account? 22. What by the Balance account? 23. What is the second step? 24. When the inventories are all entered to the proper accounts, what will be shown by the Ledger? 25. What is the third step? 26. When the balances have been properly transferred, what will the "Loss and Gain" account show? 27. What the "Balance" account? 28. What is the fourth step? 29. Of what use is the "Second Trial Balance?" 30. What is the fifth step? 31. When the net gain or loss has been transferred to Stock or Partners' accounts, what will those accounts show? 32. Why must the balance of these accounts agree with the balance of Balance account? 33. What is the sixth step? 34. What will the Balance account show when complete?

GENERAL REMARKS.

35 What is shown by the Balance account in Set I? 36. Have we sufficient data here to enable us to open a new set of books? 37. How can we represent the state of our affairs in the present Ledger? 38. Has this result been shown? 39. Was there really any necessity for opening a Balance account? 40. Why was it done? 41. Is this account often exhibited on the Ledger in actual business? 42. How are its contents otherwise shown? 43. Why does not the transferring of balances from one account to another disturb the equilibrium of the Ledger? 44. What is this transferring of balances equivalent to? 45. Will you explain this by analysis? 46. Where might the balances carried to the Loss and Gain account properly be transferred? 47. Why is it not done? 48. Upon what principle are accounts "balanced?" 49. How is an account made to balance? 50. Where does this excess subsequently appear? 51. When all the balances except Stock are transferred to Loss and Gain and Balance accounts, why must these, with Stock account, contain equal debits and credits? 52. What is shown by the Stock account at this stage? 53. What by the Balance account? 54. What discrepancy is there in these two accounts? 55. Why will this discrepancy exactly tally with the difference between the sides of Loss and Gain account? 56. What will the Stock account show when this discrepancy is transferred from the Loss and Gain account? 57. Why will the Stock account now agree with Balance? 58. What particular interest is always represented by a set of books? 59. What relation does Stock account sustain towards the business? 60. If the credit side of Stock account exceeds the debit, how does it affect the business?

INDEX TO LEDGER B,—SET II.

The purpose and importance of an Index to the Ledger will be immediately apparent. Where there is a large number of accounts much time is saved by having an alphabetical list to which to refer. The example given below will be sufficient to show the general purport of an index, but does not present the best form. The form in general use is so common and so very simple, that any attempt at explanation would be useless. We have not thought it necessary to give the index in connection with any other Set, as it would merely occupy space without affording information. We have chosen this page instead of the one next preceding the Ledger, because it best answers our purpose so to do.

Index.

A.	**N.**
B. Bryant, H. B. . . . . 1 Bills Receivable . . . . 1 Bills Payable 1	**O.**
C. Cash . . . . 1 Comstock, J. D. 2	**P.** Packard, S. S. 2
D. Dawson, Warren & Hyde 2	**Q.**
E. Expense 2	**R.** Real Estate 2
F. Folsom, E. G. 1	**S.** Stratton, H. D. 1
G. Gantz, Jno. W.	**T.**
H.	**U.** Union Bank Stock . . . . 2 Union Bank 2
I. J. Ivison & Phinney 2	**V.**
K.	**W.**
L.	**X. Y.**
M. Merchandise . . . . 1 Mortgage Payable 2	**Z**

SET II.

DAY-BOOK, JOURNAL, LEDGER, CASH-BOOK, BILL-BOOK.

[*Continuation of Set I.*]

BUSINESS PROSPEROUS.

DAY-BOOK,—SET II.

NEW YORK, FEBRUARY 1, 1859.

The following Resources and Liabilities with which we commence business this day, are taken from the Balance Account of H. B. Bryant's Ledger A.*

Resources.

√	Cash in hand	$4429 75		
	Notes on hand	57 50		
	Merchandise per Inventory	1333 50		
	E. G. Folsom owes on %	115 00		
	H. D. Stratton owes on %	20 00	5955	75

Liabilities.

√	Notes outstanding	$1235 00		
	Balance due J. D. Comstock	96 00		
	H. B. Bryant's net Capital	4624 75		
		$5955 75		

"

√	Sold S. S. Packard 2 Doz. Soft Hats. . . . @ $36		72	
	Received in Payment,			
	Cash	$20		
	Balance on %	52—$72		

2

√	Received Cash of H. D. Stratton, in full of %		20	

3

√	Bought of Ivison and Phinney,			
	150 Sets Spencerian Writing Books . . . . . @ 75c .	$112 50		
	100 Copies Bryant & Stratton's Book-keeping @ $1 .	100 00	212	50
	Paid them, Cash 50 00			
	Order on E. G. Folsom 50 00			
	Balance on % 112 50	—212 50		

5

√	Bought of Dawson, Warren & Hyde, on %			
	50 "Tip Top" Gold Pens, first quality . . . . @ $1.25		62	50

7

√	Exchanged Notes with Digby V. Bell for our mutual accommodation, each drawn at 30 days		500	

8

√	Sold J. H. Goldsmith, for Cash,			
	50 Sets Spencerian Writing Books . . . . @ 85c. .	42 50		
	25 do Bryant and Stratton's Book-keeping . . @ $1.12 .	28 00		
	5 Reams Letter Paper . . . . @ $3 . .	15 00		
	1 Doz. Gold Pens . . . . @ $1.50 .	18 00	103	50
			6926	25

* Set I.

DAY-BOOK,—SET II.

NEW YORK, FEBRUARY 10, 1859.

	Amount brought Forward	6926	25
	10		
√	Bought of Wm. B. Astor, Store and Fixtures, at . . . . Paid him, Cash . . . . $1000 Bond and Mortgage for balance . . 9000—$10,000	10000	
	12		
√	Sold J. T. Calkins, on his note @ 20 days, 50 yds. Broadcloth . . . . @ $4	200	
	14		
√	Bought of S. S. Guthrie, Buffalo, on our acceptance at 60 days favor of A. M. Clapp, 200 Bbls. Flour . . . . @ $8	1600	
	15		
√	Sold D. L. Wing, Albany, for Cash, 50 Bbls. Flour . . . . @ $8.25	412	50
	16		
√	Paid Drayman's Charges in full to date	5	
	18		
√	H. B. Bryant has made the following additional investment of Resources bequeathed him by a deceased uncle, 50 Shares Union Bank Stock valued at $105 . . . . . . $5250 00 Cash deposited in Union Bank 1000 00	6250	
	20		
√	Sold for Cash to B. McGann, 20 Shares Union Bank Stock @ $108	2160	
	24		
√	Sold John W. Gantz, 100 yds. Black French Cloth . . . . @ $5.75 . . . . Received in Payment, Cash . . . . $200 Balance on % . . . . 375—$575	575	
	25		
√	Paid for repairing store, per order on E. G. Folsom	65	
	27		
√	Rec'd Cash for 5 per cent. dividend on 30 Shares Union Bank Stock	150	
	28		
√	Paid Clerk's Salary to date . . . . $50 Paid Store Rent to date 100	150	
		28493	75

JOURNAL,—SET II.

NEW YORK, FEBRUARY 1, 1859.

				Dr.		Cr.	
	Sundries	Dr.	To Sundries,*				
1	Cash			4429	75		
1	Bills Receivable			57	50		
1	Merchandise			1333	50		
1	E. G. Folsom			115			
1	H. D. Stratton			20			
1			To Bills Payable . . .			1235	
1			" J. D. Comstock . . .			96	
1			" H. B. Bryant . . .			4624	75
		″					
1	Sundries	Dr.	To Merchandise			72	
1	Cash			20			
2	S. S. Packard			52			
		2					
1	Cash	Dr.	. . . .	20			
1			To H. D. Stratton . . .			20	
		3					
1	Merchandise	Dr.	To Sundries	212	50		
1			To Cash			50	
2			" E. G. Folsom . . .			50	
2			" Ivison & Phinney . .			112	50
		5					
1	Merchandise	Dr.	. . . .	62	50		
2			To Dawson, Warren & Hyde,			62	50
		7					
1	Bills Receivable	Dr.	. . . .	500			
1			To Bills Payable			500	
		″					
1	Cash	Dr.	. . . .	103	50		
1			To Merchandise			103	50
				6926	25	6926	25

* The term "Sundries" is difficult of explanation to a beginner; and many teachers and a few authors have thought to get rid of the difficulty by ignoring the term, upon the principle often quoted, that—

"Where ignorance is bliss, 'tis folly to be wise;"

but, like most attempts of this kind, it falls very far short of its object; for, however unnecessary the term may be in journal expressions, its convenience will secure its perpetual use by practical men, and the sooner it is comprehended by the learner the better. As used in this connection, it is, as will be readily seen, merely a *caption* for the Journal entry, indicating that the entry consists of sundry debits and sundry credits. These sundry debits and credits being afterwards specifically named, and their amounts extended, it is easy to infer that "Sundries" is not used as a Ledger account, but merely as an expression. Its convenience will be more readily apparent in *posting* to the Ledger, as it affords an expression to be entered under the Ledger title. There are, in reality, four kinds of journal entries, each requiring a different expression, viz.: 1. Those consisting of one debit and one credit; 2. Those consisting of one debit and several credits; 3. Those consisting of one credit and several debits; 4. Those consisting of several debits and several credits. Each of these is illustrated in this journal, and a little careful attention will make the student sufficiently acquainted with their characteristics.

JOURNAL,—SET II.

NEW YORK, FEBRUARY 10, 1859.

L.F.	Account		Dr.		Cr.	
	Amount brought Forward		6926	25	6926	25
	10					
2	Real Estate Dr.	To Sundries	10000			
1		To Cash			1000	
2		" Mortgage Payable* . .			9000	
	12					
1	Bills Receivable Dr.		200			
1		To Merchandise			200	
	14					
1	Merchandise Dr.		1600			
1		To Bills Payable			1600	
	15					
1	Cash Dr.		412	50		
1		To Merchandise			412	50
	16					
2	Expense Dr.		5			
1		To Cash			5	
	18					
1	Sundries Dr.	To H. B. Bryant			6250	
2	Union Bank Stock		5250			
2	Union Bank		1000			
	20					
1	Cash Dr.		2160			
2		To Union Bank Stock . .			2160	
	24					
1	Sundries Dr.	To Merchandise.			575	
1	Cash		200			
2	John W. Gantz		375			
	"					
1	Expense Dr.		65			
2		To E. G. Folsom			65	
	27					
1	Cash Dr.		150			
2		To Union Bank Stock . .			150	
	28					
2	Expense Dr.		150			
1		To Cash			150	
			28493	75	28493	75

* The term "Mortgage Payable" is but another name for Bills Payable: the accounts may be kept separate or together. We have adopted the former method, for the purpose of illustrating the principle, and to express our preference. There *is* a distinction between a promissory note and a mortgage on real estate; and the majority of business men would prefer to have that distinction preserved in their accounts.

LEDGER,—SET II.

Dr. H. B. Bryant. Cr.

Date	Day		Fo.	$	cts.	Date	Day		Fo.	$	cts.
1859						1859					
Feb.						*Feb.*	1	By Sundries	1	4624	75
						"	18		3	6250	
								10374 75			

Dr. Cash. Cr.

Date	Day		Fo.	$	cts.	Date	Day		Fo.	$	cts.
1859						1859					
Feb.	1	To Sundries	1	4429	75	*Feb.*	3	By Mdse.	1	50	
"	1	Mdse.	1	20		"	10	Real Estate	2	1000	
"	1	H. D. Stratton	1	20		"	13	Expense	2	5	
"	8	Mdse.	2	103	50	"	28	"	2	150	
"	15	"	2	412	50			1205			
"	20	Union Bank	2	2160							
"	24	Mdse.	2	200							
"	27	Union Bank Stock	3	150							
		7495 75									

Dr. Bills Receivable. Cr

Date	Day		Fo.	$	cts.	Date	Day		Fo.	$	cts.
1859											
Feb.	1	To Sundries	1	57	50						
"	7	Bills Payable	2	500							
"	12	Mdse.	3	200							
		757 50									

Dr. Merchandise. Cr.

Date	Day		Fo.	$	cts.	Date	Day		Fo.	$	cts.
1859						1859					
Feb.	1	To Sundries	1	1333	50	*Feb.*	1	By Sundries	2	72	
"	3	"	2	212	50	"	8	Cash	2	103	50
"	7	Dawson, W. & Hyde	2	62	50	"	12	Bills Receivable	3	200	
"	14	Bills Payable	3	1600		"	15	Cash	3	412	50
		3208 50				"	24	Sundries	4	575	
								1363			

Dr. H. D. Stratton. Cr.

Date	Day		Fo.	$	cts.	Date	Day		Fo.	$	cts.
1859						1859					
Feb.	1	To Sundries	1	20		*Feb.*	2	By Cash.	1	20	

Dr. E. G. Folsom. Cr.

Date	Day		Fo.	$	cts.	Date	Day		Fo.	$	cts.
1859						1859					
Feb.	1	To Sundries	1	115		*Feb.*	3	By Mdse.	1	50	
						"	25	Expense	3	65	
								115			

Dr. Bills Payable. Cr.

Date	Day		Fo.	$	cts.	Date	Day		Fo.	$	cts.
						1859					
						Feb.	1	By Sundries	1	1235	
						"	7	Bills Receivable	2	500	
							14	Mdse. 3335	3	1600	

LEDGER,—SET II.

Dr. J. D. Comstock. Cr.

Date	Day	Particulars	Fol.	Amount	Date	Day	Particulars	Fol.	Amount
					1859 *Feb.*	1	By Sundries		96

Dr. S. S. Packard. Cr.

Date	Day	Particulars	Fol.	Amount	Date	Day	Particulars	Fol.	Amount
1859 *Feb.*	1	To Mdse.	1	52					

Dr. Ivison & Phinney. Cr.

Date	Day	Particulars	Fol.	Amount	Date	Day	Particulars	Fol.	Amount
					1859 *Feb.*	3	By Mdse.	1	112 56

Dr. Dawson, Warren & Hyde. Cr.

Date	Day	Particulars	Fol.	Amount	Date	Day	Particulars	Fol.	Amount
					1859 *Feb.*	5	By Mdse.	1	62 50

Dr. Real Estate. Cr.

Date	Day	Particulars	Fol.	Amount	Date	Day	Particulars	Fol.	Amount
1859 *Feb.*	10	To Sundries	2	10000					

Dr. Mortgage Payable. Cr.

Date	Day	Particulars	Fol.	Amount	Date	Day	Particulars	Fol.	Amount
					1859 *Feb.*	10	By Real Estate	2	9000

Dr. Expense. Cr.

Date	Day	Particulars	Fol.	Amount	Date	Day	Particulars	Fol.	Amount
1859 *Feb*	16	To Cash	3	5					
"	25	E. G. Folsom	3	65					
"	28	Cash 220	4	150					

Dr. Union Bank Stock. Cr.

Date	Day	Particulars	Fol.	Amount	Date	Day	Particulars	Fol.	Amount
1859 *Feb.*	18	H. B. Bryant	3	5250	1859 *Feb.*	20	By Cash	4	2160
					"	27	" 2310	•	150

Dr. Union Bank. Cr.

Date	Day	Particulars	Fol.	Amount	Date	Day	Particulars	Fol.	Amount
1859 *Feb.*	18	To H. B. Bryant	2	1000					

Dr. John W. Gantz. Cr.

Date	Day	Particulars	Fol.	Amount	Date	Day	Particulars	Fol.	Amount
1859 *Feb.*	24	To Mdse.	4	375					

GENERAL STATEMENT.

In the preceding Ledger (Set II.,) we have the current condition of H. B. Bryant's business on the 28th of February, as far as that condition can be shown by the Ledger, *without closing the accounts.* This part of the labor we leave for the student; but shall give, in this connection, a statement which will afford him efficient aid. It is essential that the principles of this statement, as also the peculiar form and method of enforcing these principles, be clearly comprehended, as herein lies the key to much that at first seems mysterious and incomprehensible. It will be seen that this statement differs from the previous one (Set I.,) only in form and arrangement.

Trial Balance.

Differences.		*Face of Ledger.*		*Ledger Accounts.*	*Face of Ledger.*		*Differences.*	
				H. B. Bryant	10874	75	10874	75
6290	75	7495	75	. Cash	1205			
757	50	757	50	. Bills Receivable				
1845	50	3208	50	. Merchandise	1363			
		20		. H. D. Stratton	20			
		115		. E. G. Folsom	115			
				Bills Payable	3335		3335	
				J. D. Comstock	96		96	
52		52		. S. S. Packard				
				Ivison & Phinney. . . .	112	50	112	50
				Dawson, Warren & Hyde .	62	50	62	50
10000		10000		. Real Estate				
				Mortgage Payable . . .	9000		9000	
220		220		. Expense.				
2940		5250		. Union Bank Stock . . .	2310			
1000		1000		. Union Bank				
375		375		. John W. Gantz				
23480	75	28493	75	. *Equilibrium*	28493	75	23480	75

Inventory of Unsold Property.

140 yds. English Broadcloth . .	@ $3.00 . .	420		
200 do Domestic Cassimere. .	@ 1.00 . .	200		
2 dozen Soft Hats	@ 24.00 . .	48		
15 reams Foolscap Paper . . .	@ 3.50 . .	52	50	
100 sets Spencerian Writing Books	@ 75 . .	75		
38 Gold Pens	@ 1.25 . .	47	50	
150 Bbls. Flour	@ 8.50 . .	1275		2118
30 Shares Union Bank Stock . .	@ 1.03⅓ .			3100
Store and Fixtures valued at				12000
				17218

Statement of Losses and Gains.—Representative Accounts.

			Losses.		Gains	
MERCHANDISE,	*Proceeds from sales*	1363 00				
	Value of that unsold (per Invoice)	2118 00				
	Total proceeds	3481 00				
	Cost	3208 50				
	Gain	272 50			272	50
REAL ESTATE,	*Value of property unsold* . . .	12000 00				
	Cost	10000 00				
	Gain	2000 00			2000	
EXPENSE,	*Outlay*		220			
UNION BANK STOCK,	*Proceeds sales and dividend* . .	2310 00				
	Value of unsold	3100 00				
	Total proceeds	5410 00				
	Cost	5250 00				
	Gain	160 00			160	
	Net Gain		2212	50		
			2432	50	2432	50

Statement of Resources and Liabilities.—Real Accounts and Inventories

			Resources.		Liabilities.	
	1st. From Inventories of Unsold Property.					
MERCHANDISE			2118			
UNION BANK STOCK			3100			
REAL ESTATE			12000			
	2d. From Ledger Accounts.					
CASH,	*Amount Received*	7495 75				
	" *Disbursed*	1205 00				
	Balance on hand	6290 75	6290	75		
BILLS RECEIVABLE,	*Notes received, and on hand*		757	50		
BILLS PAYABLE,	*Notes issued and unredeemed*				3335	
J. D. COMSTOCK,	*We owe him*				96	
S. S. PACKARD,	*He owes us*		52			
IVISON & PHINNEY,	*We owe them*				112	50
DAWSON, WARREN & HYDE	*We owe them*				62	50
UNION BANK,	*Deposits in our favor*		1000			
JOHN W. GANTZ,	*He owes us*		375			
MORTGAGE PAYABLE,	*Mortgage issued and outstanding*				9000	
H. B. BRYANT,	*His net investment*	10874 75				
	" " *gain*	2212 50				
	His present interest . .	13087 25			13087	25
			25693	25	25693	25

The theory enforced by the preceding "General Statement," is one that must perpetually govern the record of business transactions, and one that will afford ample basis for explanation to those not thoroughly familiar with the science of Double Entry. It is, simply, that *all gains or losses in business are substantiated by the actual increase or decrease of net resources.* As simple as this proposition may appear, it will require not a little well-directed mental effort to comprehend it in all its special relations and applications.

The student is now required to "Close up" the Ledger according to instructions in Set I.

EXERCISES FOR THE LEARNER.

SECOND SERIES.

Feb. 1st, Commenced business with the Resources and Liabilities shown in Balance account, Ledger A.* Sold John D. Hinde on %, 50 bbls. Flour, @ $11. Bo't of John Gundry for cash, 200 sacks Coffee, 13,000 lbs. @ 9 c. 2d, Accepted J. D. Williams' Draft on us @ 10 days, in favor of E. C. Bradford, in full of his %. 3d, Bo't of D. C. Collins 500 bbls. Flour, @ $8; Paid him cash, $1500; order on R. C. Spencer, $133.75; our note for balance, due in four months. 4th, Paid cash for sundry expenses, $15. Sold to J. A. Harper for cash, 200 bbls. Flour, @ $8.25. 5th, Received cash of Hiram A. Pryor, in full for his note of $950. 6th, Paid our note in favor of C. S. Sill, given him on the 4th ult., in cash, $150. 7th, Rec'd cash of E. B. Rockwell, in full of %. Paid Store rent in cash, $150. 8th, Sold Samuel Jones on his note, 300 bbls. Flour, @ $8.50. 10th, Sold J. H. Bell on %, 10 pieces Calico, @ $3.75. 15th, Received from the executors of my deceased father's estate, in cash, $1200. 16th, Paid cash for acceptance favor of J. D. Williams, 2d inst. 20th, Sold Henry A. Wise, 10 pieces figured Silk, @ $10. Received in payment his draft @ 10 days on John Brown. 22d, Bo't of James Buchanan on %, 6 pipes of Wine, 720 gallons, @ $3,50. 25th, Sold our sight draft on J. D. Hinde, to balance his %, for which received cash. 28th, Discounted our note of 3d inst., favor of D. C. Collins, due in four months from date. Paid for face of note, less discount for 3 months @ 7 per cent., in cash, $2324.84.

Trial Balance.

Differences.		*Face of Ledger.*			*Face of Ledger.*		*Differences.*	
				. . . Stock	7275	75	7275	75
3437	16	8897		. . . Cash	5459	84		
3547	50	8435		. . . Merchandise	4887	50		
2650		3600		. . . Bills Receivable . . .	950			
		133	75	. . . R. C. Spencer	133	75		
		250		. . . E. B. Rockwell . . .	250			
		2666	25	. . . Bills Payable	2666	25		
		150		. . . J. D. Williams . . .	150			
		550		. . . J. D. Hinde	550			
165		165		. . . Expense.				
37	50	37	50	. . . J. H. Bell				
				. . . J. Buchanan	2520		2520	
				. . . Discount	41	41	41	41
9837	16	24884	50		24884	50	9837	16

* This is, of course, the Ledger connected with the *First Series*, the result of which the student is supposed to have shown according to directions.

Inventory of Property Unsold.

25 pieces Merrimac Prints	@ $5	125
200 sacks Coffee, 13000 lbs.	@ .09 . . .	1170
6 pipes Wine, 720 gals.	@ 3.50 . . .	2520
		3815

Balance.

Resources.			Liabilities.		
Cash	3437	16	J. Buchanan	2520	
Merchandise	3815		H. B. Bryant	7419	66
Bills Receivable . . .	2650				
J. H. Bell	37	50			
	9939	66		9939	66

The student will see the importance of carrying these transactions through the necessary books to their final result, as shown in the above Balance account. Let him not omit to make out a General Statement, and close the Ledger in strict accordance with the instructions on these points.

AUXILIARY BOOKS,

We give below two of the most common and essential auxiliary books in use, the Cash Book and the Bill Book. A moment's inspection will suggest the great advantage of these books, as showing special facts not easily gathered from any other source. The Cash Book, when kept, is closed every night, and the balance—which must agree with cash items on hand—brought down as a basis for the next day's business. This necessity of having the difference between the receipts and disbursements of cash, as shown by the two sides of the Cash Book, agree with the cash on hand, is the best possible safeguard against errors and omissions, and one which we shall more fully exemplify hereafter.

Cash Book.

CASH RECEIVED.

Feb	1	To Stock, ...	*Amount invested*	4429	75		
"	"	" Mdse., ...	*Sold S. S. Packard*	20			
"	2	" H. D. Stratton, .	*Rec'd on %*	20			
"	8	" Mdse., ...	*Sold J. H. Goldsmith*	103	50		
"	15	" "	*Sold D. L. Wing*	412	50		
"	20	" Union Bank Stock,	*Sold B. McGann*	2160			
"	24	" Mdse., ...	*Sold J. W. Gantz*	200			
"	27	" Union Bank Stock,	*Rec'd for Dividend*	150		7495	75
						7495	75
		To Balance . .	*From old %*			6290	75

Bill Book.

No.	*When Rec'd.*		*Drawer or Endorser.*	*Drawee or Maker.*	*In Whose Favor.*	*For What Rec'd.*	*Where Payable.*
1	Feb.	1	B. McGann.	S. S. Packard.	H. B. Bryant.	Investment.	Our Office.
2	"	7	H. B. Bryant.	Digby V. Bell.	do do	Accommodat'n.	do do
3	"	12	H. B. Bryant.	J. T Calkins.	do do	Merchandise.	do do

Bill Book.

No.	*When Issued*		*Drawer or Endorser.*	*Drawee or Maker.*	*In Whose Favor.*	*For What Given.*	*Where Payable.*
1	Jan.	9	Francis & Loutrel.	H. B. Bryant.	F. & Loutrel	Merchandise.	College Bank.
2	"	14	Smith & Co.	do do	Smith & Co.	do	do do
3	"	10	Peter Cooper.	do do	W. H. Beebe.	To Balance %.	do do
4	Feb.	7	Digby V. Bell.	do do	Digby V. Bell.	Accommodat'n.	do do
5	"	14	S. S. Guthrie.	do do	A. M. Clapp.	Merchandise.	do do

SET II.

The Bill Book should never be omitted in any business dealings with notes, either payable or receivable; and especially is it important to keep a record of the amount and condition of notes payable.

It will be seen that the entries made in these auxiliaries are taken from the transactions of Set II., and hence the cash on hand, notes on hand, and notes outstanding, as here shown, will be found to agree with the balance shown in the proper Ledger accounts.

The forms submitted are those in general use, and are sufficiently suggestive.

Cash Book.

Cash Disbursed.

Feb	3	By Mdse., ...	*Bo't of Ivison & Phinney* . . .	50			
"	10	" Real Estate, . .	*Paid on Store and Fixtures* . . .	1000			
"	16	" Expense, . . .	*Paid Drayman in full*	5			
"	28	" " . . .	*Paid Clerk's salary and Store rent* .	150		1205	
"		" *Balance* . . .	*Amount on hand*			6290	75
						7495	75

Receivable.

Date.			Time.	When Due.													Am'nt.	When and how disposed of.		
Year.	Month.			Year.	Jan	Feb	Mar	Apr	May	Jun	Jul	Aug	Sep	Oct	Nov	Dec				
1859	Jan.	12	60 d's.	1859			13/16										57.50			
"	Feb.	7	30 d's.	1859			9/12										500			
"	"	12	30 d's.	1859			14/17										200			

Payable.

Date.			Time.	When Due.													Am'nt.	When and how redeemed.		
Year.	Month.			Year.	Jan	Feb	Mar	Apr	May	Jun	Jul	Aug	Sep	Oct	Nov	Dec				
1859	Jan.	9	90 d's.	1859				9/12									235			
1859	"	14	40 d's.	1859		23/26											1000			
1859	"	10	10 d's.	1859	20/23												500	Jan.	28	Paid.
1859	Feb.	7	30 d's.	1859			9/12										500			
1859	"	14	60 d's.	1859							15/18						1600			

QUESTIONS FOR REVIEW,—SET II.

In the previous questions under this head, we have referred, by number, to the *written* answers in the preceding remarks. We shall hereafter secure to the student the advantage of framing his own answers, aiming, however, to ask no questions upon which instructions have not been previously given.

1. Where are the Resources and Liabilities shown at the commencement of Set II. obtained? 2. Can Gains and Losses be shown at the commencement of business? 3. Why not? 4. What has become of the gain shown to have been realized in the month of January? 5. How does the interest of the proprietor at the commencement of Set II. vary from his interest at the commencement of Set I.? 6. What has effected this difference? 7. When is it proper to increase the credit side of Stock account? 8. When the debit side? 9. Is the term "Sundries" used as a Ledger account? 10. For what purpose is it used? 11. How will its convenience be most apparent? 12. How many kinds of Journal entries are there, and what are they? 13. What is meant by the term "Mortgage Payable?" 14. What is the difference *in effect* between a Mortgage Payable and a Bill Payable? 15. Is there any difference? 16. How may Ledger accounts are opened in Set II.? 17. How many of them are canceled? 18. Which of these Ledger accounts exhibit Resources? 19. Which Liabilities? 20. Which Gains? 21. Which Losses? 22. What is the distinction between the accounts of "Union Bank," and "Union Bank Stock?" 23. What will be the first step in ascertaining the gain or loss in Merchandise account? 24. If the *net cost* of merchandise exceeds the value of merchandise unsold, will the account show a *gain* or a *loss?* 25. Why do you carry the value of merchandise unsold to the *credit* of the Merchandise account? 26. Why make the entry in red ink? 27. Can you give a rule for the use of red ink entries in the Ledger? 28. In transferring a red ink entry to another account why do you always carry the amount to the *opposite* side of the new account? 29. What Ledger account in Set II. corresponds with Stock account in Set I.? 30. What does H. B. Bryant's account represent, as it stands on the Ledger? 31. How much does it fail to show his interest in the business on the 28th February? 32. Where will you get the amounts which will make up the difference? 33. Is it necessary that a "Loss and Gain" account should be opened? 34. If not opened, to what account would it be proper to carry the losses and gains at the close of business? 35. What advantages are gained by opening a "Loss and Gain" account? 36. Is it necessary to open a Balance account? 37. If a Balance account is not opened, how can the resources and liabilities be represented on the Ledger? 38. Is it customary in business to open a Balance account? 39. What is the *theory* of the "General Statement" as given in Set II.? 40. What are the auxiliary books given in connection with this set? 41. For what purpose is the Cash Book used? 42. How often is the Cash Book closed? 43. With what must the difference in the sides agree? 44. What is the advantage of the daily test? 45. For what purpose is the Bill Book used? 46. What is the particular convenience of the Bill Book?* 47. With what account in the Ledger will the uncanceled notes in the Bill Book Receivable agree? 48. In the Bill Book Payable?

---

* The Bill Books in common use have the records of Bills Payable in one part, and Bills Receivable in the other, conversely arranged, so that each seems to be at the commencement of the book. It is usual to put the last day of grace in the "When due" column, although some insist upon including the day upon which the note is written to fall due. When both dates are specified, it is done in the form of a fraction, similar to the example shown.

SET III.

DAY-BOOK, JOURNAL,

COMMISSION SALES BOOK, ACCOUNTS SALES.

[*Continuation of Set II.*]

BUSINESS ADVERSE.

DAY-BOOK,—SET III.

NEW YORK, MARCH 1, 1859.

The following Resources and Liabilities are from H. B. Bryant's Ledger B. The business to be continued under his name.

Resources.

Merchandise as per Inventory	2118 00		
Union Bank Stock, real value	3100 00		
Real Estate, estimated at	12000 00		
Cash on hand	6290 75		
Bills Receivable, notes on hand	757 50		
S. S. Packard owes on %	52 00		
John W. Gantz do	375 00		
Union Bank, amount on deposit	1000 00	25693	25

*Liabilities.**

Bills Payable, outstanding notes	3335 00		
J. D. Comstock, balance due him	96 00		
Ivison & Phinney " " them	112 50		
Dawson, Warren & Hyde, balance due them	62 50		
Mortgage Payable	9000 00	12606	

1

Shipped per Peoples' Line, and consigned to Sheldon & Co., Albany, to be sold on our % and risk,

140 yds. English Broadcloth	@ $3 50	490 00			
200 do Domestic Cassimere	@ 1 25	250 00	—740 00		
Paid drayage on same in cash			1 00	741	

2

Sold James Monroe, for cash, 2 doz. Soft Hats, @ $26	52	

"

Received per N. Y. and E. R. R., from J. R. Wheeler & Co., Buffalo, to be sold on their % and risk,

500 bbls Flour, invoiced	@ $8 00		
5000 bush. Wheat	@ $1 25		
Paid transportation charges, in cash		100	

3

Sold S. R. Gray, Albany,

50 Sets Spencerian Writing Books	@ 88c.		44 00		
15 Reams Foolscap Paper	@ $3 70		55 50		
38 Gold Pens	@ $1 50		57 00	156	50
Received in Payment Ivison & Phinney's Draft on us for	$112 50				
Cash for balance	44 00		—156 50		

4

Received Cash for rent of offices in second story	500	
	39848	75

* We have varied this statement from the former, for the purpose of illustrating the different methods of opening books. The *Liabilities* here enumerated are simply those amounts owing *outside the concern.* The amount owing to the proprietor is, of course, the difference between the sum of these outside liabilities and the sum of all the resources, and, instead of being shown in one amount, as in Set II., will be indicated by the difference between the debit and credit of the Stock, or H. B. Bryant's account.

DAY-BOOK,—SET III.

NEW YORK, MARCH 4, 1859.

Amount brought Forward		39848	75
4			
Paid J. D. Comstock Cash, in full of %		90	
5			
Sold Wm. H. Crocker, on his note @ sixty days, 500 bbls. Flour, (J. R. W. & Co.'s Consignment) @ $9		4500	
"			
Received per Steamer New World, from M. B. Scott, Cleveland, to be sold on his % and risk, 800 bush. Corn, invoiced . . . . @ 75c. . . . . 2000 do Oats, " . . . . @ 60c. . . . . 500 do Wheat, " . . . . @ $1 38 . . . . Paid Freight and Insurance, in cash		175	
6			
Sold J. C. Bryant, for cash, 5000 bush. Wheat, (J. R. W. & Co.'s consignment) @ $1 50 . . .		7500	
"			
Closed J. R. Wheeler & Co.'s Consignment, and rendered them an Account Sales of the same. Our charges for Storage and Advertising, ... Our Commission on Sales, ... J. R. Wheeler & Co.'s net proceeds	$ 25 00 300 00 11575 00	11900	
7			
Shipped per Steamer Swiftsure, and Consigned to Cobb & Co., New Haven, to be sold on our % and risk, 100 bbls. Flour from Store, valued at $9 . . . . 800 bush. Corn, (M. B. S.'s Consignment) @ 80c. . . . . Paid Cash for Insurance—premium and policy	900 00 640 00 8 70	1548	70
8			
Paid Dawson, Warren & Hyde Cash to balance %		62	50
"			
Received Cash of S. S. Packard in full of %		52	
9			
Sold Charles Claghorn, for Cash, 2000 bush. Oats, (M. B. S.'s Consignment) @ 75c. . . . 500 bush. Wheat, do do @ $1 50 . .	1500 00 750 00	2250	
"			
Closed M. B. Scott's Consignment, and rendered him an Account Sales of the same. Our charges for Storage and Advertising . . . . Our Commission on sales . . . . M. B. Scott's net proceeds, remitted in cash	40 00 72 25 2602 75	2715	
		70647	95

DAY BOOK, SET III.

NEW YORK, MARCH 10, 1859.

	Amount brought forward	70647	95
	10		
✓	Received Cash of Jno. W. Gantz, in full of %.	375	
	11		
✓	The steamer on which we shipped goods to Sheldon & Co., Albany, was sunk by collision, and our goods, which were rescued in a damaged condition, and upon which there was no insurance, were sold at auction for cash	150	
	12		
✓	Received from C. S. Dole & Co., Chicago, to be sold on their % and risk, 500 bbls. Extra Superfine Flour, 1000 do Superfine do 3000 bush. Rye, Paid Freight in Cash	300	
	13		
✓	Sold E. R. Felton, at thirty days, on %, 500 bbls Superfine Flour, (C. S. D. & Co.'s Consignment, @ $8 00 .	4000	
	"		
✓	D. V. Bell has returned our note issued Feb. 7, and we have surrendered his of the same date and amount	500	
	15		
✓	Paid Cash for Taxes on Real Estate . . . . 150 00 Also for Clerks' Salary to date 125 00	275	
	16		
✓	H. B. Bryant has drawn Cash for private use	500	
	"		
✓	Received Cash of S. S. Packard for his note now due	57	50
	17		
✓	Received Cash of J. T. Calkins in full for his note	200	
	"		
✓	Received advice from Cobb & Co., New Haven, of the sale of 150 bbls. Flour and 800 bush. Corn, shipped them on the 7th inst., Net proceeds remitted in Cash	1200	
		78205	45

DAY BOOK,—SET III.

NEW YORK, MARCH 20, 1859.

Amount brought forward		78205	45
20			
Sold John R. Penn, for cash, 500 bbls Extra Superfine Flour, (C. S. D. & Co.'s Consignment) @ $9		4500	
22			
Sold for Cash, to E. H. Bender, Albany, 30 Shares Union Bank Stock @ $100		3000	
25			
Paid our Note in Cash, favor of Smith & Co., due Feb. 26 . Interest due on same to date	1000 00 5 83	1005	83
"			
Paid Cash for our Note of the 14th ult., at five months, favor of A. M. Clapp, Face of Note . . . . Cash paid . . . . Discount off to July 18	 1565 57 34 43 1600 00	1600	
"			
Sold J. H. Goldsmith, for Cash 500 bbls. Superfine Flour, (C. S. D. & Co.'s Consignment) @ $8 50 .		4250	
"			
Accepted J. R. Wheeler & Co.'s Draft on us @ three days sight . . .		11575	
27			
Closed C. S. Dole & Co.'s Consignment, and rendered them an Account Sales—3000 bushels Rye remaining unsold, Our charges for Storage and Advertising . . . . Our Commission on Sales . . . . C. S. Dole & Co.'s net proceeds	 50 00 318 75 12081 25	12450	
"			
Paid our Note favor of Francis & Loutrel, in Cash		235	
"			
Remitted C. S. Dole & Co. Cash to balance %		12081	25
31			
Paid sundry Expenses this month, in Cash		75	
		128977	53

JOURNAL,—SET III.

NEW YORK, MARCH 1, 1859.

	Dr.		Cr.	
Sundries Dr. To H. B. Bryant			25693	25
Merchandise				
Union Bank Stock	2118			
Real Estate	3100			
Cash	12000			
Bills Receivable	6290	75		
S. S. Packard	757	50		
Jno. W. Gantz	52			
Union Bank	375			
	1000			
〃				
H. B. Bryant Dr. To Sundries	12606			
" Bills Payable			3335	
" J. D. Comstock . . .			96	
" Ivison & Phinney . . .			112	50
" Dawson, Warren & Hyde			62	50
" Mortgage Payable . .			9000	
〃				
Shipment to Albany Dr. To Sundries	741			
" Merchandise			740	
" Cash			1	
"Shipment to Albany" is a new account, opened to represent a particular enterprise, and although it relates to merchandise, it is distinct from the merchandise *in store*, and is given this new name to mark that distinction. It is as though we had sold our merchandise for $740, and immediately invested the same in this adventure. The account is debited with its cost, and merchandise and cash credited, as per *formula* on page 17.				
2				
Cash Dr. . . . . To Merchandise	52			
			52	
〃				
J. R. Wheeler & Co.'s Consignment . . . . . . To Cash	100			
			100	
The account here opened—J. R. Wheeler & Co.'s Consignment—is precisely the same, in effect, as would be an account with J. R. Wheeler & Co., although it really represents the *property* of that firm, which we receive, as commission merchants, to sell. Instead, therefore, of debiting the Consignment account with the value of the property, we debit it only with what it has cost us.				
3				
Sundries Dr. To Merchandise.			156	50
Ivison & Phinney	112	50		
Cash	44			
Ivison & Phinney's draft on us is simply their order for the amount we owe them, and for which they stand credited on our books. If we accept or pay the draft, we must, of course, debit them, which will close their account.				
4				
Cash Dr. . . . . To Real Estate	500			
			500	
	39848	75	39848	75

JOURNAL,—SET III.

NEW YORK, MARCH 4, 1859.

Date	Account		Dr.		Cr.	
	Amount brought Forward		39848	75	39848	75
4	J. D. Comstock	Dr.	96			
		To Cash.			96	
"	Bills Receivable	Dr.	4500			
		To J. R. Wheeler & Co.'s Consignment			4500	
"	M. B. Scott's Consignment	Dr.	175			
		To Cash			175	
6	Cash	Dr.	7500			
		To J. R. Wheeler's Consignment			7500	
"	J. R. Wheeler & Co.'s Consignment	Dr. To Sundries.	11900			
		To Storage and Advertising			25	
		" Commission.			300	
		" J. R. Wheeler & Co. .			11575	

The entry above is made for the purpose of exhibiting on our books the net amount owing to J. R. Wheeler & Co., as the result of our business with them so far; and as their Consignment account was used to show the facts connected with the sale of their property, we can ascertain from this account how much they are entitled to, as net proceeds, which must be the difference between the sides of that account, when its entire cost and proceeds are properly shown; in this case, $11575. The effect of this entry will be to close the Consignment account, and carry its results to the account of J. R. Wheeler & Co.

Date	Account		Dr.		Cr.	
"	Shipment to New Haven	Dr. To Sundries	1548	70		
		To Merchandise			900	
		" M. B. Scott's Consignment			640	
		" Cash			8	70
8	Dawson, Warren & Hyde	Dr.	62	50		
		To Cash			62	50
"	Cash	Dr.	52			
		To S. S. Packard			52	
9	Cash	Dr.	2250			
		To M. B. Scott's Consignment			2250	
"	M. B. Scott's Consignment	Dr. To Sundries.	2715			
		To Storage and Advertising			40	
		" Commission.			72	25
		" Cash			2602	75
			70647	95	70647	95

NEW YORK, MARCH 10, 1859.

		Dr.		Cr.	
Amount brought Forward		70647	95	70647	95
10					
Cash Dr.		375			
	To J. W. Gantz			375	
11					
Cash Dr.		150			
	To Shipment to Albany			150	
Shipment to Albany is treated precisely as any property or representative account; having been debited with its cost, we now credit it with its proceeds. The difference will be, in this case, our loss.					
"					
C. S. Dole & Co.'s Consignment Dr.		300			
	To Cash			300	
13					
E. R. Felton Dr.		4000			
	To C. S. Dole & Co.'s Consignment			4000	
"					
Bills Payable Dr.		500			
	To Bills Receivable			500	
15					
Sundries Dr.	To Cash			275	
Real Estate		150			
Expense		125			
16					
Private Account Dr.		500			
	To Cash			500	
According to the principles already expressed, it would be proper to debit H. B. Bryant with this amount, as he has drawn it from the business for his own private use. "Private Account," then, is simply a subdivision of H. B. Bryant's, or Stock Account, and should, eventually, be closed into this account.*					
"					
Cash Dr.		57	50		
	To Bills Receivable			57	50
"					
Cash Dr.		200			
	To Bills Receivable			200	
		77005	45	77005	45

*Some authors teach the propriety of opening a "Private Expense" account for transactions of this kind, closing it into Loss and Gain, the same as the general Expense account of the business. It requires no great tact to see the fallacy of this reasoning—if, indeed, it is properly so called—as, in such a case, the prosperity or adversity of the business would depend, not on the real amount of *gain or loss*, but upon how much was drawn out for private use. There is no more justice in debiting Loss for sums drawn from a concern by the *sole* proprietor, than there would be for sums drawn by a partner. The authors who propagate this fallacy, usually give *two* rules for journalizing--both "infallible,"—one for *stock* books, and another, and different one, for *partnership* books.

JOURNAL,—SET III.

NEW YORK, MARCH 27, 1859.

		Brought forward, ...	104136	28	104136	28
		27				
C. S. Dole & Co.'s Consignment	Dr.	To Sundries	12450			
		" Storage and Advertising .			50	
		" Commission			318	75
		" C. S. Dole & Co. . .			12081	25
		30				
Bills Payable	Dr.	. . . .	235			
		To Cash			235	
		"				
C. S Dole & Co.	Dr.	. . . .	12081	25		
		To Cash			12081	25
		31				
Expense	Dr.	. . . .	75			
		To Cash			75	
			128977	53	128977	53

We have thought proper to omit the Ledger in this Set, believing the student to be fully capable to post the accounts without assistance of this kind. We shall adhere to this plan hereafter, except in cases where some new principle or application may be otherwise more clearly shown. The result of this business will differ from that shown in the preceding Sets, exhibiting, instead of a net *gain*, a net *loss*. This fact will of course, be apparent in the Loss and Gain account—the debit side of that account being the larger—which will be closed "*By* Stock," and the result carried to the debit side of Stock (H. B. Bryant's) account. Before attempting to show the result of the business, by closing the Ledger or making a Statement, the student must not forget to close "Private Account" into H. B. Bryant's (Stock) account, it having already been explained that Private Account was merely a subdivision of Stock account. This might have been done, and very properly, too, by a regular Journal entry, but the result is the same, and the method here suggested, besides being more simple and direct, is equally intelligible.

In order, however, that the student may be made familiar with the various methods of closing Ledger accounts, we shall exemplify in the succeeding Set the manner of producing all the results through the Journal. This latter method is practised to considerable extent in business houses, and particularly in joint stock concerns.

We have here a somewhat novel feature, indicated in the Inventory as "Interest Payable, due on Mortgage." This represents the interest which has accumulated and is unpaid on the mortgage held against us; and is as much a liability as the mortgage itself. In closing up the Interest account, this amount ($84) should be brought in on the debit side in red ink "To Interest Payable," and carried to the Balance account as a liability Were the business to be continued under the same proprietorship, this accumulating interest might be allowed to run on without mention until paid, when it would be charged to Interest %, thereby decreasing the gains; but as it is necessary to show the exact state of the business at this time, *all* the liabilities must be shown.

The student will please make his Ledger conform to the following Trial Balance, and close it in accordance with the Statement which follows.

NEW YORK, MARCH 27, 1859.

		Brought forward, ...	104136	28	104136	28
		27				
C. S. Dole & Co.'s Consignment	Dr.	To Sundries	12450			
		" Storage and Advertising .			50	
		" Commission			318	75
		" C. S. Dole & Co. . .			12081	25
		30				
Bills Payable	Dr.	. . . .	235			
		To Cash			235	
		//				
C. S Dole & Co.	Dr.	. . . .	12081	25		
		To Cash			12081	25
		31				
Expense	Dr.	. . . .	75			
		To Cash			75	
			128977	53	128977	53

We have thought proper to omit the Ledger in this Set, believing the student to be fully capable to post the accounts without assistance of this kind. We shall adhere to this plan hereafter, except in cases where some new principle or application may be otherwise more clearly shown. The result of this business will differ from that shown in the preceding Sets, exhibiting, instead of a net *gain*, a net *loss*. This fact will of course, be apparent in the Loss and Gain account—the debit side of that account being the larger—which will be closed "*By* Stock," and the result carried to the debit side of Stock (H. B. Bryant's) account. Before attempting to show the result of the business, by closing the Ledger or making a Statement, the student must not forget to close "Private Account" into H. B. Bryant's (Stock) account, it having already been explained that Private Account was merely a subdivision of Stock account. This might have been done, and very properly, too, by a regular Journal entry, but the result is the same, and the method here suggested, besides being more simple and direct, is equally intelligible.

In order, however, that the student may be made familiar with the various methods of closing Ledger accounts, we shall exemplify in the succeeding Set the manner of producing all the results through the Journal. This latter method is practised to considerable extent in business houses, and particularly in joint stock concerns.

We have here a somewhat novel feature, indicated in the Inventory as "Interest Payable, due on Mortgage." This represents the interest which has accumulated and is unpaid on the mortgage held against us; and is as much a liability as the mortgage itself. In closing up the Interest account, this amount ($84) should be brought in on the debit side in red ink "To Interest Payable," and carried to the Balance account as a liability. Were the business to be continued under the same proprietorship, this accumulating interest might be allowed to run on without mention until paid, when it would be charged to Interest %, thereby decreasing the gains; but as it is necessary to show the exact state of the business at this time, *all* the liabilities must be shown.

The student will please make his Ledger conform to the following Trial Balance, and close it in accordance with the Statement which follows.

Trial Balance.

Balances.		Total Footings.		Ledger Accounts.	Total Footings.		Balances.	
		12606		H. B. Bryant	25693	25	13087	25
269	50	2118		Merchandise	1848	50		
100		3100		Union Bank Stock	3000			
11650		12150		Real Estate	500			
11337	65	30421	25	Cash	19083	60		
4500		5257	50	Bills Receivable	757	50		
		52		S. S. Packard	52			
		375		J. W. Gantz	375			
1000		1000		Union Bank				
		3335		Bills Payable	14910		11575	
		96		J. D. Comstock	96			
		112	50	Ivison & Phinney	112	50		
		62	50	Dawson, Warren & Hyde	62	50		
				Mortgage Payable	9000		9000	
591		741		Shipment to Albany	150			
		12000		J. R. Wheeler & Co.'s Consignment	12000			
		2890		M. B. Scott's Consignment	2890			
348	70	1548	70	Shipment to New Haven	1200			
		12750		C. S. Dole & Co.'s Consignment	12750			
4000		4000		E. R. Felton				
		5	83	Interest	34	43	28	60
				Storage and advertising	115		115	
				Commission	691		691	
		11575		J. R. Wheeler & Co.	11575			
200		200		Expense				
500		500		Private Account				
		12081	25	C. S. Dole & Co.	12081	25		
34496	85	128977	53		128977	53	34496	85

INVENTORY.

Property Remaining Unsold, March 31.

50 sets Spencerian Writing Books	37	50
Real Estate, valued at	12000	

Liabilities not shown on Ledger.

Interest Payable. Due on Mortgage	84

Losses and Gains.

				Losses.		Gains.	
MERCHANDISE,	*Cost*		2118 00				
	Proceeds from sales .	1848 50					
	Mdse. unsold (per Inv.)	37 50	1886 00				
	Loss		232 00	232			
UNION BANK STOCK,	*Cost*		3100 00				
	Proceeds		3000 00				
	Loss		100 00	100			
REAL ESTATE,	*Proceeds from rent* .	500 00					
	Value of unsold . .	12000 00	12500 00				
	Cost		12150 00				
	Gain		350 00			350	
SHIPMENT TO ALBANY,	*Cost*		741 00				
	Proceeds		150 00				
	Loss		591 00	591			
INTEREST,	*Cost*		89 83				
	Proceeds		34 43				
	Loss		55 40	55	40		
STORAGE & ADVERTISING,	*Proceeds*					115	
COMMISSION,	"					691	
EXPENSE,	*Cost*			200			
SHIPMENT TO NEW HAVEN,	*Cost*		1548 70				
	Proceeds		1200 00				
	Loss		348 70	348	70		
	Net Loss					871	10
				1527	10	1527	10

Resources and Liabilities.

				Resources.		Liabilities.	
	1st. *Property Unsold.*						
MERCHANDISE,	*Per Inventory*			37	50		
REAL ESTATE	. . . .			12000			
	2d. *Ledger Accounts.*						
CASH,	*Amount on hand*			11337	65		
BILLS RECEIVABLE,	" "			4500			
UNION BANK,	*Amount on Deposit*			1000			
BILLS PAYABLE,	*Outstanding Notes*					11575	
MORTGAGE PAYABLE,	" "					9000	
INTEREST PAYBLE,	" "					84	
E. R. FELTON,	*Owes us on %*			4000			
H. B. BRYANT,	*Capital Invested (net)*		13087 25				
	Drawn out (Private %) .	500 00					
	Net loss.	871 10	871 10				
	Present interest in the concern . .		12216 15			12216	15
				32875	15	32875	15

H. B. BRYANT'S BOOKS CLOSED.

From the foregoing statement the student will be enabled to close up this Ledger with certainty, and to produce the results in his Balance account which are exhibited under the head of Resources and Liabilities there shown. The only difference between this and the preceding sets is, that the business has been a losing instead of a prosperous one, and that, consequently, the net resources of the concern are diminished.

Mr. Bryant now proposes to change his business, and to take in a partner, Mr. H. D. Stratton, who is to furnish an equal amount of capital. The new concern will commence with a cash capital and with no liabilities. A new set of books will be opened. This will leave Mr. Bryant to close up his old business in his own books.

The Memoranda below are for that purpose, and the student is required to write up the transactions given, and produce a Balance Sheet of the result before commencing the next set.

In closing up the business of H. B. Bryant, as per memoranda, it will not, of course, be necessary to open a new Ledger, nor even new accounts in the old Ledger; particularly, if there be sufficient space under the old accounts for the few necessary entries. The opening entries below, enumerating resources and liabilities are supposed to be taken from the last Balance account. The same purpose would be effected by bringing the balances down under their proper accounts, instead of transferring them to the Balance account. This method is shown at length in the succeeding set.

Memoranda—H. B. Bryant's Books Continued.

April 1. The following is a statement of the Resources and Liabilities of H. B. Bryant's private books, as taken from the Balance account of his Ledger:

Resources.—Mdse on hand, $37.50; Real Estate, $12000; Cash, $11337.65; Bills Receivable, $4500; Union Bank, $1000; E. R. Felton's indebtedness, $4000.

Liabilities.—Bills Payable outstanding, $11575; Mortgage Payable, $9000; Interest due on same, $84; Bryant's net investment, $12216.15.

1. Invested in the concern of Bryant and Stratton, Cash, $10000,* 2. Received Cash of E. R. Felton, in full of %, $4000. 3. Sold Bryant & Stratton Store and Fixtures for $12500. Transferred Mortgage for $9000; Interest due on same, $84; received Cash for balance, $3416. 3. Paid our acceptance favor of J. R. Wheeler & Co., $11575. Gave in payment W. H. Crocker's Note, due May 7, $4500, less discount off 34 days, $29.75; Cash for balance, $7104.75.† 10. Sold James Atwater, Lockport, for Cash, 50 sets Spencerian Writing Books, @ 80 cents, $40. 15. Deposited in Union Bank, Cash, $1688.90. 30. Drew from Union Bank, and invested in Bryant & Stratton's concern, $2688.90.

---

* The account with Bryant & Stratton should be treated in H. B. Bryant's books the same as any personal account. Mr. Bryant has, in reality, *lent* this money to Bryant & Stratton. He, therefore, should debit them and credit cash. See corresponding entry on Bryant & Stratton's Books, Set IV.

† The note which we hold against W. H. Crocker is really worth its face, less the interest for the time it has yet to run, and will be received only for its real value, $4470.25. In this transaction, therefore, we pay for our note, $11575, and for the discount on W. H. Crocker's note, $29.75. Our entry, then, is,—*Debits:* Bills Payable, $11575; Interest, $29.75—*Credits:* Bills Receivable, $4500; Cash, $7104.75.

Trial Balance.

Differences.		Footings.			Footings.		Differences.	
				. . H. B. Bryant	12216	15	12216	15
		37	50	. . Merchandise	40		2	50
		12000		. . Real Estate.	12500		500	
		18793	65	. . Cash	18793	65		
		4500		. . Bills Receivable . . .	4500			
		2688	90	. . Union Bank	2688	90		
		11575		. . Bills Payable	11575			
		9000		. . Mortgage Payable . .	9000			
		4000		. . E. R. Felton	4000			
12688	90	12688	90	. . Bryant & Stratton . .				
29	75	29	75	. . Interest				
12718	65	75313	70		75313	70	12718	65

Balance Account.

Resources.			Liabilities.		
Bryant & Stratton . . .	12688	90	H. B. Bryant	12688	90

The above Balance account shows the final result of the three months' business of H. B. Bryant, embraced in the foregoing three Sets, and most clearly demonstrates the fundamental principle for which we have contended. It will be apparent that this result could as well, and much more easily, have been shown without closing the Ledger at the end of each month, but the student, if he has faithfully followed his instructions, will not find it necessary to inquire why this was not done. We might have presented a greater variety of transactions had we chosen a different kind of business for each Set; but that would have deprived us of one of our chief objects—that of exhibiting the method of opening a new set of Books from the Balance account of an old Ledger, and the continuation of the same business from one set to another. Having, as we think, faithfully accomplished this part of our design, we shall seek new attractions and illustrations in other channels.

COMMISSION BUSINESS.

SALES BOOK AND ACCOUNTS SALES.

On the three following pages we give a few brief examples of the special forms necessary in a Commission business. They are not submitted as models, but as forms most commonly in use. The Commission Sales Book on pages 72 and 73 contains all the particulars connected with the three consignments which comprise a large share of our business in Set III., and the Accounts Sales on the opposite page are simply abstracts of those special sales, such as the commission merchant sends to his principal upon the "closing out" of a consignment. We have varied the form in these Accounts Sales, that the student may become familiar with the different methods of expressing the same result, in use among business men.

Account Sales of {500 bbls. Flour, 5000 bush. Wheat,} on % and risk of J. R. Wheeler & Co.

Mar.	5	Sold Wm. H. Crocker, on his Note @ sixty days, 500 bbls Flour, @ $9	4500 00	
	6	Sold J. C. Bryant, for Cash, 5000 bush. Wheat, @ $1.50	7500 00	12000
		Charges.		
	2	Paid Freight, in Cash	100 00	
	6	Storage and Advertising	25 00	
		Commission, 2½ % on $12000	300 00	425
		J. R. W. & Co.'s net proceeds . . . . Due by Equation, March 30.		11575
		E. E. NEW YORK, *March* 6, 1859.	H. B. BRYANT, *per Packard.*	

M. B. Scott—In Account Sales with H. B. Bryant.

1859 Mar.	5	To Cash paid Freight and Ins. . .	175		1859 Mar.	7	By 800 bush. Corn, @ 80 c.		640
	9	" Storage and Advertising . . .	40				Taken to our account.		
		" Commission 2½ % on $2890. .	72	25		9	By Cash, Sold C. Claghorn,		
		" M. B. Scott's net proceeds . .	2602	75			2000 bush. Oats @ 75 c.	$1500	
		Remitted herewith.					500 bush. Wheat @ $1 50	750	2250
		E. E. NEW YORK, *March* 9, 1859.	2890				H. B. BRYANT, *per Packard.*		2890

Sales of {500 bbls. Extra Superfine Flour, 1000 do. Superfine do.,} for % of C. S. Dole & Co.

By H. B. BRYANT

			Barrels Ex. Sup. Flour.	Barrels Super. Flour.					
Mar	13	E. R. Felton, @ thirty days		500	@ $8 00			4000	
	20	Cash	500		@ 9 00			4500	
	25	Cash		500	@ 8 50			4250	
			500	1000				12750	
		Charges.							
	12	Paid Freight in Cash				300			
	27	Storage and Advertising				50			
		Commission on Sales, 2½ % on $12750				318	75	668	75
		Net proceeds to C. as cash, March 29						12081	25
		E. & O. E.	H. B. BRYANT, *per Packard.*						

Commission

This Book is used for the convenience of the Commission Merchant, that he may be able to see, at a glance, the condition of each Consignment.

J. R. Wheeler & Co.'s

1859	Bbls. Flour.	Bush. Wheat.						
Mar. 2	500	5000	*Per N. Y. & E. R. R.*					
			To Cash,	*Paid Transp't'n Charges*	100			
" 6			Storage & Advertising,		25			
			Commission,	2½ % *on* $12000. . . .	300		425	
			J. R. Wheeler & Co.,	*Net Proceeds*			11575	
	500	5000		*Due by Equation Mar.* 30*			12000	

M. B. Scott's

1859	Bush. Corn.	Bush. Oats.	Bush. Wheat.						
Mar. 5	800	2000	500	*Per Steamer New World.*					
				To Cash,	*Paid Freight and Ins.* .	175			
" 9				Storage & Advertising,		40			
				Commission,	2½ % *on*	72	25	287	25
				Cash,	*Net Proceeds remitted* .			2602	75
	800	2000	500					2890	

C. S. Dole & Co.'s

1859	Bbls. Ex. Flour	Bbls S. F. Flour	Bush. Rye.						
Mar. 12	500	1000	3000	*Per People's Line.*					
				To Cash,	*Paid Freight* . . .	300			
" 27				Storage & Advertising,		50			
				Commission,	*On* $12750 @ 2½ % .	318	75	668	75
				C. S. Dole & Co.,	*Net Proceeds* . . .			12081	25
					Due by Equation Mar. 29				
	500	1000	3000					12750	

* The method of equating time is fully explained in that portion of the work devoted to "Commercial Calculations."

SET III.

Sales Book.

It will be seen that the entries on this Book correspond with those on the Day Book, and its use in this connection will, it is hoped, give the student a better understanding of the nature of Commission transactions.

Consignment.

1859	Bbls. Flour.	Bush. Wheat.						
Mar. 5			By Bills Receivable,	*Sold W. H. Crocker on his Note @ 60 days,*				
	500			@ $9 00	4500			
" 6			By Cash,	*Sold J. C. Bryant,*				
		5000		@ $1 50	7500		12000	
	500	5000					12000	

Consignment.

1859	Bush. Corn.	Bush. Oats.	Bush. Wheat.						
Mar. 7				By Ship't. to N.H.,	*Assumed and Ship'd Cobb & Co.*				
	800				@ 80 cts.			640	
" 9				By Cash,	*Sold C. Claghorn,*				
		2000			@ 75 cts.	1500			
			500		@ $1 50	750		2250	
	800	2000	500					2890	

Consignment.

1859	Bbls S. F. Flour	Bbls. S. Flour	Bush. Rye.						
Mar. 13				By E. R. Felton,	*Sold him @ 30 days,*				
		500			@ $8 00. . . .	4000			
" 20				Cash,	*Sold Jno. R. Penn,*				
	500				@ $9 00. . . .	4500			
" 25				Cash,	*Sold J. H. Goldsmith,*				
		500			@ $8 50. . . .	4250		12750	
			3000	*Unsold.*					
	500	1000	3000					12750	

EXERCISES FOR THE LEARNER.

THIRD SERIES.

Memoranda.

March 1st, Commenced business with the Resources and Liabilities as shown in the Balance account of Ledger B.* 2d, Sold L. S. Bliss, for cash, 25 pieces Merrimac Prints, @ $5.75. 3d, Received from Joseph Cary, Albany, to be sold on his % and risk, 200 bbls. Flour, invoiced at $8; 10,000 lbs. canvassed Hams, invoiced at 11 c. Paid freight on same, in cash, $100. 4th, Shipped N. C. Winslow, Cleveland, to be sold on our % and risk, 200 sacks Coffee, 13,000 lbs. @ 9 c.; 6 pipes Wine, 720 gals., @ $3.50; paid cash for Insurance on same, $50. 5th, Sold W. H. Hollister, on his note at 60 days, 200 bbls. Flour, (Cary's Consignment,) @ $9. Received cash in full of John Brown's acceptance, dated Feb. 20, at 10 days, $100. 7th, Shipped per steamer Isaac Newton, and consigned to J. G. Deshler & Co., Buffalo, to be sold on our % and risk, 102 boxes Sugar, each 500 lbs. @ 5 c., which we purchased of Samuel Jones, giving in full payment therefor his note of Feb. 8, for $2550. 9th, Sold John J. Cape, at 10 days on %, 10,000 lbs. canvassed Hams, (Cary's Consignment,) @ 11 c. 12th, Closed Cary's Consignment, and rendered him an Account Sales of the same. Our charges for storage and advertising, $25; commission 2½ % on $2,900, $72.50. Joseph Cary's net proceeds, $2702.50. Due by equation April 23. 14th, Received of L. S. Paine, Tonawanda, to be sold on his % and risk, 2000 bush. Corn, invoiced at 80 c.; 1000 bush. Wheat, invoiced at $1.75; paid freight in cash, $150. 15th, Sold Stephen A. Douglas, for cash, 1,000 bush. Wheat, (Paine's Consignment,) @ $1.90; Sold Horace Greeley, for cash, 2,000 bush. Corn (Paine's Consignment,) @ 90 c. 16th, Closed Paine's Consignment, and rendered him Account Sales. Our charges for storage, etc., amount to $15. Our commission, @ 2½ % on $3700, $92.50. L. S. Paine's net proceeds remitted in cash. 20th, Received advice from N. C. Winslow, Cleveland, of the sales of Coffee and Wine shipped him on the 4th inst. Our net proceeds of the same amount to only $2500, which he has remitted us in cash. 21st, J. H. Bell pays us cash to balance %, $37.50. 22d, Paid James Buchanan's draft on us for $2520, in cash. 25th, Received advice from J. G. Deshler, Buffalo, of the sales of the sugar sent him on the 7th inst., our net proceeds of which are $2700, and for which he has remitted us his note @ 10 days from March 17th. Received cash of John J. Cape, in full of his indebtedness. 26th, Closed our % with Joseph Cary, due by equation, April 23; amount due him $2702.50; discount off, in our favor $14.70. Paid him W. H. Hollister's note, due May 7th, for $1800, less discount for 42 days. Cash for balance, $902.50.† 30th, Paid clerk hire and rent in cash, $175. Received cash in full for J. G. Deshler's note of the 17th, due this day.

---

* Second Series.

† In cases of this kind, where a debit of interest may offset a credit of the same amount, it may be optional with the accountant whether or not he make any entry to the Interest account. If it be desirable to show the total amount *received* and *paid* for interest, it will be necessary to enter all the debits and credits of the account, whether they cancel or not.

Trial Balance.

Balances.		Total Footings.			Total Footings.		Balances.	
				. . Stock.	7419	66	7419	66
		3815		. . Merchandise	3833	75	18	75
		7150		. . Bills Receivable . . .	7150			
6378	41	13718	41	. . Cash	7340			
		37	50	. . J. H. Bell	37	50		
		2520		. . J. Buchanan	2520			
		2900		. . Cary's Consignment . .	2900			
1240		3740		. . Shipment to Cleveland .	2500			
		2550		. . Shipment to Buffalo . .	2700		150	
		1100		. . John J. Cape	1100			
				. . Storage and Advertising .	40		40	
				. . Commission	165		165	
		2702	50	. . Joseph Cary	2702	50		
		3700		. . L. S. Paine's Consignment	3700			
		14	70	. . Interest	14	70		
175		175		. . Expense				
7793	41	44123	11		44123	11	7793	41

Balance Account.

Resources.			Liabilities.		
Cash	6378	41	Stock	6378	41

TO THE STUDENT.

It is presumed that you have, so far, followed out the design of the work in its practical and progressive development of the principles of Accounts, omitting nothing which has been prescribed, because you could not, for the moment, appreciate all its benefits. If you have pursued this policy, you cannot, at this stage, fail to see the advantages derived from these series of "Exercises for the Learner." Our object in instituting this feature was to shield you from the temptation of passing over the work without the trouble of *thinking*. We know the strength of such temptations, and we know, also, the utter fruitlessness of the issue, when they prevail.

We have, so far, confined our record of transactions to the old Italian method of historical Day Book, with Journal separate. We did so on account of its greater simplicity, and because we did not wish to distract the mind from more important considerations which it was necessary to enforce. As you are now more thoroughly grounded in the great truths of the science, we shall henceforth give a little attention to the more practical forms in use, and to a greater scope and variety of entries than heretofore. We wish you particularly to note the peculiar form of the Journal Day Book introduced in the following Set, that you may be able to express, in this manner, any conceivable transaction, combining all the essential points of the separate Day Book and Journal. Very few business houses adopt the old method of first entering transactions in a historical Day Book, and journalizing therefrom. Where more severely practical forms—for the purposes of condensation—are not in use, the Journal Day Book meets with great favor, as being both plain and practical.

QUESTIONS FOR REVIEW,—SET III.

1. In what particular does the statement on opening the books in this set differ from previous statements. 2. What liabilities can there be to a business except to outside parties? 3. How can you ascertain what the concern owes to the proprietors or stockholders? 4. Is this amount always apparent? 5. Why not? 6 What does the account "Shipment to Albany" represent? 7. In what particular does it differ from Merchandise account? 8. What is represented by the account "J. R. Wheeler & Co.'s Consignment?" 9. Should his account be debited with the *value* of the property consigned to us? 10. How would such an entry affect us? 11. When the property represented in "Consignment" account is disposed of, why do you cancel the account? 12. How do you determine the net proceeds of a Consignment? 13. What is represented by "Storage and Advertising" account? 14. What by "Commission?" 15. What is the nature of a draft? 16. Why do you debit Ivison & Phinney with the *face* of their draft? 17. In what particular does H. B. Bryant's "Private account" differ from his Stock account? 18. How is "Private account" sometimes closed? 19. Why is it not proper to represent the balance of such an account as a gain or a loss? 20. Would the same rule apply to Partnership as to Stock books in this regard? 21. With what amounts ought notes and cash always to be debited and credited? 22. If they are really worth more or less than the face, how ought the difference to be shown? 23. What is the chief difficulty in explaining the debit and credit of interest? 24. Will Webster's definition of "Interest" suffice as a basis for journalizing? 25. What is a *correct* definition of "Interest" as the accountant should view it? 26. Is the business represented in Set III. a gaining or losing business? 27. How can you ascertain? 28. How will a loss in business effect the proprietors' account? 29. How should the account of Bryant & Stratton be treated in Mr. Bryant's private books? 30. How should the interest due on "Mortgage Payable" have been represented at the close of the March business? 31. How could it have been done? 32. Would this have increased or decreased the loss?

GENERAL QUERIES.

33. In opening a Set of Books, what is the first consideration? 34. What will always be the difference between the resources of a concern and its *outside* liabilities? 35. Does Stock account in an individual business always represent the invested capital? 36. When does it not? 37. Will Stock account and the Representative accounts, taken together, always represent the invested capital? 38. Why are the Representative accounts so called? 39. Are they less *real* than the accounts technically so called?* 40. If the increase and diminution of resources, commonly called gains and losses, should be carried immediately to Stock or Partners' Accounts, would there exist any necessity for Representative accounts? 41. What would the difference between the debit and credit sides of Merchandise account represent in that case? 42. How many methods are there of indicating the loss or gain in business? 43. What are they? 44. In what way can these two methods be made to prove each other? 45. In a final exhibit of resources and liabilities, what becomes of the Representative accounts?

* To one who has looked carefully at the distinction between Real and Representative accounts, as shown in this treatise, it will be apparent that *Representative* accounts are temporarily used for convenience' sake, containing the gains and losses which are finally to be carried to Stock or Partners' accounts, thereby increasing or decreasing the net investment; while *Real* accounts are permanent, exhibiting perpetually, in the difference between their sides, exact resources or liabilities. While Representative accounts must always cease to exist by being absorbed into the accounts which they represent, whenever an exhibit of the *condition* of the business is necessary, Real accounts form the essential matter of all such exhibits.

SET IV.

JOURNAL DAY BOOK,

COMMISSION SALES BOOK, INVOICE BOOK, FORMS OF NOTES, DRAFTS, LETTERS, ETC.

LEDGER CLOSED WITHOUT BALANCE ACCOUNT; ALSO, BY JOURNAL ENTRIES.

PARTNERSHIP BUSINESS: PROSPEROUS.

REMARKS ON SET IV.

In the transactions of this Set, we have introduced several new features, which will require more than a passing thought from the student.

FIRST.—*The form of original entry—combining the Day Book and Journal.* This form is the most practical in use for general purposes, and is adopted, in essence, by accountants, in every department of business. Its chief advantages are in dispensing with a separate Journal, and in bringing the Day Book and Journal entries into such immediate connection as to leave no room to doubt their identity. The only objection that can be urged against it is the difficulty of making the entry intelligible, as well as symmetrical. As there can exist no transactions more difficult of expression than those given in this Set, we think this objection should have very little, if any, force. However, the student will often find his ingenuity taxed to the utmost in submitting transactions to this form.

SECOND.—*The different methods of considering Mdse. Co. transactions.* It will, of course, be understood that by "Merchandise Companies" is meant the temporary copartnerships existing between the consignor and consignee, having reference to the sale of particular consignments of merchandise. The nature of this species of copartnership differs from that of a general copartnership only in its duration, and the manner of conducting its sales. In Mdse. Co business, one of the partners—the consignee—is the commission merchant, and, in that capacity, receives and disposes of the property as he would of a simple consignment; the only difference being that he is interested in the gains and losses. The two methods alluded to, and which are fully illustrated in the two months comprising this Set, differ only as regards the opening and closing entries. In the *first* method—exemplified by the three Mdse. Co. accounts, "A," "B," and "C," in the month of April—the principle recognized is, that the *holder* of the property is responsible for it. Thus, when we receive from Logan, Wilson & Co. an invoice to be sold on joint %, we debit "Mdse. Co. A" with the invoice and expenses, and credit the consignors with the cost of the invoice, thus making ourselves responsible for the property as though it were all our own. The consignor's entry, if recognizing the same principle, will be to debit us for the entire cost of the merchandise.* In the *second* method, shown by the three Mdse. Co. accounts, "D," "E," and "F," the principle recognized is that the *owner* of the property is responsible. Thus, when we receive from Wm. K. Sadler, merchandise to be sold on joint account, we debit "Mdse. Co. D" with *our own share* only, and credit the consignor. The consignor's entry, in this case, if made to correspond with ours, would be to debit us for our share, and "Shipment in Co. to New York," for his share.

Where there are more than two parties interested, if the accounts are kept by the *first* method, the consignee should, as before, debit the Mdse. Co. account with its entire cost—invoice and expenses—and credit the consignor with their (the consignee's and consignor's) joint share, and any other party or parties with his or their share. The consignor would, in such a case, debit the consignee with their joint share, and each of the other parties with his or their share. The other parties would, if making an entry to correspond, debit the consignee and credit the consignor each for his own share.

Where there are more than two parties interested, and the accounts are kept by the *second* method, the consignee should debit "Mdse. Co." account *for his own share* and all the charges, and credit the consignor for his (the consignee's share). The consignor, on the other hand, should debit each of the parties for their respective shares, and "Ship't in Co." for his own

---

* The supposition, in all these cases, is that the consignor furnishes from his own resources the property shipped

share. Each of the other parties should debit "Shipment in Co.," and credit the consignor each for his own share.

The examples given, it is hoped, will fully illustrate these several points, and fasten the principles upon the mind of the learner. As will be seen in the results, the only difference in the two methods, is a simple matter of time. By the first method, the consignee is considered as responsible for the property *when he receives it*, and by the second, *when he has disposed of it.* The final result is the same in either case.

We do not submit these separate methods because we deem our understanding of them so essential in the conduct of Mdse Co. accounts,—although it is essential in this regard,—but because the more the learner permits himself to dwell upon these principles, and the better he comprehends them in all their bearings, the more thorough and available will be his knowledge of the science. He will learn little by copying the Journal where the opening and closing entries are made ready to hand, and the calculations upon which they are based are performed by the author, but in applying the principles in writing up the "Exercises" which follow, he will have ample opportunity to test his proficiency. We need hardly say, that, so far as absolute right and responsibility are concerned, the *second* method is the correct and philosophical one—the principle recognized being that the *owner* of the property is responsible. The only advantage possessed by the *first* method is, that the "Mdse. Co." account shows its entire cost at the commencement.

The student will, doubtless, find it difficult to classify Mdse. Co. accounts, as, in their current condition, they are neither Real nor Representative. It is for this reason, mainly, that it is deemed best to close them by a Journal entry, when the property they represent is disposed of. They might be made either Real or Representative. Thus, by debiting them with all the cost, and our share of the gain—(or, crediting with our share of the loss) the difference will represent what we owe to the parties interested, the account becoming thus Real. Or, by debiting them with all the cost and the gains of the other parties (or crediting with the loss of other parties), the difference will represent our gain or loss, and the account thus becomes Representative. The learner will gain much by looking at this matter in all its bearings.

Third.—*The different methods of closing the Ledger.* In the month of April, the Ledger is closed without the use of a Balance account, by bringing down the resources and liabilities under their proper accounts. This is the *business* method; and if each month is supposed to represent a year, this would be a fair example of the manner of closing business books at the end of each year, forming a basis of resources and liabilities for the next year's accounts. The method of closing the Ledger by Journal entries, as exemplified in the month of May, is usual in a large proportion of business houses, though requiring more labor, and possessing no advantage over the method heretofore explained. The usual entry in bringing down resources and liabilities is: "Old account, Dr. To New account," and the reverse. The "Balance" account is precisely the same as "New account."

Fourth.—*A larger variety of auxiliary forms.* We have purposely introduced a great variety of auxiliaries that the student may become familiar with forms. We shall hereafter indicate how a majority of these books might be used, in connection with the Journal, to contain the record of original entries. This practice is becoming very prevalent in the larger business houses, where it is essential for the purposes of dividing labor and avoiding unnecessary writing. For instance, one clerk may keep the Invoice Book, another the Sales Book, another the Cash Rook, etc., and each of these may be so kept as to post directly from them to the Ledger, instead of passing all the transactions through the Journal. Or, the Bookkeeper may himself prefer to keep these special books separate, and at the same time avoid unnecessary repetitions of the same entry.

JOURNAL DAY BOOK,—SET IV.

NEW YORK, APRIL 1, 1859.

L.F.	Account	Particulars	Dr.	Cr.
	H. B. Bryant and H. D. Stratton have this day entered into copartnership, under the style and firm of "Bryant & Stratton," in the prosecution of a general Commission and Grocery Business; to invest in equal amounts, and participate alike in gains and losses.			
2	CASH	Dr.	10000	
1		To. H. B. BRYANT . .		10000
		For amount of his investment.		
	1			
2	EAST RIVER BANK	Dr.	10000	
1		To H. D. STRATTON . .		10000
		For amount of his investment.		
	"			
1	STORE AND FIXTURES	Dr. To SUNDRIES	12500	
		Bo't of H. B. Bryant his store and fixtures.		
1	To MORTGAGE PAYABLE	Assumed mortgage on the property . .		9000
3	" INTEREST	Due on mortgage to date		84
2	" CASH	For balance		3416
	3			
3	MERCHANDISE	Dr.	3900	
4		To HOPE & Co.		3900
		Bo't on %,		
		5 casks Brandy, 300 gals. @ $2 . $ 600		
		200 bbls. Mess Pork, @ $9 . . 1800		
		30,000 lbs. Bacon Sides, @ 5c. . 1500		
	"			
3	EXPENSE,	Dr.	75	
2		To CASH		75
		Paid for set of Books.		
	"			
4	MDSE. Co. A.	Dr. To SUNDRIES	3900	
		Received from Logan, Wilson & Co., Pittsburgh, to be sold on our joint % and risk, each ½,		
		800 kegs Nails, @ $3 2400		
		20,000 lbs. Lead, @ 7 c. 1400		
4	To LOGAN, WILSON & Co.	Their invoice as above		3800
2	" CASH,	Paid freight		100
	4			
5	MDSE. Co. B.	Dr.	4000	
3		To NILES & KINNE,		
		Received from N. & K., Buffalo, to be sold on our joint % and risk, each ½,		
		500 bbls. Flour, @ $8		4000
	5			
2	CASH	Dr.	1400	
4		To MDSE. Co. A.,		
		Sold Wm. H. Woodbury,		
		400 kegs Nails, @ $3 50		1400
			45775	45775

JOURNAL DAY BOOK,—SET IV.

NEW YORK, APRIL 6, 1859.

L.F.	Account	Particulars	Dr.		Cr.	
		Amounts brought forward	45775		45775	
		6				
5	BILLS RECEIVABLE	Dr.	3300			
4		To MDSE. Co. A.				
		Sold Robert Haywood, on his note, @ thirty days,				
		20,000 lbs. Lead, @ 9 c. 1800				
		400 kegs Nails, @ $3 75 1500			3300	
		"				
4	MDSE. Co. A.	Dr. To SUNDRIES	800			
		Closed company sales with Logan, Wilson & Co., and rendered them an account of the same.				
5	To STORAGE & ADVER.	. . . .			10	
5	" COMMISSION	Our charges @ 2½ % on $4700			117	50
4	" LOGAN & WILSON	Their ½ net gain, ...			336	25
4	" LOSS AND GAIN	Our " "			336	25
		"				
3	NILES & KINNE	Dr. To SUNDRIES	2915			
		Shipped them to be sold on our joint %, each ½,				
		20 hhds. Sugar, 24,000 lbs. @ 5 c. 1200				
		100 bags Coffee, 14,000 lbs. @ 10 c. 1400				
		100 boxes Raisins, @ $3 300				
		Bo't of Acker, Merrall & Co., on our note at ninety days,				
5	To BILLS PAYABLE	For above note, ...			2900	
2	" CASH	Paid insurance ½ % on $3000			15	
		8				
6	CHARLES STETSON	Dr.	4500			
5		To MDSE. Co. B.				
		Sold him @ thirty days,				
		500 bbls. Flour, @ $9, ...			4500	
		"				
5	MDSE. Co. B.	Dr. To SUNDRIES	500			
		Closed sales in company with Niles & Kinne, of Buffalo, and rendered them an Account Sales.				
5	To STORAGE & ADVER.	Our charges			20	
5	" COMMISSION	2½ % on $4500			112	50
3	" NILES & KINNE	Their ½ net gain			183	75
4	" LOSS AND GAIN	Our " "			183	75
		9				
3	SUNDRIES	Dr. To MERCHANDISE,				
		Sold Austin Packard,				
		30,000 lbs. Bacon, @ 6 c.			1800	
2	CASH	Received	800			
5	BILLS RECEIVABLE	His note @ thirty days, for balance . .	1000			
			59590		59590	

JOURNAL DAY BOOK,—SET IV.

NEW YORK, APRIL 9, 1859.

	Amounts brought forward		59590		59590	
	9					
4 5	Logan, Wilson & Co.	Dr. . . . . To Bills Payable . . Accepted their draft on us @ thirty days sight, favor Geo. K. Chase & Co. in full of their %.	4136	25	4136	25
	〃					
6	Mdse. Co. C.	Dr. To Sundries . . . . Received per Merchants' Line, from Pliny Moore, Troy, to be sold on joint % of himself, S. G. Payn, Albany, and ourselves, each ⅓, as per contract, 1000 bbls. Flour, @ $8 50 . . $8500	8700			
6	To Pliny Moore	For his and our ⅔ above invoice . . .			5666	67
6	" S. G. Payn	" ⅓ " " . . .			2833	33
2	" Cash	Paid Freight			200	
	12					
6	Steamer Empire Stock	Dr. To Sundries Bo't of Daniel Drew, ⅛ Steamer Empire, for	10000			
2	To Cash	Paid in hand			5000	
5	" Bills Payable	Gave our note @ ninety days, for . . .			5000	
	13					
6	Sundries	Dr. To Mdse. Co. C. Sold Warren P. Spencer, Buffalo, 1000 bbls Flour, @ $10			10000	
5	Bills Receivable	His note @ forty days, for	7000			
2	Cash	For Balance	3000			
	〃					
6	Mdse Co. C.	Dr. To Sundries . . . . . Closed sales in company with Moore & Payn, and rendered them each an Account of the same.	1300			
5	To Storage & Adver.	Our charges			30	
5	" Commission	2½ % on $10000			250	
6	" Pliny Moore	His ⅓ net gain			340	
6	" S. G. Payn	" " "			340	
4	" Loss and Gain	Our " "			340	
	15					
2 3	Cash	Dr. . . . . To Merchandise, Sold J. W. Lusk, Cleveland, 5 casks Brandy, 300 gals., @ $3 . .	900		900	
	16					
3	Merchandise	Dr. To Sundries, Bo't of Acker, Merrall & Co. 30 hhds. Sugar, 30,000 lbs., @ 6 c.	1800			
2	To Cash	Paid in hand			800	
6	' Acker, Mer. & Co.	Balance on %			1000	
			96426	25	96426	25

JOURNAL DAY BOOK,—SET IV.

NEW YORK, APRIL 18, 1859.

L. F.	Account	Particulars	Dr. $	¢	Cr. $	¢
		Amounts brought forward	96426	25	96426	25
		18				
2	Sundries	Dr. To Cash			200	
3	Expense	Paid Clerk hire to 15th	50			
7	H. D. Stratton, Priv.	Paid him on %	150			
		20				
5	Sundries	Dr. To Bills Receivable .			1000	
		Austin Packard has discounted his note in our favor, due May 12th.				
2	Cash	Proceeds of note	995	73		
3	Interest	Discount off, 22 days	4	27		
		〃				
3	Niles & Kinne	Dr.	300			
4		To Loss and Gain . .			300	
		Received an Account Sales of the Mdse. sent them to be sold on joint account, on the 7th inst. Our $\frac{1}{2}$ net gain as above.				
		22				
	Sundries	Dr. To Sundries				
		Shipped S. G. Payn, Albany, to be sold on joint % of S. G. Payn, Pliny Moore of Troy, and ourselves, each $\frac{1}{3}$.				
		30 hhds. Sugar, 30,000 lbs. @ $6\frac{1}{2}$ c. $1950				
		Freight on same 50				
		$2000				
6	S. G. Payn	For his and our $\frac{2}{3}$ above invoice . . .	1333	34		
6	Pliny Moore	For his $\frac{1}{3}$	666	66		
3	To Merchandise	As above			1950	
2	" Cash	Paid Freight			50	
		25				
7	H. B. Bryant, Private	Dr.	200			
2		To East River Bank .			200	
		Drew on private %.				
		〃				
3	Niles & Kinne	Dr.	968	75		
2		To East River Bank .			968	75
		Paid their draft on us favor of R. Courter.				
		28				
2	Cash	Dr.	1500			
1		To Store and Fixtures			1500	
		Received rent for upper apartments, to date.				
			102595		102595	

JOURNAL DAY BOOK,—SET IV.

NEW YORK, APRIL 28, 1859.

		Dr.		Cr.	
	Amounts brought forward	102595		102595	
	— 28 —				
7 6	STEAMER EMPIRE Dr. . . . . To STEAMER EMPIRE STOCK For our share of earnings of last trip, as per statement rendered this day.	250		250	
	— 29 —				
3 2	EXPENSE Dr. . . . . To CASH . . . . Sundry expenses to date, as per Expense Book.	159		159	
	— 30 —				
4 6	LOSS AND GAIN Dr. . . . . To S. G. PAYN . . . For our ⅓ net loss on shipment of Sugar for joint % of Payn, Moore and ourselves, of the 22d inst., as per Account Sales this day received.	115		115	
	— " —				
2 1	CASH Dr. . . . . To H. B. BRYANT . . . Amount invested this day.	2688	90	2688	90
		105807	90	105807	90

NEW YORK, MAY 1, 1859.

		Dr.		Cr.	
7	MDSE CO. D. Dr. To SUNDRIES . . . . Received from Wm. K. Sadler, Philadelphia, to be sold on our joint % each ½, 100 bbls. Cider Vinegar, @ $7 — $ 700 50 do. Linseed Oil, @ $40 . — 2000 40 h'f kegs White Lead, @ $3 — 120 $2820	1460			
7 2	To WM. K. SADLER. For our ½ above invoice . . . . . " EAST RIVER BANK Paid freight per check			1410 50	
	— " —				
2 2	EAST RIVER BANK Dr. . . . . To CASH . . . . Deposited.	8500		8500	
		9960		9960	

JOURNAL DAY BOOK,—SET IV.

NEW YORK, MAY 2, 1859.

L.F.	Account	Particulars	Dr. $	¢	Cr. $	¢
		Amounts brought forward	9960		9960	
		2				
	SUNDRIES	Dr. To SUNDRIES				
		Shipped R. W. Hoadley, Philadelphia, to be sold on joint %, each ½,				
		200 bbls. Mess Pork, @ $9 . . $1800				
		Drayage charges 18				
		$1818				
7	R. W. HOADLEY	For his ½ above invoice	909			
7	SHIPMENT IN CO. 1	" our ½	909			
3	To MERCHANDISE	As above			1800	
2	" CASH	Paid drayage			18	
		3				
2	CASH	Dr.	750			
7		To MDSE. CO. D.			750	
		Sold J. R. Bigelow, 100 bbls. Cider Vinegar, @ $7 50.				
		"				
7	INSURANCE,	Dr.	37	50		
2		To CASH			37	50
		Effected insurance for $5000 on any property that may be in our warehouse.				
		"				
8	HANNA, BEASER & CO.	Dr.	2370			
7		To MDSE. CO. D.				
		Shipped them to Detroit, as per their order,				
		50 bbls. Linseed Oil, @ $45 . . 2250				
		40 h'f kegs White Lead, @ $3 . 120			2370	
		Payable @ sixty days.				
		"				
7	MDSE. CO. D.	Dr. To SUNDRIES	1660			
		Closed sales in company with Wm. K. Sadler, and rendered him an Account Sales.				
8	To CHARGES	Storage, Advertising and Insurance . . .			50	
5	" COMMISSION	2½ % on $3120			78	
7	" WM. K. SADLER,	For his ½ Invoice $1410, and net gain $61 .			1471	
4	" LOSS & GAIN,	" our ½ net gain			61	
		5				
3	EXPENSE	Dr.	150			
2		To EAST RIVER BANK . .			150	
		Paid advertising bills of New York Herald per check.				
		6				
8	MDSE CO. E.	Dr. To SUNDRIES	2500			
		Received of F. A. Boyle & Co., New Orleans, to be sold on joint % of themselves, Campbell & Strong, and ourselves, each ⅓.				
		100 hhds. Sugar @ $60 . . . . $6000				
8	To F. A. BOYLE & CO.	For our ⅓ invoice.			2000	
2	" EAST RIVER BANK	Paid freight per check			500	
			19245	50	19245	50

JOURNAL DAY BOOK,—SET IV.

NEW YORK, MAY 6, 1859.

			Dr. $	cts.	Cr. $	cts.
		Amounts brought forward	19245	50	19245	50
8	MDSE CO. F.	Dr. To SUNDRIES	4000			
		Received from H. D. Van Syckel, St. Louis, to be sold on our joint %, each ½,				
		500 bbls. Pork, @ $9 . . . . . $4500				
		250 do Lard, 50,000 lbs., @ 5 c. . 2500				
		$7000				
8	To H. D. VAN SYCKEL	Our ½ above invoice			3500	
2	" EAST RIVER BANK	Freight per check			500	
		— 8 —				
8	SUNDRIES	Dr. To MDSE. CO. E.				
		Sold Wm. A. Holley, Fort Edward,				
		100 hhds. Sugar, @ $75			7500	
5	BILLS RECEIVABLE	Received in payment, Erastus Corning s note, dated January 1, 1859, due one day after date, ...	5000			
3	INTEREST	Due to date on above note	123	47		
2	CASH,	For balance.	2376	53		
		— " —				
8	MDSE. CO. E.	Dr. To SUNDRIES	5000			
		Closed Mdse. Co. E., and rendered Account Sales of the same to F. A. Boyle and Campbell & Strong, New Orleans.				
8	To CHARGES	Storage, Advertising, etc.			50	
5	COMMISSION	2½ % on $7500			187	50
8	F. A. BOYLE	His net proceeds			2254	16
8	CAMPBELL & STRONG	Their net proceeds			2254	17
4	LOSS AND GAIN	Our ⅓ net gain			254	17
		— " —				
2	CASH	Dr.	3300			
5		To BILLS RECEIVABLE . .			3300	
		R. Haywood has paid his note, due this day.				
		— 10 —				
2	EAST RIVER BANK	Dr.	4000			
2		To CASH			4000	
		Deposited.				
		— 12 —				
2	SUNDRIES	Dr. To EAST RIVER BANK . .			4657	50
		Paid on mortgage, favor of Wm. B. Astor.				
1	MORTGAGE PAYABLE	Amount applied on mortgage	4500			
3	INTEREST	In full to date	157	50		
		— 13 —				
5	BILLS PAYABLE	Dr.	4136	25		
2		To EAST RIVER BANK . .			4136	25
		Paid our acceptance, favor Logan, Wilson & Co., due this day.				
			51839	25	51839	25

NEW YORK, MAY 13, 1859.

Fol.	Account	Particulars	Dr. $	cts.	Cr. $	cts.
		Amounts brought forward	51839	25	51839	25
4	Hope & Co.	Dr.	3900			
5		To Bills Payable . . .			3900	
		Accepted their draft on us payable @ ten days sight.				
		14				
2	Cash	Dr.	4750			
8		To Mdse Co. F.				
		Sold E. A. Charlton,				
		500 bbls. Pork, @ $9.50			4750	
		15				
8	Hanna, Beaser & Co.	Dr.	275			
4		To Loss and Gain			275	
		Received advice from H. B. & Co., Detroit, of an error in an Account Sales of last year's business, in which we were credited too little by the above amount.				
		"				
8	Sundries	Dr. To Hanna, Beaser & Co. .			2645	
		Sold our draft on them @ thirty days sight.				
2	Cash	Net proceeds	2600	05		
3	Interest	Discount and Exchange off	44	95		
		17				
2	Cash	Dr.	2000			
8		To Mdse. Co. F.			2000	
		Sold Theron W. Woolson				
		250 bbls. Lard, 50,000 lbs.,@ 4 c.				
		"				
	Sundries	Dr. To Sundries,				
		Closed "Mdse. Co. F.," and rendered H. D. Van Syckel, St. Louis, an Account Sales of the same.				
8	Mdse. Co. F.	To close %	2750			
4	Loss and Gain.	Our ½ net loss	484	37		
8	To Charges	Storage, Cooperage, etc.			50	
5	" Commission	2½ % on sales			168	75
8	" H. D. Van Syckel	His ½ invoice $3500				
		Less ½ net loss 484 38				
		Leaves net proceeds			3015	62
		"				
8	H. D. Van Syckel	Dr.	6515	62		
2		To Cash			6515	62
		Remitted him in full of %.				
		"				
2	Cash	Dr.	7000			
5		To Bills Receivable . .			7000	
		Received payment in full for W.P. Spencer's note of the 13th April.				
			82159	24	82159	24

JOURNAL DAY BOOK,—SET IV.

NEW YORK, MAY 20, 1859.

L.F.		Dr.		Cr.	
	Amounts brought forward	82159	24	82159	24
	—— 23 ——				
2	EAST RIVER BANK Dr.	10000			
2	To CASH			10000	
	Deposited.				
	—— 25 ——				
7	R. W. HOADLEY Dr.	800			
7	To SHIPMENT IN CO. 1 .			800	
	Received an Account Sales of 200 bbls. Mess Pork, shipped him on the 2d inst. Our net proceeds as above.				
	—— 26 ——				
7	WM. K. SADLER Dr.	2881			
5	To BILLS PAYABLE . .			2881	
	Accepted his draft on us @ thirty days sight, favor of B. McGann, for amount his due.				
	—— 27 ——				
5	BILLS PAYABLE Dr.	3900			
2	To CASH			3900	
	Paid our acceptance favor of Hope & Co., due this day.				
	—— 28 ——				
2	CASH Dr.	4500			
6	To CHARLES STETSON			4500	
	To Balance %.				
	—— 30 ——				
6	ACKER, MERRALL & CO. Dr.	1000			
2	To CASH			1000	
	To Balance %.				
	—— 31 ——				
1	H. B. BRYANT Dr.	200			
7	To H. B. BRYANT, Private			200	
	For amount charged to H. B. B.'s private account, now carried to his Stock account.				
	—— " ——				
1	H. D. STRATTON Dr.	150			
6	To H. D. STRATTON, Private			150	
	For amount charged to Private account, now carried to Stock account.				
	—— " ——				
3	INTEREST Dr.	15	68		
1	To H. B. BRYANT . .			15	68
	Allowed 7 % on his additional investment of April 30.				
		105605	92	105605	92

JOURNAL DAY BOOK,—SET IV.

NEW YORK, MAY 31, 1859.

——CLOSING ENTRIES.——

L.F.	Particulars	Dr. $	cts.	Cr. $	cts.
8	BALANCE Dr.	15000			
1	To STORE AND FIXTURES			15000	
	Valuation of property.				
	〃				
1	STORE AND FIXTURES Dr.	2500			
4	To LOSS AND GAIN			2500	
	For increase in value of property.				
	〃				
1	MORTGAGE PAYABLE Dr.	4500			
8	To BALANCE			4500	
	Amount due on mortgage.				
	〃				
8	BALANCE Dr.	4575	09		
2	To CASH			4575	09
	Amount on hand.				
	〃				
8	BALANCE Dr.	21337	50		
2	To EAST RIVER BANK			21337	50
	Balance on deposit.				
	〃				
3	INTEREST Dr.	18	37		
8	To BALANCE			18	37
	Amount due from us to date on mortgage.				
	〃				
8	BALANCE Dr.	146	82		
3	To INTEREST			146	82
	Amount due us to date on E. Corning's note.				
	〃				
4	LOSS AND GAIN Dr.	213	15		
3	To INTEREST			213	15
	Cost over proceeds of Interest.				
	〃				
4	LOSS AND GAIN Dr.	150			
3	To EXPENSE			150	
	Balance of Expense account.				
	〃				
8	BALANCE Dr.	5000			
5	To BILLS RECEIVABLE			5000	
	Note on hand, (E. Corning's).				
	〃				
5	COMMISSION Dr.	434	25		
4	To LOSS AND GAIN			434	25
	Gain on Commission.				
	〃				
5	BILLS PAYABLE Dr.	10781			
8	To BALANCE			10781	
	Our outstanding notes.				
		64656	18	64656	18

JOURNAL DAY BOOK,—SET IV.

NEW YORK, MAY 31, 1859.

L.F.	Particulars		Dr.		Cr.	
		Amount brought forward	64656	18	64656	18
6	PLINY MOORE	Dr.	5340	01		
8		To BALANCE			5340	01
		Amount due him.				
		//				
6	S. G. PAYN	Dr.	1954	99		
8		To BALANCE			1954	99
		Amount due him.				
		//				
8	BALANCE	Dr.	10000			
6		To STEAMER EMPIRE STOCK			10000	
		Valuation of our interest in Steamer Empire.				
		//				
8	BALANCE	Dr.	250			
7		To STEAMER EMPIRE . .			250	
		Amount due us.				
		//				
8	BALANCE	Dr.	1709			
7		To R. W. HOADLEY . .			1709	
		Balance due us.				
		//				
4	LOSS AND GAIN	Dr.	109			
7		To SHIPMENT IN CO. 1 .			109	
		Our loss on shipment.				
		//				
4	LOSS AND GAIN	Dr.	37	50		
7		To INSURANCE			37	50
		Cost of insurance.				
		//				
8	CHARGES	Dr.	150			
4		To LOSS AND GAIN . .			150	
		Gain on storage, advertising, etc.				
		//				
8	F. A. BOYLE & CO.	Dr.	4254	16		
8		To BALANCE			4254	16
		Amount due them.				
		//				
8	CAMPBELL & STRONG	Dr.	2254	17		
8		To BALANCE			2254	17
		Amount due them.				
		//				
4	LOSS AND GAIN	Dr. To SUNDRIES	2680	40		
		Net gain carried to Partners' %.				
1	To H. B. BRYANT	His ½ net gain			1340	20
1	" H. D. STRATTON	" " " "			1340	20
		//				
1	H. B. BRYANT	Dr.	15785	14		
8		To BALANCE			15785	14
		For amount his net capital.				
		//				
1	H. D. STRATTON	Dr.	13130	57		
8		To BALANCE			13130	57
		For amount his net capital.				
			122311	12	122311	12

LEDGER,—SET IV.

H. B. Bryant.

Dr.								Cr.			
1859						1859					
Apr.	31	*To Balance*	L1	14629	26	Apr.	1	By Cash	1	10000	
						"	30	"	5	2688	90
						"	30	Loss and Gain	L4	1940	36
				14629	26					14629	26
May	31	To H. B B. private	9	200		May	1	By Balance	L1	14629	26
"	31	Balance	11	15785	14	"	31	Interest	9	15	68
						"	31	Loss and Gain	11	1340	20
				15985	14					15985	14

H. D. Stratton.

Dr.								Cr.			
1859						1859					
Apr.	30	*To Balance*	L1	11940	37	Apr.	1	By East River Bank	1	10000	
						"	30	Loss and Gain	L4	1940	37
				11940	37					11940	37
May	31	To H. D. S. private	9	150		May	1	By Balance	L1	11940	37
"	"	Balance	11	13130	57	"	31	Loss and Gain	11	1340	20
				13280	57					13280	57

Store and Fixtures.

Dr.								Cr.			
1859						1859					
Apr.	3	To Sundries	1	12500		Apr.	28	By Cash	6	1500	
"	30	*Loss and Gain*	L4	1500		"	30	*Balance*	L1	12500	
				14000						14000	
May	1	To Balance	L1	12500		May	31	By Balance	8	15000	
"	31	Loss and Gain	11	2500							
				15000						15000	

Mortgage Payable.

Dr.								Cr.			
1859						1859					
May	12	Tc East River Bank	7	4500		Apr.	3	By Store Fixtures	1	9000	
"	31	Balance	8	4500							
				9000						9000	

LEDGER,—SET IV.

Dr. Cash. Cr.

1859						1859					
Apr.	1	To H. B. Bryant	1	10000		*Apr.*	3	By Store and Fixtures	1	3416	
"	5	Mdse. Co. A.	1	1400		"	"	Expense	1	75	
"	9	Mdse.	2	800		"	4	Mdse Co. A.	1	100	
"	13	Mdse. Co. C.	3	3000		"	7	Niles & Kinne	2	15	
"	15	Mdse.	3	900		"	9	Mdse. Co. C.	3	200	
"	20	Bills Receivable	4	995	73	"	12	Steamer Empire Stock	3	5000	
"	28	Store and Fixtures	4	1500		"	16	Mdse.	3	800	
"	30	H. B. Bryant	5	2688	90	"	18	Sundries	4	200	
						"	22	"	4	50	
						"	29	Expense	5	159	
						"	3	*Balance*	L 8	11269	63
				21284	63					21284	63
May	1	To Balance	L 2	11269	63	*May*	1	By East River Bank	5	8500	
"	3	Mdse. Co. D.	6	750		"	2	Sundries	6	18	
"	8	Mdse. Co. E.	7	2376	53	"	3	Insurance	6	37	50
"	9	Bills Receivable	7	3300		"	10	East River Bank	7	4000	
"	14	Mdse. Co. F.	8	4750		"	17	H. D. Van Syckel	8	6515	62
"	15	Hanna, Beaser & Co.	8	2600	05	"	23	East River Bank	9	10000	
"	17	Mdse. Co. F.	8	2000		"	27	Bills Payable	9	3900	
"	17	Bills Receivable	8	7000		"	30	Acker, Merrall & Co.	9	1000	
"	27	Chas. Stetson	9	4500		"	31	Balance	10	4575	09
				38546	21					38546	21

Dr. East River Bank. Cr.

1859						1859					
Apr.	1	To H. D. Stratton	1	10000		*Apr.*	25	By H. B. Bryant	4	200	
						"	"	Niles & Kinne	4	968	7
						"	30	*Balance*		8831	25
				10000						10000	00
May	1	To Balance	L 2	8831	25	*May*	1	By Mdse. Co. D.	5	50	
"	1	Cash	5	8500		"	5	Expense	6	150	
"	10	"	7	4000		"	6	Mdse. Co. E.	6	500	
"	23	"	9	10000		"	7	Mdse. Co. F.	7	500	
						"	12	Sundries	7	4657	50
						"	13	Bills Payable	7	4136	25
						"	31	Balance	10	21337	50
				31331	25					31331	25

Interest.

Dr.						Cr.					
1859						1859					
Apr.	20	To Bills Receivable	4	4	27	Apr.	3	By Store and Fixtures	1	84	
"	3	*Loss and Gain*	L4	79	73						
				84						84	
May	8	To Mdse. Co. E.	7	123	47	May	31	By Balance	10	146	82
"	12	East River Bank	7	157	50	"	"	Loss and Gain	10	213	15
"	5	Hanna, B. & Co.	8	44	95						
"	31	H. B. Bryant	9	15	68						
"	31	Balance	10	18	37						
				359	97					359	97

Expense.

Dr.						Cr.					
1859						1859					
Apr.	3	To Cash	1	75		Apr.	30	*By Loss and Gain*	L4	284	
"	18	"	4	50							
"	29	"	5	159							
				284						284	
May	5	To East River Bank	9	150		May	31	By Loss and Gain		150	

Niles & Kinne.

Dr.						Cr.					
1859						1859					
Apr.	6	To Sundries	2	2915		Apr.	4	By Mdse. Co. B.	2	4000	
"	20	Loss and Gain	4	300		"	8	" "	3	183	75
"	25	East River Bank	4	968	75						
				4183	75					4183	75

Merchandise.

Dr.						Cr.					
1859						1859					
Apr.	3	To Sundries	1	3900		Apr.	9	By Sundries	2	1800	
"	16	"	3	1800		"	15	Cash	3	900	
"	30	*Loss and Gain*	L4	750		"	22	Sundries	4	1950	
						"	30	*Balance*	L5	1800	
				6450						6450	
May	1	To Balance		1800		May	2	By Sundries	6	1800	

LEDGER,—SET IV.

Loss and Gain.

Dr.						Cr.					
1859						1859					
Apr.	30	To S. G. Payn	5	115		Apr.	6	By Mdse. Co. A.	2	336	25
"	"	Expense	L 3	284		"	8	Mdse. Co. B.	2	183	75
"	"	*H. B. Bryant*	L 1	1940	36	"	13	Mdse. Co. C.	3	340	
"	"	*H. D. Stratton*	L 2	1940	37	"	20	Niles & Kinne	4	300	
						"	30	Store and Fixtures	L 1	1500	
						"	"	Interest	L 3	79	73
						"	"	Mdse.	L 3	750	
						"	"	Storage and Adver.	L 5	60	
						"	"	Commission	L 5	480	
						"	"	Steamer Empire Stock	L 6	250	
				4279	73					4279	73
May	17	To Mdse. Co. F.	12	484	37	May	3	By Mdse. Co. D.	6	61	
"	31	Interest	10	213	15	"	8	Mdse. Co. E.	7	254	17
"	"	Expense	10	150		"	15	Hanna, Beaser & Co.	8	275	
"	"	Shipment in Co. 1	11	109		"	31	Store and Fixtures	10	2500	
"	"	Insurance	11	37	50	"	"	Commission	10	434	25
"	"	Sundries	11	2680	40	"	"	Charges	11	150	
				3674	42					3674	42

Hope & Co.

Dr.						Cr.					
1859						1859					
May	13	To Bills Payable	3	3900		Apr.	3	By Mdse.	1	3900	

Mdse. Co. A.

Dr.						Cr.					
1859						1859					
Apr.	4	To Sundries	2	3900		Apr.	5	By Cash	1	1400	
"	6	"	2	800		"	6	Bills Receivable	2	3300	
				4700						4700	

Logan, Wilson & Co.

Dr.						Cr.					
1859						1859					
Apr.	9	To Bills Payable	3	4136	25	Apr.	4	By Mdse. Co. A.	1	3800	
						"	6	" " "	2	336	25
				4136	25					4136	25

LEDGER,—SET IV.

Dr. Mdse. Co. B. Cr.

Date			Fol.	$	cts.	Date			Fol.	$	cts.
1859 Apr.	4	To Miles & Kinne	1	4000		1859 Apr.	8	By Chas. Stetson	2	4500	
"	8	Sundries	2	500							
				4500						4500	

Dr Bills Receivable. Cr.

Date			Fol.	$	cts.	Date			Fol.	$	cts.
1859 Apr.	5	To Mdse. Co. A.	2	3300		1859 Apr.	20	By Sundries	4	1000	
"	9	Mdse.	2	1000		"	30	*Balance*	L5	10300	
"	13	Mdse. Co. C.	3	7000							
				11300						11300	
May	1	Balance	L5	10300		May	9	By Cash	7	3300	
"	8	Mdse. Co. E.	7	5000		"	22	"	8	7000	
						"	31	Balance		5000	
				15300						15300	

Dr. Storage and Advertising. Cr.

Date			Fol.	$	cts.	Date			Fol.	$	cts.
1859 Apr.	30	*To Loss and Gain*	L4	60		1859 Apr.	6	By Mdse. Co. A.	[illegible]	10	
						"	8	Mdse. Co. B.	[illegible]		
						"	13	Mdse. Co. C.	3	50	
				60						60	

Dr. Commission. Cr.

Date			Fol.	$	cts.	Date			Fol.	$	cts.
1859 Apr.	30	*To Loss and Gain*	L4	480		1859 Apr.	6	By Mdse. Co. A.	2	117	50
						"	8	Mdse. Co. B.	2	112	50
						"	14	Mdse. Co. C.	3	250	
				480						480	
May	31	Loss and Gain		434	25	May	3	By Mdse. Co. D.	6	78	
						"	8	Mdse. Co. E.	7	187	50
						"	17	Mdse. Co. F.	8	168	75
				434	25					434	25

Dr. Bills Payable. Cr.

Date			Fol.	$	cts.	Date			Fol.	$	cts.
1859 Apr.	30	*To Balance*	L5	12036	25	1859 Apr.	6	By Niles & Kinne	2	2900	
						"	9	Logan, Wilson & Co.	3	4136	25
						"	12	Steamer Empire Stk.	3	5000	
				12036	25					12036	25
May	13	To East River Bank	11	4136	25	May	1	By Balance	L5	12036	25
"	27	Cash	14	3900		"	13	Hope & Co.	8	3900	
"	31	Balance		10781		"	26	Wm. K. Sadler	9	2881	
				18817	25					18817	25

LEDGER,—SET IV.

Dr. Charles Stetson. Cr

Date			Fol.	Amount		Date			Fol.	Amount	
1859						1859					
Apr.	8	To Mdse. Co. B.	2	4500		*May*	28	By Cash	9	4500	

Dr. Mdse. Co. C. Cr

Date			Fol.	Amount		Date			Fol.	Amount	
1859						1859					
Apr.	10	To Sundries	3	8700		*Apr.*	13	By Sundries	3	10000	
"	13	"	3	1300							
				10000						10000	

Dr. Pliny Moore. Cr.

Date			Fol.	Amount		Date			Fol.	Amount	
1859						1859					
Apr.	22	To Sundries	4	666	66	*Apr.*	10	By Mdse. Co. C.	3	5666	67
"	30	*Balance*	L 6	5340	01	"	14	" " "	3	340	
				6006	67					6006	67
May	31	To Balance		5340	01	*May*	1	By Balance	L 6	5340	01

Dr. S. G. Payn. Cr.

Date			Fol.	Amount		Date			Fol.	Amount	
1859						1859					
Apr.	22	To Sundries	4	1333	34	*Apr.*	10	By Mdse. Co. C.	3	2833	33
"	30	*Balance*	L 6	1954	99	"	14	" " "	3	340	
						"	30	Loss and Gain	5	115	
				3288	33					3288	33
May	31	To Balance	15	1954	99	*May*	1	By Balance	L 6	1954	99

Dr. Steamer Empire Stock. Cr.

Date			Fol.	Amount		Date			Fol.	Amount	
1859						1859					
Apr.	12	To Sundries	3	10000		*Apr.*	28	By Steamer Empire	6	250	
"	30	*Loss and Gain*	4	250		"	30	*Balance*	L 6	10000	
				10250						10250	
May	31	To Balance		10000		*May*	31	By Balance	13	10000	

Dr. Acker, Merrall & Co. Cr.

Date			Fol.	Amount		Date			Fol.	Amount	
1859						1859					
May	30	To Cash	9	1000		*Apr.*	16	By Mdse.	3	1000	

Dr. H. D. Stratton—Private. Cr.

Date			Fol.	Amount		Date			Fol.	Amount	
1859						1859					
Apr.	18	To Cash	4	150		*May*	31	By H. D. S., Stock	9	150	

LEDGER,—SET IV.

Dr. H. B. Bryant—Private. Cr.

1859 Apr	25	To East River Bank	4	200		1859 May	31	By H. B. B., Stock	9	200	

Dr. Steamer Empire. Cr.

1859 Apr.	28	To Steamer Empire Stk.	5	250		1859 May	31	By Balance	11	250	

Dr. Mdse. Co. D. Cr.

1859 May	1	To Sundries	5	1460		1859 May	3	By Cash	6	750	
"	4	"	6	1660		"	4	Hanna, B. & Co.	6	2370	
				3120						3120	

Dr. Wm. K. Sadler. Cr.

1859 May	26	To Bills Payable	9	2881		1859 May	1	By Mdse. Co. D.	5	1410	
						"	4	" " "	6	1471	
				2881						2881	

Dr. R. W. Hoadley. Cr.

1859 May	2	To Sundries	6	909		1859 May	31	By Balance	11	1709	
"	25	Shipment in Co. 1	9	800							
				1709						1709	

Dr. Shipment in Co. 1. Cr.

1859 May	2	To Sundries	6	909		1859 May	25	By R. W. Hoadley	9	800	
						"	31	Loss and Gain	11	109	
				909						909	

Dr. Insurance. Cr.

1859 May	3	To Cash	6	37	50	1859 May	31	By Loss and Gain	11	37	50

Dr. Hanna, Beaser & Co. Cr.

1859 May	4	To Mdse. Co. D.	6	2370		1859 May	15	By Sundries	8	2645	
"	15	Loss and Gain	8	275							
				2645						2645	

Charges.

Dr.						Cr.					
1859 May	31	To Loss and Gain	11	150		1859 May	4	By Mdse. Co. D.	6	50	
						"	8	Mdse. Co. E.	7	50	
						"	18	Mdse. Co. F.	8	50	
				150						150	

Mdse. Co. E.

Dr.						Cr.					
1859 May	6	To Sundries	6	2500		1859 May	8	By Sundries	7	7500	
"	8	"	7	5000							
				7500						7500	

F. A. Boyle & Co.

Dr.						Cr.					
1859 May	31	To Balance	11	4254	16	1859 May	6	By Mdse. Co. E.	6	2000	
						"	8	" " "	7	2254	16
				4254	16					4254	16

Mdse Co. F.

Dr.						Cr.					
1859 May	7	To Sundries	7	4000		1859 May	15	By Cash	8	4750	
"	18	"	8	2750		"	18	"	8	2000	
				6750						6750	

H. D. Van Syckel.

Dr.						Cr.					
1859 May	17	To Cash	8	6515	62	1859 May	7	By Mdse. Co. F.	7	3500	
							18	" " "	8	3015	62
				6515	62					6515	62

Campbell & Strong.

Dr.						Cr.					
1859 May	31	To Balance	16	2254	17	1859 May	8	By Mdse. Co. E.	7	2245	17

Balance.

Dr.						Cr.					
1859 May	31	To Store and Fixtures	10	15000		1859 May	31	By Mortgage Payable	10	4500	
"	"	Cash	10	4575	09	"	"	Interest Payable	10	18	37
"	"	East River Bank	10	21337	50	"	"	Bills Payable	10	10781	
"	"	Interest Receivable	10	146	82	"	"	Pliny Moore	11	5340	01
"	"	Bills Receivable	10	5000		"	"	S. G. Payn	11	1954	99
"	"	Steamer Empire Stk.	11	10000		"	"	F. A. Boyle	11	4254	16
"	"	Steamer Empire	11	250		"	"	Campbell & Strong	11	2254	17
"	"	R. W. Hoadley	11	1709		"	"	H. B. Bryant		15785	14
						"	"	H. D. Stratton		13130	57
				58018	41					58018	41

Trial Balance—April.

Balances.		Total Footings.			Total Footings.		Balances.	
				H. B. Bryant (Stock)	12688	90	12688	90
				H. D. Stratton (Stock)	10000		10000	
11000		12500		Store and Fixtures	1500			
				Mortgage Payable	9000		9000	
11269	63	21284	63	Cash	10015			
8831	25	10000		East River Bank	1168	75		
		4	27	Interest	84		79	73
284		284		Expense				
		4183	75	Niles & Kinne	4183	75		
1050		5700		Merchandise	4650			
		115		Loss and Gain	1160		1045	
				Hope & Co.	3900		3900	
		4700		Mdse. Co. A.	4700			
		4136	25	Logan, Wilson & Co.	4136	25		
		4500		Mdse. Co. B.	4500			
10300		11300		Bills Receivable	1000			
				Storage and Advertising	60		60	
				Commission	480		480	
				Bills Payable	12036	25	12036	25
4500		4500		Charles Stetson				
		10000		Mdse. Co. C.	10000			
		666	66	Pliny Moore	6006	67	5340	01
		1333	34	S. G. Payn	3288	33	1954	99
9750		10000		Steamer Empire Stock	250			
				Acker, Merrall & Co.	1000		1000	
150		150		H. D. Stratton (Private)				
200		200		H. B. Bryant (Private)				
250		250		Steamer Empire				
57584	88	105807	90		105807	90	57584	88

INVENTORY.

Property Unsold April 30.

Store and Fixtures, valued at cost	12500
Mdse. on hand	1800
Steamer Empire Stock, at cost	10000

Trial Balance—May.

Balances.		Footings.*			Footings.		Balances.	
		200		H. B. Bryant	14644	94	14444	94
		150		H. D. Stratton	11940	37	11790	37
12500		12500		Store and Fixtures				
		4500		Mortgage Payable	9000		4500	
4575	09	38546	21	Cash	33971	12		
21337	50	31331	25	East River Bank	9993	75		
341	60	341	60	Interest				
150		150		Expense				
		484	37	Loss and Gain	590	17	105	80
5000		15300		Bills Receivable	10300			
				Commission	434	25	434	25
		8036	25	Bills Payable	18817	25	10781	
				Pliny Moore	5340	01	5340	01
250		250		Steamer Empire				
1709		1709		R. W. Hoadley				
109		909		Shipment in Co. 1	800			
37	50	37	50	Insurance				
				Charges	150		150	
				F. A. Boyle	4254	16	4254	16
				Campbell & Strong	2254	17	2254	17
				S. G. Payn	1954	99	1954	99
10000		10000		Steamer Empire Stock				
56009	69	124445	18		124445	18	56009	69

INVENTORY.

Resources and Liabilities not shown in Ledger Accounts.

Store and Fixtures, valued at		15000	
Steamer Empire Stock		10000	
Interest due us on Notes	$146.82		
Less, interest due from us	18.37	128	45

* The amounts in this column do not comprise, like those in the preceding balances, the footings of a. the Ledger accounts, but such only as do not balance or cancel. The footings of this column and its opposite will not, therefore, tally with the footings of the Journal, as has been the case with the Trial Balances heretofore. The method here adopted is the one most in use with accountants, but does not afford so sure a test of the correctness of the Ledger.

BALANCE SHEETS.

We give on the following pages two of the most condensed and perfect forms of statement known, the first representing the business of a single proprietor, as exhibited in Set I, and the second showing the result of the partnership business of Set IV. The symmetry of these Balance Sheets will commend them to the favor of all systematic accountants, while the fullness of their illustrations must satisfy all interested parties. This form of statement has been used, with more or less variation, for the last twenty years, but has never been adopted to any great extent by business houses; the chief objection being its inadequency to contain long lists of personal accounts. This objection can be overcome, in all cases where the general result alone is wanted, by using, instead of the persons' names, the general titles,—"Accounts Receivable," and "Accounts Payable." In most kinds of business this will reduce the number of accounts within the limits of this form.

A degree of ingenuity, and some patience, are necessary in preparing these Balance Sheets; but a little practice will overcome all such obstacles. The following brief explanation will enable the student to prepare this form.

Get a sheet of paper of the proper size, and for a border rule double red lines around the margin.*

First, rule the parallel head-lines, leaving proper space for the double captions, as in the example. Next, ascertain the number of Ledger accounts to be represented. This will, of course, embrace all the accounts in the Trial Balance that do not cancel. If the business is that of a single proprietor, usually called "Stock business," rule, in pencil, as many lines as will contain all the accounts, and *five* additional. If it be a partnership business, with two or more partners, rule three additional lines for each partner. Thus: for "Stock" business *five* lines more than all the accounts; for two partners, *eight* lines more than all the accounts; for three partners, *eleven* lines more, and so on.

Next, lay off proper spaces for debit and credit money columns; first, for the footings of Ledger accounts, second, for Gains and Losses, third, for Stock—or if partners, for each partner—and fourth, for Resources and Liabilities; also, for a *single* money column for Inventories, and for the Ledger titles and their Ledger folios. The position of these columns you will see in the example given. These spaces can best be appropriated by using a pair of dividers, and giving each of the captions its just proportion.

After denoting the proper space for each heading—which can best be done with pencil—commence to rule in red ink at the right hand, and bring all the lines of the first two captions—Real Accounts and Stock, or one of the partners—down to the lower pencil line. For the other partner drop two lines. For Losses and Gains drop two lines for Stock business, and an additional line for each partner.

Next, rule the foot-lines as shown, and the schedule will be ready to receive the accounts.

The process of showing results is precisely similar in its order, and the results the same as in "closing the Ledger," and will need no explanation aside from the example given.

As this form of statement, neatly done, will always challenge the admiration of a systematic business man, no student should permit himself to pass over it without fastening all its peculiarities indelibly upon his mind; and as no one qualification is more essential to the proper appearance of a Set of Books or a Business Statement than clean ruling, the student can hardly choose a better exercise than that of preparing these Balance Sheets.

* The border may be made either plain or ornamental, as best suits the taste of the accountant; but we would recommend in this, as well as all *business* statements, the utmost neatness, and the avoidance of that kind of affectation or display vulgarly known as "gingerbread work."

H. B. BRYANT'S BALANCE SHEET,—SET I.*

Taken January 31, 1859.	L. Folio.	Trial Balance. Dr.		Trial Balance. Cr.		Inventory.		Representative. Loss.		Representative. Gain.		Stock. Dr.		Stock. Cr.		Real. Resources.		Real. Liabilities.	
Stock		500	..	5000	..	....	..	....	..	....	..	....	..	4500	..				
Cash		6518	75	2084	..	....	..	....	..	....	..	....	..	....	..	4429	75		
Merchandise		2731	..	1706	25	1333	50	....	..	308	75	....	..	....	..	1333	50		
H. D. Stratton		40	..	20	..	....	..	....	..	....	..	....	..	....	..	20			
Bills Payable		500	..	1735	..	....	..	....	..	....	..	....	..	....	..	....	..	1235	
Bills Receivable		57	50	....	..	....	..	....	..	....	..	....	..	....	..	57	50		
Expense		184	..	....	..	....	..	184	..	....	..	....	..	....	..	....			
E. G. Folsom		115	..	....	..	....	..	....	..	....	..	....	..	....	..	115			
J. D. Comstock		....	..	96	..	....	..	....	..	....	..	....	..	....	..	....	..	96	
		10641	25	10641	25														
To Stock—net gain								124	75	....	..	....	..	124	75				
								308	75	308	75								
To Balance—net capital.												4624	75	....	..	....	..	4624	75
												4624	75	4624	75	5955	75	5955	75

* The Trial Balance from which this Statement is made will be found on Page 27.

BRYANT & STRATTON'S BALANCE SHEET,—SET IV.

Taken N. Y., May 31, 1859.	L Folio	Trial Balance. Dr.	Trial Balance. Cr.	Inventory.	Representative. Losses.	Representative. Gains.	H. B. Bryant. Dr.	H. B. Bryant. Cr.	H. D. Stratton. Dr.	H. D. Stratton. Cr.	Real. Resources.	Real. Liabilities.
H. B. Bryant	1	200	14644 94					14444 94				
H. D. Stratton	1	150	11940 37							11790 37		
Store and Fixtures	1	12500		15000		2500					15000	
Mortgage Payable	1	4500	9000									4500
Cash	2	38546 21	33971 12								4575 09	
East River Bank	2	31331 25	9993 75								21337 50	
Interest	3	341 60		128 45	213 15						128 45	
Expense	3	150			150							
Loss and Gain	4	484 37	590 17			105 80						
Bills Receivable	5	15300	10300								5000	
Commission	5		434 25			434 25						
Bills Payable	5	8036 25	18817 25									10781
Pliny Moore	6		5340 01									5340 01
Steamer Empire	7	250									250	
R. W. Hoadley	7	1709									1709	
Shipt. in Co. 1	7	909	800		109							
Insurance	7	37 50			37 50							
Charges	8		150			150						
F. A. Boyle	8		4254 16									4254 16
Campbell and Strong	8		2254 17									2254 17
S. G. Payn	8		1954 99									1954 99
Steamer Empire Stock	9	10000		10000							10000	
		124445 18	124445 18									
H. B. Bryant's net gain					1340 20			1340 20				
H. D. Stratton's net gain					1340 20					1340 20		
					3190 05	3190 05						
H. B. Bryant's present Interest							15785 14					15785 14
							15785 14	15785 14				
H. D. Stratton's present Interest									13130 57			13130 57
									13130 57	13130 57	58000 04	58000 04

AUXILIARIES TO SET IV.

We give herewith a few of the auxiliary books and documents which would be proper in connection with the transactions of Set IV.

We have already remarked that "the number and character of auxiliary books depend upon the nature and extent of the business, and the amount and kind of information desired;" we might have added, and upon the taste and ingenuity of the accountant. Perhaps there is no way in which a business man can more satisfactorily exhibit the lucidness of his own thoughts than by such methodical arrangement of the separate facts embraced in his transactions as are afforded in auxiliary forms. The only objection that can properly be urged against a multiplicity of auxiliary books is the additional labor required; and in large establishments even this objection is removed by the use of special books and forms containing characteristic portions of original entries; thus, all transactions involving the receipt or disbursement of cash are entered alone in the Cash Book, and posted from that book directly to the Ledger. In the same manner, all sales of merchandise are first entered and posted from the Sales Book, etc. This method we shall hereafter briefly illustrate.

We have already given, in connection with the preceding Set, (III.), one form of a Commission Sales Book. It is the form commonly in use, and is happily suggestive of the nature of the business. In this connection we give a different form, discarding the special columns for *quantities* of merchandise. The business also differs, the sales in this case being on joint account of the commission merchant and the consignor, and the net proceeds, shown both in the Sales Book and the Account Sales are made to correspond therewith.

We also give a brief exposition of the books containing our Bank Account, and the usual method of showing, perpetually, the balance on deposit. These books are too simple to need much explanation.

The letters and notes are not submitted as absolute models in their way. It would, in fact, be as difficult to afford a model of a business letter—one, we mean, which it would be proper for every one to *copy*—as it would for an artist to produce a cast of features that *everybody* would consider perfect. And that class of humane authors who aim to bless the world by doing all the *thinking*, as well as *talking*, for their generation, furnishing to hand "ready letter writers," apt "poetical quotations," and "rhyming dictionaries," should find little favor with persons competent to think for themselves.

To be able to write a *good* business letter is no small accomplishment, nor can it be acquired by studying models, although much aid may be secured in this way, pertaining to form, arrangement, and even style, if undertaken with no undue surrender of individuality; for a good business letter should be neither more nor less than the transcript of a man's thoughts, or what he would say were he to speak with care and deliberation. Now, as no two men ever think or talk exactly alike, so no two could be expected to write alike. Hundreds of men, doing business for years with each other, enjoy the most intimate and satisfactory acquaintanceship through their correspondence alone; having, it is possible, never met face to face, they, nevertheless, learn each other's peculiarities with as much certainty as if reared in the same family. All proper business letters, therefore, will differ in their general aspect, form, tone, and construction, as their authors differ in those characteristics which mark their individuality.

While all this is emphatically true, there are certain qualifications in business letters which are equally essential to all, and with reference to which, general instructions may be given.

We will enumerate a few of these points:

First. A business letter, like all other documents in manuscript, should be, chirographically, *well written.* We have no particular reference to any "System of Penmanship," meaning, rather, by a "well written" document, one which, in its general appearance, as well as upon closer inspection, will at once commend itself to the reader. Neatness and legibility are the chief requisites in a hand-writing.

Second. The grammatical construction should be faultless; and, above all, no document should be *disfigured* with misspelled words.

Third. The subject matter should be immediately apparent, stated without circumlocution, and in terms not to be misconstrued. One important characteristic in a business document is *brevity;* but brevity should never be secured at the cost of perspicuity. The briefest are sometimes the most unsatisfactory of communications, and an affectation of brevity is as reprehensible as an unnecessary display of words. The rule on this point should be, to speak plainly and directly upon the topics discussed, avoiding unnecessary repetitions, and leaving no part of the instruction or information to be guessed at or inferred.

There are other points which we might enumerate, but they are all subordinate to the three above-named; besides, there is little fear that any one will be proficient in these, and deficient in the others.

We cannot too strongly urge upon young men looking forward to a life of usefulness and honor, the importance of this department of their education, as there is no qualification which will more surely commend one to the favor of an employer than proficiency in Business Correspondence.

It is scarcely possible, in a treatise of these dimensions, to give, in detail, all the documents and forms which would enter into actual transactions such as are here recorded. We have supplied this necessity in a measure in the latter part of the work, but have not attempted a complete list. The forms of Deeds, Bonds, Mortgages, etc., vary in the different states; the printed blanks of which can be procured at any ordinary book or stationery establishment. The forms of Notes, Drafts, Receipts, etc., will be found on page 118.

It should not be taken for granted that any of the forms here introduced are the best that could be invented. They will certainly answer the purpose, and, in the absence of better, will do to adopt; but we would advise every intelligent accountant to learn to *depend upon himself*, and to ascertain and administer to his own wants. One of the most common objections urged against works on Book-keeping and Commercial Schools, is that the forms and illustrations thus inculcated are inefficient, from the fact that no two business houses use the same forms. If this argument proves any thing, it proves too much, as it would also render futile, knowledge acquired *in the counting-room*, as well as in the school-room, and the private studio. The fact is, different *forms* are but the different methods of expressing the same great truths, and are to be estimated according to the degree of explicitness with which they announce these truths.

An accountant, possessed of the least originality or energy, will be better able to prescribe his own forms than any person unacquainted with all the details of his particular business, however well versed in any other specialty of the science.

Mdse. Co. A.

1859					
Apr.	3	To Logan, Wilson & Co.	Received from L. W. & Co., Pittsburgh, to be sold on our joint % and risk each ½ 800 kegs Nails, @ $3 . . . . . . $2400 20,000 lbs. Lead, @ 7 c. 1400	3800	
		" Cash	Paid freight	100	
"	6	" Storage and Adver.	Our charges	10	
		" Commission	2½ % on $4700	117	50
		" Logan, Wilson & Co.	Their ½ net gain	336	25
		" Loss and Gain	Our " " "	336	25
				4700	
		Errors excepted.	Account Sales rendered April 6. L. W. & Co.'s net proceeds, $4136.25. Due May. 2.		

Mdse. Co. B.

1859					
Apr.	4	To Niles & Kinne	Received from N. & K., Buffalo, to be sold on our joint % and risk, each ½, 500 bbls. Flour, @ $8	4000	
"	8	" Storage and Adver.	Our charges	20	
		" Commission	2½ % on $4500	112	50
		" Niles & Kinne	Their ½ net gain	183	75
		" Loss and Gain	Our " " "	183	75
				4500	
		Errors excepted.	Account Sales rendered April 8. N. & K.'s net proceeds, $4183.75. Due May 6		

Mdse. Co. C.

1859					
Apr.	10	To Pliny Moore	Received per Merchants' Line, from Pliny Moore, Troy, to be sold on joint % of himself, S. G. Payn, Albany, and ourselves, each ⅓, 1000 bbls. Flour, @ $8.50 . . . $8500 P. Moore and our ⅔ invoice furnished by him .	5666	67
		" S. G. Payn	His ⅓ invoice as above	2833	33
"	13	" Cash	Paid Freight	200	
		" Storage and Adver.	Our charges	30	
		" Commission	2½ % on $1000	250	
		" Pliny Moore	His ⅓ net gain	340	
		" S. G. Payn	His " " "	340	
		" Loss and Gain	Our " " "	340	
				10000	
		Errors excepted.	Account Sales rendered April 13. P. Moore's net proceeds . . . . . . $6006.67 S. G. Payn's " " . . . . . . 3173.33 Due May 14.		

Sales.

1859				
Apr.	5	By Cash	Sold Wm. H. Woodbury, 400 kegs Nails @ $3.50	1400
"	6	" Bills Receivable	Sold Robert Haywood, on his note @ thirty days, 20,000 lbs. Lead, @ 9 c. . . . . . $1800 400 kegs Nails, @ $3.75 . . . 1500	3300
				4700

Sales.

1859				
Apr.	8	By Charles Stetson	Sold him, @ thirty days, on %, 500 bbls Flour, @ $9	4500
				4500

Sales.

1859				
Apr.	13	By Bills Receivable	Sold Warren P. Spencer, 1000 bbls. Flour, @ $10.00 . . . $10,000 Received his note, @ forty days, for	7000
		" Cash	Balance in cash	3000
				10000

Mdse. Co. D.

				$	cts.
1859 May	1	To Wm. K. Sadler	Received from W. K. S., Philadelphia, to be sold on our joint %, each ½,		
			100 bbls. Cider Vinegar, @ $7, . . $700		
			50 do Linseed Oil, @ $40 . . 2000		
			40 h'f kegs White Lead, @ $3 . . 120		
			Our ½ invoice $2820	1410	
"	3	" East River Bank	Paid freight, per check	50	
		" Charges	Storage, advertising and insurance	50	
		" Commission	2½ % on $3120	78	
		" Wm. K. Sadler	His ½ invoice, $1410, and net gain, $61 . . .	1471	
		" Loss and Gain	Our ½ net gain	61	
				3120	
		E. & O. E.	Account Sales rendered May 3d. W. K. S.'s net proceeds, $1471. Due by equation, June 20.		

Mdse. Co. E.

				$	cts.
1859 May	6	To F. A. Boyle & Co.	Received of F. A. B. & Co., New Orleans, to be sold on joint % of themselves, Campbell & Strong, and ourselves, each ⅓,		
			100 hhds. Sugar, @ $60 . . . . . . $6000		
			Our ⅓ above invoice	2000	
"	8	" East River Bank	Paid freight per check	500	
		" Charges	Storage, advertising, etc., ...	50	
		" Commission	2½ % on $7500	187	50
		" F. A. Boyle	His ⅓ invoice $2000, and net gain $254.16 . .	2254	16
		" Campbell & Strong	Their ⅓ invoice $2000, and net gain $254.17 . .	2254	17
		" Loss and Gain	Our ⅓ net gain	254	17
				7500	
		E. & O. E.	Account Sales rendered May 8. F. A. Boyle & Co.'s net proceeds, $2254.16. Campbell & Strong's " " 2254.17. Due by equation, May 8.		

Mdse. Co. F.

				$	cts.
1859 May	10	To H. D. Van Syckel	Received from H. D. V. S., St. Louis, to be sold on our joint %, each ½,		
			500 bbls. Pork, @ $9 . . . . . . $4500		
			250 do Lard, 50,000 lbs., @ 5 c. . . 2500		
			Our ½ invoice $7000	3500	
"	14	" East River Bank	Paid freight per check	500	
		" Charges	Storage, cooperage, etc	50	
		" Commission	2½ % on $6750	168	75
		" H. D. Van Syckel	His ½ invoice $3500, less his net loss $484.38 .	3015	62
				7234	37
		E. & O. E.	Account Sales rendered May 14. H. D. Van Syckel's net proceeds . $3015.62 Due by equation, May 16.		

Sales.

Date		Account	Particulars	$	cts.
1859 *May*	3	By Cash	Sold J. R. Bigelow, 100 bbls. Cider Vinegar, @ $7.50 . .	750	
"	"	" Hanna, Beaser & Co.	Shipped them to Detroit, per their order, 50 bbls. Linseed Oil, @ $45 . . . . $2250; 40 h'f kegs White Lead, @ $3 . . . 120; Payable at sixty days.	2370	
				3120	

Sales.

Date		Account	Particulars	$	cts.
1859 *May*	8	By Bills Receivable	Sold Wm. A. Holley, Fort Edward, 100 hhds. Sugar, @ $75 . . . . . . Received in payment a note against Erastus Corning for	5000	
		" Interest	Interest due on same to date	123	47
		" Cash	For balance	2376	53
				7500	

Sales.

Date		Account	Particulars	$	cts.
1859 *May*	14	By Cash	Sold E. A. Charlton, 500 bbls. Pork, @ $9.50	4750	
"	17	" Cash	Sold Theron W. Woolson, 250 bbls. Lard, 50,000 lbs., @ 4 c. . . .	2000	
		" Loss and Gain	Our net loss	484	37
				7234	37

Account Sales of { 800 kegs Nails, 20000 lbs. Lead, } on joint % of Logan, Wilson & Co., and ourselves, each ½.

1859					
Apr.	5	Sold for Cash,			
		400 kegs Nails, @ $3.50		1400	
"	6	Sold R. Haywood, on his note @ 30 days,			
		20,000 lbs. Lead, @ 9 cents	$1800		
		400 kegs Nails, @ $3.75	1500	3300	
				4700	
		Charges.			
"	3	Paid Cash for Freight	100		
"	6	Storage and Advertising	10		
		Commission, 2½ % on $4700	117.50		
		Our ½ net gain on Sales	336.25	563	75
		Logan, Wilson & Co.'s net proceeds		4136	25
		Invoice, 800 kegs Nails, @ $3	2400		
		20,000 lbs. Lead, @ 7 cents	1400		
		½ net gain	336.25		
		Net proceeds as above	$4136.25		
		E. E.			
		Due by Equation, May 2.			
		BRYANT & STRATTON, per *Packard.*			
		NEW YORK, *April* 6, 1859.			

Account Sales of 500 Bbls. Flour on joint % of Niles & Kinne and ourselves, each ½.

1859					
Apr.	8	Sold Charles Stetson @ 30 days, on %,			
		500 bbls. Flour, @ $9		4500	
		Charges.			
"	8	Storage and Advertising	$20		
		Commission, 2½ % on $4500	112.50		
		Our ½ net gain	183.75	316	25
				4183	75
		Invoice, 500 bbls. Flour, @ $8	4000		
		½ net gain	183.75		
		Net proceeds as above	$4183.75		
		E. E.			
		Due by Equation, May 6.			
		BRYANT & STRATTON, per *Packard.*			
		NEW YORK, *April* 8, 1859.			

Sales of 1000 bbls. Flour, on joint % of Pliny Moore, Troy, S. G. Payn, Albany, and ourselves, each ⅓.

1859					
Apr.	13	Sold Warren P. Spencer,			
		1000 bbls. Flour, @ $10		10000	
		Cash, $3000—Note @ forty days, $7000.			
		Charges.			
"	10	Paid Freight, in cash	$200		
"	12	Storage and Advertising	30		
		Commission 2½ % on $10000	250		
		S. G. Payn's net proceeds	3173.33		
		Our ½ net gain	340	3993	33
		P. Moore's net proceeds*		6006	67
		Invoice 1000 bbls. Flour @ $8.50	8500		
		Your and our ⅔ of above	5666.67		
		" ⅓ net gain	340		
		Net proceeds as above	$6006.67		
		Due by Equation, May 14.			

E. E.

BRYANT & STRATTON,
per Packard.

NEW YORK, *April* 13, 1859.

Sales of {100 bbls. Cider Vinegar, 50 do Linseed Oil, 40 h'f kegs White Lead,} on joint % of W. K. Sadler and ourselves, ea ½.

1859				
May	3	Sold J. R. Bigelow, for cash,		
		100 bbls. Cider Vinegar, @ $7.50		750
"	3	Assumed and shipped on our own %, @ sixty days,		
		50 bbls. Linseed Oil, @ $45	$2250	
		40 h'f kegs White Lead, @ $3	120	2370
				3120
		Charges.		
"	1	Freight per check	50	
	3	Storage, Advertising and Insurance	50	
		Commission 2½ % on $3120	78	
		Our ½ net gain	61	239
		W. K. Sadler's net proceeds		2881
		Invoice 100 bbls. Cider Vinegar, @ $7	700	
		50 do Linseed Oil, @ 40	2000	
		40 h'f kegs White Lead, @ $3	120	
			2820	
		Net gain	61	
		Net proceeds as above	$2881	
		Due by Equation, June 20.		

E. E.

BRYANT & STRATTON,
per Packard.

NEW YORK, *May* 3, 1859.

* A duplicate of this statement is sent to S. G. Payn.

Sales of 100 hhds. Sugar on joint % of F. A. Boyle & Co., N. O., Campbell & Strong, and ourselves, each $\frac{1}{3}$.

1859					
May	8	Sold Wm. A. Holley, Fort Edward, 100 hhds. Sugar, @ $75		7500	
		Charges.			
"	6	Paid Freight	$500		
"	8	Storage, Advertising, etc.	50		
		Commission $2\frac{1}{2}$ % on $7500	187.50		
		Campbell & Strong's net proceeds	2254.17		
		Our $\frac{1}{3}$ net gain	254.17	3245	84
		F. A. Boyle & Co.'s net proceeds*		4254	16
		Invoice, 100 hhds. Sugar, @ $60	$6000		
		Your and our $\frac{2}{3}$ invoice	4000		
		Your $\frac{1}{3}$ net gain	254.16		
		Net proceeds as above	$4254.16		
		E. E. Due by Equation, May 8.			
		BRYANT & STRATTON.			
		NEW YORK, *May* 8, 1859.			

Sales of {500 bbls. Pork, 250 do Lard,} on joint % of H. D. Van Syckel, St. Louis, and ourselves, each $\frac{1}{2}$.

1859						
May	14	Sold for cash, 500 bbls. Pork, @ $9.50			4750	
"	17	Sold for cash, 250 bbls. Lard, 50,000 lbs., @ 4 c.			2000	
					6750	
		Charges.				
"	6	Paid Freight	$500			
"	17	Storage and Cooperage	50			
		Commission $2\frac{1}{2}$ % on $6750	168.75	718.75		
		Less our $\frac{1}{2}$ net loss		484.37	234	38
		H. D. Van Syckel's net proceeds			6515	62
		Invoice 500 bbls. Pork, @ $9		4500		
		250 do Lard		2500		
		R. E.		7000		
		Less your $\frac{1}{2}$ net loss		484.38		
		Net proceeds as above		$6515.62		
		Due by Equation, May 16.				
		BRYANT & STRATTON.				
		NEW YORK, *May* 17, 1859.				

* A duplicate of this statement is sent to Campbell & Strong.

OUTWARD INVOICE BOOK.

This Book contains copies of invoices of merchandise shipped by us, whether on our own account or that of the consignee, or on joint % of both. These copies are usually taken with a copying press, and are, therefore, exact *facsimiles* of the invoices sent. The forms here given are those most commonly in use.

Invoice of Merchandise Shipped by Bryant & Stratton, to be sold on joint % of Niles & Kinne, Buffalo, and themselves, each ½

△	20 hhds. Sugar, 24000 lbs., @ 5 c.	$1200	
△	100 bags Coffee, 14000 lbs., @ 10 c.	1400	
△	10 boxes Raisins, @ $3	400	2900
	Charges.		
	Insurance ½ % on $3000		15
			2915

BRYANT & STRATTON,
per Packard.

New York, *May* 6, 1859.

E. E.

Invoice of Mdse. shipped S. G. Payn, Albany, by Bryant & Stratton to be sold on joint % of S. G. Payn, Pliny Moore, and themselves, each ⅓.

30 hhds. Sugar, 30,000 lbs., @ 6½ c.	1950
Charges.	
Freight on same	50
	2000

BRYANT & STRATTON
per Packard.

New York, *April* 22, 185[illegible]

E. E.

Invoice of Merchandise shipped R. W. Hoadley, Philadelphia, to be sold on joint %, each ½.

◈	200 bbls. Mess Pork, @ $9	1800	
	Charges.		
	Paid Drayage	18	—
	R. R.	1818	—

BRYANT & STRATTON,
per Packard.

New York, *May* 2, 1859.

Invoice of Merchandise shipped Hanna, Beaser & Co., as per their order.

◈	50 bbls. Linseed Oil, @ $45	2250		
◈	40 h'f kegs White Lead, @ $3	120	2370	

Payable @ sixty days.

BRYANT & STRATTON,
per Packard.

New York, *May* 3, 1859.

R. R.

Invoice of Tea.

Kinsey & Hinde, *Cincinnati.*

Bought of Stephen V. Albro & Co.

Terms: 4 Months.

72 *Chests Young Hyson Tea.*

108	100	115	105	119	110	
109	119	108	100	120	112	
112	122	109	112	121	115	
120	120	106	113	117	102	
103	118	105	110	104	108	
117	119	119	117	111	109	
102	117	115	115	111	112	
115	104	117	119	108	114	
112	102	109	106	115	118	
108	112	109	120	112	120	
107	120	108	104	100	119	
105	100	112	100	109	107	
1318	1353	1332	1321	1347	1346	8017

Tare, 20 % off	1603			
		6414 @ 30c.	1924	20
Charges.				
Drayage		5		
Insurance		10	15	—
			1939	20

New York, *Jan.* 13, 1860.

Straw Goods.*

NEW YORK, *February* 13, 1860.

Messrs. JOHN CALDWELL & Co.

Bought of T. J. G. CLARK.

Terms: 8 Months. Note to your own order.

No.	33 *Cases assorted goods.*			
342	36 Fine English split Straw Bonnets	@ $2.37½	85	50
516	42 " " "	2.00	84	
271	62 Embroidered Hair and Lace Bonnets	1.87½	116	25
403	16 Neapolitan Bonnets	1.75	28	
233	16 Pamela "	2.00	32	
453	42 15 End Braid "	0.87½	36	75
423	42 11 " "	0.75	31	50
543	42 Tulip and Coburg Braid Bonnets	1.62½	68	25
603	36 Hair " " "	2.25	81	
321	42 " Rustic " "	2.25	94	50
214	62 Pedal Braid Bonnets	0.42½	26	35
218	50 Florence " "	1.85	92	50
311	22 Fancy Lace Braid Bonnets	3.12½	68	75
372	42 " " over Frame Braid Bonnets.	1.87½	78	75
412	3½ doz. Canton Braid Riding Hats	5.50	19	25
415	$3\frac{8}{12}$ " Pedal Braid Bloomers	6.50	23	83
425	$3\frac{3}{12}$ " Hair and Fine split Straw Riding Hats	18.75	60	94
549	5 " Open Hair Lace Riding Hats	16.50	82	50
629	6 " Coburg and Hair "	19.62	117	72
456	5 " Fine split Straw R. H. (trimmed).	24.50	122	50
327	5 " Pamela and Tulip " "	30.00	150	
454	$6\frac{2}{12}$ " " Coburg " "	35.00	215	83
517	$3\frac{3}{12}$ " Fine Pedal " "	15.00	48	75
612	$4\frac{8}{12}$ " " Brown Lace " "	21.00	98	
4512	$5\frac{7}{12}$ " Men's English Dunstable Hats	42.00	234	50
3857	6 " Mixed Sennets " "	16.50	99	
3672	$4\frac{8}{12}$ " Colored " " "	18.00	84	
2837	$3\frac{7}{12}$ " White Leghorn " "	21.00	68	25
2856	4 " Assorted " " "	24.00	96	
3756	$3\frac{8}{12}$ " Canton R. Brim Hats	10.50	38	50
4289	$5\frac{2}{12}$ " Maracaibo Hats	27.00	139	50
2432	3 " Carracao "	21.00	63	
3162	$4\frac{3}{12}$ " Palm Leaf "	0.95	4	04
			$2690	21

E. K.

* This and the preceding Invoice are not connected with the transactions of this Set, but are submitted, in this connection, for the purpose of exhibiting a greater variety.

All Banks of Deposit furnish their dealers with the necessary blanks for keeping a Bank Account. These are, mainly, a Check-Book, a Pass-Book. and Deposit-Checks, all of which are here exhibited.

THE CHECK-BOOK,

As will be seen, is a book of blank-checks, with a margin for memoranda, containing, in brief, the Bank Account. The checks are filled and torn off, leaving the memoranda. By adding deposits and deducting checks, the balance in bank is always apparent. Many houses keep no other bank account than this, in which case, the balance in bank is always included in the Cash Account.

THE PASS-BOOK,

Exhibited below, is a simple memorandum of deposits, in which the receiving teller of the bank enters the date and amounts deposited, and as often as required the checks drawn are entered up, showing the balance in bank. This is our Receipt-Book with the bank.

The following example is intended to illustrate a folio, or two pages:

Dr. East River Bank in %				with Bryant & Sratton. *Cr.*			
1859				1859			
Apr 1	To Cash....S	10000		*Ap.* 25	By Cash. Ck. 1	200	
May 1	" .....S	8500		" 25	" ..Ck. 2	968	75
" 10	" .....S	4000		*May* 1	" ..Ck. 3	50	
" 28	" .....S	10000		" 5	" ..Ck. 4	150	
				" 6	" ..Ck. 5	500	
				" 7	" ..Ck. 6	500	
				" 12	" ..Ck. 7	4657	50
				" 13	" ..Ck. 8	4136	25
				" 13	Balance	[illegible]	[illegible]
		32500				32500	
	Balance	21337	50				

DEPOSIT-CHECKS

Accompany the deposits, and contain a memorandum of the kind of funds and the total of each deposit. The receiving teller compares these items, and if correct, enters the amount in the Pass-Book.

Deposited in EAST RIVER BANK,

By Bryant & Stratton.

New York, *Apr.* 1, 1859.

Bank Bills....................................	6000
Specie..	2500
Checks...	950
"	550
	10000

East River

1859				
Apr.	1	*Deposited*	10000	
"	25	*Check No. 1*	200	
			9800	
"	25	*Check No. 2*	968	75
			8831	25
May	1	*Check No. 3*	50	
			8781	25
"	1	*Deposit*	8500	
			17281	25
"	5	*Check No. 4*	150	
			17131	25
"	6	*Check No. 5*	500	
			16631	25
"	7	*Check No. 6*	500	
			16131	25
"	10	*Deposit*	4000	
			20131	25
"	12	*Check No. 7*	4657	50
			15473	75
"	13	*Check No. 8*	4136	25
			11337	50
"	23	*Deposit*	10000	
			21337	50

CHECK-BOOK.

Bank.

Stub	Dollars	Cents	Check
No. 1. *H. B. Bryant on private %* *April 25, 1859.*	200		No. 1. *New York, April 25, 1859.* **EAST RIVER BANK,** Pay to *H. B. Bryant,* or Bearer, *Two Hundred* $\frac{00}{100}$ Dollars. $200. *Bryant & Stratton.*
No. 2. *R. Courter, Niles & Hinne's Draft* *April 25.*	968	75	No. 2. *New York, April 25, 1859.* **EAST RIVER BANK,** Pay to *R. Courter,* or Bearer, *Nine Hundred and Sixty-Eight* $\frac{75}{100}$ Dollars. $968 $\frac{75}{100}$. *Bryant & Stratton.*
No. 3. *W. R. Jones, Freight* *May 1.*	50		No 3. *New York, May 1, 1859.* **EAST RIVER BANK,** Pay to *W. R. Jones,* or Bearer, *Fifty* $\frac{00}{100}$ Dollars. $50. *Bryant & Stratton.*
No. 4. *New York Herald, for Advertising,* *May 5.*	150		No. 4. *New York, May 5, 1859.* **EAST RIVER BANK,** Pay to *New York Herald,* or Bearer, *One Hundred and Fifty* $\frac{00}{100}$ Dollars. $150. *Bryant & Stratton.*
No. 5. *Western Tr. Co., Freight* *May 6.*	500		No. 5. *New York, May 6, 1859.* **EAST RIVER BANK,** Pay to *Western Transportation Co.* or Bearer, *Five Hundred* $\frac{00}{100}$ Dollars. $500. *Bryant & Stratton.*
			No. New York, ______ 18 **EAST RIVER BANK,** Pay to ______ or Bearer, ______ $\frac{00}{100}$ Dollars. $ ______

NOTES, DRAFTS, ETC.,—SET IV.

Receivable.

$3300.

New York, *April* 6, 1859.

Thirty days after date, for value received, I promise to pay Bryant & Stratton, or order, Thirty-three Hundred Dollars, at the East River Bank.

Robert Haywood.

$5000.

Albany, *January* 1, 1859.

One day after date, I promise to pay to William A. Holley, at the Bank of the Capitol, Five Thousand Dollars, value received.

Erastus Corning.

$1000.

New York, *April* 9, 1859.

Thirty days after date, I promise to pay to the order of Bryant & Stratton, at my office, No. 79 Cedar street, One Thousand Dollars, value received.

Austin Packard.

$7000.

Buffalo, *April* 13, 1859.

Forty days from date, I promise to pay Bryant & Stratton, or order, at the International Bank of Buffalo, Seven Thousand Dollars, value received.

Warren P. Spencer.

Payable.

$2900.

New York, *April* 6, 1859.

For value received, ninety days from date, we promise to pay to the order of Acker, Merrall & Co., Twenty-nine Hundred Dollars, at the East River Bank.

Bryant & Stratton.

$5000.

New York, *April* 12, 1859.

Ninety days from date, we promise to pay Daniel Drew, or order, Five Thousand Dollars, value received.

Bryant & Stratton.

$4136 $\frac{25}{100}$.

Pittsburg, *April* 7, 1859.

At thirty days sight, pay to the order of Geo. K. Chase & Co., at their Banking House, 13 Cooper Institute, Forty-one Hundred Thirty-six $\frac{25}{100}$ Dollars, value received, and charge to account of

Logan, Wilson & Co.

To Bryant & Stratton, New York.

NOTES, DRAFTS, ETC.—SET IV.

$3900. NEW YORK, *May* 13, 1859.

At ten days sight, pay to the order of George A. Crocker Thirty-nine Hundred Dollars, and charge to account of

HOPE & Co.

To Bryant & Stratton, New York.

Accepted May 13, 1859. Bryant & Stratton.

$2881. PHILADELPHIA, *May* 25, 1859.

At thirty days sight, pay to the order of B. McGann, Twenty-eight Hundred Eighty-one Dollars, at the Metropolitan Bank, value received, and charge to account of

WM. K. SADLER.

To Bryant & Stratton, New York.

Accepted May 26, 1859. Bryant & Stratton.

LETTER BOOK.

PITTSBURG, *April 1st*, 1859.

Messrs. Bryant & Stratton,
New York:

GENTLEMEN:—As per our agreement of the 30th ult., we ship you this day, (Invoice enclosed), 800 kegs Nails and 20,000 lbs. Lead, to be sold on our joint %.

We shall leave it entirely at your option to push them upon the market, or to await better prices. Your reputation and experience afford sufficient guarantee that whatever course you may see fit to pursue will be the best.

Very truly, yours,
LOGAN, WILSON & Co.

BUFFALO, *April 2d*, 1850.

Messrs. Bryant & Stratton,
New York:

GENTLEMEN:—Enclosed you will find Invoice of 500 bbls. Flour, which we ship you this day on joint %. You will, perhaps, find it best to take advantage of the present demand in your city to close out the sales at an early day. However, we leave that matter to your own good judgment.

Please keep us advised as to the indications.

Yours,
NILES & KINNE.

NEW YORK, *April 6th*, 1859.

Logan, Wilson & Co.,
Pittsburg:

GENTLEMEN:—We enclose you Account Sales of the Nails and Lead shipped us on the 1st inst. Your net gain, as shown, is $336.23. We think the present a favorable time for this class of sales, and shall be happy to join you in any reasonable amount.

Let us hear from you soon.

Respectfully,
BRYANT & STRATTON.

Messrs. Niles & Kinne, New York, *April 7th*, 1859.
Buffalo:

Gentlemen:—You will please find, enclosed, Invoice of 20 hhds. Sugar, 100 bags Coffee, and 100 boxes Raisins, to be sold, as per our agreement, on joint %.

We have an excellent opportunity, in prospect, of purchasing, to advantage, in this line, and shall be happy to learn from you that the demand will warrant a fair investment. We await your farther advices.

Respectfully,
Bryant & Stratton.

Messrs. Niles & Kinne, New York, *April 8th*, 1859.
Buffalo:

Gents:—Enclosed please find Account Sales of the Flour shipped us on the 2d inst. We feel satisfied with the returns, particularly as since our sales were effected, prices have materially declined. The uncertainty of European affairs renders the provision market extremely unstable, and all prognostications, at this time, unreliable. We have no doubt, however, that the ultimate tendency will be favorable to investments, and do not hesitate to advise you to secure any *good bargains* which the present seeming depression may throw in your way.

Truly, yours,
Bryant & Stratton.

Messrs. Bryant & Stratton, Troy, *April 10th*, 1859.
New York:

Gents:—I ship you to-day, as per Invoice enclosed, 1000 bbls. Flour, to be sold on joint % of yourselves, S. G. Payn, Albany, and myself, each one-third. You will please open an account with Mr. Payn, and render him an Account Sales of his one-third, as per our agreement. I have charged you for your one-third invoice. Please keep me advised.

Yours,
Pliny Moore.

Pliny Moore, Esq., New York, *April 13th*, 1859.
Troy:

Sir:—We send you, enclosed, Account Sales of Flour shipped us on the 10th, having effected the sale in less time than we had anticipated. We trust the result will be satisfactory. You now stand credited on our Books $6,006.67. We have communicated with Mr. Payn. We think the present a favorable time to invest in Flour, and shall be happy to join you in speculation, or to sell for you on commission. We await your further orders.

Respectfully,
Bryant & Stratton.

S. G. Payn, New York, *April 13th*, 1859.
Albany:

Sir:—Enclosed please find Account Sales of Flour, shipped us by Pliny Moore of Troy, as per our understanding. Your one-third net gain is $340, which gives you a total credit on our books of $3,173.33.

Respectfully, yours,
Bryant & Stratton.

Messrs. Bryant & Stratton,
New York:

BUFFALO, *April* 18, 1859.

GENTS:—We enclose you Account Sales of the Sugar, Coffee and Raisins, shipped us on the 7th inst. Your net proceeds from Sales, including Invoice and Gain, is $3215, which we have entered to your credit.

We shall be happy to hear from you.

Respectfully,
NILES & KINNE.

S. G. Payn, Esq.,
Albany:

NEW YORK, *April* 22, 1859.

SIR—We ship you this day, per Merchants' Line, 30 hhds. Sugar as per enclosed Invoice, to be sold on joint % of yourself, Pliny Moore, Troy, and ourselves, each $\frac{1}{3}$. We have advised Mr. Moore, and he will look to you for an account of the sales.

Please write to us.

Truly yours,
BRYANT & STRATTON.

Pliny Moore,
Troy:

NEW YORK, *April* 22, 1859.

DEAR SIR—We enclose you Invoice of 30 hhds. Sugar, shipped this day to S. G. Payn, Albany, to be sold on joint % as per arrangement. We have charged you with your $\frac{1}{3}$ Invoice, and advised Mr. Payn to account to you for the sales.

Very respectfully,
BRYANT & STRATTON.

Messrs. Bryant & Stratton,
New York:

ALBANY, *April* 29, 1859.

GENTLEMEN—I send you enclosed an account of the sales of Sugar shipped by you on the 22d inst. Your $\frac{1}{3}$ loss on sales as per statement, is $115, which reduces your net proceeds to $1218.34.

I regret the result, but have done the best I could, under the circumstances. The rapid decline in Sugar could not have been foreseen, and had I delayed the sales another day the result would have been far less satisfactory.

Respectfully yours,
S. G. PAYN.

Messrs. Bryant & Stratton,
New York:

PHILADELPHIA, *April* 30, 1859.

GENTS.—I ship you this day, as per arrangement, 100 bbls. Cider Vinegar, 50 do. Linseed Oil, and 40 h'f kegs White Lead, to be sold on joint %. I have charged you $\frac{1}{2}$ the enclosed invoice, according to agreement. Please exercise your own judgment in the matter of sales.

Respectfully yours,
WM. K. SADLER.

R. W. Hoadley, Esq.,
Philadelphia:

NEW YORK, *May* 2, 1859.

DEAR SIR—We enclose you Invoice of 200 bbls. Pork, shipped you this day, to be sold on our joint %. Your $\frac{1}{2}$ Invoice (charged) is $909. We shall trust entirely to your judgment in effecting sales.

Truly yours,
BRYANT & STRATTON.

Hanna, Beaser & Co.,
Detroit:

NEW YORK, *May* 3, 1859.

GENTS.—Enclosed we send you Invoice of Oil and Lead, shipped you this day, as per your order of the 28th ult. We possess extraordinary facilities for purchasing to advantage in this line, and shall be happy to merit your patronage. We trust we need not assure you that your orders shall receive the most prompt attention.

Your ob't serv'ts,
BRYANT & STRATTON

Wm. K. Sadler, Esq.,
Philadelphia:

NEW YORK, *May* 3, 1859.

DEAR SIR—We enclose you Account Sales of Vinegar, Oil and Lead shipped us on the 1st inst. We think we were fortunate in effecting the sales, and have no doubt, in the present state of the market, that, should you invest pretty heavily at your former figures you would not regret it. We will join you in any amount, or sell for you on commission.

Truly yours,
BRYANT & STRATTON.

Bryant & Stratton,
New York:

NEW ORLEANS, *April* 26, 1859.

GENTLEMEN—Your favor of the 18th is just at hand. Your proposition for a special copartnership strikes us favorably, and we have, without delay, shipped you as per Invoice enclosed, 100 hhds. Sugar, to be sold on joint % of yourselves, Campbell & Strong of this city, and ourselves, each $\frac{1}{3}$. Campbell & Strong are advised of the arrangement, and you will please communicate with them. We send you their card, and beg to say that you will find them, in all respects, first-class business men. Your references are unexceptionable, and it shall not be our fault if our mutual interests cease with this experiment. You will please exercise your own judgment in conducting sales, and have no delicacy in indicating how we may be of service to you in any direction. We are,

With much respect,
Yours,
F. A. BOYLE & CO.

Messrs. Bryant & Stratton,
New York:

ST. LOUIS, *May* 1, 1859.

GENTLEMEN—Your Mr. Stratton called on me to-day, and effected arrangements for a special partnership in the purchase and sale of provisions. I have formerly consigned on my own account to John J. Cape of your city, but shall be glad to join you in speculation. I have accordingly shipped, as per enclosed Invoice, 500 bbls. Pork, and 200 bbls. of Lard, one-half of which I have charged to your account.

Hoping that the result of this small adventure may be such as to encourage a more extensive and permanent arrangement, I beg to subscribe myself,

Very truly yours,
H. D. VAN SYCKEL.

F. A. Boyle & Co., NEW YORK, *May* 8, 1859.
New Orleans:

GENTLEMEN—We enclose you Account Sales of the Sugar shipped us on the 26th ult. There can be no trouble in disposing of such a grade at fair rates, and, if acceptable to you, we should like the experiment and risk of a much larger Invoice.

Very truly yours,
BRYANT & STRATTON.

Messrs Bryant & Stratton, DETROIT, *May* 13, 1859.
New York:

GENTLEMEN—We send you enclosed Account Sales of the Oil and Lead, shipped us the 3d inst. Your net proceeds, as per statement, has been carried to your credit.

Respectfully yours,
HANNA, BEASER & Co.

H. D. Van Syckel, NEW YORK, *May* 17, 1859.
St. Louis:

DEAR SIR—Enclosed please find Account Sales of the Pork and Lard shipped us on the 1st inst. The result has been, greatly to our regret, unfavorable, but we cannot attribute it to any fault of our own. Had we had, from indications, any reason to expect a more favorable turn of the market, we should, of course, have held on; but we chose to secure both ourselves and you against a greater sacrifice, by submitting to a lesser. You will see from the present quotations that we did not err in judgment.

Yours to command,
BRYANT & STRATTON.

Messrs. Bryant & Stratton, PHILADELPHIA, *May* 24, 1859.
New York:

GENTS.—I send you enclosed Account Sales of the Pork shipped me on the 2d inst.

Hoping you will find the result satisfactory, I remain,

Yours truly,
R. W. HOADLEY.

GENERAL LETTER OF INTRODUCTION.

BRYANT, STRATTON & PACKARD'S MERCANTILE COLLEGE,
18 COOPER INSTITUTE, NEW YORK, *May* 31, 1859.

To Whom it may Concern:

The bearer, Mr. John F. Simmons, is well known to us as a most estimable young man, and one possessing qualifications which will render him serviceable in any position of trust. He is a thorough accountant, and unusually expert and correct in calculations. We have no hesitation in recommending him to the public.

Very respectfully,
S. S. PACKARD, *Resident Principal.*

EXERCISES FOR THE LEARNER.

FOURTH SERIES.

In the following transactions we have endeavored to present the prominent features of the preceding Set, leaving the student to apply the principles without any special instruction The two months' business will represent two years' as in Set. IV., bringing down the balances at the end of the first year and closing finally by Journal entries. As in Set IV. also, the two methods of keeping Mdse. Co. Accounts are represented, to which the attention of the student is particularly called.

Memoranda for April.

April 1. J. H. Goldsmith and ————,* have this day entered into co-partnership, each investing $8000 Cash. The firm assumes to pay for J. H. Goldsmith, a note in favor of H. W. Ellsworth, dated Jan. 15, with interest @ 6 % from date; face of note $300; interest due to date, $3.75. **2.** Paid Cash for Store Fixtures, $1500, and for rent, six months in advance, $750. **3.** Bo't of H. G. Reeve & Co., 8 bags Rio Coffee, 1280 lbs., @ 10 c.; 6 chests Young Hyson Tea, 297 lbs., @ 65 c.; 10 boxes Virginia Tobacco, 350 lbs., @ 40 c. Accepted their draft, @ 60 days, favor of Chas. Strong, for the amount. **4.** Received from James Atwater, Lockport, to be sold on his and our joint %, each ½, 500 bbls. Flour, @ $8; 1000 bush. Wheat, @ $1.50; paid freight on same, in cash, $400. **5.** Received from D. L. Wing, Albany, to be sold on joint % of himself, J. Walker, Schenectady, and ourselves, each ⅓, 1000 bbls., "Julian Mills" Flour, @ $8.50; paid Freight, in cash, $100. **6.** Sold W. H. Beebe, for cash, 1000 bush. Wheat, (Mdse. Co. A. Atwater's Consignment,) @ $1.83. **7.** Sold J. W. Lusk, on %, @ 60 days, 2 chests Young Hyson Tea, 100 lbs., @ 75 c.; Sold J. C. Beale, on his note @ 10 days, 500 bbls. Flour, (Mdse. Co. A.,) @ $9; Closed Mdse. Co. A., and rendered James Atwater an Account Sales. Our charges for Storage, Advertising and Cooperage, $75; Commission 2½ % on sales $——; our ½ net gain, $98.37; James Atwater's do. $98.38. **8.** Shipped John R. Penn, Green Bay, Wis., to be sold on our joint %, each ½, the following merchandise, bought on our note, @ 4 months, of H. G. Reeve & Co., 30 hhds. N. O. Sugar, 32,000 lbs., @ 6½ c.; 40 bbls. N. O. Molasses, 1442 gals., @ 40 c.; charges for Drayage and Insurance, paid in cash, $75. **10.** Deposited with Geo. K. Chase & Co., Bankers, cash $10,000. **12.** Sold for cash, to J. & J. Wynkoop, 1000 bbls. "Julian Mills" Flour, (Mdse. Co. B.,) @ $9.50; Closed Mdse. Co. B., and rendered Account Sales of the same to D. L. Wing, Albany, and J. Walker, Schenectady. Our Charges, $75; Commission on Sales, 2½ %. D. L. Wing's ⅓ net gain, $195.83; J. Walker's do. $195.83; our do. $195.84. **15.** Paid cash for James Atwater's draft on us, at sight, $1000. **16.** Shipped Robt. C. Spencer, St. Louis, to be sold on joint % of himself, John Atwater, Chicago, and ourselves, each ⅓, the following Invoice of Merchandise, bought of A. T. Stewart & Co., for cash: 20 pieces dark blue Circassian, @ $12; 50 pieces green do. @ $10; 10 pieces Satinet, 300 yds., @ 90 c.; 15 pieces Jeans, 450 yds., @ $1.25. Deposited cash, $10,000. **17.** Shipped Stephen A. Douglas, Chicago, pursuant to his order, 8 bags Coffee, 1280 lbs., @ 11 c. **20.** Received

---

* Let the student use his own name.

cash in full for J. C. Beale's note of the 7th inst. **21.** Paid J. Walker's Draft @ sight, in full of his %, per check on Geo. K. Chase & Co. **25.** Received Account Sales from John R. Penn, Green Bay, of the Mdse. shipped him on the 8th inst. Our ½ net gain, $250. **30.** Received from R. C. Spencer, St. Louis, Account Sales of the Mdse. shipped him on the 16th inst. Our ⅓ net loss, $125. Paid cash in full for J. H. Goldsmith's note and interest—face of note $300, interest due to date, $5.25

Memoranda for May.

May 1. Received from John R. Penn, Green Bay, to be sold on his and our joint %, each ½, 3000 bush. Wheat, invoiced @ $1; paid Freight per check, $350. **2.** Bought on our note at sixty days, of Claflin, Mellen & Co., 10 pieces Broadcloth, 1000 yds, @ $4.50; 20 pieces, Cassimere, 1500 yds, @ $2. **3.** Shipped T. W. Woolson, Mt. Pleasant, Iowa, to be sold on our joint %, each ½, 10 pieces Broadcloth, 1000 yds, @ $4.75, 10 pieces Cassimere, 750 yds, @ $2.25; paid charges per check, $75. Received Cash of John Atwater, in full of %. **4.** Sold J. C. Bryant, on his note @ ten days, 3000 bush. Wheat, (Mdse. Co. C—Penn's Consignment), @ $ 1.50. Closed Mdse. Co. C., and rendered J. R. Penn an Account Sales of the same: Our charges for Storage, Advertising, etc., $150; our Commission, 2½ % on Sales, $——. J. R. Penn's net proceeds, $1943.75. Our ½ net gain, $——. **5.** Discounted our acceptance favor of H. G. Reeve & Co., due June 5th.; discount off thirty-one days, @ 7 %. Paid Cash for the face of the note, less the interest for the above time, $——. **6.** Shipped Chester Packard, Milwaukee, to be sold on joint % of himself, D. V. Bell, Chicago, and ourselves, each ⅓, 4 chests Young Hyson Tea, 197 lbs., @ 75 c.; 10 boxes Virginia Tobacco, 350 lbs., @ 50 c.; 100 sacks Rio Coffee, 16,000 lbs., @ 10 c. The Tea and Tobacco were from our store; the Coffee was purchased of Acker, Merrall & Co., on our acceptance @ ten days Our ⅓ the above Invoice, $640.91; C. Packard's do., $640.92; D. V. Bell's do., $640.92. **7.** Received from H. B. Tuttle, Cleveland, to be sold on joint % of himself, N. C. Winslow, and ourselves, each ⅓, 1000 bbls. Flour, invoiced @ $7; paid Transportation charges per check, $450. Our ⅓ invoice, $2333.33. **10.** Paid James Atwater in full of % per check, $——. **12.** Sold Chas. E. Carryl 10 pieces Cassimere, 750 yds, @ $2.50. Received in payment James Hill's Note, dated Jan. 1, 1859, with interest at 7 % from date, $1500. Interest on same to date, $38.21. Cash for balance, $——. **15.** Sold W. H. Clark for cash, 1000 bbls. Flour, (Mdse. Co. D.), @ $8.50. Closed Mdse. Co. D, and rendered H. B. Tuttle and N. C. Winslow each an account of the sales. Our charges for Storage, Advertising, etc., $150; our Commission 2½ % on sales, $——. H. B. Tuttle's net proceeds, $2562.50; N. C. Winslow's, $2562.50; our net gain, $229.17. **16.** Remitted H. B. Tuttle cash in full of %, $; deposited in Bank $9000. **17.** Received cash of Stephen A. Douglas, in full of %, $—— Received cash of J. C. Bryant, for his note of May 4th, due this day, $——. **19.** Paid our acceptance of the 6th inst., favor of Acker, Merrall & Co., due this day, in cash, $——. **20.** Received from T. W. Woolson, Mt. Pleasant, an Account Sales of the Mdse. shipped him the 3d inst., to be sold on our joint %. Our net proceeds, remitted in cash, $4000. **25.** Received from Chester Packard, Milwaukee, an Account Sales of the Mdse. shipped him the 6th inst, for % and risk of himself, D. V. Bell, Chicago, and ourselves, each ⅓. Our net proceeds $750. **28.** Paid N. C. Winslow's draft on us, in full of his %, $——; our draft on D. V. Bell, for $640.92; Cash for balance. $——. **30.** Received Cash of R. C. Spencer, in full of %, $——; paid John R. Penn cash, in full of %, $——; paid D. L. Wing cash, in full of %, $——.

Inventory of Property on hand, April 30.

4 Chests of Young Hyson Tea, 200 lbs. @ 63 c.	126	
10 Boxes Virginia Tobacco, 350 lbs., @ 40 c.	140	
Store Fixtures, $1400; unexpired Rent, $625, (charged to Expense)	2025	
	2291	

Inventory, May 31.

Store and Fixtures, $1400—Unexpired Rent, $500	1900	
Interest due on J. Hill's note	43	75
	1943	75

Resources and Liabilities, April 30.

Merchandise	266		Bills Payable	3117	85
Expense*	2025		James Atwater	4598	38
Cash	6127	25	D. L. Wing	5862	50
J. W. Lusk	75		J. H. Goldsmith	8075	86
I. R. Penn	2981	80	———	8379	60
Geo. K. Chase & Co.	16970	84			
R. C. Spencer	923	33			
John Atwater	524	17			
Stephen A. Douglas	140	80			
	30034	19		30034	19

Resources and Liabilities, May 31.

Expense	1900		Bills Payable	10156	80
Interest	43	75	J. H. Goldsmith	9527	53
Cash	852	21	———	9831	26
J. W. Lusk	75				
Geo. K. Chase & Co.	20497	46			
T. W. Woolson	3256	25			
Chester Packard	1390	92			
Bills Receivable	1500				
	29515	59		29515	59

* Fixtures and unexpired rent.

SET V.

JOBBING AND IMPORTING BUSINESS,

EMBRACING AS PRINCIPAL BOOKS,

CASH BOOK, DOMESTIC AND FOREIGN INVOICE BOOKS, SALES BOOK AND JOURNAL;

AND AS AUXILIARIES,

INVENTORY BOOK AND BILL BOOK,

WITH A ROUTINE OF TRANSACTIONS TAKEN FROM ONE OF THE MOST EXTENSIVE BUSINESS HOUSES IN NEW YORK.

REMARKS ON SET V.

In the following set we have illustrated a practical method of keeping the accounts of an Importing and Jobbing business. The particular feature in this set consists of the manner and form of original entries, which are made in separate books,—elsewhere used as auxiliaries,—from which they are either journalized, or passed directly to the Ledger at stated periods. This method has many advantages over consecutive entries in the Day Book, and in one form or other, is adopted generally in all large establishments. The labors of the Book-keeper are thus divided up, and the separate departments of the business receive such special record as to present all the facts in their clearest light. Thus, if any particular information is desired respecting purchases, all the facts can be shown at once from the Invoice Book; and, in the same manner, the fact and condition of the sales can be shown from the Sales Book, the receipts and disbursements of cash from the Cash Book, etc.

In the previous sets these books are represented, but they are used only as auxiliaries, the entries of the business being made in the other books without reference to them. This plan, it will be evident, although possessing some merits, involves a large amount of unnecessary labor, which would prove a great objection in extensive houses. The special books themselves, however, are so essential to every well-regulated business, that they would receive favor, even at the expense of this additional labor. If, therefore, they can be used without additional labor, and even at a reduction of labor, it would seem that no farther argument would be needed to secure their adoption.

The only difficulty in the way of using special books for original entries lies in the danger of making the entries in the different books conflict with each other upon the Ledger. For example: if a Cash Book is used, it should be competent to show all receipts and disbursements of cash. This purpose is very easily effected by placing the receipts on one side, and the disbursements on the other—the difference, of course, being, at any time, the amount on hand. But this does not cover the entire utility of the Cash Book. At the same time that cash received is entered upon the debit side of the Cash Book, the object or cause *for which* it is received may also be stated; in which case a double entry is effected, although but one amount shown. The same principle will hold in entering the disbursements of cash; as, when cash is paid, the object or cause for which it is paid is properly expressed. The appropriate caption for the debit side of the Cash Book, then, would be "Cash Dr. To Sundries;" the debit of cash being the total amount received at any specified time, and the credit of sundries being the separate amounts produced by the different causes represented; and, on the other hand, the caption for the credit side would be "Sundries Dr. To Cash," cash being credited for the total disbursement as shown, and the sundry causes for which cash was paid debited for their separate amounts. It will thus be seen that the *debit* side of the Cash Book contains the *credits* of all accounts producing cash; and the *credit* side, the *debits* of all accounts costing cash.

Upon the same principle the Invoice Book, which sustains the same relation to merchandise that the debit side of the Cash Book does to cash, while it shows, in total, the entire cost of merchandise, will also exhibit the separate credits producing merchandise; and the Sales Book, which sustains the same relation to merchandise that the credit side of the Cash Book does to cash, while it shows, in total, the proceeds of merchandise, exhibits also the separate debits produced by the sales. The difficulty of which we have spoken will now be apparent; as, in every case involving any two of these books, the tendency will be to debit and credit the same accounts *twice*—effecting thus a *double* entry not contemplated by projectors of the science, and of course not warranted by the facts in the case. Thus, all cash receipts being entered, at specified periods, in total, from the debit side of the Cash Book, and all cash disbursements from the credit side, it would be erroneous to enter cash from any other book; and the same theory will apply with equal force to the Invoice and Sales Books.

If, therefore, the peculiar rights of each of these books be respected, viz.: permitting all cash entries to be taken to the Ledger from the Cash Book, and all purchases and sales of merchandise from the Invoice and Sales Book, it would preclude the entering of cash in the Invoice or Sales Book, and also of merchandise in the Cash Book. Take a single example: Suppose the entry to be "Cash Dr. To Merchandise." All cash receipts must appear on th debit side of the Cash Book, and the entry on that book would be "To Merchandise," extending the amount into the debit column. When the Cash Book is posted, this amount will, of course, be included in the total cash debit, and must comprise one of the opposite, or credit entries. So cash would be debited and merchandise credited both from the Cash Book. Again, all sales of merchandise must be entered in the Sales Book, and when entered the corresponding debit—in this case, cash—must also be expressed. When the Sales Book is posted, the total for which merchandise is credited will include this amount (already entered and posted from the Cash Book), to correspond with which, and to secure the necessary condition of equal debits and credits, cash must again be debited. According to this standard, therefore, in every case where merchandise is either bought or sold for cash, and the fact expressed through these special books, this error of duplicating debits and credits would occur.

To avoid this difficulty—the only one which stands in the way of classified original entries—two methods have been successfully used; one of which places the books upon an equality, using "neutralizing" accounts for the conflicting entries, and the other acknowledges the supremacy of some one or more books, to which, in all matters of conflict, the others must yield. To be more explicit: In the case before instanced, "Cash Dr. To Merchandise." If the Cash Book and Sales Book were upon an equality, the one claiming to furnish all cash entries for the Ledger and the other all merchandise sales, it would be improper to write Cash as a Ledger title in the Sales Book or Merchandise in the Cash Book, for the reasons adduced; but a neutralizing account might be opened, to take the place of cash in the Sales Book and merchandise in the Cash Book, thus receiving a debit and credit of the same amount, which would, of course, cancel it. Suppose the merchandise to be sold to A, for cash: In the Sales Book the entry would be "A" Dr., and in the Cash Book, "A" Cr. The result would be the same as if A had purchased on account, and subsequently paid the amount in cash, thus closing his account. But suppose we acknowledge the supremacy of the Cash Book in all cases where the two are concerned. When merchandise is sold for cash, the entry in the Cash Book will be "Cash Dr. To Merchandise," both of which—the debit of cash and the credit of merchandise—will go to the Ledger from the Cash Book. The same entry can be made in the Sales Book, *but not posted.* For this purpose a special column may be used—as in the following examples—which, at such times as the general result may need to be shown, can be extended into the other column, which in the total footing will embrace all the sales.

Each of the above methods has its advantages; the latter, however, is generally preferred as being more brief and direct, if not more in keeping with the spirit of the times.

The Invoice Books, and the Sales Book which follow, contain all purchases and sales of merchandise, with the conditions thereof. All sales and purchases *not made for cash* pass from these books to the Ledger; all others, from the Cash Book.

The transactions of this s[illegible], and most of the forms, are taken from one of the largest Importing and Jobbing Houses in New York, and may be relied upon as eminently practical.

ROUTINE AND EXPLANATIONS.

That the student may get the full advantage of this Set, it will be necessary that he pay strict attention to the routine of transactions as indicated below. Let him make the entries in the different books precisely in the order given. Let the invoices be copied with care, and all the calculations and extensions made by himself. It is thus alone that the design of the Set will be carried out. The exercises connected with the Foreign Invoice Book, involving compound numbers, and reduction of currencies, are highly essential. In reducing sterling to federal currency, we have taken the Custom House standard of $4.84 to the £ sterling. We have also added to each foreign invoice, the duties, which being paid in cash, are not extended with the invoice, but posted from the Cash Book. In most importing houses, the duties are not extended in the Invoice Book, but only in the Cash Book. For strong reasons, we prefer the method here adopted.

ROUTINE FOR JULY.

1. The books are opened, as per first Journal entry. (Inventory Book copied—Cash Book commenced with balance on hand—Bill Book written up to show the notes, receivable and payable, as indicated in Journal entry.)....Bought of C. F. Spalding, on note @ 4 months, Invoice of Sheeting, $553.57, (Dom. I. B.—B. B.)....Received per steamer Edinburgh, Invoice of Jaconets from S. B. Higgins & Co., $1,252.55; Paid duties in cash, $300 61, (For. I. B.—C. B.)....Bought of B. S. Olmstead for cash, Invoice of Prints, etc., $1,303.76, (Dom. I. B.—C. B.)....Sold Gordon Bailey, Buffalo, on note @ 8 months, Invoice of Jaconets, $891.35, (S. B.—B. B.)....Sold Ira Packard, Peru, Ind., on note @ 6 months, Invoice of Hose and Gloves, $273.52, (S B.—B. B.)....Sold Mdse. this day, per Petty Cash Book, $97.50, (C. B.)....Received cash on % of John Lewis, $500, (C. B.)

3. Paid Francis & Loutrel for Stationery, $16.75, (C. B.).....Lent J. E. Jenkins, for one day, $1,000, (C. B.)....Sold Mdse. per Petty Cash Book,, $125, (C. B.)

5. Sold Hiram Newell, Tonawanda, on his note @ 6 months, Invoice of Sheetings, $697.54, (S. B.—B. B.)....Received of J. E. Jenkins, return loan, $1,000, (C. B.)....Paid cash for Postage Stamps, etc., $8, (C. B.)....Paid S. S. Packard, on private %, $100, (C. B.)

6. Received cash of J. H. Lewis, in full of %, $1,200, (C. B.)

7. Paid Richard Beal cash, in full of %, $185, (C. B.)

8. Sold Mdse. per Petty Cash Book, $157, (C.B.)

10. Bought of John Walker & Co., on our note @ 8 months, Invoice of Cotton, $1,006.64, (Dom. I. B.—B. B.)....Received per steamer Manchester, from Johnson, Quigley & Co., Manchester, Invoice of Cotton and Silk Goods, $221.11; Paid duties in cash, $44.21, (For. I. B.—C. B.)....Bought of Claflin, Mellen & Co., for cash, Invoice of Prints, $2,312.52, (Dom. I. B.—C. B.) .. Sold W. P. Pratt, Cincinnati, for cash, Invoice of Jaconets, 714.28, (S. B.—C. B.)....Sold Baldwin, Laundon & Co., Elyria, O., on their note @ 8 months, Invoice of Shirting, $869.38, (S. B.—B. B.)

11. Received cash of W. Pennel, in full of %, $483.50, (C. B.).

12. Sold Charles Claghorn, Homer, Ill., Invoice of Cloths, $433.12, (S. B.—C. B.)......Paid cash for Drayage and Porterage, $55, (C. B.)

14. Received cash in full of John Gundry's note, 1,580, (C. B.—B. B.)

15. Received per steamer Ætna, from A. & J. Bailey, Bradford, Invoice of Goods, $246.38; Paid duties in cash, $46.80, (For. I. B.—C. B.)....Sold E. Mussey & Co., Amherst, O., on their note @ 6 months, Invoice of Shirting, $923.25, (S. B.—B. B.)....Sold Mdse. for cash, as per Petty Cash Book, $115.75, (C. B.)

18. S. S. Pomroy's note discounted, $1,000; Discount off, $16.92, (C. B.—B. B.)

20. Bought of E. Lambert & Co.. on our note @ 8 months, Invoice of Bleached Shirtings, $660.73, (Dom. I. B.—B. B.)....Sold Starr & Co., Elyria, O., on their note, @ 6 months, Invoice of Prints, $1,425.48, (S. B.—B. B.)....Paid J. T. Calkins on private %, $150, (C. B.)

21. Sold Mdse. for cash, per Petty Cash Book, $127.50, (C. B.)

22. Sold M. Shipley & Co., Cincinnati, on his note @ 8 months, Invoice of Bleached Shirting, $1,460.14, (S. B—B. B.)

23. Paid cash in full of note, favor of H. G. Smith, $4,000, (C. B.—B. B.)

25. Sold Bidwell & Co., Adrian, Michigan, for cash, Invoice of Goods, $400, (S. B.—C. B.)....Starr & Co.'s note discounted; Face of note, $1,425.48. Discount off, $50.44, (C. B.—B. B.)....Received per steamer Halifax, from S. T. Horton, Glasgow, Invoice of Goods, $440.14; Paid duties in cash, $105.63. (For I. B.—C. B.) ...Bought of A. T. Stewart & Co., for cash, Invoice of Prints, $893.63, (D. I. B.—C. B.)..Paid clerk hire in cash, $65, (C. B.)

27. Sold Mdse. for cash, as per Petty Cash Book, $275, (C. B.)

28. Sold E. C. Packard, Crystal Lake, Wis., on his note @ 8 months, Invoice of Goods, $171. 04, (S. B —B. B.)

29. Paid D. V. Bell, on private %, $175, (C. B.)

30. Sold Mdse. as per Petty Cash Book, $83, (C. B.)

31. Received cash of R. Barker, in full of %, $1000.

ROUTINE FOR AUGUST.

1. Sold O. C. & E. C. Wright, Lockport, N. Y., on their note @ 6 months, Invoice of Goods, $1432.89 S. B.—B. B.)....Paid cash for Drayage and Porterage, $17.50, (C. B.)

2. Lent J. H. Tobitt, $500, (C. B.)

3. Sold C. R. Caulkins, Delaware, O., for cash, Invoice of Prints, $739.63, (S. B.—C. B.).....Sold Mdse. as per Petty Cash Book, $89.27, (C. B.)

5. Discounted our Note, favor of Geo. A. Crocker; face of note $1426. Discount off, $19.41, (C. B.—B. B.) ....Sold D. S. Hoadley, Berlin, O., on his note @ 8 mos., Invoice of Goods, $527, (S. B.—B. B.)

6. O. C. & E. C. Wright's note discounted; face of note, $1432.89. Discount off, $49.60, (C. B)

7. Sold Mdse. as per Petty Cash Book, $150, (C. B.)

8. Sold J. D. Hinde & Co., Cincinnati, on their note @ 8 months, Invoice of Mdse. $752.57, (S. B—B. B.)

10. Received per steamer Australia, from Wm. Thornton & Co., Bradford, Invoice of Goods, $1454.64. Duties paid in cash, $276.38, (For. I. B.—C. B.)....Sold Geo. A. Crocker, Rochester, for cash, Invoice of Prints, $912.75, (S. B.—C. B.)......Bought of Wilson G. Hunt, on our note @ 8 months, Invoice of Cloths, $708.40, (D. I. B—B. B.)

12. Sold Mdse as per Petty Cash Book, $218.50, (C. B.)....Paid cash for Drayage, $100, (C. B.)

15. Sold W. H. Woodbury, Chicago, Ill., on his note @ 8 months, Invoice of Goods, $908.29, (S. B.—B. B.)....Paid J. C. Bryant cash on private %, $150.

17. Sold C. C. Jones, Peoria, Ill., on his note @ 6 months, Invoice of Goods, $945.94, (S. B.—B. B.)... Sold Mdse. as per Petty Cash Book, $375, (C. B.)

20. Received per steamer Lebanon, from J. Muir & Sons, Manchester, Invoice of Goods, $188.62. Paid duties in cash, $45.27, (For. I. B.—C. B.)...Bought of Arnold & Constable, on our note @ 8 months, Invoice of Cloths, $1926.14, (Dom. I. B.—B. B.)......Bought of Grinnell & Minturn, for cash, Invoice of Goods, $1492.58, (Dom. I. B.—C. B.)....Sold Paul Roberts, Buffalo, for cash, Invoice of Goods, $923.40, (S. B.—C. B.)

23. Sold Mdse. as per Petty Cash Book, $175, (C. B.)

25. Sold M. Tompkins & Co., Lasalle, Ill., for cash, Invoice of Gloves, $460.75, (S. B.—C. B.).....C. C. Jones' note discounted; face of note, $945.94. Discount off, $32.19, (C. B.)....Paid Postage, Porterage, etc., in cash, $13, (C. B.).....Sold C. J. Dietrich, Bellefontaine, Ind., on his note @ 8 months, Invoice of Goods, $402.50, (S. B.—B. B.)...Sold Baldwin & Co., Cleveland, on their note @ 8 months, Invoice of Prints, $717.47, (S B.—B. B.)

27. Sold Ubsdell Pierson & Co., St. Louis, on their note @ 8 months, Invoice of Mixtures, $3303.71, (S. B.—C. B.)

28. Sold Raymond & Co., Cleveland, on 8 months note, Invoice of Goods, $641.72, (S. B.—B. B.)

30. Sold Jonas Stratton, Amherst, O., on note @ 8 months, Invoice of Goods, $457, (S. B.—B. B.)

31. Sold Mdse. per Petty Cash Book, $115, (C. B.)......Paid cash in full of Drayage %, $50.75, (C. B.)

DOMESTIC INVOICE BOOK.

THIS book contains copies of all invoices of merchandise purchased from importers and others in this country, with the conditions of all such purchases. Each lot and package is distinguished by some peculiar mark, which is transferred to the invoice, thus serving an important purpose in checking the articles, adjusting disputes, etc.

The purchases on time, for which notes are given, are passed to the Ledger from this book; those for cash, from the Cash Book.

JULY 1, 1860.

Mark	No.	Particulars			Amount	$	¢	$	¢
		C. F. Spalding & Co.,		4 months.					
	18	2 ps. 10-4 Sheeting,	92^3	@ 55c.	51.01				
	14	2 " "	92^3	60	55.65				
	16	2 " "	91^3	65	59.64				
	18	2 " "	92^1	70	64.58				
	20	1 " "	45^2	75	34.12				
	14	1 " "	46^3	65	30.39				
	16	1 " "	46^1	70	32.38				
	18	1 " "	44^1	75	33.19				
	20	1 " "	45^2	80	36.40				
	16	1 " "	46	75	34.50				
	18	1 " "	45^3	80	36.60				
	20	1 " "	45^2	90	40.95				
	22	1 " "	46	96	44.16			553	57
		Note @ 4 months from July 5.							
		B. S. Olmstead,		6 months.					
		5 Cases Columbian Prints,							
A. T	596	2137^2							
A. S	587	1913^3							
X.	351	1935							
	341	1886^3							
A. C	411	1742	9615 yds.	@ 8c. less $\frac{1}{2}$ c.	721.13				
		1 Bale $2\frac{1}{4}$lb. Black Wadding 30 yds. @ 40c.			12.00				
		2 Bales Brown Globe Drills,							
	1141	1032^3							
	1147	1029	2061^3	@ $7\frac{5}{8}$	157.21				
		4 Cases Harop Prints,							
M.	481	246	1331^3						
C.	491	1262	1581^3						
M.	509	1108	1222						
M.	97	1276	1715^2	5851 @ $8\frac{1}{2}$c less $2\frac{1}{2}$ %	482.91				
					1373.25				
		Less 5 %			68.67				
					1304.58				
		M. 97—1276, short 34 yds.			2.82				
					1301.76				
		Add error in extending Harop Prints,			2.00				
		C. B.			1303.76	1303	76		
		Amounts forward,				1303	76	553	57

JULY 10, 1860.

		Amounts forward,		1303	76	553	57
	◇C	John Walker & Co., 8 months.					
	794	40 ps. Duck Drilling, 1411^2 @ 17c.	239.96				
	800	40 " " 1389^2 18	250.11				
	834	36 Brown " 1415^2 25	353.88				
	704	42 W. B. Diaper, 2169^1 7½	162.69			1006	64
		Note @ 8 months from July 10.					
		"					
		Clafflin, Mellen & Co., 8 months.					
	9355	50 ps. Prints, # 875 1782					
	9500	52 " 813 1831^3 3613^3 yds. @ 10c.	361.37				
	8615	55 " 812 1845^1					
	9424	52 " 817 1803^1					
	9737	54 " 814 1870^2 5519 " 9½c.	524.30				
	9024	61 " 816 2112^1					
	7906	59 " 822 2033^2					
	8158	57 " 879 1996^3 6142^2 " 9c.	552.83				
	9629	56 " 818 1945^1 " 9c.	175.07				
	199	63 " 820 2249^2					
	238	60 " 821 2140 4389^2 " 7½c.	329.21				
	493	60 " 824 2164^1					
	888	59 " 823 2059^1 4223^2 " 7½c.	316.76				
	9095	58 " 825 1970^3 " 9c.	177.37				
			2436.91				
		Deduct 5%	121.84				
			2315.07				
		Less 1 ps. short 35^3 @ 7½c. 5% off	2.55				
		C. B.	2312.52	2312	52		
		20					
		Edward Lambert & Co., 8 months.					
		4 Cases 4-4 Bleached Shirting,					
	750	40 1732^2					
	751	40 1736					
	753	40 1755					
	754	40 1731^2 6955 yds @ 9½c.				660	72
		Note @ 8 months from July 20.					
		25					
		A. T. Stewart & Co.,					
C. M.	3892	52 Prints, # 973 1858					
E. A.	5788	52 " 965 1834					
E. A.	6202	53 " 967 1895^1 5587^1 y'ds @ 8c.	446.98				
D. C.	4187	51 " 972 1924^2					
E. N.	5630	49 " 968 1954^2					
E. O.	5685	49 " 971 1929 5808 @ 8½c.	493.68				
			940.66				
		Discount off 5%	47.03				
		C. B.	893.63	893	63		
		Purchases on time (taken to Ledger),				2220	94
		Cash Purchases (entered from C. B.),				4509	91
		Total for the month,				6730	85

DOMESTIC INVOICE BOOK,—SET V.

NEW YORK, AUGUST 10, 1860.

Wilson G. Hunt, 8 months,

22 ps. 3-4 Doeskin,

#163	728	28$\frac{7}{8}$	#163	899$\frac{3}{4}$	22$\frac{1}{8}$
	870	29		748	29
	754	28$\frac{3}{4}$		894	28$\frac{1}{8}$
	864	28$\frac{1}{8}$		835	28$\frac{5}{8}$
	860	29$\frac{5}{8}$		834	28$\frac{1}{2}$
	755	29$\frac{1}{8}$		729	28$\frac{3}{4}$
	759	28$\frac{3}{4}$		861	28
	750	27$\frac{5}{8}$		233	28$\frac{1}{4}$
	822	29$\frac{1}{8}$		716	27$\frac{1}{2}$
#162	554	28$\frac{3}{4}$		805	29$\frac{5}{8}$
163	833	28$\frac{7}{8}$		899$\frac{3}{4}$	21$\frac{7}{8}$—616 yds. @ $1.15

Note @ 8 months from Aug. 10. — 708 | 40

— 20 —

Arnold & Constable, 10 months,

No.	Description		Yds.	Amount
1877	30 Belgian Cass.		1091	
1881	30	"	1178^{3}	
1896	30	"	1137	
1915	28	"	1094^{2}	
1903	30	"	1151^{2}	
1737	33 World's Fair		1268	
1775	30	"	1168	
1823	33	"	1279^{3}	
1834	33	"	1261^{2}	
1845	30	"	1147	
1906	30 Sebastopol Checks		1168^{3}	
1913	27 " "		1245^{2}—14191 yds. @ 13$\frac{1}{2}$c.	1915.78
	Cooperage,			3.00
				1918.78
	Add 77 yds. @ 13$\frac{1}{2}$c.		10.39	
	Less Freight,		3.03	7.36

Note @ 8 months. — 1926 | 14

— 〃 —

Grinnell & Minturn, 8 months,

Mark	No.	Yds.		Amount
S. M. A.	733	1240^{3}		
	734	1239^{2}	"Springfield,"	
	735	1234^{3}		
H.M.C A.	539	1208		
	540	1233		
		5 Cases 4-4 Bleached Sheeting, 6156 yds. @ 10$\frac{1}{2}$c.		646.38
S. M. D.	169	1202^{2}		
	170	1197^{1}		
	171	1223^{3}		
	172	1171^{1}		
	173	1212^{2}		
H. M. C. D.	492	1239		
	500	1254		
	501	1234		
		8 Cases 33 in Bleached Sheeting, 9734^{1} yds. @ 9$\frac{1}{2}$c.		924.75
				1571.13
C. B.		Discount off 5%		78.55

Cash: 1492 | 58

Purchases on time (taken to Ledger),	2634	54
Cash purchases (posted from Cash-Book),	1492	58
Total for the month,	4127	12

FOREIGN INVOICE BOOK.*

NEW YORK, JULY 1, 1860.

			Sterling Currency.						Federal Currency			
			£	s.	d.	£	s.	d.	$	cts	$	cts
	◇R	S. B. Higgins & Co., Glasgow, per Steamer "*Edinburgh*," June 3, 1860.										
	205	50 ps. 9-8 printed Jaconets, 2572 yds. @ 4¾*d.*	50	18	1							
		Making up, Casing, etc.	1	11		52	9	1				
	206	50 ps. 9-8 printed Jaconets, 2540.2 yds. @ 4¾*d.*	50	5	7							
		Making up, Casing, etc.	1	11		51	16	7				
	207	50 ps. 9-8 printed Jaconets, 2561.2 yds. @ 4¾*d.*	50	13	11							
		Making up, Casing, etc.	1	10	9	52	4	8				
	208	60 ps. 9-8 10 B. and W. Jaconets @ 5*s.* 5*d.* 1 1 1 8 2 34 4 9 4 1 21 22½ 23 24 24½ 25 25½ 26 26½ 27	16	5								
		Making up, Casing, etc.	1	4		17	9					
	209	58 ps. 9-8 10 B. and W. Jaconets @ 5*s.* 5*d.* 2 2 42 5 6 1 23½ 24 25 25½ 26 26½	15	14	2							
		Making up, Casing, etc.	1	3	8	16	17	10				
	210	56 ps. 9-2 12⁰⁰ B. and W. Jaconets @ 7*s.* 3*d.* 1 1 4 38 11 1 18½ 23 24 25 25½ 26	20	6								
		Making up, Casing, etc.	1	3	4	21	9	4				
	211	56 ps. 9-2 12⁰⁰ B. and W. Jaconets @ 7*s.* 3*d.*	20	6								
		Making up, Casing, etc.	1	3	4	21	9	4				
	212	54 ps. 9-8 14⁰⁰ printed Jaconets @ 8*s.* 9*d.* 1 1 8 3 34 9 1 1 1 14½ 23 24 24½ 25 25½ 26 27 33	23	12	6							
		Making up, Casing, etc.	1	3		24	15	6				
						258	11	4				
		Discount off 1½ %				3	17	7				
						254	13	9				
		Cartage		2	9							
		B. L., etc.		5								
		Commission 1½ %	3	14	4	4	2	1				
						258	15	10			1252	55
	C. B.	Duties 24 % — Paid in Cash.							300	61		
		10										
P. B. & Co.		Johnson, Quigley & Co., Manchester, per Str. "*Manchester*," June 4, 1860.										
	71	25 doz. Ladies' white Cotton Hose @ 2*s.* 9*d.*	3	8	9							
		20 " " " 3*s.*	3									
		29 " " " 2*s.* 10*d.*	4	2	2							
	46	1 doz. Ladies' Pearl Spun Silk Hose, 8½ 20*s.*	1									
	46	1 " " " 9 20*s.*	1									
	1	4 " black " 9 19*s.*	3	16								
	6	2 " pearl " 9 53*s.*	5	6								
	6	½ doz. Men's Novi Silk Shirts 39*s.*		19	6							
	62	1 " " " 50*s.*	2	10								
	120	1 " " " 55*s.*	2	15								
	66	1 " " " 62*s.*	3	2								
	68	8 doz. Ladies' Lisle Gauntlets 11*s.* 6*d.*	4	12								
	100	5 " " " 12*s.* 6*d.*	3	2	6							
	101	5 " " " 22*s.*	5	10								
		103½ " Inland Carriage		2	10							
		Cases, Oil Cloth, etc.		13	6							
			45		3							
		Commission 1½ %		13	5	45	13	8			221	11
		Duties, 24 % on Cotton and 15 % on Silk Paid in Cash.							44	21		
	C. B.											
		Amounts forward							344	82	1473	66

* Copies of Foreign Invoices, with Import Duties added.

FOREIGN INVOICE BOOK,—SET V.

NEW YORK, JULY 15, 1860.

			Sterling Currency.						Federal Currency.			
			£	s.	d.	£	s.	d.	$	cts	$	cts
		Amounts forward							344	82	1473	66
		A. & J. Bailey, Bradford,										
		per Steamer "*Etna*," June 15, 1860										
P. B & Co.	54	60¼ Laveilas assorted, 3028² @ 3⅞d.	48	17	11							
		Making up, Casing, etc.	2	6	10							
			51	4	9							
		Discount 1¼ %		12	9							
			50	12								
		Carriage to Liverpool		6								
		C. B. Duties 19 %—Paid in Cash.				50	18	0	46	80	246	86
		25										
		S. T. Horton, Glasgow,										
		per Steamer "*Halifax*," June 20, 1860.										
P. B & Co. 520	70	400 9-8 14⁰⁰ Robes a Les, 10 yds. each 4s. 6d.	90	0	0							
		Off 36 ps. No 1, 9s., and 1¼ % £1 7s.	1	16	0							
			88	4	0							
		Card 4s., Box 17s., Com. etc., £1 12s.	2	13	0	90	17	0				
		Cartage				0	1	9				
		C. B Duties 24 %—Paid in Cash				90	18	9			440	14
									105	63		
		Total Imports for the month							497	25	2160	16
		Duties on the same									497	25
											2657	41
		August 10										
P. B. & Co.		William Thornton & Co., Bradford,										
		per Str. "*Australia*," July 1, 1860.										
	29	60¼ Mohair Mixtures, 2996 @ 3⅛d.	39	0	2							
		Case, Pkg, etc., 14s., Com. 19s. 6d.	1	13	6	40	13	8				
	30	60¼ Bye Cloths assorted, 2969 @ 3d.	37	2	3							
		Case, Pkg, etc., 13s., Com. 18s. 6d.	1	11	6	38	13	9				
	31	60¼ Bye Cloths assorted, 2973 @ 3d.	37	3	3							
		Case, Pkg, etc., 13s., Com. 18s. 7d.	1	11	7	38	14	10				
	32	60¼ Bye Cloths assorted, 2965 @ 3d.	37	1	3							
		Case, Pkg, etc., 13s., Com. 18s. 6d.	1	11	6	38	12	9				
	33	60¼ Bye Cloths assorted, 2966 @ 3d.	37	1	6							
		Case, Pkg, etc., 13s., Com. 18s. 6d.	1	11	6	38	13	0				
	34	60¼ Bye Cloths assorted, 2965² @ 3d.	37	1	4							
		Case, Pkg, etc., 13s., Com. 18s. 6d.	1	11	6	38	12	10				
	35	60¼ Fine Mohair Mixtures, 2877² 5½d.	65	18	10							
		Case, Pkg, etc., 12s. 6d. Com. 32s. 11d.	2	5	5	68	4	3				
						302	5	1				
		1¼ % discount				3	15	7				
						298	9	6				
		Carriage to Liverpool				2	1	5				
		C. B. Duties 19 %—Paid in Cash				300	10	11			1454	64
									276	88		
		20										
P. B & Co.		James Muir & Sons, Manchester,										
		per Str "*Lebanon*" July 10, 1860.										
	674	25 ps. White Piques, 324 @ 2s. 4d.	37	16	0							
		Discount off		9	2							
			37	6	10							
		Charges, Commission, etc.	1	12	7	38	19	5				
		C. B. Duties 24 %—Paid in Cash									188	32
									45	27		
		Total imports for the month									1643	26
		Duties on same									321	65
		Total costs of imports									1964	91

SALES BOOK.

This book contains all the regular sales, either for cash or on time; the cash sales being extended in the inner column, are, of course, not included in the amount for which merchandise is credited from the Sales Book. These sales, together with the petty sales not entered on the Sales Book, are posted from the Cash Book. The total credit of the merchandise account for the month will agree, in amount, with the monthly recapitulation in the Sales Book

NEW YORK, JULY 1, 1860.

		Gordon Bailey, Buffalo, N. Y.					
(E)	205	50 ps. 9-8 Printed Jaconets, 2572 yds. @ 15c.	$385.80				
	208	60 ps. 9-8 10 B.&W. " 1509½ " 10c.	150.95				
	209	58 ps. " " 1455 " 10c.	145.50				
	210	56 ps. " " 1394 " 15c.	209.10			891	35
		Note @ 8 months from July 1.					
		"					
		Ira Packard, Peru, Ind.					
I. P.	71	25 doz. Ladies' White Cotton Hose, @ $1	$25.00				
		20 " " 1.25	25.00				
		29 " " 1.13	32.77				
	46	1 doz. Pearl Spun Silk Hose, 8½	8.00				
	46	1 " " 9	8.00				
	1	4 doz. Black " 9 $7.50	30.00				
	6	2 doz. Pearl " 20.00	40.00				
	100	8 doz. Ladies' Lisle Gauntlets, 4.50	36.00				
	101	5 " " 4.75	23.75				
	15	5 " " 9.00	45.00			273	52
		Note @ 6 months from July 1.					
		5					
		Hiram Newell, Tonawanda, N. Y.					
(T)	13	2 ps. 10-4 Sheeting, 92¾ yds. @ 70c.	$64.93				
	14	2 " " 92¾ " 75c.	69.56				
	16	2 " " 91¾ " 80c.	73.40				
	18	2 " " 92¼ " 85c.	78.41				
	20	1 " " 45½ " 90c.	40.95				
	14	1 11-4 " 50⅕ " 84c.	42.17				
	16	1 " " 46¼ " 90c.	41.62				
	18	1 " " 44¼ " 95c.	42.04				
	20	1 " " 45½ " $1	45.50				
	16	1 12-4 " 46 " 95c.	43.70				
	18	1 " " 45¾ " $1	45.75				
	20	1 " " 45½ " $1.15	52.32				
	22	1 " " 45¾ " $1.25	57.19			697	54
		Note @ 6 months from July 5.					
		10					
		W. P Pratt & Co., Cincinnati,					
	206	50 ps. Printed Jaconets, 2540½ yds. @ 14c.	$355.67				
	207	50 " " 2561½ " 14c.	358 61	714	28		
		Received Cash.					
		Amounts forward,		714	28	1862	41

SALES BOOK,—SET V.

NEW YORK, JULY 10, 1860.

		Amounts forward,	714	28	1862	41
B.L.&Co		Baldwin, Laundon & Co., Elyria, O.				
		4 Cases Bleached Shirting,				
		#750 40 1732^1				
		751 40 1736				
		753 1745^1				
		754 40 1741^2 6955 yds. @ 12½c.			869	38
		Note @ 8 months from July 10.				
		12				
		Charles Claghorn & Co., Homer, Ill.				
		10 ps. Black Doeskin,				
		#163 728 28⅞				
		870 29				
		754 28¾				
		864 28¾				
		860 28⅛				
		755 28⅞				
		759 29⅜				
		750 29⅛				
		822 28¾				
		833 29⅛ 288¾ yds. @ $1.50	433	12		
		Received Cash.				
		15				
		E. Mussey & Co. Amherst, O.				
		5 cases Bleached Shirting,				
	733	1240^1				
	734	1239				
	735	1234^2				
	539	1208				
	540	1233 6155 yds. @ 15c.			923	25
		Note @ 8 months.				
		20				
		Starr & Co., Elyria, O.				
C. M	3892	52 Prints, 973 1858				
E. A	5788	52 " 965 1834				
E. A.	6202	53 " 967 1895 5587 yds. @ 12c. $670 44				
D. C	4187	51 " 972 1924^2				
E N.	5630	49 " 968 1954				
E O.	5685	49 " 971 1929^2 5808 yds. @ 13c. 755.04			1425	48
		Note @ 6 months.				
		22				
		Murray Shipley & Co., Cincinnati, O				
		8 cases 33in Bleached Shirting,				
	169	1202^2 1212^2				
	170	1197^1 1239				
	171	1223^3 1254				
	172	1171^1 1234 9734¼ yds. @ 15c.			1460	14
		Note @ 8 months.				
		Amounts forward,	1147	40	6540	66

SALES BOOK,—SET V.

NEW YORK, JULY 25, 1860.

				Cash $	¢	Time $	¢
		Amounts forward,		1147	40	6540	66
		Bidwell & Co., Adrian, Mich.					
520	7	200 9-8 14^{00} Robes a Les (10 yds.)	@ $2.00	400			
		Received Cash.					
		28					
		Edwin C. Packard, Crystal Lake, Wis.					
674	14	6 White Piques, 119^1 @ 75c.	$89.44				
	16	2 " 87^3 @ 80c.	30.20				
	17	4 " 64^1 @ 80c.	51.40			171	04
		Note @ 8 months from date.					
		Sales on time,				6711	70
		Sales for Cash, entered herein but posted from C. B.		1547	40		
		Petty sales, entered alone on C. B.		980	75	2528	15
		Total sales for the month,				9239	85
		August 1					
		O. C. & E. C. Wright, Lockport, N. Y.					
H. M.		1 bale Brown Sheeting, 563^3 yds. @ 14c.	$78.89				
	62	50 doz. Gent's Linen Hdkfs. @ $5.	250.00				
R. X		1 case Cotton Damask, 540 yds. @ 20c.	108.00				
	231	16 pcs. Blk Bombasin, 568 yds. @ $1.25	710.00			1432	89
		1 case Silecia, 2200 yds. @ 13c.	286.00				
		Note @ 6 months.					
		3					
		C. R. Caulkins, Delaware, O.					
	9355	50 ps. Prints, 875 1782					
	9500	50 " 813 1831^3 3613^3 yds. @ 15c.	$542.06				
	9095	58 " 825 1970^3 " 12c.	236.49				
			778.55				
		5 % off,	38.92	739	63		
		Received Cash.					
		5					
		David S. Hoadley, Berlin, O.					
	231	10 pcs. Black Bombasin, 350 yds. @ $1.10	$385.00				
	19	20 pcs. Duck, 710 " 20c.	142.00			527	
		Note @ 8 months.					
		8					
		J. D. Hinde & Co., Cincinnati.					
		1 bale Stark Brown Sheetings, 829 yds. @ 10c.	$82.90				
B.		1 bale 4-4 Shaker Flannel, 337^2 " 50c.	168.75				
		12 pcs. Green Veil Barege, 200 35c.	70.00			752	57
	1066	1 case Solid Check Ginghams, 2394 " 18c.	430.92				
		Note @ 8 months.					
		Amounts forward,		739	63	2712	46

SALES BOOK,—SET. V.

NEW YORK AUGUST 10, 1860.

		Amounts forward,		739	63	2712	46
		Geo. A. Crocker, Rochester,					
		5 cases Columbian Prints,					
A. T.	596	958 2130^{3}					
A. S.	587	959 1913^{3}					
X.	351	1935					
	341	1886^{2}					
A. C.	411	1742 9608 yds. @ 10*c*.	$960.80				
		5 % off,	48.05	912	75		
		Received Cash.					
		15					
		Wm. H. Woodbury, Chicago, Ill.					
		4 cases Harop Prints,					
M.	481	246 1331^{3}					
C.	491	1262 1581^{3}					
M.	509	1108 1222					
M.	97	1276 1715^{2} 5851 yds. @ 12*c*.	$702.12				
		2 bales Brown Globe Drills,					
		1141 1032^{3}					
		1147 1029 2061^{3} yds. @ 10*c*.	206.17			908	29
		Note @ 8 months.					
		17					
		C. C. Jones, Peoria, Ill.					
L. ⓧ P		1 case Paper Cambrics, 2000 yds. @ 10*c*.	$200.00				
	8	21 pairs White Blankets, @ $3.63	76.23				
	197	17 pcs. Black Satinet, 469 yds. @ 75*c*.	351.75				
	19	17 pcs. Duck, 662 @ 20*c*.	132.40				
A. B.		1 case Cottonades, 687^{1} @ 27*c*.	185.56			945	94
		Note @ 6 months.					
		20					
		Paul Roberts, Buffalo, N. Y.					
		9 cases Cotton Damask, 4860 yds. @ 20*c*.	$972.00				
		5 % off,	48.60	923	40		
		Received Cash.					
		25					
		M. Tompkins & Co., Lasalle, Ill.					
		90 doz. Ladies' Lisle Gauntlets, @ $5	$450.00				
		5 " Kid Gloves, @ $7	35.00				
			485.00				
		5 % off,	24.25	460	75		
		Received Cash.					
		"					
		C. J. Dietrich, Bellefontaine, Ind.					
		1 case Linseys, 1266 yds. @ 20*c*.	$253.20				
		1 case Corset Jeans, 1493 " 10*c*.	149.30			402	50
		Note @ 8 months.					
		Amounts forward,		3036	53	4969	19

SALES BOOK,—SET V.

NEW YORK, AUGUST 25, 1860.

		Amounts forward,		3036	53	4969	19
		Baldwin & Co.,	Cleveland, O.				
239	8615	55 ps. Prints, 812 1845^1					
	9426	52 " 817 1803^1					
	9737	54 " 814 1870^2 5519 yds.	@ 13c.			717	47
		Note @ 8 months.					
		27					
		Ubsdell, Pierson & Co.,	St. Louis,				
U P.&Co	29	$60\frac{3}{4}$ ps. Mohair Mixtures, 2996 @ 15c.	$449.40				
	30	$60\frac{3}{4}$ " " 2969 @ 14c.	415.66				
	31	$60\frac{3}{4}$ " " 2973 @ 14c.	416.22				
	32	$60\frac{3}{4}$ " " 2965 @ 14c.	415.10				
	33	$60\frac{3}{4}$ " " 2966 @ 14c.	415.24				
	34	$60\frac{3}{4}$ " " 2965^2 @ 14c.	415.17				
	35	$60\frac{3}{4}$ ps. Fine M. Mixtures, 2877^2 @ 27c.	776.92			3303	71
		Note @ 8 months.					
		28					
		Raymond & Co.,	Cleveland,				
674	18	4 ps. White Piques, 75^1 @ $1.00	$75.25				
	19	1 " 15 @ $1.25	18.75				
	20	8 ps. Welts, 158 @ .40c.	63.20				
	54	$60\frac{3}{4}$ ps. Lavelles, 3028^1 @ .16c.	484.52			641	72
		Note @ 8 months.					
		30					
		Jonas Stratton,	Amherst, O.				
	62	½ doz. Men's Novi Silk Shirts, @ $20	$10				
	120	1 " " 25	25				
	66	1 " " 30	30				
	68	1 " " 35	35				
	211	56 Printed Jaconets " 3	168				
	212	54 " " 3.50	189			457	
		Note @ 8 months.					
		Sales on time,				10089	09
		Sales for cash, entered here and posted from C. B.		3036	53		
		Petty sales entered alone on C. B.,		1122	77	4159	30
		Total sales for the month,				14248	39

CASH BOOK,—

This is the most convenient form for a Cash-Book to be kept in connection with a general merchandise business; the feature of *special columns* may be extended, if desirable. It will be seen that *all* cash entries, debit and credit, are taken to the Ledger, either through the Journal or directly, from this book, together with all accounts producing or costing cash. The amounts distinguished as "per petty Cash-Book," are entered here from a book contain-

Dr.

Cash.

					Mdse.		Sundries.		Balances.	
1860										
July	1			*Amount on hand*					6725	20
	1		Mdse.	Sales, per petty Cash-Book .	97	50				
	1	√	J. H. Lewis	Received on %			500			
	3		Mdse.	Sales, per petty Cash-Book .	125					
	5	√	Loan	Return from J. E. Jenkins .			1000			
	6	√	J. H. Lewis	Received in full of % . . .			1200			
	8		Mdse.	Sales, per petty Cash-Book .	157					
	10		Mdse.	Sold W. P. Pratt, Cin'ti, (S. B.)	714	28				
	11	√	W. Pennel	In full of %			483	50		
	12		Mdse.	Sold C. Claghorn, Illinois, (S.B.)	433	12				
	14	√	Bills Rec'ble	John Gundry's note due . .			1580			
	15		Mdse.	Sales, per petty Cash-Book .	115	75				
	18	√	Bills Rec'ble	S. S. Pomroy's note discounted			1000			
	21		Mdse.	Sales, per petty Cash-Book .	127	50				
	25	√	Bills Rec'ble	Starr & Co.'s note discounted			1425	48		
	25		Mdse.	Sold Bidwell & Co., Adrian(S.B.)	400					
	27		Mdse.	Sales, per petty Cash-Book .	275					
	30		Mdse.	Sales, per petty Cash-Book .	83					
	31	√	R. Barker	Rec'd in full of %			1000			
					2528	15	8188	98		
				Mdse. Sales for Cash . .			2528	15		
				Total Cash received during month			10717	13	10717	13
									17442	33
Aug	1			Balance on hand					6613	06
	3		Mdse.	Sold C. R. Caulkins, Del., (S. B.)	739	63				
	3		Mdse.	Sales, per petty Cash-Book .	89	27				
	5	√	Interest	Discount on note favor G. A. C.			19	41		
	6	√	Bills Rec'ble	Disc. O. C. & E. C. Wright's note			1432	89		
	7		Mdse.	Sales, per petty Cash-Book .	150					
	10		Mdse.	Sold Geo. A. Crocker, per S. B.	912	75				
	12		Mdse.	Sales, per petty Cash-Book .	218	50				
	17		Mdse.	Sales, per petty Cash-Book .	375					
	20		Mdse.	Sold Paul Roberts, per S. B. .	923	40				
	23		Mdse.	Sales, per petty Cash-Book .	175					
	25	√	Bills Rec'ble	Discounted C. C. Jones's note .			945	94		
	25		Mdse.	Sold M. Tompkins, per S. B. .	460	75				
	31		Mdse.	Sales, per petty Cash-Book .	115					
					4159	30	2398	24		
				Mdse. Sales for Cash . . .			4159	30	6557	54
				Total Cash rec'd during month			6557	54	13170	60

ing sales too insignificant to be entered on the regular Sales Book. The column headed "Balances," will be found very convenient for the purposes for which it is used. The Check-marks, in the column following dates, are made to indicate that the amounts opposite in the "Sundries" column have been journalized. Were these amounts posted directly to the Ledger, the Ledger-page would be written instead of the Check-marks.

Cash. Cr.

					Mdse.		*Sundries.*	
1860 July	1		Mdse.	Paid duties, per Foreign I. B.	300	61		
	1		Mdse.	Olmstead's Invoice, per Dom. I. B. . .	1303	76		
	3	√	Expense	Francis & Loutrel's Stationery Bill . . .			16	75
	3	√	Loan	Lent J. E. Jenkins for one day			1000	
	5	√	Expense	Postage Stamps, $3; Drayage, $5 . . .			8	
	5	√	S. S. Packard	Paid him on Private %			100	
	7	√	Richard Beale	Paid him in full of %			185	
	10		Mdse.	Duties, as per Foreign I. B.	44	21		
	10		Mdse.	Clafflin, Mellen & Co.'s Inv., per Dom. I. B.	2312	52		
	12	√	Expense	Drayage and Porterage			55	
	15		Mdse.	Duties, as per Foreign I. B.	46	80		
	18	√	Interest	Discount on Pomeroy's note			16	92
	20	√	J. T. Calkins	On Private %			150	
	23	√	Bills Payable	Note favor H. G. Smith due			4000	
	25		Mdse.	Duties, per Foreign I. B.	105	63		
	25		Mdse.	A. T. Stewart & Co.'s Invoice, per Dom. I. B.	893	63		
	25	√	Expense	Clerk hire, $40; $25			65	
	25	√	Interest	Discount on Starr & Co.'s note			50	44
	29	√	D. V. Bell	On private %			175	
					5007	16	5822	11
				Mdse. purchased for Cash			5007	16
				Total Cash paid out during the month . .			10829	27
				Balance on hand			6618	06
							17442	33
Aug	1	√	Expense	Paid Drayage, $10; Porterage, $7.50 . .			17	50
	2	√	Loan	Lent J. H. Tobitt			500	
	5	√	Bills Payable	Discounted Note favor Geo. A. Crocker .			1426	
	6	√	Interest	Discount on O. C. & E. C. W.'s note . .			49	60
	10		Mdse.	Duties, as per Foreign I. B.	276	38		
	12	√	Expense	Paid Drayage, on %			100	
	15	√	J. C. Bryant	Paid on private %			150	
	20		Mdse.	Duties, as per Foreign I. B.	45	27		
	20		Mdse.	Bot. of Grinnell, M. & Co., per Dom. I. B.	1492	58		
	25	√	Expense	Porterage, $5; Postage, $3; Charity, $5 .			13	
	25	√	Interest	Discount on C. C. Jones' note			32	19
	31	√	Expense	Paid Drayage in full			50	75
					1814	23	2339	04
				Mdse. purchased for Cash			1814	23
				Total Cash paid for the month			4153	27
				Balance on hand			9017	33
							13170	60

BILL BOOK,—SET V.

THE Bill Book can never, with advantage, be made a *principal* book, from which to post; although some authors have attempted so to use it. The form presented below is the best for general purposes, although the arrangement in the former example is more comprehensive

Bills Receivable.

No.	*When Rec'ed.*	*Drawer or Endorser.*	*Drawee or Maker.*	*Date.*	*Time.*	*When Due.*	*Amount.*		*When and How Disposed of.*		
				1860		1860	$	cts			
1	July 1	H. W. Ellsworth	John Gundry . .	Jan. 11	6 mo.	July 14	1580	00	July	14	Paid.
2	" 1	Daniel Atwood .	S. S. Pomroy. . .	Mar. 12	8 mo.	Nov. 15	1000	00	"	13	Disc'td.
3	" 1	P. B. & Co. . .	Gordon Bailey . .	July 1	8 mo.	1861 Mar. 4	891	35			
4	" 1	H. B. Bryant . .	Ira Packard . . .	" 1	6 mo.	Jan. 4	278	52			
5	" 5	Paul Roberts . .	Hiram Newell . .	" 5	6 mo.	" 8	697	54			
6	" 10	H. D. Stratton .	Baldwin, L. & Co. .	" 10	8 mo.	Mar. 13	869	38			
7	" 15	P. B. & Co.. . .	E. Mussey & Co. .	" 15	8 mo.	" 18	923	25			
8	" 20	J. G. Reid . . .	Starr & Co. . . .	" 20	6 mo.	Jan. 23	1425	48	July	25	Disc'td.
9	" 22	Jno. D. Hinde .	Murray, S. & Co. .	" 22	8 mo.	" 25	1460	14			
10	" 28	Wm. P. Eaton .	E. C. Packard . .	" 28	8 mo.	Mar. 31	171	04			
11	Aug. 1	James Atwater .	O. C. & E. C. Wright	Aug. 1	6 mo.	Feb. 4	1432	89	Aug.	6	Disc'td.
12	" 5	P. B. & Co. . .	David S. Hoadley .	" 5	8 mo.	April 8	527	00			
13	" 8	do . . .	J. D. Hinde & Co. .	" 8	8 mo.	" 11	752	57			
14	" 15	J. O. Eaton . .	W. H. Woodbury .	" 15	8 mo.	" 18	908	29			
15	" 17	P. B. & Co. . .	C. C. Jones . . .	" 17	6 mo.	Feb. 20	945	94	Aug.	25	Disc'td.
16	" 25	do . . .	C. J. Dietrich . .	" 25	8 mo.	Apr. 28	402	50			
17	" 25	do . . .	Baldwin & Co. . .	" 25	8 mo.	" 28	717	47			
18	" 27	do . . .	Ubsdell, P. & Co. .	" 27	8 mo.	" 30	3303	71			
19	" 28	do . . .	Raymond & Co.. .	" 28	8 mo.	May 1	641	72			
20	" 30	do . . .	Jonas Stratton . .	" 30	8 mo.	" 3	457	00			

Bills Payable.

No.	*When Issued.*	*Drawer or Endorser.*	*Drawee or Maker.*	*Date.*	*Time.*	*When Due.*	*Amount.*		*When and How Redeemed.*		
						1860	$	cts			
1	Jan. 20	H. G. Smith & Co.	P. B. & Co. . . .	Jan. 20	6 mo.	July 23	4000	00	July	23	Paid.
2	Mar. 1	A. S. Prentiss . .	do . . .	Feb. 26	8 mo.	Oct. 29	3500	00			
3	Apr. 12	Geo. A. Crocker .	do . . .	Apr. 12	6 mo.	Oct. 15	1426	00	Aug.	5	Disc'td.
4	July 5	C. F. Spalding .	do . . .	July 5	4 mo.	Nov. 8	553	57			
5	" 10	J. Walker . . .	do . . .	" 10	8 mo.	1861 Mar. 13	1006	64			
6	" 20	E. Lambert & Co.	do . . .	" 20	8 mo.	" 23	660	72			
7	Aug.	W. G. Hunt . .	do . . .	Aug. 10	8 mo.	Apr. 13	708	40			
8	"	Arnold & Co. . .	do . . .	" 20	8 mo.	" 23	1926	14			

INVENTORY BOOK.

THIS book is used to enumerate the different articles of unsold merchand se, at such times as may be deemed desirable. It is, in this instance, purely an auxiliary, the amount of merchandise on hand being included in the opening journal entry. Inventories are frequently copied into one of the Invoice Books; but a separate book is preferable.

Mdse. on hand, July 1, 1860.

Marks.	*Nos.*		*Yds*	*Price*	*Amount.*	
◇A R.	49	1 case Prints	1905	.10	190	50
		60 pieces Doeskin	1842	1.35	2486	70
H. M.		1 bale Brown Sheetings	563^2	.11	61	98
(B)	192	1 case Black Tabby Velvet	796	$.26^3$	212	93
L. ◇B B.	1	1 case Paper Cambrics	2000	$.06^1$	125	
	8	21 pairs White Blankets		3.43	72	03
B.		1 bale Denims	569	$.10^2$	59	74
		41 pcs. Blk and Wht Tweeds	1369^2	.25	342	37
	1072 1060 1085	3 pcs. Blk Doeskin	70	$.92^2$	64	75
		21 " Fancy Cassimeres	576^1	.60	345	75
	197	17 " Blk Satinet	469	$.52^2$	246	22
Y.◇A W.		1 case Printed Jaconets	2010	$.12^2$	251	25
◇A F.		1 " Woolen Shawls	60	4.89	293	40
	231	26 pcs. Blk Bombasin	900	$.87^2$	787	50
	19	37 " Duck	1392	.15	208	80
		2 bales Blk Wadding doz.	80	.22	17	60
	1289	110 Robes		1.50	165	
[A. B.]		1 case Cottonades	687^1	.22	154	63
R. & X.		10 cases Cotton Damask	5400	.16	864	
	62	150 doz. Gent's Linen Hdkfs		4.50	675	
	M.	150 pcs. Diaper		.90	135	
		50 $\frac{7}{8}$ Blay Linens	1931^2	.17	328	35
A. S. B		1 case Delaines	1300	.25	325	
	190	1 " Blk Alpacas	910	$.27^2$	250	25
	4	1 " Opera Flannel	750	$.37^2$	281	25
	3024	1 " D. Bege	864	.11	95	04
		100 doz. Men's Gloves		2.50	250	
		140 " Ladies' Lisle Gauntlets		4.46	624	40
		5 " " Kid Gloves		6.25	31	25
		1 bale Stark Brown Sheetings	829	$.08^2$	70	46
	130	1 " 4-4 Shaker Flannel	337^2	.45	151	88
		12 pcs. Green Veil Barege	200	.29	58	
	1066	1 case Solid Check Ginghams	2394	.14	335	16
		25 pcs. Coburgs	525	.50	262	50
		1 case Silecia	2200	$.09^1$	203	50
	4595	1 " Linseys	1266^2	$.17^2$	221	64
		1 " Corset Jeans	1725^1	.06	103	51
(B) E S.		1 bale Eagle Ticks	700	$.11^2$	80	50
					11432	84

JOURNAL,—SET V.

NEW YORK, JULY 1, 1860.

Account	Particulars	Dr. $	cts.	Cr. $	cts.
Sundries	To Sundries				
	Resources and Liabilities of S. S. Packard, D. V. Bell, J. C. Bryant, and J. T. Calkins, partners in the firm of "Packard, Bell & Co.," doing a general Jobbing and Importing business in the City of New York; as taken from the Balance Sheet of their last Ledger:				
Cash	Amount on hand, per Cash Book . . .	6725	20		
Merchandise	" " Inventory Book .	11432	84		
Bills Receivable	Notes on hand, per Bill Book	2580			
Store Rent	Advance payment for rent	2000			
John Lewis	Balance of %	1700			
Robert Barker	"	1000			
William Pennel	"	483	50		
To Bills Payable	Notes outstanding, per Bill Book . . .			8926	
" R P. Beale	Balance of %			185	
" S. S. Packard	Net Investment			4202	63
" D. V. Bell	"			4202	63
" J. C. Bryant	"			4202	64
" J. T. Calkins	"			4202	64
	31				
Merchandise	To Sundries	4381	10		
To Bills Payable	For the following Invoices per Dom. I. B.: From C. F. Spalding, July 5, $553.57; " J. Walker & Co. " 10, 1006.64; " E. Lambert & Co. " 20, 660.73			2220	94
To S. B. Higgins	Invoice of July 1, per For. I. B. . . .			1252	55
" Johnson, Q. & Co.	" 10, " . . .			221	11
" A. & J. Bailey	" 15, " . . .			246	36
" S. T. Horton	" 25, " . . .			440	14
	"				
Bills Receivable	To Merchandise	6711	70		
	Sales for the month, per Sales Book: Gordon Bailey, July 1, $891.35; Ira Packard, " 1, 273.52; Hiram Newell, " 5, 697.54; Baldwin, L. & Co. " 10, 869.38; E. Mussey & Co. " 15, 923.25; Starr & Co. " 20, 1425.48; M. Shipley & Co. " 22, 1460.14; Edwin C. Packard " 28, 171.04			6711	70
	"				
Cash	To Sundries	10717	13		
	Receipts per Cash Book:				
To Mdse.	Total Sales for Cash			2528	15
" John H. Lewis	Rec'd on %, $500; $1200			1700	
" Loan	Return from J. E. Jenkins			1000	
" Wm. Pennel	In full of %			483	50
" Bills Rec'ble	Rec'd on Notes, $1580; $1000; $1425.48			4005	48
" Robert Barker	In full of %			1000	
		47731	47	47731	47

JOURNAL,—SET V.

NEW YORK, JULY 31, 1860.

Account	Particulars	Dr. $	Cts.	Cr. $	Cts.
Sundries	To Cash			10829	27
	Disbursements per Cash Book:				
Mdse.	Purchases, etc., for Cash	5007	16		
Expense	As per Items, $16.75; $8; $55; $65 .	144	75		
Loan	Lent J. E. Jenkins	1000			
S. S. Packard	Paid on private %	100			
Richard Beale	In full of %	185			
Interest	Per Items, $16.92; $50.44	67	36		
J. T. Calkins	Paid on private %	150			
Bills Payable	Redeemed note favor J. H. Smith .	4000			
D. V. Bell	Paid on private %	175			
	Aug. 31				
Mdse.	To Sundries	4277	80		
To Bills Payable	Invoices per Dom. I. B.				
	From Wilson G. Hunt, Aug. 10, $708.40				
	" Arnold & C. " 20, 1926.14			2634	54
" Wm. Thornton	Invoice of Aug. 10, per F. I. B. . . .			1454	64
" J. Muir & Sons	" " 20, " . . .			188	62
	"				
Bills Rec'ble	To Mdse.	10089	09		
	Sales for the month, as per Sales Book:				
	O. C. & E. C. Wright, Aug. 1, $1432.89				
	David S. Hoadley, " 5, 527.00				
	J. D. Hinde & Co., " 8, 752.57				
	Wm. H. Woodbury, " 15, 908.29				
	C. C. Jones, " 17, 945.94				
	C. J. Deitrich, " 30, 402.50				
	Baldwin & Co., " 25, 717.47				
	Ubsdell, Pierson & Co. " 27, 3303.71				
	Raymond & Co., " 28, 641.72				
	Jonas Stratton, " 30, 457.00			10089	09
	"				
Cash	To Sundries	6557	54		
	Receipts, per Cash Book:				
To Mdse.	Total Sales for Cash			4159	30
" Interest	Discount on note favor G. A. C. . . .			19	41
" Bills Rec'ble	Received on notes, $1432.89; $945.94 .			2378	83
	"				
Sundries	To Cash			4153	27
	Disbursements, per Cash Book:				
Mdse.	Purchases, etc., for Cash	1814	23		
Expense	Per Items, $17.50; $100; $13; $50.75	181	25		
Loan	Lent J. H. Tobitt	500			
Bills Payable	Discounted note favor G. A. C. . . .	1426			
Interest	Per Items, $49.60; $32.19	81	79		
J. C. Bryant	Paid on private %	150			
		35906	97	35906	97

PACKARD, BELL & CO.'S BALANCE SHEET,—SET V.

Taken New York, August 31 1860.	L Fol.	Trial Balance Dr.	Trial Balance Cr.	Inventory.	Representative Losses.	Representative Gains.	S. S. Packard Dr.	S. S. Packard Cr.	D. V. Bell Dr.	D. V. Bell Cr.	J. C. Bryant Dr.	J. C. Bryant Cr.	J. T. Calkins Dr.	J. T. Calkins Cr.	Real Res'rces.	Real Liab'ties.
S. S. Packard			4202 68					4202 68								
D. V. Bell			4202 68							4202 68						
J. C. Bryant			4202 64									4202 64				
J. T. Calkins			4202 64											4202 64		
Cash		28999 87	14982 54												9017 33	
Bills Receivable		19380 79	6384 31												12996 48	
Mdse.		26918 13	23488 24	8000		4575 11									8000	
Store Rent		2000		1500	500										1500	
Bills Payable		5426	13781 48													8355 48
S. B. Higgins			1252 55													1252 55
J. Quigley & Co.			221 11													221 11
A. & J. Bailey			246 36													246 36
S. F. Horton			440 14													440 16
Loan		1500	1000												500	
Expense		326			326											
S. S. Packard (Priv.)		100													100	
Interest		149 15	19 41		129 74											
J. T. Calkins (Priv.)		150													150	
D. V. Bell (Priv.)		175													175	
Wm. Thornton			1454 64													1454 64
J. Muir & Sons			188 62													188 62
J. C. Bryant (Priv.)		150													150	
		80269 94	80269 94													
S. S. Packard's ½ net gain					904 84			904 84								
D. V. Bell's " "					904 84					904 84						
J. C. Bryant's " "					904 84							904 84				
J. T. Calkins " "					904 85									904 85		
					4575 11	4575 11										
S. S. Packard's net capital							5107 47									5107 47
							5107 47	5107 47								
D. V. Bell's net capital									5107 47							5107 47
									5107 47	5107 47						
J. C. Bryant's net capital											5107 48					5107 48
											5107 48	5107 48				
J. T. Calkins's net capital													5107 42			5107 49
													5107 49	5107 49	82588 81	82588 81

QUESTIONS FOR REVIEW,—SETS IV. AND V.

REMARKS.—PAGE 78.

1. What are the peculiar characteristics of Set IV? 2. What advantage does the Day-Book in Journal form have over the Historical Day-Book? 3. What objection can be urged against it? 4. What is meant by "Merchandise Companies?" 5. In what particulars does this species of copartnership differ from general co-partnerships? 6. Wherein do the two methods of keeping Mdse. Co. accounts, as shown in this set differ? 7. What is the principle recognized in the *first* method? 8. What in the *second* method? 9. Give an illustration of each. 10. By the first method, when more than two parties are interested, what entry should the *consignee* make on receipt of the property to be sold on joint %? 11. What the *consignor* upon shipping the property? 12. What the other parties? 13. By the second method when three or more parties are interested, what entry will the *consignee* make on receiving property to be sold on joint %? 14. What the *consignor?* 15. What the other parties? 16. Is there any difference in the final result by these separate methods? 17. When is the *consignee* considered responsible by the first method? 18. When, by the second? 19. Which method is absolutely correct? 20. What advantage has the other? 21. Are Mdse. Co. %'s to be classified as *Real* or *Representative?* 22. How may they be made *Real?* 23. How *Representative?* 24. What different method of closing the Ledger is shown in Set IV? 25. Is there any necessity for a *Balance* account? 26. How can its place be filled? 27. What is the usual entry in bringing down balances of resources and liabilities? 28. What is the advantage of using auxiliary books? 29. Can special books of entry be so used as to dispense with the Journal?

BALANCE SHEETS, AND AUXILIARIES.—PAGES 101 AND 104.

30. Explain the method of ruling the Balance Sheet. 31. What advantages has this form over any other in use? 32. What objection may be urged against a multiplicity of auxiliary books? 33. How is this objection removed in large establishments? 34. What are the essential points in a good business letter? 35 Can a sufficient knowledge of business correspondence be learnt from models?

REMARKS ON SET V.—PAGE 128.

36. What species of business is represented by this set? 37. What is its peculiar feature? 38. Has this method any advantages over that of consecutive entries, hitherto exhibited in this work? 39. Wherein do such advantages consist? 40. What difficulty lies in the way of using the various books of original entries as principal books, from which to post or journalize? 41. What should the Cash-Book show? 42. How is it made to show all receipts and disbursements? 43. What will the difference between the two sides of the Cash-Book represent? 44. When cash is debited on the Cash-Book, what is credited? 45. Is every entry made on either side of the Cash-Book really a *double* entry? 46. What would be a proper caption for the debit side of the Cash-Book? 47. What for the credit side? 48. What credits are shown on the debit side of the Cash-Book? 49. What debits on the credit side? 50. Does the same principle hold with reference to the Sales Book and Invoice Books? 51. Will you now state the difficulty likely to occur in transactions required to be entered in two of these books? 52. If the peculiar rights of each book is respected, will it be proper to post cash from the Sales or Invoice Book, or merchandise from the Cash-Book? 53. What would be the effect of such posting? 54. How many methods are there of avoiding this difficulty? 55. What is the first? 56. What the second? 57. Which of these two methods is preferable? 58. Which is adopted in this Set? 59. What does the Inventory Book in this Set contain, and how is it used? 60. What does the Domestic Invoice Book contain? 61. What entries are passed to the Ledger from this book? 62. What does the Foreign Invoice Book contain? 63. The Sales Book? 64. With what will the total credit of Merchandise account for the month agree? 65. Will you explain the characteristics and use of the Cash-Book? 66. Are all the debits and credits appearing on the Cash-Book posted? 67. What amounts are entered in the "Sundries" column? 68. How are these amounts posted? 69. What does the check-mark, opposite these amounts denote? 70. What would be written instead of the check-marks were the amounts posted *directly* from the Cash-Book? 71. Can the Bill Book be used to advantage as a *principal* book?

SINGLE ENTRY

CHANGED TO DOUBLE ENTRY,

WITH AMPLE ILLUSTRATIONS AND EXPLANATIONS,

EMBRACING

TWO DISTINCT SETS OF BOOKS BY SINGLE ENTRY,

ONE REPRESENTING THE BUSINESS OF A RETAIL MERCHANT AND THE OTHER THAT OF A BUILDER, BOTH OF WHICH ARE

CHANGED TO DOUBLE ENTRY, AND THE BUSINESS CONTINUED.

N THE LA TER SET A DISSOI TION OF COPARTNERSHIP TAKES PLACE, AND THE STUDENT IS REQUIRED TO WRITE P ORIGINAL TRANSACTIONS TO COMPLETE THE SET.

CHANGING SINGLE, TO DOUBLE ENTRY.

We have, so far, omitted any special instruction in Single Entry Book-keeping for the reasons, first, that we desired not to distract the mind from the more important considerations bearing upon the science of Accounts, and secondly, that we deemed it much more easy to explain the characteristic features of Single Entry, to one thoroughly familiar with the principles of Double Entry.

We have distinguished Double Entry Book-keeping as the "science of Accounts," because its theory rests on scientific principles, and its work is susceptible of scientific analysis. Single Entry, although, by no means, devoid of excellences as a system, cannot properly be called a science. It is, however, the *beginning* of a science; bearing about the same relation to Double Entry that the three terms of a compound ratio do to the proportion fully expressed.

We are not among the number who can see no merit in a system that does not square in all respects with our notions of symmetry and perfectness; and we are, therefore, quite ready to accord to Single Entry Book-keeping, all the merits it may possess. But the chief difficulty in the matter is to decide upon the fact and extent of Single Entry; and this difficulty becomes the more intense the more we seek its solution by any standard afforded in actual business. While all scientific accountants by Double Entry must agree as to the necessity of equal debits and credits—no matter through what forms expressed, Single Entry accountants differ in this regard, according to the amount of light they may have, or the condition of the precedents which they follow. Thus, while some would represent on the Ledger only accounts with individuals, others who have had the ingenuity to concoct, or the good sense to observe, find an advantage in dealing in the same manner with the other various kinds of resources and liabilities. This is, sometimes, carried so far by intelligent accountants that, although without any suspicion on their part, their books will be found to contain nearly all the requisites of Double Entry. It is from this fact that we find it difficult adequately to define Single Entry.

The term "*Single* Entry," as distinct from "*Double* Entry," has reference more particularly to the fact, that for every separate Day Book entry but one posting is made to the Ledger; but to what extent these single Day Book entries shall be carried, or how much real information contain, has never yet been decided by authors, teachers, or business men. It is usually understood, however, that the difference in the two systems consists mainly in the fact that while the Single Entry Ledger contains only accounts with *persons*, Double Entry deals also, and in like manner, with *property* and *causes*.

We have shown in the previous lectures that Double Entry Book-keeping, or the "Science of Accounts," comprises a *perfect* and continual record of resources and liabilities; and we may now say, contradistinctively, that Single Entry comprises an *imperfect* record of resources and liabilities; or, rather, a record of only a *portion* of them. Whenever this deficiency is supplied the requisitions of Double Entry are met. Therefore,

To convert Single, to Double Entry Books, *open such additional accounts in the Ledger as are necessary to exhibit the entire resources and liabilities of the concern.*

If accounts have been previously opened with the partners, or an account with Stock, as the case may be, representing investments and sums withdrawn, it will, of course, be necessary first to carry the gain or loss of the business to those accounts, as a perfect record of resources and liabilities cannot otherwise be made. The method of ascertaining such gain or loss will be shown in the succeeding statement.

It will thus be seen that Double Entry is but a continuation of Single Entry; traveling with it hand in hand, as far as it goes, but carrying out its principles to their full symmetry and perfection. Those who array formal objections against the practice of Double Entry, on account of its intricacy, its additional labor, or its departure in any sense, from the recognized principles of debits and credits as practised in Single Entry, evidently do not know of what they speak. In changing a set of books from Single to Double Entry, it is not necessary to disturb any account already opened in the Ledger, nor to keep any such account differently thereafter. This fact will be clearly shown in the illustrations given.

In the exercises which follow, we have, first, a set of Single Entry Books, comprising a Cash Book, Day Book, and Ledger. The Cash Book is for the same purpose, and kept somewhat upon the same principle as the Double Entry Cash Book. the only difference being in the *form* of recording entries. As we neither journalize nor post from the Single Entry Cash Book, it is not necessary to specify Ledger titles, as in Double Entry; the object of the Single Entry Cash Book being simply to complete the record of transactions omitted in the Day Book, and to keep the necessary check upon receipts and disbursements of cash.

It is also customary, in connection with Single Entry Books, to keep a Bill Book, for the purpose of recording Bills Receivable and Bills Payable. If, in addition to these, we should keep an Invoice Book and a Sales Book, either separate or together, for the purpose of recording purchases and sales of merchandise, we should embrace nearly all the requisites of Double Entry; the chief difference being that instead of showing the entire result upon the Ledger, we divide the honor among these various auxiliaries.

In the illustrations given we have shown first, a Single Entry Ledger, containing only personal accounts, and next, the additional accounts necessary to constitute a Double Entry Ledger. In the student's manuscript these two parts will, of course, be united, forming together a Double Entry Ledger, fulfilling the requisites of equal debits and credits, and, consequently, equal resources and liabilities. The intervening statement preparatory to changing, should be closely examined, and thoroughly understood.

The memoranda of transactions following, are intended, of course, to be regularly written up and posted to the Ledger as changed; and the general results exhibited according to the principles already laid down.

To one who fully appreciates the advantages of Double Entry, no argument nor illustration will be necessary to enforce its entire superiority over any other system, notwithstanding the crude notions sometimes expressed by those whose very position should render ignorance on so vital a point, inexcusable; but it should, nevertheless, be the aim of every intelligent accountant to place himself beyond the pale of prejudice, and let him not insist, because he esteems his own way best, that there can be no merit in any other.

It is but natural that men who have, for a lifetime been familiar with a certain routine of transactions, expressed through a certain medium, should become unalterably attached to both, and should look with jealousy upon any thing savoring of innovation. It is the duty of the accountant, who acts simply as such, to humor prejudices of this kind, rather than abuse them, and thus show his own superiority, by making even inadequate forms convey more substantial and extended information than their friends and advocates have claimed for them.

The chief advantages of Double, over Single Entry, consist, first, in the security afforded by the Trial Balance test and next, in designating the particular channels through which gains and losses come. The *fact* of gains and losses, and the exact amount of either can be as well ascertained by Single Entry, provided we have the means of knowing that the work is correct.

CASH BOOK,—SINGLE ENTRY.

1860. Receipts.

			$	cts
Jan.	1	James Mason's Investment	3000	
	1	Robert Walker's Investment	1000	
	3	John Simmons,—Coat, $20; Pants, $9.50; Vest, $7	36	50
	3	Joseph Kinsey, on %	15	
	3	Miscellaneous Sales, per tickets	58	25
	5	W. H. Beebe,—Overcoat, $35; Vest, $7.50; Cravat, $1.50	44	
	5	Miscellaneous Sales, per tickets	39	63
	7	John Mason, Invoice ready-made Clothing	175	
			4368	38
	9	Balance on hand	4156	38
	9	Robert Hall,—6 yards blue Broadcloth, @ $5	30	
	10	Wm. H. Joeckel,—Business Suit	23	
	12	Bill of Goods ordered by P. T. Barnum	350	
	13	1 doz. Hdkfs. $3; 3 doz. Cravats, $30; 2 doz. Collars, $5	38	
	15	A. B. Butts,—Dress Suit	40	
	15	Miscellaneous Sales, this week, per tickets	450	
			5087	38
	16	Balance on hand	5003	63
	16	Bill of Goods to P. Evans, Cincinnati	375	
	17	3 doz. Cravats, $40; 5 doz. standing Collars, $13.50	53	50
	20	Assortment ready-made Clothing,—J. Allen, Pittsburg	500	
	22	Miscellaneous Sales for the week, per tickets	378	95
			6311	08
	23	Balance on hand	6175	58
	23	2 doz. Cravats, $30; 6 Vest patterns, $35	65	
	25	1 pair Pants, $9; 1 dress Coat, $25; 1 Cravat, $1.50	35	50
	25	Bill of ready-made Clothing—C. S. Sill, Troy	175	
	27	6 doz. Hdkfs, $20; 8 doz. French Yoke Shirts, $170	190	
	27	Ira Packard,—Dress Suit	36	50
	30	Miscellaneous Sales, this week, per tickets	322	15
			6999	73
	31	Balance on hand	6834	73

CASH BOOK,—SINGLE ENTRY.

Disbursements.

1860.				
Jan	3	Stationery, $10; Painting and Cleaning, $15	25	
	7	Seamstress's wages, $27; Clerk hire, $10	37	
	7	John Jones, on %	50	
		Balance on hand	4156	8
			4368	38
	13	Sundry expenses, per Expense Book	15	75
	14	Seamstress's wages, $50; Clerk's hire, $18	68	
	14	*Balance on hand*	5006	63
			5087	38
	19	Sundry expenses, per Expense Book	12	50
	20	Seamstress's wages, $75; Clerk hire, $18	93	
	21	Office Desk and Chair	30	
	21	*Balance on hand*	6175	58
			6311	08
	25	Sundry expenses, per Expense Book	15	
	30	Seamstress's wages and Clerk hire	75	
	30	Cutter's wages for the month	75	
	30	*Balance on hand*	6834	73
			6999	73

SINGLE ENTRY DAY BOOK.

PHILADELPHIA, JAN. 1, 1860.

James Mason and Robert Walker unite in copartnership in a Gentlemen's Furnishing establishment. They invest equally, and share equally in gains and losses.

James Mason,	Cr.		
By Cash invested	$3000		
" Merchandise, per Inventory	4500		
" Sundry Notes, per B. B.	750	8250	
James Mason,	Dr.		
To Balance due John Jones		500	
Robert Walker,	Cr.		
By Cash invested	$1000		
" Store and Fixtures	6750	7750	
John Jones,	Cr.		
By amount owing him by J. Mason		500	
2			
William Patterson,	Dr.		
To 1 Pair Doeskin Pants	$ 9		
" 1 Blue Broadcloth Coat	22		
" 1 Figured Satin Vest	7 50		
" 12 Pocket Handkerchiefs, @ 50 c.	6	44	50
3			
Joseph Kinsey,	Dr.		
To 1 doz. Fancy Neckties	$12		
" $1\frac{1}{2}$ doz. Byron Collars, @ $3	4 50		
" 6 Vest Patterns, assorted	35		
" 8 yds. Farmer's Satin	6		
" 3 doz. Pairs Gent's Hose	9	66	50
Contra,	Cr.		
By Cash on %		15	
4			
James M. Dooley,	Dr		
To 1 doz. Fine Shirts	$24		
" 3 " Lamb's Wool Undershirts, @ $15	45		
" 3 " Pairs Flannel Drawers, @ $15	45	114	
5			
Sumner Packard,	Dr.		
To 3 yds. Fine French Broadcloth, @ $5	$15		
" 12 " English Cassimere, @ $2	24	39	
7			
John Jones,	Dr.		
To Cash Paid on %		150	

SINGLE ENTRY DAY BOOK.

PHILADELPHIA, JAN. 9, 1860.

Folio	Entry	Items	Dollars	Cents
	Jabez Dunham, Dr.			
2	To Wedding Suit, per contract		59	
	10			
	James M. Dooley, Cr.			
1	By 10 Tons Coal for use of the store @ $5		50	
	12			
	Robert S. Hayward, Dr.			
	To 1 Frock Overcoat	$30		
2	" 1 Dress Coat	25		
	" 1 Pair French Cassimere Pants	10	65	
	14			
	Erastus Young, Dr.			
	To Making Dress Coat	$9		
2	" " Vest	3		
	" Repairing Coat	2	14	
	16			
	Robert S. Hayward, Cr.			
2	By his Note @ 30 days to Balance %		65	
	17			
	David T. Fuller, Dr.			
	To 1 Frock Coat	$30		
2	" 1 Vest	5 50		
	" 1 Overcoat for Master Frank	12	47	50
	18			
	Charles Claghorn, Dr.			
	To 6 Shirts, (French Yoke), @ $2.50	$15		
2	" 10 Pairs Socks, @ 25 cts.	2 50		
	" Drawers and Undershirts, 2 each, $1. 25	5	22	50
	20			
	Henry Dwight, Dr.			
3	To Frock and Pants for Master Silas		10	
	21			
	Schuyler Corbit, Dr.			
	To 1 Dress Coat	$23		
3	" 2 Neck Ties	3		
	" 6 Pocket Handkerchiefs	1 50	27	50
	25			
	Wilson G. Hunt & Co. Cr.			
3	By Bill of Cloths, per Invoice		575	
	30			
	Henry Shaft, Dr.			
	To 1 Pair Pants	$ 9		
3	" 1 Dress Coat	25	34	

LEDGER,—SINGLE ENTRY.

Dr. James Mason. Cr.

Date				$	cts.	Date				$	cts.
1860 *Jan.*	1	To Balance Due J. J.	1	500		1860 *Jan.*	1	By Investment	1	8250	
								" ½ net gain		681	61

Dr. Robert Walker. Cr.

Date				$	cts.	Date				$	cts.
						1860 *Jan.*	1	By Investment	1	7750	
								" ½ net gain		681	62

Dr. John Jones. Cr.

Date				$	cts.	Date				$	cts.
1860 *Jan.*	7	To Cash	1	150		1860		By Balance due him		500	

Dr. Wm. Patterson. Cr.

Date				$	cts.	Date				$	cts.
1860 *Jan.*	2	To Sundries	1	44	50						

Dr. Joseph Kinsey. Cr.

Date				$	cts.	Date				$	cts.
1860 *Jan.*	8	To Sundries	1	66	50	1860 *Jan.*	8	By Cash	1	15	

Dr. James M. Dooley. Cr.

Date				$	cts.	Date				$	cts.
1860 *Jan.*	4	To Sundries	1	114		1860 *Jan.*	10	By 10 Tons Coal	1	50	

Dr. Sumner Packard. Cr.

Date				$	cts.	Date				$	cts.
1860 *Jan.*	5	To Sundries	1	39							

Dr. Jabez Dunham. Cr.

Date				$	cts.	Date				$	cts.
1860 *Jan*	9	To Wedding Suit	1	59							

LEDGER,—SINGLE ENTRY.

Dr. Robert S. Hayward. Cr.

1860 *Jan.*	12	To Sundries	2	65		1860 *Jan.*	16	By Note @ 30 days.	2	65	

Dr. Erastus Young. Cr

1860 *Jan.*	14	To Making and Repairing	2	14							

Dr. David T. Fuller. Cr

1860 *Jan.*	17	To Sundries.		47	50						

Dr. Charles Claghorn. Cr.

1860 *Jan.*	18	To Sundries	2	22	50						

Dr. Henry Dwight. Cr.

1860 *Jan.*	20	To Frock and Pants.	2	10							

Dr. Schuyler Corbit. Cr.

1860 *Jan.*	21	To Sundries	2	27	50						

Dr. Wilson G. Hunt. Cr.

						1860 *Jan.*	25	By Mdse.	2	575	

Dr. Henry Shaft. Cr.

1860 *Jan.*	30	To Sundries	2	34							

PROCESS OF CHANGING.

The intelligent learner need not, at this stage, be told that the first requisition in opening a Set of Double Entry Books is a statement of resources and liabilities. This statement is also necessary in Single Entry as often as it is desirable to know the progress or condition of the business; either with a view to apportioning gains and losses, or for any other purpose whatever. In the preceding Ledger we have a systematic record of such of the resources and liabilities as consist of personal accounts,—the remainder must be ascertained from some other source.

Inasmuch as the partners were credited, each for his net investment, we are enabled to know from their accounts what was the original capital. If there be now, either more or less net resources than this original investment, the result will show a gain or loss, as the case may be. If a gain, the partners should, of course, be credited in their proportionate shares; and if a loss, they should be debited. This will, again, equalize the resources and liabilities, and give us sufficient data for a Double Entry Ledger.

To this end we present the following

Preparatory Statement.

Statement of the Resources and Liabilities of James Mason and Robert Walker, who have this day changed their Books from Single to Double Entry.				
Resources.				
Personal Accounts Receivable (already posted) . .	413	50		
Notes Receivable on hand per Bill Book	815			
Cash, per Cash Book	6834	73		
Merchandise, per Inventory	2975			
Store and Fixtures, per cost	6750		17788	23
Liabilities.				
Personal Accounts Payable (already posted) . . .	925			
James Mason, Net Investment	7750			
Robert Walker, "	7750		16425	
Total net gain in business			1363	23
James Mason's ½ $681.61				
Robert Walker's ½ 681.62				

From this schedule it will be evident that when the above resources and liabilities are duly entered upon the Ledger—the resources to the debit, and the liabilities to the credit of the accounts representing them—they will lack just the amount of net gain ($1363.23) of balancing. If this amount, then, be entered to the credit of the partners, where it properly belongs, and the additional accounts opened, we shall have the commencement of a Double Entry Ledger.

We now complete this process, crediting the partners each for his ½ gain, and opening accounts in the extended Ledger with the additional resources: Bills Receivable, Cash, Merchandise and Store and Fixtures. These four new accounts constitute the "change," and will serve, very clearly, to show the exact difference in the two systems, so far as the Ledger is concerned.

LEDGER,—DOUBLE ENTRY.

Dr. Bills Receivable. Cr.

1860 Jan.	31	Notes on hand.		815					

Dr. Cash. Cr.

1860 Jan.	21	On hand		6834	73				

Dr. Merchandise. Cr.

1860 Jan.	31	On hand		2975					

Dr. Store and Fixtures. Cr.

1860 Jan.	31	Valuation.		6750					

It is always proper before commencing the current record of business in Double Entry Books, to ascertain if the Ledger balances. With this view we submit the following

Trial Balance.

Balances. Dr.		Balances. Cr.			Face of Ledger. Dr.		Face of Ledger. Cr.	
		8431	61	James Mason	500		8931	61
		8431	62	Robert Walker			8431	62
		350		John Jones	150		500	
44	50			Wm. Patterson	44	50		
51	50			Joseph Kinsey	66	50	15	
64				James M. Dooley	114		50	
39				Sumner Packard	39			
59				Jabez Dunham	59			
14				Erastus Young	14			
47	50			David T. Fuller	47	50		
22	50			Charles Claghorn	22	50		
10				Henry Dwight	10			
27	50			Schuyler Corbit	27	50		
		575		Wilson G. Hunt			575	
34				Henry Shaft	34			
815				Bills Receivable	815			
6834	73			Cash	6834	73		
2975				Merchandise	2975			
6750				Store and Fixtures	6750			
17788	23	17788	23		18503	23	18503	23

The books are now to be continued in Double Entry, from the following transactions.

HISTORICAL DAY BOOK,—DOUBLE ENTRY.

PHILADELPHIA, FEBRUARY 1, 1860.

Particulars	Rate	Items	Dollars	Cents
Sold Robert Milburn for Cash,				
1 doz. Suspenders		$ 4 50		
4 " Cravats	@ $15	60		
$3\frac{1}{2}$ " French Yoke Shirts (fine)	@ $30	105		
10 " Standing Collars	@ $1 80	18	187	50
2				
Received Cash for rent of upper story, one month			50	
″				
Paid Robert Walker Cash on private %			100	
3				
Accepted John Jones's draft on us @ 30 days, favor A. B. Butts			350	
5				
Bought of Dunham & Brokaw, on our note @ 60 days, Mdse, per Invoice			700	
7				
Sold Wm. Patterson* on %,				
3 doz. Vest Patterns	@ $50	$150		
10 yds. Blue Broadcloth	@ $6	60		
20 yds. French Cassimere	@ $4	80	290	
8				
Received of James M. Dooley, Cash in full of %			64	
″				
Paid the following expenses in Cash:				
Clerk hire		$ 25		
Seamstress's wages		115	140	
10				
Sold R. C. Davis & Co., Albany, on their Note @ 4 months, Mdse, per Invoice			500	
12				
Bought of James Dunham, for the private use of Robert Walker,				
1 Firkin Butter, 100 lbs.	@ 25 cts.	$25		
1 Bbl. "Seek no Further" Apples		6		
1 do Cider Vinegar		8		
Paid him per order on Sumner Packard.			39	
13				
Received Cash of Joseph Kinsey, in full of %			51	50
15				
Sold Edwin Forrest, on % 1 Suit Fine Broadcloth			50	
17				
Paid Advertising Bill in Cash			75	

* Be careful not to open the same account *twice*.

HISTORICAL DAY BOOK,—DOUBLE ENTRY.

PHILADELPHIA, FEBRUARY 20, 1860.

Entry	Items	Dollars	Cents
Paid Cash for Insurance on store and contents, $\frac{3}{4}$ % on $4000.* (Manhattan Insurance Co.)		30	
25			
Received Cash of Jabez Dunham, in full of %		59	
"			
Paid Expenses of store to date, per Expense Book.		150	
26			
Our store and contents were this day consumed by fire:			
Value of Store and Fixtures	$5000†		
Mdse on hand	2800		
Manhattan Insurance Co. owe us per policy		4000	
28			
Received Cash in full for R. S. Hayward's Note, due the 18th inst . .		65	
"			
Received Cash of the following persons:			
Erastus Young, in full of %	$14		
David T. Fuller "	47 50		
Charles Claghorn "	22 50		
Henry Dwight "	10		
Schuyler Corbit "	27 50		
Henry Shaft "	34		
		155	50
"			
Paid Cash to Wilson G. Hunt, in full of %		575	
"			
Received Cash of Manhattan Insurance Co.		4000	

* As this insurance is to be applied proportionately on the store and the merchandise it may contain, it will be more simple to charge it to Expense account, or to open a separate account with "Insurance."

† It is purposed to include in this insurance both Store and Fixtures and Merchandise at their proportionate value. It is the student's business to ascertain how much of the $4000 should be credited to Store and Fixtures account, and how much to Merchandise. This cannot be difficult, as the basis of valuation is given.

Trial Balance, Feb. 28.

				James Mason	8431	61	8431	61
		139		Robert Walker	8431	62	8292	62
10397	23	11467	23	Cash	1070			
1211	60	3675		Mdse.	2463	40		
4135	90	6750		Store and Fixtures	2614	10		
				Bills Payable	1050		1050	
395		395		Expense				
334	50	334	50	William Patterson				
50		50		Edwin Forrest				
1250		1315		Bills Receivable	65			
17774	23	24125	73		24125	73	17774	23

Inventory, Feb. 28.

Store Lot, valued at	$2000.00

Losses in Business.

On Merchandise		1211.60
" Store and Fixtures		2135.90
By Expense		395.00
James Mason's ½ net loss	$1871.25	3742.50
Robert Walker's "	1871.25	

Present Condition of Business.

Resources.

Cash	$10397.23
Store Lot	2000.00
Bills Receivable	1250.00
William Patterson	334.50
Edwin Forrest	50.00
	14031.73

Liabilities.

Bills Payable			$1050.00
James Mason, Investment		$8431.61	
" ½ net loss		1871.25	
" Present Interest			6560.36
Robert Walker, Investment		8431.62	
" Amount drawn	139.00		
" ½ net loss	1871.25	2010.25	
" Present Interest			6421.37
			14031.73

EXERCISES FOR THE LEARNER.

FIFTH SERIES.

The following memoranda of transactions will serve as material for a Set of Single Entry Books, which the student is requested to write up. Let him record the receipts and disbursements of cash in the Cash Book, adopting the form used in the previous Set; also, rule up a Bill Book, after the form on pages 54 and 55, in which enter the Bills, Receivable and Payable. Should he choose, in addition, to keep a Sales Book and an Invoice Book, in which to record receipts and sales of merchandise, it will much facilitate the labor of collecting resources preparatory to deciding upon the gain or loss in business. We have here an important change in the business, occurring at the end of the first month. One of the partners retires from the concern, his interest having been purchased by the remaining partner, who continues the business in the same books. This is a most important matter for the student to understand, both because of involving in itself principles having a general application to the science, and for the reason that such events in actual business are of the most frequent occurrence.

The first thing to be considered in buying or selling the interest of a partner in business is to know the exact pecuniary amount of that interest, or how much of the net resources of the concern belong to him. His *prospective* interest, or the "good will" of the concern, is an after and separate consideration. The interest which any sole or partial proprietor has in a concern is equal to his net investment, *plus* his share of the gain, or *minus* his share of the loss. Consequently, if he has already been credited with his net investment, it is only necessary to ascertain his share in the gain or loss, which, carried to the credit or debit side of his account, as the case may be, will make that account express his real interest in the business. This principle will, of course, need no enforcement here, as it has already been so frequently applied in its various bearings. The method of ascertaining gains and losses, where books are kept by Single Entry, is neither so direct nor satisfactory as the process by Double Entry, but it can be done, nevertheless, with certainty and exactness. That the student may learn the real difference in the two systems, he is requested to write up the following series, first in Single, and next in Double Entry form. This process will afford a more appreciable distinction between the two systems than could be otherwise obtained.

Memoranda—Partnership Books.

Buffalo, Nov. 1, 1859.—W. P. Spencer and E. R. Felton unite in copartnership for the purpose of conducting the business of Building. Each to receive interest on his average investment, and the gain or loss to be divided as follows: W. P. Spencer, $\frac{6}{10}$; E. R. Felton, $\frac{4}{10}$

W. P. Spencer Invests:

Cash deposited in N. Y. and Erie Bank, $5000;* Bills Receivable as follows: Note of A. M. Clapp's, favor of J. C. Bryant, dated July 1, @ 6 mo's, with interest @ 7% from date, $500; Wm. T. Bush's accepted draft, drawn by H. Newell, Nov. 1, 1859, @ 90 d's, for $1500;† Personal accounts, viz.: Robert Vail, $175; Henry Gray, $280; J. Pinner, $300; Cash, $259.58.

---

* If it is deemed proper to keep a Bank account in the Ledger, it will, of course, be subject to the same conditions as any personal account; for such it is.

† In determining the exact investment, it is necessary to reckon these notes at their *real* value; hence, the

E. R. Felton Invests:

Cash, $1500; Tools, Implements and Materials, $1000; Unfinished Contract with Smith and Sons—present value, $5000.*

2d. Received from Smith & Sons, cash on %, 1750; Deposited the same in N. Y. & E. Bank. 3d. Paid laborers cash as per Receipt Book, $375; Paid petty expenses, as per Expense Book, $10.75. 4th. Bo't horse and dray for use of business, for which gave check on N. Y. and E. Bank, $250; Contracted with A. H. Tracy to build for him on Delaware Street, a brick residence; amount of contract, $15,000. Received cash, in advance, as per agreement, $5000. Deposited the same in Bank.† 5th. Paid plumber's bill on Smith & Sons' house, per check, $375; Paid masons and laborers on Smith & Sons' house, per check, $150. 6th. Finished small job for J. C. Gansevoort, on South Division Street, for which he owes us $540.64. 7th. Received cash of J. C. Gansevoort on account, $300. 9th. Entered into contract with Millard Fillmore, to build for him a cottage on Niagara Street, for $9000; Received cash on contract, $1000. 10th. Paid cash to C. Kohler for 100 M. pressed brick, @ $11 per M.; Bo't of Seth Pierce, Lockport, on %, 20 bbls. cement, @ $1.50. 12th. Paid Dean Richmond's draft on W. P. Spencer, per check, $500; Paid carpenter's bill on Smith & Sons' house, per check, $1500. 13th. Finished Smith & Sons' contract, and delivered them the keys of the house. Rendered bill for the same, as per contract, $7500, which was accepted.‡ 15th. Paid laborers and masons cash, as per Receipt Book, $475; Paid cash for sundry expenses, as per Expense Book, $25. 18th. Received of Smith & Sons, note @ 60 days, to balance %, $5750. 20th. Received cash for small jobs this week, $400. 21st. Received cash of J. Pinner on %, $150; also, of Henry Gray, in full of %, $280. 22d. Paid laborers, per Receipt Book, cash, $500; Paid sundry expenses in cash, as per Cash Book, $35. 25th. Paid E. R. Felton, cash, on %, $500. 25th. Finished job of repairing outhouse for Jacob Van Brunt, for which he owes us, as per bill of items, $175. 28th. Paid cash to laborers in full to date, $378.50. 30th. Paid office rent in cash, $50; Paid Book-keeper to date, per check, $125.

---

former ($500) having already been on interest 4 months, is worth its face and the interest to date; while the latter ($1500), being drawn without interest, is worth its face, less the current rate of interest for 90 days—the date of its maturity. (We shall, in this case, assume the legal rate of interest allowed by the State to be the *current* rate, which is 7%.) Therefore, in giving Mr. Spencer credit for his investment, we will estimate the value of the first note at its face, $500, *plus* the interest on $500 for 4 mo's, @ 7%, $11.67, making in all $511.67; and the second, at its face, $1500, *minus* the interest on $1500 for 90 days, @ 7%, $26.25, making $1473.75. In the Single Entry Set it will be necessary only to credit Mr. Spencer with these real values, and enter the notes in the Bill Book. In Double Entry it will be proper also to open accounts with Interest Receivable and Interest Payable, representing the two amounts, which should be arranged under those titles.

* It is customary, in business of this kind, to enter into written contract with the parties for whom work is to be performed, and either receive pay by regularly fixed instalments, or at the completion of the contract. In all such cases, it would be eminently proper to keep a book containing a transcript of such agreements, and a separate account with each job. This is often done, even where the books are kept by Single Entry. The estimated value of this "Unfinished Contract" is, of course, based upon the actual labor performed, and not paid for, and the approximate gain thus far realized. The anticipated gain in the farther completion of the work should, of right, be shared by the partners, the same as gains accruing from new contracts.

† It would not, of course, be proper to charge Mr. Tracy, directly, with the amount of this contract, as the work is not yet completed. We should, however, credit him on account for the $5000 advanced.

‡ Smith & Sons now owe us $7500, less what they have paid on %, and with which they have already been credited. It is therefore proper to charge them this amount.

Dissolution of Copartnership.

The copartnership heretofore existing between W. P. Spencer and E. R. Felton is this day dissolved by mutual consent, Mr. Spencer retiring from the firm. The conditions of the dissolution are, that the retiring partner shall receive for his interest, (as shown by his account after being credited with his share of the gain,) one-half cash, and one-half note, payable in six months, with interest from date.

The Resources and Liabilities of the Concern at this time are as follows:

Resources.

Cash on hand, per C. B. . .	440	33
Balance in Bank	8850	
Notes on hand	7750	
Interest due on same	14	58
Balance due on personal accounts	740	64
Horse and Dray	250	
Tools and Implements . . .	1000	
Valuation of unfinished contracts	3500	
	22545	55

Liabilities.

Balance due on personal accounts		6030	
Interest for unexpired time on Bush's acceptance .	17.50		
Do. on Smith & Sons' note	53.67	71	17*
W. P. Spencer, net investment . .	7500		
Int. on same .	44.92†	7544	92
E. R. Felton, net inv.	$7000		
Int. on same .	43.26	7043	26
Total net gain		1856	20
W. P. Spencer $\frac{6}{10}$.	1113.72		
E. R. Felton $\frac{4}{10}$.	742.48		
		22545	55

From the above schedule we are enabled to arrive at the exact amount of Mr. Spencer's present interest in the concern, which is the interest to be purchased. The partners should now be credited each with the interest on his average capital, and also his share of the gain. When this is done, their individual accounts will show their separate interests in the concern.

The business will now be continued, in the same books, under the sole proprietorship of Mr. Felton.

---

* It may not be strictly true that the concern *owes* this amount of interest; and yet, should we desire to get the two notes cashed, or to receive their net value in any other commodity, we should be obliged to abate thus much from their face. In other words, we have estimated the notes as resources at *more* than their present value, (for the purpose of expressing the value written upon them,) and we must now offset this excess of resources by a corresponding liability. The same effect could have been wrought by reckoning the notes at their *real* value. The present form would be essential in a statement drawn from a Double Entry Ledger, where notes, either receivable or payable, are always reckoned at their *written* value.

† According to the partnership contract, each partner is to receive interest on his "*average* investment." As the method of ascertaining the average capital is more fully explained in its appropriate place, we shall only indicate, in this connection, that the most simple and direct method of obtaining this result is to reckon interest on all sums invested from the date of investment to the date of settlement, from which deduct the interest on all sums withdrawn from the date of withdrawal to that of settlement. The *difference* will be the interest on the average investment.

Memoranda—Individual Books.

December 1, 1859.—E. R. Felton has this day purchased the interest of his former partner W. P. Spencer, in the concern of "Spencer and Felton," and proposes to continue the business in his own name. Paid for the same, check on N. Y. & E. Bank, $4329.32; Note @ 6 mo's, with interest from date, $4329.32. 2d. Received cash in full for principal and interest on A. M. Clapp's Note, due Jan. 1, 1860; Note, $500; Interest to date, $14.58. 3d. Paid cash for tinman's bill, for roof and leaders on Mr. Fillmore's cottage, $150; Paid Charles Ely's bill in cash, for sills and lintels for A. H. Tracy's cellar, $50. 5th. Paid workmen to date in cash, $438.50. 6th. Completed job for S. G. Haven, as per bill of items, for which he owes $430. 7th. Paid cash for ton of hay, $20; and for 50 bushels oats, @ 75c., $37.50. 9th. Bo't of Jacob Van Brunt, on %, 10,000 feet pine lumber, @ 15c., $1500. 10th. Rec'd cash for job of mason-work, done for Peter Greiner, $125. 12th. Paid workmen to date, per check, $1475. 15th. Finished job of mason-work for Urial Driggs, Tonawanda, for which he owes $275. 20th. Completed contract with Millard Fillmore, and rendered him bill for the same, $9000. 22d. Paid laborers' wages, per check, to date, $1450. 23d. Passed our note, @ 60 d's, to Merritt Crandell, for bill of Lumber to date, $3000. 25th. Received cash of Urial Driggs, in full of %, $275. 26th. Received cash of J. C. Gansevoort, in full of %, $240.64. 27th. Paid workmen in full to date, per check, $563. 30th. Paid sundry expenses in cash, as per Expense Book, $175.

Changing to Double Entry.

Mr. Felton now proposes to change his books to Double Entry, preparatory to which he makes the following statement of the condition of his business:*

Resources.			*Liabilities.*		
Cash on hand, per C. B.	724	55	Due on personal accounts	6355	
Balance in Bank	1032	68	" notes	7329	32
Tools and Implements	1000		E. R. Felton, net investment	7785	74
Notes on hand	7250		" net gain	1542	17
Due on personal accounts	8755				
Horse and Dray	250				
Value of unfinished contracts	4000				
	23012	23		23012	23

The student is requested to enter up these accounts in the Ledger, according to the examples given in the previous Set, and to continue the business in Double Entry form, for one month, originating his own transactions, and closing his Ledger at the end of the month, according to the principles of Double Entry.

* It will be evident, from these frequent statements, that just as often as it is necessary, for any purpose, to know the exact condition of the business, the account or accounts representing the capital—usually called Stock Account, or Partners' Accounts—must be made to agree with the difference between the absolute resources of the concern and its outside liabilities. In Double Entry Books this is done by carrying to these accounts the result of the Representative accounts, which is the net gain or loss. As there are no such accounts in Single Entry, the same object is attained by taking the difference between the capital at commencing and at closing, which must, of course, be the net gain or loss. Any statement showing resources and liabilities will afford all the necessary material for Double Entry Books, or for any purposes of negotiation where partners' interests are concerned.

FARM ACCOUNTS:

INCLUDING

PRACTICAL FORM OF JOURNAL,

AND

OTHER NEW FEATURES

FARM ACCOUNTS.

In the exercises which follow, we have sought to illustrate, briefly, the business of farming It is, of course, impossible, in so short a space, to give the daily routine of what might be expected to occur in connection with this business; but we have endeavored to make each record as much as possible the representative of a class, and thus, without unnecessary repetition, to indicate and enforce in this department of industry the principles which we have found applicable generally to business transactions.

In certain essential particulars all departments of business assimilate; and any peculiarities which may exist will be found to depend, not upon a change of the principles, nor a difference in the application of those principles, but in the forms and methods of expression growing out of the transactions themselves.

The conditions common to all business enterprises may be briefly stated, as follows:

1. Investment.—Capital, of some kind, is essential. It may consist in *valuable resources*, such as cash, notes, merchandise, real estate, live stock, personal indebtedness, etc.; or, in *productive power*, such as professional ability, talent, industry, a good name, etc.; or in both.

2. Production.—The prime object of all business is *gain*; or, what is the substantial proof of gain, *increase of resources*. Something must produce this increase, whether it be financial capital, or enterprise, or both combined. In various kinds of business this producing power is properly represented under distinct titles, usually subdivisions of the general account. For instance, in common mercantile business, the entire gain or loss may be shown in a general "Merchandise" account, or through a variety of correlative accounts, such as, "Shipment," "Adventure," "Expense," "Loss and Gain,"* and the specific titles of the different kinds of merchandise, such as, "Corn," "Wheat," "Flour," "Cloth," "Sugar," etc. In a banking business the most common titles given to producing agents are, "Interest," which shows gains and losses accruing from money loaned, and "Exchange," showing similar results in buying and selling uncurrent or premium funds. In a purely commission business, "Commission" account is used for this purpose, and in any professional business, "Profession," "Service," or "Labor," would answer the same ends.

In short, it requires no great effort of the imagination to supply these terms, in advance, for any department of business; and it is only necessary to know the routine of transactions to be able to prescribe, with great accuracy, both appropriate titles and forms.

In the business before us we have no transactions which are not easily subjected to the general principles already advanced; and even the forms, although exceedingly practical, and containing the very essence of concentration, need only be examined to be readily and thoroughly understood.

One essential point with the farmer is to be able to dispense with all unnecessary books; in other words, to do as *little* writing as possible. The "Practical" Journal given in this connection will, if adopted, secure to him this advantage in an essential degree. This form, usually called the "Six Column Journal," is one of the most practical and comprehensive in use, and is applicable to any kind of business. Its principal feature—that of affording special columns for the accounts most used—may be carried to any extent desirable. The result is a vast saving of time in posting, and additional security as to the correctness of the work. The "Six-column Journal" is extensively used in retail dry goods establishments.

The subdivision of the "Farm" account, as shown in this connection, is also a feature of some importance, and may be adopted or not, at pleasure.

---

* See concluding remarks on page 30.

Cash Memorandum Book.

The advantages of a Cash Book in business cannot be overrated; and, to a thorough business man, any argument in favor of its use would be superfluous. It is the great conservator of Finance, and is alike essential to the merchant, the mechanic, the farmer, the professional man, and the man of leisure. It not only serves as a check on extravagant expenditures, but, from its frequent comparisons with actual results, guards, in an essential degree, against errors and omissions. To those who feel the force of these facts, but find it difficult to reduce the theory to practice through any of the rigid forms in use, we commend the following simple form as possessing all the necessary qualities of a Cash-Book, besides being so simple and practical that a child may comprehend it. A small pocket memorandum book, such as all stationers keep, is sufficient for this purpose, and the writing may be done either with pencil or ink. It should be carried *constantly*, that no excuse may exist for omitting the entry of receipts and disbursements of cash, which should always be entered *at the time.* The balancing may be done daily or weekly, as most convenient.

In the form below we have exhibited the cash transactions for one month, which is sufficient tc show the use of the form.

Riverdale Farm, March 1, 1860.

				Rec'd.		*Paid.*	
Mar.	1	Amount on hand		120			
	1	Received for 10 lbs. Butter, $2; 10 doz. Eggs, $2		4			
	5	Paid for Johnny's Boots, $3; Cap for Harry, 75c.				3	75
	6	Sold 10 bushels Wheat, @ $1.50		15			
	6	Paid for set of Harrow Teeth, $3; Shoeing Horse, $1.50				4	50
	7	Paid G. F. Wright & Co.'s Grocery Bill				17	50
	10	Paid hired man for services to date, as per receipt	154.00			10	
	10	Received for 15 bushels Potatoes, @ $1	85.75	15			
		Balance on hand	118.25				
	12	Sold 2 year old Colt to L. S. Bliss, for		125			
	13	Paid premium for Insurance on Farm Buildings				12	50
	15	Paid Mrs. M. for household expenses				5	
	16	Sold C. S. Clark & Co. 20 bushels Oats, @ 75c.	258.25	15			
	17	Shoes for Netty, $1.25; Toys for Harry, 50c.	19.25			1	75
		Balance on hand	239.00				
	19	Paid for one year's subscription to Hampshire Gazette				1	50
	19	" yearly contribution to Poor Fund, $25; Pew Rent, 1 quarter, $5				30	
	20	" Dr. Jones for filling Teeth, $5; Bridgman & Childs, for Books, $1				6	
	23	Sold Hillman & Graves 10 Sheep, for	261.00	20			
	24	Received for Poultry sent to market	87.50	2			
		Balance on hand	223.50				
	26	Deposited in Holyoke Bank				150	
	27	Received for Butter, $4; Cheese, $2.50; Apples, $3.75		10	25		
	28	Paid for repairing Implements	233.75			3	25
	31	" Charles Jones for painting House	178.25			25	
		Balance on hand	55.50			55	50
				326	25	326	25

FARM ACCOUNTS,—HISTORY OF TRANSACTIONS.

Riverdale Farm, Northampton, March 1, 1860.

The following List embraces the real and personal property and debts of William Mitchell, farmer who is sole proprietor of "Riverdale Farm," in the town of Northampton, Mass.

Resources.

75 acres cultivated land, @ \$300; 10 do. woods pasture, @ \$350; dwelling-house, out-buildings, and improvements, \$2500; 2 carriage horses, \$400; 2 work horses, \$275; 1 colt \$100; 3 milch cows, \$100; 1 yoke oxen, \$125; 10 hogs, \$75; 30 sheep, \$50; 2 calves, \$5; 50 chickens, \$10; 6 turkeys, \$5; 10 geese, \$6; farming utensils, \$250; 1 family carriage, \$200; household furniture, \$600; 200 bushels wheat, \$350; 500 do. corn, \$375; 125 do. oats, \$110; 10 tons hay, \$120; 50 bushels potatoes, \$37.50; feed, \$25; 50 shares Connecticut River R. R. Stock, \$5000; cash in hand, \$120; do. deposited in Holyoke Bank, \$1200.

Liabilities.

Mortgage on farm, due in five years, from January 1, 1859, with annual interest, @ 6% \$4000; interest unpaid to date, on same, \$40; Due Samuel Hill on %, \$75.

"

Bo't of Lewis H. Bartlett, on %, 1 two-horse wagon, for \$75; Sold for cash, 10 lbs. butter \$2; 10 doz. eggs, \$2.

4

Bo't of Jonathan Dawes, 10 head of stock cattle for feeding and grazing, for \$650; Paid him check on Holyoke Bank, \$300; note @ 30 d's for balance.

5

Paid cash for the following articles: Boots for Johnny, \$3; Cap for Harry, 75c.

6

Sold James Banks for cash, 10 bushels wheat, @ \$1.50 per bushel; Paid cash for set of harrow teeth, \$3; Shoeing horse, \$1.50.

7

Paid cash for G. F. Wright's grocery bill, \$17.50.

10

Paid hired man cash for services to date, as per receipt, \$10; Sold for cash, 15 bushels potatoes, @ \$1 per bushel.

12

Sold L. S Bliss, Hatfield, 2 year old colt, for \$125 cash.

13

Paid cash for premium for insurance on farm buildings, \$12.50.

15

Paid Mrs. Mitchell cash for household expenses, \$5.

16

Sold C. S. Clark & Co., for cash, 20 bushels oats, @ 75c. per bushel.

17

Paid cash for shoes and toys for children, \$1.75; Bo't of S. C. Parsons, on %, ½ ton Peruvian guano, for \$30.

Riverdale Farm, Northampton, March 19, 1860.

Paid one year's subscription to Hampshire Gazette, in cash, $1.50; Yearly contribution to poor fund, $25; Pew rent, 1 quarter, $5.

20

Paid Dr. Jones cash for filling teeth, $5; Paid cash to Bridgman & Childs, for books, $1

23

Sold Hillman & Graves, for cash, 10 sheep, @ $2 per head.

24

Received cash for poultry sent to market, $2.

26

Deposited in Holyoke Bank, cash, $150.

27

Received cash for butter, cheese, and eggs, $10.25.

29

Paid E. L. Kingsley, cash, for repairing farm implements, $3.25.

31

Paid Charles Jones, cash, for painting house, $25.

April 1

Received cash for marketing, as follows: 25 lbs. butter, @ 25c.; 10 bush. potatoes, @ $1

13

Paid Theo. Rust, cash, for 1 ton plaster, $8.

25

Paid cash for winter's school bill, books, &c., $17.50.

26

Bo't of James Hubbard, on %, 32 bushels oats for seed, @ 60c. per bushel.

30

Paid hired hands in full to date, $40.

May 1

Received cash for dividend on Conn. Riv. R. R. stock, 5% on $5000.

15

Paid cash for 1 new plow, $10; For repairing old plow, $3.

25

Exchanged horses with E. T. Wood; Paid difference in cash, $25.

June 1

Paid hired hands to date, cash, $55.

15

Bo't for our own use, 1 rosewood piano, for $275; Paid for the same, check on Holyoke Bank, $75; note @ 6 mo's for balance.

July 1

Paid hired hands to date, $60.

5

Sold, for cash, 3 bushels cherries, @ $4 per bushel; 6 do. currants, at $1.

Riverdale Farm, Northampton, July 10, 1860.

Paid cash for groceries, $4.75; dress pattern, $8; Stoddard & Lincoln's bill for dry goods, $17.50.

20

Finished cutting and harvesting hay, which has been estimated at 75 tons, worth, on an average, $10 per ton.*

25

Bo't of Henry Claghorn, for Cash, 2 Berkshire pigs, $15.

30

Sold for cash, 3 hogs, $25; 4 lambs, $10; 2 calves, $4.

31

Paid cash to hired hands, $37.50.

Aug. 1

Received cash of Benjamin Claghorn, in full for the rental of 10-acre lot, as per contract, $200.

5

Received cash for pasturage, to date, $175.

10

Sold Graves Bro's, Florence, 10 tons hay, @ $11; received cash, $50; balance on %.

20

Finished threshing grain, and have put in bins, as the result, 250 bushels wheat, worth $1.50 per bushel; 300 do. oats, @ 75c.; 50 do. rye, @ 60c.

30

Paid hired hands cash, to date, $50.

Sept. 5

Sold for cash, 30 bushels wheat, @ $1.63.

10

Finished harvesting potatoes, the result of which is, that we have in cellar 75 bushels, worth 75c. per bushel.

15

Sold for cash, 20 bushels potatoes, @ 87½c.

30

Have gathered from orchard, 100 bushels apples, worth 50c. per bushel.

Oct. 5

Sold for cash, the following produce: 200 bushels wheat, @ $1.50; 300 do. corn, @ 75c. 40 do. potatoes, @ 1; 35 do. apples, @ 50c.

10

Paid hired hands to date, cash, $75.

15

Received cash for pasturing 15 head of cattle, $75; 10 horses, $60

* Should we keep but one general producing account for the farm, this entry could not properly be made in the journal, as it would necessitate both a debit and a credit to that one account, inasmuch as there has been nothing disposed of, and, consequently, nothing actually produced. If, however, we desire to keep up the distinctions between the different subdivisions of the general account, as in the Ledger form given, the entry in this case will be: "Produce" Dr. to "Real Estate," as each of the subdivisions should show its cost and proceeds, the same as any general account.

Riverdale Farm, Northampton, Oct. 18, 1860.

Paid Samuel Hill, jr., cash, in full of %, $75.

21

Paid cash in full for note, favor Jonathan Dawes, due April 6. Face of note, $350; Interest to date, $11.37.

25

Sold Thayer & Sergeant, 4 fat cattle, for $350, cash.

28

Sold Alvan N. Claghorn, on %, 5 tons hay, @ $10 per ton.

30

From inventory taken, we are prepared to estimate the amount consumed by family and live stock since March 1, which is as follows: FAMILY EXPENSES—Mutton, $15; pork, $17; poultry, $18; eggs and milk, $10; flour, $40; potatoes, $10. LIVE STOCK—Corn, $50; hay, $75; feed, $25; oats, $37; pasturage, $50.

31

Upon careful estimation, the apportionment of expense, as charged in the "Expense" %, ($329,*) should be as follows: To real estate, $164.50; live stock, $82.25; produce, $82.25.

SIX-COLUMN JOURNAL.

THE peculiar characteristics of the practical Journal here introduced will be immediately understood and appreciated. Its advantages may be briefly stated, as follows:

First—A vast saving of time and space in posting.

Second—Embracing the principles of *four* books in *one*, viz.: Cash Book, Invoice Book, Sales Book and Journal.†

Third—Showing monthly totals of the principal accounts in the Ledger that the same may be compared year after year.

Fourth—Affording an opportunity to post personal accounts immediately, the debits and credits appearing separately in the "Sundries" column.

Fifth—Giving additional security of the correctness of the Ledger, there existing no probability of omitting debits and credits of the same amount.

Want of space will prevent the giving of more than one month's transactions through this form. The student is requested to write up the remainder as given in the memoranda putting the months of April, May, June and July together as one month, and August, September and October as one.

The method of posting from this Journal is extremely simple. The separate items in the "Sundries" column are posted the same as from the common Journal, while the *amounts* of the "Cash" and "Farm" columns are posted at the close of each month.

This idea of special columns is *not* original with any modern author, as variously claimed, but has been in use, to a greater or less extent, for a quarter of a century. The principle can be carried to any desirable extent; and in some jobbing-houses as many as *eight* special debit and credit columns are used. The form given in this connection is sufficient to indicate the principle.

* Paid for services and horseshoeing.

† This is the case when the form is used in a general merchandise business: in which case the *special* columns, debit and credit, would be "Cash," and "Mdse."

FARM ACCOUNTS,—JOURNAL,—PRACTICAL FORM.

RIVERDALE FARM, MARCH 1, 1860.

Drs. Farm.	Drs. Cash.	Drs. Sundries.	L. F.				L. F.	Crs. Sundries.	Crs. Cash.	Crs. Farm.
				SUNDRIES	Dr. To Stock			38038 50		
					Amount invested as follows:					
28500				REAL ESTATE	75 acres Cultivated Land, @ $300 . .	$22 500				
					10 acres Woods Pasture @ $350 . . .	3 500				
					Dwelling-house, Out-buildings, and Improvements	2 500				
1151				LIVE STOCK	5 Horses, viz.: 2 Carriage Horses, $400; 2 Work Horses, $275; 1 Colt, $100 . .	775				
					3 Milch Cows, $100; 1 yoke Oxen, $125	225				
					10 Hogs, $75; 30 Sheep, $50; 2 Calves, $5	130				
					50 Chickens, $10; 6 Turkeys, $5; 10 Geese, $6	21				
1050				FIXTURES AND IMPLEMENTS	Farming Utensils	250				
					1 Family Carriage	200				
					Household Furniture	600				
1017 50				RODUCE	200 bush. Wheat, $350; 500 do. Corn, $375	725				
					125 do. Oats, $110; 10 tons Hay, $120	230				
					50 bush. Potatoes, $37.50; Feed, $25 .	62 50				
		5000		C. R. R. R. STOCK	50 Shares, $100 each					
	120			CASH	Amount on Hand					
		1200		HOLYOKE BANK	On Deposit					
31718 50	120	6200			. . . . Amounts fc rward			38038 50		

31718	50	120	6200			Amounts forward	38038	50			
						〃					
			411		STOCK	Dr. To SUNDRIES					
						Liabilities as follows:					
					To MORTGAGE PAYABLE	Amount of Mortgage, given January 1, 1859, due in five years, with annual interest @ 6 %	4000				
					To INT. PAYABLE	Interest on same to date	40				
					" S. HILL, JR.	Due him on %	75				
						〃					
75					FIXT'S AND IMP'S	Dr. To LEWIS H. BARTLETT	75				
						Bought of him on % 1 Two-Horse Wagon.					
						〃					
		4			CASH	Dr. To LIVE STOCK					4
						10 lbs. Butter, $2; 10 doz. Eggs, $2.					
						4					
650					LIVE STOCK	Dr. To SUNDRIES					
						Bought of Jonathan Dawes 10 Head Stock Cattle.					
					To HOLYOKE B'K.	Check in part payment	300				
					" BILLS P'ABLE	Note @ 30 days	350				
						5					
			3	75	FAMILY EXPENSES	Dr. To CASH			3	75	
						Boots for Johnny, $3; Cap for Harry, 75 cts.					
						6					
		15			CASH	Dr. To PRODUCE					15
						Sold James Banks 10 bushels Wheat @ $1.50.					
						〃					
					SUNDRIES	Dr. To CASH			4	50	
			1	50	EXPENSE	Shoeing Horse					
3					FIXT'S AND IMP'S	Set of Harrow Teeth					
32446	50	139	10320	25		Amounts forward	42878	50	3	25	19

FARM ACCOUNTS,—JOURNAL,—PRACTICAL FORM.

RIVERDALE FARM, MARCH 6, 1860.

Drs. Farm.		Drs. Cash.	Drs. Sundries.		L. F.		L. F.	Crs. Sundries.		Crs. Cash.		Crs. Farm.
32446	50	139	10320	25		. . . . Amounts forward		42878	50	8	25	19
			17	50		Family Expenses Dr. To Cash . . . . G. F. Wright's Grocery Bill.				17	50	
						10						
			10			Expense Dr. To Cash . . . . Paid hired man to date.				10		
						"						
		15				Cash Dr. To Produce . . . . . . Sold 15 bushels Potatoes @ $1.						15
						12						
		125				Cash Dr. To Live Stock . . . . Sold L. S. Bliss, Hatfield, 2 year old Colt.						125
						13						
12	50					Real Estate Dr. To Cash . . . . . . Paid Insurance Premium on buildings.				12	50	
						15						
			5			Family Expenses Dr. To Cash . . . . Paid Mrs. Mitchell.				5		
						16						
		15				Cash Dr. To Produce . . . . . Sold C. S. Clark 20 bushels Oats @ 75 cts.						15
32459		294	10352	75		. . . Amounts forward		42878	50	53	25	174

$	c	$	c	$	c		$	c	$	c	$	c
32459		294		10352	75	. . . Amounts forward .	42878	50	53	25	174	
						17						
				1	75	FAMILY EXPENSES Dr. To CASH . . . . Shoes and Toys for children.			1	75		
						"						
30						PRODUCE Dr. To S. C. PARSONS. . . . Bought of him on % ½ ton Peruvian Guano.	30					
						19						
				31	50	FAMILY EXPENSES Dr. To CASH . . . . 1 year's subscription Hampshire Gazette . $ 1 50 Contribution to Poor Fund . . . . . . 25 1 quarter's Pew Rent 5			31	50		
						20						
				6		FAMILY EXPENSES Dr. To CASH . . . . . . Dr. Jones, filling teeth . . . . $5 Bridgman & Childs School-books . . . 1			6			
						23						
		20				CASH Dr. To LIVE STOCK . . . . . Sold Hillman & Graves 10 Sheep @ $2.					20	
						24						
		2				CASH Dr. To LIVE STOCK . . . . . Received for Poultry sent to market.					2	
						26						
				150		HOLYOKE BANK Dr. To CASH . . . . Deposited.			150			
						27						
		10	25			CASH Dr. To LIVE STOCK . . . . . Received for Butter, Cheese, and Eggs.					10	25
						29						
3	25					FIXT'S AND IMPL'S Dr. To CASH . . . . Paid E. L. Kingsley for repairing.			3	25		
32492	25	326	25	10542		. . . . Amounts forward	42908	50	245	75	206	25

FARM ACCOUNTS,—JOURNAL,—PRACTICAL FORM.

RIVERDALE FARM, MARCH 31, 1860.

Drs. Farm.		Cash.		Sundries.		L. F.		L. F.	*Crs.* Sundries.		Cash.		Farm.	
32492	25	326	25	10542			. . . . Amounts forward		42908	50	245	75	206	25
25							REAL ESTATE Dr. To CASH . . . . Paid Charles Jones for painting house.				25			
32517	25	326	25	10542			Total for the Month.		42908	50	270	75	206	25
				326	25		*Dr.* . . . . CASH . . . . *Cr.*		270	75				
				32517	25		*Dr.* . . . . FARM . . . . *Cr.*		206	25				
				43385	50				43385	50				
							Subdivision,—Farm Account.							
				28537	50		*Dr.* . . . . REAL ESTATE . . . . *Cr.*							
				1801			. . . . LIVE STOCK		161	25				
				1131	25		. . . . FIXTURES AND IMPLEMENTS							
				1047	50		. . . . PRODUCE		45					
				32517	25				206	25				

Form of Principal Ledger Account.

FARM.

Dr.

1860.			R. Estate.		Live Stock.		Fixt. & Imp.		Produce.		Total.	
Mar.	31	Monthly Footing	28537	50	1801		1131	25	1047	50	32517	25
July	31	" "	8		40		288		769	20	1105	20
Oct.	31	" "	164	50	31[illegible]	25			643	50	1127	25
		To Loss and Gain	1611	[illegible]	554	[illegible]			245	95	3111	45
			30321	25	2414	50	1419	25	2706	15	36861	15
		To Balance . .	28500		1798		1825		1537	25	33160	25

Cr.

1860.			R. Estate.		Live Stock.		Fixt. & Imp.		Produce.		Total.	
Mar.	31	Monthly Footing			161	25			45		206	25
July	31	" "	750		45	25			28		823	25
Oct.	31	" "	1071	25	410				1095	90	2577	15
		By Balance	28500		17[illegible]		1825		1537	[illegible]	[illegible]	95
		Loss and Gain					94	25			96	25
			30321	25	2414	50	1419	25	2706	19	36861	15

Trial Balance.

Balances.					Face of Ledger.			
		33923	50	Stock	4115		38038	50
4750				C. R. R. R. Stock	5000		250	
975				Holyoke Bank	1350		375	
		4000		Mortgage Payable			4000	
		40		Interest Payable			40	
		75		L. H. Bartlett			75	
		200		Bills Payable	350		550	
223	25			Family Expense	223	25		
		30		S. C. Parsons			30	
1075	03			Cash	2208	40	1133	37
50				A. N. Claghorn	50			
31143	05			Farm	34749	70	3606	65
		19	20	J. A. Hubbard			19	20
60				Graves Brothers	60			
11	37			Interest	11	37		
38287	70	38287	70		48117	72	48117	72

Inventory.

Real Estate,	85 acres Land, valued at	26000			
	Dwelling-House and Improvements	2500		28500	
Live Stock.	4 Horses, $700; 3 cows, $100	800			
	1 yoke Oxen, 125; 5 Hogs, $40	165			
	12 Sheep, $20; 16 Lambs, $18	38			
	2 Calves, $20; Poultry, $25	45			
	10 head Stock Cattle	750		1798	
Fixtures and Implements,	Farming Utensils	250			
	1 Family Carriage, $200; 1 two-horse Wagon, $75	275			
	Household Furniture	800		1325	
Produce,	220 bush. Wheat @ $1.50	330			
	162 " Corn " 75	121	50		
	355 " Oats " 75	266	25		
	50 " Rye " 60	30			
	25 " Potatoes " 80	20			
	65 " Apples " 50	32	50		
	67 tons Hay " 11.00	737		1537	25
				33160	25
Conn. River R. R. Stock				5000	
Interest due to date on Mortgage Payable,				$200	

STATEMENT,—FARM ACCOUNTS.

The following form of Statement has the quality of brevity and plainness; and though less satisfactory in detail than previous forms, it will sufficiently indicate the condition of the business on the date of rendering the Trial Balance and Inventory.

	Losses.		*Gains.*		*Resources.*		*Liabilities.*	
. . Conn. River R. R. Stock .			250		5000			
. . Holyoke Bank					975			
. . Bills Receivable					350			
. . Mortgage Payable . . .							4000	
. . Interest Payable	160						200	
. . L. H. Bartlett							75	
. . Bills Payable							550	
. . Family Expense	223	25						
. . S. C. Parsons							30	
. . Cash					1075	03		
. . A. N. Claghorn					50			
. . Farm			2017	20	33160	25		
. . J. A. Hubbard							19	20
. . Graves, Brothers					60			
. . Interest	11	37						
Net Gain .	1872	58						
	2267	20	2267	20				
Stock, Investment . . $33,923 50								
Net Gain . . . 1872 58								
Present Interest .							35796	08
					40670	28	40670	28

PRACTICAL HINTS FOR FARMERS.

1.—Measuring Grain.

By the United States standard, 2150 cubic inches make a bushel. Now, as a cubic foot contains 1728 cubic inches, a bushel is to a cubic foot as 2150 to 1728; or, for practical purposes, as 4 to 5. Therefore, to convert cubic feet to bushels, it is necessary only to multiply by $\frac{4}{5}$.

Example.—How much grain will a bin hold which is 10 feet long, 4 feet wide, and 4 feet deep?

Solution.—$10 \times 4 \times 4 = 160$ cubic feet. $160 \times \frac{4}{5} = 128$, the number of bushels.

To measure grain on the floor.

Make the pile in form of a pyramid or cone, and multiply the area of the base by one-third the height. To find the area of the base, multiply the square of its diameter by the decimal .7854.

EXAMPLE.—A conical pile of grain is 8 feet in diameter, and 4 feet high, now many bushels does it contain?

Solution.—The square of 8 is 64; and $64 \times .7854 \times \frac{4}{3} = 83.776$, the number of cubic feet. Therefore,

$$83.776 \times \frac{4}{5} = 67.02 \text{ bushels.} \quad \textit{Answer.}$$

2.—To Ascertain the Quantity of Lumber in a Log.

Multiply the diameter in *inches* at the small end by one-half the number of inches, and this product by the length of the log in *feet*, which last product divide by 12.

EXAMPLE.—How many feet of lumber can be made from a log which is 36 inches in diameter and 10 feet long?

Solution.—$36 \times 18 = 648$; $648 \times 10 = 6480$; $6480 \div 12 = 540$. *Answer.*

3.—To Ascertain the Capacity of a Cistern or Well.

Multiply the square of the diameter in inches by the decimal .7854, and this product by the depth in inches; divide this product by 231, and the quotient will be the contents in gallons.

EXAMPLE.—What is the capacity of a cistern which is 12 feet deep and 6 feet in diameter?

Solution.—The square of 72, the diameter in inches, is 5184; $5184 \times .7854 = 4071.51$; $4071.51 \times 144 = 586297.44$, the number of cubic inches in the cistern. There are 231 cubic inches in a gallon, therefore, $586297.44 \div 231 = 2538+$, gallons. To reduce the number of gallons to barrels, divide by $31\frac{1}{2}$.

4.—To Ascertain the Weight of Cattle by Measurement.

Multiply the girth in feet, by the distance from the bone of the tail immediately over the hinder part of the buttock, to the fore part of the shoulder-blade; and this product by 31, when the animal measures *more than* 7 *and less than* 9 *feet in girth;* by 23, when *less than* 7 *and more than* 5; by 16, when *less than* 5 *and more than* 3; and by 11, when *less than* 3.

EXAMPLE.—What is the weight of an ox whose measurements are as follows; girth, 7 feet 5 inches; length, 5 feet 6 inches?

Solution.—$5\frac{1}{2} \times 7\frac{5}{12} = 40\frac{57}{72}$; $40\frac{57}{72} \times 31 = 1264+$. *Answer.*

A deduction of one pound in 20 must be made for half-fatted cattle, and also for cows that have had calves. It is understood, of course, that such standard will at best, give only the *approximate* weight.

5.—Measuring Land.

To find the number of acres of land in a rectangular field, multiply the length by the breadth, and divide the product by 160, if the measurement is made in rods, or by 43560 if made in feet.

EXAMPLE.—How many acres in a field which is 100 rods in length, by 75 rods in width?

Solution.—$100 \times 75 = 7500$; $7500 \div 160 = 46\frac{7}{8}$. *Answer.*

To find the contents of a triangular piece of land, having a rectangular corner, multiply the two shorter sides together, and take one-half the product.

QUESTIONS FOR REVIEW.

CHANGING SINGLE TO DOUBLE ENTRY,—PAGE 152.

1. Why should Double-Entry Book-keeping be distinguished as the "*science*" of Accounts? 2. May Single Entry be properly called a science? 3. Why not? 4. What relation does Single Entry sustain to Double Entry? 5. What is the chief difficulty in defining and treating Single Entry? 6. In what particulars do Single Entry Book-keepers differ among themselves? 7. What does the term Single Entry denote? 8. What is usually understood to be the difference between Single and Double Entry? 9. What is the rule for converting Single to Double Entry? 10. If an account has been kept with Stock, or accounts with the partners, what must be done with the gain or loss? 11. Do you consider Double Entry more intricate or laborious than Single Entry? 12. What, in your opinion are the principal advantages of Double over Single Entry? 13. In changing Single to Double Entry, is it necessary to disturb the accounts already shown on the Single Entry Ledger? 14. What are the usual books in Single Entry? 15. For what purpose, and how is the Single Entry Cash-Book used? 16. What is the difference between the Single Entry and the Double-Entry Cash-Book? 17. Is it customary to journalize or post the Single Entry Cash-Book? 18. What other books than the Day Book, Cash-Book, and Ledger are used in Single Entry? 19. When all these auxiliaries are kept in Single Entry, how will it differ from Double Entry? 20. Can the gains and losses in business be ascertained by Single Entry? 21. How?

FARM ACCOUNTS,—PAGE 170.

22. Upon what do the peculiarities of business chiefly depend? 23. What conditions are common to all business enterprises? 24. What do you understand by *Investment?* 25. Can anything properly be called an investment except tangible resources? 26. Can you explain how professional ability, talent, a good name, etc., may be considered capital? 27. What is the prime object of business enterprises? 28. What is the substantial proof of gain? 29. How is the increase of resources effected? 30. How is the producing power in business variously represented? 31. What are the general producing accounts in a mercantile business? 32. In a banking business? 33. In a commission business? 34. In a professional business? 35. Is it difficult to supply the appropriate terms in any kind of enterprise? 36. What is the essential point in Farm Books? 37. Can you explain the "Six Column Journal," as used in this set? 38. What are the advantages of a Cash-Book in business? 39. What is the peculiarity of the Cash-Book used in this connection? 40. What are the five points of excellence claimed for the practical Journal used on this set? 41. How are the separate items posted from this Journal? 42. How the amounts of the "Farm" and "Cash" columns? 43. Can this form be used in any other kind of business than farming? 44. When used in mercantile business, what will be the titles to the special columns? 45. Can the number of special columns be increased? 46. What kind of business is peculiarly adapted to special columns? 47. How many debit and credit columns are sometimes used in jobbing houses?

PRACTICAL HINTS FOR FARMERS,—PAGE 182.

48 What rule have you for measuring grain in a bin? 49. How many cubic inches in a bushel? 50 Can you measure grain upon the floor? 51. How? 52. Give the rule for ascertaining the quantity of lumber in a log? 53. What is the rule for ascertaining the capacity of a well or cistern? 54. How can you get the approximate weight of cattle by measurement? 55. What is the rule for measuring land?

AGENCIES.

BOOKS OF AN ADMINISTRATOR:

HISTORICAL DAY-BOOK, JOURNAL, LEDGER.

EXHIBITING THREE DISTINCT METHODS

OF KEEPING THE ACCOUNTS OF AN AGENT.

AGENCIES.

An Agent, in common acceptation, is "one who acts for another." A broader definition, and one which would better suit the accountant's purposes, would be "*one who acts;*" for, although, the idea of *agent* presupposes that of *principal,*—the one executing the will of the other—it is by no means impossible that both functions should coexist in the same person—in other words, that a man may be *his own agent.* This view of the case we have fully recognized, and sought to enforce in the preceding lessons, by constantly keeping in view the distinction between the proprietor and his business. The analogy between the records of the two classes of agencies—if they may be so called—will be apparent in the following sets, representing various departments of business, conducted by one person, in the name and for the interest of others.

An agency, as recognized by law, is "the substitution of one for another in some matter of business." It is based upon a contract, either expressed or implied, by which one confides to the other the management of some business, to be transacted, either in his name, or on his account, and by which the other assumes to do the business, and to render an account of it.

Agencies are divided into two general classes, *Special* and *General.* A Special Agency consists in a delegation of authority to do a single act. A General Agency is such delegation to do all acts and things, connected with a particular business or employment. These classes are subdivided into *Limited* and *Unlimited.* A Limited Agent is one who is bound by specific instructions as to the manner of his acts; an Unlimited Agent is one who is permitted to use his own discretion as to the means employed for the specific end.

There are, also, different kinds of agencies having reference specially to commerce; such as the *Factor,* who is an agent for the sale of property, and is therefore intrusted with the possession; and the *Broker,* who simply negotiates sales, having no custody of the property sold.

The principles which regulate the relations of principal and agent, both as between each other, and as regards third persons, are among the most important in Mercantile Law. We have space only for a few general rules:

1. The agent is bound to obey instructions; and when explicit, they preclude the exercise of discretion. But when the thing to be done is such that two or more different modes of doing it will answer equally well, he may choose either one, provided no other has been particularly prescribed.

2. He is bound to use all ordinary diligence and care in the execution of his trust. In the absence of specific instructions, he must pursue the accustomed course of the particular business in which he is employed. As he receives compensation for his services, he is bound to bring to his undertaking such a degree and amount of skill and knowledge as would, in ordinary cases, insure its successful accomplishment.

3. His liability for negligence or neglect of duty is not limited to the direct injury occasioned to the property of the principal. He is also liable to make good all injuries which his own act as agent has occasioned to the property of others, and which the principal has been called upon to pay; hence a verdict obtained against the principal for the act of his agent is the measure of damages in favor of the former against the latter.

4. He is not chargeable with a breach of instructions in any of the three following cases: 1. Where an unforeseen necessity arises not originally contemplated by the parties. 2. Where the circumstances are such that a strict compliance is impossible. 3. Where a compliance would have been, in effect, the perpetration of a fraud upon others.

5. A factor, or other agent, in the possession of property, is responsible, to a certain extent, for its safety and preservation. He is bound, at least, to bestow the same amount of care and attention upon the goods of his principal, as he would, under similar circumstances, upon those of his own; or as much as a man of *average prudence* would bestow in the keeping of his own.

6. He is bound to keep the property of his principal insured while in his possession under the following circumstances: 1. Where the principal has effects in his hands and directs their application to such insurance. 2. Where there are *no effects* in the hands of the agent, but the course of dealing between them is such that the one has been accustomed to send orders to insure, and the other to execute them. He is bound to continue to obey such orders until he gives notice to discontinue that course of dealing. 3. Where bills of lading come to the agent with an order to insure, this being the implied condition of their acceptance. 4. Where the general usage of trade requires him to insure.

The regulations above quoted apply more particularly to *commercial* agents, more generally known as commission merchants or consignees. The business of such agents is fully exemplified in the "Commission" and "Forwarding" sets, hereinafter presented.

ADMINISTRATOR'S BOOKS.

An Administrator is a person legally appointed to settle the affairs of an intestate—or a person dying without a will. His duties, which are specifically prescribed in the statutes, pertain, first, to the liquidation of outstanding debts, and the collection of amounts due the estate; and next, to the proper distribution of net assets among the heirs and legal representatives.

So far as his accounts are concerned, they do not differ in principle from those of a commercial agent or consignee; and the same general rules of accountability will apply equally to both. The nature of the business is, however, essentially different; the one being, in its intent and scope, speculative, and the other having reference solely to liquidation. It is not impossible, however, that, in the vigilant and faithful discharge of his duties, an administrator may increase the value of the property held in trust, and by that means realize a gain for the ultimate owners; and, on the other hand, circumstances over which he has no control may tend to depreciate the property, resulting in a loss. The accounts may be kept in such a manner as to show these fluctuations, or they may show only the general *final* results.

If the gains and losses are shown, the system will not differ in theory from that of a regular mercantile business, having a single proprietor; and in the set which follows, we have used this hint to enforce more clearly the relation sustained by the accountant to the business whose continued changes and fluctuations he records.

To this end we have suggested *three* distinct methods of treating the subject, each founded upon a separate theory, yet all resulting alike. Let the student carefully observe the distinctions.

The **First Method** is based upon the general theory pertaining to the business of a single proprietor; the resources and liabilities being exhibited on the Ledger at the commencement, and all changes shown in appropriate accounts. The account representing the undivided interest of the heirs—"Park's Estate"—is treated precisely as a Stock account, the gains and losses which have accumulated and been represented under proper heads being finally closed into this account; but without passing through a general Loss and Gain account, as is customary.

The **Second Method** embodies the theory of equal resources and liabilities which has been so carefully put forth in the previous lessons. The *agent*, whose records these are, stands perpetually between the forces of this perfect equilibrium, having upon one hand the *resources*, and upon the other the *liabilities*, which, being always equal, are susceptible of canceling each other. This is the practical fact which the agent must have constantly in view—viz.: that whatever may be the result of his administration, if he acts within the line of his duty, he is responsible, or *liable*, to the parties for whom he acts, in just the amount of the property or *resources* which he has in trust; so that, at whatever moment he may be called upon to account, the one will exactly offset the other. In carrying out this theory to the letter, there should be no accumulation of gains or losses; as that would temporarily destroy the equilibrium. Therefore, as fast as gains or losses occur, they are *immediately* taken to the Estate account; thus increasing or diminishing the liability in this direction in the exact proportion of the increase or diminution of resources.

This method necessitates much care and precision, and an exact knowledge of the special gains or losses, as they occur. The same principle could be carried out in a general business, if it were possible to know the exact margin of gain or loss attending each transaction.

The **Third Method** recognizes no liability for any thing but *cash;* and consists, therefore, of only such records as grow out of cash transactions. The Estate account is credited for all cash received, and debited for all paid out; and as the result of the liquidation is to reduce every thing to a cash basis, the final result of this method is precisely the same as that of the other two.

The business represented is very brief, and the value of the set consists mainly in the theories enforced.

1

ADMINISTRATOR'S DAY BOOK.

Albany, January 2, 1860.

I have this day entered upon the duties of Administrator for the Estate of James Park, deceased. As prescribed in the Letters of Administration, I am to assume possession of all the personal property of the Estate, including cash, notes, personal debts, farm implements, live stock, etc. to pay off all just liabilities and necessary contingencies, and, after converting the surplus resources into cash, and deducting my commission, to divide the remainder equally among five heirs.

The following is a list of such resources and liabilities as are ascertainable at this time:

Resources.

James Monroe owes on %			575	
Orlando Warren do. do.			400	
Peter Deshong do. do.			120	
Edward Gurney do. do.			600	
James Truman do. do.			75	83
Robert Paton owes on note	$500			
E. C. Bradford do. do.	700			
Charles Pettingill do. do.	800			
L. S. Bliss, do. do.	450		2450	
Interest due on Paton's note	$15	75		
do. do. Bradford's do.	27	50		
do. do. Pettingill's do.	17	25		
do. do. Bliss's do.	10	17	70	67
Farming Implements, as per schedule			575	
Live Stock, as per valuation			3000	
Cash in hand			250	
do. in Farmers' Bank			1500	
			9616	50

Liabilities.

W. D. Packard, on %			400	
E. M. Hale, do.			375	
Charles Williams, do.			250	
Note favor of S. Willard	$360			
do. do. P. Horton	800		1160	
Interest due on note favor of S. Willard	5	75		
do. do. do. P. Horton	32	80	38	55
			2223	55

3

Paid the following expenses in cash:				
Undertaker's Bill	$ 75			
Livery Bill—carriages for funeral	150			
Probate Judge's Fees	10		235	

4

Collected the following amounts in cash:				
James Monroe, in full of %	$575			
Edward Gurney do.	600			
James Truman do.	75	83	1250	83

ADMINISTRATOR'S DAY BOOK.

Albany, January 5, 1860.

Particulars			$	cts.
Sold at public auction the Farming Implements enumerated in schedule, for cash			500	
6				
Paid tne following heirs, on %, in cash:				
Robert Park		$100		
James Park, Jr.		75		
Jennie Park		50	225	
7				
The following amounts due the Estate were not enumerated in the original list:				
Abraham Cuyler, on %		$123		
William Jones, do.		15 20		
Alex. Buttre, do.		75	213	20
9				
Paid the following liabilities, in cash:				
W. D. Packard		$400		
E. M. Hale		375		
Charles Williams		250	1025	
10				
Sold Live Stock for cash			3500	
11				
The following notes, with the interest thereon, were this day paid in cash:				
Robert Paton's	$500			
Charles Pettingill's	800	$1300		
Interest on Paton's to date	$16 50			
do. Pettingill's to date	18 45	$34 95	1334	95
12				
Paid Doct. Benson cash for medical attendance			65	
13				
Paid the following notes, with interest due thereon, in cash:				
Note favor S. Willard	$360			
do. P. Horton	800	$1160		
Interest favor S. Willard's to date	$6 50			
do. P. Horton's do.	$34 40	$40 90	1200	90
14				
Peter Deshong has compromised for the payment of the amount due us @ 75 %.				
Received cash		$90		
Lost the balance		30	120	
16				
Received cash in full for the following notes and interest thereon:				
E. C. Bradford's	$700			
L. S. Bliss's	450	$1150		
Interest on Bradford's	$29 25			
do. Bliss's	11 30	$40 55	1190	55

ADMINISTRATOR'S DAY BOOK.

Albany, January 17, 1860.

Received Cash of Orlando Warren, in full of %	400	
18		
Received Cash of the following persons in full of %:		
Abraham Cuyler $123		
William Jones 15 20		
Alex. Buttre 75	213	20
19		
Appropriated Cash for my services as Administrator	150	
20		
Deposited Cash in Farmers' Bank	5828	63
21		
Having converted the resources of the Estate into cash, and discharged all its liabilities, I am now able to declare a dividend in favor of the heirs. By reference to their representative account, "Park's Estate," I discover their undivided net proceeds to be	7553	63
The dividend to the credit of each heir is as follows:		
Robert Park $1510 72		
James Park, Jr. 1510 72		
Jennie Park 1510 73		
John Watson, guardian for the heirs of William Park deceased 1510 73		
Elizabeth Dewitt 1510 73		
I have already paid to heirs on %, as per record . . . . $ 225		
Balance to my credit in Farmers' Bank 7328 63		
$7553 63		

It is particularly desired that the relation which the account "Park's Estate" bears to Stock account in individual books, or to any account representing capital invested, will not be lost sight of. The inquisitive student will, in a moment, discover that inasmuch as the names of these separate heirs, as also their respective shares in the property administered upon, were known, it would have been proper to open a separate account with them, giving each credit for his or her share at the commencement, thus dispensing with the general account, "Park's Estate." This process of reasoning will bring him safely to the right conclusion, viz.: that "Park's Estate" account merely represents the undivided interest of the separate heirs, until the preliminaries of converting the resources into cash are accomplished. The great convenience of the account is in saving the trouble and perplexity of dividing into fifths each separate receipt and disbursement—for all cash received and paid out, in transacting the business, is for each of the heirs equally. "Park's Estate," in this sense, is precisely similar to "Capital Stock" account in a joint-stock association, representing the heirs precisely as "Capital Stock" account represents the undivided interests of all the separate stockholders; and the distribution which we now propose to make, based upon the net proceeds, ($7553.63), is exactly equivalent to a final dividend to stockholders. An entry might have been made, paying off the heirs, and thereby closing up the accounts, but it is not deemed necessary, since it can be easily seen that the amount in bank (7328.63) is just sufficient to discharge these liabilities. This would probably be the condition of the Administrator's accounts at the time of rendering his statement to the Probate Judge. The student, should he so desire, may make the necessary entry for closing all the accounts, which would be simply to pay off each heir the balance shown to be due in his or her account, by giving each a check on the Farmers' Bank.

Albany, January 2, 1860.

			$	¢	$	¢
	FIRST METHOD.					
Sundries	Dr.	To Park's Estate . . .			9616	50
James Monroe			575			
Orlando Warren			400			
Peter Deshong			120			
Edward Gurney			600			
James Truman			75	83		
Bills Receivable			2450			
Interest Receivable			70	67		
Farming Implements			575			
Live Stock			3000			
Cash			250			
Farmers' Bank			1500			
	SECOND METHOD.					
Same as first.						
	THIRD METHOD.					
Cash	Dr.	To Park's Estate . . .	250		250	
	〃					
	FIRST METHOD.					
Park's Estate	Dr.	To Sundries	2223	55		
		W. D. Packard . . .			400	
		E. M. Hale . . .			375	
		Charles Williams . .			250	
		Bills Payable . . .			1160	
		Interest Payable . . .			38	55
	SECOND METHOD.					
Same as first.						
	THIRD METHOD.					
No entry.						
	3					
	FIRST METHOD.					
Expense	Dr.	To Cash	235		235	
	SECOND METHOD.					
Park's Estate	Dr.	To Cash	235		235	
	THIRD METHOD.					
Same as second.						
	4					
	FIRST METHOD.					
Cash	Dr.	To Sundries	1250	83		
		James Monroe . . .			575	
		Edward Gurney . . .			600	
		James Truman . . .			75	83
	SECOND METHOD.					
Same as first.						
	THIRD METHOD.					
Cash	Dr.	To Park's Estate . . .	1250	83	1250	83
			15061	71	15061	71

ADMINISTRATOR'S JOURNAL.

Albany, January 5, 1860.

		FIRST METHOD.				
Cash	Dr.	To Farming Implements	500		500	
		SECOND METHOD.				
Sundries	Dr.	To Farming Implements			575	
Cash			500			
Park's Estate			75			
		THIRD METHOD.				
Cash	Dr.	To Park's Estate	500		500	
		6				
		FIRST METHOD.				
Sundries	Dr.	To Cash			225	
Robert Park			100			
James Park			75			
Jennie Park			50			
		SECOND METHOD.				
Same as first.						
		THIRD METHOD.				
Same as first.						
		7				
		FIRST METHOD.				
Sundries	Dr.	To Park's Estate			213	20
Abram Cuyler			123			
William Jones			15	20		
Alex. Buttre			75			
		SECOND METHOD.				
Same as first.						
		THIRD METHOD.				
No entry.						
		9				
		FIRST METHOD.				
Sundries	Dr.	To Cash			1025	
W. D. Packard			400			
E. M. Hale			375			
Charles Williams			250			
		SECOND METHOD.				
Same as first.						
		THIRD METHOD.				
Park's Estate	Dr.	To Cash	1025		1025	
			4063	20	4063	20

Albany, January 10, 1860.

			Dr. $	cts.	Cr. $	cts.
	First Method.					
Cash	Dr.	To Live Stock	3500		3500	
	Second Method.					
Cash	Dr.	To Sundries	3500			
		Live Stock			3000	
		Park's Estate . . .			500	
	Third Method.					
Cash	Dr.	To Park's Estate . . .	3500		3500	
	11					
	First Method.					
Cash	Dr.	To Sundries	1334	95		
		Bills Receivable . .			1300	
		Interest Receivable .			34	95
	Second Method.					
Cash	Dr.	To Sundries	1334	95		
		Bills Receivable . . .			1300	
		Interest Receivable* .			33	
		Park's Estate . . .			1	95
	Third Method.					
Cash	Dr.	To Park's Estate . . .	1334	95	1334	95
	12					
	First Method.					
Expense	Dr.	To Cash	65		65	
	Second Method.					
Park's Estate	Dr.	To Cash	65		65	
	Third Method.					
Same as second.						
	13					
	First Method.					
Sundries	Dr.	To Cash			1200	90
Bills Payable			1160			
Interest Payable			40	90		
	Second Method.					
Sundries	Dr.	To Cash			1200	90
Bills Payable			1160			
Interest Payable†			38	55		
Park's Estate			2	35		
			17036	65	17036	65

* This account was originally debited with the real value of Interest due on Notes, and is now credited with that value; the excess ($1.95) has accumulated since the notes came into our possession, and if not carried as a liability to the credit of the Estate, would remain in the Interest Receivable Account, making it show a gain.

† The remarks respecting Interest Receivable will apply with equal force to this entry.

Albany, January 13, 1860.

Account		Particulars	Dr. $	cts.	Cr. $	cts.
		Third Method.				
Park s Estate	Dr.	To Cash	1200	90	1200	90
		14				
		First Method.				
Sundries	Dr.	To Peter Deshong . . .			120	
Cash			90			
Loss and Gain			30			
		Second Method.				
Sundries	Dr.	To Peter Deshong . . .			120	
Cash			90			
Park's Estate			30			
		Third Method.				
Cash	Dr.	To Park's Estate . . .	90		90	
		16				
		First Method.				
Cash	Dr.	To Sundries	1190	55		
		Bills Receivable . .			1150	
		Interest Receivable . .			40	55
		Second Method.				
Cash	Dr.	To Sundries	1190	55		
		Bills Receivable . .			1150	
		Interest Receivable .			37	67
		Park's Estate . . .			2	88
		Third Method.				
Cash	Dr.	To Park's Estate . . .	1190	55	1190	55
		17				
		First Method.				
Cash	Dr.	To Orlando Warren . .	400		400	
		Second Method.				
Same as first.						
		Third Method.				
Cash	Dr.	To Park's Estate . .	400		400	
		18				
		First Method.				
Cash	Dr	To Sundries	213	20		
		Abram Cuyler . . .			123	
		William Jones . . .			15	20
		Alex. Buttre . . .			75	
			6115	55	6115	55

Albany, January 18, 1860.

	Second Method.				
Same as first.					
	Third Method.				
Cash	Dr. To Park's Estate . . .	213	20	213	20
	— 19 —				
	First Method.	150		150	
Expense	Dr. To Cash				
	Second Method.	150		150	
Park's Estate	Dr. To Cash				
	Third Method.				
Same as second.					
	— 20 —				
	First Method.				
Farmers' Bank	Dr. To Cash	5828	63	5828	63
	Second Method.				
Same as first.					
	Third Method.				
Same as first.					
	— 21 —				
	First Method.				
Park's Estate	Dr. To Sundries	7553	63		
	Robert Park			1510	72
	James Park, Jr. . . .			1510	72
	Jennie Park			1510	73
	John Watson . . .			1510	73
	Elizabeth Dewitt . .			1510	73
	Second Method.				
Same as first.					
	Third Method.				
Same as first.					
		13895	46	13895	46

ADMINISTRATOR'S LEDGER.

First Method.

Dr. PARK'S ESTATE. Cr.

Dr.				Cr.			
Jan.	2	2223	55	Jan.	2	9616	50
"	20	30		"	7	213	20
"	20	450		"	20	4	83
"	20	2	35	"	20	500	
"	20	75					
"	21	7553	63				
		10334	53			10334	53

Dr. CASH. Cr.

Dr.				Cr.			
Jan.	2	250		Jan.	3	235	
"	4	1250	83	"	6	225	
"	5	500		"	9	1025	
"	10	3500		"	12	65	
"	11	1334	95	"	13	1200	90
"	14	90		"	19	150	
"	16	1190	55	"	20	5828	63
"	17	400					
"	18	213	20				
		8729	53			8729	53

Dr. JAMES MONROE. Cr.

Dr.			Cr.		
Jan.	2	575	Jan.	4	575

Dr. ORLANDO WARREN. Cr.

Dr.			Cr.		
Jan.	2	400	Jan.	17	400

Dr. PETER DESHONG. Cr.

Dr.			Cr.		
Jan.	2	120	Jan.	14	120

Dr. EDWARD GURNEY. Cr.

Dr.			Cr.		
Jan.	2	600	Jan.	4	600

Dr. JAMES TRUMAN. Cr.

Dr.				Cr.			
Jan.	2	75	83	Jan.	4	75	83

Dr. BILLS RECEIVABLE. Cr.

Dr.			Cr.		
Jan.	2	2450	Jan.	11	1300
			"	16	1150
		2450			2450

Dr. INTEREST RECEIVABLE. Cr.

Dr.				Cr.			
Jan.	2	70	67	Jan.	11	34	95
"	[illegible]	[illegible]	[illegible]	"	16	40	55
		75	50			75	50

Dr. W. D. PACKARD. Cr.

Dr.			Cr.		
Jan.	9	400	Jan.	2	400

Dr. E. M. HALE. Cr.

Dr.			Cr.		
Jan.	9	375	Jan.	2	375

Dr. CHARLES WILLIAMS. Cr.

Dr.			Cr.		
Jan.	9	250	Jan.	2	250

Dr. FARMING IMPLEMENTS. Cr.

Dr.			Cr.		
Jan.	2	575	Jan.	5	500
			"	[illegible]	[illegible]
		575			575

Dr. BILLS PAYABLE. Cr.

Dr.			Cr.		
Jan.	13	1160	Jan.	2	1160

Dr. ROBERT PARK. Cr.

Dr.			Cr.			
Jan.	6	100	Jan.	21	1510	72

Dr. JAMES PARK, JR. Cr.

Dr.			Cr.			
Jan.	6	75	Jan.	21	1510	72

Dr. LIVE STOCK. Cr.

Dr.			Cr.		
Jan.	2	3000	Jan.	10	3500
"	[illegible]	[illegible]			
		3500			3500

Dr. EXPENSE. Cr.

Dr.			Cr.		
Jan.	3	235	[illegible]		[illegible]
"	12	65			
"	19	150			
		450			450

First Method—*Continued.*

Dr. INTEREST PAYABLE. Cr.

Jan.	13	40	90	*Jan.*	2	38	55
				"	[illegible]	[illegible]	[illegible]
		40	90			40	90

Dr. JENNIE PARK. Cr.

Jan.	6	50		*Jan.*	21	1510	73

Dr. ABRAM CUYLER. Cr.

Jan.	7	123		*Jan.*	18	123	

Dr. WILLIAM JONES. Cr.

Jan.	7	15	20	*Jan.*	18	15	20

Dr. FARMERS' BANK. Cr.

Jan.	21	1500					
"	20	5828	63				

Dr. ALEX. BUTTRE. Cr.

Jan.	7	75		*Jan.*	18	75	20

Dr. LOSS AND GAIN. Cr.

Jan.	14	30		[illegible]	[illegible]	[illegible]	

Dr. JOHN WATSON. Cr.

				Jan.	21	1510	73

Dr. ELIZABETH DEWITT. Cr.

				Jan.	21	1510	73

Second Method.

Dr. PARK'S ESTATE. Cr.

Jan.	2	2223	55	*Jan.*	2	9616	50
"	3	235		"	7	213	20
"	5	75		"	10	500	
"	12	65		"	11	1	95
"	13	2	35	"	16	2	88
"	14	30					
"	19	150					
"	21	7553	63				
		10334	53			10334	53

Dr. INTEREST RECEIVABLE. Cr.

Jan.	2	70	67	*Jan.*	11	33	
				"	16	37	67
		70	67			70	67

Dr. W. D. PACKARD. Cr.

Jan.	9	400		*Jan.*	2	400	

Dr. CASH. Cr.

Jan.	2	250		*Jan.*	3	235	
"	4	1250	83	"	6	225	
"	5	500		"	9	1025	
"	10	3500		"	12	65	
"	11	1334	95	"	13	1200	90
"	14	90		"	19	150	
"	16	1190	55	"	20	5828	63
"	17	400					
"	18	213	20				
		8729	53			8729	53

Dr. E. M. HALE. Cr.

Jan.	9	375		*Jan.*	2	375	

Dr. CHARLES WILLIAMS. Cr.

Jan.	9	250		*Jan.*	2	250	

Dr. JAMES MONROE. Cr.

Jan.	2	575		*Jan.*	4	575	

Dr. FARMING IMPLEMENTS. Cr.

Jan.	2	575		*Jan.*	5	575	

ADMINISTRATOR'S LEDGER.

Second Method—*Continued.*

Dr. ORLANDO WARREN. **Cr.**

Jan.	2	400		*Jan.*	17	400	

Dr. PETER DESHONG. **Cr.**

Jan.	2	120		*Jan.*	4	120	

Dr. EDWARD GURNEY. **Cr.**

Jan.	2	600		*Jan.*	4	600	

Dr. JAMES TRUMAN. **Cr.**

Jan.	2	75	83	*Jan.*	4	75	83

Dr. BILLS RECEIVABLE. **Cr.**

Jan.	2	2450		*Jan.*	11	1300	
				"	16	1150	
		2450				2450	

Dr. INTEREST PAYABLE. **Cr.**

Jan.	13	38	55	*Jan.*	2	38	55

Dr. ABRAM CUYLER. **Cr.**

Jan.	7	123		*Jan.*	18	123	

Dr. FARMERS' BANK. **Cr.**

Jan.	21	1500					
	20	5828	63				

Dr. JOHN WATSON. **Cr.**

				Jan.	21	1510	73

Dr. BILLS PAYABLE. **Cr.**

Jan.	13	1160		*Jan.*	2	1160	

Dr. ROBERT PARK. **Cr.**

Jan.	6	100		*Jan.*	21	1510	72

Dr. JAMES PARK, JR. **Cr.**

Jan.	6	75		*Jan.*	21	1510	72

Dr. LIVE STOCK. **Cr.**

Jan.	2	3000		*Jan.*	10	3000	

Dr. JENNIE PARK. **Cr.**

Jan.	6	50		*Jan.*	21	1510	73

Dr. WILLIAM JONES. **Cr.**

Jan.	7	15	20	*Jan.*	18	15	20

Dr. ALEX. BUTTRE. **Cr.**

Jan.		75		*Jan.*	18	75	

Dr. ELIZABETH DEWITT. **Cr.**

				Jan.	21	1510	73

CASH STATEMENT,

INVOLVING ALL THE ENTRIES IN THE "THIRD METHOD."

Jan	2	Amount on hand		250			
	3	Paid Expenses, viz.: Undertaker's Bill				75	
		Livery Bill, Carriages for Funeral				150	
		Probate Judge's Fees				10	
	4	Rec'd on Personal Accounts, viz.: James Monroe		575			
		Edward Gurney		600			
		James Truman		75	83		
	5	Rec'd for Farming Implements,—Auction Sale		500			
	6	Paid Heirs on Account, viz: Robert Park				100	
		Jas. Park, Jr.				75	
		Jennie Park				50	
	9	Paid on Personal Accounts, viz: W. D. Packard				400	
		E. M. Hale				375	
		Chas. Williams				250	
	10	Received for Live Stock		3500			
	11	Received on Notes, viz.: Robert Paton	$500 00				
		Interest on same	16 50	516	50		
		Chas. Pettingill	$800 00				
		Interest on same	18 45	818	45		
	12	Paid Dr. Benson, for Medical Attendance				65	
	13	Paid the following notes: S. Willard	$360 00				
		Interest on same	6 50			366	50
		P. Horton	$800 00				
		Interest	34 40			834	40
	14	Rec'd of Peter Deshong, as per compromise		90			
	16	Received on Notes, viz.: E. C. Bradford	$700 00				
		Interest on same	29 25	729	25		
		L. S. Bliss	$450 00				
		Interest on same	11 30	461	30		
	17	Rec'd of O. Warren, in full of account		400			
	18	Rec'd on Personal Accounts, viz: Abram Cuyler		123			
		Wm. Jones		15	20		
		Alex. Buttre		75			
	19	Appropriated for Services				150	
	20	Deposited in Bank				5828	63
				8729	53	8729	53

EXERCISES FOR THE LEARNER.

NOTE.—The following Narrative comprises a series of transactions in a regular Produce Business, designed to be written up in a manner similar to the previous set. In this case the proprietor is his own agent, and the business is conducted for his own benefit. He thus occupies a double relation to the business, viz.: as *principal*, and as *agent*. His interests as *principal* are represented by the Stock account; and his care as an *agent* should be, as in the previous case, to know that the resources and liabilities are perpetually equal.

The transactions are so arranged that the special gains and losses are made apparent as they occur, so that the different methods suggested in the previous set may be carried out in this. The teacher can make use of these transactions to perfect the student in the different methods of exhibiting gains and losses, as well as in developing the Science of Accounts. Let the student be required first to write up the set in the ordinary manner, retaining the gains and losses in the proper representative accounts, until the close of the business; and then carry them through the general Loss and Gain account to Stock. Next, let him carry each separate loss or gain directly to the Loss and Gain account, *when it occurs*, and from thence in a net amount to Stock; and, finally, let him take each separate loss or gain *directly* to the Stock account. This will teach him, in the most unequivocal manner, the *theory* of gains and losses, and the convenience of permitting all fluctuations to remain in their proper accounts during the current condition of the business.

NARRATIVE.

July 1. Commenced business with $10,000 cash capital...... Bo't of H. R. Munger, @ 10 ds., 500 Bbls. Genesee Flour, @ $10...... Bo't of James E. Jenkins, for cash, 700 Bush. Oats, @ 60¢...... Sold John J. Anderson, on his note @ 10 ds., 300 Bbls. Flour, @ $10.50...... Sold Frederick Wintle, for cash, 200 Bush. Oats, @ 75¢.

2. Bo't of W. A. Miller, for cash, 300 Bbls. Toronto Mills Flour, @ $10.25..... Paid cash for Store Expenses, $75...... Sold Thos. C. Latto, on %, 100 Bbls. Genesee Flour, @ $11...... Bo't of Samuel Martin, for cash, 1000 Bush. Corn, @ 65¢.

3. Sold James E. Day, on %, 300 Bush. Oats, @ 78¢...... Bo't of Edward C. Rice, for cash, 3000 Bush. Milwaukee Club Wheat, @ $1...... Sold Henry C. Spencer, for cash, 500 Bush. Corn, @ 73¢.

4. Bo't of John McMullen, on %, 4000 Bush. Chicago Spring Wheat, @ 85¢..... Sold G. Bailey, for cash, 1500 Bush. Milwaukee Club Wheat, @ $1.10...... Sold H. P. Perrin, for cash, 200 Bbls. Toronto Mills Flour, @ $11.50...... Received Cash of Thos. C. Latto, in full of %, $——.

5. Paid H. R. Munger Cash on %, $2500...... Bo't of Samuel Lathrop, for Cash, 2000 Bush. Rye, @ 70¢...... Sold J. Gundry, for Cash, 1500 Bush. Milwaukee Club Wheat, @ $1.20.

6. Sold Henry Eaton, for cash, 2000 Bush. Chicago Spring Wheat, @ 90¢...... Sold James Conner, for cash, 200 Bush. Oats, @ 75¢.

7. Sold Philip Kearney, for cash, 100 Bbls. Genesee Flour, @ $10.75; 100 Bbls. Toronto Mills Flour, @ $11.

10. Paid J. McMullen, cash in full of %, $——...... Sold J. Simpson, for cash, 2000 Bush. Chicago Spring Wheat, @ 92¢; 500 Bush. Corn, @ 75¢.

12. Sold J. Hollister, for cash, 2000 Bushels Rye, @ 60¢...... Received Cash in full for John J. Anderson's note of the 1st inst., $——...... Received Cash of Jas. E. Day in full of %, $——...... Paid H. R. Munger, Cash in full of %, $——.

Statement at Closing.

Cash on hand		11269			
Capital at commencing	$10000				
Net Gain	1269			11269	
		11269		11269	

COMMISSION:

EMBRACING, AS PRINCIPAL AND AUXILIARY BOOKS,

RECEIVING BOOK, SALES BOOK, CASH BOOK, JOURNAL AND LEDGER;

TOGETHER WITH

THE MOST PRACTICAL FORMS IN USE.

REPRESENTING BUSINESS AS IT OCCURS IN FIRST CLASS

COMMISSION HOUSES.

COMMISSION.

A COMMISSION MERCHANT is an agent for the sale of property consigned to his care, and is expected to carefully consult the interests of his consignors. He should not be interested in the purchase or sale of articles similar to those consigned to him on commission. The consignor may limit the price at which his property shall be sold, or withhold it from market, or may leave everything to the judgment and discretion of the Commission Merchant. If, however, explicit directions are given by the consignor as to the management of the property, the consignee must obey them to the letter. Sales on commission must be made for cash, unless the article is such as is usually sold on time, or the consignor has authorized time to be given. A departure from these restrictions will render the consignee liable for any damage which may result. He may, in fact, require payment to be made before delivery of the property sold, and should do so where any doubt exists as to the business integrity of the purchaser.

There are various methods of keeping the accounts of a Commission Merchant, so far as the consignments are concerned. Some keep no account with the different consignments, but enter all transactions relating thereto in the consignor's account; others keep a general consignment % for each consignor under the title of "Consignments," "Sales," or some other appropriate name; while others keep a separate account with each consignment, carrying the separate results as "net proceeds" to the account of the consignor.

The latter method is the one here adopted.

The books in common use with Commission Merchants are those illustrated in this set. Their distinct uses, although apparent upon their face, may be briefly stated, as follows:

THE RECEIVING BOOK

contains the copies of Bills of Lading sent with the consignments, and embraces all the necessary facts as to the quantity and kind of merchandise, by whom and how sent, on whose account to be sold, etc. It also contains the amount of freight due, and usually the receipts of the Transportation Agent for freights paid. This is a purely auxiliary book, the essential facts which it contains being properly classified in other books, and from thence posted to the Ledger

THE SALES BOOK

is the book of principal record for the Commission Merchant. It embraces the particulars of each consignment, so arranged as to present at a glance the progress of the business, and of each part thereof. It is, in effect, a Ledger of the consignment accounts; and although, as in this instance, a general Sales % may be kept in the Ledger proper, the Sales Book is indispensable to show the facts connected with each consignment. This book is sometimes journalized, but more frequently posted direct, as here shown. The only difficulty the student is likely to encounter in posting direct from the Sales Book will be that of obtaining a Trial Balance readily. The Commission Sales Book, unlike the Sales Book in a general merchandise business, is a schedule of different sales accounts in various stages of completion; so that, should we select any particular period for carrying the result to the Ledger, such as, for instance, the last of each month, it would be impossible to make the entry complete from the fact that some of the accounts would represent the sales entirely closed out, while others would exhibit only partial results, leaving space for future entries which might not occur for months; while, if we should delay the posting of the amounts in the general column of the credit side of the Sales Book until the sales are closed, our Ledger would fail to show the indebtedness of parties who have purchased on account. (It is, in fact, this necessity of keeping the personal accounts posted that leads to all the difficulty which besets us in the matter of a Trial Balance.) We cannot, therefore, as in the Sales Book connected with Set V., foot up the sales at the end of the month, carrying the amount to the credit of the Sales %, to balance the corresponding debit entries already posted, and we must either leave the sales unposted until the several consignments are closed, keeping the Ledger thus much out of balance, or collect the amount of sales up to the period at which the Trial Balance is wanted, and credit it to Sales %. The only objection to the latter method is the carrying of an amount to the Ledger which does not appear in the book of original entry, thereby rendering it difficult to check the work in case the Ledger does not balance. The trouble from this source, however, should not discourage the accountant, but should only make him the more vigilant in guarding against possible errors in collecting the items from the Sales Book.*

---

* It will be seen that we have avoided this difficulty by making in the Journal a memorandum entry at the end of each month, showing the total sales not posted from the Cash Book. This amount, though not extended into the regular money column, is posted to the credit of Sales account, and the difficulty in checking is avoided.

The debit side of the Sales Book, and the Cash column of the credit side will lead to no difficulty of this sort, from the fact that the debit of each consignment is posted only when the consignment is closed out, and the entry complete. Sales % is then debited, and the several items making the total, credited; preserving, thereby, the necessary equilibrium. The entries in the Cash column of the credit side are also made in the Cash Book, and posted from thence at the end of each month, being balanced by an equal amount of cash which is included in the cash total.

It is not deemed necessary to have a separate column for Cash on the debit side of the Sales Book, from the fact that there would generally be but one item to enter in it from each consignment, viz., the amount paid for Transportation. We have therefore made a *neutralizing* entry of this amount, crediting Transportation from the Sales Book, and debiting it from the Cash Book, after the method indicated in the second paragraph on p. 129.

THE CASH BOOK

differs in no essential particular from other Cash Books shown in this work. The special columns will be readily understood.

THE JOURNAL

contains only such records as may not properly be entered in the other books. It will explain itself.

THE LEDGER

differs from the Ledgers already shown, only in the form of entry, the explanations being more full and satisfactory.. This feature is one which we would commend to the careful attention of the student.

The NARRATIVE OF TRANSACTIONS preceding the books of entry should be carefully studied, and all *the entries* made therefrom, instead of copying them from the books themselves. We briefly indicate the order of entry.

The first regular transaction of the business is that of May 12th, relating to the 550 bbls. Flour received by the boat "Sam Miller."

The first entry to be made is in the Receiving Book, stating the date of arrival, and copying from the Bill of Lading the name of the vessel, railroad, or other mode of transportation, and all the essential facts as to the quantity and kind of property, by whom forwarded, at what date, on whose account to be sold, the charges accrued, etc. Careful attention should be given to the quantity and condition of the property, to see that it corresponds with the Bill of Lading, and if it varies in either particular, the facts should be noted immediately on the Receiving Book, that reference may be had to it in the final settlement. Upon paying the freight, a receipt is taken (generally in the Receiving Book), and the amount entered to Transportation %.

The Sales Book is then opened, and under the name of the owner an entry is made, on the left hand or debit page, of the property received, specifying the same particulars as in the Receiving Book. Other charges, such as Storage, Insurance, Commission, etc., will be entered as they occur. When the property is all disposed of, these charges, of course, are to be deducted from the gross amount of the sale, and the "net proceeds" placed to the credit, or made subject to the order of the owner.

The cash paid for freight ($93.50) must, of course, be entered in the Cash Book, and as "Transportation" % is credited in the Sales Book, it will now be debited in the Cash Book, the amount being carried to that special column, and included in the total at the end of the month.

It will be readily seen that the entries thus made in the Transportation Account must cancel or *neutralize* each other. The use of such accounts becomes necessary where conflicting entries are made from different books. In this case, the account is something better than a mere necessity, as it shows the amount we have paid on Transportation.

This set is designed to give the student a practical idea of the best method of keeping Commission Books as practised in the first Commission Houses along the great central thoroughfare, extending from the Atlantic to the Mississippi. This and the Forwarding Set which follows are made up from transactions, furnished by Mr. H. B. TUTTLE, of Cleveland, to whom we are indebted for most of the arrangement, and the practical hints touching the customs in this department of trade.

The first two months' transactions are entered up in detail in the proper books. The last two are left for the student to enter, and are relied upon mainly for practical instruction.

We are confident that no better forms are before the public, or in use among business men.

NARRATIVE OF TRANSACTIONS.

May 1. Commenced a general Commission business, occupying the office and warehouse rented of H. Harvey, River Street, at $800 per annum. Appropriated $10,000 as capital, which is now paid in. (C. B.) - - - - Paid Cash for Office Furniture, $38. (Furniture %, C. B.)

3. Paid Cash for Stationery and Blank Books, $9.95. (Expense %, C. B.) Also for Iron Safe (Furniture %, $230, C. B.)

4. Paid Cash for sundry articles for office and warehouse use, $3.25. (Expense %, C. B.)

12. Received by Boat "S. Miller," from Monroe Mills Co., Akron, O., 550 bbls. Flour, to be sold on their account. The brands are as follows: 440 bbls. "Monroe Mills Extra," 85 bbls. "Summit Mills," and 25 bbls "A. Potter." Paid Canal Freight, 17¢ per bbl. in Cash. (R. B.; S. B.; C. B.) - - - - Procured Fire Insurance in the Commercial Mutual Ins. Co., Cleveland, to cover any property in store to the amount of $5,000, @1½ ₩ ct. prem. Paid Premium in Cash.* (C. B.) - - - - Sold P. Anderson, from Monroe Mills Co.'s Consignment, 300 bbls. "Monroe Extra" Flour, @ $8 per bbl. - - - - Also sold A. M. Perry & Co. 40 bbls., same brand, @ 8.12½, both payable on presentation of bill.† (S. B.)

13. Rec'd by Boat "Cuyahoga," from R. M. Ashley, Cuyahoga Falls, 100 bbls. Linseed Oil, for % of Henry Wetmore; paid Freight, 37½ ¢ per bbl. in Cash. (R. B.; S. B.; C. B.) - - - - Sold, for Cash, 25 bbls. "A. Potter" Flour, Monroe Mills Co.'s Const., @ $5. (S. B.; C. B.) - - - - Sold H. Steller, 85 bbls. "Summit Mills" Flour Monroe Mills Co.'s Const., @ 7.50. (S. B.)

14. Sold, for Cash, 10 bbls. Linseed Oil, 403 gallons, @ 95¢—Wetmore's Const.—(S. B.; C. B.) - - - - Sold Gaylord & Co. 30 bbls. Linseed Oil, 1200 gallons, @ 92¢—same Const.—(S. B.) - - - - Received of P. Anderson, Cash for Bill of Flour of 12th inst. (C. B.)

15. Sold, for Cash, 100 bbls. "Monroe Extra" Flour, Monroe Mills Co.'s Const., @ $8. (S. B.; C. B.) - - - - Also 5 bbls. Linseed Oil—H. Wetmore's Const.—201½ gals. @ 95 ¢. (S. B; C. B.)

17. Received, per C. C. & C. R. R., from New London Station, for % J. H. Luther, Ashland, O., 100 bbls. "Ashland Mills" Flour; paid R. R. chgs. on same, $22.47; Drayage, $2.50. (R. B.; S. B.; C. B.) - - - - Rec'd Cash of A. M. Perry & Co. for amount of their bill of 12th inst. (C. B.) - - - - Also, of H. Steller, for amount of his bill of 13th inst. (C. B.) - - - - Sold A. M. Perry & Co. 100 bbls. "Ashland" Flour—J. H. Luther's Const.—@ $7.75. (S. B.) - - - - Closed Monroe Mills Co.'s Const., and rendered them % sales of the same. Our charges (aside from Transportation, already entered) are as follows: Storage, $13.50; Insurance, $10.72; Commission, 2½ % on total sales, $107.19; net proceeds credited to Monroe Mills Co. (S. B.) ‡

18. Rec'd Cash of Gaylord & Co. for amount of their bill of 14th inst. (C. B.) - - - - Sold for Cash, 55 bbls. Linseed Oil—H. Wetmore's Const.—2200 gals. @ 90¢ (S. B.; C. B.)

19. Paid Cash for H. Wetmore's sight draft on me, favor A. Gray, $1400. (C. B.) - - - - Procured a Cargo for Schr. Lavinia, as requested; Freight amounting to $850; my Commission on same, 5 %, chgd. to Schr. Lavinia (J.).

21. Rec'd Cash of A. M. Perry & Co., for amt. of bill of 17th inst. (C. B.) - - - - - Paid Cash for Monroe Mills Co's. sight draft on me, favor H. B. Hurlbut, Cashr., $2000. (C. B.)

24. Closed H. Wetmore's Consignment, and rendered him an % Sales of the same: Our chgs. (aside from Transportation, already entered) are as follows: Storage, $8; Insurance, $9.14; Cooperage, $2.50; Commission, $91.46.—Net Proceeds to be credited to H. Wetmore. (S. B.)

25. Rec'd, per Boat "Cataract" from Haughey & Byers, Newark, O., for % of Consignors, 1915 bush. Wheat. Paid Freight in Cash, 8½¢ per bush. (R. B.; S. B.; C. B.) - - - - - Also per Boat "C. Delano," from same parties, and for their %, 2006 bush. Wheat, being 6 bush. over the Bill of Lading, for which we paid the

---

* It is customary for Commission Merchants to effect a general Insurance on all property that may be in their warehouse, making the amount large enough to cover all probable risks, and then charge consignors a sufficient percentage to cover their outlay. They thus become insurers to their consignors, and in turn transfer their risks to some reliable Insurance Company, not unfrequently realizing a small margin of gain in this way.

† Nearly all Cash sales to regular customers are made in this way, the bills not being presented for two or three days after the purchase. In all such cases the purchaser should be charged immediately, the same as if the sale were on account.

‡ It is proper that a Consignment account in the Sales Book be closed immediately upon disposing of the property. In this case, although the last sale was effected on the 15th, the account is not closed until the 17th, the date of payment of the two bills due for previous sales. The reason for this delay is obvious, as the consignee does not consider himself as owing the consignor until he holds in his hands the avails of the sales. When the account sales is received by the consignor, he can draw for the amount, it being in the hands of his agent, the consignee.

Capt. the market price of $1.20 per bush.;* also paid Freight on the 2000 bush., as per Bill of Lading, @ 8½¢ (R. B.; S. B.; C. B.) - - - - Sold C. Hickox, 1915 bush. Wheat—Haughey & Byers' Const.—@ $1.20. (S. B.) - - - - Also, sold Harvey & Witt, 2006 bush. Wheat, same Const., @ $1.20. (S. B.) - - - - Paid Cash for Cooperage, $2.50. (C. B.)

26. Paid Cash for H. Wetmore's sight draft for E. Comstock, Cashr., $2200. (C. B.) - - - - - Closed J. H. Luther's Consignment, and rendered him an % Sales: Our charges (aside from Transportation already entered) are as follows: Storage, $3; Insurance, $1.94; Commission, $19.37; Net Proceeds remitted in Cash.† (S. B.; C. B.)

27. Rec'd, per Steamer "Ocean," from C. A. Trowbridge, Detroit, for % of Thos. Paxton, 100 bbls. White Fish; paid Freight, @ 12½¢ per bbl. (R. B.; S. B.; C. B.) - - - - Rec'd. per Schr. Lavinia, from Ames & Merriam, Oswego, (May 19) 600 bbls. Water Lime, for % of H. M. Ames. Freight, @ 18¢ per bbl., credited Schr. Lavinia. (R. B.; S. B.; J.)

29. Rec'd, per Str. "Ocean," from C. A. Trowbridge, Detroit, for % of Thos. Paxton, 100 hf. bbls. Fish. Paid Freight, @ 6¼¢ per hf. bbl. (R. B.; S. B.; C. B.) - - - - Accepted Thos. Paxton's draft, dated 24th inst., @ 1 month from date, for $1000.‡ (J.)

30. Rec'd Cash of C. Hickox for bill of Wheat of the 25th inst. (C. B.) - - - - Also of Harvey & Witt for bill of Wheat, same date. (C. B.)

31. Paid Inspection bill of T. Paxton's Fish, $57.50. (C. B.)—One hf. bbl. over on inspection.§ - - - - Paid Warehouseman's wages this month, $25. (C. B.) - - - - Closed Haughey & Byers' Consignment, and rendered them an % Sales. Our charges (aside from Transportation already entered) are as follows: Commission, 1¢ per bush., $39.21—Net Proceeds to credit of Haughey & Byers. (S. B.) - - - - Closed Cash Book, and posted results to the Ledger: Total Transportation paid this month, $507.50; Total Expense for the month, $40.70.—Balance Cash on hand, $16144.36. - - - - Also transferred to Journal the Sales not entered from Cash Book, viz.: "Monroe Mills Co.," $3362.50; H. Wetmore, $1104; J. H. Luther, $775; Haughey & Byers, $4705.20: Total, 9946.70.‖

June 2. Sold Gordon, McMillan & Co., @ 10 ds., from Paxton's Const., 51 bbls. White Fish, @ $8; 82 hf. bbls. do., @ $4.25. (S. B.) - - - - Sold Hubby, Hughes & Co., from Ames' Const., 300 bbls. Water Lime, @ $1.25. (S B.) - - - - Drew on H. Wetmore for balance of %, $90.32.¶ (C. B.)

5. Paid Cash for Monroe Mills Co's. Draft on me, favor T. P. Handy, Cashr., $2062.59. (C. B.) - - - - Rec'd. per C. & P. R. R., from Akron, O., for % of J. B. Woods, 250 bbls. Flour, "Phenix Mills." Paid Freight, 14¢ per bbl., $35; Drayage, $6.25. (R. B.; S. B.; C. B.) - - - - Sold Bradburn & Fisher, from Ames' Const., 300 bbls. Water Lime, @ $1.25 (S. B.)

6. Sold Gordon, McMillan & Co., from Paxton's Const., 49 bbls. Inspected Fish, @ $5, and 19 hf. bbls. same, @ $2.75. (S. B.) - - - - Rec'd., per C. C. & C. R. R., for % of Baldwin & Payne, Franklin, Ind., 500 bbls. "Pearl Mills" Flour; paid Freight to Union, 36¢ per bbl.; from Union to Cleveland, 40¢ per bbl.; Total Freight, $380; Drayage, 2½¢ per bbl., $12.50. (R. B.; S. B.; C. B.)

---

* The master of a vessel, boat, or other public vehicle, is held responsible for the safe delivery of goods as entered on his Bill of Lading. If the quantity falls short, he must make good the deficiency, and, on the other hand, if it overruns, custom allows him to appropriate the excess. In this case we pay the captain the regular market price for 6 bush. over, and charge the same to the owners.

† In ordinary cases, we should scarcely deem it necessary to open an account with a consignor, when we remit him his net proceeds in cash; but, as we must enter the cash in the Cash Book, and post it from thence to the Ledger, we are obliged to make of this a neutralizing entry, the same as we do of Transportation. We therefore credit the consignor for his net proceeds rom the Sales Book, and debit him for the remittance from the Cash Book.

‡ It is customary for consignors to draw against their consignments, making the draft payable far enough ahead to allow the consignee to realize on the property before the draft matures. There is no risk in accepting a draft when we have sufficient property belonging to the drawer.

§ In this case, the "over" is not discovered until the property is inspected, and is not therefore claimed by the transporter. We simply add it to the number already entered, and give the consignor the benefit.

‖ If the student will carefully examine his Sales Book, he will discover that these amounts, comprised in the total amount carried to the Ledger as "other sales" (than cash) for the month, he will see that a corresponding debit for each one in the shape of a personal account has been already posted; and, of course, if this credit to Sales were omitted, the Ledger would fail thus much of balancing. It may be optional with him to post the amount to the Ledger at this time, or to post the separate sales *when they are closed out*, always keeping in mind that, in the latter case, there will be a deficiency in his Trial Balance of the amount of credit sales unposted.

¶ Business houses do the most of their collecting through the Bank where their deposits are made. As this is a sight draft, and will be paid on presentation, we deposit it the same as cash. The Bank will of course send it on immediately for collection. We keep no Bank account in our Ledger, reckoning the amount on deposit as cash.

8. Paid Cash for Haughey & Byers' sight draft, favor of H. B. Hurlbut, Cashr., $2116.07. - - - - Also, per their order, remitted to R. Mead & Co., N. Y., $2198.95. Exchange on above, ½ % prem., $ 10.99.* (C. B.) - - - - Sold for Cash, from J. B. Wood's Const., 200 bbls. "Phenix Mills" Flour, @ $8.20; and 50 bbls. do., @ $8.25. (S. B.; C. B.) - - - - Rec'd, per C. C. & C. R. R., from Baldwin & Payne, Franklin, Ind., 200 bbls. "Pearl Mills" Flour, and 50 do. "Fine" Flour. Paid Freight to Union, 36¢ per bbl.; from Union to Cleveland, 40¢ per bbl.; Total Freight, $190; Drayage, 2½¢, $6.25. (R. B.; S. B.; C. B.) - - - - Rec'd, per C. & P. R. R., for % of J. B. Woods, Akron, O., 50 sacks Wool, 7500 lbs. Paid Freight, @ 10¢ per 100 lbs., $7.50; Drayage, 5 loads, @ 25¢, $1.25. (R. B.; S. B.; C. B.) - - - - Rec'd, from Boat "Tornado," for % of H. Meek, Coshocton, O., 200 kegs Butter, 22,410 lbs. Paid Freight, @ 18¢ per 100 lbs., $40.34. (R. B.; S. B.; C. B.) - - - - Sold N. Sackrider, from Baldwin & Payne's Const., 500 bbls. "Pearl Mills" Flour, @ $7.50. (S. B.) - - - - Closed J. B. Wood's Const., of June 5, and rendered % Sales of same.—Our charges not previously entered are as follows: Storage $7.50; Insurance, $2; Commission, 2½ % on $2052.50=$51.31. Net Proceeds to credit of J. B. Woods (S. B.)

9. Rec'd Cash of Hubby, Hughes & Co. for bill of Water Lime, of 2d inst. (C. B.) - - - - Paid Cooperage, $3. (C. B.)

12. Rec'd Cash of Bradburn & Fisher for bill of Water Lime, of 5th inst (C. B.) - - - - Rec'd Cash of Gordon, McMillan & Co. for bill of Fish, from Paxton's Const. of June 2, and June 6, due this day. (C. B.) - - - - Drew at sight on N. Sackrider, for $3235.50. (C. B.) - - - - Remitted Cash to J. A. Carlton, Cinci., for % of J. B. Woods, $1500. (C. B.) - - - - Closed Ames' Const., and rendered % Sales of same. Our charges, not already entered, are as follows: Storage, 8¢ per bbl., $48; Insurance, $1.50; Cooperage, $3; Commission, 12½¢ per bbl. on 600 bbls., $75. Net Proceeds to credit of H. M. Ames. (S. B.) - - - - Remitted H. M. Ames, for his net proceeds above, my sight draft on N. Sackrider, Ogdensburg, N. Y. (J.) - - - - - Closed Baldwin & Payne' Const., of June 6, and rendered % Sales of same. Our charges, not already entered, are, for our Commissions, @ 15¢ per bbl. on 500 bbls. Flour, $75. Net Proceeds to credit of Baldwin & Payne. (S. B.) - - - - - Accepted H. Meek's draft of June 9th, @ 2 months from date, for $1500, payable at Commercial Bank. (J.)

15. Rec'd, per Boat "S. Miller," from Monroe Mills Co., for % of Shipper, 544 bbls. Flour, of the following brands: 400 bbls. "Monroe Extra," 125 bbls. "Summit Mills," and 19 bbls. "A Potter." Paid Freight, 16¢ per bbl., $87.04. 10 bbls. Wet; Damage appraised and deducted, $10.† (R. B; S. B.; C. B.)

16. Remitted Baldwin & Payne, as per their request, Cash to balance %, $3282.50. (C. B.) - - - - Received per Boat "Beacon," from N. T. Claypole, Nashport, O., of June 12, for % of W. Lynn & Co., 120 pieces Bacon, 3204 lbs. Paid Freight, 18¢ per 100, $5.76. (R. B.; S. B.; C. B.)

18. Rec'd, per Schooner "Lavinia," from Ames & Merriam, Oswego, of June 11, for % of H. M. Ames, 500 bbls. Water-Lime; Freight, 18¢ per bbl., credited Schr. "Lavinia." (R. B.; S. B.; J.) - - - - Also, per same vessel from H. C. Wright, Oswego, for % of Shipper, 250 bbls. Coarse Salt, and 1000 bbls. Fine Salt; Freight 15¢ per bbl., credited Schr. "Lavinia." (R. B.; S. B.; J.)

19. Procured cargo for Schr. "Lavinia," freight amounting to $1425, for which we charge her, as per agreement, 5%. (J.) - - - - Sold for Cash, from J. B. Woods' Const., 50 sacks Wool, 7250 lbs., @ 35¢. (S. B.; C. B.) - - - - Closed J. B. Wood's Const., and rendered % Sales of same. Our Charges not already entered are: Storage, $7.50; Insurance, $6.34; Commission, 1¢ per lb., 72.50. Net Proceeds to credit of J. B. Woods. (S. B.) - - - - Sold, for Cash, from H. Meeks' const., 50 kegs Butter, 5100 lbs. @ 18¢. (S. B.: C. B.) - - - - Received, per Schr. "Marquette," from Hinckley & Handy, Chicago, for % of Shippers, 14,000 bush. Oats, stored in Erie Warehouse. Paid Freight, 5¢ per bushel. (R. B.; S. B.; C. B.) - - - - Paid J. B. Woods, Cash to balance %, $2892.85. (C. B.) - - - - Sold Gordon, McMillan & Co., from H. M. Ames' Const., 500 bbls. Water Lime, @ $1.20. (S. B.) - - - - Sold R. T. Lyon, on his note, @ 30 ds., from H. C. Wright's Const., 250 bbls. Coarse Salt, @ $2, and 1000 bbls Fine do., @ $1.50. (S. B.)

20. Closed H. M. Ames Const. of June 19, and rendered % Sales of the same. Our Charges not already posted are: Commission, 12½¢ per bbl., $62.50. Net Proceeds to credit of H. M. Ames. (S. B.) - - - - Remitted H. M. Ames sight draft on New York, for his net proceeds as above, less ½ % prem. - - - - Closed H. C. Wright's Const., and rendered % Sales of the same. Our charges not already entered, are: Commission on 1250 bbls.

*** Unless otherwise agreed, the net proceeds of sales on commission are payable in the currency of the place where the sales are effected. To send money to New York, which will be current there, we are obliged to pay ½ per ct. premium, and, as this is done at the request of the consignor, the premium is as much chargeable to him as the face of the draft.**

† As the carrier engages to deliver property in "good condition," he is responsible for any damage which may accrue through his neglect. The amount of damage, in this case, as agreed upon by the parties, is $10, which is deducted from the freight. The Commission Merchant owes it to his principal to guard against all losses which his vigilance may avert; and is, in fact, legally responsible for the result of oversight or negligence.

Salt, @ 6¢, $75. Net Proceeds credited H. C. Wright, to be paid upon collection of note for which property was sold. and which matures July 22.*

24. Procured Fire Insurance on 14,000 bush. Oats stored in Erie Warehouse, as requested by the consignors, to the value of $400, in Com. Mut. Ins. Co.; Policy No. 3210; paid premium on same, $10.50.† (J.; C. B.)

27. Paid Cash for our acceptance of T. Paxton's dft., dated May 24, due this day, $1,000. (C. B.) - - - - Closed T. Paxton's Const. of May 27 and 29, and rendered % Sales of same. Our charges not already posted are: Inspection, $57.50; Storage, $13.05; Insurance, $2.50; Commission, 2½ % on $1053.75. Net Proceeds to credit of Thos. Paxton. (S. B.)

29. Procured additional Fire Insurance for three months on property in warehouse to the value of $5000 Paid Premium, $25. (J.; C. B.)

30. Rec'd. of Gordon, McMillan & Co., Cash to balance %. (C. B.) - - - - Paid Warehouseman's wages thi month, $25; also, for extra labor, $6.50. (C. B.) - - - - Paid H. C. Wright, Cash to balance %, $1737.50, less $10.62 for interest on charges advanced.‡ - - - - Closed Cash Book and posted results. Cash on hand, $8611.71. Total Transportation paid this month, $1461.89; total Expense, $34.50. Also, entered in Journal, total sales credit not entered from Cash Book, as follows: Thos. Paxton, $1053.75; H. M. Ames, $750; do., $600; Baldwin & Payne, $3750; H. C. Wright, $2000. Total, $8153.75.

MEMORANDA OF TRANSACTIONS

TO BE WRITTEN UP BY THE STUDENT.

July 2. Rec'd, per Boat "Eagle," from R. M. Ashley, Cuyahoga Falls, 100 Bbls. Whiskey, for % of W. Deming & Co., which I refuse to sell. Paid Freight on same, $25, and placed it in store subject to owner's orders. - - - - - - - - Sold P. Anderson, from Monroe Mills Co.'s Const., 400 Bbls. "Monroe Extra" Flour, @ $8.30; 19 Bbls. A. Potter Fine Flour, @ $5:—from Baldwin & Payne's Const., 200 Bbls. Pearl Mills Flour, @ $8.00; 50 do. Pearl Mills Fine Flour, @ $4.90.

3. Sold for Cash, from H. Meek's Const., 100 Kegs Butter, 9120 ℔., @ 17¢. - - - - Rec'd, per Schooner "Coral," from Randall & Gilbert, Oswego, 8000 Bags Dairy Salt, ea. 20 ℔.; 5000 do., ea. 14 ℔. Paid Freight on same, 115 tons, @ $2.00 per ton.

5. Sold A. M. Perry & Co., from Monroe Mills Co.'s Const., 125 Bbls. Summit Mills Flour, @ $7.50. - - - - - Bo't for H. Meek, per his order, and paid Cash, Invoice of Mdse. amounting to $815.50, for which I charge him Commission @ 2½ % - - - - Rec'd, per C. C. & C. R. R., from New Orleans, via Cincinnati, for % Reynolds, Ely & Co., Chicago, 100 Hhds. Sugar. Paid Freight on same, $825; Drayage, $25. - - - - Sold for Cash, from Randall & Gilbert's Const., 3000 Bags 20 ℔ Salt, @ 13¢; 1000 do. 14 ℔ Salt, @ 10¢. - - - - Rec'd Cash of P. Anderson on % of Bill of Flour of 2d inst., $3415.

6. Sold for Cash, from Randall & Gilbert's Const., 5000 Bags 20 ℔ Salt, @ 12¢; 4000 do. 14 ℔ Salt, @ 10¢. - - - - Rec'd Cash of P. Anderson, for balance of Bill of Flour of 2d inst., $1845. - - - - Closed Randall & Gilbert's Const., and rendered them % Sales of same. Our charges not already entered, are Commission on Sales ($1490), @ 5%. Net proceeds to credit of Randall & Gilbert. - - - - Sold Randall & Gilbert, from Hinckley & Handy's Const., 14,000 Bush. Oats, @ 40¢. - - - - Rec'd Cash of Randall & Gilbert to balance %, $4414 50. - - - - Closed Hinckley & Handy's Const., and rendered them % Sales. Our Charges, not already posted, are, Interest on Advance Freight, $700, for 17 ds., @ 6 %, $1.98; Insurance, $10.50; Storage, Erie Warehouse bill, $140; Commission, 1¢ per Bush., $140. Net proceeds credited Hinckley & Handy.

---

* As this sale was made *on time*, at the instance of the consignor, he must wait for the net proceeds due him until the note matures.

† The plan of keeping a "Memorandum" account in the Ledger, after the manner of the one shown in this connection, is most admirable, and its general adoption in business would go far towards remedying the countless evils which grow out of a treacherous memory.

‡ There are two ways of making this entry; one, to be made entirely from the Cash Book, crediting Cash for the whole amount ($1737.50), and debiting it for the interest ($10.62); and the other to be divided between the Cash Book and Journal, debiting the party, and crediting Cash from the Cash-Book with the net amount paid ($1726.88), and debiting the party, and crediting Interest from the Journal for the abatement ($10.62). We prefer, and have adopted the former.

10. Rec'd Cash of A. M. Perry & Co., for Bill of Flour of 5th inst., $937.50. - - - - Sold for Cash from W. Lynn & Co.'s Const., 120 Pcs. Bacon, 3190 ℔., @ 9¢. - - - - Paid Cash for Hinckley's sight draft on us for $4607.52. - - - - Paid Cash for Erie Warehouse Bill of Storage, $140. - - - - Closed Monroe Mills Co.'s Consignment, and rendered % Sales of same. Our charges not already posted are, Storage, $16.32; Insurance, $10.88; Commission, $108.81. Net proceeds credited Monroe Mills Co., $4139.45. - - - - Closed Baldwin & Payne's Const., and rendered them % Sales. Our charges not already entered are, Interest on Advance Freight, 79¢; Storage, $7.50; Insurance, $4.61; Commission, $37.50. Net Proceeds to Baldwin & Payne's credit, $1598.35.

12. Paid Monroe Mills Co. Cash to balance %, $4139.45. - - - - Closed W. Lynn & Co.'s Const., and rendered them % Sales of same. Our charges not already entered are, Commission, @ 5%. including Storage and Insurance, $14.35. Net proceeds to their credit, $266.99. - - - - Purchased of Bradburn & Fisher, for Baldwin & Payne, as per order of the 10th inst., Invoice of Groceries, amounting to $1260. Charged 2½ % for my Commission.- - - - Sold W. Lynn & Co., from Reynolds, Ely & Co.'s Const., 2 Hhds. Selected Sugar, 2160 ℔., @ 8¢.

15. Sold Bradburn & Fisher (@ 4 mos.), from Reynolds, Ely & Co.'s Const., 50 Hhds. Sugar, 49,500 ℔., @ 7¢. - - - - Rec'd from Schr. Marquette, 500 Bbls. Fine Salt, to sell for % of vessel and owners. Advanced Cash on same, $500. - - - - Sold for Cash, from H. Meek's Const., 50 Kegs Butter, 5090 ℔., @ 17½¢.

16. Rec'd from Bradburn & Fisher, to balance %, their note, dated June 15, @ 4 mos., for $3465, payable at Merchants' Bank. - - - - Closed H. Meek's Const., and rendered % Sales of same. Our charges not already entered are, Commission (5 % including Storage and Insurance), $167.95. Net proceeds to H. Meek's credit.

19. Paid Bradburn & Fisher Cash for Bill of Groceries of 12th inst., 1260. - - - - Received by Teams from Ethan Allen Twinsburg, on % of Alling & Co., 119 Boxes Cheese. Transportation Chgs. paid by Consignor.

22. Rec'd Cash for R. T. Lyon's note, due this day, $2000.

26. Sold Reynolds, Ely & Co., from Alling & Co.'s Const., 119 Boxes Cheese, 4284 ℔., @ 9¢; also, purchased for them bill of Cheese, amounting to $1982, for Cash; my commission for purchasing, 2½ %, $49.55. - - - - Closed Alling & Co.'s Const., and rendered them % Sales. Our charges are for Commission, @ 5 %, $19.28. Net Proceeds to credit of Alling & Co.

29. Sold for Cash, from Schr. Marquette and Owner's Const., 250 Bbls. Fine Salt, @ $1.80. - - - - Paid Cash for Alling & Co.'s order fav. Gordon, McM. & Co. for net proceeds of Cheese, $366.28. - - - - Sold J. B. Woods, from Reynolds, Ely & Co.'s Const., 15 Hhds. Sugar, 12.825 ℔., @ 7½¢; also, from Schr. Marquette and Owner's Const., 250 Bbls. Salt, @ $1.80. - - - - Sold Gordon, McM. & Co., from Reynolds, Ely & Co.'s Const., 33 Hhds. Sugar, 28,215 ℔., @ 6¾¢. - - - - - Rec'd, per Schr. Lavinia, from Crawford & Co., Ogdensburg, for % of Hammond & Co., Crown Point, 150 Gro. tons. Pig Iron. Lake Freight, $218.40; previous charges, $353 Credited to Schr. Lavinia.

30. Procured Freight for Schr. Lavinia, amounting to $1455. Charged her 5 % commission.

31. Paid Cash to Schooner Lavinia, to balance %, $770.40. - - - - - Closed Schr. Marquette's Const., and rendered % Sales of same. Our charges are, for Storage, $15; Commission, 7¢ per Bbl., $35. Net Proceeds to credit, $850. - - - - Paid Schr. Marquette, to balance %, Cash, $345. Interest on advance, $5*. - - - - Paid Cash for Warehouseman's wages this month, $25; also, to H. Harvey, for rent of warehouse, 3 mos., $200. - - - Sent to Baldwin & Payne, Franklin, Ind., per express, Cash to balance %, $306.85. - - - - Prepaid my acceptance of H. Meek's draft, due Aug. 12, $1500. - - - - Credited H. Meek, $10.70, for balance of interest due him on current %. - - - - Paid Cash for draft on New York, and premium, and remitted same to H. Daw & Son, Buffalo, per order and for % of H. Meek. Face of draft, $814.43; premium, $11.25.

Memorandum.—Have this day discontinued business. Disposed of my lease to Coleman & Co., to have possession Aug. 1, and who take office furniture @ 5 % less than cost. - - - - Closed Cash Book, and posted results to Ledger. Total Transportation paid this month, $1105; Total Expense, $225; Balance Cash on Hand, $7003.28. Also, transferred to Journal the Sales not entered in Cash Book, as follows: Monroe Mills Co., $4352.50; Baldwin & Payne, $1845; Hinckley & Handy, $5600; Reynolds, Ely & Co., $6504.16; Schooner Marquette, $450; Alling & Co., $385.56.

---

* It is customary for Commission Merchants to *advance* on goods consigned to them: in other words, to lend the Consignor funds for which the goods are security. In all such cases, of course, it is proper to charge the Consignor with interest.

COMMISSION.

August 1. Rec'd Cash of Gordon, McMillan & Co., for balance of %, $1904.51. - - Rec'd Cash of J. B. Woods, for Bill of Sundries, 29th ult., $1411.87. - - - - Charged Coleman & Co., for Office Furniture, $268, less 5 %, $254.60; for sundry articles Stationery, $2.80. - - - - Closed Reynolds, Ely & Co.'s Const., and rendered % Sales of the same. Our charges not already entered are, Interest on Freight advanced, $3.56; Storage, $37.50; Insurance, $10.84; Commission, $162.60. Net Proceeds to their credit, $5439.68.

2. Paid Cash for W. Lynn & Co.'s sight draft, $94.19.

3. Rec'd Cash of T. Paxton, to balance %, $64.39. - - - - Sold Carpenter, Geary & Co., from Hammond & Co.'s Const., 150 Tons Pig Iron, @ $40, for which they are to pay charges already accrued in Cash, balance in six months.

4. Rec'd Cash for freight, $25, and storage, $10, on 100 Bbls. Whiskey, stored July 2, for W. Deming & Co., and now forwarded by their order to Buffalo. - - - - Rec'd Cash of Carpenter, Geary & Co., on % of Pig Metal purchased 3d inst., $758.90; also their note, dated Aug. 3, @ 6 mos., to the order Hammond & Co., for $5241.10. - - - - Closed Hammond & Co.'s Const., and rendered them % Sales of same. Our charges not already entered are, Storage, $75; Commission, $112.50. Net Proceeds to their credit, $5241.10. Remitted them in payment Carpenter, Geary & Co.'s note, as above.

7. Charged Coleman & Co. balance of Insurance Policy transferred, $50.

8. Rec'd Cash of Coleman & Co., to balance %, $307.40.

9. At Reynolds, Ely & Co.'s request, I have assumed Bradburn & Fisher's note, @ 4 mos., for $3465, received July 15, for 50 Hhds. Sugar, and have rendered them an % current. Balance of interest to their debit, $55.50.

10. Purchased for Cash, and remitted to Reynolds, Ely & Co., sight draft on New York to balance %. Face of draft, $2952.31; Premium, $14.76.

The following balances are carried to Loss and Gain %, viz.: *Debits*, Furniture, $13.40; Expense, $291.90 *Credits*, Insurance, $10.47; Commissions, $1855.30; Storage, $261.87; Interest, $66.75.

Statement of Business at Closing.

Resources.				
Cash on hand	8424	09		
Bills Receivable, due Nov. 18	3465		11889	09
Liabilities.				
Capital Stock at Commencement	10000			
Net Gain during Business	1889	09	11889	09

NOTE.—The natural order for the books of this set would be:

1. RECEIVING BOOK; 2. SALES BOOK; 3. CASH BOOK; 4. JOURNAL; 5. LEDGER.

An economical use of space has made it necessary to place the Journal *first*. However, as each book is distinct by itself, the order of preference is a matter of little importance.

JOURNAL,—COMMISSION.

Cleveland, May 19, 1861.

Fol.	Particulars	Dr. $	cts.	Cr. $	cts.
24	SCHR. LAVINIA To COMMISSION	42	50		
7	For procuring Cargo of Freight, of $850 @ 5%.			42	50
	— 28 —				
4	TRANSPORTATION To SCHR. LAVINIA . . .	108			
24	For Freight of 600 Bbls. Water Lime from Oswego, @ 18¢ .			108	
	— 29 —				
15	THOS. PAXTON To BILLS PAYABLE . . .	1000			
13	For acceptance of dft. of May 24, favor R. Gauson, @ 1 month from date (payable at our office, June 27)			1000	
	The above dft. is made against 100 Bbls. and 100 Hf. Bbls. Fish, received on Consignment.				
	— 31 —				
	Mem.—The following Sales on %, during the month, already debited to purchasers from Sales Book, are now posted to credit of Sales:				
	From Monroe Mills Co. . . . . . S. B. Folio 1, $3362.50				
	" H. Wetmore . . . . . . " " 2, 1104				
	" J. H. Luther . . . . . . " " 3, 775				
9	" Haughey & Byers . . . . " " 4, 4705.20 $9946.70				
	— **June 12** —				
31	H. M. AMES To N. SACKRIDER . . .	514	50		
30	For my draft on Sackrider remitted to Ames for proceeds of Water Lime, as per % Sales			514	50
	— " —				
33	H. MEEK To BILLS PAYABLE .	1500			
13	For acceptance of draft of June 9, @ 2 months from date, payable @ Commercial Bk., Aug. 12			1500	
	— 18 —				
4	TRANSPORTATION To SCHR. LAVINIA . . .	277	50		
	For Frt. of 500 Bbls. Water Lime, @ 18¢ $90				
24	" " " 1250 " " " " 187.50			277	50
	— 19 —				
24	SCHR. LAVINIA To COMMISSION	71	25		
7	For procuring Freight, of $1425 @ 5%			71	25
	— " —				
35	**Mem.**—Procured Insurance on 14000 Bush. Oats stored in Erie Warehouse, on a value of $4000, in Com. Mut. Ins. Co.—Policy No. 3210.				
	— 29 —				
35	**Mem.**—Procured additional Insurance on property in Warehouse to the to the amount of $5000, for 3 mo., in Home Ins. Co. of N. Y. Policy No. 2641.				
	— 30 —				
	Mem.—The following are the Sales on % for the month:				
	Thos. Paxton . . . . S. B. Folio 5, $1053.75				
	H. M. Ames . . . . " " 6, 1350				
	Baldwin & Payne . . . . . " " 8, 3750				
9	H. C. Wright . . . . . . " " 11, 2000 $8153.75				
		3513	75	3513	75

RECEIVING BOOK.

Cleveland, Ohio, May 12, 1861.

1861 May	12	% MONROE MILLS CO. Care H. B. TUTTLE, *Cleveland, O.*	**Canal Boat "S. Miller."** *From "Monroe Mills Co.," May* 10. 440 Bbls. Flour, "Monroe Mills Extra." 85 " " "Summit Mills." 25 " " "A. Potter." 550 Canal Frt. 17¢ ℔ Bbl. . . Rec'd Frt. May 12, ELI SHERMAN.			93	50	Sales. Fol. 1.
"	13	% HENRY WETMORE. *Cuyahoga Falls.*	**Canal Boat "Cuyahoga."** *From R. M. Ashley, Cuyah'a Falls, May* 11. 100 Bbls. Linseed Oil . . 35,000 lb Frt. 37½¢ ℔ Bbl. . . . . . Rec'd Frt. May 13, ISAAC LEWIS.			37	50	Sales. Fol. 2.
"	17	% of J. H. LUTHER. *Ashland, O.*	**C. C. & C. Rail Road.** *From New London.* 100 Bbls. Flour, "Ashland Mills." R. R. charges . . . . Drayage . . . . Charges paid per Receipt.	22 2	47 50	24	97	Sales. Fol. 3.
"	25	% HAUGHEY & BYERS, *Newark, O.*	**Canal Boat "Cataract."** *From Haughey & Byers, Newark, O., May* 19. 1915 Bush. Wheat. Freight 8½¢ ℔ Bush. . . . . Rec'd Frt. May 26, S. SWEEKART, Capt.			162	78	Sales. Fol. 4.
"	26	% of Shippers.	**Canal Boat "C. Delano."** *From Haughey & Byers, Newark, O., May* 17. 2000 Bush. Wheat. Canal Frt. 8½¢ ℔ Bush. . . . 6 Bush. over . . @ $1.20 Rec'd in full, W. WILSON, Master.	170 7	 20	177	20	Sales. Fol. 4.
"	27	% THOS. PAXTON, *Detroit, Mich.*	**Steamer "Ocean."** *From C. A. Trowbridge, Detroit, May* 26. 100 Bbls. White Fish. Lake Frt. 12½¢ ℔ Bbl. . . . Rec'd Frt. May 27, V. McDONALD, Clk.			12	50	Sales. Fol. 5.

RECEIVING BOOK.

Cleveland, Ohio, May 27, 1861.

1861								
May	27		**Schooner "Lavinia."**					
			From Ames & Merriam, Oswego, May 19.					
		% H. M. Ames,	600 Bbls. Water Lime.					
		Oswego, N. Y.	Frt. 18¢ ℔ Bbl.			108		Sales. Fol. 6
			Credited Schr. Lavinia, May 28.					
"	29		**Steamer "Ocean."**					
			From C. A. Trowbridge, Detroit, May 28.					
		% Thos. Paxton,	100 Hf. Bbls. White Fish.					
		Detroit, Mich.	Lake Frt. $6\frac{1}{4}$¢ ℔ Bbl.			6	25	Sales. Fol. 5.
			Rec'd Frt. May 29,					
			V. McDonald, Clk.					
June	5		**C. & P. Rail Road.**					
			From Akron, Ohio.					
		% J. B. Woods,	250 Bbls. Flour, "Phœnix Mills."					
		Akron, O.	Frt. 14¢ ℔ Bbl.	35				
			Drayage	6	25	41	25	Sales. Fol. 7.
			Charges paid per Receipt.					
"	6		**C. C. & C. Rail Road.**					
			From Baldwin & Payne, Franklin, Ind.					
		% Baldwin & Payne,	500 Bbls. Flour, "Pearl Mills."					
		Franklin, Ind.	Frt. to Union, 36¢ ℔ Bbl. . .	180				
			" from " 40¢ " " . . .	200				
			Drayage, $2\frac{1}{2}$¢ " " . . .	12	50	392	50	Sales. Fol. 8.
			Charges paid per Receipt.					
"	8		**Same.**					
		% of Same.	200 Bbls. Flour, "Pearl Mills."					
			50 " " "Fine."					
			250 R. R. Frt. to Union, 36¢ .	90				
			" " Cleve., 40¢ .	100				
			Drayage	6	25	196	25	Sales. Fol. 8.
"	"		**C. & P. Rail Road.**					
			From Akron, Ohio.					
		% of J. B. Woods,	50 Sacks Wool, ... 7500 lb					
		Akron, O.	R. R. Frt. 10¢ ℔ 100	7	50			
			Drayage, 5 loads	1	25	8	75	Sales. Fol. 7
			Paid per Receipt.					

RECEIVING BOOK.

Cleveland, Ohio, June 9, 1861.

1861 June	9	% H. Meek, *Coshocton, O.*	**Canal Boat "Tornado."** *From R. W. Thompson, Roscoe, June 8.* 200 Kegs Butter . . . . 22,410 lb Frt. 18¢ ℔ 100 . . . . . . Rec'd Freight, R. Welsh.			40	34	Sales. Fol. 9
"	15	% of Shippers.	**Canal Boat "S. Miller."** *From Monroe Mills Co., June 13.* 400 Bbls. Flour, "Monroe Mills Extra." 125 " " "Summit Mills." 19 " " "A. Potter." 544 Canal Frt. 16¢ ℔ Bbl. . .	87	04			
			10 Bbls. wet;—Damage appraised and deducted	10		77	04	Sales. Fol. 9.
			Rec'd in full, Eli Sherman.					
"	16	% W. Lynn & Co.,	**Canal Boat "Beacon."** *From A. F. Claypoole, Nashport, June 12.* 120 Pieces Bacon . . . . 3204 lb Frt. 18¢ ℔ 100 . . . . . . Rec'd Freight, J. M. Ten Eyck.			5	76	Sales. Fol. 10
"	18	% of H. M. Ames,	**Schooner "Lavinia."** *From Ames & Merriam, Oswego, June 10.* 500 Bbls. Water Lime. Frt. 18¢ ℔ Bbl.			90		Sales. Fol. 6.
"	"	% of Shippers.	**Same Vessel.** *From H. C. Wright, Oswego, June 11.* 250 Bbls. Coarse Salt. 1000 " Fine " 1250 Lake Frt. 15¢ ℔ Bbl. . . Credited Schr. Lavinia, June 19.	C. C.		187	50	Sales Fol. 11
"	19	% of Shippers. *Stored with F. Burnham in Erie Warehouse.*	**Schooner "Marquette."** *From Hinckley & Handy, Chicago, June 11.* 14,000 Bush. Oats. Lake Frt. 5¢ ℔ Bush. . . . . Rec'd Freight, June 21, E. Day, Master.			700		Sales. Fol. 12

1 Monroe Mills Co.—(*Akron, O.*)

			Bbls. Monroe Extra Flour.	Bbls. Summit Mills Flour.	Bbls. A. Pot'r Fine Flour.		L.F.				
1861											
May	12	Boat S. Miller	440	85	25	Transp., 17¢ ℘ Bbl.	4	93	50		
"	17					Storage, of 450 Bbls.	8	13	50		
"	"					Insurance, ¼ %	6	10	72		
"	"					Commission, 2½ %	7	107	19	224	91
"	"					Net Proceeds to Cr. May 17	22			4062	59
			440	85	25		9			4287	50
June	15	Boat S. Miller	400	125	19	Transp., $87.04; deduct $10		77	04		

2 Henry Wetmore.—(*Cuyahoga Falls, O.*)

			Bbls. Linseed Oil.								
1861											
May	13	Boat Cuyahoga	100			Transp., 37½¢ ℘ Bbl.	4	37	50		
"	24					Storage	8	8			
"	"					Insurance	6	9	14		
"	"					Expense (Cooperage)	5	2	50		
"	"					Commission, 2½ %	7	91	46	148	60
"	"					Net Proceeds, averaging as cash, May 18,	21			3509	68
			100				9			3658	28

3 J. H. Luther.—(*Ashland, O.*)

			Bbls. Ashl'd Mills Flour.								
1861											
May	17	C. C. & C. R. R.	100			Transp.	4	24	97		
"	24					Storage, 3¢ ℘ Bbl.	8	3			
"	"					Insurance,	6	1	94		
"	"					Commission, 2½ %	7	19	37	49	28
"	"					Net Proceeds to Cr. May 24	23			725	72
			100				9			775	00

4 Haughey & Byers.—(*Newark, O.*)

			Bush. Wheat.								
1861											
May	25	Boat Cataract	1915			Transp., 8½¢ ℘ Bush.	4	162	78		
"	26	" C. Delano	2000			Do. do.	4	170			
"	"		6	over		Paid Capt. & chgd. Consgrs.					
"	30					Commission, 1¢ ℘ Bush.	7	39	21	371	99
"	"					Net Proceeds to Cr. May 31	26			4333	21
			3921				8			4705	20

Monroe Mills Co. 1

			Bbls. Monroe Extra Flour.	Bbls. Summit Mills Flour.	Bbls. A. Pot Fine Flour.		L.F.	On Account.		Cash.		Total.	
1861													
May	12	P. Anderson	300			@ $8	15	2400					
"	"	A. M. Perry & Co.	40			" $8\frac{1}{8}$	16	325					
"	13	H. Steller		85		" $7\frac{1}{2}$	17	637	50				
"	"	Cash			25	" 5				125			
"	15	"	100			" 8				800			
			440	85	25			3362	50	925		4287	50

Henry Wetmore. 2

			Bbls. Linseed Oil.					L.F.	On Account.		Cash.		Total.	
1861														
May	14	Cash	10			403 Gals.	95¢				382	85		
"	"	Gaylord & Co.	30			1200 "	92¢	18	1104					
"	15	Cash	5			$201\frac{1}{2}$ "	95¢				191	43		
"	18	"	55			2200 "	90¢				1980			
			100						1104		2554	28	3658	28

J. H. Luther. 3

			Bbls. Ashl'd Mills Flour.				L.F.	On Account.		Cash.		Total.	
1861													
May	17	A. M. Perry	100			$7 75	16	775					
			100					775				775	

Haughey & Byers. 4

			Bush. Wheat.				L.F.	On Account.		Cash.		Total.	
1861													
May	25	C. Hickox	1915			$1 20	19	2298					
"	"	Harvey & Witt	2006				20	2407	20				
			3921					4705	20			4705	20

5 Thos. Paxton.—(*Detroit, Mich.*)

			Bbls. Fish.	Hf. Bls. Fish.			L.F.				
1861											
May	27	Steamer Ocean	100			Transp., 12½¢ ⅌ Bbl.	4	12	50		
"	29	Do.		100		Do. 6¼ "	4	6	25		
"	3	(On Inspection) over		1		Inspection	5	57	50		
June	27					Storage, 8¢ & 5¢	8	13	05		
"	"					Insurance on $1000	6	2	50		
"	"					Commission, 2½%	7	26	34	118	14
						Net Proceeds to Cr. June 12	25			935	61
			100	101			9			1053	75

6 H. M. Ames.—(*Oswego, N. Y.*)

			Bbls. Water Lime.								
1861											
May	27	Schr. Lavinia	600			Transp., 18¢ ⅌ Bbl.	4	108			
June	9					Expense (Cooperage)	3	3			
"	12					Storage, 8¢ ⅌ Bbl.	8	48			
"	"					Insurance	6	1	50		
"	"					Commission, 12½¢ ⅌ Bbl.	7	75		235	50
"	"					Net Proceeds to Cr. June 12	31			514	50
			600				9			750	
June	18	Schr. Lavinia	500			Transp., 18¢ ⅌ Bbl.	4	90			
"	20					Commission, 12½¢ ⅌ Bbl.	7	62	50	152	50
"	"					Net Proceeds to Cr. June 20	31			447	50
							9			600	

7 J. B. Woods.—(*Akron, O.*)

			Bbls. Phenix Flour.	Sacks Wool.							
1861											
June	5	C. & P. R. R.	250			Transp.	4	41	25		
"	8					Storage	8	7	50		
"	"					Insurance	6	2			
"	"					Commission, 2½%	7	51	31	102	06
"	"					Net Proceeds to Cr. June 8	12			1950	44
"	"	Same		50		Transp.	4	8	75		
"	19					Storage	8	7	50		
"	"					Insurance, ¼%	6	6	34		
"	"					Commission	7	72	50	95	09
						Net Proceeds to Cr. June 19	12			2442	41
			250	50			9			4590	

Thos. Paxton. 5

			Bbls. Fish.	Hf. Bls. Fish.			L.F.	On Account.		Cash.		Total.	
1861													
June	2	Gordon, McM. & Co.	51			White F. @ $8 00	29	408					
"	"	"		82		" " " 4 25	29	348	50				
"	6	"	49			Trout " 5 00	29	245					
"	"	"		19		" " 2 75	29	52	25				
			100	101				1053	75			1053	75

H. M. Ames. 6

			Bbls. Water Lime.				L.F.	On Account.		Cash.		Total.	
1861													
June	2	Hubby, Hughes & Co.	300			@ $1 25	27	375					
"	5	Bradburn & Fisher	300			" 1 25	23	375					
			600					750				750	
June	19	Gordon, McM. & Co.	500			F'm ves'l, @ $1 20	29	600					
			500					600				600	

J. B. Woods. 7

			Bbls. Phenix Flour.	Sacks Wool.			L.F.	On Account.		Cash.		Total.	
1861													
June	8	Cash	200			@ $8 20				1640			
"	"	"	50			" 8 25				412	50	2052	50
"	19	"		50		7250 lb " 35¢				2537	50	2537	50
			250	50						4590		4590	

8 Baldwin & Payne.—(*Franklin, Ind.*)

			Bbls. Pearl Flour.	Bbls. Fine Flour.							
1861											
June	6	C. C. & C. R. R.	500			Transp.	4	392	50		
"	12					Commission, 15¢ ℔ Bbl.	7	75		467	50
"	"					Net Proceeds to Cr. June 12	32			3282	50
"	8		500				9			3750	
June	8	Same	200	50		Transp.		196	25		

9 H. Meek.—(*Coshocton, O.*)

			Kegs Butter.								
1861											
June	19	Boat Tornado	200			Transp.		40	34		

10 W. Lynn & Co.—(*Nashport, O.*)

			Pieces Bacon.								
1861											
June	6	Boat Beacon	120			Transp.		5	76		

11 H. C. Wright.—(*Oswego, N. Y.*)

			Bbls. Coarse Salt.	Bbls. Fine Salt.							
1861											
June	18	Schr. Lavinia	250	1000		Transp., 15¢ ℔ Bbl.	4	187	50		
"	20					Commission	7	75		262	50
						Net Proceeds to Cr. June 20	34			1737	50
			250	1000		As Cash, when note is due	9			2000	

12 Hinckley & Handy.—(*Chicago, Ill.*)

			Bush. Oats.								
1861											
June	19	Schr. Marquette	14000			Transp.		700			

Baldwin & Payne. 8

			Bbls. Pearl Flour.	Bbls. Fine Flour.				On Account.	Cash.	Total.
1861 June	8	N. Sackrider	500			From Cars, $7 50	30	3750		3750
			500					3750		3750

H. Meek. 9

			Kegs Butter.							
1861 June	19	Cash	50			5100 ℔ @ 18¢			918	

W. Lynn & Co. 10

			Pieces Bacon.							

H. C. Wright. 11

			Bbls. Coarse Salt.	Bbls. Fine Salt.						
1861 June	19	Bills Receivable	250			R. T. Lyon n. Jn. 19 @ 1 mo. for $2000	14	2000		
	"	" "		1000						
			250	1000				2000		2000

Hinckley & Handy. 12

			Bush. Oats.							

Cleveland, May, 1861.——Receipts.

1861				LF.	General.		Sales.	
May	1	*Cash, Dr.*	*To Sundries*					
	"	Capital Stock	Amt. Invested	1	10000			
	13	Sales	Monroe Mills Co.'s Const.				125	
	14	"	H. Wetmore's "				382	85
	"	P. Anderson	Bill of Flour, 12th inst.	14	2400			
	15	Sales	Monroe Mills Co.'s Const.				800	
	"	"	H. Wetmore's "				191	43
	17	A. M. Perry & Co.	Bill of Flour, 12th inst.	16	325			
	"	H. Steller	" " 13th "	17	637	50		
	18	Gaylord & Co.	" Oil, 14th "	15	1104			
	"	Sales	H. Wetmore's Const.				1980	
	21	A. M. Perry & Co.	Bill of Flour, 17th inst.	16	775			
	30	C. Hickox	" Wheat, 25th "	19	2298			
	"	Harvey & Witt	" " 26th "	20	2407	20		
		SALES	*Total for the Month*	9	3479	28	3479	28
			Total Cash Received	11	23425	98		
					23425	**98**		

BOOK.

Cleveland, May, 1861.——Disbursements.

1861				L.F.	General.		Transp.		Expenses.	
May	1	*Sundries, Dr.* . .	. *To Cash*							
	"	Furniture . . .	. Office Furniture, per Bill .	2	38					
	3	Expense. . . .	. Stationery, etc.						9	95
	"	Furniture . . .	. Iron Safe	2	230					
	4	Expense. . . .	. Sundry Items, per P. C. B. .						3	25
	12	Transportation	. Monroe Mills Co.'s Const. .				93	50		
	"	Insurance . . .	. Prem. on $5000	6	75					
	13	Transportation	. H. Wetmore's Const. . . .				37	50		
	17	"	. J. H. Luther's "				24	97		
	19	H. Wetmore . .	. Paid st. dft. fav. A. Gray .	21	1400					
	21	Monroe Mills Co.	" " " " H. B. Hurlbut	22	2000					
	25	Transportation	. Haughey & Byers' Const. .				162	78		
	"	"	. " " " .				170			
	"	Haughey & Byers	6 Bush. over—Paid Capt. .	26	7	20				
	"	Expense. . . .	. Cooperage						2	50
	26	H. Wetmore . .	. Paid st. dft. fav. E. Comstock	21	2200					
	"	J. H. Luther . .	. Remitted to Balance % . .	23	725	72				
	27	Transportation	. Paxton's Const.				12	50		
	29	"	. " "				6	25		
	31	Inspection . . .	" "	5	57	50				
	"	Expense. . . .	. Warehouseman's Wages . .						25	
	"	EXPENSE . . .	. *Total for the Month* . . .	3	40	70			40	70
	"	TRANSPORTATION.	" " . . .	4	507	50	507	50		
			Total Cash Paid	11	7281	62				
			Balance on hand		16144	36				
					23425	98				

Cleveland, June, 1861.——Receipts.

1861				LF.	General.		Sales.	
June	1	*Cash Dr.*	*To Sundries*					
	2	H. Wetmore	Dft. on him to Balance % . . .	21	90	32		
	8	Sales	J. B. Woods' Const.				1640	
	"	"	" " "				412	50
	9	Hubby, Hughes & Co.	Bill of Water Lime, 2d inst. . .	27	375			
	12	Bradburn & Fisher .	" " " 5th inst. . .	28	375			
	"	Gordon, McM. & Co. .	" Fish, due this day . . .	29	1053	75		
	"	N. Sackrider	Dft. on him fav. T. P. Handy, Cash	30	3235	50		
	19	Sales	J. B. Woods' Const.				2537	50
	30	"	H. Meeks' "				918	
	"	Gordon, McM. & Co. .	To Balance %	29	600			
	"	Interest	Discount on H. C. Wright's %, $1737.50, 10% off at his request	10	10	62		
	"	SALES	*Total for the Month*	9	5508		5508	00
			Total Cash received	11	11248	19		
			Balance on hand from May . . .		16144	36		
					27392	**55**		

Cleveland, June, 1861.——Disbursements.

1861				L.F.	*General.*		*Transp.*		*Expenses*	
June	1	*Sundries* Dr. .	. To Cash							
	5	Monroe Mills Co. .	Pd. st. dft. for T. P. Handy .	22	2062	59				
	"	Transportation	. J. B. Woods' Const. . . .				41	25		
	6	"	. Baldwin & Payne's do. . .				392	50		
	8	Haughey & Byers	Pd. st. dft. for H. B. Hurlbut	26	2116	07				
	"	"	. Remitted R. Mead & Co. . .	26	2198	95				
	"	"	. Exchange on above ½ %. .	26	10	99				
	"	Transportation	. Baldwin & Payne's Const. .				196	25		
	"	"	. J. B. Woods' " .				8	75		
	9	"	. H. Meeks' " .				40	34		
	"	Expense . . .	. Cooperage						3	
	12	J. B. Woods .	. Remitted J. A. Carlton . .	12	1500					
	15	Transportation	. Monroe Mills Co.'s Const. .				77	04		
	16	Baldwin & Payne	Remitted per Express . .	32	3282	50				
	"	Transportation	. W. Lynn & Co.'s Const. . .				5	76		
	19	"	. Hinkley & Handy's Const. .				700			
	"	J. B. Woods .	. To Balance %	12	2892	85				
	20	H. M. Ames .	. Remitted dft. to N. Y. . .	31	445	28				
	"	"	. Exchange on same ½ % . .	31	2	22				
	24	Insurance . . .	. On Hinkley & Handy's Oats	6	10	50				
	27	Bills Payable .	. Accepted T. Paxton's Dft. .	13	1000					
	29	Insurance . . .	. Additional on Prop. in Store	6	25					
	30	Expense . . .	. Warehouseman's Wages . .						25	
	"	" . . .	. Extra Labor						6	50
	"	H. C. Wright .	. Amount due July 22 . . .	34	1737	50				
	"	EXPENSE . . .	. *Total for the Month* . . .	3	34	50			34	50
	"	TRANSPORTATION.	" " . . .	4	1461	89	1461	89		
			Total Cash Paid	11	18780	84				
			Balance on hand		8611	71				
					27392	55				

LEDGER,—COMMISSION.

1 Capital Stock.

							1861						
							May	1	By Cash invested	C. B.	1	10000	

2 Furniture.

1861													
May	1	To Sundries	C. B.	1	38								
"	3	" Safe	C. B.	1	230								

3 Expense.

1861							1861						
May	31	To Cash	C. B.	1	40	70	May	24	By H. Wetmore's Const.	S. B.	1	2	50
June	30	" "	C. B.	2	34	50	June	12	" H. M. Ames' "	S. B.	6	3	

4 Transportation.

1861							1861						
May	28	To Schr. Lavinia	J.	1	108		May	17	By Monroe Mills Const.	S. B.	1	93	50
"	31	" Cash	C. B.	1	507	50	"	24	" Luther's "	S. B.	3	24	97
June	18	" Schr. Lavinia	J.	1	277	50	"	"	" Wetmore's "	S. B.	2	37	50
"	30	" Cash	C. B.	2	1461	89	"	30	" Haughey & B.'s "	S. B.	4	170	
							"	31	" Do. "	S. B.	4	162	78
							June	8	" J. B. Woods' "	S. B.	7	41	25
							"	12	" H. M. Ames' "	S. B.	6	108	
							"	"	" Baldwin & P.'s "	S. B.	8	392	50
							"	19	" J. B. Woods' "	S. B.	7	8	75
							"	"	" H. M. Ames' "	S. B.	6	90	
							"	20	" H. C. Wright's "	S. B.	11	187	50
							"	27	" T. Paxton's, 12.50; 6.25,	S. B.	5	18	75

5 Inspection.

1861							1861						
May	31	To Cash	C. B.	1	57	50	June	27	By Paxton's Const.	S. B.	2	57	50

6 Insurance.

1861							1861						
May	12	To Cash	C. B.	1	75		May	17	By Monroe Mills Const.	S. B.	1	10	72
June	24	" "	C. B.	2	10	50	"	24	" Luther's "	S. B.	3	1	94
"	29	" "	C. B.	2	25		"	"	" Wetmore's "	S. B.	2	9	14
							June	8	" J. B. Woods' "	S. B.	7	2	
							"	12	" H. M. Ames' "	S. B.	6	1	50
							"	19	" J. B. Woods' "	S. B.	7	6	34
							"	27	" Paxton's "	S. B.	5	2	50

Commission. 7

				$	cts.					$	cts.
						1861					
						May	17	By Monroe Mills Const. S. B.	1	107	19
						"	19	" Schr. Lavinia J.	1	42	50
						"	24	" J. H. Luther's Const. S. B.	3	19	37
						"	"	" Wetmore's " S. B.	2	91	46
						"	30	" Haughey & B.'s " S. B.	4	39	21
						June	8	" J. B. Woods' " S. B.	7	51	31
						"	12	" H. M. Ames' " S. B.	6	75	
						"	"	" Baldwin & P.'s " S. B.	8	75	
						"	19	" Schr. Lavinia J.	1	71	25
						"	"	" J. B. Woods' Const. S. B.	7	72	50
						"	20	" H. M. Ames' " S. B.	6	62	50
						"	"	" H. C. Wright's " S. B.	11	75	
						"	27	" Thos. Paxton's " S. B.	5	26	34
								808 63			

Storage. 8

				$	cts.					$	cts.
						1861					
						May	17	By Monroe Mills Const. S. B.	1	13	50
						"	24	" Luther's " S. B.	3	3	
						"	"	" Wetmore's " S. B.	2	8	
						June	8	" J. B. Woods' " S. B.	7	7	50
						"	12	" H. M. Ames' " S. B.	6	48	
						"	19	" J. B. Woods' " S. B.	7	7	50
						"	27	" Thos. Paxton's " S. B.	5	13	05
								100 55			

Sales. 9

				$	cts.					$	cts.
1861						1861					
May	17	To Monroe Mills Const. S. B.	1	4287	50	May	31	By Cash Sales C. B.	1	3479	28
"	24	" J. H. Luther's " S. B.	3	775		"	"	" Other " J.	1	9946	70
"	"	" H. Wetmore's " S. B.	2	3658	28	June	30	" Cash Sales C. B.	2	5508	
"	28	" Haughey & B.'s " S. B.	4	4705	20	"	"	" Other " J.	1	8153	75
June	12	" H. M. Ames' " S. B.	6	750				27087 73			
"	"	" Baldwin & P.'s " S. B.	8	3750							
"	19	" J. B. Woods' " S. B.	7	4590							
"	20	" H. M. Ames' " S. B.	6	600							
"	"	" H. C. Wright's " S. B.	11	2000							
"	27	" Thos. Paxton's " S. B.	5	1053	75						
		26169 73									

Interest. 10

				$	cts.					$	cts.
						1861					
						June	30	By Cash C. B.	2	10	62

Cash. 11

				$	cts.					$	cts.
1861						1861					
May	31	To Sundries this mo. C. B.	1	23425	98	May	31	By Sundries this mo. C. B.	1	7281	62
June	30	" " " " C. B.	2	11248	19	June	30	" " " " C. B.	2	18780	84
		34674 17						26062 46			

12 J. B. Woods.

1861							1861						
June	12	To Cash	C. B.	2	1500		June	8	By Net Proceeds	S. B.	7	1950	44
"	19	" "	C. B.	2	2892	85	"	19	" " "	S. B.	7	2442	41
			4392 85							4392 85			

13 Bills Payable.

1861							1861						
June	27	To Thos. Paxton's Dft.	C. B.	2	1000		May	29	By Thos. Paxton's Dft.	J.	1	1000	
							June	12	" H. Meek's "	J.	1	1500	
										2500 00			

14 Bills Receivable.

1861													
June	19	To R. T. Lyon's note	S. B.	11	2000								

15 P. Anderson.

1861							1861						
May	12	To 300 Bbls. Flour	S. B.	1	2400		May	14	By Cash	C. B.	1	2400	

16 A. M. Perry & Co.

1861							1861						
May	12	To 40 Bbls. Flour	S. B.	1	325		May	17	By Cash	C. B.	1	325	
"	17	" 100 " "	S. B.	3	775		"	21	" "	C. B.	1	775	

17 Henry Steller.

1861							1861						
May	13	To 85 Bbls. Flour	S. B.	1	637	50	May	17	By Cash	C. B.	1	637	50

18 Gaylord & Co.—*City.*

1861							1861						
May	14	To 30 Bbls. Lins. Oil	S. B.	2	1104		May	18	By Cash	C. B.	1	1104	

19 C. Hickox.—*City.*

1861							1861						
May	25	To 1915 Bush. Wheat	S. B.	4	2298		May	29	By Cash	C. B.	1	2298	

LEDGER,—COMMISSION.

Harvey & Witt.—*City.* 20

1861 May	26	To 2006 Bush. Wheat	S. B.	4	2407	20	1861 May	30	By Cash	C. B.	1	2407	20

Henry Wetmore.—*Cuyahoga Falls, O.* 21

1861							1861						
May	19	To paid your draft	C. B.	1	1400		May	24	By Net Proceeds	S. B.	2	3509	68
"	26	" Cash	C. B.	1	2200		June	2	" Dft. on you	C. B.	2	90	32

Monroe Mills Co.—*Akron, O.* 22

1861							1861						
May	21	To paid your Draft	C. B.	1	2000		May	17	By Net Proceeds	S. B.	1	4062	59
June	5	" " " "	C. B.	2	2062	59							

J. H. Luther.—*Ashland, O.* 23

1861 May	26	To Cash	C. B.	1	725	72	1861 May	24	By Net Proceeds	S. B.		725	72

Schr. Lavinia. 24

1861							1861						
May	19	To Commissions	J.	1	42	50	May	28	By Transportation	J.	1	108	
June	19	" "	J.	1	71	25	June	18	" "	J.	1	277	50
		113 75							385 50				

Thos. Paxton. 25

1861 May	29	To Bills Payable	J.	1	1000		1861 June	27	By Net Proceeds Fish,	S. B.	5	935	61

Haughey & Byers.—*Newark, O.* 26

1861							1861						
May	26	To 6 Bush. Wheat,	C. B.	1	7	20	May	30	By Net Proceeds	S. B.	4	4333	21
June	18	" paid your draft	C. B.	2	2116	07							
"	"	" Cash, $2198.95; 10.99	C. B.	2	2209	94							
		4333 91											

Hubby, Hughes & Co.—*City.* 27

1861 June	2	To 300 Bbls. Lime	S. B.	6	375		1861 June	9	By Cash	C. I	2	375	

28 Bradburn & Fisher.—*City.*

Date	Day	Particulars	Ref.	Fol.	$	cts.	Date	Day	Particulars	Ref.	Fol.	$	cts.
1861 June	5	To 300 Bbls. Lime	S. B.	6	375		1861 June	12	By Cash	C. B.	2	375	

29 Gordon, McMillan & Co.—*City.*

Date	Day	Particulars	Ref.	Fol.	$	cts.	Date	Day	Particulars	Ref.	Fol.	$	cts.
1861 June	2	To Bill of Fish	S. B.	5	756	50	1861 June	12	By Cash	C. B.	1	1053	75
"	6	" " " "	S. B.	5	297	25	"	"	" "	C. B.	2	600	
"	19	" " " Lime	S. B.	6	600								
		1653 75							1653 75				

30 N. Sackrider.—*Ogdensburg, N. Y.*

Date	Day	Particulars	Ref.	Fol.	$	cts.	Date	Day	Particulars	Ref.	Fol.	$	cts.
1861 June	8	To 500 Bbls. Flour	S. B.	8	3750		1861 June	12	By Dft. fav. H. M. Ames	J.	1	514	50
							"	"	" " " Handy	C. B.	2	3235	50
									3750 00				

31 H. M. Ames.—*Oswego, N. Y.*

Date	Day	Particulars	Ref.	Fol.	$	cts.	Date	Day	Particulars	Ref.	Fol.	$	cts.
1861 June	12	To Dft. on N. Sackrider	J.	1	514	50	1861 June	12	By Net Proceeds	S. B.	6	514	50
"	20	" " " N.Y. & Exch.	C.B.	2	447	50	"	20	" " "	S. B.	6	447	50

32 Baldwin & Payne.—*Franklin, Ind.*

Date	Day	Particulars	Ref.	Fol.	$	cts.	Date	Day	Particulars	Ref.	Fol.	$	cts.
1861 June	16	To Cash	C. B.	2	3282	50	1861 June	12	By Net Proceeds	S. B.	8	3282	50

33 H. Meek.—*Coshocton.*

Date	Day	Particulars	Ref.	Fol.	$	cts.	Date	Day	Particulars	Ref.	Fol.	$	cts.
1861 June	12	To Bills Payable	J.	1	1500								

34 H. C. Wright.—*Oswego, N. Y.*

Date	Day	Particulars	Ref.	Fol.	$	cts.	Date	Day	Particulars	Ref.	Fol.	$	cts.
1861 June	30	To Cash	C. B.	2	1737	50	1861 June	20	By Net Proceeds	S. B.	11	1737	50

35 Memoranda.

Date	Day	Particulars	Ref.	Fol.	$	cts.	Date	Day	Particulars	Ref.	Fol.	$	cts.
1861 Nov.	19	Insurance on Oats	J.	1									
"	29	Do. " Property	J.	1									

ACCOUNTS SALES.

The following are presented as among the best forms for Accounts Sales. These are rendered to the Consignor immediately upon the closing out of each Consignment. The average time of payment is given as the *date* of the credit of the net proceeds.

The student should be required to render a similar Account for each Consignment.

Account Sales of 550 Bbls. Flour, per Canal Boat "S. Miller," for % and risk of Monroe Mills Co., Akron, O.

			Bbls. Monroe Extra.	Bbls. Summit Mills.	Bbls. A. Pot'r Fine.					
1861										
May	12	P. Anderson	300			@ $8	2400			
"	"	A. M. Perry & Co.	40			" $8\frac{1}{8}$	325			
"	13	H. Steller		85		" $7\frac{1}{2}$	637	50		
"	"	Cash			25	" 5	125			
"	15	"	100			" 8	800		4287	50
			440	85	25					
		Charges.								
May	12	Transportation, 550 Bbls., @ 17¢					93	50		
		Storage of 450 Bbls., @ 3¢					13	50		
		Insurance, $\frac{1}{4}$ %					10	72		
		Commission, $2\frac{1}{2}$ %					107	19	224	91
		Net Proceeds to Cr., May 17							4062	59

Account Sales of 100 Bbls. and 101 Hf. Bbls. Fish, per Str. "Ocean," for % and risk of Thos. Paxton, Detroit.

			Bbls. Fish.	Hf. Bls. Fish.					
1861									
June	2	Gordon, McMillan & Co.	51		@ $8	408			
"	"	" "		82	" $4\frac{1}{4}$	348	50		
"	6	" "	49		" 5	245			
"	"	" "		19	" $2\frac{3}{4}$	52	25	1053	75
			100	101					
		Charges.							
May	27	Transportation, $12\frac{1}{2}$¢ per Bbl.; $6\frac{1}{4}$¢ per Hf. Bbl.				18	75		
"	"	Inspection				57	50		
June	27	Storage, 8¢ and 5¢				13	05		
		Insurance on $1000				2	50		
		Commission, $2\frac{1}{2}$ %				26	34	118	14
		Net Proceeds to Cr., June 12						935	61

FORWARDING:

EMBRACING

RECEIVING BOOK, CASH BOOK, AND LEDGER

TOGETHER WITH THE MOST APPROVED FORMS OF

WAREHOUSE RECEIPTS, BILLS OF LADING, Etc.,

WITH FULL INSTRUCTIONS

CONCERNING THE DETAILS OF THE BUSINESS.

FORWARDING.

A FORWARDER is an agent for the transshipment and delivery of goods. His place of business is usually at the termini of various Transportation lines, and his principal duties are to *receive* goods from one line and *deliver to* another, or to the owner or consignee, direct, charging a commission for his services. To conduct the business properly, he must have dockage and warehouse room, where property will be safe while *in transitu*, or may be stored during the pleasure of the owner or consignee. The general rates for handling and storing goods are fixed by usage, and are as uniform as rates of commission, insurance, etc.

All persons engaged in the Forwarding or Transportation of property, are held by law responsible for its delivery to the proper parties in as good order and condition as when received (except for decay of perishable articles, or for acts which their watchfulness could not have prevented), and this must be done without unnecessary delay. It becomes necessary, therefore, that a systematic record be kept, which will show at a glance from whom, when, and in what condition, each article was received, and to whom, when, and in what condition delivered.

The FORWARDER and the CARRIER has each a lien on the property while in his possession, for all necessary and equitable charges which may have accrued thereon, including a proper remuneration for his own care, labor, and responsibility.

If either voluntarily parts with the possession of the goods, he loses his lien, and is not authorized by law to reclaim them: but if he has been induced to part with possession by false and fraudulent representations, such delivery will not amount to a waiver of his lien. So, also, a lien may be created and retained after delivery, *by agreement of the parties.*

The books necessary for the Forwarder (beside the Journal, Cash Book, and Ledger, which are incident to all departments of business) are as follows:

RECEIVING BOOK,
WAREHOUSE DELIVERY,
VESSEL DELIVERY,
RAIL ROAD DELIVERY,
CANAL DELIVERY.
} at places where these respective modes of transportation exist.

The RECEIVING BOOK is that upon which the first entries are made, and exhibits all property received, specifying the quality, condition, from whom received, to whom destined, and all charges thereon. The entries in this book are made from the Bills of Lading (B/L), and are in all essential particulars transcripts of those bills. Any additions of our own, such as our own charges, and remarks as to the condition and delivery of the property, are made in red ink, that they may be readily distinguishable.

If any articles are shipped to the Forwarder noted on the B/L as in "bad order," or "damaged," it must be similarly noted on the Receiving Book. These entries being in *black ink*, will be easily distinguished from the notings of "damages" and "bad order" discovered while receiving the property, which should be written in *red ink*, and for which the Forwarder should hold the Carrier responsible.

All amounts paid for freight, drayage, and other charges, which have accrued upon the property before receiving it may be charged to Transportation %; and when the property is delivered and the amounts refunded, Transportation should be credited. Thus, when all the property is delivered or forwarded, and the charges collected, Transportation % will balance. The excess of the debit side of this account, when it does not balance will represent the advances made by the Forwarder on property which he still holds.

The Forwarder's own charges for doing the business are frequently called "our charges," and when anything is realized in this way, a special account should be credited, which will show the earnings of the business. This account is variously designated "Storage," "Dockage," "Charges," "Forwarding," "Storage and Forwarding," etc. We have selected the term "Charges" as being both brief and comprehensive. The credit side of Charges % will show what has been produced by handling and storing goods, and the debit side the cost to us of the labor and facilities necessary to do the business.

Insurance % is used to represent what we have advanced for the insurance of goods passing through our hands, which sums are to be refunded by the owner or consignee. This account, like Transportation, will balance, when the transactions giving rise to its entries are complete; or, in other words, when our advances are refunded.

The transactions in this set comprise a month's business, and are intended to embrace as much of a variety as possible. The business itself, like all special departments of trade, is monotonous, the transactions of one day being nearly a duplicate of those of any other.

The only books shown entire are the Receiving Book, the Cash Book, and the Ledger. The Cash Book contains all the entries that are to appear upon the Ledger, and may be said to embrace the functions of the Cash Book and Journal. The Ledger differs somewhat from the preceding Ledgers in this treatise, in the form of the Entry. It is not closed, but presents at a glance, the result of the business.

To give the student as correct an idea as possible of the regular routine of receiving and delivering goods, we will take one transaction, and follow it carefully through all its entries. Let it be the first in order upon the Receiving Book, relating to the coffee received by the Propeller Cataract.

The clerk of the propeller hands us a B/L, of which the following (except the receipt across its face in red ink) is an exact copy:

No. 35. Buffalo, N. Y., *April 30, 1861.*

Shipped, *In good order and well conditioned, by* **THE AMERICAN TRANSPORTATION COMPANY,** *as Agents and Forwarders, for account and risk of whom it may concern, on board the* Propeller Cataract, Duncan, *Master, now lying in the Port of* Buffalo, *and bound for* Cleveland, O., *the following articles, marked and numbered as in the margin, and which are to be delivered in like good order and condition, (the dangers of navigation, fires and collision excepted,) without delay unto Consignees as per margin, or to* their *assigns at* Cleveland, O., they *paying freight.*

In witness whereof, *the Master of said Vessel hath affirmed unto* two *Bills of Lading, all of this tenor and date, one of which being accomplished, the other to stand void. Property on deck at risk of vessel and owners.*

G. McM. & Co.							
GORDON, McMILLAN & Co.,	120 Bags Rio Coffee	14.460					
Cleveland, O.	Freight from N. Y. to Cleveland .		35			50	61
	Amer. Transp. Co.,						
	per NELSON.						

Rec'd May 1, *and paid freight $50.61.*
BRYANT & STRATTON.

From this we copy, in our Receiving Book, enough of the *exact words* to express, and ever afterwards to show, all essential information, *viz.*, by what conveyance the coffee was received, who consigned it to us, at what date, to whom destined, the quantity and kind of property, weight, and rate of freight to be paid thereon, etc. (See Receiving Book entry.) A memorandum of the quantity and marks is then made in the Tally Book of our dock clerk, who proceeds to note (while the coffee is being landed) whether the quantity is correct, and every bag in good order. Upon his report that all is correct, we pay the freight ($50.61), which we charge to Transportation %, in our Cash Book (see entry), and the clerk acknowledges the payment by his signature on the Receiving Book.

As it is necessary that the Propeller shall preserve a voucher that it has properly delivered the property to us, we acknowledge its receipt by writing (with red ink generally) across the face of the Bill of Lading, "Rec'd, May 1 1861, and paid freight, $50.61, Bryant & Stratton," and return the B/L to the clerk.

DELIVERY TO VESSELS.

The 3 boat-loads of corn, received from Chillicothe, and consigned to H. Daw & Son, Buffalo, N. Y., must be shipped by vessel. For this purpose we bargain with the master of the Schr. Ironsides for freight of same to Buffalo, at 4 cents per bushel. We hand him our order on the Erie Warehouse (where the corn was stored) for the quantity—5761 bushels. When he has received it on board, we give him a bill of lading, as follows:

No. 127. Cleveland, Ohio, *May 7, 1861.*

Shipped, *In good order and well conditioned, by* **BRYANT & STRATTON,**

as Agents and Forwarders, for account and risk of whom it may concern, on board the Schr. Ironsides, Grover, *Master, now lying in the Port of* Cuyahoga, *and bound for* Buffalo, *the following articles, marked and numbered as in the margin, and which are to be delivered in like good order and condition, (the dangers of navigation, fires and collision excepted,) without delay unto Consignees as per margin, or to* their *assigns at* Buffalo, they *paying freight.*

In witness whereof, *the Master of said Vessel hath affirmed unto* two *Bills of Lading, all of this tenor and date, one of which being accomplished, the other to stand void. Property on deck at risk of vessel and owners.*

H. Daw & Son,	5761 Bushels Corn.				
Buffalo, N. Y.	Freight to Cleveland	691	60		
	Erie Warehouse storage . . . . 1¢	57	61		
For % of J. Madeira,	Our charges . . . . 1¢	57	61		
Chillicothe, O.					
	For which we have made our Dft. at 3 days' sight			806	82
	Captain collect Lake Freight only, 4¢ per bush.				
	Bryant & Stratton.				

A duplicate of the above is made in our Shipping Book, which is signed by the captain, and which is our voucher for the proper shipment of the property. He also signs another, precisely similar, which we mail to Daw & Son, as notice to them.

If the captain had been in possession of sufficient funds to have paid the charges on the corn, he might have done so, and collected them with his freights at Buffalo, but this not being the case, we draw on the consignees for the charges, and the captain is to collect only his freight.

WAREHOUSE DELIVERY.

The party (Gordon, McMillan & Co.) to whom the coffee is destined being city residents, are notified of its arrival, and send an order for its delivery to their drayman. In doing so, the number of the bags is tallied as they pass out from our possession. The written order of Gordon, McMillan & Co., retained by us, is our voucher for its having been delivered to them; but we may also require a more formal receipt, as in a form given below.

We may, if we choose, require payment of all charges accumulated before delivery, which would, in this instance, be the freight $50.61, and " our charges" for receiving, paying freight, storage, (if any,) and delivery, which charges vary in different localities, or by special agreement, but are generally $1 per ton.

Theoretically, the business is done strictly for cash, but, practically, short credits arise with responsible parties, or those with whom we have reciprocal transactions. Connecting transportation companies or lines keep an open account with each other, and settle weekly or monthly.

In this instance the charges were paid to us, at the time, which were credited as follows:

Transportation %, charges of G., McM. & Co.	$50 61
Charges %, our charges, ...	7 23

A common form of receipt for property delivered is as follows:

Cleveland, Ohio, May 3, 1861.

Received *of* BRYANT & STRATTON, *in good order, and paid charges thereon.*

Marks.	Articles.	Weight.	Charges.			
G. McM. & Co.	120 Bags Rio Coffee	14.460				
	Freight from N. Y.		50	61		
	Cleveland charges		7	23		
	GORDON, MCMILLAN & Co.				57	84

They also requre, from us, a receipt for the payment of the charges, which is usually in a form similar to the following:

Cleveland, Ohio, May 3, 1861.

Delivered *to* GORDON, McMILLAN & CO., *in good order, for which they have paid the charges thereon.*

Marks.	Articles.	Weight.	Charges.			
G. McM. & Co.	120 Bags Rio Coffee	14.460				
	Prop. Cataract charges		50	61		
	Our charges		7	23		
	Rec'd in full, May 3, BRYANT & STRATTON.				57	84

We then note on the right-hand margin of our Receiving Book, and opposite to the entry of this property, "Warehouse Delivery, May 3," and the entire transaction is completed.

Should any dispute hereafter arise relative to it, we have preserved evidence throughout of our having properly executed our duties.

DELIVERY TO RAIL ROADS.

EXAMPLE.—Goods for James Goodwin, Columbus, (see Receiving Book.)

Form of Rail Road Bill of Lading.

Cleveland, Ohio, May 11, 1861.

Forwarded *by* BRYANT & STRATTON, *in good order, by the* CLEVELAND, COLUMBUS, AND CINCINNATI RAIL ROAD, *the following property, to be delivered in like condition and as consigned.*

James Goodwin, Columbus, Ohio.

20	Boxes Goods	7.300				
10	Bales "	3.000				
		10.300				
	Charges to Cleveland		28	84		
	Drayage		1	25		
	Cleveland Charges		5	15		
	BRYANT & STRATTON.				35	24

A duplicate, in our book for R. R. delivery, is signed by the Receiving Clerk of the R. R. Co., which is preserved as our voucher. The R. R. Co. pays the charges, on receipt of the goods, which amount is credited to the respective accounts.

FORM FOR CANAL SHIPPING.

No. -------- Cleveland, Ohio, -------------------- *186*

Shipped, *by* **BRYANT & STRATTON**, *on board the Canal Boat* ---------------- *whereof* ------------------ *is Master, in good order, the following articles, to be delivered in like good order to Consignees, without delay.*

NARRATIVE.

The following are the transactions embraced in this Set. Let the student follow them through the various books in the order indicated on page 233.

May 1. Cash Balance on hand, $5,682. - - - - The Propeller Cataract arrived, with B/L from the American Transportation Co., Buffalo, dated April 30, of 120 bags Rio Coffee, to our care, for % of Gordon, McMillan & Co. (City), weight 14.460 lb. Freight from N. Y. to Cleveland, 35¢ per 100 lb.=$50.61.

2. The coffee landed in good order. Paid freight. - - - - Canal-boat America arrived with B/L of 1800 bush. corn, from Chillicothe, shipped by J. Madeira, April 24th, on his own %, and consigned to H. Daw & Son, Buffalo. Freight to Cleveland, 12¢ per bush. By advices from the consignor, two other boat-loads are on the way, and all are to arrive before we forward the corn from Cleveland, and special instruction is given to omit procuring insurance. Ordered the corn into the Erie Warehouse.

3. Delivered Gordon, McMillan & Co.'s coffee, and collected the charges thereon, as follows: Transportation, $50.61; our charges (credited to "Charges" %), $7.23. Paid Boat America freight on corn, $216. - - - - Canal-boat Nautilus arrived with B/L of 2000 bush. corn from J. Madeira, April 25. Freight at 12¢ per bush. Ordered to Erie Warehouse.

4. Boat Nautilus unloaded, and falls short 2 bushels. Deducted the value of 2 bush. (at market price of 40¢ per bush.) from the freight ($240), and paid captain in full, $239.20. - - - - Canal-boat Grenada arrived, and is the third and last load advised by J. Madeira, and was shipped by him April 26. Freight 12¢ per bush. Ordered to Erie Warehouse. - - - - Received this day the last of a lot of 1200 bars of R. R. iron, from Stone, Chisholm & Jones (City), to be forwarded to the Chicago and North-Western R. R. Co., Chicago. Total weight, 403,200 lb.

6. Boat Grenada unloaded, and overruns 3 bushels. Paid freight, $235.20, and for the 3 bush., at 40¢ per bush., $1.20. - - - - Propeller "Gov. Cushman" arrived from Dunkirk (N. Y. & Erie R. R. Co.), and landed goods for Bradburn & Fisher (City); weight, 44,935 lb. Freight from N. Y. to Cleveland, 35¢ per 100 lb.=$157.27. - - - - Contracted Schr. Ironsides to take J. Madeira's corn to Buffalo at freight of 4¢ per bushel, and gave her an order on the Erie Warehouse therefor.

7. Paid Propeller Gov. Cushman's freight on goods delivered yesterday, $157.27. Schr. Ironsides being loaded, gave her B/L 5761 bush. corn, consigned to H. Daw & Son, Buffalo, N. Y., for % of J. Madeira, Chillicothe, freight to be collected by captain, at 4¢ per bushel. Made our draft on H. Daw & Son favor D. P. Eells, Cashier, @ 3 days, for charges on the corn, as follows: Transportation (paid on the 3 boat-loads), $691.60; Storage in Erie Warehouse, 1¢ per bush., $57.61; Do. (our charges), 1¢ per bush., $57.61=$806.82. Drew. Deposited the draft in the Commercial Bank to our credit. - - - - Received charges on Bradburn and Fisher's goods: Transportation, $157.27; storage (our charges), $22.47. - - - - Shipped the 1200 bars R. R. iron, by Barque Naomi, to the Chicago & Northwestern R. R. Co., Chicago, at a freight of $1.25 per ton. Paid extra labor loading the same, $21.15. Received our charges (Storage %), $1.00 per ton=$201.60.

10. Received 1000 bbls. flour, "Beacon Mills Extra," from Cleveland and Pittsburg R. R. for % of J. B Woods, Akron, to be forwarded to Bryant, Stratton, & Packard, New York. Paid R. R. freight, 15¢ ($150), and drayage from depot, 2¢ per barrel=$20.

11. Shipped J. B. Woods' flour, by Propeller Gov. Cushman, through to New York, by N. Y. & Erie R. R. Co., from Dunkirk, at 85¢ per bbl. Procured Lake Insurance thereon for $4500, in Etna Ins. Co., Carlton's Agency. Paid Insurance prem., $22.50. Received charges on the flour, as follows: Transportation, $170; Insurance, $22.50; Storage, $50. Received of Schr. Farwell, from Oswego, 5th instant, 20 boxes and 10 bales goods for James Goodwin, Columbus, O.; weight, 10,300 lb. Freight 28¢ per 100 lb. to Cleveland. Paid freight, and sent the goods immediately to the C. C. & C. R. R. Co.'s depot, and paid the drayage, $1.25.

13. Collected charges of the C. C. & C. R. R. Co., as follows: Transp., $30.09; Storage (our charges), $5.15.

16 Received 300 bags coffee, from Prop. "Fountain City," shipped by Amer. Transp. Co., 15th inst., for % Gordon, McMillan & Co. (City); weight, 39,000 lb. Freight, N. Y. to Cleveland, 35¢=$136.50. Of these, 15 bags were found to have been damaged by water, and by agreement between the owners of the coffee and the Propeller, $3.00 per bag, or $45, was estimated as the measure of damages. Deducted $45 from the freight of the coffee, and paid balance, $91.50. Coffee delivered to owners.

17. Rec'd of Gordon, McMillan & Co., charges on coffee, as follows: Transp., $91.50; our chgs., $19.50.

RECEIVING BOOK

Cleveland, May, 1861.

1861								
Month	Day	Consignee	Particulars	$	¢	$	¢	Remarks
May	1	GORDON, MCMILLAN & CO., *Cleveland, O.*	**Propeller "Cataract."** *From Am. Transp. Co., Buffalo, Apr. 30.* 120 Bags Rio Coffee, ... 14,460 lb Freight from N. Y. . . . 35¢ Rec'd Freight, May 2, P. RICHARDS, Clerk.	50	61	50	61	*Delivered, May 3.*
"	2	For % of Shippers, H. DAW & SON, *Buffalo, N. Y.* *Stored in Erie Warehouse.*	**Canal Boat "America."** *From J. Madeira, Chillicothe, Apr. 24.* 1800 Bush. Corn. Canal Frt. to Cleveland . . . 12¢ Rec'd May 3, ISAAC LEWIS, Capt.	216		216		B/L 127
"	3	Same as above. *Stored in Erie Warehouse.*	**Canal Boat "Nautilus."** *From J. Madeira, Chillicothe, Apr. 25.* 2000 Bush. Corn. Canal Frt. to Cleve. . . . . . 12¢ 2 Bush. short; deduct 40¢ per Bu. Rec'd in full, May 4, JOHN MATTHEWS, Capt.	240	 80	239	20	B/L 127
"	4	Same as above. *Stored in Erie Warehouse.*	**Canal Boat "Grenada."** *From J. Madeira, Chillicothe, Apr. 26.* 1960 Bush. Corn. Canal Frt. to Cleve. . . . . . 12¢ 3 Bush. over: add 40¢ per Bu. Rec'd in full, May 6, GEO. WATERS, Capt.	235 1	20 20	236	40	B/L 127
		CHICAGO & NORTH WESTERN R. R. CO., *Chicago.*	**Stone, Chisholm & Jones.** *Cleveland, (By Team.)* 1200 Bars T R. R. Iron . . . 408,200 lb					B/L 128

RECEIVING BOOK.

Cleveland, May, 1861.

1861 May	6	BRADBURN & FISHER, *Cleveland, O.*	**Prop. "Gov. Cushman."** *N. Y. & E. R. R., Dunkirk, May 4.* 20 Bbls. Syrup . . . . 6.500 lb 10 " Refined Sugar . . . . 2.500 20 " P. R. " . . . . 22.000 40 Bags Coffee . . . . 6.150 35 Chests Tea . . . . 2.520 40 Hf. Chests Tea . . . . 1.410 20 Boxes Tobacco . . . . . . 1.900 5 Bbls. " . . . . . . 540 50 Boxes Raisins . . . . 1.415 44.935 lb Frt. from N. Y., per Contract . . 35¢ Rec'd Frt., May 7, D. SCOTT, Master.	157	27	157	27	*Delivered, May 7.*
"	10	For % J. B. WOODS, BRYANT, STRATTON & PACKARD, *New York.*	**Cleve. & Pitts. R. R. Co.** 1000 Bbls. Flour, "Beacon Mills, Extra." R. R. Frt. per Bbl., ... 15¢ Drayage from Depot . . . Paid Chgs. May 10, per Receipts	150 20		170		B/L 129
"	11	JAMES GOODWIN, *Columbus, O.*	**Schr. "Farwell."** *J. Fitzhugh, Oswego, May 5.* 20 Bxs. Goods . . . . 7.300 lb 10 Bales " . . . . 3.000 10.300 lb Frt from N. Y. to Cleve. . . 28¢ Rec'd, May 12, G. W. JONES, Owner.	28	84			*C. C. & C. R. R May 11.*
"	16	GORDON, MCMILLAN & CO., *Cleveland, O.*	**Prop. "Fountain City."** *Am. Transp. Co., Buffalo, May 15.* 300 Bags Coffee . . . . 39.000 lb Frt. from N. Y. to Cleve. . . 35¢ 15 Bags damaged—Deduct as agreed. Rec'd in full, CHAS. BUTTS, Clk.	136 45	50	91	50	*Delivered, May 17.*

CASH

Cleveland, May, 1861.—Receipts.

1861				Transp.		Charges.		General.	
May	1		*Amount on hand from Apr.*					5682	
	3	Transportation .	Frt. Chgs. on 120 Bags Coffee .	50	61				
	"	Charges . . .	Our " " " " . .			7	23		
	7	Transportation .	Frt. Chgs. on 5761 Bush. Corn .	691	60				
	"	Charges . . .	Storage paid Erie Warehouse . .			57	61		
	"	" . . .	Our Storage on above Corn . .			57	61		
	"	Transportation .	Frt. on Bradburn & Fisher's Goods	157	27				
	"	Charges . . .	Our Charges on same			22	47		
	"	" . . .	" " " 1200 bars T Rail			201	60		
	11	Transportation .	Frt. on 1000 Bbls. Flour . . .	170					
	"	Insurance . .	Ins. on same					22	50
	"	Charges . . .	Our Chgs. on same			50			
	13	Transportation .	Frt. of C. & C. R. R. Co. . .	30	09				
	"	Charges . . .	Our Chgs. on same			5	15		
	17	Transportation .	Frt. on 300 Bags Coffee . . .	91	50				
		Charges . . .	Our Chgs. on same			19	50		
			Transportation, Total	1191	07			1191	07
			Charges, "			421	17	421	17
								7316	74

Cleveland, May, 1861.—Disbursements

1861			Transp.		Charges.		General.	
May	2	Commercial B'k Deposited					4500	
		Transportation . Freight, Prop. Cataract	50	61				
	3	" . " Boat America	216					
	4	" . " " Nautilus	239	20				
	6	" . " " Grenada	236	40				
	7	Charges . . . Erie Warehouse, 5761 Bu. Corn .			57	61		
	"	" . . . Extra Labor on R. R. Iron . .			21	15		
	"	Transportation . Freight Prop. Gov. Cushman . .	157	27				
	"	Commercial B'k Deposited Dft. on Daw & Son .					806	82
	10	Transportation . Freight, Flour, C. & P. R. R. . .	150					
	"	" . Drayage to " . . .	20					
	11	Insurance . . Prem. on 1000 Bbls. Flour . . .					22	50
		Transportation . Freight, Schr. Farwell	28	84				
	13	" . Drayage to Depot	1	25				
	17	" . Freight Prop. Fountain City .	91	50				
		Transportation. Total . . .	1191	07			1191	07
		Charges, "			78	76	78	76
		Balance on hand					717	59
							7316	74

LEDGER,—FORWARDING.

Stock.

Dr.						Cr.					
						1861					
						May	1	Amount Invested,	1	5682	

Cash.

Dr.						Cr.					
1861						1861					
May	17	Total for the month	1	7316	74	May	17	Total for the month		6599	15

Transportation.

Dr.						Cr.					
1861						1861					
May	17	Total for the month	1	1191	07	May	17	Total for the month	1	1191	07

Charges.

Dr.						Cr.					
1861						1861					
May	17	Total for the month	1	78	76	May	17	Total for the month	1	421	17

Insurance.

Dr.						Cr.					
1861						1861					
May	11	Paid on 1000 Bbls. Flour	1	22	50	May	11	Refunded	1	22	50

Commercial Bank.

Dr.						Cr.					
1261											
May	2	Deposited	1	4500							
"	7	"	1	806	82						

BANKING:

EMBRACING, AS PRINCIPAL BOOKS,

DEBIT JOURNAL, CREDIT JOURNAL, AND GENERAL LEDGER;

AND AS AUXILIARIES,

DEPOSIT LEDGER, DISCOUNT REGISTER, COLLECTION REGISTER, DOMESTIC TICKLER, FOREIGN TICKLER, AND PASSED COLLECTIONS;

WITH FORMS OF

CASH BOOK, STOCK LEDGER, TRANSFER BOOK, OFFERING BOOK, STATEMENT BOOK, ETC.

ALSO

The most approved forms of the various kinds of Bank Paper.

COMPRISING TWELVE DAYS' BUSINESS, REPRESENTING AS MANY MONTHS, AND EMBRACING A SUFFICIENT NUMBER AND VARIETY OF TRANSACTIONS TO FULLY ILLUSTRATE THE BUSINESS OF BANKING AS IT IS CONDUCTED IN THE GREAT MAJORITY OF BANKING INSTITUTIONS IN THE COUNTRY.

BANKING.

THE business of BANKING is so inwoven in all our commercial relations, that any attempt to apply the principles of Book-keeping to the specialties of trade which should ignore this department, or fail to make it prominent, would be justly entitled to censure as falling short of the public demand.

In presenting the subject in this connection, however, the authors disclaim any dictatorial rights pertaining either to substance or form; but would respectfully state that, after a careful examination of all the published works on the general theme of BANKING, as well as those having more particular reference to Bank Book-keeping; and after consulting many prominent bankers, and examining carefully the books of various banking institutions in our large commercial cities, east and west, they have settled upon the following forms as being best adapted to the business as it is conducted in the great majority of banks throughout the country, and as presenting, in the most concise manner, the characteristic transactions of those banks which combine in their operations the various departments of finance.

It is well known that in large commercial centers the tendency of trade is to specializing and centralizing; so much so that the cities themselves become divided up into homogeneous business communities, the limits of which may be almost as distinctly defined as the wards or election districts. So, also, each establishment is specialized into *departments*, and the labor so divided as to give to each employé specific and monotonous duties. This can be done, however, only where the business is so extensive as to render each separate department a business of itself. Thus, in a large metropolitan banking house, fifty clerks may be necessary to do labor embracing no greater variety than that of a country bank whose duties devolve on one man. This massing of business begets the necessity of such divisions and subdivisions as shall secure the most perfect system of operation, and the most effectual application of the peculiar talents of employés.

In the smaller centers of trade such divison of labor becomes impracticable from want of magnitude in the business itself; and hence, commercial houses asssume a more general character, and the duties of clerks become more diversified.

It is evident, therefore, that the forms for business record which would be appropriate in a large establishment, where each department is distinct, would not answer so well in a house where all the departments are merged in one.

In presenting the subject of BANK BOOK-KEEPING, we have not been unmindful of these difficulties, and have tried to meet them in a manner best calculated to benefit the general student, and to afford information of the most practical kind.

The business represented is that of a *medium* institution; and the transactions such as generally occur at the counters of the great majority of banks throughout the country. The locality is central, affording thus a more extended variety of transactions in Exchange, and a favorable opportunity of illustrating the system of correspondence which constitutes so important a feature of Banking.

Before referring to the details of the business, it may be well to speak in general terms of some of the more important characteristics of banks, and the offices they perform in the communities by whose patronage they thrive.

THE SPHERE OF BANKS.

A BANK is a perfected system of organizing capital with a view to securing the best interests of the two great classes of community, *borrowers* and *lenders*. The private means of individuals are united in a general fund which is loaned out on interest to those who need it, and can afford to pay for its use.

In this view, a bank is simply an agency for the promotion of the public weal; and when properly conducted, there is no one agency which will do so much for the material prosperity of a community. It is scarcely to be expected, however, that the desire, alone, to benefit community would induce men to employ their time and means; or that the majority of men will consent to use their capital, whether of money or brains, without adequate compensation; and we are strengthened in this impression with reference to banks and bank owners, by the fact that while the law in most states restricts the interest on loans to 6 or 7 per cent. per annum, the yearly profits of many banking institutions exceed 12 per cent., while the majority of them are able to declare annual dividends of from 7 to 10 per cent.; notwithstanding the fact that the current expenses for conducting the business, such as rent, fuel, salaries for officers and clerks, etc., etc., amount often to a heavy percentage on the capital.

It may be well, therefore, to look at some of the sources of profits enjoyed by banks, as also at the legitimate means employed to secure their prosperity.

Most banks in operation in this country are joint stock corporations, chartered by the Legislatures of the several states in which they are located, and privileged, under certain restrictions, to receive money on deposit; to loan money on interest; to buy and sell money, and negotiable funds; to collect paper at maturity; and to issue notes which, being redeemable in coin at their own counter, pass as money, and constitute the great currency of the country. Private individuals or companies, however, may engage in the business of banking—except that of issuing notes—with no more restrictions or privileges than those incidental to other business enterprises.

We will consider briefly these separate characteristics of banks:

1. DEPOSITS AND DISCOUNT.

As places of deposit, banks afford to the community a most convenient and safe custody for money; which, being deposited and drawn out at the pleasure of the owner, enjoins upon the banker not only the necessity of keeping a strict account with each dealer, but the responsibility of having always on hand current funds with which to meet the drafts he is bound to pay upon presentation. The great improbability, however, that all or any considerable proportion of the depositors will demand their money *at the same time*, renders it perfectly safe for the bank to loan a portion of such funds at interest, thereby receiving compensation for the trouble and responsibility attending depositors' accounts. The original capital or stock of the bank is also employed in this manner, the bank exacting ample security for all money loaned with the legal rate of interest, which is usually taken *in advance*, or computed upon the face of the obligation, and deducted therefrom when the money is loaned.

The advantages to a business man of keeping a bank account, can scarcely be overrated. They may be briefly enumerated as follows:

1. If the bank be, in all respects, responsible, his money is safer than in his own hands.
2. The payment of bills by checks on his banker, besides being much more convenient, enables him to keep trace of his money transactions, affording him vouchers for money paid, and avoiding errors that might otherwise occur without detection.
3. By making his own notes payable at the bank where his deposits are, he is saved the trouble and annoyance of hunting them up at maturity; and by depositing his bills receivable, he throws the trouble and responsibility attending their collection upon his banker.
4. By doing his business through a bank, he acquires habits of promptness and order, which will render him more efficient in all his business relations; is better able to establish his credit among business men, and enjoys more extended facilities for knowing the financial standing of those with whom he deals.

2. EXCHANGE.

Banks located in the interior usually keep funds on deposit at the principal centers of trade, against which they draw in amounts to suit customers, charging therefor a certain percentage of premium, known as the "rate of *exchange*" between the two points. The amount of this premium is variable, and subject to contingencies which we have not space in this connection to discuss. Suffice to say, that when the *intrinsic* value of the currency or "money of account" is the same at any two given points, the rate of exchange between them can not greatly exceed the cost and risk of transporting coin, no matter what may be the preponderance of the "balance of trade." *

Another important item of bank profits arises from dealing in uncurrent and premium funds, the position occupied by banks giving them the advantage, both in purchases and sales, over private individuals. In large cities, however, the regular banks do not deal in *uncurrent* funds, leaving that department of finance to a class of private bankers known as Exchange Brokers.† We have, nevertheless, incorporated the feature in this set, as we desire to make the instruction as comprehensive as possible.

3. COLLECTION.

The complete system of correspondence which banks are forced to put in practice and maintain, enables them with the greatest facility to collect money falling due at various points. This they can afford to do for their regular dealers at a small charge independent of the rate of exchange. For other collections they charge a small additional compensation, usually a percentage on the amount collected.

---

* Perhaps on no one subject do Political Economists differ more widely than that of Currency; and more particularly as to the causes which lead to fluctuations in exchange. For a clear statement of the best points put forth by one class, we refer the student to the article on "Exchange," in Bryant & Stratton's Commercial Arithmetic, by J. B. Meriam, Esq., Cashier of Cleveland City Bank.

† In many of the states banks are prohibited by law from dealing in uncurrent funds.

4. ISSUE, OR CIRCULATION.

The function of issuing paper money, is at once the most delicate and important which banks possess, and is the peculiar feature of *incorporated* institutions.

The conditions upon which banks are permitted to issue notes to circulate as money, aim to secure the prompt redemption of such notes in gold or silver whenever demanded; and the intrinsic value of the paper currency thus created, depends upon the certainty of this redemption. If a bank were obliged to keep always on hand an amount of specie equal to its circulation, there would be no profit from circulation except what would accrue from the destruction or loss of its notes, or their failure to be presented for payment, which does not ordinarily exceed the rate of one-tenth of one per cent. per annum; while, on the other hand, if banks were permitted to issue notes without being obliged to keep idle capital with which to redeem them, they would enjoy the use of so much additional capital at no expense save that incidental to the manufacture of the notes themselves.

To secure these advantages to banks as far as possible, without weakening the basis of redemption, the Legislatures of the different states have passed such laws relating to the subject as have seemed at the time most promotive of these ends. The particular conditions prescribed in these statutory grants are various, and, in many cases, local; the general provisions, however, may be summed up into three distinct lines of policy, viz., the *specie* basis, the *safety fund* basis, and the *stock* basis. The latter is more generally known as the "free banking" principle.

The SPECIE basis requires a certain proportion of the capital to be retained in coin, limits the amount of circulation in proportion thereto, and holds the assets of the bank, with the private means of its stockholders, as liable for the redemption of its notes.

The SAFETY FUND system requires each of several banks to deposit in the State Department a certain percentage of its capital or circulation, which is invested in good securities and retained as a common fund for the redemption of the notes of any insolvent contributing bank.

The STOCK or "free banking" basis requires the bank to deposit in the State Department, State or United States stocks equal to its entire circulation, the stocks to be estimated not above their market value, and to be made equal to stocks producing, in some states five, and in others six per cent. per annum. The interest on these stocks is paid over to the bank, unless they are permitted to run below the required standard; but if the bank refuses to redeem its notes, the notes may be protested, and the stocks sold to meet the payment. In some states, as in New York, it is made optional with the bank to furnish public stocks for the entire amount of security, or to deposit one half in stocks, and one half in bonds and mortgages on real estate; the land to be unencumbered and in a state of cultivation, and the mortgage not to exceed two-thirds of its appraised value.

This is called the "*free* banking" law, as it enables any person or association to engage in the business of banking who will conform to its requirements; no *special* act of legislature being necessary to confer a charter.

It will be seen that any of the above systems secures to the bank the privilege of increasing its working capital by issuing its own promissory notes payable on demand without interest; and that under the "free banking law" which is illustrated in this set, although an equal amount of producing stocks must be pledged to secure the notes, yet the bank receives the interest on these stocks, while, at the same time, it uses the notes in its regular business, thereby obtaining the benefit of a double use of its capital.*

Let us now briefly estimate the probable earnings of a bank under the franchises above enumerated.

First, it has a nominal capital stock, which is the amount originally paid in by its stockholders, and which must remain as a permanent investment. This is the amount upon which dividends are paid. This capital can, of course, be used in the legitimate business of the bank, and should produce in the various channels, at least six per cent.

Next, the continual balance kept by dealers on deposit will not usually fall short of the original capital. In

* One great evil which has attended the working of the "Free Banking Law," especially in the Western States, is the inflation and consequent depreciation of paper currency. Banks are located in out-of-the-way places, having none of the facilities for a legitimate banking business except that of *issuing* notes. A limited capital is invested in stocks, which being deposited with the proper state officer, a corresponding issue of bank notes is authorized; these notes are immediately employed in purchasing other stocks, which in turn are deposited, and additional issues authorized, and thus repeating the process until the premium paid for stocks has so diminished the capital as to render farther attenuation unprofitable. The difficulty of presenting these notes for redemption at the counters of the banks issuing them, keeps them constantly in circulation, and while every thing is prosperous, and the currency of the country is not subjected to those severe tests precipitated by revulsions and panics, the interest on the stocks, thus doubled and redoubled, will make a generous dividend on the *investment*. If, however, any considerable quantity of the funds are pressed home for payment, the bubble bursts, and the *bank*, which never existed in fact, ceases to exist in name. This evil is securely guarded against in New York, and other States, where the free banking law prevails, by forcing the "country banks" to redeem their currency at certain points of commercial importance. All New York State banks have established agencies for redemption at New York City, Albany, and Troy. The New England banks redeem at Boston.

some banks it greatly exceeds the capital. This may also safely be used for short loans, and in fact forms a part of the working capital of the bank.

Next, the securities deposited with the State Department produce a regular percentage of interest to which the bank is entitled.

Assuming that the original capital of the bank is invested in stocks, for the face of which its notes are issued, and that the continued balance of deposits is equal to the paid-in capital, we have a *producing* capital three times as large as the nominal capital. If we can safely keep employed two-thirds of this amount at six per cent., the earnings from these sources alone will amount to 12 per cent. on the capital stock.

If, then, our earnings from collections and exchange can be relied on to pay the current expenses of the bank, our stockholders will have no just occasion to complain of the non-productiveness of their investment.

ORGANIZATION.

The preliminary steps for organizing a bank are duly prescribed in the law which confers its charter. The general course may be thus briefly stated:

Articles of Association are drawn up, giving the name of the institution, the amount of capital to be subscribed, and such other facts as are necessary to be known to stockholders. It is usual to mention the names of the first directors in this document, their election being secured by the act of subscription. The stockholders subscribe to these articles, each placing opposite his name the number of shares he is willing to take; the payment of which is divided into convenient instalments as agreed upon. When the amount of capital is fully subscribed, a certificate of organization is filed with the proper State officers, and also in the County Clerk's office of the county where the bank is located. The final act of organization is the deposit in the State Department of the necessary securities; which, in the State of New York, can not be less in value than one hundred thousand dollars. As soon as this deposit is made, the bank is authorized to do business; and until its own bills are ready for use, it can use the bills of other banks and such other currency as its depositors may pay in.

MANAGEMENT.

The management of the bank is vested in a

BOARD OF DIRECTORS,

who are annually chosen by the stockholders from their own number. Directors are required by some banks to hold a certain number of shares of the stock, upon the ground that the greater their pecuniary interest, the more carefully will they look after the welfare of the institution. The directors appoint one of their number as

PRESIDENT,

whose duty it is to preside at their meetings, and to act upon their authority during the recesses of the Board. He is, in fact, the chief executive officer of the bank, and, so far as the public is concerned, is the *bank itself.* The President usually devotes his whole time to the interests of the institution which he represents, and is not expected to engage in any pursuit which may distract his attention and sympathies therefrom.

A Bank President should be the soul of honor; in his private relations above reproach, and in his public character a man of known integrity. He should possess that happy equanimity of temperament which will guard him from inconsiderate action, and that ready discernment of character which will save him alike from the deep-laid schemes of dishonest tricksters without, and from the influence of parties and cliques within. He, more than any other person connected with the bank, imparts to it his own character, as the public are quite apt to judge of an institution by what they know of its acknowledged representative and head.

The duties of the Board of Directors have reference more to the general management of the bank in respect to its relations with the public, than to its internal workings, about which they are expected to know little.

OPERATION.

The machinery of the bank is under the immediate supervision and direction of

THE CASHIER,

who is its acting financial officer. He is assisted in the various departments by a larger or smaller number of clerks, according to the amount and classification of the business. The Cashier is selected with reference to his ability, and is not necessarily a stockholder. In fact, he is not usually permitted to have any private dealings with the bank, even as a depositor. He is expected to hold himself aloof from the petty schemes and private differences of the friends of the institution. Although appointed by the Board of Directors, and subject to its control, he is more particularly the representative and trustee of the stockholders, and is so considered by them. It is his prerogative to guard the financial interests of the bank, and if necessary in the discharge of this sacred trust, he may authoritatively interpose before the acts of the Directors themselves.

The duties and responsibilities of a Cashier differ in different institutions. In the smaller ones, known as "Country Banks," he is the *factotum;* often combining in his person the dignity and duties of the Board of Management with the more onerous labors of Teller, Book-keeper, and subordinate clerk. In the larger metropolitan houses his duties are more circumscribed, but not less important. Standing, as he does, at the head of the operative functions of the bank, he is, in the greatest measure, responsible for the workings of its machinery. Being brought into immediate contact with dealers, he is supposed to know all about their business and their standing. Conversant, both with the theory and practice of financial operations, his judgment is consulted in matters requiring the nicest discrimination, and compassing the most important results. He is the mouthpiece of the institution to the public. All its correspondence is conducted in his name, and all its important documents bear his signature. If the institution is prosperous, its success is, in great part, attributed to his prudent management; if unsuccessful, he can not escape his corresponding share of responsibility.

If it is essential to the continued prosperity of a bank that its chief officers should be capable and trustworthy, it is not the less so that the more minute details of the business should be in charge of competent assistants. When the business is such as will warrant the employment of a special clerk for each department, the division of labor is somewhat as follows:

THE FIRST, OR PAYING TELLER

pays out all monies, takes charge of the vault and its contents, attends to the Clearing House exchanges, certifies checks, issues certificates of deposit, etc. His transactions are recorded in a book called the "Paying Teller's Cash Book," or "Debit Journal." The latter title is given it from the fact that all debits, except cash, which appear in the Ledger are first entered here.

The responsibilities attached to the duties of this department are of the gravest nature, and call for a kind and degree of talent out of the usual order. The frauds so continually practiced, in one way and another, upon banks; the frequent temptations presented for stepping aside from the plain path of duty, and the necessity of keeping constantly in mind the condition of dealers' accounts, requires in the person having charge of bank disbursements, keen perception, mature judgment, unfaltering memory, and incorruptible honesty.

THE SECOND, OR RECEIVING TELLER

receives all monies paid into the bank, keeping a proper account of the same. His records are made in a book called the "Receiving Teller's Cash Book," or "Credit Journal."

His duties, though not so responsible as those of the Paying Teller, are by no means sinecure; requiring great facility and correctness in counting money and adding columns of figures, as also a thorough familiarity with currency. The rapidity with which an accomplished Bank Teller will count money, is truly astonishing to the uninitiated; and the ease and certainty with which he will detect a spurious bank note, not the less so.

The duties of the Receiving Teller are sometimes divided between two clerks, called Deposit and Note Tellers; the one having charge of all receipts from depositors, and the other from notes, either discounted or left for collection.

THE DISCOUNT CLERK

has charge of all paper offered for discount, as well as that which has been discounted. His records are made in three different books: the "Offering Book," the "Discount Register," and the "Tickler." The Offering Book contains an alphabetical list of the persons offering paper for discount, with a description of the paper, amount, collaterals, etc. This book, with the offerings themselves, is submitted to the Board at its regular meetings, where each offering is passed upon, and the result noted by the Cashier opposite each name, the letter "A" signifying "Accepted," and the letter "R," "Rejected." If it is deemed best to refer any of the offerings to some member of the Board or to the Cashier with power to act, upon sufficient information, the abbreviation "Ref" will properly designate such. The book and papers are returned to the Discount Clerk, who immediately proceeds to transcribe the *accepted* paper in the Discount Register, and Tickler; the one containing a description of each bill discounted, numbered in proper order, and the other exhibiting, in the most convenient form for reference, the date of its maturity. The discounted paper is properly filed, and remains in the custody of the Discount Clerk until paid or protested. The net proceeds or present worth is immediately credited as a deposit to the person for whom the discount was obtained. The rejected paper is, of course, returned to the owners.

BANKING.

THE BOOK-KEEPER

has charge of the Ledgers, of which there are two, one containing depositors' accounts only, and the other the general accounts of the business. The depositors in some banks are so numerous as to require two or three Ledgers, with a separate clerk for each. When such is the case, the alphabet is divided so as to apportion the names properly, giving each Ledger its due share. Very little knowledge of the principles of Book-keeping is necessary to transcribe the facts connected with depositors' accounts; but the utmost correctness and promptness will be found essential. To be able, at a moment's notice, to give the standing of any one of five hundred dealers requires not only quick discernment and a retentive memory, but order in arrangement, and a *habit* of having every day's transactions written up to time. As moderate as are these requirements, many banks have just cause to complain of the inefficiency of their Book-keepers.

The duties connected with the General Ledger are more diversified, and require a better knowledge of the *Science* of Accounts. When this book is kept by a separate clerk he is called

THE GENERAL BOOK-KEEPER.

The items which make up the accounts in the General Ledger are taken from the Tellers' Journals, where they are arranged with a view to the proper debits and credits. One important item in the duties of the General Book-keeper is to keep the accounts with corresponding banks, charging them with notes sent for collection—when such notes are paid—and crediting them with remittances and the proceeds of notes collected for them. This duty often requires a vast amount of correspondence. He has also charge of the Stock Ledger and Transfer Books, and is obliged to render periodical statements of the current condition of the business, for the information both of stockholders and the public. Having frequent access to the books of the various departments, he becomes the repository of all the important facts connected with the business. His position brings him into confidential relations with the officers of the bank, who defer to his judgment in matters pertaining to the general condition of its affairs.

Besides the clerks already enumerated, who may properly be styled heads of departments, most large banks employ various other assistants, such as

THE ASSISTANT TELLER,

whose principal duty is to aid the Paying and Receiving Tellers, in counting and assorting funds;

THE CHECK CLERK,

who keeps the check-list, and assorts the checks preparatory to their entry on the Debit Journal;

THE RUNNER,

who is the Mercury of the bank, and whose duty it is to collect notes and drafts, present drafts for acceptance, serve notices of the maturity of paper, etc., etc.; and last, though not least,

THE PORTER,

who carries the keys of the bank and its sacred depositories, and is its general custodian and special policeman. The Porter is a kind of general assistant of the clerks, but his duties are more intimately connected with the Paying Teller's department. He has much to do with the handling of coin, and becomes very expert in counting it, and detecting base pieces. All valuable packages to be conveyed to and from the Clearing House, Express, or Post Office, are entrusted alone to him. Though lowest in the grade of regular bank employés, he is the peer of the highest in the responsibility and importance of his position; and his selection and retention in office are the best possible recommendations for strict honesty and fidelity.

THE DAILY ROUTINE.

The transactions which daily occur at the bank counter, though varying somewhat in their method and details, produce a monotonous record; one day's business being almost a transcript of every other day. A few hints upon this point may better enable the student to comprehend the "Narrative" which follows.

1. DEPOSITS.

A person desiring to become a depositor or dealer with a bank, first obtains an introduction to the Cashier, who learns from him his business, and the probable nature and extent of his future dealings with the bank. These preliminaries are mutually advantageous to the parties, and, so far as the bank is concerned, are necessary for various reasons; the chief of which is, that the dealers of a bank are the main borrowers of its capital; the relative average of deposits being, other things equal, the basis of "accommodation." If the introduction is satisfactory, the dealer is requested to leave the signature which will be adopted by him in all his future dealings with the bank, and is furnished with the necessary auxiliaries for keeping his own bank account, consisting of a blank Check Book, a Pass Book, and a package of Deposit Checks. Examples of these and the methods of their use are shown in connection with Set IV., Pages 116 and 117.

A man in active business usually makes his deposits once a day. Each deposit is accompanied with the Pass Book and a Deposit Check, the latter enumerating the kind of funds and amount of the deposit. If, upon examination, the Teller finds the amount to be right, and the funds satisfactory, he enters the amount in the Pass Book, and files the check for future record upon his own book. The entry upon the Pass Book, accompanied, as it is, with the Teller's initial signature, serves as the depositor's receipt. The Deposit Checks which thus accumulate on the Teller's file, are taken from time to time by a special clerk, and entered on the Credit Journal, or are allowed to accumulate until the close of the day's business, and entered up by the Teller. So, also, the checks of dealers, which are usually much more frequent than their deposits, are cashed by the Paying Teller, and filed until the close of the day's business, when they are collected, assorted, and entered up in proper order; those of each dealer being enumerated together, and extended in one amount to the deposit column. This arrangement enables the Tellers to attend to their business with less hindrance as also to secure a more symmetrical entry, by classifying their transactions.

2. DISCOUNTS.

Paper to be discounted is first presented as an offering to the Board of Directors, who hold regular sessions for that purpose, usually twice a week. It then comes in charge of the Discount Clerk, or, if there be no special clerk for this department, of one of the Tellers, who enters it on the Discount Register, and, if payable at home, in the Domestic Tickler; or, if sent abroad for collection, in the Domestic Exchange Book. Bills Receivable is then debited in the Debit Journal (under the title of "Bills Discounted," or "Domestic Exchange," as the case may be), for the face of the bill, and "Interest," and the person for whom discounted, credited in the Credit Journal for the discount and net proceeds. If the net proceeds is paid in cash, Interest alone is credited.

3. COLLECTIONS.

When notes are received for collection, they are entered in the order of their receipt on the Collection Register and also on the Ticklers; if payable at home, on the Domestic Tickler, if abroad, on the Foreign Tickler. If left by a regular dealer, the note is first entered in his Pass Book, but not extended into the Cash column until paid. If left by a stranger or one having no dealings with the bank, it is entered only in the Collection Register and Tickler. When paid, the amount less charges for collection is paid over to the owner, no entry being made in the main books, except as relating to the amount received for collection.

PRINCIPAL BOOKS.

The principal books of a bank, or those necessary to record the general results of the business, embrace necessarily only the Tellers' Journals and the General Ledger, all of which are here briefly explained.

1. THE DEBIT JOURNAL,

or Paying Teller's Cash Book, contains the record of all cash paid out, with the corresponding debits of accounts for which it is paid. The "Interest and Exchange" column, in the example given, contains the items of expense from these sources, which are posted in total at the end of each day to the debit of that account. The "Deposit" column contains the amounts paid out on depositors' checks, the total of which is posted each day to the debit of Deposit account in the General Ledger, and the separate amounts to the debit of each depositor's account in the Deposit Ledger. This book is equivalent to the credit side of a Cash Book, the footing being posted to the credit of Cash account in the Ledger, and the amounts composing it to the debit of other accounts.

2. THE CREDIT JOURNAL,

or Receiving Teller's Cash Book, contains the record of all cash received, with the corresponding credits of accounts producing it. The "Interest and Exchange" column in this Journal contains the items of profits from these sources, the total of which is posted each day to the credit of that account. The "Deposit" column contains the separate deposits of dealers, the total of which is posted each day to the credit of Deposit account in the General Ledger, and the separate amounts to the credit of the individual depositors in the Deposit Ledger. This book is equivalent to the debit side of a Cash Book, the footings being posted to the debit of Cash account, and the separate amounts to the credit of other accounts.

The difference between these two Journals when the balances are carried forward, should always agree with the Cash on hand.

3. THE GENERAL LEDGER

Is the grand book of results, and differs in no important respect from the Ledger in other kinds of business. The style of expression, under the separate accounts here adopted, is deemed preferable to the conventional form of "opposite Journal expressions," because more explanatory. The student will observe that the *explanation* used in the Journal is transferred to the Ledger, making the process of posting extremely simple. The entries in this book are posted directly from the Debit and Credit Journals, comprising only the amounts extended in the "general" column. Some banks divide the General Ledger into two or three separate books, for purposes of classification; others accomplish similar ends by devoting different parts of the book to the different classes of accounts.

AUXILIARY BOOKS.

The following auxiliary books, which are used in this connection, are sufficient for a limited business. A more thorough subdivision of labor, however, would require, perhaps, a larger number, and a different classification of entries.

1. THE DEPOSIT LEDGER.

This book contains only dealers' accounts. Its items are posted from the deposit columns of the Debit and Credit Journals, the totals of which go to the deposit account in the General Ledger. An important feature is introduced into the Deposit Ledger here shown, which will commend itself to the practical, viz.: exhibiting in a separate column the *balances* on deposit each day to the credit of each depositor. The practice is pursued in many of the larger banking houses, and is highly commended for the facility it affords in estimating the average business of individual depositors. The balances are usually written in *pencil;* and instead of being entered on the *opposite* side when checks are drawn and no deposits made, as is here practised for convenience' sake, they are usually interlined. It needs no special hint to enforce the importance of this book.

2. THE DISCOUNT REGISTER.

This is simply a Bill Book, somewhat more formal and extensive than those used in connection with general mercantile business, but identical in its main design.

In this book are recorded, in the order of discount, the notes which become the property of the bank, with such facts pertaining to them as are necessary to be known. These notes or bills are classified in the Ledger under two heads, viz.: "Bills Discounted" and "Domestic Exchange," the former embracing those payable at home, or in the place where the bank is located, and the latter payable elsewhere in the country. Some banks class them all under the general title of "Bills Receivable."

The records made in this book are collected each day, and properly entered on the principal books.

3. THE COLLECTION REGISTER.

This book contains a consecutive record of notes and bills left with the bank for collection, with such facts as are necessary to be known. No entry is made of these on the principal books until they are paid, when, if belonging to a dealer, he is credited with the proceeds as a deposit; and if to a stranger or non-dealer it is either remitted immediately or retained as a *special* deposit until called for by the owner. When bills come into our hands payable abroad, whether they are our own discounted bills or those left with us for collection, they are immediately sent forward, either to the bank where they fall due or to our most convenient correspondent, who will act in the matter as our agent. If sent to a correspondent we either await his advices, and when notified of payment, charge him with the amount, or, after waiting the due course of mail and receiving no notice of protest, consider the payment made, and make the entry accordingly. If sent to a bank *not* a correspondent, the remittance should accompany the advice of payment.

4. THE DOMESTIC TICKLER.

The Tickler is a book containing a classified record of bills, under their date of maturity, with the names of the principal parties, in order that if not promptly paid they may be protested, and the owner be able to hold the endorsers.

The *Domestic* Tickler contains the record of all bills, whether discounted or left for collection, falling due *at home.* There are different methods of separating the discounts and collections. Some adopt the plan of entering one in black ink and the other in red, while others set aside separate spaces under each date. The plan here adopted is both simple and explicit, having the discounts on one side of the folio and the collections on the other. In actual business it would be well to divide each page into *three* dates, having the first working day of the week come always at the head of the page. This arrangement greatly facilitates the reckoning of time and is generally beneficial.

5. THE FOREIGN TICKLER.

This book contains the record of both discounts and collections due *abroad*, and is similar in all essential respects to the Domestic Tickler. When bills are sent forward for collection they are entered in the Foreign Tickler under the date of maturity, usually adding from one to three days, according to the distance and the contingency of the mails. When the time elapses and no notice comes to hand of failure to pay, the bill is assumed to have been paid, and the proper entry made. Of course if subsequent advices should vary the result, the error would need to be corrected, which can easily be done by counter entries. This plan is adopted by most banks as preferable to that of waiting advices, both on account of the uniform system of which it is susceptible, and the saving of labor in correspondence.

6. THE PASSED COLLECTIONS.

This book contains a record of such collections as have been paid. They are *passed* from the Collection Register, or, more properly, from the Ticklers, for the purpose of effecting a more regular entry into the Ledger where the results are shown. As the main purpose of the book is to arrange the amounts to be debited or credited to dealers and correspondents, which grow out of collections, it would be quite unnecessary to record herein the paper left by strangers and non-dealers, which is to be paid at the bank and the proceeds immediately remitted. The general plan and utility of the book will be readily apparent.

The following additional auxiliaries, though not essential to the complete rendering of general results, are, nevertheless, important, and are used, in some form, in nearly all banks:

7. THE INDIVIDUAL LIABILITIES, OR STANDING LEDGER.

This is a convenient book of reference for the officers of the bank, as it illustrates, in a simple manner, the *standing* of the principal parties whose names appear on discounted paper, as to their liability to the bank and their claims as depositors. It is freely consulted in deciding as to the merits and claims of offerings.

8. THE CASH BOOK,

As shown in this connection, is simply an enumeration of the different items of cash embraced in the amount on hand, and affords a test of the correctness of the cash entries. It is used also, under different forms, as a settlement book between the tellers, each of whom is obliged to prove the correctness of his own work by the vouchers which he holds. Of course it has no vital force except in connection with actual transactions, as there can be no means of knowing the different kinds of cash items except in the actual count

9. THE STOCK LEDGER

Contains a complete list of the stockholders, with the amount of stock held by each. It is auxiliary to the General Ledger, and sustains the same relation to the Capital Stock % that the Deposit Ledger does to the Deposit %. As the stockholders of a bank are constantly changing, some system of recording the changes, so that the actual stockholders may at any time be shown, is necessary; and as no stock can be legally transferred without being entered upon the books of the bank, the process of keeping the Stock Ledger becomes very simple.

10. THE TRANSFER BOOK

Is a book of printed forms, which are filled up with the necessary points of information upon the occasion of the transfer of stock from one stockholder to another. All changes occurring in the Stock Ledger after the original entries, are taken from this book.

11. THE OFFERING BOOK

Contains a consecutive list of all the "offerings" submitted to the directors for loans. This book is used at the meetings of the Discount Board, when the merits of the various offerings are duly discussed, and the final decisions recorded. The "accepted" offerings are transferred to the Discount Register.

12. THE STATEMENT BOOK

Shows the periodical condition of the bank, and is useful both to the stockholders who are more immediately interested in the prosperity of the institution, and the public who hold its credits and have a right to know its condition.

In most of the large cities banks are required by law to render such statements as will serve to enlighten the public as to their condition, as often as once or twice a month; in the smaller cities, villages, and rural districts, once in two or three months.

We present two kinds of statements in this connection, both prescribed by the banking laws of the State of New York—the former to be published semi-monthly by the banks of the city of New York, and the latter to be published quarterly, and sent to the Bank Department, by all the banks in the State.

BANKING.

DIRECTIONS FOR WRITING UP.

In the preparation of material for this set, the author has been governed by the leading impulse of making the instruction full on every essential point, and covering sufficient ground in the transactions to fully illustrate the business.

In carrying out this plan it has been found necessary to submit an extensive variety of transactions, and to resort to a constant repetition of the more ordinary details comprising the daily routine of banking. But this necessity has given to the work a character which will be appreciated by practical minds, and which is mainly relied upon to secure public favor—that of representing business *as it actually occurs.* The supposition upon which the work was commenced, and has been completed, was, that whoever should have the courage and desire to avail themselves of its lessons, would be satisfied with nothing less than a complete exposition of the business, both in its general principles and its characteristic details.

Instead, therefore, of selecting a few representative transactions with the sole purpose of evolving the general theory of banking, we have chosen the more natural, and, as we believe, more efficient plan of first submitting the few general principles peculiar to banking, and then fully establishing them in the record of such transactions, arranged in their natural order, as occur daily at the counters of the class of banks intended to be represented. We are aware that this plan will subject the student, as it has the author, to more labor than a less thorough one, but we fully believe that the efficiency of the instruction is so much more enhanced.

In treating upon the general subject of banking, as well as in enforcing its principles by "Explanatory Notes" referring to specific entries, the aim has been to leave as little as possible to the student's mere conjecture; and this idea has been carried out through the entire work, even at the risk of verbosity and tediousness.

The hints given in this connection are intended to furnish all necessary information as to the character of the transactions, and the order and manner of entry in the various books. It is believed that if they are thoroughly understood and applied, there is no record suggested in the "Narrative" which may not readily be made.

TIME AND DATES.

The business comprises the labor of *twelve* days, so arranged as to cover the space of one year; the first six months of which are written up in full, exhibiting all the necessary principal and auxiliary books, forms, etc.

In the nature and order of the transactions, each day's business is designed to represent such a series of entries as would naturally occur on any one day in a bank; while in the time supposed to elapse for the maturity of paper, etc., each day is made to represent a month. Thus the twelve days' business comprises twelve months' time, affording sufficient opportunity to show the maturity of paper, to declare dividends, and accomplish other characteristic results.

In reckoning time on discounts and collections, as great exactness is used as in actual business; but in noting the date of maturity in the Ticklers, such precision is impossible, from the fact that the year contains but *twelve* business days, neither of which, it might happen, would be the exact day upon which paper would mature. This seeming difficulty is very easily adjusted by considering all paper as due upon the day representing the *month* in which its exact date of maturity would fall; hence, all paper falling due *on any day of the month* would be reckoned as due on the same day. This plan, which we have adopted and carried out, secures all the advantages of exact reckoning without the necessity of representing every business day in the year.

COUNTER-CHECKING.

The system of checking adopted in this set has reference mainly to *transferring* from the original books of entry those results which require a different classification, the more readily to be shown in the general statement of the business.

To give a definite idea of the plan, we will take the books in their order.

1. The Debit and Credit Journals.—The first column is used for checking, and contains simply the Ledger pages to which the results are posted. The amounts in the "General" column are taken to the General Ledger, the check mark showing the page, and those in the "Deposit" column to the Deposit Ledger in the same way. When the entry is made alone in the "Collection and Exchange" column, the check mark (✓) indicates that the amount forms part of a total which is extended into the "General" column, and from thence posted to the General Ledger.

2. The General and Deposit Ledgers.—The check column in these books is next to the money column on either side, and refers to the page of the Journal from which the amounts are taken.

3. The Discount Register.—The check marks in the last column of this book, refer to the credits of net proceeds from discounts (the amounts of which are in the preceding column), and indicate that the proper parties have been credited. The check marks preceding the column footings indicate that the amounts have been properly transferred—"Bills Discounted" and "Domestic Exchange" to the *debit* of those accounts, and "Interest" and "Collection and Exchange" to the *credit* of those accounts. It will be observed that the sum

of the first two columns will equal that of the last three, proving the total net proceeds to be the difference between the face of the paper discounted and our charges for Interest and Collection and Exchange. Although the amounts marked as credited to "Cash" are checked the same as the others, they do not appear in the Journal or Ledger, this discrepancy marking the exact amount of cash actually paid out, which will appear in the general results of the Journals.

4. THE COLLECTION REGISTER.—The check marks in this book indicate that the collections are entered in the Ticklers, under the proper dates of maturity.

5. THE DOMESTIC TICKLER.—As the Ticklers mark the maturity of paper, the results to be transferred from them arise from the payment or protest of notes falling due. When discounts falling due at our bank are paid, we have only to credit Bills Discounted. The check mark "Paid and Entered" indicates that this entry has been made. If the paper is protested, it is so checked. The checks for Collections—"Passed," and "Remitted" —indicate that such payments as are to be credited to other parties are carried to the Passed Collections Book for that purpose; while such as are to be paid over immediately to owners are set aside for that purpose, or remitted, as the case may be. Those amounts which are to be remitted are marked "special."

6. THE FOREIGN TICKLER.—As the paper recorded in this book falls due abroad, and when paid, is usually to be charged to correspondents, a system of double checking seems to be necessary for the discounts; one to indicate the *credit* of Domestic Exchange, and the other the *debits* of correspondents to whom paid. The remarks "Paid and Entered" would in this case be unnecessary, save as to confirm the other checks. The check "Passed" on the collection side has reference to the results being taken to the Passed Collection Book, as in the Domestic Tickler.

7. THE PASSED COLLECTIONS.—The checks in the last column of this book refer to the credits of proceeds to parties for whom collected; those immediately preceding the names of correspondents under the head of "By whom Collected," indicate that those parties are debited; while that preceding the footing of the "Collection and Exchange" column, indicates that amount as credited.

CORRESPONDENCE.

That part of the business conducted by correspondence will be found at once the most difficult and instructive; both on account of the entries growing out of it and the adjustment of inland exchange, which comprises so important a feature in the business relations between different parts of the same country.

There is no feature of banking more important to the community and to banks themselves than the system of agencies which is found necessary in conducting that portion of the business of each bank which is beyond its own immediate reach. By a mutual arrangement, two banks in different parts of the state or country, undertake to do each for the other such business as comes within its own immediate province. This, of course, necessitates a correspondence, and generally a running account between the banks, which, if not kept in tolerable equilibrium by mutual collections, is adjusted from time to time as the parties may desire.

Each bank has its own cluster of such mutual agents—in business language, *correspondents*—located at such points as will best serve its own interest, and is thus enabled, with little trouble, and no risk, to do the foreign business of its dealers, and at rates both remunerative to itself and satisfactory to all parties.

The great advantage to the community growing out of this system, aside from the facilities afforded for the ready adjustment of foreign business, lies in the safety of making remittances, by substituting bank credits for money. One or two examples will sufficiently illustrate this point:—

A, who is a dealer at our bank, has a note falling due in Buffalo. To collect this note himself would subject him to the trouble and uncertainty of sending it to some bank or person in that city, upon whom he may rely to attend to the collection and remit him the funds. It is thus a constant care to him until the funds are in his hands. Instead of this process, however, he simply leaves the note with us, for which we give him an informal receipt—entering it in regular order upon his Pass Book, but not extending the amount into the deposit column. He has now no farther trouble or anxiety in the matter. We send the note to our Buffalo correspondent, who attends to the collection at maturity, and credits us with the amount. When we are satisfied that the note is paid, we charge our Buffalo correspondent, and extend the amount in *A's* Pass Book, the same as a regular deposit; also crediting him in our main books. Thus the whole transaction is conducted without delay or uncertainty, and without the handling of money. Again, suppose *A* wishes to pay a debt in New York, and would avoid the trouble and risk of sending current funds. He simply draws his check on us, for which we give him a draft on our New York correspondent, payable to the order of his creditor. When the draft comes to hand, and is endorsed by the proper party, it will be redeemed upon presentation, or received as cash by any bank in the city. The transaction is simple, incurring no risk and very little trouble.

But there is another important question connected with bank correspondence which it will be more difficult for the student to comprehend, but which, when understood, will afford him the means of pleasant and profitable study. We allude to

DOMESTIC, OR INLAND EXCHANGE.

Without presuming even to enter upon the philosophy, we shall merely state the fact that, owing to sufficient causes, the currency, or "money of account" of different localities differs in value; in other words, that the kind of funds which will pass readily at par in Cleveland are at a discount in New York; and that, consequently, for a debtor residing in Cleveland to discharge a debt due in New York, he will need to remit either New York funds for the exact amount, or sufficient Cleveland funds to cover the debt and discount.

It will be borne in mind that the transactions of this set are predicated upon the condition of public finances, which existed previous to the remarkable changes wrought by the civil war. It is, of course, impossible to predict what may be the final effect of the success of our arms, or the measures of the government, upon this great question of currency; and it is therefore deemed best in preparing a text-book, the prime object of which is to teach the theories of business record, to adopt something near the standard which existed during the normal condition of public affairs, and which affords the readiest means of illustrating some of the most vital points in the science of Bookkeeping.

This state of facts affords to banks through their extensive system of agencies the opportunity of realizing a small per centage in the adjustment of exchange, a feature which the student will fully understand in writing up the transactions of the set.

The chief point of difficulty, however, will be the adjustment of accounts between correspondents where the money of account differs: thus, if we keep our New York correspondent's account in our own currency, and he keeps ours in his currency, there will always exist a discrepancy equal to the rate of exchange between the points. It will, therefore, be evident that we must adopt some *standard* in our mutual dealings, by which we may always agree in our counter entries.

In order to give the student the benefit of uniformity, we have assumed *certain* rates of exchange to exist between ourselves and the several correspondents with whom we deal, and who are enumerated in this connection; and further, have adopted a *standard* of account which must be strictly observed.

The following is our list of correspondents, with the rates of exchange and standard of account:

Localities.	*Correspondents.*	*Rate of Exchange.*	*Standard of %.*
New York,	Duncan, Sherman & Co.,	1 % prem.,	New York Currency.
Albany,	Bank of Capitol,	1 % prem.,	Albany Currency.
Philadelphia,	Girard Bank,	1 % prem.,	Philadelphia Currency.
Buffalo,	Exchange Bank,	½ % prem.,	Buffalo Currency.
Pittsburg,	Iron City Bank,	½ % prem.,	Pittsburg Currency.
Cincinnati,	Lafayette Bank,	par,	Cleveland Currency.
Columbus,	Franklin Bank,	par,	do.
Toledo,	Toledo Branch Bank,	par,	do.
Sandusky,	Moss Brothers,	par,	do.
Elyria,	Lorain Bank,	par,	do.
Ashtabula,	Farmers' Branch Bank,	par,	do.
Detroit,	Farmers & Mechs' Bank,	½ % discount,	do.
Chicago,	Burkam & Sons,	½ % discount,	do.

CHARGES FOR COLLECTION, ETC.

For the sake of uniformity, the following rates for Collection and Exchange have been strictly adhered to throughout the transactions: For collecting paper due at our bank or in the city, no charge is made either to dealers or others. For collecting that due abroad, whether for dealers or others, and whether it be paper for discount or for collection only, we charge ¼ % in addition to the rate of exchange, *when exchange is at a discount.* For all collections due at points where exchange is at a premium, no charge is made—the advantage in exchange being considered an equivalent for the trouble of collection.

In keeping accounts with correspondents whose currency differs in value from our own, the *better* currency is adopted as the standard; and when payments are made on either side the value of the currency in which such payments are made is always considered.

In writing up the set the student will follow the order of the Narrative, making the entries in the books as indicated by the initials. The small reference figures refer to corresponding numbers in the "Explanatory Notes" where specific instruction is given in connection with such entries as seem to demand it.

NARRATIVE OF TRANSACTIONS.

— JANUARY. —

THE **Commercial College Bank** of Cleveland was this day organized under the "Act to incorporate Free Banks in the State of Ohio," passed March 21, 1851. (1)

— STOCKHOLDERS. —

H. D. STRATTON	100	Shares, $100 each.	Cf. No. 1	$10,000
H. B. BRYANT	100	do.	" " 2	10,000
J. B. MERIAM	100	do.	" " 3	10,000
DUNCAN, SHERMAN & Co. .	200	do.	" " 4	20,000
PARKER HANDY	200	do.	" " 5	20,000
HENRY IVISON	250	do.	" " 6	25,000
JOHN R. PENN	100	do.	" " 7	10,000
PETER COOPER	200	do.	" " 8	20,000
JAS. W. LUSK	100	do.	" " 9	10,000
W. H. CLARK	250	do.	" " 10	25,000
J. H. GOLDSMITH	100	do.	" " 11	10.000
A. C. TAYLOR	150	do.	" " 12	15,000
M. B. SCOTT	150	do.	" " 13	15,000
	2000	Shares @ $100		200,000

— BOARD OF OFFICERS. —

H. D. STRATTON,
H. B. BRYANT,
J. B. MERIAM,
M. B. SCOTT,
PETER COOPER, } DIRECTORS.

H. D. STRATTON, ... PRESIDENT.
S. S. PACKARD, ... CASHIER.

THE Stockholders have this day paid in the first instalment of 60% of the Capital Stock, amounting to $120,000; among which are the following Bills of Exchange on N. Y., which we have remitted Duncan, Sherman & Co. to be entered to our credit, viz.: H. B. Bryant's draft on Ocean Bank for $5000; J. B. Meriam's do. on Continental Bank for $7500; Metropolitan Bank's certificate of deposit, favor of H. Ivison, for $10000; W. H. Clark's draft on Duncan, Sherman & Co. for $15000. (2) (Dr. J.; Cr. J.)

Received the following deposits: (3) N. C. Winslow, $1000; E. R. Felton, $1750; Jacob Hoornbeek, $5000; M. B. Scott, $900; J. W. Lusk, $2500; Lewis R. Morris, $3000; John S. Woolson, $1500; T. P. Handy, $4700; E. L. Jones, $975; James Richards, $1750; Alonzo Mitchell, $2000; Asa Mahan, $1200; Robert Brown, $1000; Ingham & Bragg, $3750; Chas. Hickox, $1325. (Cr. J.)

Sold N. C. Winslow, on his check, (4) our draft on Duncan, Sherman & Co. for $500 @ 1% prem. (Cr. J.)

Paid Cash for Blank Books, Stationery, and sundry expenses, $150. (Dr. J.)

Paid the following checks to-day: (5) N. C. Winslow, $505, 100; E. R. Felton, $18.75, 25, 130, 125; Jacob Hoornbeck, $500, 175, 25.50, 19, 12, 110; J. W. Lusk, $175, 125.50, 13.75, 112, 200; Lewis R. Morris, $118, 12.50, 142, 19.30; John S. Woolson, $14.50, 110; T. P. Handy, $1500, 500; James Richards, $113, 19.60, 144, 12; Alonzo Mitchell, $200, 120, 13.75; Robert Brown, $12, 190; Chas. Hickox, $190; H. B. Bryant, $3000; John R. Penn, $2500. (Dr. J.)

Purchased at ½% prem. T. P. Handy's draft on Ocean Bank, N. Y., for $30,000. Remitted same to Duncan, Sh. & Co. for our credit. (Dr. J.)

NARRATIVE.

Discounted the following paper:

For H. B. Bryant: His draft for \$5000 @ 60 ds. (6) on Wright, Gillett & Rawson, N. Y., endorsed by H. D. Stratton; proceeds to credit of H. B. B. as deposit. Remitted same to Duncan, Sh. & Co. for collection. (7) (Dis. R., For. Tic.)

For John R. Penn: Peter Cooper's note of \$4000 @ 60 ds., endorsed by William B. Ogden, payable at our bank; net proceeds to J. R. P.'s credit. (Dis. R.; Dom. Tic.)

The Discount Register is now closed, and the results carried to the Debit and Credit Journals, as follows: *Debits*—Bills Discounted, \$4000; Domestic Exchange, \$5000. *Credits*—H. B. Bryant, \$4947 50; John R. Penn, \$3958; Interest, \$94 50.)

—— FEBRUARY. ——

Bot. per our draft on Duncan, Sh. & Co., N. Y., 20 Shares U. S. 6% Stocks, ea. \$1000, @ 92%; 20 Shares Ohio State 6% Stocks, ea. \$1000, @ 90%. (8) (Cr. J.; Dr. J.) Remitted same to State Department as basis of circulation. (9)

Received from Board of Control for circulation, our registered notes of various denominations, amounting to \$35,000. (10) (Cr. J.)

Bot. the following Bills on N. Y. @ ½% prem., and remitted same to Duncan, Sh. & Co. for our credit: E. R. Felton's draft on Exchange Bank for \$5000; M. B. Scott's do. on Ocean Bank for \$1200; Ctfct. Dep. on Met. Bank, fav. Chas. Hickox, \$2500; John R. Penn's draft on East River Bank, \$500; James Moore's do. on Duncan, Sh. & Co., \$3000. (Dr. J.)

Received the following Bills for Collection:

From Duncan, Sherman & Co.: Ivison, Phinney & Co.'s draft for \$1500 on Ingham & Bragg, @ 30 ds. sight, payable at City Bank. (Col. R., Dom. Tic.) Peter Cooper's draft on D. P. Eells for \$2000 @ 60 ds. from Feb. 1, payable at Commercial Branch Bank. (Col. R.; Dom. Tic.) James Shaw's note of \$2500, fav. W. H. Crocker, dated Jan. 1, @ 90 ds., payable at City Bank. (Col. R.; Dom. Tic.) W. H. Beebe's draft @ 10 ds. from Feb. 1, on T. Dwight Eells, for \$3000, payable at Bank of Cleveland. (Col. R.; Dom. Tic.)

From W. H. Clark: T. P. Handy's note at 30 ds., from Jan. 15, for \$1500, payable at our bank. (Col. R.; Dom Tic.) James Smith's accepted draft for \$2000, drawn by W. H. C., @ 30 ds. sight, and accepted Feb. 1, payable at Merchants' Bank. (Col. R.; Dom. Tic.)

From Lewis R. Morris: His draft for \$900, @ 10 ds. sight, on R. M. Bartlett, Cincinnati—sent to Lafayette Bank for collection. (Col. R.; For. Tic.) J. W. Lusk's note for \$500, @ 30 ds. from Feb. 1, payable at our bank. (Col. R.; Dom. Tic.)

From Jacob Hoornbeek: James McAllister's note for \$1200, @ 60 ds. from Jan. 1, payable at our bank. (Col. R.; Dom. Tic.) His draft on Peter Aiken, Sandusky, for \$475, @ 20 ds. sight—sent Moss Brothers, Sandusky, for collection. (Col. R.; For. Tic.)

Received the following deposits: John R. Penn, \$3000; Geo. A. Crocker, \$1500; Jno. D. Williams, \$1200; John S. Woolson, \$2500; T. P. Handy, \$1175 50; Jacob Hoornbeek, \$4000; E. L. Jones, \$900; Ingham & Bragg, \$875; Henry Ivison, \$1700; Lewis R. Morris, \$1200; H. B. Bryant, \$1200; Asa Mahan, \$2500; Chas. Hickox, \$1700. (Cr. J.)

Sold drafts on Duncan, Sh. & Co., @ 1% prem., as follows: M. B. Scott, \$3000; Robert Smith, \$1500; John S. Woolson, \$750; John R. Penn, \$2500; T. P. Handy, \$1975. (Cr. J.)

Paid the following checks to-day: M. B. Scott, \$3030, 150, 19 75; T. P. Handy, \$1994 75, 120; John S. Woolson, \$757 50, 113, 15 75; John R. Penn, \$2525, 183 75, 144; Asa Mahan, \$325, 450, 19 75, 50; James Richards, \$110, 120, 300, 43 75; Alonzo Mitchell, \$138, 26, 44 90, 300; Chas. Hickox, \$400, 120, 19 34; H. B. Bryant, \$900, 13 75, 122, 75; Robt. Brown, \$115, 26, 35 20, 75; Lewis R. Morris, \$17, 25, 19, 83 25; Jacob Hoornbeek, \$150, 12, 46, 75, 18 75; Jas. W. Lusk, \$29, 34 50, 129; E. L. Jones, \$190, 12 38, 115; Ingham & Bragg, \$50, 120, 38 90; E. R. Felton, \$170, 123, 19 50. (Dr. J.)

The following paper left with us for collection has been paid: (11) *Domestic*—No. 4, T. Dwight Eells, for D., Sh. & Co., \$3000; (12) No. 5, T. P. Handy, for W. H. Clark, \$1500; (13) (Pas. Col., Dom. Tic.) *Foreign*—No. 7, R. M. Bartlett, for Lewis R. Morris, \$900; No. 10, Peter Aiken, for Jacob Hoornbeek, \$475. (Pas. Col.; For. Tic.)

Discounted the following paper:

For Alonzo Mitchell: One note for \$5000, @ 30 ds., from Feb. 1, signed by A. J. Comstock, and endorsed by A. Mitchell; and one for \$3000, @ 40 ds. from Feb. 1, signed by N. Bidwell, and endorsed by William Cook; both payable at Metropolitan Bank, N. Y. Net proceeds to be credited to Alonzo Mitchell. (Dis. R.; For. Tic.)

NARRATIVE.

For Jas. W. Lusk: His draft for $2500, @ 90 ds. from Jan. 15, drawn on and accepted by John R. Penn, payable at Mercantile Bank, N. Y. Net proceeds to credit. (Dis. R.; For. Tic.)

For E. R. Felton: T. P. Handy's note for $1600, @ 4 mos. from Jan. 21, endorsed by D. P. Eells, payable at Commercial Br. Bank, Cleve.; James Richard's acceptance for $3500, @ 60 ds. from Feb. 1, payable at our bank. Net proceeds to credit. (Dis. R.; Dom. Tic.)

For M. B. Scott: Chas. Hickox's acceptance for $7000, @ 90 ds. from Jan. 3, favor of Jacob Hinds, payable at Commercial Br. Bank, Cleve. Net proceeds credited. (Dis. R.; Dom. Tic.)

(The Passed Collections Book and Discount Register are now closed for the day, and the proper amounts transferred to the Debit and Credit Journals. From the Passed Collections the following results are obtained: *Debits*—Lafayette Bank, Cincinnati, $900; Moss Bros., Sandusky, $475. *Credits*—Duncan, Sh. & Co., N. Y., $2970; W. H. Clark, $1500; Lewis R. Morris, $897 75; Jacob Hoornbeek, $473 81; Collection and Exchange, $33 44. From the Discount Register the following results: *Debits*—Bills Discounted, $12100; Domestic Exchange, $10500. *Credits*—A. Mitchell, $4972 50, 2978 50; Jas. W. Lusk, $2468 33; E. R. Felton, $1570 14, 3463 25; M. B. Scott, $6925 34; Interest, 221 94.)

—— MARCH. ——

The following discounts, sent Duncan, Sherman & Co. for collection, have been paid and entered to our credit: No. 1. Wright, Gillet & Rawson, $5000; No. 3. A. J. Comstock, $5000; No. 4. N. Bidwell, $3000. (For. Tic.; Dr. J.; Cr. J.)

Sold Jas. W. Lusk draft on Duncan, Sh. & Co., for $3000, @ 1% prem. (Cr. J.)

Bot. @ 1% discount, $7500 in Canada Funds, which we have sent for our credit to Farmers and Mechanics' Bank, Detroit, paying express charges, $3 75 in cash. (14) (Dr. J.; Cr. J.)

Bot. @ 2% discount, $10000 Government 7 3/10% Treasury notes, for which gave draft on Duncan, Sherman & Co. (15) (Dr. J.; Cr. J.)

Bot. @ 1/4% prem. $5000 New England Bank notes, which we have remitted to Duncan, Sherman & Co., N. Y., to be entered to our credit @ 1/8% discount; Express charges paid in cash, $3 75. (Dr. J.)

Received the following paper for collection:

From Duncan, Sherman & Co., N. Y.: D. Appleton & Co.'s draft on Bryant, Stratton & Co., Cleve., for $2500, dated Feb. 15, @ 30 ds. (Col. R.; Dom. Tic.) Smith & McDougal's draft on J. B. Cobb, Cleve., for $3000, dated Feb. 1, @ 60 ds. (Col. R.; Dom. Tic.) Parker Handy's draft for $6000 on Commercial Br. Bank, Cleve., @ 10 ds.' sight from Mar. 1. (Col. R.; Dom. Tic.)

From W. H. Clark: James Stanton's note for $3000, endorsed by Albert Wellslager, @ 60 ds. from Feb. 15, payable at our bank. (Col. R.; Dom. Tic.)

From J. B. Meriam: D. P. Eells' draft on Handy, Gillett & Co., N. Y., for $1500, @ 30 ds. from Mar. 1. (Col. R.; For. Tic.) M. B. Scott's draft on R. M. Bartlett, Cincinnati, for $2000, @ 60 ds. from Mar. 1. (Col. R.; For. Tic.)

From Lafayette Bank, Cincinnati: Note for $6000, signed by John Gundry and endorsed by D. C. Collins, @ 90 ds. from Jan. 1, payable at Commercial Br. Bank, Cleve. (Col. R.; Dom. Tic.) Murray Shipley's draft on James Parker, Cleve., for $3000, @ 30 ds. from Mar. 1. (Col. R.; Dom. Tic.)

From Lewis R. Morris: E. R. Felton's note for $3000, payable at our bank, endorsed by James Richards, @ 4 mos. from Dec. 1, 1861. (Col. R.; Dom. Tic.) James W. Lusk's note for $1575, endorsed by H. B. Bryant, @ 60 ds. from Feb. 1, payable at our bank. (Col. R.; Dom. Tic.)

From Jacob Hoornbeek: H. C. Spencer's note for $1250, endorsed by P. R. Spencer, Jr., @ 3 mos. from Jan. 15, payable at City Bank, Cleve. (Col. R.; Dom. Tic.)

Received the following deposits: J. W. Lusk, $1530; E. R. Felton, $1900; John R. Penn, $375; H. B. Bryant, $4375 29; John D. Williams, $1500; Robert Brown, $575; James Richards, $2500; Austin Packard, $500; Hiram A. Pryor, $1250; John S. Woolson, $2000; E. L. Jones, $375; Ingham & Bragg, $975; Jacob Hoornbeek, $1500; Geo. A. Crocker, $1900; Lewis R. Morris, $1750; N. C. Winslow, $3750; Asa Mahan, $1400; M. B. Scott, $1300; T. P. Handy, $1100; Alonzo Mitchell, $3750; Henry Ivison, $1200; Joseph P. Walter, $900; Chas. Hickox, $2900. (Cr. J.)

Paid the following checks: H. B. Bryant, $90, 75, 18 20, 138, 143 75; John R. Penn, $118, 120, 35 80, 19 23, 150; John S. Woolson, $112 50, 125, 142, 18 75, 119, 12 50; Asa Mahan, $150, 200, 38 50, 192; John D. Williams, $175; T. P. Handy, $115, 275, 87 50, 90; Lewis R. Morris, $130, 12 75, 18, 110; E. L. Jones, $90, 125, 116, 25 50; Chas. Hickox, $225, 75, 12 50; Alonzo Mitchel, $125, 132 25, 16 75, 300; James Richards, $500, 300; J. W. Lusk, $138, 500, 19 50, 12, 115, 3030 Ingham & Bragg, $132, 119, 12 75, 25, 1500. (Dr. J.)

Discounted the following paper:

For William T. Brooks: Note for $5000, signed by Clarence Shook, and endorsed by L. J. Lyman, dated Jan.

15, @ 90 ds., payable at City Bank, Cleve. (Dis. R.; Dom. Tic.) Jas. W. Lusk's draft on Claflin, Mellen & Co., N. Y., @ 10 ds.' sight [16] for $4000; net proceeds credited. (Dis. R.; For. Tic.)

For James W. Lusk: Note for $6000, @ 60 ds. from Feb. 1, signed by M. B. Scott, and endorsed by Jas. W. Lusk, payable at our bank: net proceeds credited. (Dis. R.; Dom. Tic.)

For J. B. Meriam: Note for $2500, @ 30 ds. from Mar. 1, signed by H. B. Tuttle, and endorsed by N. C. Winslow, payable at Exchange Bank, Buf.: net proceeds paid in cash. (Dis. R.; For. Tic.)

For James Richards—proceeds credited: Draft of James Eells on Ivison, Phinney & Co., N. Y., for $6000, @ 30 ds. from Mar. 1. (Dis. R.; For. Tic.) Note for $2500, signed by W. H. Clark, and endorsed by E. R. Felton, @ 60 ds. from Feb. 1, payable at Lafayette Bk., Cincinnati, charging ¼% for collection. (Dis. R.; For. Tic.)

For M. B. Scott—proceeds credited: Draft of T. P. Handy on Parker Handy, N. Y., for $7000, @ 60 ds. from Feb. 15. (Dis. R.; For. Tic.) Draft of Chas. Hickox on James Armstrong, Buffalo, for $3000, @ 30 ds. from Mar. 1. (Dis. R.; For. Tic.)

For J. B. Cobb: Draft of T. Dwight Eells on Winslow, Lanier & Co., N. Y., for $2500, @ 30 ds. from Mar. 1; net proceeds paid in cash. (Dis. R.; For. Tic.)

For John R. Penn: Note for $12000, @ 90 ds. from Feb. 1, signed by W. B. Ogden, and endorsed by H. B. Bryant, payable at E. I. Tinkham's Bank, Chicago: net proceeds credited. [17] (Dis. R.; For. Tic.)

For E. R. Felton: Draft of H. D. Stratton on D. Appleton & Co., N. Y., for $3000, @ 60 ds. from Mar. 1, payable at Metropolitan Bank: net proceeds credited. (Dis. R.; For. Tic.)

The following collections payable in this city, as per Domestic Tickler, have been paid and entered in the Passed Collections: No. 8, for Lewis R. Morris, $500; No. 9, for Jacob Hoornbeek, $1200; No. 1, for Duncan, Sh. & Co., $1500; No. 6, for W. H. Clark, $2000; No. 11, for Duncan, Sh. & Co., $2500; No. 13, for Duncan, Sh. & Co., $6000. (Dom. Tic.; Pas. Col.)

Discount No. 2, for $4000, has been paid in cash. (Dom. Tic.; Cr. J.)

Discount No. 10, for $4000, sent Duncan, Sh. & Co., N. Y., for collection, has been paid and entered to our credit. (For. Tic.; Dr. J.; Cr. J.)

(The Passed Collection Book and Discount Register are now closed, and the results entered in the Debit and Credit Journals, viz.: FROM PASSED COLLECTIONS—*Credits:* Duncan, Sh. & Co, $1485, 2475, 5940; W. H. Clark, $2000; Lewis R. Morris, $500; Jacob Hoornbeek, $1200; Collection and Exchange, $100. FROM DISCOUNT REGISTER—*Debits:* Bills Discounted, $11000; Domestic Exchange, $42500. *Credits:* W. T. Brooks, $4960, 4000; Jas. W. Lusk, $5965; Jas. Richards, $5967, 2479 17; M. B. Scott, $6942 83, 2983 50; John R. Penn, $11780; E. R. Felton, $2968 50; Interest, $385 25. Collection and Exchange, $96 25.)

— APRIL. —

Issued for John R. Penn, Certificate of Deposit, favor of Thos. Hunter, N. Y., for $3000. (Cr. J.) Also certified J. R. Penn's check for $575. [18] (Cr. J.; Dr. J.)

Discounted for Sumner Packard: his note for $4000, endorsed by James Eaton, @ 60 ds. from April 1, payable at our bank; gave him in payment of net proceeds our draft on Duncan, Sh. & Co., N. Y., @ 1% prem. [19] (Dis. R.; Dom. Tic.; Cr. J.)

Paid cash for Bill Furniture and Fixtures, $575. [20] (Dr. J.)

Received from Duncan, Sh. & Co., per express, $10000 in gold. Paid express charges in cash, $50. (Cr. J.; Dr. J.)

Received the following paper for collection:

From Duncan, Sh. & Co.: E. W. Mason's note, favor of Claflin, Mellen & Co., for $5000, dated Jan. 1. @ 5 months, payable at our bank. (Col. R.; Dom. Tic.) E. R. Felton's note, favor of A. T. Stewart & Co., for $3500, dated Mar. 10, @ 60 ds., payable at our bank. (Col. R.; Dom. Tic.) Bryant & Stratton's draft on J. B. Meriam, for $7000, @ 60 ds. from Mar. 5, payable at City Bank. (Col. R.; Dom. Tic.)

From Lafayette Bank, Cin.: D. C. Collins' draft on E. G. Folsom, Cleve., for $1750, @ 30 ds. from Apr. 1. (Col. R.; Dom. Tic.)

From Burkam & Sons, Chic.: M. B. Scott's note, favor of C. Dunham, for $4000, dated Feb. 10, @ 3 mos., payable at Merchants' Bank, Cleve. (Col. R.; Dom. Tic.) E. Hill's draft on Ingham & Bragg, Cleve., for $3750, @ 60 days from Mar. 10. (Col. R.; Dom. Tic.)

From Wm. Mason, Cleve.: Jacob Hoornbeek's note for $900, dated Feb. 12, @ 90 ds., payable at our bank. (Col. R.; Dom. Tic.)

From E. G. Folsom, Cleve.: A. S. Wheeler's note for $1500, @ 2 mos. from Mar. 15, payable at our bank (Col. R.; Dom. Tic.)

NARRATIVE.

From Exchange Bank, Buf.: J. R. Wheeler's draft on J. B. Cobb, Cleve., for $1000, @ 30 ds. from Apr. 1. (Col. R.; Dom. Tic.)

From Franklin Bank, Columbus: H. Stillman's note, favor of Robert Parker, for $750, @ 4 mos. from Feb. 17, payable at City Bank, Cleveland. (Col. R.; Dom. Tic.)

From E. R. Felton, Cleve.: His draft on J. H. Goldsmith, Detroit, @ 60 ds. from March 20, for $2000—sent Farmers and Mechanics' Bank, for collection. (Col. R.; For. Tic.)

From M. B. Scott, Cleve.: His draft on James Madison, Dayton, Ohio, for $1500, @ 90 ds. from Feb. 20—sent Lafayette Bank, Cincinnati, for collection. (Col. R.; For. Tic.)

From D. P. Eells, Cleve.: James Smith's note, Eells' favor, for $700, @ 60 ds. from Mar. 15, payable at Sandusky—sent Moss Brothers for collection. (Col. R.; For. Tic.)

Discounted the following paper:

For W. H. Clark: His note endorsed by Lewis R. Morris for $5000, @ 60 ds. from Apr. 1, payable at our bank; proceeds credited. (Dis. R.; Dom. Tic.)

For H. D. Stratton: Peter Cooper's note for $15000 endorsed by Wilson G. Hunt, @ 90 ds. from Mar. 25, payable at Commercial Branch Bank, Cleve.; proceeds credited. (Dis. R.; Dom. Tic.)

For J. B. Meriam: N. C. Winslow's note of $7000 endorsed by T. P. Handy, @ 90 ds. from Mar. 1, payable at our bank; proceeds credited. (Dis. R.; Dom. Tic.)

For Charles Baker: His note for $20000 endorsed by John Simmons, @ 60 ds. from Mar. 3, payable at our bank. In addition to the endorsement, Mr. Baker gives us as collateral security, Cleveland and Erie Railroad bonds amounting to $25000; proceeds paid in Cash. [21] (Dis R.; Dom. Tic.)

For E. G. Folsom: H. Bishop's note, his favor for $3000, @ 30 ds. from Apr. 1. payable at our bank; proceeds credited. (Dis R.; Dom. Tic.)

For M. B. Scott: His note, favor of Chauncey Prentiss, endorsed by Jacob Hinds for $10000, @ 60 ds. from Apr. 1, payable at Niagara River Bank, Buffalo; proceeds credited. (Dis R.; For. Tic.)

For John R. Wheeler: R. M. Bartlett's note, his favor endorsed by John Gundry for $3000, @ 90 ds. from Mar. 10, payable at Citizens' Bank, Cin.; charges for collection, ¼%; proceeds paid in cash. (Dis. R.; For. Tic.)

For George M. Penn: His note, favor of E. P. Dolbear, endorsed by H. D. Stratton for $5000, @ 60 ds. from Mar. 31, payable at E. I. Tinkham's Bank, Chicago; Collection and Exchange, ¾%; proceeds credited. (Dis. R.; For. Tic.)

For James Richards: His accepted draft on Austin Packard endorsed by Zalmon Richards for $3500, @ 60 ds from Apr. 1, payable at Fulton Bank, N. Y.; proceeds credited. (Dis. R.; For. Tic.)

For George S. Eaton: W. D. Packard's note, his favor, endorsed by Wm. B. Ogden, for $4000, @ 90 ds. from Apr. 1, payable at Mercantile College Bank, Chicago; Collection and Exchange, ¾%; proceeds paid in draft on Duncan, Sh. & Co., N. Y. (Dis. R.; For. Tic.; Cr. J.)

For John S. Woolson: His draft on Woolson & McFarland, Mt. Pleasant, Iowa, for $3000, accepted Mar. 25, @ 90 ds.' sight, payable at A. & W. A. Sanders, Mt. Pleasant—sent to Burkam & Sons, Chicago, for collection. Col. & Exch. ¾%; proceeds credited. (Dis. R.; For Tic.)

Received the following deposits: M. B. Scott, $900; Jacob Hoornbeek, $750; E. R. Felton, $525; Geo. M. Penn, $1500; E. G. Folsom, $1000; N. C. Winslow, $795: T. P. Handy, $850; John S. Woolson, $782; Lewis R. Morris, $563; Jas. W. Lusk, $1000; Alonzo Mitchell, $1500; E. L. Jones, 1500; James Richards, $500; H. B. Bryant, $675; Robert Brown, $1500; Chas. Hickox, $3000; Ingham & Bragg, $975; John R. Penn. $1200; John D. Williams, $784; Henry Ivison, $1500; Austin Packard, $1275; Joseph P. Walter, $1500; Wm. T. Brooks, $500; W. H. Clark, $1200; Hiram A. Pryor, $3000. (Cr. J.)

Paid the following checks: Chas. Hickox, $7000: H. B. Bryant, $1500, 125, 87 50, 100; James Richards, $3500, 1750, 25; Ingham & Bragg, $175, 238, 500, 75, 115; Robert Brown, $150, 125, 75, 400, 138 50; Asa Mahan, $900, 75, 250; Alonzo Mitchell, $6000, 750, 125, 400; E. L. Jones, $475, 300, 175, 87 50, 12 75; T. P. Handy, $2000, 175, 187 50; John S. Woolson, $75, 137 50; Lewis R. Morris, $156 25, 400, 115, 375; Jas. W. Lusk, $1575, 2000, 175, 125; John R. Penn, $5000, 3000, 1500, 750; Geo. A. Crocker, $500; John D. Williams, $1200, 150; Henry Ivison, $500, 75, 250; Austin Packard, $400, 125; M. B. Scott, $1500, 2000, 135, 120; Jacob Hoornbeek, $750; E. R. Felton, $3000, 2500, 450; N. C. Winslow, $500. (Dr. J.)

The following discounts, payable in the city, as per Dom. Tic., have been paid: No. 7, J. Richards, $3500; No. 8, Chas. Hickox, $7000; No. 9, C. Shook, $5000; No. 11, M. B. Scott, $6000.

The following discounts, sent Duncan, Sh. & Co., for collection, have been paid and credited to us: No. 5, J. R. Penn, $2500; No. 13, I. P. & Co., $6000; No. 15, P. Handy, $7000; No. 17, Winslow, L. & Co., $2500.

Discount No. 12, $2500, H. B. Tuttle, sent Exchange Bank, Buf., for collection, has been paid and entered to our credit. (For. Tic.; Dr. J.; Cr. J.)

Discount No. 16, $3000; M. B. Scott, sent to Exchange Bank, Buffalo, has been protested for non-payment. Expense of protest charged us by Exch. Bk. $1. [22] (For. Tic.; Cr. J.; Dr. J.)

NARRATIVE.

Discount No. 14, W. H. Clark, $2500—sent Lafayette Bank, Cin.; has been paid and entered to our credit (For. Tic.; Dr. J.; Cr. J.)

The following City Collections, due this day, as per Domestic Tickler, have been paid: For Duncan, Sh. & Co., No. 2, $2000; No. 3, $2500; No. 12, $3000; For. W. H. Clark, No. 14, $3000: For Lafayette Bank, Cin., No. 17, $6000; No. 18, $3000; For Lewis R. Morris, No. 19, $3000; No. 20, $1575; For Jacob Hoornbeck, No. 21, $1250. (Pas. Col.; Dom. Tic.)

Collection No. 15, $1500, for J. B. Meriam—sent Duncan, Sh. & Co.; due this day, as per Foreign Tickler, is assumed to have been paid and credited to us. (Pas. Col.; For. Tic.)

(The Passed Collection Book and Discount Register exhibit the following results:—PASSED COLLECTIONS—*Credits*—Duncan, Sh. & Co., $1980, 2475, 2970; W. H. Clark, $3000; Lafayette Bank, Cin., $6000, 3000; Lewis R. Morris, $3000, 1575; Jacob Hoornbeek, $1250; J. B. Meriam, $1500; Collection and Exchange, $75. *Debits*—Duncan, Sh. & Co., $1500. DISCOUNT REGISTER.—*Credits*—W. H. Clark, $4947 50; H. D. Stratton, $14785; J. B. Meriam, $6927 67; E. G. Folsom, $2983 50; M. B. Scott, $9895; George M. Penn, $4910 83 James Richards, $3463 25; John S. Woolson, $2934 50; Interest, $845 58; Collection and Exchange, $97 50. *Debits*—Bills Discounted, $54000; Domestic Exchange, $28500.)

— MAY. —

Received from stockholders final instalment of 40% on Capital Stock, amounting to $80000. (Cr. J.)

Sent Duncan, Sherman & Co. the following funds received from stockholders: A. C. Taylor's draft on Ivison, Phinney & Co. for $6000; J. H. Goldsmith's do. on Bryant, Stratton & Co., $4000; James W. Lusk's do. on Parker Handy, $4000; John R. Penn's do. on East River Bank, $4000; Duncan, Sh. & Co.'s Ctfct. Dep., favor S. S. Packard, Cashier, $8000. (Dr. J.)

Received from State Department semi-annual interest on State Stocks (3% on $20000), $600; and on U. S. Stocks, $600. (Cr. J.)

Paid rent of Banking-House, in cash, to date, $333 34. (Dr. J.)

Received the following paper for Collection:

From W. H. Clark: Solomon Jones' note for $3000, endorsed by Robert Sweetzer, @ 3 mos. from Mar. 25, payable at Adrian, Mich.—sent Toledo Br. Bank for collection. (Col. R.; For. Tic.)

From P. R. Spencer—to be remitted when paid: His draft on H. D. Stratton, Cleve., for $1500, accepted Apr. 30, @ 30 ds., payable at our bank. (Col. R.; Dom. Tic.)

From Duncan, Sherman & Co.: Thomas Smith's note, favor John W. Gantz, for $750, @ 3 mos. from Mar. 20, payable at Ashtabula, O.—sent Farmers' Branch Bank for collection. (Col. R.; For. Tic.) Wm. H. Crocker's draft on J. Rhodes, Oberlin, O., for $900, accepted Apr. 10, @ 60 ds.—sent Lorain Bank, Elyria, for collection. (Col. R.; For. Tic.) Wm. H. Beebe's note, favor of Henry C. Spencer, for $1200, @ 3 mos. from Mar. 15, payable Xenia, O.—sent Lafayette Bank, Cincinnati, for collection. (Col. R.; For. Tic.)

From Merchants' Bank, Massillon—to be remitted when paid: Ezra Jones' note, favor of Robert Dean, for $1000, payable at our bank, @ 30 ds. from May 1. (Col. R.; Dom. Tic.)

From J. B. Meriam: Peter Cook's note, favor of Jacob Hinds, for $750, @ 30 ds. from Apr. 15, payable at Merchants' Bank, Cleveland. (Col. R.; Dom. Tic.) Emerson E. White's draft on E. G. Folsom for $900, @ 10 ds. from Apr. 30, payable at City Bank, Cleve. (Col. R.; Dom. Tic.)

From John R. Penn: Abram Van Wyck's note, favor of John D. Hinde, for $1750, @ 60 ds. from Apr. 25, payable at Ocean Bank, N. Y. (Col. R.; For. Tic.) E. W. Mason's accepted draft, drawn by H. D. Stratton, @ 30 ds. from May 1, for $7000, payable at our bank. (Col. R.; Dom. Tic.)

From George A. Crocker: Charles Jones' note for $750, payable at N. Y. & E. Bank, Buffalo, @ 30 ds. from Apr. 15. (Col. R.; For. Tic.)

From George M. Penn: His draft on Walkden & Co., Toledo, for $2000, @ 30 ds. from May 1. (Col. R.; For. Tic.) Note of James Garrett, endorsed by Robert Lincoln, for $1500, @ 60 ds. from Apr. 15, payable at our bank. (Col. R.; Dom. Tic.)

From James W. Lusk: John Holbrook's note for $2000, endorsed by D. W. Fish, @ 90 ds. from Feb. 15, payable at City Bank, Cleve. (Col. R.; Dom. Tic.) C. B. Stout's note for $500, endorsed by T. S. Quackenbush, @ 30 ds. from Apr. 30, payable at Citizens' Bank, Cincinnati. (Col. R.; For. Tic.)

Received from Farmers & Mechanics' Bank, Detroit, their sight draft on Metropolitan Bank, N.Y., for $3000, the same to be entered to their credit, @ ½% prem. (Cr. J.) Sent the same to Duncan Sh. & Co., for our credit. (Dr. J.)

Received Cash from M. B. Scott in full payment of James Armstrong's note and protest fees, $3001. (Cr. J.)

NARRATIVE.

Issued the following Certificates of Deposit: No. 2, for Lewis R. Morris, to the credit of Robert Smith, Detroit, \$3000; No. 3, for Wm. T. Brooks, to the credit of H. B. Bryant, Buffalo, \$7000; No. 4, for E. G. Folsom, to credit of Geo. Eddy, Albany, \$1000. (Cr. J.)

Chas. Baker's note—Disc. No. 24, for \$20000 has been protested for non-payment; protest fees paid in cash \$1. (Dom. Tic.; Dr. J.; Cr. J.) In accordance with the written permission of Mr. Baker, we have ordered the Railroad Bonds left by him as collateral security, sold at public auction for our benefit; the surplus, if any, to be paid over to him. [23]

Received from Knox Co. Bank, Mt. Vernon, sight draft on H. Bishop, Cleveland, for \$1500, which we have collected, and remitted them the proceeds in our draft on Duncan, Sh. & Co., N. Y., as per their request, at the current rate of exchange. (Cr. J.)

Received from East River Bank, N. Y., our Certificate of Deposit, No. 1, \$3000, issued for John R. Penn. Remitted in payment thereof our draft on Duncan, Sh. & Co., less current exchange. (Dr. J.; Cr. J.)

The Railroad Bonds held by us as collaterals for Discount No. 24, were this day sold at public auction for \$18000, we becoming the purchasers. Auctioneers commissions, ¼% (\$45), paid in cash. (Dr. J.; Cr. J.) [24]

Discounted the following paper:

For E. G. Folsom—proceeds credited: His note for \$4000, endorsed by Jas. Cruikshank, @ 90 ds. from May 1, payable at our bank, *with exchange.* [25] (Dis. R.; Dom. Tic.)

For E. R. Felton—proceeds credited: Barnaby Rudge's note for \$10000, endorsed by Nicolas Nickleby, @ 60 ds. from April 15, payable at Metropolitan Bank, N. Y. (Dis. R.; For. Tic.)

For John S. Woolson—proceeds credited: Smith & Nixon's acceptance for \$6000, @ 60 ds. from April 30, payable at Kinney, Espy & Co.'s, Cincinnati. (Dis. R.; For. Tic.) James Bradley's note for \$5000, endorsed by Robert Peel, @ 90 ds. from April 1, payable at our bank. (Dis. R.; Dom. Tic.)

For J. B. Meriam—proceeds credited: H. D. Stratton's note for \$7500, endorsed by H. D. Clark, @ 60 ds. from May 1, payable at City Bank, Columbus. (Dis. R.; For. Tic.) John R. Penn's note for \$6000, endorsed by Peter Cooper, @ 2 mos. from April 25, payable at East River Bank, N. Y. (Dis. R.; For Tic.)

For J. G. Fox—proceeds in cash: W. H. Clark's note, endorsed by J. G. F., for \$10000, @ 60 ds. from April 1, payable at our bank *with exchange.* (Dis. R.; Dom. Tic.)

For Geo. A. Crocker—proceeds credited: A. Stager's acceptance for \$7000, endorsed by Chas. Jones, @ 3 mos. from Apr. 1, payable at N. Smith's Banking Office, Buffalo. (Dis. R.; For. Tic.) S. S. Packard's note for \$3000, endorsed by W. P. Spencer, @ 60 ds. from Apr. 20, payable at Merchants' Bank, Cleveland. (Dis. R.; Dom. Tic.)

For Chas. Hickox—proceeds credited: His note for \$1500, endorsed by J. Kennedy, @ 90 ds. from Apr. 25, payable at Merchants' Bank, Cleveland. (Dis. R.; Dom. Tic.) Jonathan Gillett's accepted draft, Hickox's favor for \$7000, @ 60 ds. from Apr. 30, payable at Ocean Bank, N. Y. (Dis. R.; For. Tic.)

For Victor M. Rice—proceeds in cash: E. W. Keyes' note for \$8000, @ 30 ds. from Apr. 28, payable at Commercial Bank, Albany. (Dis. R.; For. Tic.)

For E. P. Selmser—proceeds in cash: J. G. Deshler's note for \$15000, endorsed by Hiram Niles, @ 60 ds. from Apr. 15, payable at Geo. Smith & Co.'s Bank, Chicago. (Dis. R.; For. Tic.)

For H. B. Bryant—proceeds credited: R. C. Spencer's note for \$3500, endorsed by James Hamilton, @ 60 ds. from Apr. 10, payable at Farmers & Mechanics' Bank, Detroit. (Dis. R.; For. Tic.) William Smith's acceptance, Robert Davis' favor for \$7000, @ 90 ds. from Apr. 1, payable at City Bank, Troy. Sent Bank of Capitol, Albany, for collection. (Dis. R.; For. Tic.)

For T. P. Handy—proceeds credited: H. B. Tuttle's acceptance for \$10000, @ 30 ds. from May 1, payable at Merchants' Bank, Cleveland. (Dis. R.; Dom. Tic.) E. R. Morgan's note for \$4000, endorsed by William Butts, @ 60 ds. from Apr. 15, payable at Franklin Bank, Columbus. (Dis. R.; For. Tic.)

For John Simmons—proceeds in cash: James Smiley's note for \$8000, endorsed by John Rogers, @ 30 ds. from Apr. 30, payable at our bank. (Dis. R.; Dom. Tic.)

Received the following deposits: N. C. Winslow, \$1500; Jacob Hoornbeek, \$700; M. B. Scott, \$800; Jas. W. Lusk, \$1500; Lewis R. Morris, \$750; E. L. Jones, \$3000; James Richards, \$975; Alonzo Mitchell, \$500; Asa Mahan, \$1500; Robert Brown, \$2000; Ingham & Bragg, \$1700; John R. Penn, \$1200; John D. Williams, \$1350; Henry Ivison, \$2575; Austin Packard, \$758; Hiram A. Pryor, \$1500; Joseph P. Walter, \$900; Geo. M. Penn, \$1500; E. G. Folsom, \$738. (Cr. J.)

Paid the following checks: Lewis R. Morris, \$3000, 5000, 175; Wm. T. Brooks, \$7000, 915, 75; E. G. Folsom, \$1000, 175, 123 75, 94 63; N. C. Winslow, \$700, 83 33, 19 75, 12 50; E. R. Felton, \$9000, 185; Jacob Hoornbeek, \$6750, 1983 25, 12 75, 150; M. B. Scott, \$120, 3000, 5000, 329 83; John S. Woolson, \$5000, 133, 762, 18 50; James W. Lusk, \$217, 25, 172 93, 125; E. L. Jones, \$975, 150; Asa Mahan, \$400, 595, 12 50;

NARRATIVE.

Alonzo Mitchell, $3000, 150, 19^{63}; James Richards, $275, 1250, 318; Ingham & Bragg, $125, 1200; Robert Brown, $125, 25^{73}, 180, 19^{75}; H. B. Bryant, $75, 128^{90}; John R. Penn, $195, 63^{50}, 128; Geo. A. Crocker, $189, 12^{75}, 312^{50}; John D. Williams, $129, 17^{50}, 193^{75}; Henry Ivison, $400, 123, 85^{50}; W. H. Clark, $8000, 2750, 129; Austin Packard, $300, 129, 87^{50}; Hiram A. Pryor, $500, 129, 17^{50}; Joseph P. Walter, $129, 700, 12^{50}; Geo. M. Penn, $900, 127, 13^{75}; H. D. Stratton, $8000, 4000; J. B. Meriam, $3750, 128, 17^{50}; T. P. Handy, $1600, 10000. (Dr. J.)

The following discounts due this day, as per Domestic Tickler, have been paid: No. 6, T. P. Handy, $1600; No. 25, H. Bishop, $3000. (Dom. Tic.; Cr. J.)

The following discounts due this day, as per For. Tickler, are assumed to have been paid, and entries made accordingly: No. 18, W. B. Ogden, $12000, sent Burkam & Sons, Chicago; No. 19, D. Appleton & Co., $3000, sent Duncan, Sh. & Co.; No. 43, E. W. Keyes, $8000, sent Bank of Capitol, Albany. (Dr. J.; Cr. J.)

The following city collections, due this day, as per Dom. Tickler, have been paid: *For Duncan, Sh. & Co.:* No. 23, E. R. Felton, $3500; No. 24, J. B. Meriam, $7000. *For Lafayette Bk., Cin.:* No. 25, E. G. Folsom, $1750. *For Burkam & Sons, Chicago:* No. 26, M. B. Scott, $4000; No. 27, Ingham & Bragg, $3750. *For William Mason* (special): [26] Jacob Hoornbeek, $900. *For E. G. Folsom:* No. 29, A. S. Wheeler, $1500. *For Exchange Bank, Buf.:* No. 30, J. B. Cobb. $1000. *For J. B. Meriam:* No. 41, Peter Cook, $750; No. 42, E. E. White, $900. *For Jas. W. Lusk:* No. 48, John Holbrook, $2000. (Dom. Tic.; Pas. Col.)

The following foreign collections due to-day, as per Foreign Tickler, are assumed to have been paid: *For J. B. Meriam:* No. 16, R. M. Bartlett, $2000, sent Lafayette Bk., Cin. *For E. R. Felton:* No. 32, J. H. Goldsmith, $2000, sent Farmers & Mechanics' Bk., Detroit. *For M. B. Scott:* No. 33, James Madison, $1500, sent Lafayette Bk., Cin. *For D. P. Eells:* No. 34, James Smith, $700, sent Moss Bros., Sandusky. *For Geo. A. Crocker:* No. 45, Chas. Jones, $750, sent Exchange Bank, Buffalo. (For. Tic.; Pas. Col.)

(The Passed Collections Book and Discount Register exhibit the following results:

Passed Collections—*Credits:* Duncan, Sh. & Co., $3465, 6930; Lafayette Bank, Cin., $1750; Burkam & Sons, Chicago, $4000, 3750; E. G. Folsom, $1500; Exchange Bk., Buffalo, $995; J. B. Meriam, $750, 900, 1995; Jas. W. Lusk, $2000; E. R. Felton, $1985; M. B. Scott, 1496^{25}; D. P. Eells, 698^{25}; Geo. A. Crocker, $750; Collection and Exchange, 135^{50}. *Debits:* Lafayette Bk., Cin., $2000, 1500; Farmers & Mech.'s Bank, Det., $2000; Moss Bros., Sandusky, $700; Exchange Bank, Buf., $750.

Discount Register—*Debits:* Bills Discounted, $41500; Domestic Exchange, $81000. *Credits:* E. G. Folsom, $3938; E. R. Felton, 9921^{67}; John S. Woolson, $5923, 4947^{50}; J. B. Meriam, 7402^{50}, 5942; Geo. A. Crocker, 6925^{33}, 2974; Chas. Hickox, 1478^{25}, 6927^{67}; H. B. Bryant, 3449^{25}, 6926^{50}; T. P. Handy, $9945, 3958^{67}; Interest, 1025^{83}; Col. and Exch., 182^{50}.)

—— JUNE. ——

Paid Lafayette Bk. Cin.'s draft on us, favor James Moore, for $1500. (Dr. J.)

Received from Moss Bros., Sandusky, currency in full of their %, $1175. (Cr. J.)

Sold John S. Woolson, at par, our draft for $1800 on Exchange Bk., Buffalo. (Cr. J.)

Received from Duncan, Sh. & Co. $5000 in Ohio State currency, on which they allowed us ¾% discount. (Cr. J.) Paid Express chgs. in case, 3^{75}. (Dr. J.)

Remitted Duncan, Sh. & Co., in N. Y. State currency, $7500, @ ½% discount. Paid Express chgs., $4 (Dr. J.)

Received of W. H. Clark $1000 in gold, as a special deposit. [27]

Received from Toledo Branch Bank $7070 in our own notes, to be invested in New York exchange, at current rates. Sent them our draft on D. Sh. & Co. for net amount. (Cr. J.)

Received the following paper for collection:

From H. D. Stratton: J. C. Bryant's note for $1500, endorsed by Jacob Reifsnider, @ 30 ds. from May 15, payable at Amherst, O. Sent Lorain Bank. (Col. R.; For. Tic.)

From Kinney, Espy & Co., Cincinnati—proceeds to be remitted: John D. Hinde's note of $3000, endorsed by Joseph Kinsey, @10 ds. from May 30, payable at our bank. (Col. R.; Dom. Tic.)

From Penney & Co., Newark—proceeds to be remitted: E. M. Hale's draft on Thomas Irwin for $3500, @ 60 ds. from Apr. 15, payable at our bank. (Col. R.; Dom. Tic.)

From Duncan, Sh. & Co., N. Y.: Daniel Slote's note of $750, endorsed by Joseph Russell, @ 30 ds. from May 10, payable at Clinton Bank, Columbus. Sent Franklin Bk. (Col. R.; For. Tic.) Ivison, Phinney & Co.'s accepted draft, favor of Smith & McDougal, for $500, @ 60 ds. from May 15, payable at Merchants, Bank, Cleve. (Col. R.; Dom. Tic.) Bryant, Stratton & Co.'s draft on J. B. Meriam for $1750, accepted June 1, @ 30 ds., payable at our bank. (Col. R.; Dom. Tic.) A. C. Taylor's note of $500, endorsed by

J. W. Lusk, @ 30 ds. from May 20, payable at Bucyrus Bank. Sent Toledo Branch Bk. (Col. R.; For. Tic.)

From M. B. Scott: S. S. Pomroy's note of $2500, endorsed by C. L. Skeels, @ 60 ds. from May 20, payable at Niagara County Bank, Lockport, N. Y. Sent Exchange Bank, Buf. (Col. R.; For. Tic.) Hiram Newell's note for $350, endorsed by William T. Bush, @ 30 ds. from May 12, payable at Manchester & Rich's Bank, Buffalo. Sent Exchange Bk., Buf. (Col. R.; For. Tic.)

From Bank of Marysville—proceeds to be remitted: John Cook's draft on James Moses for $600, accepted May 10, @ 30 ds., payable at E. B. Hale's Bank, Cleveland. (Col. R.; Dom. Tic.)

From James Richards: Benjamin Carpenter's note of $1700, endorsed by Roderick Dhu, @ 60 ds. from May 12, payable at City Bank, Cleve. (Col. R., Dom. Tic.)

From W. H. Clark: J. G. Fox's note of $750, endorsed by James Romney, @ 30 ds. from May 25, payable at Kraus & Smith's Bank, Toledo. Sent Toledo Br. Bk. (Col. R.; For. Tic.)

From John S. Woolson: Thomas Minturn's draft on Robt. Smith for $1200, accepted Apr. 25, @ 90 ds., payable at Niagara River Bk., Buffalo. Sent Exch. Bk., Buf. (Col. R.; For. Tic.) John Simson's note for $500, endorsed by James Sweeney, @ 30 ds. from May 25, payable at H. Norman Smith's Bk., Buffalo. Sent Exch. Bk., Buf. (Col. R.; For. Tic.)

From Jacob Hoornbeek: E. R. Felton's note of $750, endorsed by A. S. Wheeler, @ 60 ds. from May 18, payable at our bank. (Col. R.; Dom. Tic.)

From Lafayette Bk., Cin.: Jacob Hoornbeek's note of $600, endorsed by Charles Stratton, @ 60 ds. from May 10, payable at Sandusky. Sent Moss Bros. (Col. R.; For. Tic.)

From Exchange Bank, Buffalo: Charles Reynold's note of $700, endorsed by Robert Minturn, @ 20 ds. from May 25, payable at our bank. (Col. R. Dom. Tic.) Henry P. Smith's draft on M. B. Scott for $3500, @ 60 ds. from Apr. 25, payable at City Bank, Cleve. (Col. R.; Dom. Tic.)

From George M. Penn: Henry Stratton's note of $600, endorsed by Abram Vinton, @ 60 ds. from Apr. 10, payable at our bank. (Col. R.; Dom. Tic.)

Sold H. D. Stratton Cleveland & Erie Rail Road Bonds for $23500; receiving in payment thereof his draft on C. V. Culver, New York, which we have remitted Duncan, Sh. & Co. (Dr. J.; Cr. J.)

The following city collections due this day, as per Dom. Tic., have been paid: *For Duncan, Sh. & Co.:* No. 22, E. W. Mason, $5000. *For Franklin Bank, Columbus:* No. 31, H. Stillman, $750. *For P. R. Spencer*—to be called for: No. 36, H. D. Stratton, $1500. *For Merchants' Bank, Massillon*—to be remitted: No. 40, Ezra Jones, $1000. *For John R. Penn:* No. 44, E. W. Mason, $7000. *For Geo. M. Penn:* No. 47, James Garrett, $1500; No. 68, Henry Stratton, $600. *For Kinney, Espy & Co., Cin.*—to be remitted: No. 51, J. D. Hinde, $3000. *For Penney & Co., Newark, O.*—to be remitted: No. 52, Thomas Irwin, $3500. *For Bank of Marysville*—to be remitted: No. 59, James Mason, $600. *For Exchange Bank, Buffalo:* No. 66, Charles Reynolds, $700; No. 67, M. B. Scott, $3500. (Pas. Col.; Dom. Tic.)

The following foreign collections due at this time, as per For. Tic., are assumed to have been paid: *For W. H. Clark:* No. 35, Solomon Jones, $3000, sent Toledo Branch Bank. *For Duncan, Sh. & Co.:* No. 37, Thos. Smith, $750, sent Farmers' Br. Bk., Ashtabula. No 38, J. Rhoades, $900, sent Lorain Bank, Elyria. No. 39, W. H. Beebe, $1200, sent Lafayette Bk, Cincinnati. *For John R. Penn:* No. 43, Abram Van Wyck, $1750, sent Duncan Sh. & Co., N. Y. *For Geo. M. Penn:* No. 46, Walkden & Co, $2000, sent Toledo Br. Bank. *For Jas. W. Lusk:* No. 49, C. B. Stout, $500, sent Lafayette Bk., Cincinnati. *For H. D. Stratton:* No. 50, J. C. Bryant, $1500, sent Lorain Bk., Elyria. *For Duncan, Sh. & Co.:* No. 53, Daniel Slote, $750, sent Franklin Bk. Columbus. No. 56, A. C. Taylor, $500, sent Toledo Br. Bank. *For M. B. Scott:* No. 58, Hiram Newell, $350, sent Exch. Bk. Buffalo. *For W. H. Clark:* No. 61, J. G. Fox, $750, sent Toledo Br. Bank. *For John S. Woolson:* No. 63, James Sweeney, $500, sent Exch. Bk., Buffalo. (Pas. Col.; For. Tic.)

The following discounts payable in the city, due this day, as per Dom. Tic., have been paid: No. 20, Sumner Packard, $4000; No. 21, W. H. Clark, $5000; No. 22, Peter Cooper, $15000; No. 23, N. C. Winslow, $7000; No. 38, W. H. Clark, $10000, with exchange added $100; No. 40, S. S. Packard, $3000; No. 47, H. B. Tuttle, $10000. (Cr. J.) No. 49, J. Smiley, has been extended to July 2, interest to be added.

The following discounts sent abroad for collection, due this day, as per For. Tic., are assumed to have been paid: No. 26, M. B. Scott, $10000, sent Exch. Bk. Buf.; No. 27, R. M. Bartlett, $3000, sent Lafayette Bk., Cin.; No. 28, Geo. M. Penn, $5000, sent Burkam & Sons. Chic.; No. 29, Austin Packard, $3500, sent Duncan, Sh. & Co., N. Y.; No. 31, Woolson & McFarland, $3000, sent Burkam & Sons, Chic.; No. 33, Barnaby Rudge, $10000, sent Duncan, Sh. & Co., N. Y.; No. 37, John R. Penn, $6000, sent Duncan, Sh. & Co., N. Y.; No. 44, J. G. Deshler, $15000, sent Burkam & Sons, Chic.; No. 45, R. C. Spencer, $3500, sent Farmers & Mechanics' Bk., Det.; No. 48, E. R. Morgan, $4000, sent Franklin Bk., Col. Burkam & Sons, Chicago, advise us that our Discount, No. 30, W. D. Packard, for $4000, due July 3, has been paid. (For Tic.; Dr. J.; Cr. J.)

NARRATIVE.

Discounted the following paper:

For N. C. Winslow—proceeds credited: Geo. M. Strong's note of \$3000, endorsed by James Mallory, @ 60 ds. from June 1, payable at our bank. (Dis. R.; Dom. Tic.) Edward Savery's note of \$1500, endorsed by T. P. Handy, @ 90 ds. from May 31, payable at City Bank, Cleve. (Dis. R.; Dom. Tic.)

For Lewis R. Morris—proceeds credited: Philip Seaton's note of \$5000, endorsed by James Smiley, @ 60 ds. from May 3, payable at H. Norman Smith's Banking Office, Buffalo. Sent Exchange Bank. (Dis. R.; For. Tic.) Peter Stone's acceptance for \$4750, endorsed by E. G. Folsom, at 60 ds. from May 27, payable at our bank. (Dis. R.; Dom. Tic.)

For T. P. Handy—proceeds credited: Thomas Jones' note of \$7500, endorsed by Hiram Dixon, @ 3 mos. from May 31, payable at East River Bank, N. Y. (Dis. R.; For. Tic.) Jacob Harrison's note of \$1500, endorsed by Charles Eaton, @ 60 ds. from June 1, payable at Merchants' Bank, Cleve. (Dis. R.; Dom. Tic.)

For E. L. Jones—proceeds credited: W. H. Woodbury's accepted draft for \$6000, endorsed by Joseph Arnold, @ 3 mos. from May 15, payable at Dayton Bank. Sent Lafayette Bank, Cin. (Dis. R.; For. Tic.) W. T. Sherman's note of \$3750, endorsed by Childs and Peterson, @ 6 mos. from Mar. 15, payable at Bank of Commerce, Phila. Sent Girard Bank, Phila. (Dis. R.; For. Tic.)

For Asa Mahan—proceeds credited: E. R. Finney's note of \$600, endorsed by H. B. Bryant, @ 60 ds. from May 10, payable at Alleghany Bank, Pittsburg. Sent Iron City Bank. (Dis. R.; For. Tic.)

For Robert Brown—proceeds credited: Samuel Rand's note of \$6750, endorsed by Peter McGrath, @ 8 mos. from Jan. 15, payable at City Bank, Cleve. (Dis R.; Dom. Tic.)

For Ingham & Bragg—proceeds credited: John Pelton's acceptance for \$1800, endorsed by Robert Martin, @ 4 mos. from May 12, payable at Bank of Galena, Ill. Sent Burkam & Sons, Chic. (Dis. R.; For. Tic.) Horace Holden's note for \$1500, endorsed by Thomas Foulke, @ 60 ds. from May 15, payable at our bank. (Dis. R.; Dom. Tic.)

For John D. Williams—proceeds credited: William Gray's acceptance for \$900, endorsed by Henry C. Spencer, @ 3 mos. from May 25, payable at C. V. Culver & Co.'s Banking Office, N. Y. (Dis. R.; For. Tic.) E. W. Mason's note for \$1500, endorsed by C. R. Wells, @ 4 mos. from Apr. 10, payable at Bank of Po'keepsie. Sent Duncan, Sh. & Co. (Dis R.; For. Tic.)

Received the following deposits: T. P. Handy, \$700; D. P. Eells, \$745; Wm. T. Brooks, \$1275; George M. Penn, \$900; E. G. Folsom, \$1560; H. D. Stratton, $\$3763^{75}$; Joseph P. Walter, \$1960; Hiram A. Pryor, \$3750; Austin Packard, \$670; W. H. Clark, \$1200; Henry Ivison, \$800; Geo. A. Crocker, \$500; John R. Penn, \$700; H. B. Bryant, \$300; Charles Hickox, \$1700; Alonzo Mitchell, \$1500; Asa Mahan, \$700; Robert Brown, \$962; James Richards, \$1500; E. L. Jones, \$900; John S. Woolson, \$400; James W. Lusk, $\$1832^{98}$; M. B. Scott, \$936; Jacob Hoornbeek, \$406; E. R. Felton, \$729; N. C. Winslow, \$300. (Cr. J.)

Paid the following checks: N. C. Winslow, \$3750, 400, 110; M. B. Scott, \$6000, 125, 146^{32}, 154; Jacob Hoornbeek, \$900, 18^{75}; E. R. Felton, \$213, 180, 25, 37^{50}; E. L. Jones, \$4000, 3718, 125; James W. Lusk, \$416, 253^{75}, 15, 22^{50}; T. P. Handy, \$6000, 194, 212^{75}; John S. Woolson, \$1800, 400, 239, 212^{50}; Lewis R. Morris, \$90, 12^{50}, 28, 19^{25}, 142; Ingham & Bragg, \$1500, 170, 12^{50}, 13^{25}, 50; Robert Brown, \$5000, 112^{50}; Asa Mahan, \$300, 112^{50}, 97^{75}; James Richards, \$4000, 137^{50}, 19^{75}; John D. Williams, \$1200, 17^{50}, 26, 38^{25}, 14^{75}; Geo. A. Crocker, \$8000, 125, 210; John R. Penn, \$125, 12^{50}, 16; Charles Hickox, \$1275, 182, 100; H. B. Bryant, \$150, 2000, 1200; Joseph B. Walter, \$275, 117, 142^{50}; Hiram A. Pryor, \$90, 110, 12^{75}, 125; Austin Packard, \$112, 145, 19; W. H. Clark, \$110, 112; Henry Ivison, \$500, 123, 17^{50}; Geo. M. Penn, \$125, 12^{75}, 18; W. T. Brooks, \$175, 19, 12; E. G. Folsom, \$19, 120, 117; H. D. Stratton, \$125, 19, 12^{50}, 20; J. B. Meriam, \$12000, 150, 119; D. P. Eells, \$150, 19^{75}, 112. (Dr. J.)

Received interest on Treasury Notes from Mar. 1, to June 1, \$184. (Cr. J.)

Received from Duncan, Sh. & Co., their semi-annual account current, by which it appears that our average balance on deposit with them during the five months ending June 1, is $\$38204^{95}$; for which we are credited interest @ 3% per annum, as per agreement, $\$477^{56}$.[28] (Dr. J.; Cr. J.)

Received certified check of \$575 issued J. R. Penn, May 1, for which gave draft on Duncan, Sh. & Co. favor of J. L. Dawes, at current rate of exchange. Premium paid in cash. (Dr. J.; Cr. J.)

Certificate of Deposit, No. 2, for \$3000, is returned to us by Farmers & Mechanics' Bank, Detroit, to apply on their %. (Dr. J.; Cr. J.)

The Passed Collections Book and Discount Register exhibit the following results.

PASSED COLLECTIONS—*Credits*—Duncan, Sherman & Co, \$4950, 740^{62}, 888^{75}, 1185, 740^{62}, 493^{75}; Franklin Bk. Col., \$750; John R. Penn, \$7000, 1750; Geo. M. Penn, \$1500, 600, 1995; Exchange Bk., Buf., $\$696^{50}$, 3482^{50}; W. H. Clark, $\$2992^{50}$, 748^{12}; Jas. W. Lusk, $\$498^{75}$; H. D. Stratton, $\$1496^{25}$; M. B. Scott, \$350; John S. Woolson, \$500; Collection and Exchange, $\$141^{64}$. *Debits*—Toledo Br. Bk., \$3000, 2000, 500, 750;

Farmers' Br. Bk., Ashtabula, $750; Lorain Bank, Elyria, $900, 1500; Lafayette Bk., Cin., $1200, 500; Duncan, Sh. & Co., $1750; Franklin Bk. Col., $750; Exchange Bk., Buf., $350, 500.

DISCOUNT REGISTER:—*Credits:* N. C. Winslow, $2968 50, 1477; Lewis R. Morris, $4971 67, 4704 08; T. P. Handy, $7382 50, 1484 25; E. L. Jones, $5907, 3681 88; Asa Mahan, $595 90; Robert Brown, $6627 38; Ingham & Bragg, $1754 70, 1488 50; John D. Williams, $886 80, 1481 75; Interest, $609 59; Col. and Exch., $28 50. *Debits:* Bills Discounted, $19000; Domestic Exchange, $27050.

Paid officers and clerks' salaries, as follows: President, $1000; Cashier, $750; First Teller, $600; Second Teller, $500; Book-keeper, $500; Assistant Book-keeper, $400; Porter, $200. (Dr. J.)

(It is now proposed to ascertain the current condition of the business, with a view to declaring the first semi-annual dividend. The following accounts are closed into Loss and Gain: Collection and Exchange, *credit* balance, $837 01; Expense, *debit* balance, $4478 34; Interest, *credit* balance, $5044 25; C. & E. R. R. Bonds, *credit* balance, $5500. [29] By transferring these amounts to the Loss and Gain account, we ascertain our net gain to be $4946 99. Upon this state of affairs being reported to the Directors, who are also satisfactorily assured that the resources shown on the Ledger are real and available, it is decided to declare a semi-annual dividend of 2% from the earnings. [3

—— JULY. ——

NOTE.—The transactions which follow complete the year, and furnish the material for another fiscal period; thereby affording the student sufficient practice to establish him thoroughly in the principles and applications contemplated by the set. It is presumed that the very elaborate instructions given in connection with the previous entries will render it wholly unnecessary to point out the special channels through which the remaining transactions are to find their way into the book of *results*. From this point forward the student must trust to himself; and if he has been thus far faithful, the difficulties which he will encounter will be few and easily surmounted. He will, of course, use the same books as for the previous entries, and in the same manner. If his work is right, the results can not differ materially from those submitted at the close of this narrative.

Received from Farmers' Branch Bank, Ashtabula, $750 in currency.

Paid the following dividends in cash: H. D. Stratton, $200; H. B. Bryant, $200; Parker Handy, $400; Henry Ivison, $500; W. H. Clark, $500; M. B. Scott, $300.

Remitted Duncan, Sh. & Co. our draft on them for their dividend ($400), less the current discount. [31]

Received per express, from Duncan, Sh. & Co., $6000 in Ohio currency, @ ¼% discount. Paid express charges in cash, $4 50.

Paid the following dividends in cash: J. B. Meriam, $200; John R. Penn, $200; James W. Lusk, $200; J. H. Goldsmith, $200.

Paid the following dividends by drafts on Duncan, Sh. & Co., at current exchange: Peter Cooper, $400; A. C. Taylor, $300.

Received the following paper for collection:

From Lafayette Bank, Cin.: Shepard Hamlin's draft on P. Conover, Ashtabula, for $575, accepted June 15, @ 60 ds. sight, payable at Farmers' Branch Bank.

From Duncan, Sherman & Co., N. Y.: Ivison, Phinney & Co.'s note of $3700, endorsed by H. C. Spencer, @ 60 ds. from June 10th, payable at our bank; W. W. Harder's accepted draft of $360, favor of Robert Spellman, @ 30 ds. from June 16, payable at Merchants' Br. Bank, Cleve.

From Charles Hickox: Thomas Curtis' note of $3000, endorsed by William Dooley, @ 60 ds. from June 12, payable at Springfield, Ill. Sent Burkam & Sons, Chicago.

From Geo. A. Crocker: W. B. Jameson's accepted draft of $3000, drawn by James Maxwell, @ 90 ds. from May 10, payable at City Bank, Cincinnati. Sent Laf. Bk.

From Joseph P. Walter: James Cook's note of $1500, endorsed by W. W. Birdsall, @ 60 ds. from June 25, payable in Detroit. Sent Farmers & Mechs.' Bk.

From Hiram A. Pryor: Edwin C. Packard's note of $900, endorsed by Stetson Eaton, @ 60 ds. from June 12, payable at Waupacca, Wis. Sent Burkam & Sons, Chic.

From Franklin Bk., Columbus: W. Burton's draft on H. B. Bryant for $1500, accepted June 10, @ 30 ds., payable at City Bk., Cleve.; W. T. Coggeshall's draft on Ingham & Bragg for $700, accepted June 25, @ 30 ds., payable at our bank.

From Exchange Bk., Buffalo: James Sweeney's draft on Bryant, Stratton & Co. for $7000, accepted June 16, @ 60 ds., payable at Elyria. Sent Lorain Bk.; N. Hucker's draft on Peter Van Dusen for $3750, @ 3 mos. from Apr. 15, payable at City Bank, Cleve.

The following discounts, payable in the city, due this day, have been paid: No. 35, James M. Bradley,

$5000; No. 41, Chas. Hickox, $1500; No. 49, James Smiley, $8000; interest on same, $40; No. 53, Peter Stone, $4750; No. 60, H. Holden, $1500.

The following discounts, payable abroad, are assumed to have been paid: [32] No. 34, Smith & Nixon, $6000, sent Lafayette Bk., Cin.; No. 36, H. D. Stratton, $7500, sent Franklin Bk., Col.; No. 39, Chas. Jones, $7000, sent Exch. Bk., Buf.; No. 42, Jonathan Gillett, $7000, sent Duncan, Sh. & Co., N. Y.; No. 46, William Smith, $7000, sent Bank of Capitol, Albany; No. 52, Philip Seaton, $5000, sent Exchg. Bk., Buffalo; No. 58, E. R. Finney, $600, sent Iron City Bk., Pittsburg.

Discounted the following paper:

For E. W. Mason—proceeds credited: J. C. Hall's note of $2000, endorsed by Robert C. Bangs, @ 60 ds. from June 18, payable at Providence, R. I. Sent Duncan, Sh. & Co., N. Y.

For W. W. Harder—proceeds remitted in cash: His draft on H. B. Bryant, Chicago, for $2500, accepted June 25, @90 ds., payable in N. Y. Sent D., Sh. & Co.

For Jacob Hoornbeek—proceeds credited: W. P. Pratt's note for $1500, endorsed by D. C. Collins, @ 90 ds. from July 1, payable at Cincinnati. Sent Lafayette Bk.

For D. P. Eells—proceeds credited: W. G. Morton's accepted draft of $2300, @ 60 ds. from June 30, payable at our bank; R. C. Spencer's note of $5000, @ 6 mos. from May 10, endorsed by B. McGann, payable at Merchants' Bk., Cleve.

For W. Dwight Packard—proceeds remitted: Ivison, Phinney & Co.'s note for $1575, endorsed by H. D. Stratton, @ 4 mos. from June 12, payable at New York. Sent D. Sh. & Co.

For M. B. Scott—proceeds credited: J. Sackrider's note of $4500, endorsed by M. B. S., @ 3 mos. from June 12, payable at Merchants' Bk., Cleve.: N. C. Winslow's accepted draft, M. B. S.'s favor, for $2750, @ 60 ds. from June 30, payable at Xenia. Sent Lafayette Bk., Cin.

For E. G. Folsom—proceeds credited: Thomas Brown's note of $2758, endorsed by Wm. Burnett, @ 6 mos. from June 10, payable at Galena, Ill. Sent Burkam & Son, Chic.

For James Richards—proceeds credited: His note of $1960, endorsed by J. G. Deshler, @ 3 mos. from July 1, payable at our bank.

For Ira Packard—proceeds remitted: Wm. Bryant's note of $500, @ 90 ds. from June 30, payable at Ann Arbor, Mich. Sent Farmers & Mechs.' Bk., Det.

Received the following deposits: H. B. Bryant, $500; Robert Brown, $750; E. W. Mason, $3000; J. P. Walter, $975; Hiram A. Pryor, $700; W. H. Clark, $750; H. Ivison, $1575; J. D. Williams, $838 75; Asa Mahan, $938 50; Jacob Hoornbeek, $1200; N. C. Winslow, $837 50; Geo. A. Crocker, $718 25; Austin Packard, $1563 75; W. T. Brooks, $946; Jas. W. Lusk, $439.

Paid the following checks: Chas. Hickox, $1500, 700, 125, 14 75; M. B. Scott, $4000, 1563 25, 112, 19 75; Lewis R. Morris, $4365, 120, 118, 46 58; John S. Woolson, $1500, 125, 144; H. B. Bryant, $3695, 123 75, 144, 209; John R. Penn, $6000; Geo. M. Penn, $112, 134, 3263 19; J. B. Meriam, $1200, 154 63, 219, 275; E. G. Folsom, $1500; T. P. Handy, $175, 1200, 375, 14 95; Jas. Richards, $144, 12 75, 164 29; Ingham & Bragg, $1200, 193, 400, 175; Geo. A. Crocker, $124, 19, 206 25; Hiram A. Pryor, $127, 19 65, 144 38; J. W. Lusk, $127, 13 50, 144, 18 75.

The following foreign collections due this day, as per Foreign Tickler, are assumed to have been paid, and we now transfer them to the Passed Collections Book: *For M. B. Scott:* No. 57, S. S. Pomroy, $2500, sent Exch. Bk., Buf. *For John S. Woolson:* No. 62, Robert Smith, $1200, sent Exch. Bk., Buf. *For Lafayette Bk., Cin.:* No. 65, Jacob Hoornbeek, $600, sent Moss Bros., Sandusky.

The following home collections have been paid, and results transferred to Passed Collections: *For Duncan, Sh. & Co.:* No. 54, Ivison, Ph. & Co., $500; No. 55, J. B. Meriam, $1750, No. 71, W. W. Harder, $360. *For James Richards:* No. 60, Benj. Carpenter, $1700. *For Jacob Hoornbeek:* No. 64, E. R. Felton, $750. *For Franklin Bk., Col.:* No. 76, H. B. Bryant, $1500; No. 77, Ingham & Bragg, $700. *For Exchange Bk., Buf.:* No. 79, Peter Van Dusen, $3750.

The following results are taken from the Passed Collection Book and Discount Register:

PASSED COLLECTIONS—*Debits:* Exchange Bk., Buf., $2500, 1200; Moss Bros., Sandusky, $600. *Credits:* M. B. Scott, $2500; John S. Woolson, $1200; Lafayette Bk., Cin., $598 50; Duncan, Sh. & Co., $495, 1732 50, 356 40; Jas. Richards, $1700; Jacob Hoornbeek, $750; Franklin Bk., Col., $1500, 700; Exch. Bk., Buffalo, $3731 25; Col. & Exch., $46 35.

DISCOUNT REGISTER—*Debits:* Bills Discounted, $13760; Domestic Exchange, $13583. *Credits:* E. W. Mason, $1983 33; Jacob Hoornbeek, $1473; D. P. Eells, $2276 23, 4887 50; M. B. Scott, $4443, 2714 70; E. G. Folsom, $2661 49; Jas. Richards, $1928 97; Interest, $440 21; Col. & Ex., 35 05.

NARRATIVE.

—— AUGUST. ——

Sold James Richard's draft on Duncan, Sh. & Co. for $4000, at current rate of exchange.

Issued Certificate of Deposit, favor of Thomas Jones, for $3000.

Received from Exchange Bk., Buf., for their credit, sight draft on Merchants' Bk., Cleve., for $15000. [33]

Purchased at ½% prem. the following N. Y. drafts, which we have remitted Duncan, Sh. & Co. on %: W. P. Pratt on Metropolitan Bk., $3500; W. W. Harder on Culver & Penn, $2000; Ctfct. Dep. on Chemical Bk., $3750; J. B. Meriam on P. Handy & Co., $1275; H. D. Stratton on Peter Cooper, $5600.

Purchased, @ ¾% discount, D. P. Eells' sight draft on J. H. Goldsmith, Detroit, for $3000. Sent the same to Farmers & Mechanics' Bank for our credit. [34]

Received from Burkam & Sons, Chicago, on %, $10000 in New York State bank notes, @½% prem. Remitted the same to Duncan, Sh. & Co., N. Y., @ ¼% discount. Paid express chgs. in cash, $5. [35]

Purchased, per draft on Duncan, Sh. & Co., $50000 in U. S. 6% Stocks, @ $1 02. Sent the same to State Department as basis for new issue of circulation.

Received the following deposits: Jas. W. Lusk, $900; Lewis R. Morris, $1275; T. P. Handy, $738; E. L. Jones, $1027; Jas. Richards, $745; Ingham & Bragg, $839; Chas Hickox, $2940; Geo. M. Penn, 967 32; H. D. Stratton, $642 50; E. W. Mason, $1575; J. B. Meriam, $2675; W. W. Harder, $1000.

Received the following paper for collection:

From Exchange Bank, Buffalo: H. P. Smith's draft on M. B. Scott, accepted July 1, @ 45 ds., for $4000, payable at Merchants' Bank, Cleve.; J. P. Warner's note of $2500, endorsed by James Sweeney, at 60 ds. from June 15, payable at City Bank.

From Bank of Capitol, Albany: B. F. Payn's draft on J. Holbrook, Elyria, for $1500, accepted July 15, @ 30 ds. Sent Lorain Bank, Elyria.

From T. P. Handy: Calvin S. Sill's note for $1255, endorsed by G. S. Berry, @ 2 mos. from June 20, payable at our bank; Henry Morgan's note of $3500, endorsed by John Baxter, @ 60 days from July 25, payable at City Bank.

From H. D. Stratton: John R. Penn's note of $1200, endorsed by W. H. Clark, @ 30 ds. from July 17, payable at our bank; Alonzo Mitchell's note of $3750, endorsed by J. J. Newell, @ 60 ds. from July 27, payable at Adrian, Mich. Sent Toledo Branch Bank.

From Farmers & Mechs.' Bank, Detroit: J. H. Goldsmith's draft on H. B. Bryant, for $3000, accepted June 14, @ 60 ds, payable at our bank.

From Chas. Hickox: Abram Van Wyck's note of $3700, endorsed by Robert Schuyler, @ 2 mos. from July 17, payable at Dayton, O. Sent Lafayette Bk., Cin.

From Ira Packard—proceeds to be remitted: Charles Willard's draft on Hubby & Hughes for $2000, accepted May 17, @ 90 ds., payable at our bank.

Discounted the following paper:

For Edwin C. Packard—proceeds remitted in draft on D. Sh. & Co., N. Y.: John Brewster's note of $3000, endorsed by John Wentworth, @ 90 ds. from July 22, payable in Chicago. Sent Burkam & Sons. [36]

For John S. Woolson—proceeds credited: Lewis J. Lyman's note of $1250, endorsed by C. Shook, @ 3 mos. from July 27, payable at City Bank.

For W. W. Harder—proceeds credited: S. S. Packard's draft on H. D. Stratton for $4000, accepted July 19, @ 90 ds., payable at Metropolitan Bk., N. Y. Sent D., Sh. & Co.

For J. B. Meriam—proceeds credited: E. C. Benedict's note of $3700, endorsed by J. B. M. @ 60 ds. from Aug. 1, payable at our bank.

For Jacob Hoornbeek—proceeds credited: Samuel Sly's note of $1500, endorsed by Thomas Perrin @ 4 mos. from July 22, payable at Sandusky. Sent Moss Bros.

For James Richards—proceeds credited: Cyrus Ford's note of $2700, endorsed by Reuben Hitchcock, @ 4 mos. from July 28, payable in Detroit. Sent Farmers & Mechs.' Bk.

For E. G. Folsom—proceeds credited: Samuel Slick's accepted draft E. G. F.'s fav. for $1794, @ 90 ds. from July 10, payable at Chicago. Sent Burkam & Sons.

For J. C. Bryant—proceeds paid in cash: W. P. Spencer's note of $1900, endorsed by Gerritt Smith, @ 3 mos. from July 12, payable at Buffalo. Sent Exchange Bk.

The following discounts due at home, as per Domestic Tickler, have been paid: No. 32, E. G. Folsom, $4000—Exchange $40; No. 50, Geo. M. Strong, $3000; No. 55, Jacob Harrison, $1500.

The following discounts due abroad, as per Foreign Tickler, are assumed to have been paid: No. 56, W. H. Woodbury, $6000, sent Laf. Bk., Cin.; No. 62, William Gray, $900, sent Duncan, Sh. & Co., N. Y.; No. 63, E. W. Mason, $1500, sent Duncan, Sh. & Co., N. Y.; No. 64, J. C. Hall, $2000, sent Duncan, Sh. & Co., N. Y. [37]

The following collections, payable in the city, as per Domestic Tickler, have been paid: For *D., Sh. & Co.*

No. 70, $3700. *For Exchg. Bk., Buf.*, No. 80, $4000; No. 81, $2500. *For T. P. Handy*, No. 83, $1255. For *H. D. Stratton*, No. 85, $1200. *For Far. & Mechs.' Bk., Det.*, No. 87, $3000. *For Ira Packard*, (special), No. 89, $2000.

The following collections, payable abroad, are assumed to have been paid: *For Lafayette Bk., Cin.*, No. 69, $575, sent Farmers' Br. Bk., Ash. *For Chas. Hickox*, No. 72, $3000, sent Burkam & Sons, Chic. *For Geo. A. Crocker*, No. 73, $3000, sent Laf. Bk., Cin. *For Joseph P. Walter*, No. 74, $1500, sent F. & Mechs.' Bk., Det. *For Hiram A. Pryor*, No. 75, $900, sent Burkam & Sons, Chic. *For Exch. Bk., Buf.*, No. 78, $7000, sent Lorain Bk., Elyria. *For Bank of Cap., Albany*, No. 82, $1500, sent Lorain Bk., Elyria.

Paid the following checks: N. C. Winslow, $500, 425; E. R. Felton, $118, 25^{63}, 194, 123^{75}; Jacob Hoornbeek, $119, 154, 12^{75}; E. L. Jones, $194, 183^{75}, 125^{60}, 1500; Alonzo Mitchell, $2000; Asa Mahan, $196, 187^{50}, 38^{93}; M. B. Scott, $4000, 125; Henry Ivison, $3700, 149, 87^{63}; H. D. Stratton, $1200, 125, 194, 317; H. B. Bryant, $3000, 129, 128, 78^{63}; Robert Brown, $196; J. D. Williams, $110, $$144^{75}$; W. H. Clark, $175, 393^{75}, 126, 87^{50}; Austin Packard, $194, 163^{50}, 1200; W. T. Brooks, $175, 129, 14^{50}.

The following results are taken from the Discount Register and Passed Collections:

Discount Register—*Debits:* Bills Discounted, $4950; Domestic Exchange, $14894. *Credits:* John S. Woolson, $$1231^{25}$; W. W. Harder, $$3946^{67}$; J. B. Meriam, $$3661^{15}$; Jacob Hoornbeek, 1467^{25}; James Richards, $$2624^{85}$; E. G. Folsom, $$1759^{32}$; Interest, $$281^{31}$; Col. & Exch., $$59^{95}$.

Passed Collections—*Debits:* Farmers' Br. Bk., Ash., $575; Burkam & Sons, Chic., $3000, 900; Lafayette Bk., Cin., $3000; F. & Mech.'s Bank, Det., $1500; Lorain Bank, Elyria, $7000, 1500. *Credits:* Duncan, Sh. & Co., $3663; Exch. Bk., Buf., $3980, 2487^{50}, 6947^{50}; T. P. Handy, $1255; H. D. Stratton, $1200; Far. & Mechs.' Bk., Det., $3000; Laf. Bk., Cin., $$573^{56}$; Chas. Hickox, $$2977^{50}$; Geo. A. Crocker, $$2992^{50}$; Joseph P. Walter, $$1488^{75}$; Hiram A. Pryor, $$893^{25}$; Bank of Capitol, Albany, $$1481^{25}$; Col. and Exch., $$190^{19}$

—— SEPTEMBER. ——

Sold W. E. Crocker for cash at par, our draft of $2000, on Farmers & Mechs.' Bank, Detroit. [38]

Received from Burkam & Sons, Chicago, our Ctfct. Dep. No. 3, $7000, issued May 1, fav. H. B. Bryant

Received from Duncan, Sh. & Co., $3000 in unassorted Ohio State currency, at $1\frac{1}{2}$% discount. [39]

Issued Ctfct. Dep. fav. of R. C. Spencer, Chicago, for $3000.

Received from Farmers & Mechs.' Bk., Detroit, $5000 in Cleveland city funds, for which we give them draft on D., Sh. & Co., N. Y., at current rate of exchange.

Received from Lafayette Bk., Cin., per express, $7500 in N. Y. State currency, @ $\frac{1}{2}$% prem. Sent the same to Exchange Bk., Buf., at par. Paid Express chgs. in cash, $2.

Received the following deposits: E. R. Felton, $1575; N. C. Winslow, $2550; M. B. Scott, $$1354^{29}$; Alonzo Mitchell, $2738; Asa Mahan, $1835; Robert Brown, $$2793^{50}$; H. B. Bryant, $2363; John R. Penn, $1456; J. D. Williams, $$564^{28}$; H. Ivison, $1200; W. H. Clark, $1358; Austin Packard, $2700; Wm. T. Brooks, $1340; D. P. Eells, $1490; E. W. Mason, $1293; W. W. Harder, $1496; Geo. M. Penn, $1200; H. D. Stratton, $1278; Chas. Hickox, $1000.

Paid rent of Banking House in cash, $$333^{33}$.

Received the following paper for collection:

From Duncan, Sh. & Co.: J. Hardinge's note of $7000, endorsed by Robert C. Biddle, @ 90 ds. from July 20, payable in Detroit. Sent Farmers & Mechs.' Bk. Ivison, Phinney & Co.'s draft on Ingham & Bragg for $1500, accepted Aug. 12, @ 30 ds., payable at Merchants' Bk., Cleve.

From Lafayette Bk., Cin.: D. C. Collins' draft on P. Hoadley for $3750, accepted July 12, @ 60 ds., payable at our bank; John Fitzsimmons' sight-draft, for $2500, on P. R. Spencer, payable at Ashtabula. Sent Farmers' Br. Bk.

From Burkam & Sons, Chic.: D. V. Bell's draft on S. Sheldon for $1750, accepted Aug. 12, @ 30 ds., payable at Oberlin. Sent Lorain Bk., Elyria. Thos. Hewes' note of $2700, endorsed by James Thompson, @ 40 ds. from Aug. 15, payable at City Bk., Cleve.

From John R. Penn: C. V. Culver's note of $1700, endorsed by James Watson, @ 30 ds. from Aug. 15, payable at Philadelphia. Sent Girard Bank.

From T. S. Quackenbush—proceeds to be remitted in cash: C. B. Stout's draft on J. B. Cobb & Co., for $3000, accepted May 10, @ 4 mos., payable at our bank.

From J. B. Meriam: His sight-draft on R. C. Spencer, Chicago, for $2500. Sent Burkam & Sons.

From Farmers & Mechs.' Bank, Det.: J. H. Goldsmith's sight-draft on Bryant, Stratton & Co., Cleve., for $3700.

From N. C. Winslow: His draft for $1700 on R. M. Bartlett, Cincinnati, at 10 ds. from Sept. 1. Sent Laf. Bk., Cin.

Issued Ctfct. Dep. for John R. Penn, fav. of N. Frederick, Philadelphia, for $3975.

NARRATIVE.

Received from Bank of Capitol, Albany, our Ctfct. Dep. No. 4, fav. Geo. Eddy, Albany, for $1000.*

Discounted the following paper:

For Jacob Hinds—proceeds remitted in cash: Silas M. Burroughs' note of $1500, endorsed by J. Murdock, @ 60 ds. from Aug. 25, payable at Albion, N. Y. Sent Exch. Bk., Buf.

For H. D. Stratton—proceeds credited: His draft on Ivison, Phinney & Co., N. Y., for $1500, @ 30 ds. from Sept. 1. Sent Duncan, Sh. & Co., N. Y.

For E. W. Mason—proceeds credited: T. Wolcott's note of $1375, endorsed by Roger Williams, @ 90 ds. from Aug. 25, payable in N. Y. Sent Duncan, Sh. & Co.

For Nelson Frederick—proceeds remitted in cash: T. B. Peterson's note of $1675, endorsed by Jno. R. Penn, @ 60 ds. from Aug. 18, payable at Philadelphia. Sent Girard Bk.

For Geo. A. Crocker—proceeds credited: James Montgomery's note of $1850, endorsed by N. Hucker, @ 90 ds. from August 20, payable in Buffalo. Sent Exchange Bank.

For E. R. Felton—proceeds credited: James Smith's note of $3500, endorsed by Joseph Cutter, @ 60 ds. from Aug. 12, payable at Dayton. Sent Lafayette Bk., Cin.

For W. H. Clark—proceeds credited: A. W. Smith's note of $3700, endorsed by C. E. Delevan, @ 4 mos. from Aug. 16, payable at our bank.

For A. C. Taylor—proceeds in draft on N. Y.: Ivison, Phinney & Co.'s note of $2700, endorsed by A. C. T., @ 4 mos. from Sept. 4, payable at our bank. [46]

For T. P. Handy—proceeds credited: M. B. Scott's acceptance favor Jonathan Gillett, for $4500, @ 60 ds. from August 19, payable at Merchants' Bk., Cleve.

For Jacob Hoornbeek—proceeds credited: James Ellison's note of $4300, endorsed by Thomas Brooks, @ 3 mos. from September 1, payable at our bank.

For W. W. Harder—proceeds credited: J. Simpson's note of $2750, endorsed by Joseph Guild, @ 45 ds. from Sept. 1, payable in Buffalo. Sent Exchange Bk.

Paid the following checks: Ingham & Bragg, $1500, 175, 125; Jas. W. Lusk, $114, 125, 317^{50}, 128; Lewis R. Morris, $1100, 1500, 175; John S. Woolson, $3000, 2500, 128^{75}, 144^{48}; T. P. Handy, $146, 192, 238, 1400; Jas Richards, $5160, 200, 19^{38}; Chas. Hickox, $3715, 125, 194^{63}; Jno. R. Penn, $2500, 183^{94}; 1600; Geo. A. Crocker, $$1297^{38}$, 1400, 215^{75}; Hiram A. Pryor, $1500, 125, 187^{50}; J. P. Walter, $$146^{75}$, 1200, 134^{98}; Geo. M. Penn, $195, 143^{82}, 168; E. G. Folsom, $198, 275, 5000; J. B. Meriam, $1500, 126^{75}, 134; D. P. Eells, $1600, 173^{25}, 194, 126; E. W. Mason, $1200, 139, 146^{70}; W. W. Harder, $175, 250, 268^{93}, 314^{50}.

The following discounts, payable at home, have been paid: No. 51, Edward Savage, $1500; No. 59, Samuel Rand, $6750; No. 67, W. G. Morton, $2300; No. 70, J. Sackrider, $4500.

The following discounts, payable abroad, are assumed to have been paid: No. 54, sent Duncan, Sh. & Co., $7500; No. 57, sent Girard Bk., Phila., $3750; No. 60, sent Burkam & Sons, Chic., $1800; No. 65, sent Duncan, Sh., & Co., N. Y., $2500; No. 71, sent Laf. Bk., Cin., $2750.

The following *home* collections, due this day, as per Domestic Tickler, have been paid: *For T. P. Handy*, No. 84, $3500. *For D., Sh. & Co.*, No. 91, $1500. *For Laf. Bk., Cin.*, No. 92, $3750. *For Burkam & Sons, Chic.*, No. 95, $2700. *For T. S. Quackenbush, (special)* No. 97, $3000. *For F. & Mechs.' Bk., Det.*, No. 99, $3700.

The following *foreign* collections, due at this time, as per Foreign Tickler, are assumed to have been paid: *For H. D. Stratton*, No. 86, $3750, sent Toledo Br. Bk. *For Chas. Hickox*, No. 88, $3700, sent Laf. Bk. Cin.; No. 93, $2500, sent Far. Br. Bk., Ash. *For Burkam & Sons, Chic.*, No. 94, $1750, sent Lorain Bk., Elyria. *For John R. Penn*, No. 96, $1700, sent Girard Bank. *For J. B. Meriam*, No. 98, $2500, sent Burkam & Sons, Chic. *For N. C. Winslow*, No. 100, $1700, sent Laf. Bk., Cin.

The following results are taken from the Discount Register and Passed Collections:

DISCOUNT REGISTER—*Debits:* Bills Discounted, $15200; Domestic Exchange, $14150. *Credits:* H. D. Stratton, $$1491^{75}$; E. W. Mason, $$1355^{29}$; Geo. A. Crocker, $$1825^{03}$; E. R. Felton, 3466^{17}; W. H. Clark, $$3632^{79}$; T. P. Handy, $$4462^{50}$; Jacob Hoornbeek, $$4232^{63}$; W. W. Harder, $2728; Interest, $$357^{37}$; Col. & Ex., $$8^{75}$.

PASSED COLLECTIONS—*Debits:* Toledo Br. Bk., $3750; Laf. Bk., Cin., $3700, 1700; Far. Br. Bk., Ash., $2500; Lorain Bk., Elyria, $1750; Girard Bk., Phil., $1700; Burkam & Sons, Chic., $2500. *Credits:* T. P. Handy, $3500; Duncan, Sh. & Co., $1485; Laf. Bk., Cin., $3750, 2493^{75}; Burkam & Sons, Chic., $2700, 1745^{62}; F. & Mechs.' Bk., Det., $3700; H. D. Stratton, $$3740^{62}$; Chas. Hickox, $$3690^{75}$; John R. Penn, $1700; J. B. Meriam, $$2481^{25}$; N. C. Winslow, $$1695^{75}$; Col. & Exch., $$67^{26}$.

---

* Bank of Albany should be credited, *less exchange.*

NARRATIVE.

— OCTOBER. —

Received from Board of Control $45000 in our registered notes, which we have had properly signed and put in circulation.

Sold T. P. Handy, for his draft on Ocean Bk., N. Y., $10000 7$\frac{3}{10}$ Treasury notes, @ 1^{15}, with back interest added, $244. Remitted the draft, for our credit, to Duncan, Sh. & Co. [41]

Sold the following drafts on Duncan, Sh. & Co., at the current rate of exchange: E. R. Felton, $2000; Jacob Hoornbeek, $5000; John R. Penn, $4370; Geo. M. Penn, $2500.

Sold H. D. Stratton draft on Lorain Bk., at par, $7500.

Received from Franklin Bk., Col., in Cleveland City Bank notes, $5000.

Received from Girard Bk., Phil., our Certificate of Deposits No. 7, issued N. Frederick, $3975. [42].

Sold J. B. Meriam, at par, our draft on Toledo Br. Bank for $6700.

Received the following paper for collection:

From Duncan, Sh. & Co., N. Y.: Claffin, Mellen & Co.'s draft of $2750 on Henry W. Phillips, @ 30 ds. sight, payable at our bank; [43] A. T. Stewart's draft of $4675 on James Otis, @ 10 ds. sight, payable at Merchants' Bk., Cleve.

From Far. Br. Bk., Ashtabula: Henry W. Seymour's note of $3000, endorsed by T. W. Blake, @ 3 mos. from July 10, payable at Toledo. Sent Toledo Br. Bk.

From E. W. Mason: His sight draft on Thomas Higgins, Cincinnati, for $1900. Sent Lafayette Bk.

From Geo. A. Crocker: His draft, @ 30 ds. sight, on Thomas Merrill, Buffalo, for $3750. Sent Exchange Bk.

From Edwin C. Packard—proceeds to be paid in cash: J. B. Meriam's note of $500, @ 3 mos. from July 15, payable at our bank.

From John R. Penn: L. Fairbanks' note of $1200, endorsed by Thos. Swain, @ 60 ds. from Sept. 15, payable at Sandusky. Sent Moss Bros.; W. P. Spencer's accepted draft of $4000, @ 30 ds. from Sept. 10, payable at Buffalo. Sent Exchange Bank.

From Ingham & Bragg: J. Hollister's note of $2000, endorsed by Philip McGuire, @ 30 ds. from Sept. 20, payable at our bank; their sight draft of $3000 on W. B. Ogden, Chicago. Sent Burkam & Sons.

From Burkam & Sons, Chicago: R. C. Spencer's sight draft on H. B. Bryant, Cleve., for $1500; Thos. Milligan's note of $1700, endorsed by H. Bradley, @ 60 ds. from Aug. 12, payable at City Bank, Cleve.

Discounted the following paper:

For T. P. Handy—proceeds credited: His note for $15000, @ 60 ds. from Oct. 1, endorsed by N. C. Winslow, and payable at Merchants' Bk., Cleve.

For Jacob Hinds—proceeds remitted in cash: Thomas Jewett's note of $6000, @ 3 mos. from Sept. 30, endorsed by P. Roberts, payable at N. Y. & E. Bank. Sent Exchange Bk.

For J. P. Walter—proceeds credited: C. V. Culver's note of $6000, @ 90 ds. from Sept. 25, endorsed by J. R. Penn, payable at Culver & Brooke's Bank, Phil. Sent Girard Bank.

For J. D. Williams—proceeds credited: H. C. Spencer's note of $4750, endorsed by Jas. W. Lusk, @ 2 mos. from Oct. 1, payable at East River Bank, N. Y. Sent Duncan, Sh. & Co.

For Ingham & Bragg—proceeds credited: Ivison, Phinney & Co.'s note of $7000, endorsed by Ingham & Bragg, @ 4 mos. from August 25, payable at Mercantile Bank, N. Y. Sent Duncan, Sh. & Co.

For Alonzo Mitchell—proceeds credited: E. Pomroy's note of $5700, endorsed by C. B. Jones, @ 3 mos. from Sept. 30, payable at Adrian, Mich. Sent Toledo Br. Bk.

For Robert Brown—proceeds credited: Philip Sampson's note of $2500, endorsed by Thomas Mason, @ 3 mos. from Sept. 20, payable at our bank; John Simpson's note of $1500, endorsed by Robert Brown, @ 60 ds. from Oct. 1, payable at Sandusky. Sent Moss Bros.

For E. L. Jones—proceeds credited: H. P. Smith's note of $6000, endorsed by Alex. Kent, @ 4 mos. from Sept. 1, payable at Buffalo, sent Exchange Bank; Henry Martin's note of $2000, endorsed by J. Moore, @ 90 ds. from Sept. 25, payable at City Bank, Cleve.

Received the following deposits: J. W. Lusk, $1500; Lewis R. Morris, $1975; John S. Woolson, $2500; E. L. Jones, $2725; Jas. Richards, $4000; Ingham & Bragg, $4379; H. A. Pryor, $1700; J. P. Walter, $1475; E. G. Folsom, $4300; E. R. Felton, $2000; T. P. Handy, $2750; Alonzo Mitchell, $2000; J. R. Penn, $1500; H. Ivison, $1750; Chas. Hickox, $2400; W. H. Clark, $1800; Geo. M. Penn, $1575; H. D. Stratton, $2750; W. W. Harder, $1825.

Received from Duncan, Sh. & Co. our Certificate of Deposit No. 5, issued Aug. 1, fav. Thos. Jones, $3000.

Certified John R. Penn's check for $425.

Paid the following checks: N. C. Winslow, $125, 175^{23}, 212^{50}, 1025; E. R. Felton, $2020, 500, 1275, 210; Jacob Hoornbeek, $5050, 112^{50}, 500; M. B. Scott, $975, 124^{75}, 112^{50}, 200; E. L. Jones, $175, 144, 1200;

NARRATIVE.

Alonzo Mitchell, \$230, 195, 417^{50}; Asa Mahan, \$170, 129, 312^{50}, 183^{25}; Robert Brown, \$185, 125, 800; H. B. Bryant, \$129, 14^{56}, 125, 317; J. D. Williams, \$194, 125, 100; H. Ivison, \$145, 217, 359^{40}; W. H. Clark, \$119, 148^{50}, 129^{75}; Austin Packard, \$119, 144^{50}, 500; J. P. Walter, \$217, 250, 319^{50}; W. T. Brooks, \$500, 129, 127^{50}; H. D. Stratton, \$7500, 194^{63}, 229^{80}, 112^{50}, 400; D. P. Eells, $\$144^{50}$, 128, 1200; E. W. Mason, \$175, 219, 515, 163^{50}; W. W. Harder, \$500, 438^{95}, 127^{50}; J. R. Penn, $\$4413^{70}$; Geo. M. Penn, \$2525; J. B. Meriam, \$6700, 148, 112^{50}.

The following discounts payable at home, as per Domestic Tickler, have been paid: No. 73, \$1960; No. 76, \$1250; No. 78, \$3700; No. 91, \$4500.

The following discounts payable abroad, as per Foreign Tickler, are assumed to have been paid: No. 66, \$1500; No. 69, \$1575; No. 74, \$500; No. 75, \$3000; No. 77, \$4000; No. 81, \$1794; No. 82, \$1900; No. 83, \$1500; No. 84, \$1500; No. 86, \$1675; No. 88, \$3500; No. 93, \$2750. (44)

The following *home* collections due this day, as per Domestic Tickler, have been paid: No. 102, \$4675; No. 106, \$500; No. 109, \$2000; No. 111, \$1500; No. 112, \$1700.

The following *foreign* collections due this day, as per Foreign Tickler, are assumed to have been paid: No. 90, \$7000; No. 103, \$3000; No. 104, \$1900; No. 108, \$4000; No. 110, \$3000.

The following results are taken from the Discount Register and Passed Collections:

DISCOUNT REGISTER—*Debits:* Bills Discounted, \$19500; Domestic Exchange, \$36950. *Credits:* T. P. Handy, $\$14842^{50}$; J. P. Walter, \$5913; J. D. Williams, $\$4699^{33}$; Ingham & Bragg, $\$6897^{34}$; Alonzo Mitchell, $\$5583^{16}$; Robert Brown, $\$2465^{42}$, 1480^{50}; E. L. Jones, \$5905, 1971; Int., $\$753^{51}$; Col. & Ex., $\$32^{25}$.

PASSED COLLECTIONS.—*Debits:* F. & Mechs.' Bank, Det., \$7000, 2955; Toledo Br. Bk., \$3000; Laf. Bk., Cin., \$1900: Exch. Bk., Buf., \$4000; Burkam & Sons, \$3000. *Credits:* Duncan, Sh. & Co., $\$4628^{25}$, 6877^{50}; Ingham & Bragg, \$2000, 2977^{50}; Burkam & Sons, \$1500, 1700; E. W. Mason, $\$1895^{25}$; J. R. Penn, \$4000; Col. & Ex., \$204.

—— NOVEMBER. ——

Sold J. B. Meriam draft on Exch. Bk., Buf., @ ½% prem., \$1500.

Recd. from Farmers & Mechs.' Bk., Det., \$5000 in N. Y. State currency, @ ½% prem. Sent the same to Duncan, Sh. & Co., N. Y., per express, @ ¼% discount. Paid Express chgs. in cash, $\$2^{50}$.

Sold J. C. Bryant, for cash at current rate of exchange, our draft on Duncan, Sh., & Co., for \$3500.

Certified M. B. Scott's check of \$3000.

Received from Lafayette Bk., Cin., Cleveland city notes, \$10000.

Sold the following drafts on Duncan, Sh. & Co., at current rate of exchange: Jacob Hoornbeek, \$2000; Jas. Richards, \$5600; Alonzo Mitchell, \$3500; T. P. Handy, \$10000.

Issued the following Certificates Deposit: Geo. A. Crocker, for C. Jones, Buf., \$2000; J. D. Williams, for J. Gray, N. Y., \$1500; Ingham & Bragg, for J. W. Lusk, N. Y., \$4000.

Received the following paper for collection:

From Duncan, Sh. & Co., N. Y.: Peter Snyder's note of \$5700, endorsed by Ivison, Ph. & Co., N. Y., @ 3 mos. from Sept. 1, payable at Toledo. Sent Toledo Br. Bk. M. B. Scott's accepted draft of \$3000, favor of D. W. Fish, @ 30 ds. from Oct. 1, payable at our bank.

From Lafayette Bk., Cin.: D. C. Collins' sight-draft on Robert Smith, of Cleveland, for \$1500.

From Toledo Br. Bk.: Ira Packard's note of \$3750, endorsed by James Richards, @ 30 ds. from October 10, payable at Merchants' Bank, Cleve.

From Exchange Bk, Buf.: James Cook's note of \$1450, endorsed by F. J. Fithian, @ 6 mos. from June 15, payable at Commercial Br. Bank, Cleve.

From D. P. Eells: His draft at 30 ds. from Oct. 1, on Smith & Nixon, Cin., for \$7000. Sent Laf. Bk., Cin.

From Asa Mahan: Timothy Smith's note of \$5000, endorsed by Robert Rantoul, @ 60 ds. from Sept. 15, payable at our bank.

From Lewis R. Morris: H. Sullivan's note of \$3500, endorsed by Jacob Simmons, at 3 mos. from August 12, payable at City Bk., Cleve.

From Ira Packard—proceeds to be remitted in cash; J. C. Bryant's note of \$900, @ 2 mos. from Sept. 20, payable at our bank.

Discounted the following paper:

For Alonzo Mitchell—proceeds credited: William Hubbard's note of \$3000, endorsed by Chas. King, @ 4 mos. from Nov. 1, payable at Oswego. Sent Bank of Capitol, Albany.

For Chas. Hickox—proceeds credited: His draft of \$6000 on John R. Wheeler, Buffalo, @ 60 ds. from Nov. 1. Sent Exchange Bk., Buf. J. Hind's note of \$1500, endorsed by H. Newell, at 3 mos. from Oct. 27, payable at Tonawanda, N. Y. Sent Exchange Bk., Buf.

NARRATIVE.

For Jennison C. Hall—proceeds remitted in cash: His note of $4000, endorsed by Crocker & Guild, @ 90 ds. from Oct. 29, payable at Providence, R. I. Sent Duncan, Sh. & Co., N. Y.

For J. D. Williams—proceeds credited: P. C. Schuyler's note for $7000, endorsed by Clark, Austin & Maynard, @ 3 mos. from October 20, payable at our bank.

For Henry Ivison—proceeds credited: A. C. Taylor's note of $7500, endorsed by C. B. Stout, @ 2 mos. from Nov. 1, payable in New York. Sent Duncan, Sh. & Co.

For Austin Packard—proceeds credited: His note of $3500, endorsed by Packard & Seymour, @ 3 mos. from Oct. 18, payable at City Bank, Cleve.; H. L. Dawes' note of $3000, endorsed by A. Packard, at 4 mos. from Nov. 1, payable at Fulton Bk., N. Y. Sent Duncan, Sh. & Co.

For George A. Crocker—proceeds credited: John W. Gantz' note of $4500, endorsed by John H. Williams, @ 3 mos. from October 15, payable at our bank.

For Geo. M. Penn—proceeds credited: Thos. Seymour's note of $4000, endorsed by Jacobs & Smollett, @ 6 mos. from Oct. 10, payable at Com. Br. Bk., Cleve.

For E. G. Folsom—proceeds credited. His note of $6000, endorsed by Philip Garrett, @ 3 mos. from Nov. 1, payable at our bank; James Seaton's note of $2700, endorsed by Thomas Handel, @ 3 mos. from Oct. 25, payable at R. K. Swift's Bank, Chicago. Sent Burkam & Sons.

Received the following deposits: N. C. Winslow, $1500; Jacob Hoornbeek, $3750; M. B. Scott, $975; Asa Mahan, $1735; H. B. Bryant, $1230; Geo. A. Crocker, $2900; Austin Packard, $1975; W. T. Brooks, $1325; J. B. Meriam, $2500; D. P. Eells, $3000; E. R. Felton, $460; J. W. Lusk, $475; Lewis R. Morris, $635; John S. Woolson, $1400; Jas. Richards, $1400; John R. Penn, $1500; Chas. Hickox, $1230.

Paid the following checks: J. B. Meriam, $1515, 230, 140; J. Hoornbeek, $2020, 195, 14^{75}; J. Richards, $5656, 2000, 125; Alonzo Mitchell, $3535, 175, 144; T. P. Handy, $10100, 1500; Geo. A. Crocker, $2000, 1700; J. D. Williams, $1500, 134, 18^{75}; Ingham & Bragg, $4000, 2500, 1350; Henry Ivison, $1400, 125, 140; Chas. Hickox, $15000, 1275; Robert Brown, $12000, 560, 129; E. G. Folsom, $7000, 500, 150; Geo. M. Penn, $1400, 3000, 125; J. P. Walter, $3000, 2000, 175, 195; W. W. Harder, $5000, 150; M. B. Scott, $4000, 175, 1250; E. L. Jones, $10000, 145, 125; Jas. W. Lusk, $8000, 2750; John S. Woolson, $2400, 125, 175, 18^{60}.

The following discounts, due to-day, as per Ticklers, have been paid: *Domestic*—No. 68, $5000. *Foreign*—No. 79, $1500; No. 85, $1375; No. 87, $1850.

The following collections, due this day, as per Ticklers, have been paid: *Domestic*—No. 101, $2750; No. 114, $3000; No. 115, $1500; No. 116, $3750; No. 119, $5000; No. 120, $3500; No. 121, $900. *Foreign*—No. 105, $3750; No. 107, $1200; No. 118, $7000.

The following results are taken from the Discount Register and Passed Collections:

Discount Register—*Debits:* Bills Discounted, $25000; Domestic Exchange, $27700. *Credits:* Alonzo Mitchell, 2938^{50}; Chas. Hickox, $5937, 1477^{50}; J. D. Williams, 6903^{17}; H. Ivison, $7420; Austin Packard, 3452^{75}, 2938^{50}; Geo. A. Crocker, 4441^{50}; Geo. M. Penn, 3891^{33}; E. G. Folsom, $5905, 2640^{15}; Interest, 794^{35}; Col. and Exch., 20^{25}.

Passed Collections—*Debits:* Exch. Bk. Buf., $3750; Moss Bros., Sandusky, $1200; Lafayette Bk., Cin., $7000. *Credits:* Duncan, Sh. & Co., 2722^{50}, 2970; Laf. Bk., Cin., $1500; Tol. Br. Bk., $3750; Asa Mahan, $5000; L. R. Morris, $3500; Geo. A. Crocker, $3750; J. R. Penn, $1197; D. P. Eells, 6982^{50}; Col. & Ex., $78.

—— DECEMBER. ——

Received from Burkam & Sons, Chic., our Ctfct. Deposit, No. 6, fav. R. C. Spencer, $3000.

Received from Girard Bank, Phila., J. R. Penn's Certified Check of Oct. 1, $425.

Paid Cash for M. B. Scott's Certified Check of Nov. 1, $3000.

Received the following deposits: W. W. Harder, $3700; H. D. Stratton, $2750; J. R. Penn, $1760; Robt. Brown, $5000; Jas. Richards, $1500; T. P. Handy, $1275; Jas. W. Lusk, $5600; M. B. Scott, $4500; N. C. Winslow, $1500; E. G. Folsom, $1700; W. T. Brooks, $3000.

Received the following paper for collection:

From Duncan, Sh. & Co.: Francis & Loutrel's note of $3000, endorsed by Ivison, Phinney & Co., at 60 ds. from Nov. 17, payable at Oberlin. Sent Lorain Bank, Elyria. W. E. Crocker's draft of $3000 on Ingham & Bragg, Cleve., @ 10 ds. from Nov. 25; J. H. Johnston's draft of $1500 on Simeon Jones, Ashtabula, @ 30 ds. from Nov. 15. Sent Farmers' Br. Bk., Ash.

From Burkam & Sons, Chic.: Wm. H. Denison's note of $3000, endorsed by Philip Jones, at 60 ds. from Oct. 10, payable in Cleveland.

NARRATIVE.

From Franklin Bank, Col.: Thaddeus Stevens' note of $1200, endorsed by J. H. Baker, @ 30 days from Nov. 10, payable at Merchants' Bk., Cleve.

From Lafayette Bk., Cin.: Thomas McCook's draft of $1000 on Peter Simpkins, Cleveland, @ 10 ds. from Nov. 28.

From Exchange Bk., Buffalo: Chas. Jones' draft of $1500 on A. Stager, Cleveland, @ 60 ds. from Oct. 15.

From Iron City Bk., Pittsburg: James Wood's note of $1750, endorsed by Hiram A. Pryor, @ 3 mos. from Sept. 19, payable at our bank.

From E. R. Felton: James McCormick's draft of $2000 on Smith & McCormick, Chicago, at 30 ds. from Dec. 1. Sent Burkam & Sons, Chic.

From John S. Woolson: His draft on Woolson & McFarland, Mt. Pleasant, Iowa, for $2500, @ 60 ds. from Nov. 12. Sent Burkam & Sons, Chic.

Discounted the following paper:

For W. W. Harder—proceeds credited: His note of $15000, endorsed by Theo. W. Dwight, @ 4 mos. from Dec. 1, payable at our bank.

For E. W. Mason—proceeds credited: J. C. Hall's note of $12000, endorsed by Simeon Jones, @ 90 ds. from Nov. 20, payable at Providence, R. I. Sent Duncan, Sh. & Co., N. Y.

From D. P. Eells—proceeds credited: Samuel Jackson's note of $7000, endorsed by Patrick Gallagher, @ 3 mos. from Nov. 30, payable at our bank.

For Theron W. Woolson—proceeds in cash: John Simson's note of $8000, endorsed by Urial Driggs, @ 4 mos. from Nov. 20, payable at Niagara River Bank, Buffalo. Sent Exchange Bk.

For B. M. Worthington—proceeds in cash: Thos. King's note of $7500, endorsed by Chas. West, at 60 ds. from Dec. 1, payable at Portland, Me. Sent Duncan, Sh. & Co.

For H. A. Pryor—proceeds credited: B. K. Phillip's note of $6000, endorsed by Jones & Tillinghast, @ 4 mos. from Nov. 12, payable at Pittsburg. Sent Iron City Bank.

For W. H. Clark—proceeds credited: His draft of $5000 on Bryant, Stratton & Co., Brooklyn, at 60 ds. from Dec. 1. Sent Duncan, Sh. & Co.

For W. T. Brooks—proceeds credited: Bradford & Renick's note of $8000, endorsed by H. D. Stratton, @ 3 mos. from Nov. 20, payable at Hartford, Conn. Sent Duncan, Sh. & Co.

For Robert Brown—proceeds credited: Samuel Smiley's note of $10000, endorsed by H. Norman Smith, at 3 mos. from Dec. 1, payable at our bank.

For Edwin C. Packard—proceeds in cash: Stetson Eaton's note of $7500, endorsed by Philip Carr, @ 90 ds. from Dec. 1, payable at Milwaukee. Sent Burkam & Sons, Chic.

The following discounts, due this day, as per Ticklers, have been paid: *Domestic*—No. 89, $3700; No. 92, $4300; No. 94, $15000; No. 100, $2500; No. 103, $2000. *Foreign:* No. 72, $2758; No. 80, $2700; No. 96, $6000; No. 97, $4750; No. 98, $7000; No. 101, $1500.

The following collections, due this day, as per Ticklers, have been paid: *Domestic*—No. 117, $1450; No. 123, $3000; No. 125, $3000; No. 126, $1200; No. 127, $1000; No. 128, $1500; No. 129, $1750. *Foreign*—No. 113, $5700; No. 124, $1500.

The following checks have been paid: T. P. Handy, $15000; Ingham & Bragg, $3000, 575, 1400, 212^{50}; W. W. Harder, $12000, 750, 112^{75}; E. W. Mason, $10000; D. P. Eells, $7000, 125; H. A. Pryor, $3000, 1200, 325^{67}; W. H. Clark, $200, 3000, 19^{75}; W. T. Brooks, $1750, 2300, 118^{75}; Robert Brown, $5000, 1750, 12^{38}; Geo. M. Penn, $1500, 175; E. G. Folsom, $2000, 175, 187^{50}; J. B. Meriam, $1400, 112^{75}, 238^{50}; Jacob Hoornbeek, $500, 175, 1275, 39^{67}; Alonzo Mitchell, $2000, 129^{63}, 1750; H. B. Bryant, $10000; E. L. Jones, $8500, 212^{50}; M. B. Scott, $1200.

The following results are taken from the Discount Register and Passed Collections:

Discount Register—*Debits:* Bills Discounted, $32000; Domestic Exchange, $54000. *Credits:* W. W. Harder, $14690; E. W. Mason, $11836; D. P. Eells, $6892^{67}; H. A. Pryor, $5896; W. H. Clark, $4947^{50}; W. T. Brooks, $7888; Robert Brown, $9845; Interest, 1349^{16}; Collection and Exchange, $56^{25}.

Passed Collections—*Debits:* Toledo Br. Bk., $5700; Far. Br. Bk., Ashtabula, $1500. *Credits*; Exch. Bk., Buf., $1442^{75}, 1492^{50}; Duncan, Sh. & Co., $2970, 5628^{75}, 1481^{25}; Burkam & Sons, Chic., $3000; Franklin Bk., Col., $1200; Lafayette Bk., Cin., $1000; Iron City Bk., Pitts., $1741^{25}; Collection & Exchange, $143^{50}.

Received from Duncan, Sh. & Co., statement of our % with them for the past six months. Our average of deposits amounts to $45028^{05}, for which they allow us $1\frac{1}{2}$% interest, $675^{42}.

Received from State Department semi-annual interest on Public Stocks, 3% on $90000.

Received from Farmers & Mechs.' Bk., Detroit, currency to balance %, $7824.

Sold P. Hood draft on Exch. Bk., Buf., @ $\frac{1}{2}$% prem., $568^{50}.

Received from Burkam & Sons, Chic., Cleve. currency on %, $5000.

NARRATIVE.

Received from Moss Bros., Sandusky, currency to balance %, $4800.

Paid Salaries as follows: President, $1000; Cashier, $750; First Teller, $600; Second Teller, $500; Bookkeeper, $500; Assistant do., $400; Porter, $200.

The several accounts showing gains and losses are now closed into the general Loss and Gain account, preparatory to declaring the second semi-annual dividend. The condition of these accounts is as follows: *Showing Gain*—Treasury Notes, $1700; Collection and Exchange, $1432 [51]; Interest, $7635 [35]. *Showing Loss*—Expense, $4283 [33]. The net gain during six months is $6484 [53].

Declared dividend of 2%, setting the amount aside in the Dividend %, and transferring the balance to Reserved Profits %.

The General Ledger now exhibits the following balances:

Resources.			*Liabilities.*		
Duncan, Sh. & Co.	5078	96	Capital Stock	200000	
Bills Discounted	59700		Deposits	297551	20
Domestic Exchange	99400		Office Notes	80000	
Cash	259582	16	Dividend	4000	
Lafayette Bank, Cin.	11965	44	Reserved Profits	3431	45
Public Stocks	87400		Iron City Bank, Pitts.	1141	25
Exchange Bank, Buf.	9000				
Fixtures	575				
Burkam & Sons	14042	62			
Bank of Capitol	12528	65			
Toledo Branch Bank	8250				
Far. Br. Bk., Ashtabula	1582	50			
Franklin Bank, Col.	3100				
Lorain Bank, Elyria	5150				
Girard Bank, Philadelphia	8768	57			
	586123	90		586123	90

The Deposit Ledger shows the following balances:

Balances on Deposit.			*Brought Forward*	206425	75
N. C. Winslow	11230	44	J. P. Walter	6097	52
E. R. Felton	11645	60	W. T. Brooks	11784	25
Jacob Hoornbeek	6277	02	Geo. M. Penn	6601	97
M. B. Scott	7228	77	E. G. Folsom	12050	57
J. W. Lusk	6715	88	H. D. Stratton	11448	44
Lewis R. Morris	12652	32	Certificate Deposit	7500	
J. S. Woolson	7239	42	J. B. Meriam	6363	94
T. P. Handy	4726	47	D. P. Eells	15999	65
Jas. Richards	6614	22	E. W. Mason	10379	67
Alonzo Mitchell	8023	24	W. W. Harder	9298	04
Asa Mahan	12019	22			
Robert Brown	7436	74		303949	80
Ingham & Bragg	5634	14			
Chas. Hickox	8435	45			
John R. Penn	11792	58			
Geo. A. Crocker	14864	98	*Overdrafts.*		
J. D. Williams	14719	83			
H. Ivison	11322	97	H. B. Bryant	2068	50
W. H. Clark	14576	16	E. L. Jones	4330	10
Austin Packard	12194	50	Balance	297551	20
Hiram A. Pryor	11075	80			
				303949	80
Amount Forward	206425	75			

EXPLANATORY NOTES.

(1) This Act provides, among other things, as follows:

[*Capital to be paid in.*]

SEC. 4. "Every such banking company, before commencing business, shall have paid in and remaining in its possession, *bona fide*, the property of such company, for the sole purposes of such company, *sixty per centum* of its entire capital stock, and the residue shall be paid in in such installments as may be required by the directors of any such company.

[*Basis of Issue.*]

SEC. 7. Whenever any company, formed for the purpose of Banking under the provisions of this Act, shall lawfully transfer to the Auditor of State any portion of the public stock issued or to be issued by the State of Ohio, or by the United States, such company shall be entitled to receive from the Auditor an equal amount of such circulating notes of different denominations, registered and countersigned as aforesaid: but such public stock shall in all cases be, or be made to be equal to a stock of this State producing at least five per centum interest per annum; and it shall not be lawful for the Auditor to take such stock at a rate above its par value, or above its current market value—provided that the Auditor shall not furnish to such company circulating notes to an amount more than *three times* the amount of the capital stock of such company actually paid in. and remaining in such bank undiminished by losses. * * * * *

[*To Circulate as Money.*]

SEC. 8. Every such company is hereby authorized, after having executed such circulating notes, in the manner herein required, to make them obligatory promissory notes payable on demand, at its place of business within the State; to loan and circulate the same as money, according to the ordinary course of banking business. * * * *

[*Coin for Redemption.*]

SEC. 19. Each company shall, at all times, have on hand, in gold and silver coin, or their equivalent—one half, at least, of which shall be in gold and silver coin—in its vault, an amount equal to *thirty per centum* of the amount of its outstanding notes of circulation.

(2) As one great source of our profits will be the selling of drafts on New York at a premium, it becomes essential that we should get as large a credit with our New York correspondent, and at as little cost as possible. It will, in fact, often happen, that we can make debts which are to mature at our bank, payable in New York currency, without any extra consideration, which should, of course, be done. It is quite customary in discounting paper to make the amount *payable in New York*, which is equivalent to an additional rate of interest; and which, if voluntarily paid, does not subject the bank to the penalties for usury.

(3) When deposits are made they are accompanied with "Deposit Checks," an example of which may be seen on page 116. These checks are usually filed by the Receiving Teller during banking hours. When the Journals are written up, which is usually done after the bank is "closed" to customers, the deposit checks are taken from the file, and entered, one after the other, to the credit of the parties whose names appear thereon. This plan enables the Teller to attend more promptly to customers, and avoids the liability to err in entering up deposits during the confusion of business. In banks doing sufficient business to employ assistant Tellers, the same object is attained by having one person receive the money and another enter up the credits. In very extensive houses even this labor is subdivided.

(4) This check ($505) will be found among those enumerated at the close of the day's business, and of course is not to be entered simultaneously with the draft. It is not thought necessary to designate, in every instance, the particular sums paid *by check*, as the facts will be apparent in the denominations of the checks entered in their proper order.

(5) When cash is paid on check, the check is filed and counts as cash during business hours. The checks are then collected and properly assorted, getting those of each dealer together, and the entries made and extended as per example in Debit Journal.

(6) Drafts may be drawn at so many days from *date*, or from *sight;* the difference being that in one case they commence maturing when *drawn*, and in the other, when *accepted*. In recording paper on the Discount Register, the student will be careful to note the date at which maturity commences, which should be entered in the "date" column. The draft here mentioned, although drawn at "60 days' sight," and not to be paid until 63 days from the date of its acceptance in New York, we have reckoned as running from the date of discount. The difference cannot exceed two days, and we can well afford to waive even a greater consideration in view of the advantage in exchange. This is the first transaction resulting in a gain to the bank, and illustrates one of its most important functions—that of loaning money on interest. Bank usage warrants us in reckoning the interest on the face of the note ($5000), while the money actually loaned is the difference between the interest thus computed and the face of the note ($4947 50). In loaning its capital the bank is actuated by two leading impulses: first, to secure the greatest good to its stockholders, and next, to accommodate its friends or dealers. Other things being equal, when discrimination is to be made in its offerings, the bank should give preference to those who have been its best cus-

tomers, or who have kept the largest and most uniform average on deposit. When discounts are made in favor of a dealer, as in this case, the net proceeds are entered to his credit as a deposit.

(7) Duncan, Sherman & Co. being our New York correspondent, we of course send them all collections and discounts payable in that city and vicinity, and also draw upon them for our New York exchange. For full instruction in this and similar cases, the student should refer to the article on "Correspondence," page 256.

(8) These stocks were purchased at less than their *nominal* value, such being the market rates. Were we to reckon them at their nominal value, and credit "Exchange" for the difference, there would *seem* to be a profit of this amount, which would not be warranted by the facts, and would be quite apt to mislead us in declaring our dividends, which the law says "must be made from the *earnings* of the institution, and not from its *capital*."

(9) Inasmuch as the stocks remain the property of the bank, though held by the Department as security for the redemption of our issue, no entry of this transfer need be made in our principal books. The property has passed from our *custody*, but not from our *possession*.

(10) It is plain that the addition of these notes to our circulation will increase our working capital by just that amount. As, however, this is not a gratuity, but simply a permission to issue and *redeem* our own paper, we can not add the amount to our *resources* without increasing our *liabilities* in the same proportion. We have simply *borrowed* $35000 on our own notes, payable "on demand." We therefore credit Bills Payable, or, what is the same in effect, "Office Notes," thereby debiting Cash.

(11) By referring to the collections in the Domestic and Foreign Ticklers, the student will see that the paper here enumerated falls due at this time. Concerning that which is payable in our own city, we of course know whether it is paid, as we receive the money; as to the foreign collections, we have to depend upon our correspondents, knowing that if the paper sent them is not met at maturity, they will notify us without delay. It is usual, therefore, to date the Foreign Tickler far enough forward to cover the usual contingency of the mails, and to assume all paper as paid of which we have received no notice of protest. The entry in this case consists of transferring these collections from the Ticklers to the "Passed Collections," charging our correspondents with the proceeds of the *foreign* collections, and crediting the parties for whom collected; or paying over the amount, as the case may be.

(12) It must be borne in mind that the paper falling due at our bank, unless by special agreement otherwise, is payable in *currency*. As our account with Duncan, Sherman & Co. is kept in the currency of New York city, we can not, of course, afford to give them credit for the *face* of payments made here; as by that process we should lose the current exchange—which we have assumed to be 1%. We therefore credit them the amount of the draft ($3000), less 1% ($30), which we credit to our own Exchange %.

(13) This note has for payer one of our dealers, and it is fair to presume that, inasmuch as he has a balance on deposit, he will not deem it necessary to send the cash. He will either draw his check for the amount, or allow us to hold the note as a check, to be charged and filed in the same manner as other checks. This latter plan is adopted by some business men, and is preferable on some accounts. The only plausible objection against it is that the sense of security it affords to the business man, may render him less vigilant in preparing for the payment of his obligations by keeping sufficient funds on deposit. However, this objection has no force if the system of business record is such as will keep these facts prominent.

(14) The *grade* of the currency in any locality is regulated in a great measure by the banks. Whatever is *bankable* passes readily at par. When banks are paying their creditors specie, it is scarcely possible for gold and silver to be at a premium, from the fact that paper money and other bank credits will command it at par. If, however, owing to the scarcity of the precious metals, or to financial revulsions and panic, specie payments are suspended, gold and silver will immediately appreciate, or, what is the same, paper currency will depreciate in value. So long, however, as paper money is used for the general purposes of trade, it will continue in circulation, and remain the *standard* of currency; as it is an inevitable law of political economy that the *poorest* currency permitted to pass at par will fill the channels of circulation to the exclusion of the more valuable. Canada money, which is at 1% discount in Cleveland, is at par in Detroit, while Detroit currency is at only ½% discount in Cleveland. It is clear, therefore, that if we buy Canada funds, and remit the same for our credit to Detroit, we shall make ½% on the amount, less the express charges; which will make our actual gain in this transaction $33.75.

(15) As these notes do not enter into circulation like the Government currency, but are held by us as a loan, we open a separate account with them, charging it with their cost. It may seem anomalous that Government securities, producing 7$\frac{3}{10}$% interest, could be had at less than their nominal value while money is freely loaned on *personal* security @ 6%. This is but one of the various phenomena presented in the financial world, and shows the influence which popular apprehension has in fixing the value of any class of credits. The "7$\frac{3}{10}$ Treasury Notes" were issued upon the authority of Congress, as a means of obtaining loans from the people to aid the Government in its efforts to put down the rebellion. The rate of interest, payable semi-annually *in specie*, was fixed unprecedentedly high, and the entire resources of the country pledged for the payment of both principal and interest; and yet, such was the reluctance of the people to try the new channel of investments, or their temporary apprehensions as to the final result of the measure, aided to a great extent by the combination of unprincipled capitalists who had a direct personal interest in reducing the rates to the lowest possible figure, that for a time this class of securities was forced far below its intrinsic value.

(16) In this case it is understood that the draft shall commence maturing from the date of its *acceptance*, which will be upon its arrival in New York. By due course of mail this would take two days. We have, therefore,

made the date March 3. This draft, being payable in New York, is worth to us, when it matures, a premium of 1%. We can well afford to take it at par, the twelve days' *interest* we lose being only one fourth of what we gain by *exchange*.

(17) This note is payable in Chicago currency, which is ½% below our own. Consequently, we charge Mr. Penn not only the regular rate of *interest*, but the regular *exchange* on the face of his note added to our charges for collection.

(18) These transactions are among the most common of bank routine, and easily understood. Their proper record requires the opening of two special accounts in the Deposit Ledger, viz., "Certified Checks" and "Certificates," both of which are mere variations of depositors' accounts. The Certificates of Deposit and Certified Checks (examples of which are given in this connection), are simply *deferred* payments on depositors' orders, and as the obligations are assumed under the signature of the proper bank officers, they become a species of bills payable, and may be grouped under collective heads, instead of appearing in the separate accounts of the actual parties at whose instance the credits are made. Were we to defer charging the drawer with this check until presented *for payment*, there might be danger of his account being overdrawn. So far as the drawer is concerned, the check is *paid* when its payment is assumed by certification; and if his own bank account is properly kept, this fact will appear. It would be admissible to file a memorandum of this check, entering it up with the "checks paid" at the close of the day. It is more usual, however, to make a separate record of such transactions, which plan we have adopted.

(19) This transaction involves a somewhat intricate entry, and, if properly studied, will exhibit to the student one of the most interesting features in banking. It is evident that two sources of profit are presented, viz., one from *interest*, in discounting the note, and the other from *exchange*, in selling the draft. The problem is exceedingly simple, involving only the plainest application of percentage. The entry is first made in the Discount Register, where the interest ($42) is credited, and the proceeds ($3958) shown as cash. This latter amount is to be invested in a draft worth 1% premium. The following is the simplest process :

$$3958 \div 1.01 = 3918.81, \text{ \textit{the face of the draft;}}$$
$$\text{Therefore, } 3958 - 3918.81 = 39.19, \text{ \textit{the premium.}}$$

The complete entry, when properly recorded, will be: Bills Discounted, Dr. $4000; Duncan, Sh. & Co., Cr. $3918.81; Interest, Cr. $42; Exchange, Cr. $39.19.

(20) This bill of expenses being for the permanent fixtures of the bank, such as counters, furniture, safe, gas fixtures, etc., it is not deemed proper to charge it to the general Expense % as a loss. In the first place, there is intrinsic value in the property, and next it remains from year to year without sensible diminution. If we should apply the amount against the first year's gains, we might be unable to declare a dividend. We have, therefore, opened a "Fixtures" %, which will remain on our books as a *resource* until our gains accumulate sufficiently to cancel it without affecting our dividends.

(21) The *one* thing about which banks should be careful, is to secure the prompt payment of the debts which accrue from loans. Ordinarily the loans are made to dealers, and the only security demanded is the endorsement of well-known responsible parties. In this case, neither the borrower nor the endorser is a dealer, and neither is sufficiently known to the bank officers to warrant the venture of so large a sum. An additional, or "collateral" security, is, therefore, required. The Railroad Bonds thus pledged are to be held by the bank until the note matures, when, if it is paid, they are delivered up. If, however, the payment fails, the bank has power to sell the bonds at public auction or otherwise, applying the proceeds to the payment of the note and all expenses legally incurred; the balance to be paid over to the proper persons. In cases of this kind it is usual for banks to take Collateral Notes, an example of which is given on page 333.

(22) This note was discounted for M. B. Scott, who is, also, one of the endorsers, and whom we hold, with others, for its payment. The expense of protest is, of course, his expense and not ours; and while our correspondent will look to us for the protest fees, we have our remedy in the parties to the note. It is true that we still hold the note in our possession, and having served the notice of protest on the proper parties, we are entitled to the benefit of their endorsements, which will, in all probability, render the payment sure. However, having failed of being paid at maturity, it is, in business language, "disgraced," and should no longer hold a place with our undoubted resources. We have, therefore, opened an account with "Protested Paper," which we debit with the amount of note and protest fees; crediting Domestic Exchange with the face of the note, and Exchange Bank with the protest fees. We are aware that this may seem a rather formal proceeding in reference to a note that will probably be paid upon being presented to its endorsers; but the opportunity is taken to illustrate a point which the student should understand, and to impress upon the mind the importance of guarding one's business reputation by promptness against the suspicions which are always engendered by suffering paper to go to protest.

(23) In the ordinary legal process, some time would elapse before realizing upon securities of this kind; but in the present case we have taken the precaution of evading the legal formalities of foreclosure in a written permission to sell *immediately* upon failure to pay. See "Collateral Note," page 333.

(24) Although by the terms of our charter we are not permitted to deal in stocks with a view to speculation, we have, nevertheless, the right to protect our own interests. In this case we have loaned $20000 cash on what we deemed ample security; but from some cause, which we have reason to believe temporary, the security has depreciated in value; so that, being exposed to public sale, it does not realize sufficient to pay our demands. It is now

optional with us to let it pass into other hands, receiving ourselves only the proceeds to apply on our claim, or to purchase it, hoping a more favorable turn of affairs. If we become the owners by purchase, under these circumstances, we have every right to sell to the best advantage.

(25) The theory of which this is an application is distinctly set forth in Note 2 of this series. The note is made payable *with exchange;* which means simply that when it is paid we shall charge, in addition to its face, 1%, or the rate of exchange on New York. The sagacious student will readily discover that this is a covert method of evading the usury law; and that the *shorter* the time allowed on this class of notes, the larger will be the percentage of interest. While the particular currency in which the note is to be paid may be expressed upon its face, it is also well to mark it in the Tickler. The simple contraction "Ex." in the "Remarks" column is sufficient.

(26) There are two classes of collections constantly maturing at our bank; one for our regular dealers and correspondents, and the other for strangers and banks with which we keep no account. When those of the former class are paid, we immediately credit the owners with the amount; the proceeds of the latter class we either immediately remit to the proper parties, or hold as a special deposit till called for. Thus no entry is made of these special collections in the main books. We are aware that this practice is not pursued by all banks; some adopting the plan of opening a temporary special account, and passing the cash through the regular channel.

(27) It is customary with banks to receive on *special* deposit from its dealers, valuable articles of various kinds, such as jewelry, plate, and even packages of money, merely for safe-keeping. Any *special* deposit is to be paid back in the *identical* article, and not in something of its kind, as when one deposits cash on account, and checks out in amounts to suit his convenience. When special deposits are made, it is not necessary that any entry should be made in the principal books, although some banks adopt the plan of entering all *cash*, whether special or otherwise, and reckoning it among cash items. We have adopted a different plan in this case; simply giving the depositor a receipt for the package, and making a memorandum in a book kept for that purpose. Upon the return of the receipt, the package will be delivered to its proper owner.

(28) The practice of paying interest on deposits is strongly discountenanced by financiers, as opposed to the true spirit and theory of banking, and as destructive of one important means of prosperity; although many banks resort to it as a method of increasing their working capital, and to compete successfully with rival institutions. It is customary and proper, however, when banks receive and keep large average balances belonging to correspondents, to pay a small percentage of interest. We have sanctioned this practice in the adjustment of our account with Duncan, Sherman & Co.

(29) The student is aware that the necessary entries for getting the special gains and losses into one account may be made either through the Journals, the same as current transactions, or by the method already fully endorsed in this work, of red ink transferring entries in the Ledger. Our choice is decidedly for the latter method, and we have used it here. We have also closed up all the running accounts having more than one entry, and brought down the balances; which, although not absolutely necessary, enables us to enter upon another semi-annual career with a simple statement of resources and liabilities, instead of the long unfooted columns of the past six months.

(30) No prudently-conducted joint-stock institution will adopt the practice either of declaring a dividend which shall entirely exhaust its earnings, or of *borrowing* the means for such dividend when the earnings have not been sufficient. The latter method is sometimes adopted for the purpose of presenting a bold front to the public, and keeping up the market value of stocks; but the practice is most pernicious, and, if persevered in, must end in embarrassment, if not in utter ruin. In fact, the law recognizes no such rights, but explicitly provides that all dividends to stockholders shall be made "from the earnings," and not from the capital. There can be no plausible excuse for departing from this plain, conservative policy, except in cases of extraordinary and temporary reverses which are morally sure to be soon counteracted; and even under such circumstances prudence would dictate the withholding of dividends to stockholders which have to be borrowed from the public. So far are those institutions which stand fair in public esteem from following this destructive policy, that they make a uniform practice of not only not declaring profits which have not been realized, but of setting aside a part of the *real earnings* to guard against future contingencies. This is a most commendable plan, as it serves the double purpose of increasing the working capital of the bank by permitting its earnings to accumulate instead of being drawn out by stockholders, and of establishing its reputation upon a sound basis, thereby increasing its usefulness and adding to the value of its stock. We have given shape to this policy by setting aside a part of the earnings ($946 92) in a "Reserved Profits" account, thereby restricting the first dividend to 2%, which, under the circumstances, should be more than satisfactory to the stockholders. The "Dividend" account, as it now stands, will, of course, show an amount owing by the bank to stockholders. As fast as the stockholders are paid dividend will be debited until the amount is exhausted and the account canceled.

(31) It must be remembered that while our account with Duncan, Sh. & Co., is kept in N. Y. currency, the bank dividends are payable in our own currency. Therefore, if we pay them in New York funds, they must stand the exchange. *The draft, with 1% added, should amount to $400.*

(32) The entries required for this in the Debit and Credit Journals are taken from the Discount side of the "Foreign Tickler." The student will not forget that the check "Pd. & Ent.," in the "Remarks" column, signifies that not only are the bills credited as paid, but the parties to whom the payments are made are properly debited for the same.

(33) This draft being payable in Cleveland currency, will not pay an equal amount in Buffalo currency, which is the standard adopted as between us and our Buffalo correspondent. The probabilities are that this draft was pur-

chased at a sufficiently large discount to make it an object for our correspondent to remit it to us on %. We credit the Buffalo bank with the amount of the draft, *less the current rate of discount* (½%) which we credit to Collection and Exchange. The effect with us is precisely similar to that of drawing a draft on Buffalo at ½% premium, and taking our pay in Cleveland currency.

(34) This draft is payable in Detroit currency, while our % with Farmers & Mechanics' Bank is kept in Cleveland currency, which is ½% prem. at Detroit. Our Detroit correspondent will, therefore, credit us with the face of the draft less ½%, while we debit him the same. Our gain in the transaction will be ½% of the face of the draft.

(35) This transaction enables our Chicago correspondent to cancel a portion of his % with us at a profit to himself—provided the N. Y. funds were received by him at par—while it enables us to get funds in the hands of our N. Y. correspondent at a cost of ½%, besides the express charges. On receipt of the money from Chicago, we credit Burkam & Sons $10025, and debit Collection and Exchange $25. On remitting to N. Y., we charge Duncan, Sh. & Co., $9975, and Collection and Exchange, $25 + 5.

(36) The previous entries of this kind will leave no doubt in the student's mind as to the process and results. There are, in this transaction, three elements of gain—first, the interest on the note; second, the charges for Collection and Exchange; and third, the premium on the N. Y. draft. In making the calculations, first ascertain the proceeds of the discounted note, in Cleveland currency; and next, the face of a draft which, with 1% premium added, will amount to said proceeds.

(37) Inasmuch as we charge our N. Y. correspondent a percentage on collections made for him out of our own city, it is but fair to presume that he will exact the same of us; for aside from the services rendered in making the collection, it is probable the funds in which it is paid are not at par in New York. For the sake of exactness, and to give the student the benefit of the variety afforded by the record, we have assumed the charges for the collection in this instance to be ½%, or $5. Duncan, Sh. & Co. then should be debited $1995, and Col. & Exch. $5.

(38) The payment of this draft by our Detroit correspondent, *in his own currency*, will not, of course, cancel an equal amount of his indebtedness to us, which is reckoned in our currency, the difference being, according to our understanding, ½%. We therefore credit Farmers & Mechs.' Bank with the face of the draft, *less the rate of exchange*, and "Collection & Exch." with the difference, thus realizing a gain of $10, the difference in exchange.

(39) In a regular banking business it is probable that transactions like this would be of very frequent occurrence. As we are the regular correspondent of Duncan, Sh. & Co. for this locality, it is much more convenient for them to send this mixed currency to us than to send it home to the various banks issuing it, with whom they have no account. It has probably been purchased by them at a much higher rate of discount than they allow us. The margin allowed us, ½% is for assorting and sending home. We can either do this or pay it out over our counter in the regular discharge of our business.

(40) This kind of transaction has been repeated so frequently that the student will need no hints as to the process of entry. The proceeds being set down in the Discount Register as "Cash, there may be danger of omitting to credit Duncan, Sh. & Co. with the draft. To avoid this omission the better plan would be to enter it *immediately*, instead of waiting for the results to be entered up from the Discount Register, as is the practice with the other credits of proceeds. In actual business there would be no such liability to omission, as when the draft was drawn the drawee would be credited.

(41) These Treasury Notes were purchased for less than their nominal value, at a time of general depression, and before the financial policy of the Government was understood, or the willingness of the people to assist in bearing the burden of suppressing the rebellion had been tested. As soon, however, as the public mind began to settle down to the new condition of things, and patriotism and confidence to displace hesitation and distrust, the advantages of this national loan become at once so apparent that almost every one who had money unemployed sought to invest it in securities which were at once so safe and remunerative. The consequence was a sudden rise in this class of stocks. We have taken advantage of this buoyancy, and realized a generous margin on our investment. The interest on these notes is payable semi-annually, accumulating at the rate of two cents per day on every hundred dollars. In disposing of them, this accumulated interest must not be lost sight of. This transaction presents two elements of gain—the appreciation of the notes and the accumulation of interest. Treasury Notes should be credited with the proceeds of the notes, and Interest with the gain from this source.

(42) Our account with Girard Bank is kept in Philadelphia currency, which is 1% better than our own. Our certificate, therefore, being payable in Cleveland currency, can be received by us only at its Philadelphia value, which is 1% discount. We credit Girard Bank with a sum which, with 1% added, will amount to $3975; and Col. and Exch. with the premium.

(43) A draft drawn at "sight," or at so many days' sight, commences maturing from the date of presentment. A bank receiving such paper for collection impliedly engages to present it *immediately*, as any delay in this particular would wrongfully keep the owner from his money. In recording paper of this kind in our Collection Register, we shall assume the *date of record* as the time from which maturity commences.

(44) Inasmuch as the student has a full description of these notes, both in his Discount Register and Ticklers, a reference to them by numbers alone is deemed sufficient. Care should be taken in recording them as paid not to omit to debit the parties to whom paid.

DEBIT JOURNAL.

Cleveland, O., January, 1862. 1

L F.			Col. & Ex.		Deposits.		General	
8	Duncan, Sh. & Co.	Remitted as follows:						
		H. B. Bryant on Ocean Bk.					5000	
		J. B. Meriam on Cont. Bk.					7500	
		Ctfct. Dep. Met. Bk. . .					10000	
		W. H. Clark on D., Sh. & Co.					15000	
7	Expense	Blank Books, Stationery, etc.					150	
1	N. C. Winslow	505, 100			605			
2	E. R. Felton	18^{75}, 25, 130, 125 . . .			298	75		
3	Jacob Hoornbeek	500, 175, 25^{50}, 19, 12, 110			841	50		
5	Jas. W. Lusk	175, 125^{50}, 13^{75}, 112, 200			626	25		
6	Lewis R. Morris	118, 12^{50}, 142, 19^{30} . . .			291	80		
7	John S. Woolson	14^{50}, 110			124	50		
8	T. P. Handy	1500, 500			2000			
10	James Richards	113, 19^{60}, 144, 12 . . .			288	60		
11	Alonzo Mitchell	200, 120, 13^{75}			333	75		
13	Robert Brown	12, 190			202			
15	Charles Hickox	. . . .			190			
16	H. B. Bryant	. . . .			3000			
17	John R. Penn	. . . .			2500			
8	Duncan, Sh. & Co.	T. P. Handy, on Ocean Bk.	150				30000	
4	Bills Discounted	Per Discount Register . .					4000	
5	Domestic Exch.	" " " . .					5000	
6	Col. & Exch.	. . . .	150				150	
2	Deposits	. . . .			11302	15	11302	15
8	*Cash Cr.*	*Total Disbursements* .					88102	15

DEBIT JOURNAL.

Cleveland, O., February. 1862.

L.F.			Col. & Ex.		Deposits.		General	
10	Public Stocks	20 Shares U. S. 6% @ 92¢.					18400	
		20 do. O. S. 6% @ 90¢.					18000	
3	Duncan, Sh. & Co.	E. R. Felton on Exch. Bk.	25				5000	
		M. B. Scott on Ocean Bk. .	6				1200	
		Ctfct. Dep. Met. Bk. . .	12	50			2500	
		J. R. Penn on East Riv. Bk.	2	50			500	
		Jas. Moore on D., Sh. & Co.	15				3000	
4	M. B. Scott	3030, 150, 19^{75}			3199	75		
8	T. P. Handy	1994^{75}, 120			2114	75		
7	John S. Woolson	757^{50}, 113, 15^{75}			886	25		
17	John R. Penn	2525, 183^{75}, 144			2852	75		
12	Asa Mahan	325, 450, 19^{75}, 50 . . .			844	75		
10	James Richards	110, 120, 300, 43^{75} . . .			573	75		
11	Alonzo Mitchell	138, 26, 44^{90}, 300 . . .			508	90		
15	Chas. Hickox	400, 120, 19^{34}.			539	34		
16	H. B. Bryant	900, 13^{75}, 122, 75 . . .			1110	75		
13	Robert Brown	115, 26, 35^{20}, 75			251	20		
6	Lewis R. Morris	17, 25, 19, 83^{25}			144	25		
3	Jacob Hoornbeek	150, 12, 46, 75, 18^{75} . .			301	75		
5	Jas. W. Lusk	29, 34^{50}, 129			192	50		
9	E. L. Jones	190, 12^{38}, 115			317	38		
14	Ingham & Bragg	50, 120, 38^{90}			208	90		
2	E. R. Felton	170, 123, 19^{50}.			312	50		
9	Lafayette Bk. Cin.	Collection, No. 7					900	
11	Moss Bro., Sand'y	" " 10					475	
4	Bills Discounted	per Discount Register . .					12100	
5	Domestic Exch.	" " " . .					10500	
6	Col. & Exch.	. . .	61				61	
2	Deposits	. . . .			14359	47	14359	47
8	*Cash Cr.*	*Total Disbursements* .					86995	47

DEBIT JOURNAL.

Cleveland, O., March, 1862. 3

L.F.			Col. & Ex.		Deposits.		General	
3	Duncan, Sh. & Co.	Disc. 1. Wright G. & R. .					5000	
		" 3. A. J. Comstock .					5000	
		" 4. N. Bidwell . . .					3000	
13	Far. & M. B., Det.	Canada Funds per Express	37	50			7462	50
√	Exchange	Exps. chgs. on above . .	3	75				
12	Treasury Notes	Bot. $10,000 @ 98¢ . . .					9800	
√	Duncan, Sh. & Co.	N. E. Bank Notes ^{5000} 6 25 .	6	25			4993	75
√	Exchange .	Pm. on above 12^{50}; Ex. 3^{75}	16	25				
16	H. B. Bryant	90, 75, 18^{20}, 138, 143^{75} .			464	95		
17	John R. Penn	118, 120, 35^{80}, 19^{23}, 150 .			443	03		
7	John S. Woolson	112^{50}, 125, 142, 18^{75}, 119, 12^{50}			529	75		
12	Asa Mahan	150, 200, 38^{50}, 192 . . .			580	50		
19	John D. Williams	175			175			
8	T. P. Handy	115, 275, 87^{50}, 90 . . .			567	50		
1	Lewis R. Morris	130, 12^{75}, 18, 110 . . .			270	75		
9	E. L. Jones	90, 125, 116, 25^{50} . . .			356	50		
15	Charles Hickox	225, 75, 12^{50}			312	50		
11	Alonzo Mitchell	125, 132^{25}, 16^{75}, 300 . .			574			
10	James Richards	500, 300			800			
5	Jas. W. Lusk	138, 500, 19^{50}, 12, 115, 3030			3814	50		
14	Ingham & Bragg	132, 119, 12^{75}, 25, 1500 .			1788	75		
3	Duncan, Sh. & Co.	Disc. 10. Claflin, M. & Co.					4000	
4	Bills Discounted	Per Discount Register . .					11000	
5	Domestic Exch.	" " " . .					42500	
6	Col. & Exch.		63	75			63	75
2	Depositors				10677	73	10677	73
8	*Cash Cr.*	*Total Disbursements* .					103497	73

DEBIT JOURNAL.

 Cleveland, O., April, 1862.

L.F.			*Col. & Ex.*		*Deposits.*		*General*	
17	John R. Penn	575, 5000, 3000, 1500, 750			10825			
17	Fixtures	Bill of Furn. and Fixtures.					575	
[illegible]	Exchange	Ex. chgs. on Gold from N.Y.	50					
15	Chas. Hickox	7000			7000			
16	H. B. Bryant	1500, 125, 87 50, 100 . .			1812	50		
10	James Richards	3500, 1750, 25			5275			
14	Ingham & Bragg	175, 238, 500, 75, 115 . .			1103			
13	Robert Brown	150, 125, 75, 400, 138 50 .			888	50		
12	Asa Mahan	900, 75, 250			1225			
11	Alonzo Mitchell	6000, 750, 125, 400 . . .			7275			
9	E. L. Jones	475, 300, 175, 87 50, 12 75.			1050	25		
8	T. P. Handy	2000, 175, 187 50. . . .			2362	50		
7	John S. Woolson	75, 137 50			212	50		
6	Lewis R. Morris	156 25, 400, 115, 375 . .			1046	25		
5	Jas. W. Lusk	1575, 2000, 175, 125 . .			3875			
18	Geo. A. Crocker	500			500			
19	John D. Williams	1200, 150			1350			
20	Henry Ivison	500, 75, 250			825			
22	Austin Packard	400, 125.			525			
4	M. B. Scott	1500, 2000, 135, 120 . .			3755			
3	Jacob Hoornbeek	750			750			
2	E. R. Felton	3000, 2500, 450			5950			
1	N. C. Winslow	500			500			
3	Duncan, Sh. & Co.	Disc. 5. Jno. R. Penn . .					2500	
		" 13. Ivison, Ph. & Co. .					6000	
		" 15. Parker Handy . .					7000	
		" 17. Wm. Lanier & Co.					2500	
16	Exch. Bk., Buf.	Disc. 12. H. B. Tuttle . .					2500	
18	Protested Paper	Disc. 16. M. B. Scott 3000 / 1 .					3001	
9	Lafayette Bk. Cin.	Disc. 14. W. H. Clark . .					2500	
3	Duncan, Sh. & Co.	Col. 15. J. B. Meriam . .					1500	
4	Bills Discounted	Per Discount Register . .					54000	
5	Domestic Exch.	" " " . .					28500	
6	Col. & Exch.		50				50	
2	Deposits				58105	50	58105	50
8	*Cash Cr.*	*Total Disbursements* .					168731	50

DEBIT JOURNAL.

L.F.			Col. & Ex.		Deposits.		General.	
3	Duncan, Sh. & Co.	A. C. Taylor on L., P. & Co.					6000	
		J. H. Goldsmith on B. & S.					4000	
		Jas. W. Lusk on P. H. . .					4000	
		John R. Penn on E. R. B.					4000	
		Ctfct. Dep. fav. S. S. P., Cashier					8000	
7	Expense	Pd. Rent of Banking Ho. .					333	34
3	Duncan, Sh. & Co.	F. & M.'s Bk., Det., on M. B.	22	50			3000	
18	Protested Paper	Disc. No. 24 protested, $^{20000}_{\ \ \ \ \ 1}$					20001	
29	Certifct. Deposit	No. 1 .			3000			
20	C. & E. R. R. Bs.	Bot. Collaterals at auction .					18000	
	Expense	Auctioneer's Charges . .					45	
21	Loss and Gain	Deficiency on Disc. 24 . .					1956	
6	Lewis R. Morris	3000, 5000, 175			8175			
25	Wm. T. Brooks	7000, 915, 75			7990			
27	E. G. Folsom	1000, 175, 123 75, 94 63 . .			1393	38		
1	N. C. Winslow	700, 83 33, 19 75, 12 50 . .			815	58		
2	E. R. Felton	9000, 185			9185			
3	Jacob Hoornbeek	6750, 1983 25, 12 75, 150 .			8896			
4	M. B. Scott	120, 3000, 5000, 329 83 . .			8449	83		
7	John S. Woolson	5000, 133, 762, 18 50 . .			5913	50		
5	Jas. W. Lusk	217, 25, 172 93, 125 . . .			539	93		
6	E. L. Jones	975, 150			1125			
[illegible]	Asa Mahan	400, 595, 12 50			1007	50		
[illegible]	Alonzo Mitchell	3000, 150, 19 63			3169	63		
[illegible]	James Richards	275, 1250, 318			1843			
[illegible]	Ingham & Bragg	125, 1200			1325			
[illegible]	Robert Brown	125, 25 73, 180, 19 75 . . .			350	48		
[illegible]	H. B. Bryant	75, 128 90			203	90		
[illegible]	John R. Penn	195, 63 50, 128			386	50		
[illegible]	Geo. A. Crocker	189, 12 75, 312 50			514	25		
[illegible]	John D. Williams	129, 17 50, 193 75			340	25		
[illegible]	Henry Ivison	400, 123, 85 50			608	50		
[illegible]	W. H. Clark	8000, 2750, 129			10879			
[illegible]	Austin Packard	300, 129, 87 50			516	50		
[illegible]	Hiram A. Pryor	500, 129, 17 50			646	50		
[illegible]	Joseph P. Walter	129, 700, 12 50			841	50		
[illegible]	Geo. M. Penn	900, 127, 13 75			1040	75		
[illegible]	H. D. Stratton	8000, 4000			12000			
[illegible]	J. B. Meriam	3750, 128, 17 50			3895	50		
[illegible]	T. P. Handy	1600, 10000			11600			
[illegible]	Burkam & Sons	Disc. 18. W. B. O. 12000 .	60				11940	
[illegible]	Duncan, Sh. & Co.	Disc. 19. D. Appleton & Co.					3000	
[illegible]	Bk. of Cap., Alb.	Disc. 43. E. W. Keyes . .					8000	
[illegible]	Lafayette Bk. Cin.	Cols. 2000, 1500					3500	
[illegible]	F. & M. Bk., Det.	Collection 2000	10				1990	
[illegible]	Moss Bro., Sand.	Collection					700	
[illegible]	Exch. Bk., Buf.	Collection					750	
[illegible]	Bills Discounted	Per Discount Register . .					41500	
[illegible]	Domestic Exch.	" " " . .					81000	
9	Col. & Exch.	. . . .	92	50			92	50
2	Deposits	. . . .			106651	98	106651	98
8	*Cash Cr.*	*Total Disbursements* .					328459	82

DEBIT JOURNAL.

Cleveland, O., June, 1862.

L. F.	Account	Particulars	*Col. & Ex.*		*Deposits.*		*General.*	
8	Lafayette Bk., Cin.	Your Dft. fav. Jas. Moore . . .					1500	
√	Exchange	Exps. Chgs. on Curr'cy from N.Y.	3	75				
3	Duncan, Sh. & Co.	N. Y. State Currency . . . 7500	18	75			7481	25
√	Exchange	Express Chgs. on above	4					
3	Duncan, Sh. & Co.	H. D. Stratton on C. V. Culver .					23500	
16	Exch. Bank, Buf.	Disc. 26, M. B. Scott					10000	
9	Lafayette Bk., Cin.	" 27, R. M. Bartlott					3000	
19	**Burkam & Sons, Ch.**	" 28, Geo. M. Penn . . 5000	25				4975	
19		" 30, W. D. Packard 4000	20				3980	
19		" 31, Woolson & McF. 3000	15				2985	
3		" 44, J. G. Deshler . . 15000	75				14925	
3	F. & M. Bk., Det.	" 45, R. C. Spencer . . 3500	17	50			3482	50
3	Franklin Bk., Col.	" 48, E. R. Morgan					4000	
1	Duncan, Sh. & Co.	" 29, Austin Packard . . .					3500	
4		" 33, Barnaby Rudge . . .					10000	
3		" 37, Jno. R. Penn					6000	
2	N. C. Winslow	8750, 400, 110			4260			
9	M. B. Scott	6000, 125, 146^{32}, 154			6425	32		
5	Jacob Hoornbeek	900, 18^{75}			918	75		
8	E. R. Felton	218, 130, 25, 87^{50}			455	50		
7	E. L. Jones	4000, 3718, 125			7843			
6	Jas. W. Lusk	416, 253^{75}, 15, 22^{50}			707	25		
14	T. P. Handy	6000, 194, 212^{75}			6406	75		
13	John S. Woolson	1800, 400, 239, 212^{50}			2651	50		
12	Lewis R. Morris	90, 12^{50}, 28, 19^{25}, 142			291	75		
10	Ingham & Bragg	1500, 170, 12^{50}, 13^{25}, 50 . . .			1745	75		
19	Robert Brown	5000, 112^{50}			5112	50		
18	Asa Mahan	800, 112^{50}, 97^{75}			510	25		
17	James Richards	4000, 137^{50}, 19^{75}			4157	25		
15	John D. Williams	1200, 17^{50}, 26, 38^{25}, 14^{75} . . .			1296	50		
16	Geo. A. Crocker	8000, 125, 210			8335			
24	John R. Penn	125, 12^{50}, 16.			153	50		
23	Chas. Hickox	1275, 182, 100			1557			
22	H. B. Bryant	150, 2000, 1200			3350			
21	Joseph P. Walter	275, 117, 142^{50}			534	50		
20	Hiram A. Pryor	90, 110, 12^{75}, 125			337	75		
26	Austin Packard	112, 145, 19			276			
25	W. H. Clark	110, 112			222			
27	Henry Ivison	500, 123, 17^{50}			640	50		
28	Geo. M. Penn	125, 12^{75}, 18			155	75		
31	Wm. T. Brooks	175, 19, 12			206			
33	E. G. Folsom	19, 120, 117			256			
3	H. D. Stratton	125, 19, 12^{50}, 20			176	50		
30	J. B. Meriam	12000, 150, 119			12269			
29	D. P. Eells	150, 19^{75}, 112			281	75		
24	Duncan, Sh. & Co.	Interest on Deposits					477	56
25	Certified Checks	J. R. Penn			575			
26	Ctfct. Deposit	No. 2, Returned			3000			
9	Toledo Br. Bk.	Cols. 3000, 2000, 500, 750					6250	
3	Farm. Br. Bk., Ash.	Collection					750	
23	Lorain Bk., Elyria	Cols. 900, 1500					2400	
16	Lafayette Bk., Cin.	Cols. 1200, 500					1700	
4	Duncan, Sh. & Co.	Collection					1750	
6	Franklin Bk. Col.	Collection					750	
7	Exch. Bank, Buf.	Cols. 350, 500					850	
	Bills Discounted	Per Discount Register					19000	
	Domestic Exch.	" " "					27050	
	Expense	**Paid Officers' Salaries, viz.:** President, 1000; Cashier, 750; First Teller, 600; Second do., 500; Bookkeeper, 500; Assistant do., 400; Porter, 200					3950	
6	**Col. & Exch.**	. . . .	179				179	
2	**Deposits**	. . . .			75108	32	75108	32
8	***Cash Cr.***	***Total Disbursements*** . . .					239543	63

CREDIT JOURNAL.

Cleveland, O., January, 1862. 1

L.F			Col. & Ex.		Deposits.		General.	
1	Capital Stock	First Instalment of 60%						
		H. B. Bryant 100 sh. 6000						
		H. D. St'tton 100 " 6000						
		J. B. Meriam 100 " 6000						
		D., Sh. & Co. 200 " 12000						
		P. Handy 200 " 12000						
		H. Ivison 250 " 15000						
		J. R. Penn 100 " 6000						
		P. Cooper 200 " 12000						
		J. W. Lusk 100 " 6000						
		W. H. Clark 250 " 15000						
		J. H. Gold'th 100 " 6000						
		A. C. Taylor 150 " 9000						
		M. B. Scott 150 " 9000					120000	
1	N. C. Winslow	1000			1000			
2	E. R. Felton	1750			1750			
3	Jacob Hoornbeek	5000			5000			
4	M. B. Scott	900			900			
5	Jas. W. Lusk	2500			2500			
6	Lewis R. Morris	3000			3000			
7	John S. Woolson	1500			1500			
8	T. P. Handy	4700			4700			
9	E. L. Jones	975			975			
10	James Richards	1750			1750			
11	Alonzo Mitchell	2000			2000			
12	Asa Mahan	1200			1200			
13	Robert Brown	1000			1000			
14	Ingham & Bragg	3750			3750			
15	Charles Hickox	1325			1325			
3	Duncan, Sh. & Co.	N. C. Winslow Dft. 1.	5				500	
16	H. B. Bryant	Disc. 4947 50			4947	50		
17	John R. Penn	Disc. 3958			3958			
14	Interest	Per Discount Register .					94	50
6	Col. & Exch.		5				5	
2	Deposits				41255	50	41255	50
8	*Cash Dr.*	*Total Receipts* . .					161855	

CREDIT JOURNAL.

Cleveland, February, 1862.

L.F.			Col. & Ex.		Deposits.		General.	
2	Duncan, Sh. & Co.	Stocks . . . Dft. 2					36400	
15	Office Notes	From B. C. for circulation					35000	
17	John R. Penn	3000			3000			
18	Geo. A. Crocker	1500			1500			
19	John D. Williams	1200			1200			
7	John S. Woolson	2500			2500			
8	T. P. Handy	1175 50			1175	50		
3	Jacob Hoornbeek	4000; Col. 473 81 . . .			4473	81		
9	E. L. Jones	900			900			
13	Ingham & Bragg	875			875			
20	Henry Ivison	1700			1700			
6	Lewis R. Morris	1200; Col. 897 75 . . .			2097	75		
16	H. B. Bryant	1200			1200			
12	Asa Mahan	2500			2500			
15	Chas. Hickox	1700			1700			
3	Duncan, Sh. & Co.	M. B. Scott . . Dft. 3	30				3000	
		Robert Smith . " 4	15				1500	
		John S. Woolson " 5	7	50			750	
		John R. Penn . " 6	25				2500	
		T. P. Handy . " 7	19	75			1975	
3	Duncan, Sh. & Co.	Collection No. 4 . . .					2970	
21	W. H. Clark	" " 5 . . .			1500			
✓	Col. & Exchange	per Passed Collect. Book	33	44				
11	Alonzo Mitchell	Discs. 4972 50, 2978 50 .			7951			
5	Jas. W. Lusk	Disc.			2468	33		
2	E. R. Felton	Discs. 1570 14, 3463 25 .			5033	39		
4	M. B. Scott	Disc.			6925	34		
14	Interest	Per Discount Register .					221	94
6	Col. & Ex.	. . . .	130	69			130	69
2	Deposits	. . . .			48700	12	48700	12
8	*Cash Dr.*	*Total Receipts* . .					133147	75

CREDIT JOURNAL.

Cleveland, O., March, 1862.

L.F.			Col. & Ex.		Deposits.		General.	
5	Domestic Exch.	Disc. 1, D., Sh. & Co. 5000						
		" 3, " 5000						
		" 4, " 3000					13000	
3	Duncan, Sh. & Co.	J. W. Lusk . . Dft. 8	30				3000	
✓	Exchange	Discount on Canada Cur.	75					
3	Duncan, Sh. & Co.	Treasury Notes Dft. 9					9800	
5	Jas. W. Lusk	1530; Discs. 5965 . .			7495			
2	E. R. Felton	1900; Discs. 2968^{50} .			4868	50		
17	John R. Penn	375; Discs. 11780 . .			12155			
16	H. B. Bryant	4375^{29}			4375	29		
19	Jno. D. Williams	1500			1500			
13	Robert Brown	575			575			
10	James Richards	2500; Ds. 5967, 2479^{17}			10946	17		
22	Austin Packard	500			500			
23	Hiram A. Pryor	1250			1250			
7	John S. Woolson	2000			2000			
9	E. L. Jones	375			375			
14	Ingham & Bragg	975			975			
3	Jacob Hoornbeek	1500; Col. 1200 . . .			2700			
18	Geo. A. Crocker	1900			1900			
6	Lewis R. Morris	1750; Col. 500 . . .			2250			
1	N. C. Winslow	3750			3750			
12	Asa Mahan	1400			1400			
4	M. B. Scott	1300; Ds. 6942^{83}, 2983^{50}			11226	33		
8	T. P. Handy	1100			1100			
11	Alonzo Mitchell	3750			3750			
20	Henry Ivison	1200			1200			
24	Joseph P. Walter	900			900			
15	Charles Hickox	2900			2900			
4	Bills Discounted	Peter Cooper . Disc. 2					4000	
5	Domestic Exch.	Disc. 10, Dunc., Sh. & Co.					4000	
3	Duncan, Sh. & Co.	Cols. 1485, 2475, 5940 .					9900	
21	W. H. Clark	Col. 2000			2000			
✓	Col. & Exch.	Pas. Col. 100; D. R. 96^{25}	196	25				
25	W. T. Brooks	Discs. 4960, 4000. . .			8960			
14	Interest	Per Discount Register .					385	25
6	Col. & Exch.	. . . .	301	25			301	25
2	Deposits	. . . .			91051	29	91051	29
8	*Cash Dr.*	*Total Receipts* . .					135437	79

CREDIT JOURNAL.

4 Cleveland, O., April, 1862.

L.F			Col. & Ex.		Deposits.		General.	
29	Ctfct. Deposit	J. R. Penn for T. Hunter			3000			
30	Certified Checks	J. R. Penn			575			
3	Duncan, Sh. & Co.	Sumner Packard, Dft. 10	39	19			3918	81
3	Duncan, Sh. & Co.	Gold by Express . . .					10000	
3	Duncan, Sh. & Co.	Geo. S. Eaton . Dft. 11	38	69			3869	31
4	M. B. Scott	900; Disc. 9895 . .			10795			
3	Jacob Hoornbeek	750; Col. 1250 . . .			2000			
2	E. R. Felton	525			525			
26	Geo. M. Penn	1500; Disc. 4910 83 . .			6410	83		
27	E. G. Folsom	1000; Disc. 2983 50 . .			3983	50		
1	N. C. Winslow	795			795			
8	T. P. Handy	850			850			
7	John S. Woolson	782; Disc. 2934 50 . .			3716	50		
6	Lewis R. Morris	563; Cols. 3000, 1575.			5138			
5	Jas. W. Lusk	1000			1000			
11	Alonzo Mitchell	1500			1500			
9	E. L. Jones	1500			1500			
10	James Richards	500; Disc. 3463 25 . .			3963	25		
16	H. B. Bryant	675			675			
13	Robert Brown	1500			1500			
15	Chas. Hickox	3000			3000			
14	Ingham & Bragg	975			975			
17	John R. Penn	1200			1200			
19	John D. Williams	784			784			
20	Henry Ivison	1500			1500			
22	Austin Packard	1275			1275			
24	Joseph P. Walter	1500			1500			
25	Wm. T. Brooks	500			500			
21	W. H. Clark	1200; C. 3000; D. 4947 50			9147	50		
23	Hiram A. Pryor	3000			3000			
	Bills Disctd.	Disc. 7, J. Richards, 3500						
		" 8, C. Hickox, 7000						
		" 9, C. Shook, 5000						
		" 11, M. B. Scott, 6000					21500	
5	Domestic Exch.	Disc. 5, D., S. & Co., 2500						
		" 13, " 6000						
		" 15, " 7000						
		" 17, " 2500					18000	
5	Domestic Exch.	Disc. 12, Exch. Bk., Buf.					2500	
5	Domestic Exch.	Disc. 16, Protested . .					3000	
16	Exch. Bk., Buf.	Protest Fees on Disc. 16					1	
5	Domestic Exch.	Disc. 14, Laf. Bk., Cin. .					2500	
3	Duncan, Sh. & Co.	Cols. 1980, 2475, 2970 .					7425	
9	Lafayette Bk., Cin.	Cols. 6000, 3000 . . .					9000	
31	J. B. Meriam	Col. 1500; Disc. 6927 67			8427	67		
√	Col. & Exch.	Pas. Col. 75; Dis. R. 97 50	172	50				
28	H. D. Stratton	Disc. 14785.			14785			
14	Interest	Per Discount Register .					845	58
6	Col. & Exch.		250	38			250	38
2	Deposits				94021	25	94021	25
8	*Cash Dr.*	*Total Receipts* . .					176831	33

CREDIT JOURNAL.

Cleveland, O., May, 1862. 5

L.F.			Col. & Ex.		Deposits.		General.	
1	Capital Stock	Final Instalment of 40 % . . .					80000	
14	Interest	Semi-an. Int. on U. S. Stks., $600 do. O. S. do. 600					1200	
13	F. & M. Bk., Det.	Remittance in N. Y. Exch. 3000 22 50					3022	50
18	Protested Paper	Disc. No. 16, Redeemed . . .					3001	
29	Ctfct. Deposit	L. R. Morris, for Robt. Smith .			3000			
29		W. T. Brooks for H. B. Bryant .			7000			
29		E. G. Folsom for Geo. Eddy .			1000			
4	Bills Discounted	Disc. No. 24, Protested . . .					20000	
3	Duncan, Sh. & Co.	Knox Co. Bank . . . Dft. 12	14	85			1485	15
3	Duncan, Sh. & Co.	East River Bank . . Dft. 13	29	70			2970	30
18	Protested Paper	Redeemed by Sale of Collaterals					20001	
1	N. C. Winslow	1500			1500			
3	Jacob Hoornbeek	700			700			
4	M. B. Scott	800; Col. 1496 25			2296	25		
5	Jas. W. Lusk	1500; Col. 2000			3500			
6	Lewis R. Morris	750			750			
9	E. L. Jones	3000			3000			
10	Jas. Richards	975			975			
11	Alonzo Mitchell	500			500			
12	Asa Mahan	1500			1500			
13	Robert Brown	2000			2000			
14	Ingham & Bragg	1700			1700			
17	John R. Penn	1200			1200			
19	John D. Williams	1350			1350			
20	Henry Ivison	2575			2575			
22	Austin Packard	758			758			
23	Hiram A. Pryor	1500			1500			
24	Joseph P. Walter	900			900			
26	Geo. M. Penn	1500			1500			
27	E. G. Folsom	738; Col. 1500; Disc. 3938 .			6176			
4	Bills Discounted	No. 6, T. P. Handy . . 1600 " 25, H. Bishop . . . 3000					4600	
5	Domestic Exch.	" 18, W. B. Ogden . 12000 " 19, D. Appleton & Co. 3000 " 43, E. W. Keyes . 8000					23000	
3	Duncan, Sh. & Co.	Cols. 3465, 6930					10395	
9	Lafayette B., Cin.	Col.					1750	
19	Burkam & Sons, C.	Cols. 4000, 3750					7750	
16	Exch. Bank, Buf.	Col.					995	
31	J. B. Meriam	C. 750, 900, 1995; D. 7402 50, 5942			16989	50		
2	E. R. Felton	Col. 1985; Disc. 9921 67 . . .			11906	67		
33	D. P. Eells	Col. 698 25			698	25		
18	Geo. A. Crocker	Col. 750; Discs. 6925 33, 2974 .			10649	33		
✓	Coll. & Exch.	From Pas. Col	135	50				
7	John S. Woolson	Discs. 5923, 4947 50			10870	50		
15	Chas. Hickox	Discs. 1478 25, 6927 67			8405	92		
16	H. B. Bryant	Discs. 3449 25, 6926 50			10375	75		
32	T. P. Handy	Discs. 9945, 3958 67			13903	67		
14	Interest	Per Discount Register					1025	83
✓	Col. & Exch.	" " "	182	50				
6	Col. & Exch.	. . . .	362	55			362	55
2	Deposits	. . . .			129179	84	129179	84
8	*Cash Dr*	*Total Receipts*					310738	17

6 Cleveland, O., June, 1862.

L. F			Col. & Ex.		Deposits.		General	
11	Moss Bros., Sandy.	Currency to bal. %					1175	
16	Exch. Bank, Buf.	Jno. S. Woolson . . . Dft. 1					1800	
3	Duncan, Sh. & Co.	Currency by Express . . . 5000	37	50			4962	56
3	Duncan, Sh. & Co.	Toledo Br. Bank . . . Dft. 14	70				7000	
20	C. & E. R. R. Bonds	Sold H. D. Stratton					22500	
4	Bills Discounted	Disc. 20, S. Packard . . . 4000						
		" 21, W. H. Clark . . . 5000						
		" 22, Peter Cooper . 15000						
		" 23, N. C. Winslow . 7000						
		" 38, W. H. Clark . . 10000	100					
		" 40, S. S. Packard . . 3000						
		" 47, H. B. Tuttle . . 10000					54000	
5	Domestic Exch.	Disc. 26, M. B. Scott . . 10000						
		" 27, R. M. Bartlett . . 3000						
		" 28, Geo. M. Penn . . 5000						
		" 29, Austin Packard . 3500						
		" 30, W. D. Packard . . 4000						
		" 31, Woolson & McF. . 3000						
		" 33, Barnaby Rudge 10000						
		" 37, Jno. R. Penn . . 6000						
		" 44, J. G. Deshler . 15000						
		" 45, R. C. Spencer . . 3500						
		" 48, E. R. Morgan . . 4000					67000	
8	T. P. Handy	700; Discs. 7382^{50}, 1484^{25} . .			9566	75		
32	D. P. Eells	745			745			
25	Wm. T. Brooks	1275			1275			
26	Geo. M. Penn	900; Cols. 1500, 600, 1995 . . .			4995			
27	E. G. Folsom	1560			1560			
28	H. D. Stratton	3763^{75}; Col. 1496^{25}			5260			
24	Joseph P. Walter	1960			1960			
23	Hiram A. Pryor	3750			3750			
22	Austin Packard	670			670			
21	W. H. Clark	1200; Cols. 2992^{50}, 748^{12}			4940	62		
20	Henry Ivison	800			800			
18	Geo. A. Crocker	500			500			
17	John R. Penn	700; Cols. 7000, 1750			9450			
16	H. B. Bryant	300			300			
15	Chas Hickox	1700			1700			
11	Alonzo Mitchell	1500			1500			
12	Asa Mahan	700; Discs. 595^{90}			1295	90		
13	Robert Brown	962; Discs. 6627^{38}			7589	38		
10	James Richards	1500			1500			
9	E. L. Jones	900; Discs. 5907, 3681^{88}			10488	88		
7	John S. Woolson	400; Col. 500			900			
5	Jas. W. Lusk	1832^{98}; Col. 498^{75}			2331	73		
4	M. B. Scott	936; Col. 350			1286			
3	Jacob Hoornbeek	406			406			
2	E. R. Felton	729			729			
1	N. C. Winslow	300; Discs. 2968^{50}, 1477 . . .			4745	50		
14	Interest	on Treasury Notes					184	
14	Interest	Duncan, Sh. & Co. on deposits .					477	56
3	Duncan, Sh. & Co.	J. L. Dawes . . . . . . Dft. 15	5	75			575	
13	F. & Mechs. B., Det.	Our Ctfct. Dep. . . . . . No. 2					3000	
3	Duncan, Sh. & Co.	C. 4950, 740^{62}, 888^{75}, 1185, 740^{62}, 493^{7}					8998	74
23	Franklin Bk. Col.	Collection					750	
16	Exch. Bank, Buf.	Cols. 696^{50}, 3482^{50}					4179	
✓	Col. & Exch.	Pas. Col. 141^{64}; Disc. Reg 28^{50}.	70	14				
6	Lewis R. Morris	Discs. 4971^{67}, 4704^{08}			9675	75		
14	Ingham & Bragg	Discs. 1754^{70}, 1488^{50}			3243	20		
19	John D. Williams	Discs. 886^{80}, 1481^{75}			2368	55		
14	Interest	From Discount Register . . .					609	59
6	Col. & Exch.	. . . .	383	39			383	39
2	Deposits	. . . .			95532	26	95532	26
8	*Cash Dr.*	*Total Receipts*					274127	04

GENERAL LEDGER.

Capital Stock.

Date		Particulars	Fol.	Amount		Date		Particulars	Fol.	Amount	
1862						1862					
June	1	Balance		200000		Jan.	1	60% paid in	1	120000	
						May	1	40% do.	5	80000	
				200000						200000	
						June	1	Balance		200000	

Deposits. 2

Date		Particulars	Fol.	Amount		Date		Particulars	Fol.	Amount	
1862											
Jan.	1	Drawn out this day	1	11302	15	Jan.	1	Deposited this day	1	41255	50
Feb.	1	" " "	2	14359	47	Feb.	1	" " "	2	48700	12
Mar.	1	" " "	3	10677	73	Mar.	1	" " "	3	91051	29
Apr.	1	" " "	4	58105	50	Apr.	1	" " "	4	94021	25
May	1	" " "	5	106651	98	May	1	" " "	5	129179	84
June	1	" " "	6	75108	32	June	1	" " "	6	95532	26
"	"	Balance		223523	11						
				499740	26					499740	26
						June	1	By Balance		223535	11

Duncan, Sherman & Co. 3

Date		Particulars	Fol.	Amount		Date		Particulars	Fol.	Amount	
1862						1862					
Jan.	1	H. B. B. on Ocean Bk.	1	5000		Jan.	1	N. C. Winslow, Dft. 1	1	500	
		J. B. M., Cont. Bk.	1	7500		Feb.	1	Stocks " 2	2	36400	
		Ctfct. Dep. Met. Bk.	1	10000				M. B. Scott " 3	2	3000	
		W. H. C. on you	1	15000				R. Smith " 4	2	1500	
		T. P. H. on Ocean Bk.	1	30000				J. S. Woolson " 5	2	750	
Feb.	1	E. R. F. on Ex. Bk.	2	5000				J. R. Penn " 6	2	2500	
		M. B. S. on Ocean Bk.	2	1200				T. P. Handy " 7	2	1975	
		Ctfct. Dep. Met. Bk.	2	2500				Collection, No. 4	2	2970	
		J. R. P. on E. Riv. Bk.	2	500		Mar.	1	J. W. Lusk, Dft. 8	3	3000	
		Jas. Moore on you	2	3000				Treas. Notes, " 9	3	9800	
Mar.	1	Disc. 1, W. G. & R.	3	5000				Collections	3	9900	
		" 2, A. J. Comst'k	3	5000		Apr.	1	S. Packard, Dft. 10	4	3918	81
		" 4, N. Bidwell	3	3000				Gold by Express	4	10000	
		N. E. Bk. Notes	3	4993	75			G. S. Eaton, Dft. 11	4	3869	31
		Disc. 10, Claf. M. & Co.	3	4000				Collections	4	7425	
Apr.	1	" 5, J. R. Penn	4	2500		May	1	Knox Co. Bk., Dft. 12	5	1485	15
		" 13, Iv., Ph. & Co.	4	6000				East Riv. Bk., " 13	5	2970	30
		" 15, P. Handy	4	7000				Collections	5	10395	
		" 17, W., L. & Co.	4	2500		June	1	Currency by Exp.	6	4962	50
		Col. 15, J. B. Meriam	4	1500				Tol. Br. Bk., Dft. 14	6	7000	
May	1	A. C. T. on I. Ph. & Co.	5	6000				J. L. Dawes " 15	6	575	
		J. H. G. on B. & S.	5	4000				Collections	6	8998	74
		J. W. L. on P. Handy	5	4000		"	"	Balance		72007	75
		J. R. P. on E. Riv. Bk.	5	4000							
		Ctfct. Dep.	5	8000							
		F. & M. B., Det. on M. B.	5	3000							
		Disc. 19, D. Ap. & Co.	5	3000							
June	1	N. Y. State Currency	6	7481	25						
		H. D. S. on C. V. C.	6	23500							
		D'sc. 29, A. Packard	6	3500							
		" 33, B. Rudge	6	10000							
		" 37, J. R. Penn	6	6000							
		Int. on Deposits	6	477	56						
		Collection	6	1750							
				205902	56					205902	56
June	1	Balance		72007	75						

GENERAL LEDGER.

4 Bills Discounted.

1862						1862					
Jan.	1	Sundries	1	4000		Mar.	1	Disc. 2	3	4000	
Feb.	1	"	2	12100		Apr.	1	Discs. 7, 8, 9, 11	4	21500	
Mar.	1	"	3	11000		May	1	Disc. 24, protested	5	20000	
Apr.	1	"	4	54000		"	"	Discs. 6, 25	5	4600	
May	1	"	5	41500		June	1	Discs. 20, 21, 22, 23, 38, 40, 47	6	54000	
June	1	"	6	19000		"	"	Balance		[illegible]	
				141600						141600	
June	1	Balance		37500							

5 Domestic Exchange.

1862						1862					
Jan.	1	Sundries	1	5000		Mar.	1	Discs. 1, 3, 4	3	13000	
Feb.	1	"	2	10500		"	"	Disc. 10	3	4000	
Mar.	1	"	3	42500		Apr.	1	Discs. 5, 13, 15, 17	4	18000	
Apr.	1	"	4	28500		"	"	Disc. 12	4	2500	
May	1	"	5	81000		"	"	Disc. 16	4	3000	
June	1	"	6	27050		"	"	Disc. 14	4	2500	
						May	1	Discs. 18, 19, 43	5	23000	
						June	1	D. 26, 27, 28, 29, 30, 31, 33, 37, 44, 45, 48	6	67000	
						"	"	Balance		61550	
				194550						194550	
June	1	Balance		61550							

6 Collection and Exchange.

1862						1862					
Jan.	1	Sundries	1	150		Jan.	1	Sundries	1	5	
Feb.	1	"	2	61		Feb.	1	"	2	130	69
Mar.	1	"	3	63	75	Mar.	1	"	3	301	25
Apr.	1	"	4	50		Apr.	1	"	4	250	38
May	1	"	5	92	50	May	1	"	5	362	55
June	1	"	6	179		June	1	"	6	383	39
"	"	Loss and Gain [L. P.]	21	[illegible]	[illegible]						
				1433	26					1433	26

7 Expense.

1862						1862					
Jan.	1	B. Bks., Stat'nery, &c.	1	150		June	1	Loss and Gain [L. P.]	21	4478	34
May	1	Rent of Bank. House	5	333	34						
"	"	Auctioneer's Bill	5	45							
June	1	Officers' Salaries	6	3950							
				4478	34					4478	34

GENERAL LEDGER.

Cash. 8

1862						1862					
Jan.	1	Receipts this day	1	161855		Jan.	1	Disbursem'nts this day	1	88102	15
Feb.	1	" " "	2	133147	75	Feb.	1	" " "	2	86995	47
Mar	1	" " "	3	135437	79	Mar.	1	" " "	3	103497	73
Apr	1	" " "	4	176831	33	Apr.	1	" " "	4	168731	50
May	1	" " "	5	310738	17	May	1	" " "	5	328459	82
June	1	" " "	6	274127	04	June	1	" " "	6	239543	63
						"	"	Balance		176806	78
				1192137	08					1192137	08
		Balance		176806	78						

Lafayette Bank,—*Cincinnati.* 9

1862						1862					
Feb.	1	Col. No. 7	2	900		Apr.	1	Cols. 6000, 3000	4	9000	
Apr.	1	Disc. 14, W. H. C.	4	2500		May	1	Collection		1750	
May	1	Collections	5	3500		June	1	Balance		2350	
June	1	Dft. fav. J. Moore	6	1500							
"	"	Disc. 27, R. M. B.	6	3000							
"	"	Collections	6	1700							
				13100						13100	
June	1	Balance		2350							

Public Stocks. 10

1862						1862					
Feb.	1	20 Shrs. U. S. 6%	1	18400		Jan.	1	Balance		36400	
		20 do. O. S. 6%	1	18000							
				36400							
June	1	Balance		36400							

Moss Bros.,—*Sandusky.* 11

1862						1862					
Feb.	1	Col. No. 10	2	475		June	1	Currency to bal. %	6	1175	
		Collection	5	700							
				1175						1175	

12 Treasury Notes.

1862											
Mar.	1	$10000 @ 98¢	3	9800							

13 Farmers' & Mechs.' Bank,—*Detroit.*

1862						1862					
Mar.	1	Canada Currency	3	7462	50	May	1	N. Y. Currency	5	3022	50
May	1	Collection	5	1990		June	1	Ctfct. Dep., No. 2	6	3000	
June	1	Disc. 45, R. C. S.	6	3482	50	"	"	Balance		6912	50
				12935						2935	
		Balance		6912	50						

14 Interest.

1862						1862					
June	1	Loss and Gain [L. F.]	21	5044	25	Jan.	1	From Discount Reg.	1	94	50
						Feb.	1	" " "	2	221	94
						Mar.	1	" " "	3	385	25
						Apr.	1	" " "	4	845	58
						May	1	On Public Stocks	5	1200	
						"	"	From Discount Reg.	5	1025	83
						June	1	On Treasury Notes	6	184	
						"	"	Duncan, Sh. & Co.	6	477	56
						"	"	From Discount Reg.	6	609	59
				5044	25					5044	25

15 Office Notes.

						1862					
						Feb.	1	Total Circulation	2	35000	

GENERAL LEDGER.

Exchange Bank,—*Buffalo.* 16

1862					1862				
Apr.	1	Disc. 12, H. B. Tuttle	4	2500	Apr.	1	Protest on Disc. 16	4	1
May	1	Collection	5	750	May	1	Collection	5	995
June	1	Disc. 26, M. B. Scott	6	10000	June	1	J. S. Woolson, Dft. 1	6	1800
"	"	Collections	6	850	"	"	Collections		4179
					"	"	Balance		7125
				14100					14100
June	1	Balance		7125					

Fixtures. 17

1862									
Apr.	1	Furniture, etc.	4	575					

Protested Paper. 18

1862					1862				
Apr.	1	Disc. 16, M. B. S.	4	3001	May	1	Disc. 16, redeemed	5	3001
May	1	Disc. 24, Chas. B.	5	20001			Disc. 24. redeemed	5	20001
				23002					23002

Burkam & Sons,—*Chicago.* 19

1862					1862				
May	1	Disc. 8, W. B. Ogden	5	11940	May	1	Collections	5	7750
June	1	Disc. 28, Geo. M. P.	6	4975	June		Balance		31055
"	"	Disc. 30, W. D. P.	6	3980					
"	"	Disc. 31, W. & McF.	6	2985					
"	"	Disc. 44, J. G. D.	6	14925					
				38805					38805
June	1	Balance		31055					

20 C. & E. R. R. Bonds.

Date						Date					
1862						1862					
May	1	Bot. at auction	5	18000		June	1	Sold H. D. Stratton	6	23500	
June	1	Loss and Gain [L. F.]	21	5500							
				23500						23500	

21 Loss and Gain.

Date						Date					
1862						1862					
May	1	Deficiency on Disc. 24	5	1956		June	1	Colls. and Ex. [L. F.]	6	837	01
June	1	Expense [L. F.]	7	4478	34	"	"	Interest [L. F.]	14	5044	25
		Dividend [L. F.]	27	4000		"	"	C. & E. R. R. Bs. [L. F.]	20	5500	
"	6	Reserved Profits [L. F.]	28	946	92						
				11381	26					11381	21

22 Bank of Capitol,—*Albany.*

Date						Date					
1862											
May	1	Disc. 43, E. W. Keyes	5	8000							

23 Franklin Bank,—*Columbus.*

Date						Date					
1862						1862					
June	1	Collection	6	750		June	1	Collection	6	750	
"	"	Disc. 48, E. R. M.	6	4000		"	"	Balance	6	4000	
				4750						4750	
June	1	Balance		4000							

GENERAL LEDGER.

Toledo Branch Bank. 24

1862											
June	1	Collections	6	6250							

Farmers' Br. Bank,—*Ashtabula.* 25

1852											
June	1	Collections	6	750							

Lorain Bank,—*Elyria.* 26

1862											
June		Collections	6	2400							

Dividend. 27

						1862					
						June	1	Loss and Gain	21	4000	

Reserved Profits. 28

						1862					
						June	1	Loss and Gain	21	946	92

General Ledger.

Debit Balances.			Credit Balances.		
Duncan, Sherman, & Co.	72007	75	Capital Stock	200000	
Bills Discounted	37500		Deposits	223535	11
Domestic Exchange	61550		Collection and Exchange	837	01
Expense	4478	34	Interest	5044	25
Cash	176806	78	Office Notes	35000	
Lafayette Bank	2350		C. & E. R. R. Bonds	5500	
Public Stocks	36400				
Treasury Notes	9800				
Farmers' and Mech's Bank	6912	50			
Exchange Bank, Buffalo	7125				
Fixtures	575				
Burkam & Sons	31055				
Loss and Gain	1956				
Bank of Capital	8000				
Franklin Bank, Collection	4000				
Toledo Branch Bank	6250				
Farmers' Branch Bank	750				
Lorain Bank	2400				
	469916	37		469916	37

Deposit Ledger.

Credit Balances.					
N. C. Winslow	5609	92	*Amount Forward*	123417	52
E. R. Felton	8610	81	John R. Penn	13802	22
Jacob Hoornbeek	3571	81	George A. Crocker	5200	08
M. B. Scott	11599	02	John D. Williams	4040	80
James W. Lusk	9539	63	Henry Ivison	5701	
Lewis R. Morris	12691	70	W. H. Clark	6487	12
John S. Woolson	11169		Austin Packard	1885	50
T. P. Handy	6244	42	Hiram A. Pryor	8515	75
E. L. Jones	6546	75	Joseph P. Walter	3884	
James Richards	6196	82	Wm. T. Brooks	2539	
Alonzo Mitchell	5339	72	George M. Penn	11709	33
Asa Mahan	3727	90	E. G. Folsom	10070	12
Robert Brown	5859	70	H. D. Stratton	7868	50
Ingham & Bragg	5346	80	Certificate	8000	
Charles Hickox	9432	08	J. B. Meriam	9252	67
H. B. Bryant	11931	44	D. P. Eells	1161	50
Forward	123417	52	*Total Net Deposits**	223535	11

* See Deposit %, General Ledger.

DEPOSIT LEDGER.

N. C. Winslow. 1

1862						1862							
Jan.	1	Cash	1	605		Jan.	1	Cash	895		1	1000	
Apr.	1	do.	4	500		Mar.	1	do.	4145		3	3750	
May	1	do.	5	815	58	Apr.	1	do.	4440		4	795	
June	1	do.	6	4260		May	1	do.	5124	52	5	1500	
						June	1	Sunds.	5609	92	6	4745	50

E. R. Felton. 2

1862						1862							
Jan.	1	Cash	1	298	75	Jan.	1	Cash	1451	25	1	1750	
Feb.	1	do.	2	312	50	Feb.	1	Discs.	6172	14	2	5033	39
Apr.	1	do.	4	5950		Mar.	1	Sunds.	11040	64	3	4868	50
May	1	do.	5	9185		Apr.	1	Cash	5615	64	4	525	
June	1	do.	6	455	50	May	1	Sunds.	8337	11	5	11906	67
						June	1	Cash	8610	81	6	729	

Jacob Hoornbeek. 3

1862						1862							
Jan.	1	Cash	1	841	50	Jan.	1	Cash	4158	50	1	5000	
Feb.	1	do.	2	301	75	Feb.	1	do.	8330	56	2	4473	81
Apr.	1	do.	4	750		Mar.	1	Sunds.	11030	56	3	2700	
May	1	do.	5	8896		Apr.	1	do.	12280	56	4	2000	
June	1	do.	6	918	75	May	1	Cash	4084	56	5	700	
						June	1	do.	3571	81	6	406	

M. B. Scott. 4

1862						1862							
Feb.	1	Cash	2	3199	75	Jan.	1	Cash	900		1	900	
Apr.	1	do.	4	3755		Feb.	1	Disc.	4625	59	2	6925	34
May	1	do.	5	8449	83	Mar.	1	Sunds.	15851	92	3	11226	33
June	1	do.	6	6425	32	Apr.	1	do.	22891	92	4	10795	
						May	1	do.	16738	44	5	2296	25
						June	1	do.	11599	02	6	1286	

Jas. W. Lusk. 5

1862						1862							
Jan.	1	Cash	1	626	25	Jan.	1	Cash	1873	75	1	2500	
Feb.	1	do.	2	192	50	Feb.	1	Disc.	4149	58	2	2468	33
Mar.	1	do.	3	3814	50	Mar.	1	Sunds.	7830	08	3	7495	
Apr.	1	do.	4	3875		Apr.	1	Cash	4955	08	4	1000	
May	1	do.	5	539	93	May	1	Sunds.	7915	15	5	3500	
June	1	do.	6	707	25	June	1	do.	9539	63	6	2331	73

DEPOSIT LEDGER.

6 Lewis R. Morris.

1862							1862						
Jan.	1	Cash		1	291	80	Jan.	1	Cash	2708 20	1	3000	
Feb.	1	do.		2	144	25	Feb.	1	do.	4661 70	2	2097	75
Mar.	1	do.		3	270	75	Mar.	1	do.	6640 95	3	2250	
Apr.	1	do.		4	1046	25	Apr.	1	do.	10732 70	4	5138	
May	1	do.		5	8175		May	1	do.	3307 70	5	750	
June	1	do.		6	291	75	June	1	Disc.	12691 70	6	9675	75

7 John S. Woolson.

1862							1862						
Jan.	1	Cash		1	124	50	Jan.	1	Cash	1375 50	1	1500	
Feb.	1	do.		2	886	25	Feb.	1	do.	2989 25	2	2500	
Mar.	1	do.		3	529	75	Mar.	1	do.	4459 50	3	2000	
Apr.	1	do.		4	212	50	Apr.	1	Sunds.	7963 50	4	3716	50
May	1	do.		5	5913	50	May	1	Discs.	12920 50	5	10870	50
June	1	do.		6	2651	50	June	1	Sunds.	11169	6	900	

8 T. P. Handy.

1862							1862						
Jan.	1	Cash		1	2000		Jan.	1	Cash	2700	1	4700	
Feb.	1	do.		2	2114	75	Feb.	1	do.	1760 75	2	1175	50
Mar.	1	do.		3	567	50	Mar.	1	do.	2293 25	3	1100	
Apr.	1	do.		4	2362	50	Apr.	1	do.	780 75	4	850	
May	1	do.		5	11600		May	1	Discs.	3084 42	5	13903	67
June	1	do.		6	6406	75	June	1	Sunds.	6244 42	6	9566	75

9 E. L. Jones.

1862							1862						
							Jan.	1	Cash	975	1	975	
Feb.	1	Cash		2	317	38	Feb.	1	do.	1557 62	2	900	
Mar.	1	do.		3	356	50	Mar.	1	do.	1576 12	3	375	
Apr.	1	do.		4	1050	25	Apr.	1	do.	2025 87	4	1500	
May	1	do.		5	1125		May	1	do.	3900 87	5	3000	
June	1	do.		6	7843		June	1	Sunds.	6546 75	6	10488	88

10 James Richards.

1862							1862						
Jan.	1	Cash		1	288	60	Jan.	1	Cash	1461 40	1	1750	
Feb.	1	do.	887 65	2	573	75	Mar.	1	Sunds.	11033 82	3	10946	17
Mar.	1	do.		3	800		Apr.	1	do.	9722 07	4	3963	25
Apr.	1	do.		4	5275		May	1	Cash	8854 07	5	975	
May	1	do.		5	1843		June	1	do.	6196 82	6	1500	
June	1	do.		6	4157	25							

DEPOSIT LEDGER.

Alonzo Mitchell. 11

1862						1862					
Jan.	1	Cash	1	333	75	Jan.	1	Cash	1	2000	
Feb.	1	do.	2	508	90	Feb.	1	Disc.	2	7951	
Mar.	1	do.	3	574		Mar.	1	Cash	3	3750	
Apr.	1	do.	4	7275		Apr.	1	do.	4	1500	
May	1	do	5	3169	63	May	1	do.	5	500	
						June	1	do.	6	1500	

Asa Mahan. 12

1862						1862					
Feb.	1	Cash	2	844	75	Jan.	1	Cash	1	1200	
Mar.	1	do.	3	580	50	Feb.	1	do.	2	2500	
Apr.	1	do.	4	1225		Mar.	1	do.	3	1400	
May	1	do.	5	1007	50	May	1	do.	5	1500	
June	1	do.	6	510	25	June	1	Sunds.	6	1295	90

Robert Brown. 13

1862						1862					
Jan.	1	Cash	1	202		Jan.	1	Cash	1	1000	
Feb.	1	do.	2	251	20	Mar.	1	do.	3	575	
Apr.	1	do.	4	888	50	Apr.	1	do.	4	1500	
May	1	do.	5	350	48	May	1	do.	5	2000	
June	1	do.	6	5112	50	June	1	Sunds.	6	7589	38

Ingham & Bragg. 14

1862						1862					
Feb.	1	Cash	2	208	90	Jan.	1	Cash		3750	
Mar.	1	do.	3	1788	75	Feb.	1	do.		875	
Apr.	1	do.	4	1103		Mar.	1	do.		975	
May	1	do.	5	1325		Apr.	1	do.		975	
June	1	do.	6	1745	75	May	1	do.		1700	
						June	1	do.		3243	20

Chas. Hickox. 15

1862						1862					
Jan.	1	Cash	1	190		Jan.	1	Cash	1	1325	
Feb.	1	do.	2	539	34	Feb.	1	do.	2	1700	
Mar.	1	do.	3	312	50	Mar.	1	do.	3	2900	
Apr.	1	do.	4	7000		Apr.	1	do.	4	3000	
June	1	do.	6	1557		May	1	Disc.	5	8405	92
						June	1	Cash	6	1700	

DEPOSIT LEDGER.

16 H. B. Bryant.

1862						1862						
Jan.	1	Cash	1	3000		Jan.	1	Disc.	1947 50	1	4947	50
Feb.	1	do.	2	1110	75	Feb.	1	Cash	2036 75	2	1200	
Mar.	1	do.	3	464	95	Mar.	1	do.	5947 09	3	4375	29
Apr.	1	do.	4	1812	50	Apr.	1	do.	4809 59	4	675	
May	1	do.	5	203	90	May	1	Discs.	14981 44	5	10375	75
June	1	do.	6	3350		June	1	Cash	11931 44	6	300	

17 John R. Penn.

1862						1862						
Jan.	1	Cash	1	2500		Jan.	1	Disc.	1458	1	3958	
Feb.	1	do.	2	2852	75	Feb.	1	Cash	1605 25	2	3000	
Mar.	1	do.	3	443	03	Mar.	1	Sunds.	13317 22	3	12155	
Apr.	1	do.	4	10825		Apr	1	Cash	3692 22	4	1200	
May	1	do.	5	386	50	May	1	do.	4505 72	5	1200	
June	1	do.	6	153	50	June	1	Sunds.	13802 22	6	9450	

18 Geo. A. Crocker.

1862						1862						
Apr.	1	Cash 2900	4	500		Feb.	1	Cash	1500	2	1500	
May	1	do.	5	514	25	Mar.	1	do.	3400	3	1900	
June	1	do.	6	8335		May	1	Sunds.	13035 08	5	10649	33
						June	1	Cash	5200 08	6	500	

19 John D. Williams.

1862						1862						
Mar.	1	Cash	3	175		Feb.	1	Cash	1200	2	1200	
Apr.	1	do.	4	1350		Mar.	1	do.	2525	3	1500	
May	1	do.	5	340	25	Apr.	1	do.	1959	4	784	
June	1	do.	6	1296	50	May	1	do.	2968. 75	5	1350	
						June	1	Discs.	4040 80	6	2368	55

20 Henry Ivison.

1862						1862						
Apr.	1	Cash	4	825		Feb.	1	Cash	1700	2	1700	
May	1	do.	5	608	50	Mar.	1	do.	2900	3	1200	
June	1	do.	6	640	50	Apr.	1	do.	3575	4	1500	
						May	1	do.	5541 50	5	2575	
						June	1	do.	5701	6	800	

DEPOSIT LEDGER.

W. H. Clark. 21

1862							1862			1500			
May	1	Cash	1768 50	5	10879		Feb.	1	Col.	3500	2	1500	
June	1	do.		6	222		Mar.	1	do.	12647 50	3	2000	
							Apr.	1	Sunds.	6496 50	4	9147	50
							June	1	do.		6	4940	62

Austin Packard. 22

1862							1862			500			
Apr.	1	Cash		4	525		Mar.	1	Cash	1250	3	500	
May	1	do.		5	516	50	Apr.	1	do.	1491 50	4	1275	
June	1	do.		6	276		May	1	do.	1885 50	5	758	
							June	1	do.		6	670	

Hiram A. Pryor. 23

1862							1862			1250			
May	1	Cash		5	646	50	Mar.	1	Cash	4250	3	1250	
June	1	do.		6	337	75	Apr.	1	do.	5103 50	4	3000	
							May	1	do.	8515 75	5	1500	
							June	1	do.		6	3750	

Joseph P. Walter. 24

1862							1862			900			
May	1	Cash		5	841	50	Mar.	1	Cash	2400	3	900	
June	1	do.		6	534	50	Apr.	1	do.	2458 50	4	1500	
							May	1	do.	3884	5	900	
							June	1	do.		6	1960	

William T. Brooks. 25

1862							1862			8960			
May	1	Cash	1470	5	7990		Mar.	1	Disc.	9460		8960	
June	1	do.		6	206		Apr.	1	Cash	2539		500	
							June	1	do.			1275	

DEPOSIT LEDGER.

26 Geo. M. Penn.

1862							1862						
May	1	Cash		5	1040	75	Apr.	1	Sunds.	[illegible]	4	6410	83
June	1	do.		6	155	75	May	1	Cash	[illegible]	5	1500	
							June	1	Sunds.	[illegible]	6	4995	

27 E. G. Folsom.

1862							1862						
May	1	Cash		5	1393	38	Apr.	1	Sunds	[illegible]	4	3983	50
June	1	do.		6	256		May	1	do.	[illegible]	5	6176	
							June	1	Cash	[illegible]	6	1560	

28 H. D. Stratton.

1862							1862						
May	1	Cash	2785	5	12000		Apr.	1	Disc.	[illegible]	5	14785	
June	1	do.		6	176	50	June	1	Sunds.	[illegible]	6	5260	

29 Certificate.

1862							1862						
May	1	No. 1.		5	3000		Apr.	1	J. R. P.	No. 1.	4	3000	
June	1	No. 2.		6	3000		May	1	L. R. M.	No. 2.	5	3000	
									W. T. B.	No. 3.	"	7000	
									E. G. F.	No. 4.	"	1000	

30 Certified Checks.

1862							1862						
June	1	J. R. P.		6	575		Apr.	1	J. R. P.		4	575	

DEPOSIT LEDGER.

J. B. Meriam. 31

1862							1862						
May	1	Cash		5	3895	50	Apr.	1	Sunds.	8427 67	4	8427	67
June	1	do.	9252 67	6	12269		May	1	do.	[illegible] 67	5	16989	50

D. P. Eells. 32

1862							1862						
June	1	Cash		5	281	75	May	1	Col.	698 25	5	698	25
							June	1	Cash	1161 50	6	745	

When Disc'd.	No.	Drawer or Endorser.	Drawee or Maker.	Where Payable.	Date.	Time.
1862						
Jan. 1	1	H. B. Bryant	Wright G. & Rawson	New York	Jan. 1	60 ds.
	2	W. B. Ogden	Peter Cooper	City	Jan. 1	60 ds.
Feb. 1	3	Alonzo Mitchell	A. J. Comstock	New York	Feb. 1	30 ds.
	4	William Cook	N. Bidwell	New York	Feb. 1	40 ds.
	5	Jas. W. Lusk	J. R. Penn	New York	Jan. 15	90 ds.
	6	D. P. Eells	T. P. Handy	City	Jan. 21	4 mos.
	7	E. R. Felton	Jas. Richards	City	Feb. 1	60 ds.
	8	Jacob Hinds	Chas. Hickox	City	Jan. 3	90 ds.
Mar. 1	9	L. J. Lyman	Clarence Shook	City	Jan. 15	90 ds.
	10	Jas. W. Lusk	Clafflin, M. & Co.	New York	Mar. 1	10 ds.
	11	Jas. W. Lusk	M. B. Scott	City	Feb. 1	60 ds.
	12	N. C. Winslow	H. B. Tuttle	Buffalo	Mar. 1	30 ds.
	13	James Eells	Ivison, Ph. & Co.	New York	Mar. 1	30 ds.
	14	E. R. Felton	W. H. Clark	Cincinnati	Feb. 1	60 ds.
	15	T. P. Handy	Parker Handy	New York	Feb. 15	60 ds.
	16	Chas. Hickox	Jas. Armstrong	Buffalo	Mar. 1	30 ds.
	17	T. Dwight Eells	Winslow, L. & Co.	New York	Mar. 1	30 ds.
	18	H. B. Bryant	W. B. Ogden	Chicago	Feb. 1	90 ds.
	19	H. D. Stratton	D. Appleton	New York	Mar. 1	60 ds.
Apr. 1	20	James Eaton	Sumner Packard	City	Apr. 1	60 ds.
	21	L. R. Morris	W. H. Clark	City	Apr. 1	60 ds.
	22	Wilson G. Hunt	Peter Cooper	City	Mar. 25	90 ds.
	23	T. P. Handy	N. C. Winslow	City	Mar. 1	90 ds.
	24	John Simmons	Chas. Baker	City	Mar. 3	60 ds.
	25	E. G. Folsom	H. Bishop	City	Apr. 1	30 ds.
	26	Jacob Hinds	M. B. Scott	Buffalo	Apr. 1	60 ds.
	27	John Gundry	R. M. Bartlett	Cincinnati	Mar. 10	90 ds.
	28	H. D. Stratton	Geo. M. Penn	Chicago	Mar. 31	60 ds.
	29	Zalmon Richards	Austin Packard	New York	Apr. 1	60 ds.
	30	W. B. Ogden	W. D. Packard	Chicago	Apr. 1	90 ds.
	31	J. S. Woolson	Woolson & McF.	Mt. Pleasant	Mar. 25	90 ds.

When Due.	*Days to Run.*	*Bills Discd.*		*Dom. Ex.*		*Interest.*		*Col. & Ex.*		*Proceeds.*		*To Whom Credited.*	*Ck.*
1862													
Mar. 5	'63			5000		52	50			4947	50	H. B. Bryant	✓
Mar. 5	63	4000				42				3958		John R. Penn	✓
		✓4000		✓5000		✓94	50			8905	50		
Mar. 6	33			5000		27	50			4972	50	A. Mitchell .	✓
Mar. 16	43			3000		21	50			2978	50	A. Mitchell .	✓
Apr. 18	76			2500		31	67			2468	33	J. W. Lusk .	✓
May 24	112	1600				29	86			1570	14	E. R. Felton .	✓
Apr. 5	63	3500				36	75			3463	25	E. R. Felton .	✓
Apr. 6	64	7000				74	66			6925	34	M. B. Scott .	✓
		✓12100		✓10500		✓221	94			22378	06		
Apr. 18	48	5000				40				4960		W. T. Brooks	✓
Mar. 14	13			4000						4000		W. T. Brooks	✓
Apr. 5	35	6000				35				5965		J. W. Lusk .	✓
Apr. 3	33			2500		13	75			2486	25	Cash . . .	✓
Apr. 3	33			6000		33				5967		Jas. Richards	✓
Apr. 5	35			2500		14	58	6	25	2479	17	Jas. Richards	✓
Apr. 19	49			7000		57	17			6942	83	M. B. Scott .	✓
Apr. 3	33			3000		16	50			2983	50	M. B. Scott .	✓
Apr. 3	33			2500		13	75			2486	25	Cash . . .	✓
May 5	65			12000		130		90		11780		John R. Penn	✓
May 3	63			3000		31	50			2968	50	E. R. Felton .	✓
		✓11000		✓42500		✓385	25	✓96	25	53018	50		
June 3	63	4000				42				3958		Cash . . .	✓
June 3	63	5000				52	50			4947	50	W. H. Clark .	✓
June 26	86	15000				215				14785		H. D. Stratton	✓
June 2	62	7000				72	33			6927	67	J. B. Meriam .	✓
May 5	34	20000				113	33			19886	67	Cash . . .	✓
May 4	33	3000				16	50			2983	50	E. G. Folsom	✓
June 3	63			10000		105				9895		M. B. Scott .	✓
June 11	71			3000		35	50	7	50	2957		Cash . . .	✓
June 2	62			5000		51	67	37	50	4910	83	Geo. M. Penn	✓
June 3	63			3500		36	75			3463	25	Jas. Richards	✓
July 3	93			4000		62		30		3908		Cash . . .	✓
June 26	86			3000		43		22	50	2934	50	J. S. Woolson	✓
		✓54000		✓28500		✓845	58	✓97	50	81556	92		

When Disctd.	No.	Drawer or Endorser.	Drawee or Maker.	Where Payable.	Date.	Time.
1862						
May 1	32	Jas. Cruikshank .	E. G. Folsom . .	City. . . .	May 1	90 ds.
	33	Nicolas Nickleby .	Barnaby Rudge .	New York .	Apr. 15	60 ds.
	34	Jno. S. Woolson .	Smith & Nixon .	Cincinnati. .	Apr. 30	60 ds.
	35	Robert Peel. . .	James Bradley. .	City. . . .	Apr. 1	90 ds.
	36	H. D. Clark. . .	H. D. Stratton . .	Columbus . .	May 1	60 ds.
	37	Peter Cooper . .	J. R. Penn . . .	New York .	Apr. 25	2 mos.
	38	J. G. Fox . . .	W. H. Clark . .	City. . . .	Apr. 1	60 ds.
	39	Chas. Jones. . .	A. Stager . . .	Buffalo. . .	Apr. 1	3 mos.
	40	W. P. Spencer. .	S. S. Packard . .	City. . . .	Apr. 20	60 ds.
	41	J. Kennedy. . .	Chas. Hickox . .	City. . . .	Apr. 25	90 ds.
	42	Chas. Hickox . .	Jonathan Gillett .	New York .	Apr. 30	60 ds.
	43	Victor M. Rice. .	E. W. Keyes . .	Albany. . .	Apr. 28	30 ds.
	44	Hiram Niles . .	J. G. Deshler . .	Chicago . .	Apr. 15	60 ds.
	45	James Hamilton .	R. C. Spencer . .	Detroit. . .	Apr. 10	60 ds.
	46	Robert Davis . .	Wm. Smith . . .	Troy . . .	Apr. 1	90 ds.
	47	T. P. Handy . .	H. B. Tuttle . .	City. . . .	May 1	30 ds.
	48	William Butts . .	E. R. Morgan . .	Columbus . .	Apr. 15	60 ds.
	49	John Rogers . .	Jas. Smiley . . .	City. . . .	Apr. 30	30 ds.
June 1	50	Jas. Mallory	Geo. M. Strong .	City. . . .	June 1	60 ds.
	51	T. P. Handy . .	Edward Savage .	City. . . .	May 31	90 ds.
	52	Jas. Smiley. . .	Philip Seaton . .	Buffalo. . .	May 3	60 ds.
	53	E. G. Folsom . .	Peter Stone. . .	City. . . .	May 27	60 ds.
	54	Hiram Dixon . .	Thomas Jones . .	New York .	May 31	3 mos.
	55	Chas. Eaton. . .	Jacob Harrison .	City. . . .	June 1	60 ds.
	56	Joseph Arnold. .	W. H. Woodbury.	Dayton . .	May 15	3 mos.
	57	Childs & Peterson.	W. T. Sherman .	Philadelphia .	Mar. 15	6 mos.
	58	H. B. Bryant . .	E. R. Finney . .	Pittsburg . .	May 10	60 ds.
	59	Peter McGrath. .	Samuel Rand . .	City. . . .	Jan. 15	8 mos.
	60	Robert Martin . .	John Pelton . .	Galena, Ill. .	May 12	4 mos.
	61	Thos. Foulke . .	Horace Holden .	City. . . .	May 15	60 ds.
	62	Henry C. Spencer.	William Gray . .	New York .	May 25	3 mos.
	63	C. R. Wells. . .	E. W Mason . .	P'keepsie, N.Y.	Apr. 10	4 mos.

When Due.	Days to Run.	Bills Disctd.	Dom. Ex.	Interest.		Col. & Ex.		Proceeds.		To Whom Credited.	Ck.
1862											
Aug. 2	93	4000		62				3938		E. G. Folsom	√
June 17	47		10000	78	33			9921	67	E. R. Felton .	√
July 2	62		6000	62		15		5923		J. S. Woolson	√
July 3	63	5000		52	50			4947	50	J. S. Woolson	√
July 3	63		7500	78	75	18	75	7402	50	J. B. Meriam .	√
June 28	58		6000	58				5942		J. B. Meriam .	√
June 3	33	10000		55				9945		Cash . . .	√
July 4	64		7000	74	67			6925	33	G. A. Crocker	√
June 22	52	3000		26				2974		G. A. Crocker	√
July 27	87	1500		21	75			1478	25	Chas. Hickox	√
July 2	62		7000	72	33			6927	67	Chas. Hickox	√
May 31	30		8000	40				7960		Cash . . .	√
June 17	47		15000	117	50	112	50	14770		Cash . . .	√
June 12	42		3500	24	50	26	25	3449	25	H. B. Bryant	√
July 3	63		7000	73	50			6926	50	H. B. Bryant	√
June 3	33	10000		55				9945		T. P. Handy .	√
June 17	47		4000	31	33	10		3958	67	T. P. Handy .	√
June 2	32	8000		42	67			7957	33	Cash . . .	√
		√41500	√81000	√1025	83	√182	50	121291	67		
Aug. 3	63	3000		31	50			2968	50	N. C. Winslow	√
Sept. 1	92	1500		23				1477		N. C. Winslow	√
July 5	34		5000	28	33			4971	67	L. R. Morris .	√
July 29	58	4750		45	92			4704	08	L. R. Morris .	√
Sept. 3	94		7500	117	50			7382	50	T. P. Handy .	√
Aug. 3	63	1500		15	75			1484	25	T. P. Handy .	√
Aug. 18	78		6000	78		15		5907		E. L. Jones .	√
Sept. 18	109		3750	68	12			3681	88	E. L. Jones .	√
July 12	41		600	4	10			595	90	Asa Mahan .	√
Sept. 18	109	6750		122	62			6627	38	Robt. Brown .	√
Sept. 15	106		1800	31	80	13	50	1754	70	Ingham & B. .	√
July 17	46	1500		11	50			1488	50	Ingham & B. .	√
Aug. 28	88		900	13	20			886	80	J. D. Williams	√
Aug. 13	73		1500	18	25			1481	75	J. D. Williams	√
		√19000	√27050	√609	59	√28	50	45411	91		

When Left	No.	Drawer or Endorser.	Drawee or Maker.	Where Payable.
1862				
February	1	Ivison, Phinney & Co. .	Ingham & Bragg . . .	City Bank . . . . .
	2	Peter Cooper	D. P. Eells	Com. Br. Bank . . .
	3	W. H. Crocker	James Shaw	City Bank . . . . .
	4	Wm. H. Beebe	T. Dwight Eells	Bank of Cleveland . .
	5	W. H. Clark	T. P. Handy	Our Bank . . .
	6	W. H. Clark	James Smith	Merchants' Bank . .
	7	Lewis R. Morris	R. M. Bartlett	Cincinnati . . . . .
	8	Lewis R. Morris . . .	Jas. W. Lusk . . .	Our Bank . . . .
	9	Jacob Hoornbeek . . .	Jas. McAllister	Our Bank . . . . .
	10	Jacob Hoornbeek . . .	Peter Aiken	Sandusky . . . .
March	11	D. Appleton & Co. . . .	Bryant & Stratton . . .	B. & S.'s Office . . .
	12	Smith & McDougal . .	J. B. Cobb	J. B. C.'s Office . .
	13	Parker Handy	Com. Br. Bank	Com. Br. Bk. . . .
	14	A. Wellslager	Jas. Stanton	Our Bank . . . .
	15	D. P. Eells	Handy, Gillett & Co. . .	New York . . .
	16	M. B. Scott	R. M. Bartlett . . .	Cincinnati . . .
	17	D. C. Collins	John Gundry	Com. Br. Bank .
	18	Murray Shipley	James Parker	J. P.'s Office .
	19	Jas. Richards	E. R. Felton	Our Bank . . . . .
	20	H. B. Bryant	Jas. W. Lusk	Our Bank . . . .
	21	P. R. Spencer, Jr. . . .	H. C. Spencer	City Bank . . . .
April	22	Clafflin, Mellen & Co. . .	E. W. Mason	Our Bank . . . . .
	23	A. T. Stewart & Co. . .	E. R. Felton	Our Bank . . . . .
	24	Bryant & Stratton . . .	J. B. Meriam	City Bank . . . . .
	25	D. C. Collins	E. G. Folsom	E. G. F.'s Office . . .
	26	C. Dunham	M. B. Scott	Merchants' Bk. . . .
	27	E. Hill	Ingham & Bragg . . .	Our Bank . . . . .
	28	Wm. Mason	Jacob Hoornbeek . .	Our Bank . . . . .
	29	E. G. Folsom	A. S. Wheeler	Our Bank . . . . .
	30	J. R. Wheeler	J. B. Cobb	J. B. C.'s Office . . .
	31	Robert Barker	H. Stillman	City Bank . . . . .
	32	E. R. Felton	J. H. Goldsmith . . .	Detroit . . . . . .
	33	M. B. Scott	Jas. Madison	Dayton . . . . . .
	34	D. P. Eells	Jas. Smith	Sandusky . .

Date.	Time.	When Due.	Amount.	For Whom Collected.	To Whom Sent.	Ck.
Feb. 1	30 ds.	Mar. 6	1500	Duncan, Sh. & Co. .	. . . .	√
Feb. 1	60 ds.	Apr. 5	2000	do. .	. . . .	√
Jan. 1	90 ds.	Apr. 4	2500	do. .	. . . .	√
Feb. 1	10 ds.	Feb. 14	3000	do. .	. . . .	√
Jan. 15	30 ds.	Feb. 17	1500	W. H. Clark . . .	. . . .	√
Feb. 1	30 ds.	Mar. 6	2000	do. . . .	. . . .	√
Feb. 3	10 ds.	Feb. 16	900	Lewis R. Morris . .	Lafayette Bk. . .	√
Feb. 1	30 ds.	Mar. 6	500	do. . .	. . . .	√
Jan. 1	60 ds.	Mar. 5	1200	Jacob Hoornbeek .	. . . .	√
Feb. 2	20 ds.	Feb. 25	475	do.	Moss Bros. . . .	√
Feb. 15	30 ds.	Mar. 20	2500	Duncan, Sh. & Co. .	. . . .	√
Feb. 1	60 ds.	Apr. 5	3000	do. .	. . . .	√
Mar. 1	10 ds.	Mar. 14	6000	do. .	. . . .	√
Feb. 15	60 ds.	Apr. 19	3000	W. H. Clark . . .	. . . .	√
Mar. 1	30 ds.	Apr. 3	1500	J. B. Meriam . . .	Duncan, Sh. & Co.	√
Mar. 1	60 ds.	May 3	2000	do. . . .	Lafayette Bk. . .	√
Jan. 1	90 ds.	Apr. 4	6000	Lafayette Bk., Cin. .	. . . .	√
Mar. 1	30 ds.	Apr. 3	3000	do. .	. . . .	√
Dec. 1	4 mos.	Apr. 4	3000	Lewis R. Morris . .	. . . .	√
Feb. 1	60 ds.	Apr. 5	1575	do. . .	. . . .	√
Jan. 15	3 mos.	Apr. 18	1250	Jacob Hoornbeek .	. . . .	√
Jan. 1	5 mos.	June 4	5000	Duncan, Sh. & Co. .	. . . .	√
Mar. 10	60 ds.	May 12	3500	do. .	. . . .	√
Mar. 5	60 ds.	May 7	7000	do. .	. . . .	√
Apr. 1	30 ds.	May 4	1750	Lafayette Bk., Cin. .	. . . .	√
Feb. 10	3 mos.	May 13	4000	Burkam & Sons, Chic.	. . . .	√
Mar. 10	60 ds.	May 12	3750	do.	. . . .	√
Feb. 12	90 ds.	May 16	900	William Mason . .	. . . .	√
Mar. 15	2 mos.	May 18	1500	E. G. Folsom . . .	. . . .	√
Apr. 1	30 ds.	May 4	1000	Exch. Bk., Buf. . .	. . . .	√
Feb. 17	4 mos.	June 20	750	Franklin Bk., Col. .	. . . .	√
Mar. 20	60 ds.	May 22	2000	E. R. Felton . . .	Farmers' & M. Bk.	√
Feb. 20	90 ds.	May 24	1500	M. B. Scott . . .	Lafayette Bk. . .	√
Mar. 15	60 ds.	May 17	750	D. P. Eells. . . .	Moss Bros. . . .	√

When Left.	No.	Drawer or Endorser.	Drawee or Maker.	Where Payable.
1862				
May	35	Robert Sweetzer . . .	Solomon Jones	Adrian, Mich. . . .
	36	P. R. Spencer	H. D. Stratton	Our Bank . . . . .
	37	John W. Gantz	Thos. Smith	Ashtabula . . . . .
	38	W. H. Crocker	J. Rhoades	Oberlin . . . . . .
	39	Henry C. Spencer . . .	Wm. H. Beebe	Xenia . . . . . .
	40	Robert Dean	Ezra Jones	Our Bank . . . . .
	41	Jacob Hinds	Peter Cook	Merchants' Bank . .
	42	Emerson E. White . . .	E. G. Folsom	City Bank . . . . .
	43	John D. Hinde	Abram Van Wyck . . .	New York . . . . .
	44	H. D. Stratton	E. W. Mason	Our Bank . . . . .
	45	Geo. A. Crocker . . .	Chas. Jones	Buffalo, N. Y. . . .
	46	Geo. M. Penn . .	Walkden & Co.	Toledo . . . . . .
	47	Robert Lincoln . .	James Garrett	Our Bank . . . . .
	48	D. W. Fish . . .	John Holbrook	City Bank . . . . .
	49	T. S. Quackenbush . .	C. B. Stout	Cincinnati . . . . .
June	50	Jacob Reifsnyder . . .	J. C. Bryant	Amherst . . . . .
	51	Joseph Kinsey	J. D. Hinde	Our Bank . . . . .
	52	E. M. Hale	Thos. Irwin	Our Bank . . . . .
	53	Joseph Russell	Daniel Slote	Columbus . . . . .
	54	Smith & McDougal. . .	Ivison, Phinney & Co. .	Merchants' Bank . .
	55	Bryant, Stratton & Co. .	J. B. Meriam	Our Bank . . . .
	56	J. W. Lusk	A. C. Taylor	Bucyrus . . . .
	57	C. L. Skeels	S. S. Pomroy	Lockport, N. Y. . . .
	58	Wm. T. Bush	Hiram Newell	Buffalo, N. Y. . . .
	59	John Cook	James Moses	E. B. Hale's Bank . .
	60	Roderick Dhu	Benj. Carpenter	City Bank . . .
	61	James Romney	J. G. Fox	Toledo . . . . .
	62	Thos. Minturn	Robert Smith	Buffalo, N. Y. .
	63	James Sweeney	John Simson	Buffalo, N. Y. . .
	64	A. S. Wheeler	E. R. Felton	Our Bank . .
	65	Chas. Stratton	Jacob Hoornbeek . . .	Sandusky . . .
	66	Robert Minturn	Chas. Reynolds	Our Bank .
	67	Henry P. Smith	M. B. Scott	City Bank
	68	Abram Vinton	Henry Stratton	Our Bank . .

Date.	Time.	When Due.	Amount.	For Whom Collected.	To Whom Sent.	Ck.
Mar. 25	3 mos.	June 28	3000	W. H. Clark . . .	Toledo Br. Bk. . .	✓
Apr. 30	30 ds.	June 2	1500	P. R. Spencer (special)	. . . .	✓
Mar. 20	3 mos.	June 23	750	Duncan, Sh. & Co. .	Farmers' Br. Bk. .	✓
Apr. 10	60 ds.	June 12	900	Duncan, Sh. & Co. .	Lorain Bk., Elyria	✓
Mar. 15	3 mos.	June 18	1200	Duncan, Sh. & Co. .	Lafayette Bk., Cin.	✓
May 1	30 ds.	June 3	1000	Mer. Bk., Mass (spec.)	. . . .	✓
Apr. 15	30 ds.	May 18	750	J. B. Meriam . . .	. . . .	✓
Apr. 30	10 ds.	May 13	900	J. B. Meriam . . .	. . . .	✓
Apr. 25	60 ds.	June 27	1750	John R. Penn . . .	Duncan, Sh. & Co.	✓
May 1	30 ds.	June 3	7000	John R. Penn . . .	. . . .	✓
Apr. 15	30 ds.	May 18	750	Geo. A. Crocker . .	Exch. Bk., Buf. .	✓
May 1	30 ds.	June 3	2000	Geo. M. Penn . . .	Toledo Br. Bk. . .	✓
Apr. 15	60 ds.	June 17	1500	Geo. M. Penn . . .	. . . .	✓
Feb. 15	90 ds.	May 19	2000	Jas. W. Lusk . . .	. . . .	✓
Apr. 30	30 ds.	June 2	500	Jas. W. Lusk . . .	Lafayette Bk., Cin.	✓
May 15	30 ds.	June 17	1500	H. D. Stratton . . .	Lorain Bk., Elyria	✓
May 30	10 ds.	June 12	3000	Kinney E. & Co. (sp.)	. . . .	✓
Apr. 15	60 ds.	June 17	3500	Penny & Co., N'k (sp.)	. . . .	✓
May 10	30 ds.	June 12	750	Duncan, Sh. & Co. .	Franklin Bk. Col. .	✓
May 15	60 ds.	July 17	500	Duncan, Sh. & Co. .	. . . .	✓
June 1	30 ds.	July 4	1750	Duncan, Sh. & Co. .	. . . .	✓
May 20	30 ds.	June 22	500	Duncan, Sh. & Co. .	Toledo Br. Bk. . .	✓
May 20	60 ds.	July 22	2500	M. B. Scott . . .	Exch. Bk., Buf. .	✓
May 12	30 ds.	June 14	350	M. B. Scott . . .	Exch. Bk. Buf. . .	✓
May 10	30 ds.	June 12	600	Bk. of Marysville (sp.)	. . . .	✓
May 12	60 ds.	July 14	1700	James Richards . .	. . . .	✓
May 25	30 ds.	June 27	750	W. H. Clark . . .	Toledo Br. Bk. . .	✓
Apr. 25	90 ds.	July 27	1200	John S. Woolson . .	Exch. Bk., Buf. .	✓
May 25	30 ds.	June 27	500	John S. Woolson . .	Exch. Bk., Buf. .	✓
May 18	60 ds.	July 20	750	Jacob Hoornbeek .	. . . .	✓
May 10	60 ds.	July 12	600	Lafayette Bk., Cin. .	Moss Bros., Sand'y	✓
May 25	20 ds.	June 17	700	Exch. Bank, Buf. .	. . . .	✓
Apr. 25	60 ds.	June 27	3500	Exch. Bank, Buf. . .	. . . .	✓
Apr. 10	60 ds.	June 12	600	Geo. M. Penn . . .	. . . .	✓

DISCOUNTS——February, 1862.

No.	Payer.	Amount.		Remarks.

March.

No.	Payer.	Amount.		Remarks.
2	Peter Cooper	4000		Paid and Entered

April.

No.	Payer.	Amount.		Remarks.
7	James Richards	3500		Pd. and Ent.
8	Chas. Hickox	7000		Pd. and Ent.
9	Clarence Shook	5000		Pd. and Ent.
11	M. B. Scott	6000		Pd. and Ent.

May.

No.	Payer.	Amount.		Remarks.
6	T. P. Handy.	1600		Pd. and Ent.
24	Chas. Baker	20000		Protested
25	H. Bishop	3000		Pd. and Ent.

COLLECTIONS——February, 1862.

No.	Payer.	Amount.		For whom Collected.	Remarks.
4	T. Dwight Eells	3000		Duncan, Sh. & Co. . . .	Passed
5	T. P. Handy	1500		W. H. Clark	Passed

March.

No.	Payer.	Amount.		For whom Collected.	Remarks.
1	Ingham & Bragg . . .	1500		Duncan, Sh. & Co. . . .	Passed
6	James Smith	2000		W. H. Clark	Passed
8	J. W. Lusk	500		Lewis R. Morris . . .	Passed
9	Jas. McAllister	1200		Jacob Hoornbeek . . .	Passed
11	Bryant & Stratton . . .	2500		Duncan, Sh. & Co. . . .	Passed
13	Com. Branch Bank . . .	6000		Duncan, Sh. & Co. . . .	Passed

April.

No.	Payer.	Amount.		For whom Collected.	Remarks.
2	D. P. Eells	2000		Duncan, Sh. & Co. . . .	Passed
3	James Shaw	2500		Duncan, Sh. & Co. . . .	Passed
12	J. B. Cobb	3000		Duncan, Sh. & Co. . . .	Passed
14	Jas. Stanton	3000		W. H. Clark	Passed
17	J. Gundry	6000		Lafayette Bk., Cin. . .	Passed
18	James Parker	3000		Lafayette Bk., Cin. . .	Passed
19	E. R. Felton	3000		Lewis R. Morris . . .	Passed
20	Jas. W. Lusk	1575		Lewis R. Morris . . .	Passed
21	H. C. Spencer	1250		Jacob Hoornbeek . . .	Passed

May.

No.	Payer.	Amount.		For whom Collected.	Remarks.
23	E. R. Felton . . .	3500		Duncan, Sh. & Co. . . .	Passed
24	J. B. Meriam	7000		Duncan, Sh. & Co. . . .	Passed
25	E. G. Folsom	1750		Lafayette Bk., Cin. . .	Passed
26	M. B. Scott	4000		Burkam & Sons, Chic. .	Passed
27	Ingham & Bragg . . .	3750		Burkam & Sons, Chic. .	Passed
28	Jacob Hoornbeek . . .	900		William Mason (special) .	Remitted
29	A. S. Wheeler	1500		E. G. Folsom.	Passed
30	J. B. Cobb	1000		Exchange Bank, Buf. .	Passed
41	Peter Cook	750		J. B. Meriam	Passed
42	Emerson E. White . . .	900		J. B. Meriam.	Passed
48	John Holbrook	2000		Jas. W. Lusk.	Passed

DISCOUNTS.——June, 1862.

No.	*Payer.*	*Amount.*	*Remarks.*
20	Sumner Packard	4000	Paid and Entered
21	W. H. Clark	5000	Pd. and Ent.
22	Peter Cooper	15000	Pd. and Ent.
23	N. C. Winslow	7000	Pd. and Ent.
38	W. H. Clark. . . . (Ex.)	10000	Pd. and Ent.
40	S. S. Packard	3000	Pd. and Ent.
47	H. B. Tuttle	10000	Pd. and Ent.
49	James Smiley, ...	8000	Extended to July 2, with interest.

July.

No.	Payer	Amount	Remarks
35	James Bradley	5000	
41	Chas. Hickox	1500	
49	James Smiley	8000	
53	Peter Stone	4750	
60	Horace Holden	1500	

August.

No.	Payer	Amount	Remarks
32	E. G. Folsom . . . (Ex.)	4000	
50	Geo. M. Strong	3000	
55	Jacob Harrison	1500	

September.

No.	Payer	Amount	Remarks
51	Edward Savage	1500	
59	Samuel Rand	6750	

COLLECTIONS.——June, 1862.

No.	Payer.	Amount.	For Whom Collected.	Remarks.
22	E. W. Mason.	5000	Duncan, Sh. & Co. . . .	Passed
31	H. Stillman	750	Franklin Bk., Columbus .	Passed
36	H. D. Stratton	1500	P. R. Spencer (special) .	Remitted
40	Ezra Jones	1000	Mer. Bk., Mass. (special) .	Remitted
44	E. W. Mason	7000	John R. Penn	Passed
47	James Garrett	1500	Geo. M. Penn	Passed
51	J. D. Hinde	3000	K., E. & Co., Cin, (special)	Remitted
52	Thos. Irwin	3500	P. & Co., Newark (special)	Remitted
59	Jas. Mason	600	Bk. of Marysville (special)	Remitted
66	Chas. Reynolds . .	700	Exch. Bk., Buf.	Passed
67	M. B. Scott . . .	3500	Exch. Bk., Buf.	Passed
68	Henry Stratton . . .	600	Geo. M. Penn	Passed

July.

No.	Payer.	Amount.	For Whom Collected.	Remarks.
54	Ivison, Ph. & Co. . . .	500	Duncan, Sh. & Co. . . .	
55	J. B. Meriam	1750	Duncan, Sh. & Co. . .	
60	Benj. Carpenter	1700	Jas. Richards . .	
64	E. R. Felton	750	Jacob Hoornbeek . . .	

August.

September.

DISCOUNTS.——February, 1862.

No.	Payer	Amount.	To Whom Sent.	Remarks.

March.

No.	Payer	Amount.	To Whom Sent.	Remarks.
1	Wright G. & Rawson .	√5000	√Duncan, Sh. & Co., N. Y. . .	Paid & Entered
3	A. J. Comstock . . .	√5000	√Duncan, Sh. & Co., N. Y. . .	Paid & Ent.
4	N. Bidwell	√3000	√Duncan, Sh. & Co., N. Y. . .	Paid & Ent.
10	Claflin, Mellen & Co. .	√4000	√Duncan, Sh. & Co., N. Y. . .	Paid & Ent.

April.

No.	Payer	Amount.	To Whom Sent.	Remarks.
5	John R. Penn . . .	√2500	√Duncan, Sh. & Co., N. Y. . .	Paid & Ent.
12	H. B. Tuttle . . .	√2500	√Exch. Bank, Buffalo. . . .	Paid & Ent.
13	Ivison, Phinney & Co.	√6000	√Duncan, Sh. & Co., N. Y. . .	Paid & Ent.
14	W. H. Clark	√2500	√Lafayette Bank, Cin. . . .	Paid & Ent.
15	Parker Handy . . .	√7000	√Duncan, Sh. & Co., N. Y. . .	Paid & Ent.
16	James Armstrong . .	√3000	√Exch. Bank, Buffalo	Protested.
17	Winslow, Lanier & Co. .	√2500	√Duncan, Sh. & Co., N. Y. . .	Paid & Ent.

May.

No.	Payer	Amount.	To Whom Sent.	Remarks.
18	W. B. Ogden	√12000	√Burkam & Sons, Chicago . .	Paid & Ent.
19	D. Appleton & Co. . .	√ 3000	√Duncan, Sh. & Co., N. Y. . .	Paid & Ent.
43	E. W. Keyes	√ 8000	√Bank of Capitol, Albany . .	Paid & Ent.

COLLECTIONS.——February, 1862.

No.	Payer.	Amount.		For Whom Collected.	To Whom Sent.	Remarks.
7	R. M. Bartlett . .	900		Lewis R. Morris .	Lafayette Bk., Cin.	Passed
10	Peter Aiken . .	475		Jacob Hoornbeek .	Moss Bros., Sand. .	Passed

March.

April.

15	Handy Gillett & Co.	1500		J. B. Meriam . .	Duncan, Sh. & Co.	*Passed

May.

16	R. M. Bartlett . .	2000		J. B. Meriam . .	Lafayette Bk., Cin.	Passed
32	J. H. Goldsmith .	2000		E. R. Felton . .	Far. & M. Bk., Det.	Passed
33	Jas. Madison . .	1500		M. B. Scott . . .	Lafayette Bk., Cin.	Passed
34	Jas. Smith . . .	700		D. P. Eells . . .	Moss Bros., Sand. .	Passed
45	Chas. Jones . . .	750		Geo. A. Crocker .	Exch. Bk., Buf. .	Passed

DISCOUNTS.—June, 1862.

No.	Payer.	Amou	To Whom Sent.	Remarks.
26	M. B. Scott	√10000	√ Exchange Bk., Buffalo . . .	Paid & Entered
27	R. M. Bartlett . . .	√ 3000	√ Lafayette Bk., Cincinnati . .	Paid & Ent.
28	Geo. M. Penn . . .	√ 5000	√ Burkam & Sons, Chicago . .	Paid & Ent.
29	Austin Packard . . .	√ 3500	√ Duncan, Sh. & Co., N. Y. . .	Paid & Ent.
31	Woolson & McFarland .	√ 3000	√ Burkam & Sons, Chicago . .	Paid & Ent.
33	Barnaby Rudge . . .	√10000	√ Duncan, Sh. & Co., N. Y. . .	Paid & Ent.
37	John R. Penn . . .	√ 6000	√ Duncan, Sh. & Co., N. Y. . .	Paid & Ent.
44	J. G. Deshler	√15000	√ Burkam & Sons, Chicago . .	Paid & Ent.
45	R. C. Spencer. . . .	√ 3500	√ Farmers & Mechs.' Bk., Det. .	Paid & Ent.
48	E. R. Morgan	√ 4000	√ Franklin Bk., Columbus . .	Paid & Ent.

July.

No.	Payer.	Amou	To Whom Sent.	Remarks.
30	W. D. Packard . . .	√4000	√Burkam & Sons, Chicago . .	Pd. & Ent. June
34	Smith & Nixon . . .	6000	Lafayette Bk., Cincinnati . .	
36	H. D. Stratton . . .	7500	Franklin Bk., Columbus . .	
39	A. Stager	7000	Exchange Bk., Buffalo . . .	
42	Jonathan Gillett . . .	7000	Duncan, Sh. & Co., N. Y. . .	
46	William Smith . . .	7000	Bank of Capitol, Albany . .	
52	Phillip Seaton . . .	5000	Exchange Bk., Buffalo . . .	
58	E. R. Finney	600	Iron City Bk., Pittsburg . .	

August.

No.	Payer.	Amou	To Whom Sent.	Remarks.
56	W. H. Woodbury . .	6000	Lafayette Bank, Cincinnati . .	
62	William Gray	900	Duncan, Sh. & Co., N. Y. . .	
63	E. W. Mason	1500	Duncan, Sh. & Co., N. Y. . .	

September.

No.	Payer.	Amou	To Whom Sent.	Remarks.
54	Thomas Jones . .	7500	Duncan, Sh. & Co., N. Y. . .	
57	W. T. Sherman . . .	3750	Girard Bk., Philadelphia . .	
60	John Pelton . . .	1800	Burkam & Sons, Chicago .	

COLLECTIONS.——June, 1862.

No.	Payer.	Amount.		For Whom Collected.	To Whom Sent.	Remarks.
35	Solomon Jones . .	3000		W. H. Clark . .	Tol. Br. Bk., Toledo	Passed
37	Thos. Smith . . .	750		Duncan, Sh. & Co.	Farm. Br. Bk., Ash.	Passed
38	J. Rhoades . . .	900		Duncan, Sh. & Co.	Lorain Bk., Elyria	Passed
39	Wm. H. Beebe . .	1200		Duncan, Sh. & Co.	Laf. Bk., Cincinnati	Passed
43	Abram Van Wyck	1750		J. R. Penn . . .	Dunc., S. & Co. N.Y.	Passed
46	Walkden & Co. .	2000		Geo. M. Penn . .	Tol. Br. Bk., Toledo	Passed
49	C. B. Stout . . .	500		Jas. W. Lusk . .	Laf. Bk., Cincinnati	Passed
50	J. C. Bryant . .	1500		H. D. Stratton . .	Lorain Bank, Elyria	Passed
53	Daniel Slote . .	750		Duncan, Sh. & Co.	Franklin Bk., Col.	Passed
56	A. C. Taylor . .	500		Duncan, Sh. & Co.	Toledo Br. Bank	Passed
58	Hiram Newell . .	350		M. B. Scott . . .	Exch. Bk., Buffalo	Passed
61	J. G. Fox . . .	750		W. H. Clark . .	Toledo Br. Bank	Passed
63	James Sweeney .	500		John S. Woolson .	Exch. Bk., Buffalo	Passed

July.

No.	Payer.	Amount.		For Whom Collected.	To Whom Sent.	Remarks.
57	S. S. Pomroy . .	2500		M. B. Scott . . .	Exch. Bk., Buf. .	
62	Robert Smith . .	1200		John S. Woolson .	Exch. Bk., Buf. .	
65	Jacob Hoornbeek .	600		Laf. Bk., Cincinnati	Moss Bros., Sand'y	

August.

No.	Payer.	Amount.		For Whom Collected.	To Whom Sent.	Remarks.

September.

No.	Payer.	Amount.		For Whom Collected.	To Whom Sent.	Remarks.

PASSED COLLECTIONS.

When Passed.	No.	Ck.	By Whom Collected.	On Whose Account.	Amount.		Col. & Ex.		Proceeds.		Ck
Feb.	4		Ourselves	Duncan, Sh. & Co.	3000		30		2970		√
	5		do.	W. H. Clark	1500				1500		√
	7	√	Laf. Bank, Cin.	L. R. Morris	900		2	25	897	75	√
	10	√	Moss Bros., Sand'y	J. Hoornbeek	475		1	19	473	81	√
					5875		√33	44	5841	56	
Mar.	1		Ourselves	Duncan, Sh. & Co.	1500		15		1485		√
	6		do.	W. H. Clark	2000				2000		√
	8		do.	L. R. Morris	500				500		√
	9		do.	J. Hoornbeek	1200				1200		√
	11		do.	Duncan, Sh. & Co.	2500		25		2475		√
	13		do.	Duncan, Sh. & Co.	6000		60		5940		√
					13700		√100		13600		
Apr.	2		Ourselves	Duncan, Sh. & Co.	2000		20		1980		√
	3		do.	Duncan, Sh. & Co.	2500		25		2475		√
	12		do.	Duncan, Sh. & Co.	3000		30		2970		√
	14		do.	W. H. Clark	3000				3000		√
	17		do.	Laf. Bank, Cin.	6000				6000		√
	18		do.	Laf. Bank, Cin.	3000				3000		√
	19		do.	L. R. Morris	3000				3000		√
	20		do.	L. R. Morris	1575				1575		√
	21		do.	J. Hoornbeek	1250				1250		√
	15		Duncan. Sh. & Co.	J. B. Meriam	1500				1500		√
					26825		√75		26750		
May	23		Ourselves	Duncan, Sh. & Co.	3500		35		3465		√
	24		do.	Duncan, Sh. & Co.	7000		70		6930		√
	25		do.	Laf. Bank, Cin.	1750				1750		√
	26		do.	Burk & Sons, Chic.	4000				4000		√
	27		do.	Burk & Sons, Chic.	3750				3750		√
	29		do.	E. G. Folsom	1500				1500		√
	30		do.	Exch. Bk., Buf.	1000		5		995		√
	41		do.	J. B. Meriam	750				750		√
	42		do.	J. B. Meriam	900				900		√
	48		do.	Jas. W. Lusk	2000				2000		√
	16	√	Laf. Bank, Cin.	J. B. Meriam	2000		5		1995		√
	32	√	F. & M. Bk., Det.	E. R. Felton	2000		15		1985		√
	33	√	Laf. Bank, Cin.	M. B. Scott	1500		3	75	1496	25	√
	34	√	Moss Bros., Sand'y	D. P. Eells	700		1	75	698	25	√
	49	√	Exch. Bk., Buf.	Geo. A. Crocker	750				750		√
					33100		√135	50	32964	50	

PASSED COLLECTIONS.

When Passed.	No.	Ck.	By Whom Collected.	On Whose Account.	Amount.		Col. & Ex.		Proceeds.		Ck.
June	22		Ourselves	Duncan, Sh. & Co.	5000		50		4950		✓
	31		do.	Franklin Bk., Col.	750				750		✓
	44		do.	John R. Penn	7000				7000		✓
	47		do.	Geo. M. Penn.	1500				1500		✓
	66		do.	Exch. Bank, Buf.	700		3	50	696	50	✓
	67		do.	Exch. Bank, Buf.	3500		17	50	3482	50	✓
	68		do.	Geo. M. Penn	600				600		✓
	35	✓	Toledo Br. Bk.	W. H. Clark	3000		7	50	2992	50	✓
	37	✓	Far. Br. Bk., Ash.	Duncan, Sh. & Co.	750		9	38	740	62	✓
	38	✓	Lorain B., Elyria	Duncan, Sh. & Co.	900		11	25	888	75	✓
	39	✓	Laf. Bank, Cin.	Duncan, Sh. & Co.	1200		15		1185		✓
	43	✓	D., Sh. & Co., N. Y.	J. R. Penn	1750				1750		✓
	46	✓	Toledo Br. Bk.	Geo. M. Penn	2000		5		1995		✓
	49	✓	Laf. Bank, Cin.	Jas. W. Lusk	500		1	25	498	75	✓
	50	✓	Lorain Bk., Elyria	H. D. Stratton	1500		3	75	1496	25	✓
	53	✓	Franklin Bk., Col.	Duncan, Sh. & Co.	750		9	38	740	62	✓
	56	✓	Toledo Br. Bk.	Duncan, Sh. & Co.	500		6	25	493	75	✓
	58	✓	Exch. Bk., Buf.	M. B. Scott	350				350		✓
	61	✓	Toledo Br. Bk.	W. H. Clark	750		1	88	748	12	✓
	63	✓	Exch. Bk., Buf.	John S. Woolson	500				500		✓
					33500		✓141	64	33358	36	

ADDITIONAL AUXILIARY BOOKS.

INDIVIDUAL LIABILITIES.

H. B. Bryant.

When Discounted		*No.*	*Other Parties Liable*	*Discounted for Him.*	*Liable as Payer.*	*Liable as Endorser.*	*When Due.*		*Remarks.*
Jan.	1	1	Wright G. & Rawson	5000		5000	Mar.	5	Paid
Mar.	1	18	W. B. Ogden			12000	May	5	Paid
May	1	45	R. C. Spencer	3500			June	12	Paid
May	1	46	William Smith	7000			July	3	
June	1	58	E. R. Finney.			600	July	12	

H. D. Stratton.

When Discounted		*No.*	*Other Parties Liable*	*Discounted for Him.*	*Liable as Payer.*	*Liable as Endorser.*	*When Due.*		*Remarks.*
Jan.	1	2	Peter Cooper			4000	Mar.	5	Paid
Mar.	1	19	D. Appleton			3000	May	3	Paid
Apr.	1	28	Geo. M. Penn			5000	June	2	Paid
May	1	36	H. D. Clark		7500		July	3	

James W. Lusk.

When Discounted		*No.*	*Other Parties Liable*	*Discounted for Him.*	*Liable as Payer.*	*Liable as Endorser.*	*When Due.*		*Remarks.*
Feb.	1	5	John R. Penn	2500		2500	Apr.	18	Paid
Mar.	1	10	Clafflin, M. & Co.			4000	Mar	16	Paid
Mar.	1	11	M. B. Scott			6000	Apr.	5	Paid

Peter Cooper.

When Discounted		*No.*	*Other Parties Liable*	*Discounted for Him.*	*Liable as Payer.*	*Liable as Endorser.*	*When Due.*		*Remarks.*
Jan.	1	2	H. D. Stratton		4000		Mar.	5	Paid
Apr.	1	22	Wilson G. Hunt		15000		June	26	Paid
May	1	37	John R. Penn			6000	June	28	Paid

T. P. Handy,

When Discounted		*No.*	*Other Parties Liable*	*Discounted for Him.*	*Liable as Payer.*	*Liable as Endorser.*	*When Due.*		*Remarks.*
Feb.	1	6	D. P. Eells		1600		May	24	Paid
Mar.	1	15	Parker Handy			7000	Apr.	19	Paid
Apr.	1	23	N. C. Winslow			7000	June	2	Paid
May	1	47	H. B. Tuttle			10000	June	3	Paid
May	1	48	E. R. Morgan	4000			June	17	Paid
June	1	51	Edward Savage			1500	Sept.	1	
June	1	54	Thomas Jones	7500			Sept.	3	
June	1	55	Jacob Harrison	1500			Aug.	3	

Charles Hickox.

When Discounted		*No.*	*Other Parties Liable*	*Discounted for Him.*	*Liable as Payer.*	*Liable as Endorser.*	*When Due.*		*Remarks.*
Feb.	1	8	Jacob Hinds		7000		Apr.	6	Paid
Mar	1	16	Jas. Armstrong			3000	Apr.	3	Protested
May	1	41	J. Kennedy	1500	1500		July	27	
May	1	42	J. Gillett	7000		7000	July	2	

ADDITIONAL AUXILIARY BOOKS.

CASH BOOK.

	Jan. 1.		Feb. 1.		March 1.		April 1.		May 1.		June 1	
City Bank Notes	36700		62817		72119		69175		85960		75060	
State "	12750		25600		27150		37240		22710		38700	
Eastern "	4283		5617		12300		13720		12900		19850	
Western "	7508		8759		17916		12916		7618		15825	
Checks, etc.	1500		5500		10130		14125	50	500		12000	
Gold	6900		7418		7340		8725		7510		8900	
Silver	3712	90	3594	15	4719	25	3627	50	4460	35	5792	33
Pennies	398	95	599	98	170	94	416	02	564	87	679	45
	73752	85	119905	13	151845	19	159945	02	142223	22	176806	78

STOCK LEDGER.

H. D. Stratton. 1

				1862			
				Jan.	1	100 Shares, 1st Instl.	6000
						2d Instl.	4000
						50 Shrs. from H. B. B.	5000
				July	1	150 Shares @ $100	15000

H. B. Bryant. 2

1862				1862			
June	1	50 Shares to H. D. S.	5000	Jan.	1	100 Shares, 1st Instl.	6000
July	1	50 Shares	5000	May	1	2d Instl.	4000
		100	10000			100	10000
				July	1	50 Shares, @ $100	5000

TRANSFER BOOK.

L.F.	June 1, 1862.	
2	H. B. Bryant, *Dr.*	
1	H. D. Stratton, *Cr.*	
	50 Shares @ $100	5000

NO. OF CERTIFICATES.

Issued.	*Redeemed.*
14	2

50 Shares. Cleveland, *June 1, 1862.*

For value received, I hereby assign and transfer to H. D. Stratton, all my right, title, and interest in Fifty Shares of the Capital Stock of the Commercial College Bank, *standing in my name on the Books of said Bank.*

H. B. Bryant.

Witness, S. S. Packard.

L. F.

NO. OF CERTIFICATES.

Issued.	*Redeemed.*

Cleveland, ... *186*

For value received .... *hereby assign and transfer to* .... *all* .... *right, title, and interest in* .... *Shares of the* Capital Stock of the Commercial College Bank, *standing in* .... *name on the Books of said Bank.*

....

Witness, ...

OFFERING BOOK.

OFFERED, FEBRUARY 1, 1862.

No	By Whom Offered.	Payers and Endorsers.	Time to Run.	Amount.		Av. Bal.		Remarks.
3	Alonzo Mitchell	A. J. Comstock	33 ds.	5000		5000		A.
4	Alonzo Mitchell	N. Bidwell, William Cook	43 ds.	3000				A.
5	Jas. W. Lusk	John R. Penn	76 ds.	2500		3000		A.
6	John Driscoll	Heman Barker	63 ds.	4000				R.
7	E. R. Felton	T. P. Handy, D. P. Eells	112 ds.	1600		3800		A.
8	E. R. Felton	Jas. Richards	63 ds.	3500				A.
9	Thos. Barrows	H. Emans & Co.	90 ds.	5000				R.
10	M. B. Scott	Chas Hickox, J. Hinds	64 ds.	7000		2800		A.
11	Horace Mahew	James Earl	79 ds.	3500				R.

STATEMENT BOOK.

SEMI-MONTHLY STATEMENT.

Date.		Discounts on Hand.		Bills of other Banks.		Due Foreign Banks.		Specie.		Circulation.		Due Depositors.	
Jan.	1	9000		34841				11011	85			29953	35
Feb.	1	31600		75676				11612	13	35000		64294	
Mar.	1	64100		102316				12230	19	35000		144667	56
Apr.	1	95100		107576				12768	52	35000		180583	31
May	1	174000		101228				12535	22	35000		203111	17
June	1	99050		123575				15371	78	35000		223535	11

QUARTERLY STATEMENT,* JUNE 1, 1862.

Resources.		
1. Loans and Discounts . . .	99050	
2. Overdrafts		
3. Due from Banks	140850	25
4. Due from Directors, $7500		
5 Due from Brokers, 88137 90		
6. Real Estate		
7. Specie	15371	78
8. Cash Items, viz.: Checks, etc.	12000	
9. Stocks, $36400; Treasury Notes, $9800	46200	
10. Bonds and Mortgages. . .		
11. Bills of Solvent Banks	123575	
12 Bills of Suspended Banks		
13. Loss and Exp. % (Fixtures)	575	
	437622	03

Liabilities.		
1. Capital	200000	
2. Circulation Registered, $35000 Less Notes on hand, 25860 Leaves Outstanding Notes .	9140	
3. Profits	4946	92
4. Due to Banks.		
5. Due to Individuals and Corporations other than Banks and Depositors		
6. Due State Treasurer . . .		
7. Due Depositors on Demand .	223553	11
8. Amt. due not included under either of above Heads . .		
	437622	03

* Form prescribed by the Banking Laws of New York.

FORMS OF BANK PAPER.

CERTIFICATE OF STOCK.

No. 3. **100 Shares.**

SHARES $100 EACH

Commercial College Bank.

This is to certify that J. B. Meriam is entitled to One Hundred Shares of ONE HUNDRED DOLLARS *each, in the Capital Stock of the Commercial Bank of Cleveland, transferable at the Bank only by him or his attorney on surrender of this certificate.*

In Witness Whereof *the Seal of said Bank is hereunto affixed, at Cleveland, this first day of January, 1862.*

S. S. Packard, *Cash^r.* H. D. Stratton, *Pres^t.*

CERTIFICATE OF DEPOSIT.

$3000 **Commercial College Bank.** No. 1.

John R. Penn has deposited in this Bank Three Thousand Dollars, payable to Thomas Hunter, or order, on return of this Certificate properly endorsed.

Cleveland, April 1, 1862. James E. Day, *Teller.*

CERTIFIED CHECK.

No.______ *Cleveland, April 1, 1862.*

Commercial College Bank.

Pay to ______ N. Frederick, ______ *or order,*

Five Hundred Seventy-five ______ *Dollars.*

$575 Jno. R. Penn

FORMS OF BANK PAPER.

BANK DRAFT.

$500 **Commercial College Bank.** No. 283.

Cleveland, Jan. 1, 1862.

At sight, pay to N. C. Winslow, or order, Five Hundred Dollars, value received.

S. S. Packard, *Cashier.*

To Duncan, Sherman & Co., New York.

NEGOTIABLE NOTE.

$4000 Cleveland, Jan. 1, 1862.

Sixty days after date, I promise to pay John R. Penn, or order, Four Thousand Dollars, at the Commercial College Bank, value received.

Peter Cooper.

ACCEPTED DRAFT.

$5000 Cleveland, Jan. 1, 1862.

At sixty days' sight, pay to the order of H. D. Stratton, Five Thousand Dollars, value received.

H. B. Bryant.

To Wright, Gillett & Rawson, New York.

FORMS OF BANK PAPER.

COLLATERAL NOTE.

$20,000 Cleveland, May 3, 18 62.

Sixty days after date, I promise to pay to the Commercial College Bank, or order, Twenty Thousand Dollars, for value received, at the rate of six per cent. per annum, having deposited with them, as Collateral security, Cleveland and Erie Railroad Bonds of the nominal value of Twenty=five Thousand Dollars, (with authority to sell the same at the Brokers' Board, or at public or private sale, or otherwise, at their option, on the non-performance of this promise, and without notice.)

Chas. Baker.

NOTICE TO DRAWER OR ENDORSER.

Buffalo, April 3, 18 62.

Sir,

Take notice, that a note for Three Thousand Dollars, made by James Armstrong, and endorsed by you, was this day protested for non-payment, and that the holder looks to you for the payment thereof, payment of the same having been this day demanded and refused.

Respectfully yours,

Samuel B. Allison,

Notary Public.

To Chas. Hickox, Cleveland.

PROTEST FOR NON-PAYMENT.

United States of America,
State of New York, } ss.:

Be it known that on the third day of April, in the year 1862, at the request of the Exchange Bank, I, Samuel B. Allison, a Notary Public, duly admitted and sworn, dwelling in the city of Buffalo, did present the original bill or note which is hereto annexed, and demanded payment thereof, which was refused: I, therefore, on the same day and year above written, and after said demand and refusal, duly notified the drawer and the several endorsers of the non-payment of the same as follows:

By serving personally on James Armstrong, at his office;

By putting in the Post Office, in this city, addressed to Charles Hickox, Cleveland, O., that being the reputed residence of the said party, and the Post Office nearest thereto.

Whereupon I, the said Notary, at the request aforesaid, have protested, and do solemnly protest, against the drawer and endorsers of said bill, and all others concerned, for all exchange, re-exchange, costs, damages, and interest incurred, by reason of the non-payment of said bill.

In witness whereof I have hereunto subscribed my name, and affixed my seal of office.

Samuel B. Allison,
Notary Public.

BROKERAGE AND EXCHANGE:

EMBRACING

CASH BOOK, GENERAL LEDGER, STOCK LEDGER, AND BLOTTER

WITH FORMS OF

GOVERNMENT AND RAILROAD STOCKS, FOREIGN BILLS OF EXCHANGE, ETC.;

WITH A FEW

GENERAL REMARKS ON CURRENCY AND STOCKS,

REPRESENTING THE BUSINESS OF A STOCK AND EXCHANGE BROKER.

BROKERAGE AND EXCHANGE.

THE exigencies of Commerce and Finance bring into requisition an almost endless variety of *middle men*, or agents, who, by devoting their entire energies each to some particular line, are enabled to accomplish results with much more certainty and dispatch than would attend the efforts of men equally efficient in other respects, who are not versed in the details of the particular departments for which special agents are properly employed.

In fact, the system of agencies or brokerage which so thoroughly pervades all departments of business, is but the natural result of legitimate causes, and is in direct accordance with the established principles of economy.

"Jack at all trades, and good at none," is a saying which has a peculiar force when applied to business; and experience has fully shown that the best interests of community, as of each individual member, are subserved by a properly adjusted division of labor.

In large commercial cities the necessities of trade have established this principle, and are daily carrying it out to greater perfection and with more complete results. In the city of New York, for instance, there is scarcely any end to special agencies; in nearly all of which the adjustment of compensation—which is usually a *pro rata* commission on services rendered—is regulated by custom, upon so just and liberal a scale, as to secure ready and remunerative patronage.

These special agents are popularly known as "Brokers," the term designating their particular line being prefixed, as: "Produce Brokers," "Cotton Brokers," "Stock Brokers," "Money Brokers," "Custom-House Brokers," etc., etc.

The term "Broker," legitimately implies an agent, or one employed to negotiate bargains for another. Such, however, is not the sense as applied to a dealer in stocks and currency—which business is chosen for the following set—for although there are Stock Brokers who do strictly a commission business, by far the greater number do not hesitate to avail themselves of favorable conditions of the market to speculate on their own account. This fact is so well understood as to render necessary some line of distinction; and so we are favored in business dialect with the tautological phrase, "Commission Brokers," which we are permitted to infer means Brokers who are *really* Brokers.

The purport of the following set is to briefly illustrate the business of Currency and Stock Brokerage, as conducted in establishments combining the two.

CURRENCY,

In its general application, means the accepted medium or standard of commercial values. When the banks of the country were paying their debts in specie—which was also the only legal tender—gold and silver constituted the standard of value, and were themselves *currency;* but when paper credits were made legal tender, thus displacing the precious metals from circulation as currency, specie at once appreciated in value, as compared with its paper representative, ceased to be considered as money, and entered into the lists of speculative values, being bought and sold the same as merchandise and stocks.

It will at once be apparent that this seeming *appreciation* of specie is, in reality, but the *depreciation* of the standard by which it is estimated; and gold and silver being the only common standard of all civilized countries, it would, perhaps, be more truthful to speak of our local currency as at a *discount*, rather than of gold and silver as at a *premium*. But whatever the theory, the practical fact still exists that so long as all values are measured by local currency, that currency must be considered as the *standard*. Thus, while in the United States, Canada currency, which is based upon specie, is at a *premium;* in Canada, United States currency, which is not at present redeemable in specie, is at a corresponding *discount*. In fact, such are the necessities of the case, that whatever may be the intrinsic value of any currency, so long as it is the recognized medium of commercial dealings, it must be acknowledged as the *standard* of all values within its jurisdiction.

This view of the case will suggest the fact, that all commodities which are bought and sold, whether having a written or nominal value, such as gold, silver, stocks, etc., or without any such extraneous conditions, such as merchandise, real estate, etc., are necessarily articles of commerce; and that the currency in which their values are estimated constitutes the cash standard in all local transactions, unless otherwise stipulated.

While a depreciated national currency increases the relative value of specie and its representatives, other causes, which have been fully explained in the preceding set, tend to affect the comparative value of the different local currencies. And although this difference is very slight—varying from $\frac{1}{8}$ to 2%—and does not seriously interfere with its par circulation in the common channels of trade, it is distinctly recognized by the banks, which are the acknowledged umpires of money values. For instance, in the eastern cities, banks will not take on deposit western or other funds which are below par value; and as such funds are always to a greater or less extent in circulation, the broker stands ready to purchase them at a remunerative rate, giving bankable currency in exchange. The uncurrent money thus purchased is sometimes sent home for redemption, sometimes disposed of at a small profit, and not unfrequently paid out at par. The margin on such transactions is necessarily small, but their frequency and extent, in well established houses, render the business on the whole profitable.*

STOCKS.

The term Stocks, as used in this country, covers a wide area of signification, embracing almost every species of obligation, from the best secured pledges of national and state indebtedness to the personal "promises to pay" of individuals.

The intrinsic value of these pledges depends, first, upon the surety of final payment, and next, upon the percentage of yearly disbursements to the holder.

Stocks may be properly divided into two classes, which, for the sake of distinction, we will denominate *Interest* and *Dividend*.

Interest Stocks are those calling for a certain fixed percentage on the amount loaned, and are secured either by pledge of the public wealth, or by mortgage on adequate intrinsic value. Of this class are government securities of all kinds, bonds of railroads and other corporations, mortgages on real estate, etc. The only influences which can effect the value of this class of stocks are the worth of money and the character of the securities upon which they rest.

Dividend Stocks are those which call for a dividend of the net earnings of certain enterprises, and are secured by the net resources and earning capacity of such enterprises. Of this class are the shares in the capital stock of railroads, banks, manufacturing and mining establishments, and other joint stock corporations. They fluctuate in value according to the pecuniary success and prospects of the business which they represent; and as the intrinsic value of all property depends upon its producing power, so the *dividends* which are declared upon these shares—if the same are known to be from the legitimate earnings of the business—regulate, in the greatest degree, their market value. Other influences may force these values out of their proper relations to this test, but if left to their legitimate course, like other commodities, the parallel between earnings and commercial value must hold good. There is, of course, a difference in the value of what we have denominated *Interest* Stocks, not dependent upon the percentage of disbursements. Such difference must of course be owing to the character of the securities themselves. For instance, when the country was at peace and the national debt inconsiderable, United States Stocks, paying only 6% per annum, were always at a premium of from 1 to 10%, while the best railroad securities, declaring from 7 to 8%, varied from 1% premium to 10% discount. At the present time the very best government securities, or those paying the highest rates of interest, command a premium of not over 5%, while the first mortgages on our northern railroads sell at from 5% to 30% premium. It requires but little reflection to assign adequate causes for this state of facts. The government is engaged in a desperate struggle for self-preservation, and the national debt is accumulating at the rate of over two millions of dollars per day; while the very business of war, shutting up as it does some of the finest channels of commerce, creates an immense carrying trade, which is monopolized by our northern railroads, giving them a degree of financial prosperity never before experienced. Stock dealers, in their relation to the government, may all be patriots of the most approved kind; but in their relation to stock dealing they are simply speculators; and in that capacity will not hesitate to use the kind of argument best calculated to promote their individual interests. While the war goes on with varied results, the bare possibility of ultimate failure, together with the certainty of an immense public debt, must keep government securities within moderate limits; while the fact that in any event, the railroads will not cease to prosper, will enable the holders of securities based upon them to maintain their superiority in the market.

The true basis of value in *Dividend* Stocks is, first, the permanent prospects of the association represented, and, next, its real net earnings. The law which makes it incumbent upon banks to publish at certain periods a sworn statement of their affairs, is eminently calculated to further the interests of the public, and if one could always be sure that things are called by their right names in these statements, the process of estimating the value of such stocks would be simple enough. Take an example: At a certain date the net reserved profits in

---

*** It is not yet demonstrated what may be the effect of the new National Banking Law, which confines the basis of circulation in all the states to pledges of United States securities; but if it subserve the design of its originators and supporters, the present local currency will be entirely displaced by a uniform national currency, which, although issued and redeemable by local institutions, will be uniformly secured, and hence not liable to those violent and disastrous fluctuations which have so affected the issues of western banks under state laws. With a uniform currency, or a local currency having a uniform basis of redemption, the rates of exchange between different parts of the country can never be excessive, nor subject to extensive fluctuations.**

the Chemical Bank of New York were $586,176, and the capital stock $300,000. During the succeeding year this bank paid to stockholders a dividend of 12%, and added to the reserved profits $42,056, which is equivalent to 14% of the capital. The net earnings during the year, therefore, were 26% on the capital stock. The question now is, What is stock worth which produces 26%? or what is its value as compared with money? The first thing be to ascertained, then, is the value of money, which, by reference to quotations at this time, we find to average about $6\frac{1}{2}$%. We have now a simple problem in proportion, viz.: *If one dollar produces $6\frac{1}{2}$ cents, how much will be required to produce 26 cents?* The solution is as follows:

$$6\tfrac{1}{2} : 26 :: 100 : 400.$$

Or,

$$26 \div 6\tfrac{1}{2} = 4.$$

The answer is: One dollar in Chemical Bank stock is worth *four dollars* in money; which was the quoted market value of the stock at this time.

Another example: The Atlantic Bank at the same period had a reserved profit of $14,642, and a capital stock of $400,000. During the year the bank declared a dividend of 7%, which *reduced* the reserved profits $8,430, being a little over 2% on the capital. The net earnings of the bank, therefore, were a little less than 5%, say $4\frac{3}{4}$. What is the value of the stock? Solution as before:

$$6\tfrac{1}{2} : 4\tfrac{3}{4} :: 100 : 73.$$

Atlantic Bank stocks were quoted at 70¢, which varies but slightly from the above result.

While it is true that upon a basis of this kind the approximate value of a large portion of the current stocks may be ascertained, the parallel will not hold good in all cases. For instance, many of the railroads were paying annual dividends of from 7 to 8%, whose stocks ruled no higher than 80%. The reason for this discrepancy between dividends and market value can exist only in a lack of confidence in the management and prospects of the corporations. It is known, in fact, that railroad dividends are often declared *without reference to earnings*, for the purpose of giving a fictitious value to the stocks. Of course, when such is the case, money for this purpose has to be borrowed, and must eventually be paid. So reckless have some railroad companies been in these matters, that the original stock, which by prudent management and a persistent course of honesty toward the public might have been kept at a low rate of discount, if not at par, has been run down to zero, carrying with it, of course, all securities based upon it. There are various ways of "cooking up" the financial affairs of a large corporation, so that those who have no means of knowing the intrinsic worth of what are called its "resources," may be easily deceived. Nothing is more deceptive than an ingenious array of sober-looking figures. Efforts have been made by the various state legislatures to infuse a little leaven of honesty into joint-stock associations, by obliging them to make periodical statements to the public of their financial condition, but such enactments, though serviceable in many ways, afford no absolute guaranty. It is a difficult matter to legislate men honest, and corporations are certainly no better in this regard than individuals.

We have given in connection with this set a few samples of government and railroad stocks, copied from the original documents, which may be found useful in giving a definite idea of their character.

STOCK BROKERAGE.

The Stock business, as it is conducted in the great commercial emporiums—and very little dealings in stocks occur elsewhere—is so intricate in detail, and subject to such a variety of contingencies, as to require in its elaboration more space than we have at disposal, and more minute investigation into the hidden springs of financial speculation than we have either the time or inclination to make. Neither would the knowledge, could it be thus obtained and imparted, be of essential service to the student of accounts. To become a successful financier — or, more properly speaking, *speculator*—requires peculiar qualifications; the first of which we believe to be *natural endowments*, which no man can acquire; and the next, *actual contact* with the business itself. There is, perhaps, no subject upon which a greater variety of theories have been evolved;—some of them as finely spun as gossamer, and as evanescent—and none which business men more pride themselves in understanding, than the general subject of Finance; and especially that department which relates to the public weal. Particularly is this true with reference to those measures intended to secure national prosperity. Every man seems blessed with a "private opinion" as to the effect of this or that line of policy—one reasoning to an inevitable conclusion that if certain plans are adopted, the country will instantly hasten to financial ruin; and another, with quite as formidable a display of logic and erudition, arriving at the very opposite result; while equally earnest and infallible guides take up positions at every possible resting-place between the two extremes.

The *practical* financier is, in this sense, no theorist. He must have, it is true, intelligent and well settled views upon all the great questions of the day, political and otherwise, which have a bearing upon his particular line He is, or should be, a careful observer of all public movements calculated, either immediately or remotely to affect the interests of the people at large; and is usually prepared to estimate the effect of such movements upon the various classes of securities in market. His mind is quick and comprehensive, enabling him to act with promptness and discrimination; while his convictions are so certain and tangible as to admit of no hesitation in following them out. True, he may fail, but failure does not discourage him. Like a true general, he looks well to the chances before entering upon an engagement; but when once fairly in the fray, he turns neither to the right nor the left, but presses straight forward. If a line wavers, he strengthens it; if a column gives way, he redoubles his vigor to overcome the disadvantage; and if, with all his efforts, disaster still comes, bringing with it defeat, he does not, like a timid foe, lie tamely down, giving up all for lost, but with what wreck he may gather from the strife, he pushes for safer shelter, congratulating himself that if he bears no other trophies from the field, he has won the guerdon of experience, which will be invaluable to him in all future contests.

No one will attempt to deny that speculation in stocks, even under favorable circumstances, is extremely hazardous; neither will any one, careful of his reputation for plain speaking, pretend to say that unworthy means are not often resorted to, for the purpose of forcing securities out of that healthy relation of supply and demand which, in theory at least, regulates all commercial and financial dealings. With this we have nothing to do, except to recognize it as a general fact; but were we permitted to arrange the good and evil in this matter on opposite sides, with reference to the effect upon public interests, we think it would not be difficult to show that the benefits resulting from systematized operations in public securities, thus bringing them to notice and creating a demand for permanent investments; stimulating public and individual enterprise, and giving healthy circulation to the nation's wealth, will very far outweigh any temporary evils to which individuals resort for their own aggrandizement. Besides, with all the opprobrium which has been heaped upon the business of stock dealing, causing it to stink in the nostrils of the public as a species of legalized gambling; throwing distrust upon quotations as in no wise indicating true values; the fact cannot be denied, that there exists no more faithful barometer of the financial condition of the country than the daily stock quotations. It is true that powerful combinations and adroit misrepresentations, by creating temporary scarcity or glut in the market, and filling the public mind with undue apprehensions, or exciting to unwarrantable hopefulness, may for a time disturb the healthful equipoise; but such disturbances are necessarily brief, and the evils which they engender, so often "like curses come home to roost," that the antidote may be said to go with the poison. Besides, the directly opposite interests, which are so differently affected by every fluctuation, secures a vigilance in the matter which renders deception for any length of time impossible. So, even the very outrages on decency and public morals, claimed to be inflicted by mythological "bulls" and "bears," may, like countless other evils to which flesh is heir, prove an ultimate good; and the vigilance induced by a sense of self-preservation, constitute the great bulwark and defense of national as well as individual prosperity.

The most reputable among the stock-dealers are members of the Stock Exchange, a regularly organized association, having for its purpose the bringing together of the two great classes of dealers—buyers and sellers, and embracing features of mutual protection and benefit.

This association holds semi-daily sessions, and controls nearly all the operations of importance in the stock market. Its transactions serve as the basis of quotations, and regulate the rate of all classes of securities.

The "regular" way of concluding sales of stocks, gold, etc., is to deliver and receive payment therefor on the day succeeding the contract. Often, however, the buyer or seller is allowed three days in which to fulfil his part. When this margin is allowed, and the fulfilment of the contract is claimed on any day previous to the last, notice must be given to the other party before two o'clock of the day chosen. "Cash" sales are deliverable and payable on the day of sale. To sell "short," is to sell without at the time owning the property sold, expecting to purchase before the date of delivery at favorable rates. To sell "flat," is to waive all considerations of commission or accrued interest; simply selling the stocks themselves at a given rate.

Stock Brokers frequently advance for parties who commission them to purchase and hold stocks. When this is done, a small deposit is usually required, which is discretionary between the parties, and is intended to cover any contingencies of depreciation. The stocks themselves are held as collateral security for the loan, upon which the regular rate of interest is charged.

The uniting of Currency Exchange with Stock business is not practiced to any great extent in the more important houses. That they are thoroughly compatible, however, will be evident to all.

It will be necessary to mark the distinction which we have drawn between money and stocks, and to notice the difference in their treatment. That which passes as currency in *any part of the United States* we treat as *cash*, counting it as such in making up our cash items at the close of the day. Gold, Silver, Canada and Sterling currency we treat as *stocks;* they having passed beyond the precincts of our own currency.

In purchasing and selling uncurrent funds, the margin of profit or loss needs particularly to be noted; and as a formal entry of purchase and sale would be quite out of taste and unnecessary, we simply indicate each little discrepancy in a kind of memorandum-book, called a "Blotter," which is fully explained hereafter.

BROKERAGE AND EXCHANGE.

THE BOOKS AND THEIR USE.

In prescribing the forms of entry for the various departments of business represented in this treatise, our plan has been, first, to examine the forms of the best houses, and selecting such as, in our judgment, were best adapted to the purpose, with such improvements of our own as the exigencies of the case seemed to suggest, to arrange the whole into such a system as would be best calculated to subserve the purposes of an economical and satisfactory record.

In the business before us there is little chance to display ingenuity; and no necessity for a large number of books, with an intricate system of counter-checking. The transactions are exceedingly simple and monotonous; and, after the first two or three entries are completed, the student will be able to proceed with little or no assistance.

The forms are simple and direct, having very few marked peculiarities; and are quite sufficient for the most extensive business of this kind.

The main book of entry is

THE CASH BOOK,

which differs in no essential particular from ordinary Cash Books, except that, like the Debit and Credit Journals in Banking, it contains *all* the entries that go to the Ledger, rendering unnecessary any other book of original entry. The difference between the two sides of this book showing the cash on hand, it has not been deemed necessary to open any Cash account in the Ledger. In taking a Trial Balance, the cash on hand will need to be included.

THE GENERAL LEDGER

contains all the accounts of the business except Cash—which has been omitted as explained—and the accounts of the various Stocks; which, owing to the necessity of some slight peculiarity in the ruling, appear in a separate book, called

THE STOCK LEDGER,

but which really is a part of the General Ledger, and may be so kept if desired. We wish to call particular attention to the convenient arrangement of this book; believing, as we do, that the improvement which we have suggested, embodying a complete and perpetual inventory of unsold stocks, with the regular account of cost and proceeds, will commend itself to all practical men.

THE BLOTTER

is an indispensable book to the dealer in currencies, and is the principal book of entry in a simple Exchange business. Its real office, as will be apparent, is to mark the discrepancies between the amount of cash *received* and *paid out* in each currency transaction. The book in this connection is rather more formal than is usual; but not too much so for intelligent record. The columns "out" and "in" are sufficiently suggestive; and it will require no great shrewdness to see that the difference in the footings of these columns will exactly tally with the increase or diminution of cash from the exchanges thus recorded. This discrepancy is carried as a loss or gain to the Cash Book each day, and thus preserves the character of this book for showing the balance of cash on hand.

Aside from these regular books of entry, the dealer carries a

MEMORANDUM BOOK,

in which are entered the conditions of sales when effected, and such general facts as are necessary to a full understanding of the transactions.

The entire work as represented, comprises but six days' business, and is intended to show the ordinary daily operations of a medium establishment. As this limited period will not allow for the fulfilment of "time" sales, the business is restricted to cash transactions. In rendering the inventories of unsold stocks and accumulated interest, we have reckoned them at their *actual worth* according to the quotations. This plan will enable us to show a gain on stocks by a rise in the market, as well as by actual sales; a feature which every student should well understand.

We are well aware that Exchange Brokers not unfrequently connect with their business the features of Discount and Collection, already so thoroughly shown up in the previous set. As the student will need no further instruction on these points, we have deemed it unnecessary to repeat them here. For similar reasons we have omitted to include in the transactions any thing relating to the expenses of conducting the business.

NARRATIVE.

Monday, March 2, 1863.—Commenced business with \$150000 cash capital...... Bo't \$2000 Illinois currency, @ 2% discount...... Bo't \$1000 Kentucky currency, @ ½% disc...... Bo't \$2000 Canada currency, @ $\$1^{53}$; 1500 do., @ $\$1^{52\frac{1}{4}}$...... Bo't \$10000 U. S. Registered 6% 1881, at par: Accumulated interest on same from Nov. 1, 1862, \$——...... Rec'd from H. R. Munger \$10000 on deposit, to be invested as per future advice...... Sold \$1000 Illinois currency, at 1½% disc...... Bo't \$15000 U. S. Coupon 6% 1881, @ $\$1^{02}$: Interest on same from Jan. 1, \$——*..... Bo't \$2500 Missouri currency, @ 2% disc...... Bo't for H. R. Munger, per instructions, \$8000 N. Y. C. R. R. stocks, @ $\$1^{18}$: Our commission, ¼% on amount invested.

Tuesday, 3.—Sold \$2500 Canada, @ $\$1^{54}$...... Bo't \$3500 N. Y. State currency, @ ¼ disc...... Bo't \$2000 Baltimore currency, @ 1% disc..... Rec'd of S. S. Packard on deposit, \$20000..... Bo't \$10000 Delaware and Lackawana 1st Mortgage, @ $\$1^{22}$, *flat*...... Sold \$10000 U. S. Reg. 6%, '81, @ $\$1^{01}$: Interest from Nov. 1, 1862, \$——...... Sold for J. E. Jenkins \$20000 N. Y. and E. R. R. 5th Mortgage, 1888, @ $\$1^{67}$, cash; for which we credit him less our ¼% commission...... Bo't \$10000 Gold, @ $\$1^{65}$...... Bo't for S. S. Packard, as per advice, \$15000 Cleveland & Toledo R. R. Stocks, @ 94½: Our commission on same, ¼%...... Bo't \$5000 N. Y. State currency, @ ¼% disc...... Bo't \$3000 on State Bk. Indiana, @ 4% disc...... Sold \$2500 Missouri, @ 1% disc.; \$1000 Kentucky, @ ¼% disc...... Sold for H. D. Stratton, \$15000 N. J. R. R. Stocks, @ $\$1^{55}$, cash; for which we credit him less our ¼% commission.

Wednesday, 4.—Bo't uncurrent money as follows; \$1000 Wisconsin, @ 1½% disc.; \$900 Michigan @ 1% disc.; \$500 Missouri, @ 2% disc.; \$300 Indiana, @ 2% disc...... Paid J. E. Jenkins, cash in full of %, \$——...... Sold for H. R. Munger, \$15000 Gold, @ $\$1^{66\frac{3}{4}}$, cash: Credited him amount less our ¼% commission...... Bo't \$15000 $7\frac{3}{10}$ Treasury Notes, @ $\$1^{04}$: Accumulated interest from Nov. 1, '62, \$——...... Sold for J. E. Jenkins, \$25000 Michigan Coupon Bonds of 1888, @ $\$1^{02}$, *flat*: Credited him amount less our 1% commission...... Bo't \$3000 Wisconsin, @ 1¾ disc...... Bo't Sterling Bill of Exchange for £2000 @ $\$1^{78}$.† ..... Bo't for J. E. Jenkins, \$50000 Gold, @ $\$1^{64}$: Our commission, by special arrangement, ⅛%...... Sold \$4000 Wisconsin, @ 1% disc...... Sold for Geo. A. Reed, \$15000 N. Y. & Erie (preferred), @ $\$1^{02}$: Remitted amount, less our ¼% commission...... Sold \$1000 Canada, @ $\$1^{55}$...... Bo't \$15000 Gold, @ $\$1^{65\frac{1}{2}}$...... Sold \$3000 State Bk. Indiana, @ 2½% disc...... Bo't for H. R. Munger, \$10000 Panama R. R. Stock, @ $\$1^{89\frac{1}{2}}$: Our commission, ¼%...... Sold \$25000 Gold, @ $\$1^{63}$...... Bo't \$25000 U. S. 1 Yr. 6% Certificates, @ $\$1^{01}$: Interest accumulated as follows: \$5000 from Jan. 1, '63, to date, \$——; \$10000 from Jan. 15 to date, \$——; \$10000 from Feb. 1 to date, \$——...... Sold \$10000 Delaware & Lackawana, @ $\$1^{25}$...... Paid H. D. Stratton, cash in full of %, \$——...... Sold £2000 Sterling Exchange, @ $\$1^{80}$...... Sold for Culver, Penn & Co., \$15000 N. Y. C. R. R. Stocks, @ $\$1^{20}$: Credited amount, less ¼% commission...... Paid Culver, Penn & Co.'s draft on us of \$10,000 favor of H. B. Bryant.

Inventory, March 4.

Interest on U. S. Coup. 6%, 1881	150 42		
" U. S. $7\frac{3}{10}$ Treas. Notes	369		
" U. S. 1 Yr. 6% Certificates	184 93	704	35
U. S. Coupon 6%, '81, 15000, @ 1^{03}		15450	
U. S. $7\frac{3}{10}$% Treasury Notes, 1500, @ 1^{04}		15600	
U. S. 1 Yr. 6% Certificates, 25000, @ 1^{01}		25250	

NARRATIVE FOR THE STUDENT.

TO BE CONTINUED IN THE SAME BOOKS.

Thursday, 5.—Sold \$1000 Illinois, @ 1% disc...... Bo't \$7500 N. Y. State, @ ¼% disc...... Sold \$15000 U. S. 6% Coupon, @ $\$1^{04\frac{1}{2}}$: Interest on same from Jan. 1, \$——...... Bo't for S. S. Packard, \$10000 N. Y. & E. 1st Mortgage, 1868, @ $\$1^{21}$: Our commission, ¼%...... Sold for Frederick W. Warner, \$15000 Gold, @ $\$1^{67\frac{1}{2}}$: Our commission, ¼%..... Bo't \$2000 Missouri currency, @ 2% disc..... Bo't \$3000 Wisconsin

* Interest on Government Stocks is always computed at the rate of 365 days to the year.

† The quotations of sterling currency are always based on the exchange value of the pound sterling, which is $\$4\ 44\frac{4}{9}$. To compute the value of sterling currency at any given rate, reduce it first to federal, at the above standard, and then proceed in the usual way.

currency, @ 1¾% disc...... Sold $300 Indiana, @ 1% disc...... Sold for J. E. Jenkins, $20000 Cleveland & Toledo R. R., @ 95¢: Our commission, ¼%......Bo't $7000 Canadian currency, @ $1 [51]..... Bo't $25000 U. S Coup. 6%, 1881, @ $1 [01½]: Interest due on same as follows: on $5000, from Nov. 1, 1862, $——; $10000, from Dec. 1, 1862, $——; $10000, from Jan. 1, 1863, $——...... Sold $900 Michigan, @ ½% disc...... Bo't uncurrent funds as follows: $1000 N. Y. State, @ ½% disc.; $3000 Indiana Free Banks, @ 2% disc.; $4000 Wisconsin, @ 1¾% disc..... Sold $5000 Wisconsin, @ 1% disc..... Sold for Ira Packard, $5000 Mich. Central Stock, @ 98½¢: Remitted him amount, less ½% commission...... Bo't for J. E. Jenkins, $10000 Gold, @ $1 [67] Our commission, ¼%.

Friday, 6.—Bo't Bill of Exchange on London for £1500, @ $1 [76½]...... Bo't $3500 N. Y. State currency @ ½% disc....... Bo't for H. R. Munger, $6000 N. Y. & Harlem, preferred, @ 78¢: Our commission, ¼%..... Sold for Chester Packard, $10000 La Crosse Land Grants, @ 31¢; Remitted him amount, less our ¼% commission...... Bo't uncurrent money, as follows: $2000 Free Indiana, @ 2% disc.; $1000 Michigan, @ 1% disc.; $2500 Iowa, @ ¾% disc...... Bo't $20000 Gold, @ $1 [67]...... Bo't for F. W. Warner, $15000 Cleveland & Toledo, @ 95¢: Our commission, ¼%...... Bo't $15000 U. S. 1 Yr. 6% Certificates, @ $1 [02]: Interest accumulated on same from Jan. 1, 1863, to date, $——...... Sold $15000 U. S. 7 3/10 Treas. Notes, @ $1 [05]: Interest on same from Nov. 1, 1862, $——...... Sold for J. E. Jenkins, $17000 Metropolitan Bank Stock, @ $1 [04]. Our commission, ¼%...... Sold uncurrent funds, as follows: $500 Missouri, @ 1% disc.; $2000 Baltimore, @ ½% disc.; $4000 Wisconsin, @ ¾% disc...... Bo't for S. S. Packard, $10000 Gold, @ $1 [67]: Our commission, ¼%. ..... Paid F. W. Warner, in full of his %, per our draft on S. S. Packard, $——...... Bo't for W. W. Harder, $25000 Galena & Chic. R. R. Stock, @92½¢: Our commission, ¼%...... Bo't $30000 U. S. 7 3/10% Treas. Notes, @ $1 [04½]: Interest due on same from Nov. 1, 1862, $——...... Received cash of J. E. Jenkins, in full of %, $——...... Sold $20000 Gold, @ $1 [68½].... Sold for S. S. Packard, $25000 Gold, @ $1 [68¼]: Our commission, ¼%...... Bo't uncurrent funds, viz.; $4000 Missouri, @ 2% disc.; $3000 Free Indiana, @ 2% disc.

Saturday, 7.—Sold $7000 Canada currency, @ $1 [54]...... Paid Culver & Penn's draft on us for $7000. ..... Bo't $10000 U. S. 1 Yr. Certificates, @ $1 [02½]: Interest on same from Dec. 16, 1862, $——..... Sold for Culver, Penn & Co., $20000 Pacific Mail Steamship Co., @ $1 [67]: Our commission, ¼%...... Bo't uncurrent funds, viz.: $5000 New England, @ ½% disc.; $4000 New York State, @ ¼% disc.; $1500 Michigan, @ 1% disc.; $2500 Kentucky, @ ½% disc...... Paid S. S. Packard's draft, favor Culver, Penn & Co., for $25000..... Sold $25000 U. S. Coupon 6%, '81, @ $1 [03½]: Interest on same, as follows: $5000 from Nov. 1, 1862, $——; $10000 from Dec. 1, 1862, $——; $10000 from Jan. 1, 1863, $——...... Sold $5000 U. S. 1 Yr. 6% Certificates, @ $1 [04]: Interest due on same, as follows: $20000 from Jan. 1, 1863, $——; $10000 from Jan. 15, '63, $——; $10000 from Feb. 1, '63, $——; $10000 from Dec. 16, 1862, $——...... Paid Culver, Penn & Co., cash to balance %, $——...... Sold £1500 Sterling Exchange, @ $1 [78]...... Sold $6000 Missouri funds, @ 1% disc.; $4000 Indiana, @ 1% disc.

Inventory, March 7

U. S. 7 3/10% Treasury Notes, $30000, @ $1 [05]	31500	
Interest on same, from Nov. 1, 1862	756	

Statement, March 7.

Resources.			
Cash	106987 24		
Interest	756		
U S. Treasury Notes	31500		
W. W. Harder	23120 15	162363	39
Liabilities.			
H. R. Munger	1797 29		
S. S. Packard	4651 47	6448	76
Net Capital		155914	63

BLOTTER.

New York, Monday, March 2, 1863.

Description.	*Rate.*	*Out.*		*Description.*	*Rate.*	*In.*	
1000 Illinois	$1\frac{1}{2}$	15		2000 Illinois	2	40	
Bal. to C. B.		80		1000 Kentucky	$\frac{1}{2}$	5	
				2500 Missouri	2	50	
		95				95	

Tuesday, 3.

Description.	*Rate.*	*Out.*		*Description.*	*Rate.*	*In.*	
2500 Missouri	1	25		3500 N. Y. State	$\frac{1}{4}$	8	75
1000 Kentucky	$\frac{1}{4}$	2	50	2000 Baltimore	1	20	
Bal. to C. B.		133	75	5000 N. Y. State	$\frac{1}{4}$	12	50
				3000 Indiana	4	120	
		161	25			161	25

Wednesday, 4.

Description.	*Rate.*	*Out.*		*Description.*	*Rate.*	*In.*	
3000 Wisconsin	1	40		1000 Wisconsin	$1\frac{1}{2}$	15	
4000 Indiana	$2\frac{1}{2}$	75		900 Michigan	1	9	
				500 Missouri	2	10	
				300 Indiana	2	6	
				3000 Wisconsin	$1\frac{3}{4}$	52	56
				Bal. to C. B.		2[illegible]	56
		115				115	

CASH

NEW YORK, MONDAY,

Day	Fol.	Account	Explanation	$	cts.	$	cts.
2	1	Stock	Amount invested	150000			
	2	H. R. Munger	Deposit	10000			
	3	Com. and Brokerage	H. R. M. on $8000 N. Y. C. R. R.	23	60		
	4	Exchange	Balance from Blotter	80		160103	60
						160103	60
			Balance brought down			119630	65
3	11	Canada Currency	2500 . . . 1.54	3850			
	5	S. S. Packard	Deposit	20000			
	12	U. S. Reg. 6 %, 1881	10000 . . . 1.01	10100			
	6	Interest	On same from Nov. 1, 1862	200	55		
	7	J. E. Jenkins	Sale of New York & Erie Bonds,				
			20000 . . @ 1.07 . . $21400 00				
			Less ¼ % Com. 53 50	21346	50		
	3	Com. and Brokerage	As above	53	50		
	3	Com. and Brokerage	S. S. P. on 15000 Cleve. & Tol.	35	44		
	8	H. D. Stratton	Sale of N. J. R. R. Stocks,				
			15000 . . @ 1.55 . $23200 00				
			Less ¼ % Com. 58 00	23142			
	3	Com. and Brokerage	As above	58			
	4	Exchange	Balance per Blotter	133	75	78919	74
						198550	39
			Balance brought down			155639	95
4	2	H. R. Munger	Sale of Gold, viz.:				
			15000 . . @ 1.66¾ . . $25012 50				
			Less ¼ % Com. 62 53	24949	97		
	3	Com. and Brokerage	As above	62	53		
	7	J. E. Jenkins	Sale of Mich. Coup., 1888,				
			25000 . . @ 1.02 . . $25500 00				
			Less ¼ % Com. 63 75	25436	25		
	3	Com. and Brokerage	As above	63	75		
	3	Com. and Brokerage	J. E. J. on $50000, Gold	102	50		
	3	Com. and Brokerage	Sale of N. Y. & E. for G. A. R.,				
			15000 . . @ 1.02 . . $15300 00				
			Our Com. ¼ %	38	25		
	11	Canada Currency	1000 . . . 1.55	1550			
	3	Com. and Brokerage	H. R. M. on 10000 Panama	47	38		
	15	Gold	25000 . . . 1.68	42000			
	14	Del. & Lack. 1st Mort.	10000 . . . 1.25	12500			
	17	Sterling Exchange	£2000=$8888.89 . . . 1.80	16000			
	9	Culver, Penn & Co.	Sale of N. Y. C. R. R. Stock,				
			15000 . . @ 1.20 . . $18000 00				
			Less ¼ % Com. 45 00	17955			
	3	Com. and Brokerage	As above	45		140750	63
						296390	58
			Balance brought down			58728	55

BOOK.

MARCH 2, 1863.

Day	Fo.	Account	Particulars	Rate	Amount	¢	Total	¢
2	11	Canada Currency	2000	1.53	3060			
			1500	1.53¼	2302	50		
	12	U. S. Reg. 6 %, 1881	10000	1.00	10000			
	6	Interest	On above, from Nov. 1, 1862		198	90		
	13	U. S. Coupon, 6 %, 1881	15000	1.02	15300			
	6	Interest	On above, from Jan. 1, 1863		147	95		
	2	H. R. Munger	8000 N. Y. C. R. R.	1.18	9440			
			Our Com. on above, ¼ %		23	60	40472	95
			Balance carried down				119630	65
							160103	60
3	14	Del. & Lack. 1st Mort.	10000	1.22	12200			
	15	Gold	10000	1.65	16500			
	5	S. S. Packard	15000 Cleve. & Tol.	94½	14175			
			Our Com. on above, ¼ %		35	44	42910	44
			Balance carried down				155639	95
							198550	39
4	7	J. E. Jenkins	To balance %		21346	50		
	16	U. S. 7 3/10 Treas. Notes	15000	1.04	15600			
	6	Interest	On above, from Nov. 1, 1862		369			
	17	Sterling Exchange	£2000=$8888.89	1.78	15822	22		
	7	J. E. Jenkins	50000, Gold	1.64	82000			
			Our Com. on above, ⅛ %		102	50		
	15	Gold	15000	1.65½	24825			
	2	H. R. Munger	10000 Panama	1.89½	18950			
			Our Com. on above, ¼ %		47	38		
	18	U. S. 1 Yr. 6 % Cert.	25000	1.01	25250			
	6	Interest	5000 from Jan. 1	51.78				
			10000 " " 15	80.55				
			10000 " Feb. 1	52.60	184	93		
	8	H. D. Stratton	To balance %		23142			
	9	Culver, Penn & Co.	Draft favor H. B. Bryant		10000			
	4	Exchange	Balance per Blotter		22	50	237662	03
			Balance carried down				58728	55
							296390	58

GENERAL LEDGER.

1 Stock. 1

Date				$	cts	Date				$	cts
1863						1863.					
Mar.	4	*Balance* . . .		152165	60	*Mar.*	2	Amount invested .		150000	
						"	4	Loss and Gain . .		2165	60
				152165	60					152165	60
						Mar.	4	Balance . . .		152165	60

2 H. R. Munger. 2

Date				$	cts	Date				$	cts
1863						1863.					
Mar.	2	8000 N. Y. C. .	1.18	9440		*Mar.*	2	Deposit.		10000	
"	"	Our ¼ % Com. . .		23	60	"	4	Proceeds of Gold .		24949	97
"	4	10000 Panama .	1.89½	18950							
"	"	Our ¼ % Com. . .		47	38						
"	"	*Balance*		6488	99						
				34949	97					34949	97
						Mar.	4	Balance		6488	99

3 Commission and Brokerage. 3

Date				$	cts	Date				$	cts
1863						1863					
Mar.	4	*Loss and Gain* .		529	95	*Mar.*	2	H. R. M. on N. Y. C.		23	60
						"	3	J. E. J. on N. Y. & E.		53	50
						"	"	S. S. P. on Clev. & Tol.		35	44
						"	"	H. D. S. on N. J. R. R.		58	
						"	4	H. R. M. on Gold. .		62	53
						"	"	J. E. J. on Mich. Coup.		63	75
						"	"	" " on Gold . .		102	50
						"	"	G. A. R. on N.Y. & E.		38	25
						"	"	H. R. M. on Panama		47	38
						"	"	C. P. & Co. on N.Y. C.		45	
				529	95					529	95

4 Exchange. 4

Date				$	cts	Date				$	cts
1863						1863					
Mar.	4	Balance pr. Blotter		22	50	*Mar.*	2	Balance from Blotter		80	
"	"	*Loss and Gain* . .		191	25	"	3	" " "		133	75
				213	75					213	75

5 S. S. Packard. 5

Date				$	cts	Date				$	cts
1863						1863					
Mar.	3	15000 Clev. & Tol.	94½	14175		*Mar*	3	Deposit.		20000	
		Our ¼ % Com. . .		35	44						
"	4	*Balance*		5789	56						
				20000						20000	
								Balance		5789	56

GENERAL LEDGER.

6 Interest. 6

Date	Day	Particulars		$	cts	Date	Day	Particulars		$	cts
1863						1863					
Mar.	2	U. S. Reg. 6 %, '81		198	90	Mar.	3	On U. S. Reg. 6 %, '81		200	55
"	"	U. S. Coup. 6 % .		147	95	"	4	*U. S. Coup.*, 6 %, '81		150	42
"	4	U. S. 7 3/10 Tr. Notes		369				*U. S. 7 3/10 Treas.* . .		369	
		U. S. 1 yr. 6 % Cert.		184	93			*U. S. 1 Yr. 6 % Cert.*		184	93
		Loss and Gain .		4	12						
				904	90					904	90
Mar.	4	Balance		704	35						

7 J. E. Jenkins. 7

Date	Day	Particulars		$	cts	Date	Day	Particulars		$	cts
1863						1863					
Mar	3	To balance % .		21346	50	Mar.	3	Proceeds N. Y. & E.		21346	50
"	4	50000 Gold . .	1.64	82000		"	4	Proceeds Mich. Coup.		25436	25
		Our 1/8 % Com. . .		102	50			*Balance*		56666	25
				103449						103449	
Mar.	4	Balance		56666	25						

8 H. D. Stratton. 8

Date	Day	Particulars		$	cts	Date	Day	Particulars		$	cts
1863						1863					
Mar.	3	To balance % . .		23142		Mar.	3	Proceeds N. J. R. R.		23142	

9 Culver, Penn & Co. 9

Date	Day	Particulars		$	cts	Date	Day	Particulars		$	cts
1862						1863					
Mar	4	Dft. fav H. H. B.		10000		Mar.	4	Proceeds N. Y. C. .		17955	
"	"	*Balance* . .		7955							
				17955						17955	
						Mar.	4	Balance		7955	

10 Loss and Gain. 10

Date	Day	Particulars		$	cts	Date	Day	Particulars		$	cts
1863						1863					
Mar.	4	*Stock* . . .		2165	60	Mar.	4	Com. and Brokerage		529	95
								Exchange		191	25
								Interest		4	12
								Canada Currency .		37	50
								U. S. Reg. 6 % . .		100	
								U. S. Coup. 6 % . .		150	
								Del. & Lack. 1st Mort.		300	
								Gold		675	
								Sterling Exchange .		177	78
				2165	60					2165	60

11 Canada Currency. 11

1863							1863					
Mar.	2	2000		1.53	3060		*Mar.*	3	2500		1.54	3850
"	4	1500	*L. & G.*	1.53½	2302	50	"	4	1000		1.55	1550
					37	50						
		3500			5400	00			3500			5400

12 U. S. Reg. 6 p. c., 1881. 12

1863							1863					
Mar.	2	10000	*L. & G.*	1.00	10000		*Mar.*	3	10000		1.01	10100
					100							
		10000			10100				10000			10100

13 U. S. Coupon, 6 p. c., 1881. 13

1863							1863					
Mar.	3	15000	*L. & G.*	1.02	15300		*Mar.*	4	15000	*Bal.* . .	1.03	15450
					150							
		15000			15450				15000			15450
Mar.	4	15000		1.03	15450							

14 Delaware and Lackawanna. 14

1863							1863					
Mar.	3	10000	*L. & G.*	1.22	12200		*Mar.*	4	10000		1.25	12500
					300							
		10000			12500				10000			12500

STOCK LEDGER.

15 Gold. 15

1863.							1863.						
Mar.	3	10000		1.65	16500		*Mar.*	4	25000		1.68	42000	
"	4	15000	*L. & G.*	$1.65\frac{1}{8}$	24825								
					675								
		25000			42000				25000			42000	

16 U. S. $7\frac{3}{10}$ p. c. Treas. Notes. 16

1863.													
Mar.	4	15000		1.04	15600								

17 Sterling Exchange. 17

1863.							1863.						
Mar.	4	£2000	$8888.89 *L. & G.*	1.78	15822	22	*Mar.*	4	£2000	$8888.89	1.80	16000	
					177	78							
		2000			16000				2000			16000	

18 U. S. 1 Yr. 6 p. c. Certificates. 18

1863.													
Mar.	4	25000		1 01	25250								

UNITED STATES "FIVE-TWENTY" COUPON BOND.

Treasurer's Department. | **Register's Office.**

1000 — No. 52351. — No. 52351. — 1000

IT IS HEREBY CERTIFIED THAT

The UNITED STATES OF AMERICA

Are indebted unto

S. S. Packard,

or Bearer, the sum of ONE THOUSAND DOLLARS, *redeemable at the pleasure of the United States after the 30th day of April, 1867, and payable on the 30th day of April, 1882, with interest from the 1st day of May, 1862, inclusive, at Six per cent per annum, payable on the first day of May and November in each year, on the presentation of the proper coupon, hereunto annexed. This debt authorized by Act of Congress, approved Feb. 25th, 1862.*

Entered ---- D. S. P.

Recorded ---- D. O.

Redeemable after Five Years,
and Payable Twenty Years from date.

Loan of Feb. 25, 1862.

Washington, May 1, 1862.

L. E. CHITTENDEN,

Register of the Treasury.

Six months' interest, due 1st May, 1882, payable with this bond.

---

30 Act of Feb. 25th, 1862. 30

THE United States of America

Will pay the bearer

THIRTY DOLLARS,

for Six Months' interest, due Nov. 1, 1881,
upon Bond 52351.

L. E. CHITTENDEN,

$1000. *Reg. U. S. Treas.*

---

30 Act of Feb. 25th, 1862. 30

THE United States of America

Will pay the bearer

THIRTY DOLLARS,

for Six Months' interest, due May 1, 1881,
upon Bond 52351.

L. E. CHITTENDEN,

$1000. *Reg. U. S. Treas.*

---

30 Act of Feb. 25th, 1862. 30

THE United States of America

Will pay the bearer

THIRTY DOLLARS,

for Six Months' interest, due Nov. 1, 1880,
upon Bond 52351.

L. E. CHITTENDEN,

$1000. *Reg. U. S. Treas.*

---

30 Act of Feb. 25th, 1862. 30

THE United States of America

Will pay the bearer

THIRTY DOLLARS,

for Six Months' interest, due May 1, 1880,
upon Bond 52351.

L. E. CHITTENDEN,

$1000. *Reg. U. S. Treas.*

U. S Registers Bond.

No.

Proceeds of the sale of Public Lands pledged to pay Principal and Interest.

$10,000.

Trea'r. Department

$10,000.

Register's Office.

LOAN OF 1847.

It is hereby certified that the UNITED STATES OF AMERICA, *are indebted to* PETER COOPER, *or his assigns, the sum of* TEN THOUSAND DOLLARS, *"after the last day of December, 1867," with interest from the 10th day of June, 1847, inclusive, at Six per cent. per annum, payable on the first days of January and July, in each year. This debt is authorized by an Act of Congress approved January 28th, 1847, and is transferable on the books of this office.*

Entered, June 10, 1847.

Recorded, June 12, 1847.

SEAL.

Signed,

REGISTER U. S. TREASURY.

Railroad Shares.

DELAWARE, LACKAWANNA & WESTERN

RAILROAD COMPANY,

STATE OF PENNSYLVANIA.

Number.

Shares

SHARES.

This is to Certify that CHARLES E. CARRYL *is entitled to*-----ONE HUNDRED----*Shares of the Capital Stock of the* DELAWARE, LACKAWANNA & WESTERN RAILROAD COMPANY, *transferable only on the Books of the Company in the City of New York by him or his Attorney, upon the surrender of this Certificate.*

In Testimony whereof, *the said Company have caused this Certificate to be signed by their President and Treasurer, and sealed with their corporate seal.*

NEW YORK, *January*, 1860.

$50 EACH.

Treasr.

Prest.

UNITED STATES OF AMERICA,

State of Pennsylvania.

No. $500

CONVERTIBLE MORTGAGE BOND OF 1881.

The Delaware, Lackawanna and Western Railroad Company.

KNOW ALL MEN BY THESE PRESENTS, *That The Delaware, Lackawanna and Western Railroad Company* acknowledge themselves indebted and bound to
paid to the said .... in the sum of **FIVE HUNDRED DOLLARS**, lawful money of the United States of America, to be
.... or his assigns, at their Office, in the City of New-York, on the First Day of March, in the year Eighteen
Hundred and Eighty-one, with interest thereon, at the rate of SEVEN PER CENT. per annum, payable semi-annually, at the office of said Company in the City of New York, on the first days of March
and September, in each year, on the presentation and surrender, as they fall due, of the annexed coupons, or interest warrants; the first payment of interest to be made on the first day of September
next ensuing the date hereof.

This Bond is one of a series of twenty-seven hundred of the like tenor and date, twenty-five hundred of which are each for One Thousand Dollars, and two hundred of which are each for
Five Hundred Dollars, in the aggregate amounting to Twenty-Six Hundred Thousand Dollars, executed and issued, or to be issued from time to time, as the wants of said Company shall
require, for the construction of a second track upon their railroad, purchasing the necessary equipment for operating the same, and other purposes; and the holder is entitled to the security to be
derived from a Mortgage bearing even date herewith upon the said railroad, constructed and to be constructed, from its connection with the New York and Erie Railroad, at Great Bend, to the crossing
of the Delaware River, (a distance of one hundred and ten miles,) including all lands, rights of way, privileges and easements in or relating to the lands occupied by said railroad, or over which the same
shall pass, also the Coal Estates and Mines of said Company, together with its corporate rights and franchises; which mortgage is executed by said Company and delivered to SAMUEL WILLETS and
SAMUEL L. MITCHILL, in trust, to secure the principal and interest of said Bonds, and duly recorded in the several counties through which said road passes, in the Commonwealth of Pennsylvania
—subject only to the prior liens of Twenty-Four Hundred Thousand Dollars; of which amount the sum of $900,000, payable January 1st, 1871, is secured by a Mortgage, executed to Samuel Marsh and
Daniel S. Miller, trustees, and the sum of $1,500,000, payable April 1st, 1875, is secured by a Mortgage executed to Moses Taylor and L. A. Von Hoffman, trustees.

And said Company hereby agree that the holder of this Bond may transfer the same at pleasure, either in person or by attorney, only upon the books of the Company, at their Office in the City
of New York, such transfer to be endorsed hereon by the Treasurer, excepting when the same has been previously transferred on said books *to Bearer*, and so endorsed hereon by the Treasurer, in
which case it will be transferable by mere delivery until the holder shall again have the same transferred on the books of the Company, to some person or persons named in such transfer; also, that said
holder of this Bond shall have the privilege, at any time before the first day of April, 1862, to convert the principal sum into the Capital Stock of the Company, at par, on surrendering the Bond with
the coupons not then due, to their Treasurer at their Office in the City of New York.

In Witness whereof, the said Company have caused this Bond to be signed in their behalf by their President and Treasurer, and their corporate Seal affixed, at
their Office in Scranton, Pennsylvania, the first day of April, in the year of our Lord one thousand eight hundred and fifty-six.

.... Treasurer. .... President.

THE DELAWARE LACKAWANNA & WESTERN Railroad Company.
Will pay the bearer hereof on the first day of March, 1881, SEVENTEEN $\frac{50}{100}$ DOLLARS, at their Office in the City of New York for interest due that day on their Bond. No. ....
$17\frac{50}{100}$ .... FOR THE TREASURER.

50

THE DELAWARE LACKAWANNA & WESTERN Railroad Company.
Will pay the bearer hereof on the first day of September, 1880, SEVENTEEN $\frac{50}{100}$ DOLLARS, at their Office in the City of New York, for interest due that day on their Bond. No. ....
$17\frac{50}{100}$ .... FOR THE TREASURER.

49

THE DELAWARE LACKAWANNA & WESTERN Railroad Company.
Will pay the bearer hereof on the first day of March, 1880, SEVENTEEN $\frac{50}{100}$ DOLLARS, at their Office in the City of New York, for interest due that day on their Bond. No. ....
$17\frac{50}{100}$ .... FOR THE TREASURER.

48

FOREIGN BILLS.

NOTE.—Foreign Bills of Exchange are usually drawn in sets of three; one of which being honored, the others become void. This precaution is used to guard against the contingencies of transmission; the separate bills being sent by different routes, or at different times.—A *single* bill is called a "sola."

We give below examples of the first and second bills of a set, and also one of a sola.

Foreign Bills are usually drawn in the currency of the country where payable, instead of that where drawn

1 **Exchange for** *New York, March 1, 1863.*

£1000. *Ten days after sight of this* FIRST *of Exchange, (second and third unpaid) pay to the order of* **ELIHU BURRITT, One Thousand Pounds Sterling,** *value received, and charge to account of*

To Messrs. N. M. Rothschild & Son,
No. 15750. London.

BRYANT, STRATTON & PACKARD.

2 **Exchange for** *New York, March 1, 1863.*

£1000. *Ten days after sight of this* SECOND *of Exchange, (first and third unpaid) pay to the order of* **ELIHU BURRITT, One Thousand Pounds Sterling,** *value received, and charge to account of*

To Messrs. N. M. Rothschild & Son,
No. 15750. London.

BRYANT, STRATTON & PACKARD

Exchange for *New York, March 5, 1863.*

Rx. 1000. *Sixty days after sight of this* SOLA *of Exchange, pay to the order of* CHESTER PACKARD, *in Bremen,* One Thousand Bremen Rix Thalers, *value received, and charge the same to account of*

To Messrs Meyer & Schmidt,
No. 127. Bremen.

BRYANT, STRATTON & PACKARD.

COMMERCIAL CALCULATIONS.

COMMERCIAL CALCULATIONS.

It will, of course, be impossible to do more than hint at a few of the most prominent questions properly embraced under this general subject; and it shall be our earnest aim to make these of the most practical kind. The very idea of accountantship is inseparable from a thorough knowledge of calculations; and all theoretical abstractions which lie at the basis of the science of accounts, will be found of little avail without he practical results which come alone through the almost magical power of figures.

ADDITION.

The simple process of addition would seem to need no enforcement or illustration; and yet there is no part of the science of numbers more important to accountants, or in which they are more apt to be deficient. We mean, of course, the process as applied to the addition of long columns of figures, which should be done with facility and correctness. Authors and teachers have shown both ability and ingenuity in their various suggestions and aids, but nothing can be of so much service to the student as *continued practice.* The most approved method of testing the correctness of addition is to add the columns in both directions, first upward and then downward, or the reverse. The philosophy of this is, that the combinations are thus varied, and the chance of committing the same error twice is avoided.

Three very simple processes of retaining the figure to be carried to the next column—a very important consideration with beginners—are shown below. The first is the usual method of writing the figure to be carried, *small,* under the unit amount of the column which produced it. The second requires the addition of each separate column to be written down on a waste space, commencing with the right-hand column, and carrying to the next column, as in the usual method; these separate amounts placed in their order one under the other, will present in their unit figures, counting upward, the general result. The third method consists of the proper arrangement of the independent sum of each column, so that being again added, the proper result is secured.

Examples.

First Process.

1829.25
743.18
2562.28
145.19
2823.25
7574.28
4291.83
25.64
19994.90
333.25

Second Process.

1st.	column	50
2d.	"	29
3d.	"	34
4th.	"	39
5th.	"	39
6th.	"	19994.90

Third Process.

```
        5 0
      2 4 ·
    3 2 · ·
  3 6 · · ·
 3 6 · · · ·
1 6 · · · · ·
-------------
1 9 9 9 4 . 9 0
```

When the student becomes more accurate and self-reliant, he may feel justified in dispensing with all such aids; and particularly if his memory is sufficient to retain the carrying figure; but until he arrives at this desirable state of perfection, it becomes him to guard himself on every hand. Great proficiency in this regard may be readily acquired by practice, some accountants being able, very readily to cast up three and four columns of figures at once.

INTEREST.

Interest, in the accountant's vocabulary, means *the use of money.* The amount received or paid *for* interest is usually a percentage on the sum used, and is fixed either by contract or statute. *Per cent.* signifies *by the hundred,* and implies, in interest, so many cents on the hundred cents, so many dollars on the hundred dollars, etc. It is usual to reckon interest by the year; but it is always proper to express the time, as it is not necessarily understood.

In calculating *per annum* interest, it is customary to reckon 360 days to the year, and 30 days to the month; although in some states the whole number, 365 days, is reckoned to the year, and any number of days as a proportion of 365. In the State of New York the basis of 360 days to the year is fixed by law. The section reads thus: "For the purpose of calculating interest, a month shall be considered a twelfth part of a year, and as consisting of thirty days; and interest for any number of days less than a month shall be estimated by the proportion which such number of days shall bear to thirty." There are those, however, who consider interest reckoned on this basis as usurious, it being $\frac{1}{73}$ more than by the basis of 365 days to the year.

In the illustrations which follow we shall adopt the usual standard of 360 days.

The rate, or *per centage* of interest is established by law in most countries and states. Any excess over this rate is termed usury, for the exaction of which various penalties are prescribed.

The rate of interest in Pennsylvania, New Jersey, (except in Jersey City and Hoboken,) Delaware, Mary land, Virginia, North Carolina, South Carolina, Tennessee, Kentucky, Ohio, Indiana, Illinois, Iowa, Missouri, Arkansas, Mississippi, Florida, the six Eastern States, the District of Columbia, and on debts due the United States, is 6 per cent. per annum.

In New York, Michigan, Wisconsin, and Georgia, it is 7 per cent.

In Alabama, 8 per cent.

In California, 10 per cent.

In Louisiana, 5 per cent.

In most of the states the law permits a higher than the established rate, in cases of special contract.

In reckoning interest, at whatever rate, it is most convenient first to obtain it, for the given time, at 6 per cent., and then add or subtract for the difference. Particularly is this the case, where 360 days are reckoned to the year; 6 being an aliquot part both of 360, the number of *days* in the year, and 12, the number of *months*.

There are many processes of reckoning interest, all more or less worthy of thought; but we shall confine our practice to the one which, under all circumstances, we consider the best.

Taking as a basis 360 days to a year, 30 days to a month, and 6 per cent. per annum, we are easily led to the following conclusion: If 12 months produce 6 per cent., 1 month will produce one-twelfth of 6, or one-half of 1 per cent., and two months, 1 per cent. One per cent. of any amount, therefore, is the interest on that amount for 2 months, or 60 days, at the rate of 6 per cent. per annum. One per cent. being the one hundredth part of any amount, is easily obtained by dividing by 100, or, what is the same, cutting off two right-hand figures.

EXAMPLE 1.—Required the interest on $3750, for 2 months, at 6 per cent. per annum.

Solution: 37 | 50; or $37.50

Having this starting point, the process of obtaining the interest for any given number of months or days becomes extremely simple.

EXAMPLE 2.—Find the interest on $4675 for 3 months, 15 days, at 6 per cent.

Solution:

2)46	75	= 2 months.
2)23	375	= 1 month.
11	6875	= 15 days.
81	8125	

REMARKS.—We first find the interest for 2 months by the process already given, which is $46.75. Dividing this amount by 2, will give us the interest for 1 month, $23.375; and this by 2 will give the interest for one-half a month, or 15 days, $11.6875. By adding these results together, we get the grand result, $81.81 +.

Should the number of days be no equal part of 60, nor of any other number for which the result is shown, it will be necessary to use such component parts as are equal parts of 60. Thus, if the number of days be 13, we can take 1 and 12, or 3 and 10; 1 being the sixtieth part, 12 the fifth; 3 the twentieth, and 10 the sixth of 60. If the number of days be 18, take 6 and 12, or 3 and 15, and so on.

From these remarks and illustrations, we are prepared to submit the following rule for reckoning interest on any given amount for any given time, at 6 per cent. per annum.

RULE.—*Cut off two figures from the right of dollars in the principal, by a perpendicular line; the result will be the interest for* 60 *days, the dollars being on the left, and the cents and mills on the right of the line. Multiply this result by one-half the number of months required, to which add, for days, that proportion of the interest for* 60 *days which the given number of days is of* 60.

The using of a perpendicular line for the separatrix is of more consequence than will appear at first view. All necessity for pointing off in the product is thus happily dispensed with, and the work is brought within the smallest possible compass. For universal use, we do not know of a better rule for computing interest than the foregoing.

If the rate of interest be any other than 6 per cent., the proper proportions added to, or deducted from, 6 per cent., will, of course, produce the result. If 5 per cent., deduct $\frac{1}{6}$; if 7 per cent., add $\frac{1}{6}$; if 8 per cent., add $\frac{2}{6}$, or $\frac{1}{3}$; if 9 per cent., add $\frac{1}{2}$, etc.

DISCOUNT

Discount is an allowance made for the payment of a debt before it is due. The *present worth* of such a debt is that sum which being put at interest for the given time, would at the end of that time amount to the face of the debt.

Thus, if I owe $106 due in one year, without interest, and money is worth 6 per cent. per annum, the *present worth* of the debt is $100; because $100 at 6 per cent. will amount in one year to $106. The *discount* would, in such case, be $6; which is the *difference* between the *present* value of the debt, and its value one year hence.

To find the *present worth* of any sum due at any given time and rate, it is only necessary to divide the sum by the amount of $1 at the given rate and time. To find the *discount*, subtract the present worth from the given sum.

Example 1.—What is the present worth of a note for $750, due in 4 months, without interest, if the use of money is worth 6 per cent. per annum?

Solution.—The amount of $1 for 4 months at 6 per cent. per annum is $1.02; therefore, $750 divided by $1.02, will be the present worth:

750 ÷ $1.02 = 735.29 + *present worth.*

The *discount* on the above note can be obtained by subtracting the present worth from the note, viz.: 750 − 735.29 = $14.71.

The rule and process above will obtain the *true* discount; but business custom varies from this standard. Business discount, as it is called, is simply interest on the face of the debt, taken in advance. Thus, if I owe $106, due in one year without interest, when money is worth 6 per cent. per annum, and I wish to discount the debt, or pay it *now*, business custom warrants me in computing the *interest* on $106 for the time, which interest is deducted from the debt, leaving the present worth, or the sum I am to pay. The interest for one year at 6 % on $106, is $6.36, which deducted from $106, leaves as present worth $99.64, instead of $100, which, as before shown, is the *true* worth.

By this method I gain 36 cents, which, it will be seen, is the interest on the *true* discount, $6 for 1 year. The difference between these two methods then, is, that by *true* discount the interest is considered due when the debt is due; while by *business* discount it is considered due when the debt is discounted.

Example 2.—What is the present worth of a note for $1500, due in 60 days without interest, when money is worth 6 % per annum; discount reckoned by the business standard?

Solution.—The interest on $1500 for 60 days at 6 %, is $15; which deducted from the face of the note, $1500, leaves the present worth, $1485.

There are various and conflicting opinions as to the legality of this mode of reckoning discount, but as it is almost universally used, both in banks and business houses, we must concede its practical authority.

EQUATION OF PAYMENTS.

Equation of Payments, or Average, as it is more frequently called, is the finding of an *average* or *mean* time for the payment of several amounts, due at different times; and also, when the *balance* of an account having both debit and credit amounts, will average due, that no loss may be sustained by either party. The philosophy of equation is based upon the compound relation of *money* and *time;* or upon a recognition of the fact that the *value* of the use of money is in proportion to the *amount* used, and the *time* for which it is used. As a simple illustration: if the use of $100 is worth a certain sum for one month, it is worth *twice* that sum for two months; or, if $100 is worth a certain sum for one month, $200 for the *same* time is worth *twice* as much.

EXAMPLE 1.—A owes B $1200, payable as follows: $100, in 30 days; $400, in 60 days; and $700 in 90 days. When will the entire debt average due?

Solution.—The question is, how long may $1200 be used, to be equivalent to the use of $100, for 30 days, $400, for 60 days; and $700 for 90 days?

The use of	$100	for	30	days is equal to the use of	$1	for	3000	days.
"	$400	"	60	" " "	$1	"	24000	"
"	$700	"	90	" " "	$1	"	63000	"
	$1200						90000	

Therefore, the use of $1 for 90000 days would be equivalent to the time to which A is entitled on his deb of $1200. We have, then, this statement:

The use of $1 for 90000 days is equal to that of $1200 for 75 days.

The *average* time for the payment of A's entire debt, is 75 days hence.

We are thus enabled to give a general rule for finding the average time of payment of several amounts, due at different times.

RULE.—*Multiply each payment by the number of days before it is due, and divide the sum of the* PRODUCTS *by the sum of the payments. The quotient will be the number of days (to be counted forward from the date of reckoning), to the average time of payment.*

EXAMPLE 2.—Abram Jones purchased of Samuel Lincoln the following bills of merchandise:

Jan. 1, 1860,	a bill amounting	$175.34
Apr. 15,	" " "	$538.25
Apr. 30,	" " "	$180.60
June 9,	" " "	$400.00

The term of credit on each purchase is 4 months. If Mr. Jones should propose to give his note for the full amount, due in 4 months from date, when should the note be dated?

NOTE.—To apply the foregoing, or any other adequate rule to a statement of this kind, it will be necessary first, to settle upon some date from which the time on each payment is to be reckoned. It is usually best to select the date, either of the *first* or *last* amount, and reckon backwards or forwards, counting the average time accordingly. As the purchases are all made on 4 months' time, and the note is to be drawn at 4 months it will not be necessary to take either fact into consideration. If, in this case, we select the *first* date from which to count, we shall have the following solution:

Amounts.		*Days before due.*		*Products.*
175.34	×	0	=	0
538.25	×	104	=	55978.00
180.60	×	119	=	21541.40
400.00	×	159	=	63600.00
$1294.19		)		141119.40 (108 + days.

The average is 108 days; which is the number to be counted *forward* from the date selected, Jan. 1. The note must be dated Apr. 19.

AVERAGING ACCOUNTS CURRENT.

AN ACCOUNT CURRENT is a statement of the transactions between two parties, showing dates, items, and amounts, both debit and credit, during a certain period.

The *balance* of an Account Current is the difference between the debits and credits; or what one party is owing the other, as indicated by the items.

To *average* an Account Current is to fix the date when the *balance* is due. The adjustment is called "Compound Equation," or "Compound Average." The usual process is, *first to average each side of the account; and then multiply the amount earliest due by the number of days between the average dates, and divide the product by the balance of the account. The quotient will be the number of days from the latest date, when the balance will average due; to be counted* FORWARD *if the amount latest due is the larger, and* BACKWARD *if the amount latest due is the smaller.*

A better process than this, we think, because more easily comprehended and practical, is the averaging by interest. Not having space to exemplify more than one method, we shall choose the latter.

EXAMPLE 1.—The following account is found on my Ledger. The amounts on each side are supposed to be due at their several dates. When is the *balance* due?

Dr. JOHN ANDERSON. *Cr.*

Jan.	15	To Mdse	275	*Feb.*	1	By Cash	500
Apr.	10	"	650			*Balance*	425
			925				925

Solution.—First assume the date of settlement to be the latest date on which any amount, debit or credit, falls due, and reckon interest on the debit and credit items to that date, viz.:

Credit.—The interest on $500 from Feb. 1 to Apr. 10, @ 6 %, is $5.75.
Debit.—The interest on $275 from Jan. 15 to Apr. 10, @ 6 %, is 3.90.
Excess of credit interest, $1.85.

It will thus appear that on the assumed date of settlement, April 10, Mr. Anderson owed me $925 of account, and $3.90 interest; while I owed him $500 of account, and $5.75 interest. In other words: he owed me the *balance* of the account ($425) less the balance of interest ($1.85). It would be very easy to settle the account at this date, provided the rate of interest was satisfactory, by deducting the balance of interest from the balance of account; but, instead of this, it is proposed that Mr. Anderson pay me the *exact balance* shown to be due by his account, *at such time* as will secure an equitable adjustment of the interest. It will be evident that were he to pay me the balance of account on the assumed day of settlement, April 10, he would be the loser of the balance of interest due him at that date. The simple question then, is, how long may he retain the balance of account ($425), to accumulate the balance of interest ($1.85)?

First ascertain how much the balance of account will accumulate in *one* day, and divide the balance of interest by it: the quotient will be the number of days which the balance may be held.

The interest on $425 for one day, at 6 % per annum, is $.0708.

Then, $1.85 ÷ $.0708 = 26 + = the number of days.

In 26 days from April 10, then, which will be May 6, Mr. Anderson will owe me, by average, the balance of his account, $425.

EXAMPLE 2.—When will the balance of the following account average due, assuming the different items to be due at their several dates?

Dr. ALONZO MITCHELL. *Cr.*

May	1	To Mdse	185	*June*	1	By Cash	400
"	15	"	750	"	15	"	200
July	1	"	475			*Balance*	810
			1410				1410

Solution.—Assuming the date of settlement to be July 1, we have:

Debit Interest.

$185 from May 1, to July 1—2 mo., $1.85
$750 " " 15, " "—1 mo. 15 da., $5.63 $7.48

Credit Interest.

$400 from June 1 to July 1— 1 mo. . . $2.00
$200 " " " " "—15 da. . . $0.50 $2.50
Leaving the excess of *debit interest*, $4.98

On July 1, the assumed date of settlement, therefore, Mr. Mitchell owes, not only his balance of account ($810) but a balance of interest, ($4.98.) It is evident, then, that the balance of account has been due long enough to accumulate this interest. What is the time required? By the process already shown, we ascertain the time to be 37 days; which reckoned back from July 1, will make the average date May 25.

From the foregoing examples, we adduce the following rule for obtaining the date when the balance of an account will average due:

RULE.—*Assume as the date of settlement the latest date at which any amount, debit or credit, falls due: ascertain the balance of interest due at that date, at any given rate, and how long it will take the balance of account to accumulate this interest, at the same rate. The answer will be the time before or after the average date. If the balance of interest, and the balance of account are on the same side, reckon* BACKWARD*; if on opposite sides, reckon* FORWARD.

NOTE.—Although to average an account is to obtain a date when *no interest* is due from either side, yet the important principle recognized is, that the use of money is valuable to the user, in the compound ratio of time and amount; and the real achievement of any correct process of average, is to make the value thus determined, on *one* side, balance that on the *other*. For this reason, the *rate* of interest is unimportant so long as the *same rate* is used on both sides. We have chosen 6 %, because it is more easily obtained.

Any other time may be assumed for the date of settlement, as well as "the latest date at which any amount falls due," but, for evident reasons, this date is preferable.

We will now apply the foregoing rule in averaging the time for the payment of *net proceeds* in a few of the Consignment and Mdse. Co. accounts in the body of the work.

EXAMPLE 3.—Account Sales of Flour and Wheat sold on % and risk of J. R. Wheeler & Co. (Page 71.)

Date.		*Article.*	*Amount.*		*Time.*	*Interest.*		*Date.*		*Article.*	*Amount.*		*Time.*	*Interest.*	
Mar.	2	To Cash . . .	100		66 da	1	10	*Mar.*	6	By Cash . . .	7500		62 da	77	50
"	6*	Storage, etc. .	325		62 da	3	36	*May*	7†	"	4500				
		Net proceeds .	11575												
		Bal. Interest .				73	04								
			12000			77	50				12000			77	50

Balance of account ($11575); and balance of interest ($73.04) on the same side. Ascertain the time it will take $11575 to accumulate $73.04, and count backward. *Ans.* 38 days before May 7, or March 30.

EXAMPLE 4.—Account Sales of Nails and Lead, sold on joint % of Logan, Wilson & Co., and ourselves, each ½. (Page 110.)

Date.		*Article.*	*Amount.*		*Time.*	*Interest.*		*Date.*		*Article.*	*Amount.*		*Time.*	*Interest.*	
Apr.	3	To Cash . . .	100		36 da		60	*Apr.*	5	By Cash . . .	1400		34 da	7	93
"	6	Storage, adv.						*May*	9	" . . .	3300				
		Com. and Gain‡	463	75	33 da	2	55								
		Net proceeds .	4136	25											
		Bal. of Interest				4	78								
			4700			7	93				4700			7	93

Balance of account, $4136.25; balance of interest, $4.78. Time from date of settlement, (May 9,) reckoned backward, 7 days. Equated time, May 2.

---

* The Commission, Storage, etc., is assumed to be due when the account is rendered.

† This is the assumed date of settlement, as the note given March 5, falls due at this time.—See Account Sales.

‡ It must not be forgotten, that although the consignee is, in this case, a partner, his account is rendered simply as an agent, or consignee. In this view, his own share of the net gain is as much a part of the "charges" as is his claim for commission. In all these statements of Company sales, we have considered the invoice furnished by the consignor as subject to the same time of settlement as the average sales. The *fact* in all such matters should properly be stated in the partnership contract. If the consignee's share of the invoice is considered due when the property is shipped, it will, of course, vary the time of equation.

EXAMPLE 5.—Account Sales of Vinegar, Linseed Oil, and White Lead, sold on joint % of W. K. Sadler and ourselves, each ½. (Page 111.)

Date.		Article.	Amount.		Time.	Interest.		Date.		Article.	Amount.		Time.	Interest.	
May	1	To Cash . . .	50		62 da		52	*May*	3	By Cash . . .	750		60 da	7	50
"	3	Storage, Adv.						*July*	3	" . . .	2370				
		Com. and Gain	189		60 da	1	89								
		Net proceeds .	2881												
		Bal. of Int. . .				5	09								
			3120			7	50				3120			7	50

Balance of Account, $2881; balance of interest, $5.09. Time from date of settlement, (July 3,) 13 days, reckoned backward 13 days. Equated time, June 20.

EXAMPLE 6.—Account Sales of Sugar, sold on joint % of F. A. Boyle & Co., N. O., Campbell & Strong, and ourselves, each ⅓. (Page 111.)

Date.		Article.	Amount.		Time.	Interest.		Date.		Article.	Amount.		Time.	Interest.	
May	6	To Cash, paid Fre't	500		2 da		17	*May*	8	By Cash, Note, etc.	7500	00			
"	8	Storage, Ad. etc.	237	50						*Bal of Int.* .					17
"	8	Our net gain .	254	17											
		Net proceeds .	6508	33											
			7500	00			17				7500	00			17

Balance of account, $6508.33; balance of interest, $0.17. The time it would take for the balance of account to accumulate this interest would be much less than one day. Equated time, May 8.

NOTE.—It must be borne in mind that the *net proceeds* above comprise the amount due to *both* of the other parties. In equating time on an Account Sales—whether the consignee is a partner or not—the net proceeds, or "balance of account" should be the difference between the charges (including the consignee's share of the gain, when he is a partner,) and the gross proceeds. This is upon the supposition that the consignee's share is subject to the same terms of payment as the net proceeds.

ACCOUNT CURRENT, AND INTEREST ACCOUNT.

The following illustrations are based upon an understanding between the parties that all amounts, debit and credit, shall draw interest after due, at a specified rate. The settlement may be effected at any time and interest adjusted as per agreement. This method is preferred by some to that of averaging payments. The form will be sufficient without specific instruction:

Dr. P. R. SPENCER, IN ACCOUNT CURRENT AND INTEREST WITH B. S. & P., April 10, 1860. *Cr.*

1860			Amount.		Days.	Interest.		1860			Amount.		Days.	Interest.	
Jan.	1	To Mdse. . . .	500		100	3	33	*Feb.*	1	By Cash . . .	675		69	7	76
"	10	" . . .	475		91	2	46	"	15	" . . .	400		55	3	68
"	15	" . . .	700		86	10	03			*Bal. of Int.* .				10	20
Mar.	1	" . . .	870		40	5	80			*Bal. Due* . .	1480	20			
		Bal. of Int. .	10	20											
			2555	20		21	62				2555	20		21	62
Apr.	10	To Balance . .	1480	20											

NOTE.—The rate of interest taken in the above is 6 %. The debit interest exceeds the credit interest on the day of settlement, $10.20, which amount is brought forward to increase the debit side of the account.

The statement on the following page is somewhat more complex, owing to the necessity of both debit and credit interest columns on each side. We think this form altogether preferable to the one used by most authors, necessitating the frequent transfer of interest from one side of the account to the other.

J. W. Lusk, in Account Current and Interest with Ivison, Phinney & Co., Sept. 1, 1860.

Dr.

1860.			Amounts.	Due.	Days.	Dr. Int.	Cr. Int.
May	1	Mdse. @ 6 months	400	Nov. 1	61		4 07
"	15	" as Cash	500	May 15	109	9 08	
June	10	" @ 4 months	475	Oct. 10	40		3 16
July	25	" @ 3 "	900	" 25	54		8 10
Aug	1	" as Cash	325	Aug 1	31	1 68	
Sep.	1	" @ 3 months	500	Dec. 1	91		7 58
		Bal. Cr. Int.				12 15	
			3100			22 91	22 91
Sep.	1	To Balance	1002 20				

Cr.

1860.			Amounts.	Due.	Days.	Dr. Int.	Cr. Int.
June	1	Cash on %	800	June 1	92		12 27
July	1	Draft at 33 days	400	Aug 3	29		2 00
Aug	15	" " 63 "	500	Oct. 17	47	3 92	
"	20	Cash on %	375	Aug 20	12		75
		Bal. Cr. Int.				11 10	
		Int. from Dr.	12 15				
		" " Cr.	11 10				
		Bal. Due	1001 75				
			3100 00			15 02	15 02

As the settlement takes place before several amounts on either side are due, interest must be *deducted* from, instead of added to, such amounts. This is effected by the double interest columns on each side, showing the *debit* interest on the *credit* side of the account, and the *credit* interest on the *debit* side. The *excess* of credit interest from both sides is carried to the credit of the account, showing the *real balance* due at settlement.

Same Account Averaged.

Dr.

1860.			Amounts.	Due.	Days.	Interest.
May	1	Mdse. @ 6 months	400	Nov. 1	30	2
"	15	" as Cash	500	May 15	199	16 58
June	10	" @ 4 months	475	Oct. 10	51	4 04
July	25	" @ 3 "	900	" 25	37	5 55
Aug	1	" as Cash	325	Aug 1	122	6 61
Sep.	1	" @ 3 months	500	Dec. 1		
Dec.	1	*Bal. Cr. Int.*				7 81
			3100			42 59
		Balance of Account	1025			

Cr.

1860.			Amounts.	Due.	Days.	Interest.
Jan.	1	Cash on %	800	June 1	183	24 40
July	1	Draft @ 33 days	400	Aug 3	120	8
Aug	15	" @ 63 "	500	Oct. 17	45	3 75
"	20	Cash on %	375	Aug 20	103	6 44
Dec.	1	*Balance of Account*	1025			
			3100			42 59
		Balance Cr. Interest				7 81

The balance of account and balance of interest being on opposite sides, the balance of account must be held until it accumulates the balance of interest, which is 46 days, nearly. The account will, then, average due in 46 days from December 1 or January 16, 1860. To make these two processes prove each other, it is only necessary to ascertain what would have been due had the account been paid, as in the previous supposition, on September 1. Deduct the interest on $1025 for 137 days, from $1025. The result will be within a fraction of the amount shown to be due at that date on the former account, $1001.74

COMMERCIAL CALCULATIONS.

PARTNERSHIP SETTLEMENTS.

The adjustment of accounts between partners involves, often, the nicest discriminations, and the most thorough appreciation of the various bearings of different entries.

The basis of all such settlements is, of course, the original agreement or contract between the parties; the terms of which should always be of the most plain and unequivocal nature.

A few points, only, need be expressed in a partnership contract; among which are:

First. The amount to be invested by each partner.

Second. The services to be rendered by each, and the compensation to be allowed therefor.

Third. The basis of gain or loss, and the proportion to be shared by each partner.

It is frequently the case that partners, desiring to have everything *expressed* in the contract, and not appreciating the full bearing of certain conditions, defeat their own purposes, by making the terms themselves incompatible. In such cases, the construction should be in accordance with the evident *intent* of the parties.

The difficulties existing in partnership settlements are so irregular, that any attempt at supplying competent rules to meet every case, would be preposterous. It is, however, possible to give such general hints and illustrations as will apply in the majority of cases; a thorough knowledge of the principles of accounts, with sufficient common sense to apply them, must do the rest.

The following general statements, although many of them are self-evident, will serve a purpose in the solutions under this head:

1. The *present worth* of a concern is its net resources; or the excess of its resources over its outside liabilities.

To find the present worth, subtract the liabilities from the resources; or, ascertain the original investment, to which add the net gain, or from which subtract the net loss.

NOTE.—If the liabilities exceed the resources, the difference is the *net insolvency.*

2. The *net investment,* in business, is the amount invested, less the amount drawn out by the partners.

3. The *average investment* is a sum which being kept in the business during the specified time, would be equivalent to the actual investments, in the compound ratio of time and amount.

To ascertain the average investment, multiply each investment by the time of its continuance in the business, and divide the sum of the products by the time for which the average is wanted. The most satisfactory proof is to compute the interest on each investment for the time of its continuance, which must be equal to that on the average investment for the specified time of average.

4. The *gain* or *loss* during a certain period of business is measured by the increase or diminution of the net resources for that time.

To ascertain the net gain or loss, get the difference between the *net investment* and the *present worth.* If the present worth is the larger, the difference is a *gain;* if smaller, a *loss.*

EXAMPLE 1.—A and B are partners, commencing with a joint capital of $10,000. The terms of the contract are that A shall receive $\frac{4}{5}$ and B $\frac{1}{5}$ of the net gain. At the close of the year, when the division is to be made, the resources and liabilities stand thus:

Resources.		*Liabilities.*	
Cash,	$5793.25	Bills Payable,	$3000
Merchandise,	3500.00	Personal Accounts,	1500
Bills Receivable,	1500.00		$4500
Personal Accounts,	5500.00		
	$16293.25		

What proportion of the net resources belongs to each partner?

Solution.—First ascertain the net gain, by subtracting the investment from the present worth, viz.:

Total Resources,	$16293.25
Less Total Liabilities,	4500
Leaves Present Worth,	$11793.25
From which subtract investment,	10000
Leaving Net Gain,	$1793.25

Then add each partner's share of the gain to his share of the investment, viz.:

$\frac{1}{4}$ of \$1793.25 = \$ 448.31, B's share of gain.
$\frac{3}{4}$ " " = 1344.94, A's " " "

A's Investment,	\$5000	
Plus his Gain,	1344.94	
Equals his Present worth,		\$6344.94
B's Investment,	\$5000	
Plus his Gain,	448.31	
Equals his Present Worth,		5448.31
Total Present Worth, as before shown,		\$11793.25

EXAMPLE 2.—C, D and E invested as follows:

C	put in \$4000,	and drew out	\$ 700
D	" 5000,	"	825
E	" 4500,	"	1000

The gain in business is \$1500, of which each is to share $\frac{1}{3}$. What is the interest of each in the business at closing? *Ans.* C's, \$3800; D's, \$4675; E's, \$4000.

EXAMPLE 3.—F, G and H are partners. They invest in equal amounts. At the close of the year their resources exceed their liabilities \$27000; and their gains have been \$4000, of which F is to share $\frac{1}{6}$ G, $\frac{2}{6}$; and H, $\frac{1}{2}$. What was the capital of each at commencing? What, at closing?

NOTE.—The capital at commencing, subtracted from the capital at closing, will equal the net gain; and, consequently, the net gain subtracted from the capital at closing, or present worth, will equal the capital at commencing, or the net investment.

Ans. to the above: F's capital at commencement, \$7666.66+; G's and H's the same. F's capital at closing, \$8333.33; G's, \$9000; H's, \$9666.67.

EXAMPLE 4.—A and B are partners, investing equally, and sharing equally in gains or losses. At commencing business, their resources and liabilities are as follows:

Resources.		*Liabilities.*	
Cash,	\$5000	Bills Payable,	\$2000
Mdse.,	1475	Personal accounts,	125
Bills Receivable,	750		\$2125
	\$7225		

At closing, as follows:

Resources.		*Liabilities.*	
Cash,	\$7000	Personal accounts,	\$1500
Bills Receivable,	2000	Bills Payable,	3000
	\$9000		\$4500

What is the whole gain or loss? What each man's net capital at closing?

EXAMPLE 5.—K and L enter into copartnership, with the understanding that the gain or loss shall be divided in proportion to the average investment. They remain in business one year, during which time they have invested and drawn out as follows:

K. *Drawn out.*		K. *Invested.*		L. *Drawn out.*		L. *Invested.*	
Jan. 15,	\$500	Jan. 1,	\$7000	Jan. 31,	\$400	Jan. 1,	\$8000
July 1,	650	Mar. 1,	6000	Apr. 15,	2000	July 1,	4000
Aug. 31,	3000			Sept. 15,	500		

At the close of the year their resources and liabilities are as follows:

Resources.		*Liabilities.*	
Cash,	$5100	Bills Payable,	$1500
Bank Stock,	6000	Personal accounts,	1750
Real Estate,	7500		
Bills Receivable,	4000		
Personal accounts,	2000		

What is each man's share of the gain? What each man's capital at closing?

NOTE.—There are two methods of obtaining a basis for the division of gains or losses under such an arrangement as the preceding: one, to ascertain, according to previous suggestions, the *exact* average capital of each partner; and the other, to compute the interest on the investments, which assume as *relative* capital. The latter is preferable, when the only object is a basis for division; first, because interest is more easily obtained than the average capital, and next, because it is more easily used when obtained. We shall briefly illustrate both methods.

First Solution.—Multiply each investment by the time of its continuance, and divide the sum of these products by the time for which the average is wanted:

K's Investments.

$7000	from January 1,	to January 15,	½	month	= $3500
6500	" " 15,	" March 1,	1½	"	= 9750
12500	" March 1,	" July 1,	4	"	= 50000
11850	" July 1,	" August 31,	2	"	= 23700
8850	" August 31,	" December 31,	4	"	= 35400
					$122350

$122350 ÷ 12 = $10195.83, K's average investment.

L's Investments.

$8000	from January 1,	to January 31,	1	month	= $8000
7600	" " 31,	" April 15,	2½	"	= 19000
5600	" April 15,	" July 1,	2½	"	= 14000
9600	" July 1,	" September 15,	2½	"	= 24000
9100	" September 15,	" December 31,	3½	"	= 31850
					$96850

$96850 ÷ 12 = $8070.83, L's average investment.

K's average investment,	$10195.83
L's " "	8070.83
Total "	$18266.66

We have, then, the familiar formula: "As the whole investment is to each man's investment, so is the whole gain or loss to each man's share of the same."

Operation.

$18266.66 : $10195.83 :: $3400 : $1897.76 = K's share.
18266.66 : 8090.82 :: 3400 : 1502.24 = L's "

Second Solution.—Compute the interest on each investment for the time of its continuance, and take the interest due each partner as his relative investment; and proceed as with the average investment.

K's Interest Account.

Interest on	$7000	from January 1,	to January 15,	½	month	= $17.50
"	6500	" " 15,	" March 1,	1½	"	= 48.75
"	12500	" March 1,	" July 1,	4	"	= 250.00
"	11850	" July 1,	" August 31,	2	"	= 118.50
"	8850	" August 31,	" December 31,	4	"	= 177.00
						$611.75

L's Interest Account.

Interest on $8000	from	January	1, to	January	31,	1	month =	$40.00
" 7600	"	"	31, "	April	15,	$2\frac{1}{2}$	" =	95.00
" 5600	"	April	15, "	July	1,	$2\frac{1}{2}$	" =	70.00
" 9600	"	July	1, "	September	15,	$2\frac{1}{2}$	" =	120.00
" 9100	"	September	15, "	December	31,	$3\frac{1}{2}$	" =	159.25
								$484.25

Taking these amounts of interest due, as relative capital, we have statement as before, viz.:

$1096 : $611.75 :: $3400 : $1897.76 = K's gain.
1096 : 484.25 :: 3400 : 1502.24 = L's "

K's net investment is, ...	$8850.00	
" " gain "	1897.76	
" " capital at closing, ...		$10747.76
L's net investment is, ...	$9100.00	
" " gain "	1502.24	
" " capital at closing, ...		$10602.24
Present worth of firm, ...		$21350.00

NOTE.—In computing the interest above, as also, in multiplying the investments by the time of their continuance, we have taken the common method of using the *exact amount* of capital, from one date to another. The same purpose may be effected by getting the value of each investment from the time invested till the end of the year; and also of each amount withdrawn from the time withdrawn to the end of the year, subtracting the latter from the former. This latter method is preferred by some, and is identical in its results, with the method shown.

The plan of dividing gains and losses in proportion to investment is not adopted, to any great extent, in general copartnerships, but is peculiar to joint-stock concerns, where it is estimated as a *percentage,* the result being precisely the same as by the above method. It is much more easy to declare a percentage dividend in joint-stock concerns, for two especial reasons: first, the capital does not fluctuate—the amount of stock which a man holds being always his *average* investment—and next the gains are not usually *all* divided; so that an *exact* percentage may be divided, leaving the balance of gain as a sinking, or accumulating fund.

The precise distinction between a general copartnership and a joint-stock association, so far as keeping the accounts is concerned, has chief reference to the basis of dividends. In *all* joint-stock concerns the gains are divided according to the capital held, while in general copartnerships the usual method is first to equalize the capital by allowing interest on net investments, and then to divide the gain or loss equally. It is also customary in copartnerships, for the partners to draw regular salaries for services the same as employés.

The more usual basis of a partnership contract is, first, to equalize the capital by allowing each partner interest on his average investment, and then to divide the net gain or loss in certain proportions independent of capital. The following examples will illustrate this point.

EXAMPLE 7.—A, B & C are partners under a contract providing that each man shall receive interest on his average capital, at the rate of 6% per annum, and the net gain be divided equally. They invest, and draw out as follows:

A.		B.		C.	
Drawn out.	*Invested.*	*Drawn out.*	*Invested.*	*Drawn out.*	*Invested.*
May 1, . $300	Jan. 1, . $4000	Jan. 15, . $150	Jan. 1, $5000		Jan. 1, $10000
	Mar. 1, . 7000	Apr. 1, . 200	April 1, 5000		

At the end of six months, July 1, they ascertain that the business has gained $1500, not reckoning the interest due on capital. To how much of the $1500 is each man entitled? and what is each man's interest in the business on the first of July?

Solution.—Ascertain the interest due each on his investment, which deduct from the gain, leaving the amount to be divided *equally.* Add each man's interest to his $\frac{1}{3}$ net gain to obtain his share of the $1500. Add each man's share thus found to his *net* investment, to obtain his interest in the business on the first of July

Operation.

A's credit interest, $4000, for 6 months	= $120.00			
7000, " 4 "	= 140.00	$260.00		
" debit " 300, " 2 "		3.00		
A's net interest,				$257.00
B's credit interest, $5000, for 6 months	= $150.00			
5000, " 3 "	= 75.00	$225.00		
" debit " 150, " $5\frac{1}{2}$ "	= 4.13			
200, " 3 "	= 3.00	7.13		
B's net interest,				217.87
C's credit interest, $10000 for 6 months,				300.00
Total interest due partners,				$774.87

$1500 − $774.87 = $725.13, net gain to be divided equally; viz.: $725.13 ÷ 3 = $241.71.

	A		B		C
A's net interest,	$257.00	B's net interest,	$217.87	C's net interest,	$300.00
" $\frac{1}{3}$ net gain,	241.71	" $\frac{1}{3}$ net gain,	241.71	" $\frac{1}{3}$ net gain,	241.71
" *share of total gain,*	498.71	" *share of total gain,*	459.58	" *share of total gain,*	541.71
" net investment,	10700.00	" net investment,	9650.00	" net investment,	10000.00
" *capital, July* 1,	$11198.71	" *capital, July,* 1,	$10109.58	" *capital, July* 1,	$10541.71

NOTE.—In a set of Double-Entry Books, a settlement like the above would be easily effected, by carrying the interest allowed the first partners directly to the debit of Loss and Gain account, the same as any other expense which would leave in the Loss and Gain account the net gain to be divided. If we take into account the fact that the investment is *borrowed* from the partners, who receive interest thereon, the same as on money loaned to other parties, the proposition is simple enough. It is always proper, whether practiced or not, to deduct the interest on investment, as well as the salaries of the partners—if they are entitled to any—from the gains, before attempting to decide upon the prosperity of the business.

EXAMPLE 8.—A, B, C, and D are partners. The contract provides that A and B are to furnish the capital, and C and D to defray the expenses. The gain is to be divided as follows: A, $\frac{1}{3}$; B, $\frac{1}{4}$; C, $\frac{1}{4}$; and D, $\frac{1}{6}$. The net gain, besides expenses, is $4000; the expenses, which have been paid from the business, are $500. How much of the net gain is each partner entitled to?

Solution.—It would seem at first view, that there is a hopeless incompatibility in the terms of this contract. It is true that if $4000 be assumed as the gain, to be divided among the four partners, injustice would be done to A and B, as they were not to participate in the expenses; and it will readily appear that if C and D had paid the expenses from their own pockets, instead of from the avails of the concern, the gain would appear $500 more. So far, then, as A and B are concerned, the net gain is $4500.

$\frac{1}{3}$ of $4500 = $1500, A's share of the gain.
$\frac{1}{4}$ " 4500 = 1125, B's " " "
$\frac{1}{4}$ " 4500 = 1125, C's " " "
$\frac{1}{6}$ " 4500 = 750, D's " " "

C and D are each to be charged with one half the expenses, $500, which deducted from their share of the gain as above, will leave the result:

$1125 − $250 = $875, C's share of the $4000.
750 − 250 = 500, D's " " "

NOTE.—There are, in reality, two distinct contracts to be regarded in the above adjustment; one for the payment of the expenses, and the other for the division of gain; and they should by no means be made to conflict. The difficulty which the tyro would be apt to encounter, would be the attempt to divide what seems to be the *net gain*—$4000. The fact is, C and D had no right to charge the expenses to a general account of the concern, thereby reducing the gains, but should have charged their own personal accounts, the same as for money drawn for any private purpose. The net gain is really $4500, and each partner should receive his appropriate share. As C and D have already received each $250, it should be deducted from their gain.

Example 9.—*Three methods of adjusting interest between partners.*—X, Y, and Z enter into equal copartnership with unequal capital, each man to receive interest on his average investment. X's interest amounts to $300; Y's, to $250; and Z's to $180. How can the adjustment be made?

First.—The total amount of interest may be charged to Loss and Gain account, which being divided equally between the three partners, each of whom are credited for their respective portions, will produce the following results

Dr. X	*Cr.*	*Dr.* Y	*Cr.*	*Dr* Z	*Cr.*
243.33	300	243.33	250	243.34	180

Second.—X's and Y's *excess* of interest over Z's may be charged to Loss and Gain account, and they credited with the same; the Loss and Gain account to be shared equally as before, viz.:

Dr. X	*Cr.*	*Dr.* Y	*Cr.*	*Dr.* Z	*Cr.*
63.33	120	63.33	70	63.34	

Third.—A Journal entry may be made direct, without taking the amount to the Loss and Gain account, viz.:

Dr. X	*Cr.*	*Dr.* Y	*Cr.*	*Dr.* Z	*Cr.*
	56.67		6.67	63.34	

It will be seen that the *net* debits and credits are the same in each of the three methods, clearly proving the essential identity of the different results. The former method is, perhaps, preferable, because more readily understood and applied.

Example 10.—A, B and C enter into copartnership with equal capital, upon the following conditions: A to receive as a salary $1500; B, $1200; and C, $1000; the gain to be divided equally. At the close of the year, the net gain, exclusive of salaries, proves to be $3000. To how much of this amount is each partner entitled?

Solution.—It will be plainly seen that had the partners received their stipulated salaries and the total been carried to Expense %., instead of a *gain* of $3000 there would have appeared a *loss* of $700. The provisions of the contract are that the "*gains* shall be divided equally;" and it may be proper to suggest, that if there be *losses* instead of *gains*, the proportion must be the same. We have, then, the following result:

A's salary, ...	$1500	
B's "	1200	
C's "	1000	$3700
From which deduct gain, ...		3000
Leaves net loss, ...		$700

A's ⅓ net loss, $233.33; B's, $233.33; C's, $233.34.
Therefore, $1500 − $233.33 = $1266.67, A's share.
1200 − 233.33 = 966.67, B's "
1000 − 233.34 = 766.66, C's "
Total, . . $3000.00

A common fallacy with reference to settlements like the above, would be to divide the $3000 in proportion to the salaries. The reasoning would be this: If there had been earned just $3700, A would have received $1500; B, $1200; and C, $1000; therefore, if there be less than enough to pay these amounts, it should be divided in the same proportion. The solution, according to this understanding, would be as follows:

$3700 : $1500 :: $3000 : $1216.22, A's share.
3400 : 1200 :: 3000 : 972.97, B's "
3700 : 1000 :: 3000 : 810.81, C's "
Total, ... $3000.00

The remedy for all such misconceptions is to understand the distinction between the separate contracts in the copartnership. The apportionment of salary, in the above case, is *absolute*, and is not at all contingent upon the gain or loss. To appreciate this fact fully, suppose the salary is to be paid to clerks instead of to the partners; the result would be a loss of $700, as shown in the first statement. The partners act in the double capacity of proprietors and employés; as employés, they *gain* each the amount of his stipulated salary; as proprietors, they *lose* each ⅓ of $700.

GENERAL HINTS AS TO DIVIDENDS.

It is customary with all establishments to declare, periodically, the gains or losses in business. Joint-stock companies usually do this twice a year, and all other concerns as often as once a year. It is well to consider, in all such cases, not only what *appears* to be the condition of the business with reference to gains and losses, but what that condition really *is*. It is not impossible that the Representative accounts should make a fair show of prosperity, while the state of available resources would plainly indicate an entirely different state of affairs. For instance, the credit side of Merchandise account may exhibit a commendable preponderance over the debit side, showing thereby a gain; while the resources which that credit produced may have a fictitious value. Suppose the merchandise to have been sold on notes and personal accounts which are not worth more than half what their Ledger titles express. It will be evident that the Merchandise account exhibits a fictitious gain of exactly the amount of such depreciation of resources; and any dividend declared on such a basis would be false to that extent: as it would fail, by so much, of being realized. The question, then, arises, Would it be best to dispose of these doubtful accounts by carrying their deficiency to Loss and Gain? Such a course would doubtless be legitimate, were it possible to determine just *how worthless* the accounts were, or how much of them it would be safe to retain as absolute resources. This uncertainty would suggest the propriety of permitting them to remain upon the Ledger until their worth could be ascertained; besides, it would scarcely be advisable to close up a personal account so long as any chance remains of realizing it. What, then, is the best method of retaining these doubtful accounts on the Ledger, and yet avoid showing a fictitious gain? The most satisfactory plan of which we have a knowledge, is to open a general account to represent liabilities; as, for instance, "Suspense," or "Sinking Fund" to the credit of which carry all doubtful resources, debiting Loss and Gain with the same. It is well understood that a liability will cancel a resource, and *vice versa.* As the "Suspense" account would thus be considered a liability, it would, of course, offset just so much of what appears elsewhere as resources; and thus permit the dividend to be made from the actual gain. In all cases, however, where resources have been thus canceled, there should be some method of knowing which they are, that if any thing is thereafter realized on them, "Suspense" account may be charged and Loss and Gain credited.

The result of this arrangement would be to guard, in the most effectual way, against excessive dividends, and to exhibit perpetually the accounts in "suspense," without exciting the suspicion of the parties from whom we may hope, eventually, to realize a fair proportion, at least, of the amounts shown to be due.

Where the object is simply to declare dividends due partners that are to continue in the same relation, it is not necessary to be very exact in these estimates; but if the purpose be to arrive at the actual condition of the business with a view to changing the relations of proprietorship, it will be necessary to estimate the *real value* of such doubtful resources, or as nearly as possible.

The plan usually adopted of closing all doubtful resources into "Suspense" is not only injurious, but utterly useless, as the Suspense account must then represent a resource or a loss. If a resource, the accounts may as well have remained under their proper titles, and if a loss, they should have been carried directly to Loss and Gain. But the chief objection to such a course would be the exhibiting of accounts as closed which are yet owing, and may be paid. If Mr. A., for instance, whom we have thus considered doubtful, should desire to see his account on our Ledger, that he may pay it, it might be awkward to inform him that, having considered his account worthless, we had carried it to Loss and Gain. He might not desire to contribute so directly to our profit.

In Joint-stock concerns, particularly, where the settled policy is, under no circumstances to decrease the capital stock, a "Suspense," or "Sinking Fund" account is exceedingly proper; and it is well, under such circumstances, to carry to such account, not only the resources which are doubtful, but a sufficient amount to cover all contingencies. It is quite as easy to estimate the real value of a "Sinking Fund" account as that of any doubtful resource, and in case an *exact* statement of the condition of the concern is wanted, any excess which may have been transferred hither may be easily restored.

VOCABULARY OF MERCANTILE TERMS.

ABANDONMENT, the surrendering of a ship or goods insured, to the insurer.
Abatement, discount allowed on damaged goods, or for the payment of money before due.
Acceptance, the formal agreement to pay a draft or bill according to its terms.
Accommodation, the loan of money or of one's name upon which money may be raised.
Account, a systematic arrangement of debits and credits under the name of a person, species of property, or cause. Book-keeping is the *science* of Accounts.
Account-Current, a running, or unsettled account.
Accountant, one skilled in Accounts, or engaged in keeping books.
Actuary, the active officer in a Life Insurance company; one skilled in the science of annuities.
Adjustment, the settlement of a loss incurred by the insured; a general settlement.
Administrator, one who administers upon an estate, by order of the Probate Court.
Adulteration, the act of debasing by mixing any spurious commodity with a genuine article.
Ad valorem, according to the value; a term used in fixing the rates of duties on imports.
Adventure, a speculation; usually applied to the shipment of goods on account of the shipper.
Advance, increase in price; money paid on goods before they are delivered.
Advice. Information given with reference to a shipment or other important matter.
Agent, one who acts; usually applied to a person who does business for, and in the name of another.
Agio, a term used to denote the difference between the real and nominal value of money.
Allowance, deduction made from weights, etc. [See *Tare*.]
Amalgamation. The operation of forming amalgam; mixing mercury with any metal.
Ante-date, to date beforehand.
Appraisal, a value set upon goods or property of any kind.
Appraiser, one who appraises.
Aqueduct, a channel or conduit for the conveyance of water.
Arbitration, the hearing of a cause between parties in controversy; estimating the value of exchange, negotiated through indirect channels.
Assay, the trial or proof of the purity of metals.
Assets, resources of any kind; available means.
Assessment, a valuation of property or profits, for the purpose of taxation.
Assessor, one who assesses or values property.
Assignee, a person properly appointed to transact business, or receive property for, or on account of any person or estate.
Assignor, one who makes an assignment or transfers property or interest.
Assignment, the act of making over property or trust to an assignee.
Association, the union of persons in company, for the transaction of business.
Assortment, a variety of sorts or kinds, adapted to various wants.
Assurance, a guarantee or indemnity. [See *Insurance*.]
Attachment, a legal warrant for seizing a man's person or goods.
Auction, a method of selling goods to the highest bidder.
Auctioneer, one who sells goods at auction.
Auditor, a person appointed and authorized to examine accounts, compare vouchers, etc.
Average, a term used to denote damages or expenses resulting from accidents at sea; the mean time for the payment of several items due at different times.
Avoirdupois, the common standard of weight for all commodities except precious metals and drugs.

BALANCE, a term used to denote the difference between the sides of an account, or the sum necessary to make the account balance; an account in the Ledger, showing resources and liabilities.
Balance of Trade, the difference between the value of imports and exports.
Ballast, a heavy substance placed in the hold of a ship to keep her steady in the water.
Banking, the business of a bank.
Bankrupt, one who is unable to pay his debts.
Bill, a general name given to a statement in writing. The following are some of the technical names of bills:
- *Bill of Exchange*, an order drawn on a person in a distant place, requesting the payment of a sum of money.
- *Bill of Entry*, a written account of goods entered at the Custom-House.
- *Bill of Right*, a form of entry at the Custom-House by which the importer may examine his goods.
- *Bill of Lading*, a list of goods shipped, having the signature of the master of the vessel, or the proper officer of the transportation company.
- *Bill of Parcels*, an account given by the seller to the buyer, of articles and prices.
- *Bill of Sale*, a writing given by the seller of personal property to the buyer, equivalent to a deed.
- *Bill of Health*, a certificate from the proper authorities as to the state of health of a ship's company on leaving port.
- *Bill of Mortality*, a certified account of the deaths at a certain place, during a certain period.
- *Bill of Credit*, a document for raising money on the credit of a state.

Board of Trade, an association of business men, for the general advancement of commercial interests.

Bona fide, in good faith.
Bond, a deed by which the party binds himself, his heirs, executors and assigns to the performance of certain conditions.
Bonded Goods, those which remain in the Custom warehouse until the duties are paid.
Bottomry Bond, a mortgage on the bottom of a vessel, that is, on the vessel itself, for the repayment of money loaned.
Broker, a trader in stocks, moneys, or other commodities.
Brokerage, the commission or percentage charged by a broker for services.

CAPITAL, investment in business.
Carat, the weight which expresses the degree of fineness of gold.
Cargo, the lading or freight of a vessel.
Cashier, one who keeps the cash account; the financial officer of a bank, railroad, or mercantile house.
Carrier, one who carries goods for another.
Charter, an instrument bestowed with form and solemnity, bestowing certain privileges and rights.
Charter-party, a contract between the owner of a ship and the freighter.
Clearance, a certificate from the Custom-House that a ship has permission to sail.
Clearing, the obtaining of permission for a ship to leave port; the exchanging of drafts and settlement of balances between different houses.
Clearing-House, the place where the operation of clearing is performed.
Coasting, the trade carried on between different ports of the same country.
Coin, pieces of metal, usually gold or silver, impressed with a public stamp, and used as money.
Commerce, the exchange of commodities.
Commission, a percentage for the sale of goods or other service.
Company, an association of persons for a common enterprise.
Compound, to settle with a creditor by paying a part only of the debt.
Compromise, an agreement embracing mutual concessions.
Consignee, one to whom goods are consigned.
Consignment, goods consigned to be sold on account.
Consignor, one who consigns goods.
Consols, an abbreviation of the term "Consolidated Funds," applied to the chief public stocks of England.
Consul, an agent for a government in a foreign land.
Contraband, an article prohibited from being imported, exported, bought or sold.
Contract, an agreement between two or more parties upon sufficient consideration, to do, or not to do a certain thing.
Contra, on the opposite side.
Copyright, the secured privilege of monopolizing the publication of any book or work.
Counterfeit, a spurious article resembling the genuine.
Coupon, a French word, signifying *cut off*. It is applied to interest warrants, attached to public stocks, bonds, etc. When paid they are cut off from the bond.
Credential, the official warrant of a delegating power, authorizing the holder to act in a specified capacity.
Credit, trust given to one who owes.
Currency, a term used to express the collective amount of money used in the business of buying and selling.
Customs, the tariff charged by law on imports or exports.
Custom-House, the office where the business connected with customs is transacted.

DAMAGED GOODS, in the language of customs, are goods subject to duties, that have received injury, either in the voyage home, or the bonded warehouse.
Days of Grace, the time allowed by law and usage between the written date of maturity of a note or draft, and the date upon which it must be paid.
Debenture, a certificate of drawback entitling the importer to return duties on goods shipped again.
Debt, an amount owing from one party to another.
Decimal, from the Latin *decem*, signifying ten; any system of counting by tens.
Decimal Fractions, fractions having any power of ten for their denominator.
Deed, a written contract, sealed and delivered.
Defalcation, diminution, deducted from.
Defaulter, one who fails to account for money or valuables entrusted to his care.
Delivery, the passing of goods or money from one to another.
Demand and Supply, terms used to denote the relations existing between consumption and production.
Demurrage, forfeit money for detaining a vessel beyond her time.
Denier, a small French copper coin.
Deviation, the departure of a vessel from the course specified in her insurance policy.
Diplomacy, the art of conducting negotiations.
Discount, consideration allowed for the payment of a debt before it is due.
Dividend, division of profits among stockholders.
Drawback, an amount remitted which has been previously paid as duties.
Draft, an order for the payment of money.
Drawee, the person on whom a draft is drawn.
Drawer, the person who draws a draft.
Duplicate, a copy or transcript of any thing.
Duty, a government tax.

EFFECTS, property of any kind.
Embargo, a prohibition laid by the government on ships to prevent their leaving port.
Embezzlement, the illegal appropriation of the funds of a principal by an agent or employee.
Emporium, a commercial center; a mart.
Endorse, to subscribe to any thing; to write one's name on the back of a note.
Engross, to monopolize; to buy up produce for the purpose of affecting the market; to copy in manuscript.
Exchange, the fundamental principle of trade; the species of paper by which debts are paid without the transmission of money; premium and discount arising from the purchase and sale of funds.
Exports, goods or produce carried abroad.
Express, a messenger or vehicle sent on a special errand; a regular convenance for packages.

FABRIC, manufactured cloth.
Face, the amount expressed on a note or draft.
Factor, an agent employed to transact business for another.
Factory, a house or place where factors reside; a building for the manufacture of goods.
Fac simile, an exact resemblance.
Failure, becoming insolvent.
Fancy Stocks, usually applied to the stocks of joint-companies, subject to fluctuation in price.
Favor, the polite term for a letter received; a note or draft is *in favor* of the person to whom it is to be paid.
Fee simple, an estate held by a person in his own right.
Finance, pertaining to money; the public revenue.

Financier, an officer of revenue; one skilled in money matters.
Firm, the general title of a copartnership.
Firkin, a measure equal to nine ale gallons.
Foreclose, to cut the mortgager off from the equity of redemption.
Forestalling, buying up produce before it gets to market, to enhance the price.
Form, a particular arrangement; a systematic method of expressing facts.
Forecastle, the part of the upper deck of a ship forward of the mast.
Folio, page of a book; usually applied to the two pages opposite each other.
Franc, a French coin, equal to about eighteen cents of American money.
Free Trade, the policy of conducting international commerce, without duties.
Freight, goods being transported; the price of transportation.
Fund, a stock or capital; a sum of money appropriated to some special enterprise; used in the plural to denote wealth, generally.

GAUGING, the art of measuring the contents of a cask or other receptacle.
Gain, profit; increase in wealth.
Gratuity, a free gift; a donation.
Guarantee, or *Guaranty*, an undertaking or engagement by a third person that the agreement between two parties shall be observed; a surety.

HARBOR, a place where ships may lie at anchorage and in safety; a port for loading and unloading.
Hawker, an itinerant pedler of merchandise.
Highway, a public road or thoroughfare.
High Seas, the waters of the ocean, without the boundaries of any country.
Honor, to accept or pay when due.
Hypothecate, to pledge as security.

IMPORT, to bring from a foreign country.
Importation, the act of importing; the thing imported.
Indemnity, a guarantee against loss.
Insolvency, the condition of bankruptcy.
Insurance, indemnity from loss; the rate paid for indemnity.
Installment, part of a sum of money paid or to be paid at a certain time.
Interest, the use of money; commonly defined as a percentage allowed by the borrower to the lender.
Inventory, a list of goods enumerated in detail.
Investment, the laying out of money in the purchase of property.
Invoice, a bill of goods bought or sold.

JETTISON, goods thrown overboard to lighten a ship in a storm.
Jointure, an estate in lands settled on a woman, in consideration of marriage.
Joint-stock, property held in common by a company.
Journal, the chief book of the current entries in business.

LEASE, a contract demising the use of property for a certain time.
Ledger, the merchant's book of accounts.
Legacy, a bequest; money or property given by will.
Letter of Credit, an open letter of request authorizing the holder to receive money on account of the writer.
Liability, a debt or claim against a person.
License, a legal permission to do a certain act such as selling goods, etc.
Lien, security on land or other property.
Lighter, a large, open, flat-bottomed boat used to carry goods to or from a vessel when loading or unloading.
Lighterage, a charge or commission for carrying goods in a lighter.
Liquidate, to pay or satisfy demands.
Loan, that which is lent for a temporary purpose.
Lucre, gain in money or goods.

MANIFEST, a list of the articles comprising a vessel's cargo.
Manufacture, the process of converting raw materials into articles of use and sale.
Manufactory, the place where goods are manufactured.
Marine, a general name for the navy of a kingdom or a state.
Maratime Law, law relating to harbors, ships, and seamen.
Mark, or *Marc*, a weight in European countries for estimating gold and silver.
Maturity, the date when a note or draft falls due.
Maximum, the highest price or rate.
Mercantile Law, law pertaining to business transactions.
Merchandise, goods; the common articles of barter.
Merchant, one who speculates in merchandise.
Minimum, the lowest price or rate.
Mint, the place where money is coined.
Monopoly, the sole right to make or use a certain article.
Monetary, relating to financial matters.
Mortgage, the transfer of property to secure the payment of a debt.
Mortgagee, the person to whom the transfer is made.
Mortgager, the one who makes the transfer.

NAVIGATION, the science of conducting ships or other vessels from one port to another.
Net, or *Nett*, that which remains of a weight or quantity after certain deductions.
Net Proceeds, the amount due a consignor, after deducting charges attending sales.
Nickel, a scarce metal resembling silver; used in the composition of the new cent coin of the United States.
Notary Public, an officer whose chief business it is to protest paper for non-payment.
Note, an incidental remark made for the purpose of explanation; a written obligation to pay money or goods.

PAR, equal in value.
Partnership, an agreement between two or more persons to share in the profit and loss of any enterprise.
Pawnbroker, a person who advances money on goods, having power to dispose of the same if the money is not refunded as per contract.
Policy of Insurance, contract between the insurer and the insured.
Portage, the amount paid by a captain in running his vessel; the price of carrying.
Premium, the sum paid for insurance; the excess of value above par.
Price Current, a list of merchandise, with market value.
Principal, an employer; the head of a commercial house; the sum loaned upon which interest accrues.
Protest, a formal notice to the sureties of a note or draft, stating that the same was not paid at maturity; or to the drawer of a draft stating that the same was not accepted upon presentment.

QUARANTINE, restraint of intercourse to which a ship is subjected, upon the supposition that she may be infected with disease.

RATE, price; amount above or below par.
Rebate, reduction for prompt payment.
Receipt, a written acknowledgment of having received money or other value.
Reprisal, the act of seizing ships or property as indemnity for unlawful seizure or detention.
Resources, effects—property of any kind.
Revenue, the annual produce of rents, excise, customs duties, etc., collected by a state or nation.

SALVAGE, an allowance made by law for the saving of a ship's cargo from wreck or fire.
Sample, a specimen.
Seaworthy, in a proper condition to venture to sea.
Seize, to take possession of by legal process.
Shipment, goods shipped; the act of loading a vessel for voyage.
Sight, the time of presenting a bill to the drawee.
Signature, the name of a person written by himself.
Solvent, sound; able to pay all liabilities.
Sounding, trying the depth of the sea, and the nature of the bottom.
Stock, capital in trade; the title of the proprietor of a business.
Stocks, shares in joint-stock companies, and negotiable debts of governments and corporations, drawing interest.
Stock jobber, one who deals in stocks.
Surety, indemnity against loss; a person bound for the performance of a contract by another.

TARE, an allowance or discount for the weight of boxes and other receptacles of merchandise.
Tariff, a list of prices; duties on imports and exports.
Teller, an officer in a bank who receives or pays money.
Tender, an offer for acceptance; a legal tender is an offer of such money as the law prescribes.
Tonnage, the weight of a ship's lading; the capacity of a vessel.
Transfer, to convey from one to another.
Trustee, a person trusted; one to whom some special business or interest is committed.

USANCE, business custom or habit which is generally conceded and acted upon.
Usury, illegal interest; formerly, any consideration for the use of money.

VEND, to sell, or transfer for a consideration.
Voucher, a written evidence of an act performed, such as the payment of money.

WAGES, compensation for services.
Warehouse, a building in which goods are stored.
Wares, merchandise of any kind.
Wharfage, money paid for the use of a wharf.
Wreck, the ruins of a ship stranded.
Wreckers, persons employed in saving property from a wreck.

ABBREVIATIONS AND CHARACTERS.

ABBREVIATIONS.

Ac t.....Account.
Am't....Amount.
Ans.....Answer.
Apr.....April.
Ass't'd...Assorted.
Aug ....August.

Bal.....Balance.
B. B....Bill Book.
Bbl.....Barrel.
B. Pay..Bills Payable.
B. Rec...Bills Receivable.
Bl'k.....Black.
Bo't.....Bought.
Bro't....Brought.

Cap......Capital.
C.-B....Cash-Book.
Co......Company.
Com.....Commission.
Cons t....Consignment.
Cr.. ....Creditor.

Dec.....December.
D'ft.....Draft.
Do......The same.
Doz.....Dozen.
Dr......Debtor.
D's......Days.

ea.......Each.
E. E....Errors excepted.
E.&O.E. Errors and omissions excepted.
Emb'd...Embroidered.
Eng.....English.
Ex.......Example.
Exch....Exchange.
Exp.....Expenses.

Fav.....Favor.
Feb......February.
Fig'd....Figured.
Fol......Folio.
For'd....Forward.

Fr't......Freight.

Gal.....Gallon.

Hhd.....Hogshead.

I. B.....Invoice Book.
Ins......Insurance.
Inst......Instant.
Int.......Interest.
Inv't....Inventory.

Jan.....January.

lbs......Pounds.
L. F.....Ledger Folio.

Mar......March.
Mdse....Merchandise.
Mo......Month.

No.......Number.
Nov.....November.

Oct......October.
O. I. B..Outward Invoice Book.

p........Page
Pay't....Payment.
P. C. B..Petty Cash Book.
Pd.......Paid.
Pkg.....Package.
Pr......Pair.
pr, per..By.
Prem...Premium
Ps.......Pieces.

Rec'd.....Received.

S. B.....Sales Book.
Sept.....September.
Ship't...Shipment.
Sunds....Sundries.

Yds.....Yards.
Yr......Year.

CHARACTERS.

@..At.
%..Account.
%..Per cent.
#...Number.
+..Sign of addition.
—..Sign of subtraction.
×..Sign of multiplication.
÷..Sign of division.
=..Sign of equality.
1¹..One and one-fourth.
1²..One and two-fourths.
1³..One and three-fourths.

TIME TABLE.

Showing the time in months or days from any day in one month to the corresponding day in any other month.

FROM	*TO*	Jan.	Feb.	Mar.	Apr.	May	June	July	Aug.	Sept	Oct.	Nov.	Dec.
JANUARY.	Months.	12	1	2	3	4	5	6	7	8	9	10	11
	Days...	365	31	59	90	120	151	181	212	243	273	304	334
FEB'UARY.	Months.	11	12	1	2	3	4	5	6	7	8	9	10
	Days...	334	365	28	59	89	120	150	181	212	242	273	303
MARCH...	Months.	10	11	12	1	2	3	4	5	6	7	8	9
	Days...	306	337	365	31	61	92	122	153	184	214	245	275
APRIL.....	Months.	9	10	11	12	1	2	3	4	5	6	7	8
	Days...	275	306	334	365	30	61	91	122	153	183	214	244
MAY......	Months.	8	9	10	11	12	1	2	3	4	5	6	7
	Days...	245	276	304	335	365	31	61	92	123	153	184	214
JUNE.....	Months.	7	8	9	10	11	12	1	2	3	4	5	6
	Days...	214	245	273	304	334	365	30	61	92	122	153	183
JULY......	Months.	6	7	8	9	10	11	12	1	2	3	4	5
	Days...	184	215	243	274	304	335	365	31	62	92	123	153
AUGUST...	Months.	5	6	7	8	9	10	11	12	1	2	3	4
	Days...	153	184	212	243	273	304	334	365	31	61	92	122
SEPT'BER.	Months.	4	5	6	7	8	9	10	11	12	1	2	3
	Days...	122	153	181	212	242	273	303	334	365	30	61	91
OCTOBER.	Months.	3	4	5	6	7	8	9	10	11	12	1	2
	Days...	92	123	151	182	212	243	273	304	335	365	31	61
NOV'MBER	Months.	2	3	4	5	6	7	8	9	10	11	12	1
	Days...	61	92	120	151	181	212	242	273	304	334	365	30
DEC'MBER	Months.	1	2	3	4	5	6	7	8	9	10	11	12
	Days...	31	62	90	121	151	182	212	243	274	304	335	365

EXPLANATIONS.

Suppose the time be required from July 10 to September 10. Find July in the left-hand column, and follow out the line to the right until you come to September; the number of months is 2, of days 62. If the date *to* which we reckon be either greater or less than the one *from* which we reckon, the difference should be added or subtracted as the case may be. For example: How many days from February 1 to August 31? By following out the February line to the August column, we find the time from February 1 to August 1 to be 181 days, to which if we add 30, the difference between 1 and 31, the time required will be 211 days. If the time be required between February 28 and August 1, we find the time from February 28 to August 28, to be 181 days, from which, if we subtract 27, the difference between 1 and 28, we get for the number of days, 154.

The Table is one of quite common use, but is none the less important. It may be used to great advantage in the processes of averaging.

www.ingramcontent.com/pod-product-compliance
Lightning Source LLC
LaVergne TN
LVHW101439200926
848483LV00004B/405